FUZZY INFERENCE SYSTEM – THEORY AND APPLICATIONS

Edited by **Mohammad Fazle Azeem**

Fuzzy Inference System – Theory and Applications
Edited by Mohammad Fazle Azeem

Published by InTech
Janeza Trdine 9, 51000 Rijeka, Croatia

Publishing Process Manager Bojan Rafaj

Technical Editor Teodora Smiljanic

Cover Designer InTech Design Team

Additional hard copies can be obtained from orders@intechopen.com

Fuzzy Inference System – Theory and Applications, Edited by Mohammad Fazle Azeem
p. cm.
ISBN 978-953-51-0525-1

For EU product safety concerns:
IN TECH d.o.o., Prolaz Marije Krucifikse Kozulić 3, 51000 Rijeka, Croatia,
info@intechopen.com or visit our website at intechopen.com.

Meet the editor

Professor Mohammad Fazle Azeem was born on 01st, July' 1966 in a reputed Qazi family of Gorakhpur, UP, INDIA. He earned his Bachelor degree in electrical engineering from MMMEC, Gorakhpur in 1987, Master degree in instrumentation & control from AMU in 1991, and Doctorate degree from Indian Institute of Technology, Delhi, INDIA in 2001. He has joined the department of electrical engineering, AMU, Aligarh, INDIA in December'1989 as lecturer. He has promoted to senior lecturer and associate professor in the year 1995 and 2000 respectively. Presently, he has been deputed to PA College of Engineering, Mangalore, Karnataka, INDIA as professor and academic director ECE/TCE since October'2007. Till date he has sixty six publications in his credit, published in international journals, international and national conferences. He has delivered more than twenty five technical talks in India and abroad. As a philanthropist his message to humanity is: "be tolerant to inculcate love for human and living being"

Contents

Preface

Evolution of global technologies has prompted increasing complexity of applications developed in both, the industry and the scientific research fields. These complexities are generally attributed to nonlinearities, poorly defined dynamics and absence of *apriori* information about the systems. Imprecision, uncertainties and vagueness in information about the system are also playing vital roles in enhancing the complexity of application. During the last five decades researchers had concentrated their efforts on providing simple and easy algorithms using different methodologies to cope with the increasing complexity of the system. The concept of fuzzy sets had been proposed in 1965 to address the issues of application complexities arising due to nonlinearities, poorly defined dynamics, absence of *apriori* information, imprecision, uncertainties and vague description of the system. After the proposition of fuzzy set theory, this field has witnessed an explosion of its application in diverse multi-discipline areas like engineering, medicine, management, behavioral science etc. The application of fuzzy sets has widen the horizon of technologies, such as fuzzification of pixel intensity values and fuzzy clustering on image processing, fuzzy clustering on classification, decision making, identification and fault detection, fuzzy controllers to map expert knowledge into control systems, fuzzy modeling combining expert knowledge, fuzzy optimization to solve design problems etc. A very interesting characteristic of the fuzzy systems is their capability to handle numeric and linguistic information in the same framework. This characteristic made these systems very useful to handle expert tasks. Making use of these characteristic fuzzy systems are applied to artificial intelligence for representing the knowledge of experts or acquired through learning process. Additionally, fuzzy systems provide a rich and robust method of building systems that include multiple conflicting, cooperating, and collaborating knowledge.

While several books are available today that address the mathematical and philosophical foundations specific to a particular application of fuzzy logic, none, unfortunately, provides the new practitioner, with capabilities and practical information about diverse inter-disciplinary fuzzy system applications. This book is an attempt to accrue the researches performed by the prominent researchers, geographically scattered on the globe, on diverse inter disciplinary field of engineering and management using Fuzzy Inference System (FIS). The book is spread over twenty two chapters carved up in seven sections covering a wide range of applications.

Section I, consists of single chapter that caters theoretical aspects of FIS. Chapter 1 deals with an introductive study about Fuzzy Logic, its differences with the other many-valued calculi and relationships with the complex sciences.

Section II deals FIS applications to management related problems by enveloping chapters 2 to 4. Chapter 2 describes the main features a fuzzy expert system for supporting risk management activities termed as RA_X FMADM (Fuzzy Multiple Attribute Decision Making) model. The support of a proactive risk management is achieved by assessing potential factors that contribute for occupational accident occurrence and by guiding on the adoption of safety measures. In its current stage a prototype was implemented for test and validation purposes. Chapter 3 introduces a new fuzzy approach to perform a more applicable risk analysis in real world applications. The introduced method is applied to two different problems. The first application is to determine the multi-purpose criticalities of activities. Whereas, second application deal with simultaneous task scheduling and path planning of rescue robots. Chapter 4 explores the potentials of the hybrid approach with the FIS to handle uncertainties in the decision making obtained from the human experts. To reduce the size of complete fuzzy rule base, because of large number of fuzzy term sets and antecedents, a rough–fuzzy approach is adopted in this chapter to form a concise fuzzy rule base with an application to reason the student performance.

Section III accumulates chapters 5 to 10 to commemorate FIS application to mechanical and industrial engineering problems. Chapter 5 presents Adaptive Neuro-Fuzzy Inference System (ANFIS) based modeling and various grip force control schemes of an intelligent robotic gripper. These schemes have been tested using simulation studies and obtained results were compared. Chapter 6 accommodates various fuzzy logic control schemes for mechatronics and automation problem like quarter car suspension system, rotary crane system automation, point to point position control, mobile autonomous robot system. Chapter 7 describes a FIS based method for the analysis of vibrations in electric machines. Chapter 8 proposes a hybrid intelligent method based on FIS to diagnose incipient and compound faults of large-scale and complex mechanical equipments like rotating machinery. Chapter 9 suggests studies on noise and its effects on industrial cognitive task performance by developing a neuro-fuzzy model for the prediction of cognitive task efficiency as a function of noise level, cognitive task type and age. Chapter 10 presents practical applications of FIS based data processing for detection of rare data in industrial applications that are capable to outperform the widely adopted traditional methods.

Section IV encompasses chapters 11 to 14 and elaborates FIS application to image processing and cognition problems. Chapter 11 describes application of FIS to image classification in the industrial field through several examples to demonstrate applicability of the FISs in industrial field because of their flexibility and the simplicity. Chapter 12 explores the superiority of FIS over the Sobel and Laplacian-of-Gaussian (LoG) operators for edge detection on some gray images. Chapter 13 presents Type-2 FIS for edge detection of gray scale images and compares the result with Type-1 FIS and magnitude gradient methods. Chapter 14 proposes a robust analysis system embedding neuron-fuzzy prediction scheme together with support vector machine in feature extraction for brain-computer interface (BCI) application.

Section V composed of chapters 15 to 17 to describe FIS application to power system engineering problem. Chapter 15 proposes a novel ANFIS based method for identifying various fault types, fault location and power restoration plan in power distribution network and evaluates the performance of proposed approach on a 47 buses practical system. Chapter 16 investigates the use of multi ANFIS to study the design of Short-Term Load Forecasting (STLF) systems for the east of Iran. The results show that temperature and the features of 2, 7 and 14 day ago have an important role in load forecast. Chapter 17 analyses the use of FIS in modeling the energy demand, improving the prediction performance and adapting the prediction to the real time effects in a specific electric network after analyzing its demand characteristics.

Section VI constitutes chapters 18 to 20 for highlighting the FIS application to system modeling and control problems. Chapter 18 explains the three-step structure designing of fuzzy knowledge based controllers, i.e., fuzzification, inference and defuzzification using a trivial, academic example involving temperature control. Chapter 19 presents an evolutionary fuzzy hybrid system for control application by proposing the strategies for membership function generation using three different evolutionary algorithms namely modified genetic algorithms (MGA), particle swarm optimization (PSO) and hybrid particle swarm optimization (HPSO). Performance of these three different evolutionary algorithms are evaluated and compared. Chapter 20 proposes self-constructing Fuzzy Cerebellar Model Articulation Controllers (SC-FCMAC) and parametric FCMAC (P-FCMAC) as improvements in FCMAC, which demonstrates state-of-the art in the field of fuzzy inference systems for system modeling and control.

Section VII accommodates chapters 21 and 22 as FIS application to civil engineering problem. Chapter 21 proposes FIS based Bridge Management System (BMS) comprised of a Diagnosis Synthesis (DIASYN) tool that is a fuzzy rule-based inference system for bridge damage diagnosis and prediction, an adaptive neuro-fuzzy inference system for bridge risk assessment, a neuro-fuzzy hybrid system for condition state evaluation of existing reinforced concrete bridges, a fuzzy concrete bridge deck condition rating method and a two stage method for structural damage identification using hybrid of ANFIS and practice swarm optimization (PSO). Chapter 22 propounds ANFIS and Artificial Neural Network (ANN) models for prediction of shear strength of ferro-cement members and concrete beams reinforced with fiber reinforced polymer (FRP) bars. The results of these models have been compared with experimental and available methods results. The comparison shows that ANFIS and ANN have the ability to predict the shear strength of ferro-cement members and the shear strength of concrete beams reinforced with FRP with a high degree of accuracy.

Professor (Dr.) Mohammad Fazle Azeem,
Department of Electronics and Communication Engineering,
PA College of Engineering,
India

Section 1

Theory

1

Fuzzy Logic, Knowledge and Natural Language

Gaetano Licata
Università degli Studi di Palermo
Italy

1. Introduction

This is an introductive study on what Fuzzy Logic is, on the difference between Fuzzy Logic and the other many-valued calculi and on the possible relationship between Fuzzy Logic and the complex sciences. Fuzzy Logic is nowadays a very popular logic methodology. Different kinds of applications in cybernetics, in software programming and its growing use in medicine seems to make Fuzzy Logic, according to someone, the "new" logic of science and technology. In his enthusiastic panegyric of Fuzzy Logic, Kosko (1993) argues that after thirty years from the birth of this calculus, it is time to declare the new era of Fuzzy Logic and to forget the old era of classical logic. I think that this point of view is too much simplistic. However, it is true that Fuzzy Logic and many valued-logics are connected with a new ontology. Quantum physics and biology of complexity push the research in the direction of a new and more complex concept of logical formalization. The ontological vagueness must be connected to the logical vagueness, the undetermined development of some natural phenomena must be treated with many-valued logic. The importance and usefulness of many-valued logic in science will be showed by two examples: i) the unforeseeability in biology (theory of Prigogine), ii) the birth of quantum mechanics and the employment of probabilistic logic in the interpretation of the wave-function. Kosko affirms that Fuzzy Logic is the solution to the fact that science proposes a linear image of a non-linear world and quotes the Heisenberg's indeterminacy principle. Moreover Kosko proposes a fuzzy alternative to the probabilistic interpretation of the equation of Schrödinger. I think that Fuzzy Logic is an important device to face the new ontology of complexity, but this does not entail that Fuzzy Logic is the solution to all the scientific problems. It is useful to understand why Fuzzy Logic created this illusion and which can be its real place in scientific methodology.

One of the most important argument employed by Kosko to underline the superiority of Fuzzy Logic (against classical and probabilistic logic) is its similarity with natural language (henceforth NL) and natural thinking. The relaxations of the pretences of logical truth, in classical sense, seem to give Fuzzy Logic the character of natural thinking, with its imprecision and its approximation, and also with its richness. In my work I will argue that Fuzzy Logic is a very useful device to treat natural phenomena and quantities in a logical way, and that Fuzzy Logic is a very versatile many-valued logic because the number of truth values can vary from few to infinite, at will of the user. Nevertheless, I will argue also that Fuzzy Logic is not the key of the formalization of NL, and that the phenomena of vagueness and the relaxations of classical logical truth, which Fuzzy Logic can treat, are only one aspect of NL. Natural Language/Thinking has a lot of aspects that a logical calculus cannot have. Being the source of Fuzzy Logic - and of all possible logical calculi –, NL gives to Fuzzy Logic some power. Our task here is to study the nature of this power. From this point of view, it is clear that the enthusiastic judgement on Fuzzy Logic, given by Kosko, should be reconsidered.

As third point of my work, I will focus the position of Fuzzy Logic in the context of the many-valued logics. Fuzzy Logic has two important characteristic which make it very versatile and very useful in technological employments: 1) the user can choose the number of truth-values from few to infinite; 2) the process of fuzzification and defuzzification requires a double kind of truth values: the "hedges" and the percent values. In the process of fuzzification the quantities to employ in the calculus must be considered as "scalar". This can be done creating a table of correspondence between the intensity of a phenomenon and the percent values. The application of fuzzy calculus to clinical diagnosis, with the fuzzification of biological parameters (the signs, the symptoms and the laboratory tests) is a good example of fuzzification of quantitative phenomena (cf. Licata, 2010). The correspondence with percent values is aimed to establish the hedges which marks the passage from a fuzzy set to another. The hedges correspond to the critical values of the quantities, those who drives the decisions of the system's user (human or artificial). Thus Fuzzy Logic has the aspect of a complex polyvalent calculus which is clearly aimed to applicative and, in particular, "engineering" solutions. From a theoretical point of view, the debate has evidenced that Fuzzy Logic is a good device to treat the linguistic vagueness, as distinct from the uncertainty (Benzi, 1997). In technical sense the "uncertainty" is the effect of an incomplete information with respect to a subjective prevision. The uncertainty is usually treated with the probabilistic logic, but some scholar (those who follows Kosko, 1993) thinks that uncertainty and casualness are aspects derived from vagueness. Fuzzy Logic, according to them, is the best way to give a mathematical account of the uncertain reasoning. With regard to this problem, I think that it is not strange to find similarities and new connections between methods which are studied to treat similar aspects of knowledge; this happens also because distinctions like uncertainty/vagueness or subjective/objective are often linguistic distinctions. Thus the study of Fuzzy Logic, in the context of Natural Language, is a good method to say what is in general Fuzzy Logic and what are its best employments.

2. Importance and usefulness of Fuzzy Logic in sciences: A classification of sciences on the basis of complexity

More and more the science of today face uncertainty, vagueness and phenomena which traditional methodologies cannot study adequately. With respect to classical ontology, an ontology of complexity is, in the last years, the object of sciences. The birth of many-valued logic is marked by the idea that classical bivalent logic has been the soul of the old scientific ontology, while the new calculi with many truth-values should be the basis of the complex ontology. In this sense, the father of classical logic and of classical ontology, Aristotle, is considered an outdated thinker (Kosko, 1993). Which is the place of Fuzzy Logic in the context of many-valued calculi? Is it true that the Aristotelian bivalence is an outdated logic? Fuzzy Logic is a very useful device to treat natural phenomena and quantities in logical way, it is a very versatile many-valued system because the number of truth values can vary from few to infinite, at will of the user. Moreover the study of probabilistic logic, and of its applications, is very important to understand Fuzzy Logic. Indeed many theorists of probability (following de Finetti, 1989) think that Fuzzy Logic is useless because all the problems treated by Fuzzy Logic can be solved by calculus of probability. On the other hand, Kosko thinks that probabilistic logic was born for the fuzzy nature of things, and that probabilistic logic can be reduced to Fuzzy Logic. In this chapter I will try to study the relationship between sciences and logical systems. In particular I will underline how the birth of an *ontology* of complexity is in correspondence with a *logic* of complexity. The starting point of the analysis, and the element which binds logical systems and sciences, can be the nomologic-deductive model of scientific explanation. I will employ this famous model of explanation (and of prediction) as a structure in which it is possible to change the different logical systems, on the basis of the different scientific ontologies considered. With the examples of the biology of complexity and of quantum mechanics, I will show that the scientific indeterminism is the natural field of many-valued logics. It is exactly in the discussion of these problems that we will find the place of many-valued logics in the context of formalized languages, and the place of Fuzzy Logic in the context of many-valued logics. The nomologic-deductive explanation of a phenomenon proposed by Popper (1935) was applied by Hempel (1942) to history. An event E is explained, from a causal point of view, if it is possible to deduce logically it from two kind of premises: a) the general scientific laws ($L_1, L_2, \ldots, L_n$), which regard the development of the event E as belonging to a class, and b) the initial conditions ($C_1, C_2, \ldots, C_n$), which are specific aspects of E in connection with the general laws. In the scheme of Hempel

	$L_1, L_2, \ldots, L_n$ (general laws) $C_1, C_2, \ldots, C_n$ (initial conditions)	} *Explanans*
(logical deduction)	________________________	
	E (event to explain)	*Eplanandum*

Fig. 1. The nomologic-deductive model of scientific explanation.

Popper proposes the following example. We have a causal explanation of "the breaking of a thread which is charged of a weight" (*Explanandum*), if we have two kind of premises: the proposition "A thread breaks when it is charged of a weight that is heavier than the weight which defines the resistance of the thread", and this has the form of a general law (L_1); and propositions which are specific of the singular event like "The weight which defines the resistance of this thread is x" (C_1) and "The thread has been charged with a weight of 2x" (C_2). Clearly this example regards a deterministic event. It can be studied with the methodologies of macroscopic physics (Galilean and Newtonian physics). On the basis of explanations similar to the scheme of Fig. 1, it is possible to make predictions which are, in principle, absolutely true. E.g. It is absolutely true that, if the thread of the previous example is charged with a weight of 0.5x, the thread will not break; or it is absolutely true that, on the basis of laws of Keplero, in 365 days and 6 hours the earth will be in the same position, with respect to the sun, of today. Buzzoni (2008) proposes an example of a probabilistic version of the nomologic-deductive model of Fig. 1. If the scientific laws, which regard the event E, are statistic and not deterministic, the scheme can be

	$L_1, L_2, \ldots, L_n$ (statistic laws) $C_1, C_2, \ldots, C_n$ (initial conditions)	} *Explanans*
(inductive-statistic inference)	==========================	
	E (event to explain)	*Eplanandum*

Fig. 2. The probabilistic version of the nomologic-deductive model.

We can explain that a person P was infected by measles (*Explanandum*), affirming, as general probabilistic law, that "The probability to be infected by measles is high when a person is exposed to contagion" (L_1); and, as initial condition, that "The person P has been exposed to contagion". In this case the event *E* is not a (absolutely true) logical consequence of the premises: the *explanans* furnishes to the *explanandum* only a certain degree of probability. An eventual prediction, based upon this kind of explanation, would be probable and not true.

These two examples of scientific explanation show the difference between natural sciences (macroscopic physics, classical chemistry) and human sciences (history, economics, politics, psychology). An intermediate case of complexity between natural sciences and human sciences could be the biology and similar sciences[1]: the complexity of biological phenomena cannot be well represented by classical logic. In the prevision of a macro-physical phenomenon it is possible to employ a two-valued logic, because knowing the physical laws and the initial conditions it is possible to make previsions with an absolute certainty. On the other hand, in the prevision of a biological phenomenon it is impossible to have an absolute certainty. At the degree of complexity of biological sciences rises the need to employ probabilistic logic. The high number of variables, the complexity of processes and the high number of possible ways give rise to the problem of unforeseeability.

Prigogine's theory and complexity in biology. Prigogine introduced in 1967 the concept of "dissipative structure" to describe some special chemical systems. Later the concept of dissipative structure was employed to describe the living organisms. In Prigogine's theory (1967, 1971, 1980), the dissipative structures are in condition of stability when they are far from thermic equilibrium; in this condition they are also able to evolve. When the flux of energy and matter, which goes through them, grows up, they can go through new phases of instability and transform in new, more complex, structures. Dissipative structures receive matter from outside; the instabilities and the jumps to new forms of organization are the result of fluctuations which are amplified by the positive feedback loops (reinforcement feedback loops). The critical points of instability, the jumps, are also called "bifurcation points", because the system can choose between different ways of evolution, out of the normal way. In an artificial machine the structure and the components are fix and immutable, on the other hand, in a living organism structure and components change continuously. A continue flux of matter goes through living organisms: every cell decomposes and synthesizes chemical structures while eliminating the rejects. In living organism there are always development and evolution. The cell can be considered a very complex kind of dissipative structure, while a very simple example of dissipative structure is the drain whirlpool. The forces which find balance in a whirlpool are mechanic and the most important is the gravity, while the forces which operate in a cell are chemical and the description of these forces is enormously more complex than the description of a whirlpool. The energetic processes of the cell are the catalytic cycles which act as feedback loops. The catalytic cycles (Eigen, 1971) are very important in metabolic processes, they can act as auto-balancing feedback loops and as reinforcement feedback loops. The auto-balancing feedback loops maintain the stability in the metabolism of the organism, the reinforcement feedback loops can push the organism more and more far from equilibrium,

[1] The case of medicine is particular, because in some aspects it can be considered a biological science (e.g. from the point of view of the development of a pathological phenomenon), while in other aspects (e.g. in psychiatry, or for the influence of consciousness in the development of some diseases) it can be considered a human science.

until the point of instability: this is the "bifurcation" point. The bifurcation points can give rise to new forms of order: they are the keys of the growing up and of the evolution of living organisms, because they are radical and unexpected transformations in which the system's behavior takes a new direction. The figure 2 shows how a system changes the trajectory of its behavior: the arrow f_1 represents the development of the system before the bifurcation point B. The arrow f_2 represents a new unexpected direction in the behavior of the system after B. The broken arrow represents the hypothetical direction of the behavior of the system if B would have not happened.

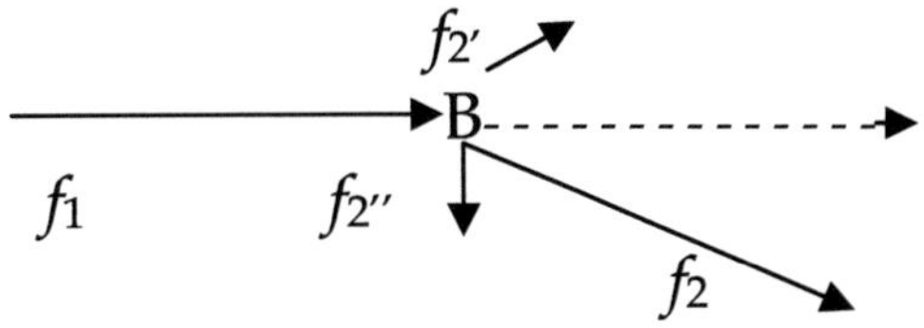

Fig. 3. The bifurcation point in the evolution of a dissipative structure.

According to Prigogine, in the point of instability the system can take different ways ($f_{2'}, f_{2''}$, …). The way that actually will be taken (f_2) depends on the history of the system and on the casual fluctuations of the system's environment, which happen in the moment of instability. In the case of living organisms this is very interesting, because a living organism is always a registration of its past and this past always influences its development. Moreover the life of organisms always depends on their environment. In the point of bifurcation the dissipative structure is very sensitive to the minimal fluctuations of the environment, because the point of bifurcation is a "crisis" of the system, in which the rules of the system can be modified. The smallest casual events can orientate the choice of the future behavior of the system. Given that all the living organisms live in environments which continuously fluctuate, and given that it is impossible to know which fluctuations will happen in the moment of maximum instability, it is impossible to foresee the future way of the system. Thus Prigogine theorizes the unforeseeability in principle of the system in the point of bifurcation.

Many-valued logics and probabilistic logic are clearly more useful than classical logic in the explanation, in the description and in the prediction of a biological phenomenon. In the human sciences the complexity reaches an higher degree, with respect to biology, because human sciences study the phenomena in which operate a multiplicity of biological subjects who has a mind. The superior complexity of this degree is given by the unforeseeability of groups. If the development of phenomena which regard a single subject is unforeseeable for the complexity of biological processes and for the influence that the consciousness of the subject has in the processes, then the phenomena which regard groups of biological subjects, and groups of minds, entail an unforeseeability of superior degree. Sciences like economy, politics and history (the so called human sciences) study phenomena in which the behavior of the group is the result of the behavior of the single biological subjects, and the result of the influences between subjects. On the basis of these distinctions, we can consider three kinds of phenomena: A) Macro-physical and chemical phenomena; B) Biological phenomena, C) Group phenomena. To each kind of phenomenon a different kind of logical system can correspond, with a different degree of complexity. It's clear that the number of truth-values and the possibility to vary the number of truth-values mark the different degree of complexity. The degrees of logical complexity will be: I) truth-false; II) truth-false + a fix number of truth values (simple polyvalence); III) truth-false + a variable number of truth values (a multiple system which contains subsystems with different numbers of truth-values: complex polyvalence). In this way we find a place for Fuzzy Logic in the context of many-valued systems. With respect to simple many-valued logical systems with a fix number of truth-values, Fuzzy Logic give the possibility to vary the number of truth-values and to build multiple logical systems for the treatment of different aspects of the phenomenon. Thus we can build the following table:

Levels of complexity	Science	Foreseeability of phenomenon	Kind of explanation	Logical system employed
1° level of complexity	Classical macroscopic Physics, classical Chemistry	Foreseeability, Always true or false	Nomologic-deductive explanation	Classical bivalent Logic
2° level of complexity	Biologic sciences (biology, istology, genetics)	Un-foreseeability of single subjects	Probabilistic-Nomologic-deducitve explanation	Polyvalent Logics (Probabilistic logic)
3° level of complexity	Human sciences (history, sociology, psicology, economics)	Un-foreseeability of groups	Different many-valued logics (Fuzzy Logic) in the Nomologic-deducitve explanation	Different many-valued logics (Fuzzy Logic) in a single phenomenon

Table 1. Increasing complexity of sciences and the adequate logical systems for their methodologies.

I think that this table can receive some critique, nonetheless it is possible that it tells something right. For instance, molecular biology is a border science between the first and the second level of complexity, because chemical reactions can be treated as phenomena of first level with a bivalent approach, while biological phenomena must be treated as phenomena of second level with a polyvalent approach. Also medicine is a border science, because it contains (biological) phenomena of second level, but it can be considered a science of third level for the influence that the consciousness has in the development of pathologic phenomena.

In the twentieth century the quantum physics theory has demonstrated that simple phenomena are not the basis of complex phenomena, and that the more you go in the microcosm to find the "elements" of reality, the more you find complexity. The theorists of quantum mechanics treated the complexity of quantum interaction employing many-valued logics. The passage from classical particles to waves corresponds to the passage from two-valued logic to many-valued logics. It is very interesting, to recall the birth of quantum physics, that the employment of probabilistic logic marks this birth, and that many-valued systems and fuzzy logic are connected to quantum paradigm.

Quantum physics and many-valued logics. Formulated at the beginning of twentieth century, undulatory mechanics theorizes that the behavior of the smallest constituent of matter can be described trough waves of frequency (ν) and lenght (λ). In the hypothesis of undulatory mechanics, variables of corpusculary kind are connected to variables of undulatory kind.

The photon, the quantum of light, is connected to the electromagnetic wave with energy E and quantity of motion p, which are given by the equations $E = h\nu$ and $p = h/\lambda$. The fundamental hypothesis of undulatory mechanics, proposed by de Broglie in 1924, is that each particle is connected to a wave described by these equations. The law of propagation of these waves of "matter" was found by Schrödinger, who in analogy with classical mechanics formulated the right wave equation. The energy of a classic particle is a function of position and of velocity, thus Born affirmed that the *probability* to find a particle of mass m in the position x at the instant t was expressed by the wave function $\psi(x, t)$ which satisfies the Schrödinger's equation

$$i\hbar\frac{\partial\psi}{\partial t} = -\frac{\hbar^2}{2m}\frac{\partial^2\psi}{\partial x^2} + V(x)\psi \tag{1}$$

Where the field of forces around the particle derives from the potential $V(x)$ and ħ is a variant of the Plank's constant h, $\hbar = h/2\pi$. The hypothesis of de Broglie, and the Schrödinger's equation, mark the birth of quantum mechanics. Undulatory mechanics permits to calculate the energetic levels of atoms and the spectral terms. In this way, the old theory of quanta based on classical principles, unable to interpret the spectrum of black body, the photoelectric effect and the atomic spectra was surpassed. Born gave to the wave-function the following probabilistic interpretation, an interpretation which was refused by Schrödinger. In a one-particle-system, with a wave function $\psi(\boldsymbol{r}, t)$, the probability to find a particle in the volume dv, centered around the point $\boldsymbol{r}_1$, is

$$\psi^*(\boldsymbol{r}_1,t)\psi(\boldsymbol{r}_1,t)dv \tag{2}$$

where ψ^* is the conjugated complex of ψ. In the same years Heisenberg theorized the mechanics of matrices, in which a dynamic variable is represented by a matrix Q. The equation of motion of mechanics of matrices is

$$i\hbar\frac{dQ}{dt} = QH - HQ \tag{3}$$

Where H is the matrix obtained from the classic Hamiltonian function, through the substitution of classic dynamic variables with the correspondent Heisenberg's matrices. The second member QH – HQ is the commutator, and it is commonly written [Q,H]. Quantum mechanics derives from the acknowledgement of the equivalence between the undulatory mechanics and the mechanics of matrices. In quantum mechanics the status of a physical system is represented by a vector of Hilbert's space. Dynamic variables are represented by linear operators in the Hilbert's space. The evolution of a physical system can be described in two ways. In the first way, proposed by Schrödinger, the operators are fixed, while the vector of status evolves in time following the equation

$$i\hbar\frac{\partial}{\partial t}\psi = H\psi \tag{4}$$

Where ψ represents the vector of the status and H is the operator of energy. In the second way, proposed by Heisenberg, the vector of status is fixed while the operators evolve in time following the equation

$$i\hbar Q' = [Q, H] \quad (5)$$

Where Q′ is the derivate respect to time of the operator Q. Over these two ways, it is possible to give an intermediate representation of the evolution of a physical system in which both the vector of status and the operators evolve in time. It is a postulate of quantum mechanics that the operators of position and of impulse of a particle satisfy the relation of commutation

$$[Q, P] = i\hbar \quad (6)$$

Thus the position and the impulse cannot be measured simultaneously with arbitrary precision. This is the principle of indetermination enounced by Heisenberg. The measure of a dynamic variable Q gives a determined and exact result q only when the vector ψ, the vector of the status of the system, satisfies the equation $Q\psi = q\psi$. In this case ψ is an auto-status of Q, which corresponds to the auto-value q. If the system is not in an auto-status of the dynamic variable measured, it is impossible to predict the result of the measure, it is only possible to assign the probability to obtain a determinate value q. For this statistic character of quantum mechanics some physicists, like Einstein, believed that this theory is not complete. Kosko (1993: 67) writes that the operator ψ represents the matter's wave in an infinitesimally little volume dV; Born interpreted the square of the absolute value of the wave, $|\psi|^2$, as a measure of probability. Thus the infinitesimal quantity $|\psi|^2$ dV measures the *probability* that a particle of matter is in the infinitesimally little region dV. This entails that all the infinitesimal particles are casual point. On the other hand, the fuzzy thinking considers $|\psi|^2$ dV as the measure of *how much* the particle is in the region dV. According to this point of view, the particles are to some extent in all the regions of the space: hence the particles are deterministic clouds. Telling that the quantum particles, in fuzzy thinking, are "deterministic" clouds, Kosko means that it is precisely determinable the measure of the quantity of matter in the volume dV; as we will see, fuzzy thinking is always connected to the precision. However, the adjective "deterministic" is too much employed to describe the old scientific paradigm, thus I prefer to say that, in this anti-probabilistic interpretation, quantum particles are *fuzzy* clouds.

Thus it is clear that, in the table 1, the first level of complexity does not contain the sciences which study the most fundamental elements of reality, or the "atoms" of the ancient science. The classification of the table 1 regards only the methodology and the kind of phenomenon considered by a science, not the *ontological level* (more or less fundamental) of the phenomena studied by a science. In quantum physics, which study the subatomic particles, we find the unforeseeability and the uncertainty that, at the level of macroscopic chemistry and of macroscopic physics, is substituted by foreseeability and bivalence. Thus quantum mechanics could be a science of second or third level of complexity in the table 1. In the classical physics of Galileo and Newton the phenomena were reduced to the properties of material and rigid bodies. From 1925, quantum mechanics showed that, at subatomic level, material bodies dissolve in undulatory schemas of probability. Subatomic particles are not understood as rigid but very little entities, they are instead relationships or interconnections between processes which can be only theoretically distinguished. The schemas of probability (or fuzziness) are not probabilities of material objects (electrons, quarks, neutrins, etc.), but probabilities of interconnections between events. Capra (1996: 41) writes that "when we move our attention from macroscopic objects to the atoms and to subatomic particles, Nature does not show isolated bricks, but it appears as a complex weft of relations between parts of an unified everything". The father of the idea of vague (fuzzy) sets, M. Black, was an expertise of quantum mechanics. And the studies of Łukasiewicz on many-valued logic, from 1920, were soon connected with the development of quantum physics. In 1936 Birkhoff and von Neumann wrote a famous essay on the logic of quantum mechanics. The fact that the Schrödinger's wave function ψ was interpreted in a probabilistic way, and the fact that the father of the idea of vague/fuzzy sets was an expertise of quantum mechanics, are very important for two reasons: they show us that i) a many-valued logic system is much more adequate to quantum physics than classical logic and that ii) a scientific theory becomes much more clear if we find an adequate logic system to explain the phenomena considered by it. Thus it is clear why it is useful to build and to improve the table 1.

Mathematic has been, especially in the last four centuries, the language of science; if logics is another useful point of view to understand natural phenomena, then Fuzzy Logic is a very good instrument to build explanations, even it is not the solution of so many problems as Kosko believes.

3. Fuzzy Logic is not the key of the formalization of Natural Language

Fuzzy Logic is not the key of a complete formalization of NL. The phenomena of vagueness and the relaxations of classical logical truth are only an aspect of NL that Fuzzy Logic is able to treat. In the essay *Vagueness: An Excercise in Logical Analysis* (1937), the work in which was proposed for first time the idea of vague sets, Black distinguished three kinds of imprecision in NL: the generality, the ambiguity and the vagueness. The generality is the power of a word to refer to a lot of things which can be very different each other. The ambiguity is the possibility that a linguistic expression has many different meanings. The vagueness is the absence of precise confines in the reference of a lot of adjectives and common names of human language, e.g. "table", "house", "tall", "rich", "strong", "young", etc. More precisely, vagueness is an approximate relation between a common name or a *quantitative* adjective[2] and the objects of the world which can be referred by this name or predicated of this adjective. Fuzzy Logic has been developed to treat in a formal way the linguistic vagueness.

The successes of Fuzzy Logic in the field of engineering (in the automatic and self-regulating processes of cybernetics) and the birth of fuzzy sets theory from the study of linguistic vagueness (cf. Black 1937, Zadeh 1965) empowered the idea that Fuzzy Logic can give solution to the problems that the bivalent logic leaves unsolved in artificial intelligence (henceforth AI). Kosko (1993) proposes the idea that an artificial system will be a good imitation of a natural system, like a brain, only when the artificial system will be able to learn, to get experience and to change itself without the intervention of a human programmer. I think that this is correct, but I believe that it is not enough to put Fuzzy Logic into a dynamic system to solve the problems of AI. Instead Kosko (cf. 1993: 185-190) hypothesizes that the employment of Fuzzy Logic is the key to give the *common sense* to a system. I think that this is not correct. The common sense is the result of so many experiences and so many complex processes of our knowledge, in social interaction, that it is not enough to substitute bivalent logic with Fuzzy Logic to obtain a system which operates on the basis of common sense. Moreover it is important to remember that classical logic is however the soul of logic, and Zadeh does not think that there is a great difference between classical and Fuzzy Logic.

---

[2] With the expression „quantitative adjective" I mean an adjective which refers to qualities which have variable intensities, i.e. qualities which can be predicated of the subject more or less.

The faith in Fuzzy Logic, with respect to the problems of AI, created the illusion that Fuzzy Logic could be the key of the formalization of NL. But, also admitting that Fuzzy Logic is the best method to formalize all kinds of linguistic vagueness, the vagueness is only one of the many aspects of NL that classical logic cannot treat. A calculus would reproduce a good part of the richness of NL only having, at least, 1) a sufficient meta-linguistic power, 2) the ability to interpret the metaphors and 3) the devices to calculate all the variables of the pragmatic context of the enunciation. The first problem is solvable with a very complicate syntax and the large employment of the set theory (cf. the use of Universal Algebra in Montague, 1974). With regard to the second problem, there are a lot of theories on the treatment of metaphor, but none of them seems to be adequate to reach the objective of a "formal" interpretation. The third problem is instead very far from a solution. The pragmatics studies of physical, cultural and situational context of linguistic expressions show only that the pragmatics is fundamental for semantics: the Wittgenstein's theory of linguistic games (1953) is the best evidence of this fact. With regard to pragmatics, today it is clear that it is impossible that an artificial cognitive system could process semantically sentences, if this system is not also capable of perception and action (cf. Marconi, 1997). The problem of vagueness is important in semantics, but I think that the solutions of the problems 1), 2) and 3) are more important and more structural to reach a good automatic treatment of NL. A good automatic treatment of NL does not necessarily require a rigorous logical formalization of NL. With regard to the formalization of NL, I believe that Tarski (1931) has demonstrated that it is, in principle, an impossible task; formalized languages are always founded on NL and their semantic richness is always a parasitical part of the semantic richness of NL. Thus the objective of the research in NLP (Natural Language Processing) and AI can be only: I) the automatic production of artificial sentences which human speakers can easily understand, and II) a sufficiently correct interpretation of sentences of NL. In a static system, which is not able to program itself, I) and II) will be realized on the basis of a formalized language, NL', which is semantically rich enough to be similar to NL, but the semantic richness of NL' is however founded on NL. In a dynamic system, projected in an advanced technological environment, are conceivable *imitations* of natural phenomena like "the extensibility of the meaning of the words", "the change of meaning of words along time" and other kinds of "rule changing creativity" or of "metaphorical attitude", on the basis of the auto-programming activity of the system. Also in dynamic systems, like the hypothetical neural nets, the substitution of bivalent logic with Fuzzy Logic is a good improvement, but it is not the key of the solution of all problems. The concept of dynamic system, understood as a system which learns and changes on the basis of experience is very important, but we are still very far form a concrete realization of a system like this, and the treatability of semantic vagueness through Fuzzy Logic is only a little solution of this task. Now it is clear how much is far from truth who thinks that Fuzzy Logic is the key of formalization of NL.

4. The position of Fuzzy Logic in the context of the many-valued logics

Often Kosko affirms, in his book (1993), that "fuzzy logic is a polyvalent logic". This is true, but this proposition hides the fact that fuzzy logic is a special kind of polyvalent logic: fuzzy logic is a polyvalent logic which is always based upon another many-valued calculus. Benzi (1997: 133) proposes a mathematical relationship between Fuzzy Logic and many-valued logics. *A fuzzy logic calculus is a logic in which the truth-values are fuzzy subsets of the set of truth-values of a non fuzzy many-valued logic*. Thus, a simple many-valued logic has a fix number of truth values (3,4, …, *n*), while a Fuzzy Logic has a free number of truth values: it will be the user who will choose, each time, how many truth values he wants to employ. The user will find the truth-values of the fuzzy system inside the evaluation set of the many-valued calculus, which is the basis of the fuzzy system. This freedom in the choice, of how many truth-values are to employ, makes Fuzzy Logic a very dynamic device to treat the complex phenomena.

Definitions. Fuzzy Logic is a logic built over a polyvalent logic. The FL system was proposed by Zadeh in 1975. The basis of FL is the system $L_{\aleph 1}$ of Łukasiewicz. $L_{\aleph 1}$ is a many-valued logic in which the set of truth values contains all the real numbers of the interval [0,1]. FL admits, as truth values, "linguistic" truth values which belong to a set *T* of infinite cardinality: *T* = {True = {Very True, Not very True, More or less True, Not True, …}, False = {Very False, Not very False, More or less False, not False, ….}, … }. Each linguistic truth-value of FL is a fuzzy subset of the set *T* of the infinite numeric truth values of $L_{\aleph 1}$. The employment of linguistic truth-values permits to formulate vague answers to vague questions. A concrete example permits to understand what is a fuzzy truth. To the question "Is John YOUNG?", I can answer "It is Very True that John is YOUNG". As we see in this example, FL works with vague sentences, i.e. with sentences which contain vague or fuzzy predicates. As in the case of truth values, the fuzzy predicates are fuzzy subsets of the universe of discussion X. The universe of discussion is a classical (non fuzzy) set which contains e.g. ages, temperatures, velocities and all kind of adjectival quantities which can have a numerical translation. In the case of our example the universe of discussion is the "age". The set A ("age") contains finite numeric values [0,120]. Inside the classical set A it is possible to define the linguistic variables (YOUNG, OLD, …) as fuzzy subsets. A = {YOUNG = {Very YOUNG, Not very YOUNG, More or less YOUNG, Not YOUNG,…}, OLD = {Very OLD, Not very OLD, More or less OLD, Not OLD,…}, …}. Given that inside the set A = {0,120}, a subset of values which can be considered internal to the vague concept of "young" is e.g. {0,35}, the employment of modifiers (Very ..., Not very…, More or less…, etc.) makes fuzzy the subset YOUNG.

Membership function. The membership function of the elements of A establish *how much* each element belongs to the fuzzy subset YOUNG[3]. The membership function $\mu_{YOUNG}(a_n) = [x]$ of the element a_n establishes that the age a_n belongs to the fuzzy set YOUNG at the degree x, which is a real number of the interval [0,1]. The interval [0,1] is called "Evaluation set". Let's make some examples. The membership degree of the age "20" to the fuzzy set YOUNG is 0,80. In symbols this is written as $\mu_{YOUNG}(20) = [0,80]$. The membership degree of the age "30" to the fuzzy set YOUNG is 0,50. In symbols this is $\mu_{YOUNG}(30) = [0,50]$. If we write the membership degree of each age of the fuzzy set YOUNG we will obtain a bend.

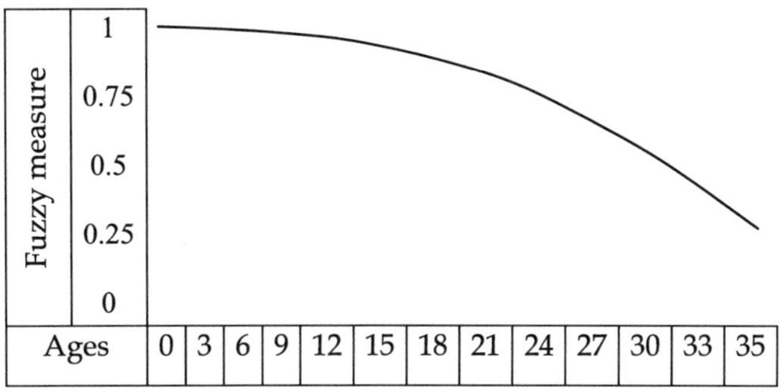

Fig. 4. Diagram of the fuzzy set YOUNG.

[3] At the end of this paragraph I will give a mathematical and graphic explanation of the membership function.

The bend gives an idea of the fuzzy membership of the elements to a fuzzy set.

Modifiers. The Zadeh's modifiers of FL are arithmetical operators on the value of the membership function of the primary terms. In this way it is possible to obtain secondary terms. If the primary term is "YOUNG", the secondary terms will be "Very YOUNG", "Not very YOUNG", "More or less YOUNG", "Not YOUNG", etc. For the application of the modifiers it is necessary to give an average value to the fuzzy set YOUNG. Let's suppose that the membership value of the average element of YOUNG is μ_{YOUNG}. The modifier "Not" will define the value "Not YOUNG" in this way:

$$\mu_{\text{Not YOUNG}} = 1 - \mu_{\text{YOUNG}} \tag{7}$$

The modifier "Very" will define the value "Very YOUNG" in this way:

$$\mu_{\text{Very YOUNG}} = (\mu_{\text{YOUNG}})^2 \tag{8}$$

The modifier "More or less" will define the value "More or less YOUNG" in this way:

$$\mu_{\text{More or less YOUNG}} = (\mu_{\text{YOUNG}})^{1/2} \tag{9}$$

The Zadeh's modifiers give a concrete idea of what is a fuzzy set, because they are the linguistic translation of the *degree* of membership of the elements. Their mathematical definition is necessary for their employment in the calculus.

In a calculus it is possible to introduce a lot of different universes discourse: "age", "strenght", "temperature", "tallness", etc. A fuzzy system can treat vague sentences like "Maria is rich enough" or "The fever of Bill is very high", or more complicated sentences like "It is not very true that an high fever is dangerous for life". In this way it is possible to build a logical system, which can be employed to translate the vague sentences of natural language in a formal calculus, and it is possible to make formal demonstrations about a scientific phenomenon. It is clear that the fuzziness of the sentence can be transferred from the predicate to the truth value. The sentence "John is Not very YOUNG" is synonym of the sentence "It is Not very True that John is YOUNG". Now it is clear how is possible to have, in a logical system, "linguistic" truth-values as fuzzy sets. These truth-values must be the subsets of a classical set: the set of truth-values of a simple many valued logic.

In (Licata 2007) and (Licata 2010) I demonstrated that it is possible to obtain a great advantage employing Fuzzy Logic in the clinical diagnosis of a concrete clinical case. In those works the linguistic variables were the so called "hedges", i.e. sets of values which are in correspondence to the numerical values of the universe of discourse. So, remaining in the example of the "age", the set A = {0,120} can be split into five subsets: A = {VERY YOUNG, YOUNG, ADULT, OLD, VERY OLD}. The 120 values of A are distributed in this five sets. VERY YOUNG = {0,18}; YOUNG = {19,35}; ADULT = {36,55}; OLD = {56,75}; VERY OLD = {76,120}. These five sets are fuzzy sets because I consider that each value belongs to a subset of A *more or less*, following a fuzzy membership function. I mean that, e.g., the element "70" has a higher degree of membership than the element "60" to the set OLD; or that the element "2" has a higher degree of membership than the element "10" to the set VERY YOUNG. With respect to Zadeh's FL, this is another way to create a correspondence between linguistic variables and fuzzy values. The unchanged matter is that, even if we work with vague predicates, this vagueness has however a precise reference to scalar values. Moreover, when the phenomenon we want to treat has no a scalar shape, we must give to this phenomenon a scalar shape following its intensity, to put this datum in a fuzzy inference. When, in my works on clinical diagnosis, I put the "pain" or the "liver enlargement" in fuzzy inferences I had to give to these factors a scalar shape, employing percent values. Thus I created tables of correspondence between "linguistic" and "numeric" intensities with the aid of bends (as in Fig. 1): a pain with value "20%" was "Light", a pain with value "50%" was "Mild"; a liver enlargement with value "15%" was "Little", a liver enlargement with value "85%" was "Very big". The employment of these tables in the premises of the diagnostic inferences gave, as result, intensity values for the diseases found in the patient; e.g. I obtained conclusions like "the patient suffers from a 'moderate-severe' Congestive Heart Failure (80%) and from a 'moderate' Congestive Hepatopathy (50%)". The great precision and richness of this new kind of diagnosis is the advantage of the use of Fuzzy Logic in clinical diagnosis. Anyway, It is important to notice here that the correspondence between linguistic and numerical values is what permits the processes of fuzzification and defuzzification. The fuzzification is the transformation of a numerical value in a linguistic value, the defuzzification is the reverse. It is clear that Zadeh's FL system doesn't need diagrams of correspondence, or fuzzification-defuzzification processes, because the linguistic variables (for predicates and for truth-values) represent fuzzy sets through the modifiers. However, also in FL system (as in all fuzzy systems) we find a precise correspondence between numerical and linguistic values. This happens because fuzzy sets can be theorized only as subsets of a classical set X, and the possibility to use linguistic vague predicates is given by the reference to a great number, or an infinite number of values into the classical set X. Thus, the "formal" vagueness of Fuzzy Logic is only the result of a great numerical precision.

An "indicator function" or a "characteristic function" is a function defined on a set X that indicates the membership of an element x to a subset A of X. The indicator function is a function μ_A: $X \rightarrow \{0,1\}$. It is defined as $\mu_A(x) = 1$ if $x \in A$ and $\mu_A(x) = 0$ if $x \notin A$. In the classical set theory the characteristic function of the elements of the subset A is assessed in binary terms according to a crisp condition: an element either belongs (1) or does not belong (0) to the subset. By contrast, fuzzy set theory permits a gradual membership of the elements of X (universe of discourse) to the subset B of X. Thus, with a generalization of the indicator function of classical sets, we obtain the membership function of a fuzzy set:

$$\mu_B : X \rightarrow [0,1] \tag{10}$$

The membership function indicates the degree of membership of an element x to the fuzzy subset B, its value is from 0 to 1. Let's consider the braces as containing the elements 0 and 1, while the square parentheses as containing the finite/infinite interval from 0 to 1. The generalization of the indicator function corresponds to an extension of the valuation set of B: the elements of the valuation set of a classical subset A of X are 0 and 1, those of the valuation set of a fuzzy subset B of X are all the real numbers in the interval between 0 and 1. For an element x, the value $\mu_B(x)$ is called *"membership degree* of x to the fuzzy set B", which is a subset of X. The universe X is never a fuzzy set, so we can write:

$$\forall x \in X, \mu_X(x) = 1 \tag{11}$$

As the fuzzy set theory needs the classical set theory as its basis, in the same way, the fundament of the logic, also of polyvalent logic, is however the bivalence.

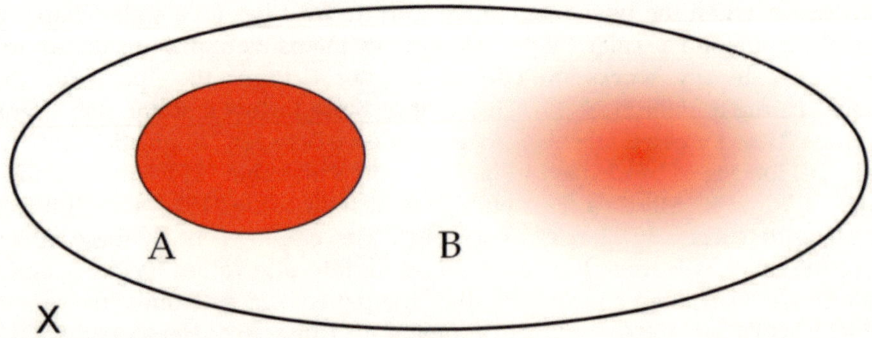

Fig. 5. A fuzzy set is always a subset of a classical set.

In conclusion, it seems that the dispute between bivalent and polyvalent logic proposed by Kosko is not a real opposition. The vagueness, the becoming of world and the plenty of points of view request polyvalence, but the Aristotelian bivalence is however fundamental in our knowledge. A lot of circumstances in our life require the bivalence. Often our decisions are choices between two alternatives, and the alternative true/false is one of the most fundamental rule of our language (Wittgenstein, 1953). As Quine (1960) underlines, the learning of a foreign language has at its basis the "yes" and the "no", as answers to sentences. Kosko, instead, affirms that the advent of Fuzzy Logic is a real revolution in science and in philosophy, also from a metaphysical point of view. When he prefers the Buddah principle of "A ∧ non A" to the Aristotle principle "A ∨ non A", he is meaning that the world can be understood only if we forget the principle of non contradiction, because always the objects of the world have in the same time opposite determinations. On the other hand, Zadeh does not think that Fuzzy Logic is so in contrast with classical logic. Zadeh and Bellman writes (1977: 109): "Although fuzzy logic represents a significant departure from the conventional approaches to the formalization of human reasoning, it constitutes - so far at least - an extension rather than a total abandonment of the currently held views on meaning, truth and inference". Fuzzy logic is just an extension of standard Boolean logic: if we keep the fuzzy values at their extremes of 1 (completely true), and 0 (completely false), the laws of classical logic will be valid. In this sense it is possible to formulate a new principle which considers the importance of bivalence and, in the same time, permits to accept the polyvalence, the Aristotle-and-Buddah principle:

$$(A \wedge \text{non } A) \text{ and } (A \vee \text{non } A)$$

In the Aristotle-and-Buddah principle I employed the conjunction "and" of natural language, and not the conjunction ∧ of a formalized language, because only the natural language has the power to maintain the conjunction between two principles which express different metaphysical systems. In the spirit of Aristotle-and-Buddah principle, bivalence can be considered a *polarization* of polyvalence, but bivalence is also the fundament of polyvalence: the evidences are that i) bivalence was born as foundation of logic while polyvalence is only a recent result, and that ii) Zadeh (1965) was able to theorize the fuzzy sets only because he considered them as subsets of a classical set. Thus it is clear that Aristotle's thought and bivalence are not outdated themes of philosophy.

5. Probabilistic and Fuzzy Logic in distinct sides of knowledge

I think that the fuzzy interpretation, proposed by Kosko, of the wave-function $|\psi|^2$ in Schrödinger's equation is very interesting. Indeed it seems to me that Schrödinger's equation regards the quantity and the quantum distribution of matter, and not the probability to find the particle in the region dV. However, in other fields of science it is not useful to try to reduce probabilistic logic to Fuzzy Logic or to treat the problems of probability with Fuzzy Logic. It is also wrong to reduce Fuzzy Logic to probabilistic logic. These two kinds of calculus have different fields of employment, different aims and give different informations about phenomena. An evidence is that probabilistic diagnosis and fuzzy diagnosis give different kinds of information about the health of the patient. In particular: probabilistic diagnosis drives in the choice of the possible diseases which could cause the symptoms, while fuzzy diagnosis gives the exact quantification of the strength of diseases. They are both useful in the study and in the cure of pathology but they do different tasks (cf. Licata, 2007). It is usual in literature to distinguish probabilistic logic from fuzzy logic, telling that the first is a way to formalize the "uncertainty" while the second is a method to treat "vagueness". In technical sense, uncertainty is the incompleteness of information, while vagueness is the absence of precise confines in the reference of *quantitative* adjectives, common names, etc. to objects of world (see §3). Nevertheless, some authors employed Fuzzy Logic to treat uncertainty (in the sense of incompleteness of information) and many theorists of probability think that probabilistic logic is a good way to treat vagueness. In general, it is clear that vagueness and uncertainty (in technical sense) can be theorized as two distinct areas of knowledge, studied by distinct methods. Given that uncertainty is understood as incompleteness of information, while vagueness regards an indefinite relationship between words and objects, it is possible to say that uncertainty and probabilistic logic fall in the area of "subjective knowledge", while vagueness and Fuzzy Logic fall in the area of "objective knowledge".

6. Acknowledgments

I thank Giuseppe Nicolaci and Marco Buzzoni for their irreplaceable help in the development of my research.

7. References

AA.VV., (1988). La Nuova Enciclopedia delle Scienze Garzanti, Garzanti editore, Milano.

Benzi, M. (1997). Il ragionamento incerto, Franco Angeli, Milano.

Bellman, R.E. & Zadeh, L. (1977). Local and Fuzzy Logics, in: *Modern Uses of Multiple-Valued Logic*, J.M. Dunn & G. Epstein, (ed.), pp. 105-165, Dodrecht.

Birkhoff G. & von Neumann J. (1936), The Logic of Quantum Mechanics, in: *Annals of Mathematics*, 37, pp. 823-843.

Black, M. (1937). Vagueness: An Excercise in Logical Analysis, In: *Philosophy of Science*, 4, pp. 427-455.

Buzzoni, M. (2008). Epistemologia e scienze umane - 1. Il modello nomologico-deduttivo, In: *Nuova Secondaria*, 8, pp. 50-52.

Capra, F. (1996). The Web of Life, Doubleday-Anchor Book, New York.

Eigen, M. (1971). Molecular Self-Organization and the Early Stages of Evolution, in *Quarterly Reviews of Biophysics*, 4, 2-3, 149.

Finetti, B. de (1989). La logica dell'incerto, edited by M. Mondadori, Il Saggiatore, Milano.

Hempel, G. (1942). The Function of General Laws in History, in: *Journal of Philosophy*, 36, pp. 35-48

Kosko, B. (1993). Fuzzy Thinking. The New Science of Fuzzy Logic, Hyperion, New York.

Licata, G. (2007). Precision and Uncertainty. Fuzzy Logic in Clinical Diagnosis, Selecta Medica, Pavia.

Licata, G. (2010). Employing Fuzzy Logic in the Diagnosis of a Clinical Case, In: *Health*, Vol. 2, 3, pp. 211-224.

Marconi, D. (1997). Lexical Competence. MIT Press, Cambridge

Montague, R. (1974). Formal Philosophy, R. Thomason (ed.), Yale University Press, New Haven.

Popper, K.R. (1935). Logik der Forschung zur Erkenntnistheorie der modernen Naturwissenschaft, Springer, Vienna 1935

Prigogine, I. (1967). Dissipative Structure in Chemical Systems, in: *Fast Reactions and Primary Processes in Chemical Kinetics*, S. Claesson (ed.), Interscience, New York.

Prigogine, I. & Glansdorff, P. (1971). Thermodynamic Theory of Structure, Stability and Fluctuations, Wily, New York.

Prigogine, I. (1980). From Being to Becoming, Freeman, San Francisco.

Quine, W.V.O. (1960). Word and Object, MIT Press, Cambridge.

Tarski, A. (1931). The Concept of Truth in formalized Languages, in: A. Tarski, *Logic, Semantics and Mathematics. Papers from 1923 to 1938*, eng. trans. J.H. Woodger, Clarendon Press, Oxford 1969.

Wittgenstein, L. (1953). Philosophische Untersuchungen, Blackwell, Oxford.

Zadeh, L., (1965). Fuzzy Sets, In: *Information and Control*, 8, pp. 338-353.

Zadeh, L., (1975). Fuzzy Logic and Approximate Reasoning, In: *Sinthese*, 30, pp. 407-428.

Section 2

Application to Management Problems

2

Applications of Fuzzy Logic in Risk Assessment – The RA_X Case

Isabel L. Nunes[1] and Mário Simões-Marques[2]
[1]*Centre of Technologies & Systems; and Faculdade de Ciências e Tecnologia, Universidade Nova de Lisboa,*
[2]*Portuguese Navy,*
Portugal

1. Introduction

Risk management for work accidents and occupational diseases is of utmost importance considering the high toll paid each year in human life, human suffering and the social and economical costs resulting from work accidents and work-related disorders. According to European Agency for Safety and Health at Work every year 5,720 people die in the European Union (EU) as a consequence of work-related accidents (EASHW, 2010). The same Agency points that the International Labour Organisation estimates that an additional 159,500 workers die every year from occupational diseases in the EU. Taking both figures into consideration, it is estimated that every three-and-a-half minutes somebody in the EU dies from work-related causes. EUROSTAT performed the Labour Force Survey 2007 regarding the situation on accidents at work and work-related health problems for the 27 EU Member States (EU-27). The main findings were (Eurostat, 2009):

- 3.2% of workers in the EU-27 had an accident at work during a one year period, which corresponds to almost 7 million workers;
- 8.6% of workers in the EU-27 experienced a work-related health problem in the past 12 months, which corresponds to 20 million persons;
- 40% of workers in the EU-27, i.e. 80 million workers, were exposed to factors that can adversely affect physical health; and
- 27% of workers, i.e. 56 million workers, were exposed to factors that can adversely affect mental well-being.

The same source notes that among workers who had an accident, 73% reported lost work days after the most recent accident, and 22% reported time off that lasted at least one month; hence, due to an accident at work, 0.7% of all workers in the EU-27 took sick leave for at least one month.

Within the context of their general obligations, employers have to take the necessary measures to prevent workers from exposure to occupational risks. This is a quite basic principle in the law of many countries. For instance, within the European Community, such principle was established by the Council Directive of 12 June 1989 on the introduction of measures to encourage improvements in the safety and health of workers at work (Directive 89/391/EEC – the Framework Directive), and then adopted by Member States' national legislations.

For this purpose employers must perform risk assessment regarding safety and health at work, including those facing groups of workers exposed to particular risks, and decide on protective measures to take and, if necessary, on protective equipment to use. Risk assessment is according to (BSI, 2007), the process of evaluating the risk(s) arising from a hazard(s), taking into account the adequacy of any existing controls, and deciding whether or not the risk is acceptable. According to OSHA an acceptable risk is a risk that has been reduced to a level that can be tolerated by the organization having regard to its legal obligations and its own occupational health and safety (OHS) policy (BSI, 2007).

In a work situation a hazard is, according to (BSI, 2007), a source, situation or act with a potential for harm in terms of human injury or ill health or a combination of these, whereas risk is defined by the same standard as a combination of the likelihood of an occurrence of a hazardous event or exposure(s) and the severity of injury or ill health that can be caused by the event or exposure(s).

Risk assessment should be integrated in a more comprehensive approach, designated as risk management, which includes also the process of performing the reduction of risks to an acceptable level. This can be achieved through the implementation of safety measures or safety controls considering the following hierarchy: engineering controls to eliminate the risk, to substitute the source of risk or at least to diminish the risk; organizational/administrative controls to diminish the workers exposure time or to sign/warn risks to workers and; as a last measure, the implementation of personnel protective equipment usage. A key aspect in risk management is that it should be carried out with an active participation/involvement of the entire workforce.

2. Risk management

Risk management is an iterative and cyclic process whose main aim is to eliminate or at least to reduce the risks according to the ALARP (as low as reasonably practicable) principle. Following the methodology PDCA (Plan-Do-Check-Act) risk management is a systematic process that includes the examination of all characteristics of the work performed by the worker, namely, the workplace, the equipment/machines, materials, work methods/practices and work environment; aiming at identifying what could go wrong, i.e. finding what can cause injury or harm to workers; and deciding on proper safety control measures to prevent work accidents and occupational diseases and implement them (i.e. risk control).

Performing risk management entails several phases, which are illustrated in Figure 1. Considering a work system under analysis, the first phase is the collection of data, usually denoted as Risk Analysis, i.e identification of hazards present in the workplace and work environment as well as the exposed workers, and identification of potential consequences of the recognized hazards - risks, i.e. the potential causes of injury to workers, either a work accident or an occupational disease. This is followed by the Risk Assessment phase, which includes the risk evaluation, the ranking of the evaluated risks and their classification in acceptable or unacceptable. At the end of this phase the unacceptable safety and health risk situations are identified. The last phase is Risk Control that includes designing/planning safety control measures to eliminate or at least to reduce risks to ALARP, followed by the implementation of safety control measures. This should be done using the following hierarchy order, first prevention measures and after protection measures (NSW, 2011) (Harms-Ringdahl, L., 2001). The safety control measures to be implemented should be based on the current technical knowledge, and good practices. Part of the risks could be transferred to insurance companies. In EU is mandatory that employers have an insurance coverage for work accidents for each worker. This way part of the risk is transferred to the insurance companies. It is very important that employers know where the risks are in their organizations and control them to avoid putting at risk the employees, customers and the organization itself.

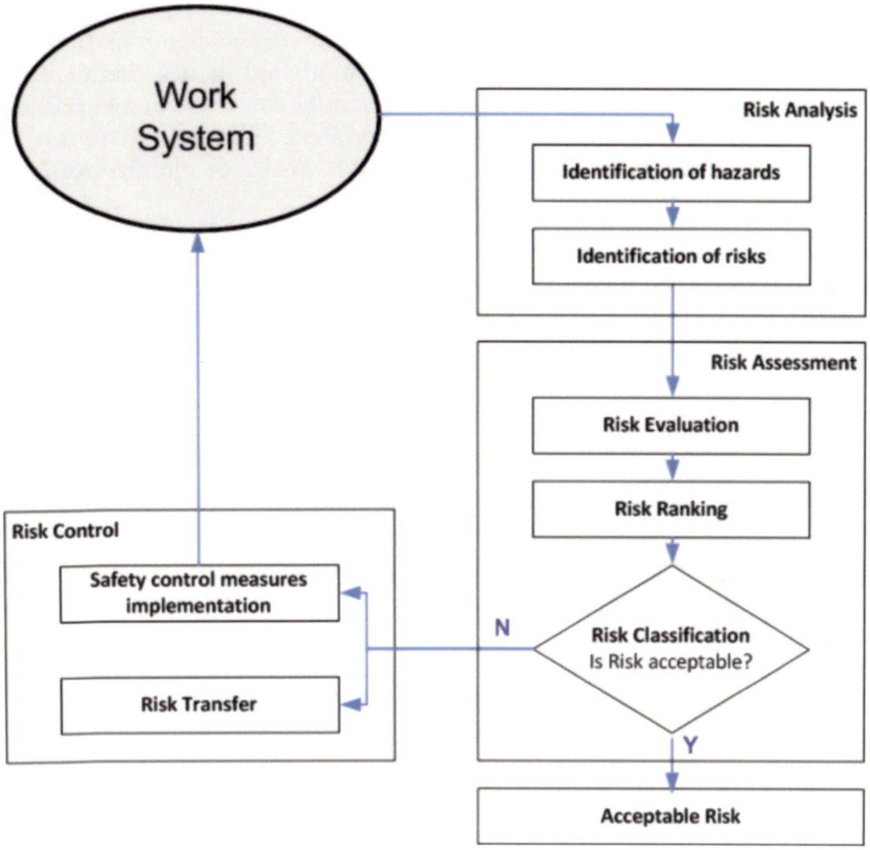

Fig. 1. Phases of the risk management process (Nunes, I. L., 2010b)

Further, in EU is a legal requirement that information and training courses are provided to workers, since workers must know the risks they are exposed to.

The standard risk assessment approach, for different risks (e.g., falls, electrical shock, burn, burying due to trench collapse, crushing) is based in the evaluation of the risk level, which results from the combination of two estimated parameters. One is the likelihood or probability of an occurrence of a hazardous event or exposure(s); and the other is severity of injury or ill health that can be caused by such event or exposure(s). These estimations are based on data regarding the presence of the hazards or risk factors in the workplace and the adequacy of the control measures implemented (prevention and protection measures).

The estimations of these parameters usually involve imprecise or vague data, incomplete information or lack of historical data that can be used to produce statistics. This is the reason why the introduction of methodologies based on fuzzy logic concepts can improve risk assessment methods.

Another important aspect in risk management is that there is no single cause (or simple sequence), but rather an interaction of multiple causes that directly and indirectly contribute to an occupational accident, the so-called cumulative act effects (Reason, J., 1997). The Reason model for the study of accident causation lies on the fact that most accidents can be traced to one or more of four levels of failure: organizational influences, unsafe supervision, preconditions for unsafe acts, and the unsafe acts themselves. The organization's defenses against these failures are modelled as a series of barriers. The barriers could be physical or organizational. The model considers active failures (unsafe acts that can be directly linked to an accident) and latent failures (contributory factors in the work system that may have been hidden for days, weeks, or months until they finally contributed to the accident) (Reason, J., 1997).

Therefore, is important to include organizational and individual factors in the risk management process. This is also in accordance with more holistic views, recognized by several authors, that consider also a host of other factors (e.g., individual, psychosocial) that can contribute to the risk (EC, 2009), (EASHW, 2002).

3. The RA_X expert system

Construction industry is one of the activities more affected by work accidents. According to European Agency for Safety and Health at Work around 1,300 workers are killed each year, equivalent to 13 employees out of every 100,000 – more than twice the average of other sectors (EASHW, 2010). As a result of its particular characteristics (e.g., projects performed only once, poor working conditions, some tasks involve particular risks to the safety and health of workers, emigrant workers, low literacy, low safety culture) construction industry has special legislation concerning the workers protection, because temporary or mobile construction sites create conditions prone to expose workers to particularly high levels of risk. Temporary or mobile construction sites means any construction site at which building or civil engineering works are carried out, which include repair and maintenance activities. In Europe the Framework Directive is complemented by the Council Directive 92/57/EEC of 24 June 1992 that addresses minimum safety and health requirements at temporary or mobile construction sites designed to guarantee a better OHS standard for workers.

Despite a steady and steep decline in the accident rates in the construction industry they remain unacceptably high, both in Europe (EASHW, 2010) and in the US (NASC, 2008). One contribution for the lowering of such accident rates could be making available tools that support the risk management activities in a simple and easy way, since there is still a lack of practical tools to support these activities. This shortfall leads to the existence of a big gap between the available health and safety knowledge and the one that is applied. Using computer-based methods could be an interesting approach to support risk assessment. The possible reasons for the lack of computer aided support tools are twofold. On one hand, the conventional software programming, based on Boolean approaches, have trouble in dealing with the inherent complexity and vagueness of the data and knowledge used in the risk assessment processes. On the other hand there are no steady and Universal rules to use for the assessment (e.g., action and threshold limit values) and the advice (e.g., regulations). These challenges call for solutions that are innovative in terms of methodologies, flexible in terms of tailoring to a specific regional context, and adaptive to deal with new or emerging risks and regulations.

The motivation for the development of the Risk Analysis Expert System (RA_X) was to make use of some emergent instruments offered by the Artificial Intelligence toolbox, namely the use of fuzzy logics in the development of a fuzzy expert system. Fuzzy Logics has been used to handle uncertainty in human-centred systems (e.g., ergonomics, safety, occupational stress) analysis, as a way to deal with complex, imprecise, uncertain and vague data. The literature review performed by (Nunes, I. L., 2010a) characterizes and discusses some examples of such applications.

Expert Systems (ES), also called knowledge-based systems, are computer programs that aim to achieve the same level of accuracy as human experts when dealing with complex, ill-structured specific domain problems so that they can be used by non-experts to obtain answers, solve problems or get decision support within such domains (Turban, E. et al., 2004). The strength of these systems lies in their ability to put expert knowledge to practical use when an expert is not available. Expert systems make knowledge more widely available and help overcome the problem of translating knowledge into practical, useful results. ES architecture contains four basic components: (a) a specialized Knowledge Base that stores the relevant knowledge about the domain of expertise; (b) an Inference Engine, which is used to reason about specific problems, for example using production rules or multiple-attribute decision-making models; (c) a working memory, which records facts about the real world; and (d) an interface that allows user-system interaction, as depicted in Figure 2.

A Fuzzy Expert System is an ES that uses Fuzzy Logic in its reasoning/inference process and/or knowledge representation scheme. For more information about Expert Systems see, for instance, (Turban, E. et al., 2010), (Gupta, J. N. D. et al., 2006), (Turban, E. et al., 2004).

The main objective of RA_X is assisting the risk management process, which is key for the promotion of safety and health at work, by identifying, assessing and controlling occupational risks and advising on the application of corrective or preventive actions. One requirement for this system is the adoption of a flexible framework that can be easily customized to the particular needs and specificities of groups of users (e.g., particular fields of activity, different national/regional legislation and standards). The underlying concept was first presented in (Nunes, I. L., 2005) and the proof of concept for the risk assessment phase was presented in (Monteiro, T., 2006).

In (Nunes, I. L., 2005) it was described the Fuzzy Multiple Attribute Decision Making (FMADM) model developed by the author for the evaluation of risk factors. This model was applied in two different risk assessment contexts, for ergonomic analysis and for risk analysis for work accidents. The ergonomic analysis FMADM model was used in the ERGO_X fuzzy expert system prototype and in the subsequent implementation of the FAST ERGO_X fuzzy expert system. To learn more about ERGO_X and FAST ERGO_X see, for instance, (Nunes, I. L., 2006a, b, 2007, 2009). This article offers a view of the current state of evolution of the FMADM model for the risk analysis for work accidents that was introduced in (Nunes, I. L., 2005) used for the development of the RA_X fuzzy expert system and presents an example applied to the risk management in the construction industry.

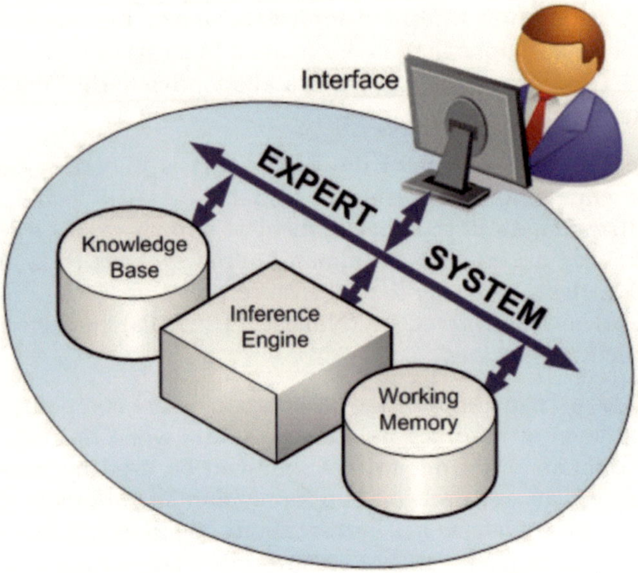

Fig. 2. Basic architecture of an Expert System

Considering the risk management context, as a very brief summary one can say that the FMADM model is used to compute the possibility of occurrence of Cases that are defined in the expert system. "Cases" are what, in classical Risk Analysis terminology, is referred as Risks (e.g., falls, electrical shock, burn, burying due to trench collapse, crushing). A given Case is assumed to be possible to occur based on the evaluation of a set of contributing "Factors". In the RA_X analysis model, three types of Factors are considered: "Hazard", "Safety Control Factors" and "Potentiating Factors". The main objective of the "Hazard" and the "Potentiating Factors" is to characterize the risk factors present on a specific work situation; and the "Safety Control Factors" purpose is to characterize the adequacy of the safety measures implemented in the workplace. Each Factor is evaluated based on a set of relevant "Attributes" that characterize in detail the work situation.

The concept and the analysis model was implemented in the RA_X, which is a fuzzy expert system prototype designed to support risk management for work accidents. This tool can facilitate the practical application of risk management at company level, targeting especially SMEs. The main objectives of the RA_X are the identification and assessment of exposure to occupational risks and the advice on measures to implement in order to control risks, i.e., to eliminate or, at least, to reduce the potential of the occupational risks for accident causation. The system also allows monitoring the evolution of risks over time, by performing trend analysis through the comparison of different risk assessment results regarding the same work situation.

3.1 General structure

RA_X lies in a FMADM model that calculates the risk level for each specific Case (i.e. Risk) based on three main factors: the Hazard itself, the effectiveness of the Safety Control measures set in the workplace, and the presence of a number of other factors, collectively referred as Potentiating Factors.

These main factors are assessed based on Attributes that characterize one particular work situation. Attribute's raw data can be of objective or subjective nature, depending if it is quantitative data obtained from measurements (e.g., height of a scaffold, depth of a trench, voltage of a power line) or qualitative data obtained from opinions of experts (e.g., adequacy, periodicity, acceptability). Figure 3 shows a schematic representation of the RA_X assessment model. The process depicted in the figure will be repeated as many times as the number of Cases to analyze (which may be the total number of cases in the Knowledge Base, or a user selected subset of those).

In this approach it is considered that the data collection phase (depicted inside the boxes in the left hand side of Figure 3) includes the gathering of raw data and their pre-processing (i.e., fuzzification and aggregation) in order to generate the fuzzy attributes that will be used as inputs in the subsequent phase (the risk assessment). Usually each risk results from a single specific hazard but its triggering is affected by different types of safety control measures and potentiating factors. Therefore, for each Case defined in the Knowledge Base the model considers one Hazard fuzzy attribute, and several Safety Control Factors and Potentiating Factors fuzzy attributes.

The risk assessment phase is depicted in the right hand side of Figure 3, illustrating the inference process that uses the attributes as criteria for the Fuzzy Rules that emulate the reasoning process used by human risk analysis experts (note that these fuzzy rules are translated into the FMADM model as discussed in subsection 3.3). The fuzzy evaluation result is defuzzified and presented in a more intelligible way to the users, for instance using sentences in natural language.

Figure 3 illustrates also the type of entities stored in the Knowledge Base (e.g., Fuzzy Sets, Fuzzy Rules) and their use in these two phases. The fuzzification of the raw data is done using continuous fuzzy sets (①) for the objective data, and linguistic variables or discrete fuzzy sets (②) for the subjective data. The objective and subjective attributes resulting from the fuzzification are aggregated using fuzzy aggregation operators (③) (e.g., fuzzy t-norm and fuzzy t-conorms) generating a unique fuzzy attribute that reflects both sources of data. The fuzzy attributes characterizing the hazards, the safety controls measures and the potentiating factors present in the workplace are aggregated according to fuzzy rules (④) that evaluate the risk. Finally the fuzzy result is defuzzified using linguistic variables (⑤) to generate conclusions expressed as natural language sentences. In addition, the conclusions can be explained to users.

The advice phase, also depicted in the right hand side of Figure 3, is performed after the conclusion of the risk assessment and is based on an inference process that uses rules (④) contained in the knowledge base, which identify potential risk control solutions and prioritize them according to the factors that were assessed as more critical in the previous phase.

Hence, building up the RA_X Knowledge Base according to the above described model required the elicitation and representation of knowledge in the risk management domain, which involved the following activities:

- Enumeration of Cases;
- Identification of the Factors that contribute to each specific Case;
- Identification of the Attributes to use in the assessment of each Factor;
- Identification of Measurements to use as data for an Objective Attribute (quantitative) related to an Attribute;
- Identification of Opinions to use as data for a Subjective Attribute (qualitative) related to an Attribute;
- Definition of continuous Fuzzy Sets used for the fuzzification of Objective Attributes;
- Definition of Linguistic Variables used for the fuzzification of Subjective Attributes;
- Definition of Generic Recommendations related to Cases;
- Definition of Specific Recommendations related with Attributes.

The knowledge acquisition is a manual process based on data available on literature, on information collected from experts and on legislation. The initial knowledge acquisition activities for the RA_X were mainly focused on the Construction industry.

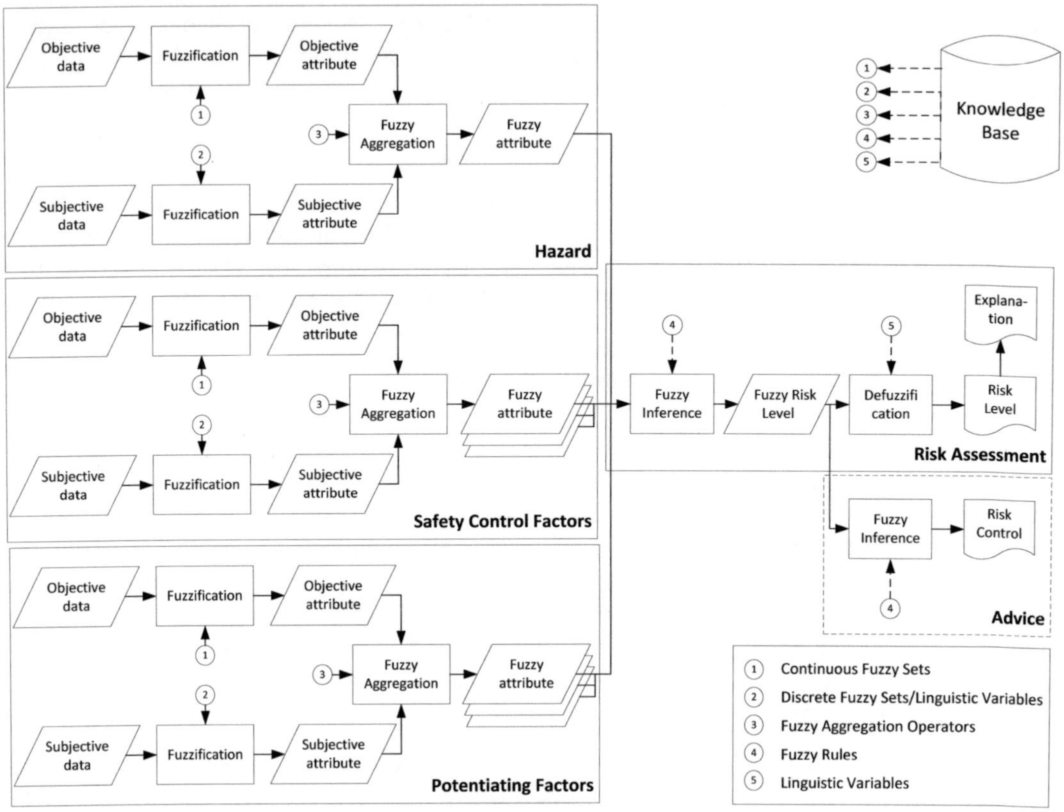

Fig. 3. Schematic representation of the risk assessment model for a Case

3.2 Data collection phase

The data collection is the phase of the process where the risk analysis raw data is gathered and pre-processed (i.e., fuzzified and aggregated) in order to generate the fuzzy attributes that will be used as inputs in the subsequent phase (the risk assessment).

As mentioned before, on a specific risk assessment situation the fuzzy attributes characterizing the three main factors of a particular Case can result from the combination of objective and subjective attributes that relate, respectively, to objective and subjective data. Objective data is typically a quantitative value that can be measured (e.g., the height in meters at which a worker operates), therefore in this model it will be designated as "measurement". Subjective data is a qualitative estimate made by an analyst (e.g., "very high", "high", "and low") and therefore in this model it will be designated as "opinion".

Using the FST principles it is possible to evaluate the degree of membership to some high-level concept based on observed data. Consider, for example, the evaluation of the risk of injury associated with falls from height based on the continuous membership function presented in Figure 4, where the input is a measured height. A low degree of membership to the "falls from height" risk concept (i.e., values close to 0) means the height is safe; while a high degree of membership (i.e., values close to 1) means the risk is unacceptable.

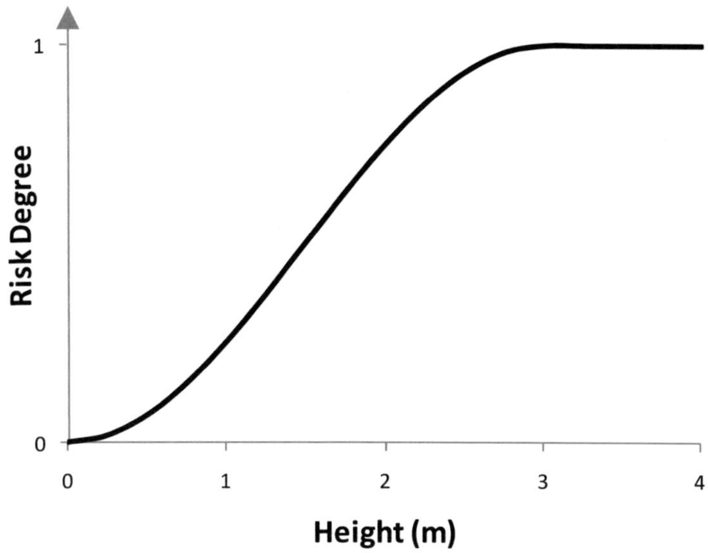

Fig. 4. Fuzzy set for the evaluation of the *risk of falls from height*

The representation of continuous fuzzy sets in the Knowledge Base is done using a parametric method that was discussed in (Nunes, I. L., 2007).

The fuzzification of opinions can use Linguistic Variables (LV). In this approach, due to considerations regarding the numerical efficiency of the computational process, the LV terms were assumed as discrete fuzzy sets. Consider, as an example, the LV "inadequacy" presented in Figure 5, which can be used to evaluate the inadequacy of the protection provided in a workplace, by the Safety Control measures implemented (Nunes, I. L., 2007). An effective protection can be classified using the term "very adequate" (i.e., a membership degree of 0), while an inexistent protection can be classified as "very inadequate" (i.e., membership degree of 1).

The result of the aggregation of the existing objective and subjective attributes is a fuzzy value assigned to the corresponding attribute. In the present model the aggregation of opinions and measurements is done using the OWA operator (Yager, R. R., 1988). With this operator it is possible to assign weights to the different input data sources. This is particularly useful when the sources of information have different levels of reliability. In this case the inputs from more reliable sources have a bigger weight than the ones coming from less reliable sources.

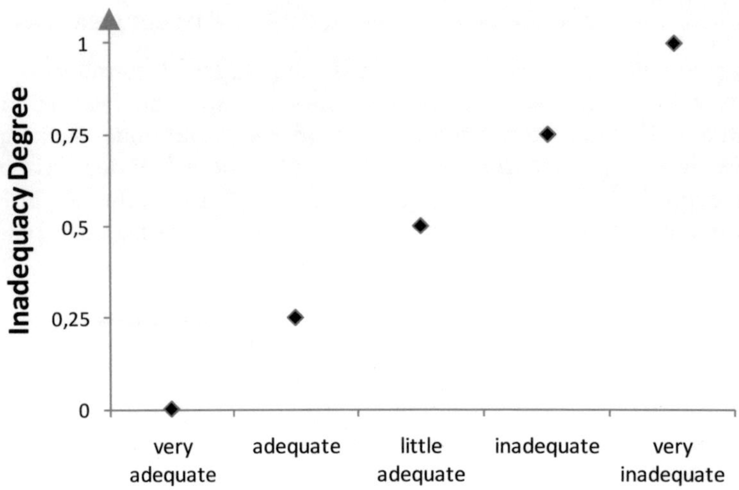

Fig. 5. Linguistic variable "inadequacy" used to evaluate "protection inadequacy"

3.3 Risk assessment phase

3.3.1 Fuzzy inference process

The risk assessment is the phase where the fuzzy attributes related to a Case are processed according to fuzzy rules evaluating the degree of risk present in the workplace. At the end of this phase the fuzzy evaluation result is defuzzified to produce the output to present to the users. The reasoning process used is discussed in this section as well as its FMADM mathematical counterpart.

The main assumption of this fuzzy risk assessment model is that if a hazard is present in a workplace and there is a lack of adequate safety control measures and there are some potentiating factors then there is risk for accident. This can be expressed by the following generic rule:

IF hazard exists **AND**
safety control is inadequate AND (R1)
potentiating factors exist
THEN risk exists

The fuzzy approach allows the use of fuzzy operators to numerically aggregate the different fuzzy attributes that characterize the criteria of the rule and assess the degree of truth of the conclusion. Considering the variety of fuzzy operators the ANDs expressed in the rule can be formulated using different intersection operators, according to desired aggregation behaviour. Therefore, rule [R1] can be translated into a mathematical formula such as:

$$\mu_r = (\mu_h \, \alpha \, \mu_p) * \mu_{pf} \quad \text{(E1)}$$

Where:

μ_r is the Fuzzy membership degree that reflects the risk level;
μ_h is the Fuzzy membership degree that reflects the hazard level for a specific risk;
μ_p is the Fuzzy membership degree that reflects the inadequacy level of the safety control measures set in place to prevent a specific risk;
μ_{pf} is the Fuzzy membership degree that reflects the level of the potentiating factors for a specific risk;
α represents a Fuzzy Intersection aggregation operator that produces a normalized fuzzy value, i.e., in the interval [0, 1]
$*$ represents a Fuzzy Intersection aggregation operator that produces a normalized fuzzy value, i.e., in the interval [0, 1]

Each criteria of the rule (the left side terms of the IF-THEN) can be the result of previous rules of an inference chain. For instance, considering that the protection provided by the safety control measures can be achieved through collective and personnel protection means the evaluation of the criteria "safety control is inadequate" can result from the use of the following rule:

IF collective protection is inadequate **AND**
personnel protection is inadequate (R2)
THEN safety control is inadequate

As before this rule can be translated into a mathematical formula, such as:

$$\mu_p = \mu_{cp} \wedge \mu_{ip} \quad \text{(E2)}$$

Where:

μ_p is the Fuzzy membership degree that reflects the inadequacy of the safety control measures set in place to prevent a specific risk;
μ_{cp} is the Fuzzy membership degree that reflects the inadequacy of the collective protection measures set in place to protect a specific risk;
μ_{ip} is the Fuzzy membership degree that reflects the inadequacy of the personnel protection measures set in place to protect a specific risk;
$\wedge$ represents a Fuzzy Intersection aggregation operator that produces a normalized fuzzy value, i.e., in the interval [0, 1]

Another example relates with the evaluation of the potentiating factors. These factors (e.g., work activity, and environmental, psychosocial and individual factors) do not represent risk by themselves but potentiate and may intensify the negative impact of a hazard. In this case the evaluation of the criteria "potentiating factors exist" can result from the use of the following rule:

IF work activity is inadequate **OR**
environmental factors are inadequate **OR**
psychosocial factors are inadequate OR (R3)
individual factors are inadequate
THEN potentiating factors exist

Naturally such inference chains can have multiple layers that address the information regarding a specific concept with difference levels of detail (i.e., complexity, vagueness and relevance). An example of the next level of the inference chain rules is the evaluation of the criteria "work activity is inadequate". One should note that this evaluation is risk dependent. Considering, for instance, the criteria to assess the "work activity" potentiating factor regarding the risk of "falls from height", the following rule could be used:

IF type of floor/tidiness is inadequate **OR**
manual materials handling exists **OR**
use of tools exists **OR** (R4)
handling of suspended loads exists
THEN work activity is inadequate

This type of rule can be assessed numerically considering the respective membership degrees using a generic assessment formula such as:

$$\mu_{pf_i} = \cup_{j=1}^{n} \mu_{f_{ij}} \tag{E3}$$

Where:

μ_{pf_i} is the Fuzzy membership degree that reflects the inadequacy level of ith potentiating factor for a specific risk;
$\mu_{f_{ij}}$ is the Fuzzy membership degree that reflects the inadequacy level of the jth factor contributing to the ith potentiating factor for a specific risk;
U represents a Fuzzy Union aggregation operator that produces a normalized fuzzy value, i.e., in the interval [0, 1]

3.3.2 Fuzzy operators selection

The selection of the aggregation operators was based on the eight selection criteria proposed by (Zimmermann, H.-J., 2001) mentioned above. Table 1 synthesizes the main fuzzy operators used in the RA_X, and also the value of the parameters adopted for the parametric operators.

Equation #	Fuzzy Operator			Parameter
E1	α	Dubois and Prade Intersection	$\mu_{A\alpha B} = \frac{\mu_A \mu_B}{\max(\mu_A, \mu_B, \alpha)}, \alpha\epsilon[0,1]$	α = 0.9
E1	*	Algebraic product	$\mu_{A.B} = \mu_A . \mu_B$	-
E2	^	Min	$\mu_{A\cap B} = \min(\mu_A, \mu_B)$	-
E3	∪	Dubois and Prade Union	$\mu_{A\alpha' B} = \frac{\mu_A + \mu_B - \mu_A\mu_B - \min(1-\alpha', \mu_A, \mu_B)}{\max(1-\mu_A, 1-\mu_B, \alpha')}, \alpha'\epsilon[0,1]$	α' = 0.6

Table 1. Fuzzy operators adopted in the RA_X model

The Dubois and Prade Intersection operator is an operator with compensation which is controlled by the α parameter. This operator was selected to aggregate two main factors, Hazard and lack of adequate Safety Control. The result of this aggregation reflects the extension of the Hazard that is not mitigated by the Safety Control (Prevention and Protection) measures implemented.

The Algebraic Product was selected to combine the result of the above aggregation with the Potentiating factors. The rationale behind this selection is that there is an identical contribution of both terms to the risk level.

The Min operator is used in the aggregation of data regarding the levels of Collective and Personnel Protection. This operator was selected because it reflects the lack of protection that is still present in the workplace after combining all the types of protective measures set in place.

The Dubois and Prade Union operator is an operator with compensation which is controlled by the α' parameter. This operator is used twice. It is used first to aggregate the Attributes that characterize each Potentiating factor, and a second time to aggregate the results of all individual Potentiating factors, producing a global result. The use of this operator allows the simulation of the synergistic effect resulting from the simultaneous presence of several Potentiating factors.

3.3.3 Defuzzification process

The risk assessment results are presented as crisp risk levels which are obtained through a defuzzification process that uses a VL like the one presented in Figure 6. Note that the definition of the defuzzification fuzzy sets has to consider the relationship between the results distribution in the [0, 1] domain and the linguistic evaluation categories. Since the evaluation process uses product operators and the terms in the interval [0, 1], the evaluation results tend to be shifted to zero; therefore, the width of the fuzzy sets that reflect each linguistic term varies to accommodate this characteristic of the evaluation process. For a

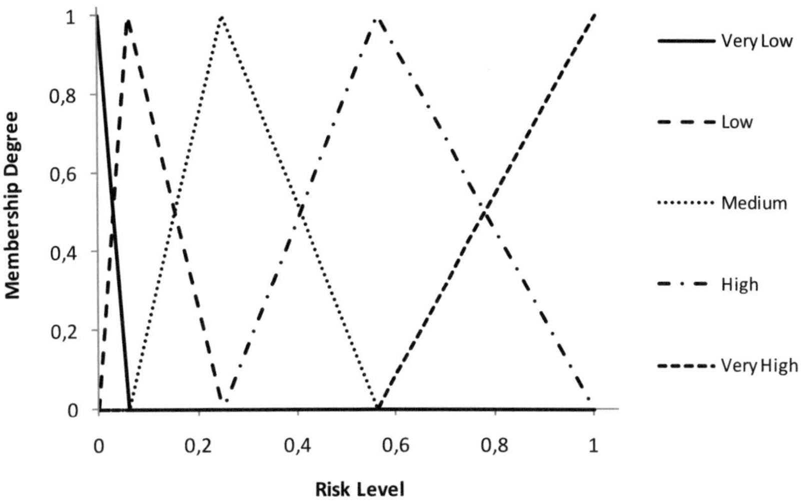

Fig. 6. Linguistic variable "risk level" used to defuzzify the risk assessment results

given fuzzy risk level the linguistic term is selected from the fuzzy set with higher membership degree. For instance, a risk level of 0.5 has a membership degree of 0.2 to "Medium" and 0.8 to "High", consequently the qualifier to use will be "High".

The selected qualifier is used for building a sentence in natural language that presents the result to the user, using the generic format:

The risk of [descriptor of risk] is [qualifier]

For instance, a result from a risk assessment can be "The risk of electrical shock is very high".

3.3.4 Explanation process

The system can also offer explanations about the results presented. This is done using a backward chain inference process that identifies, ranks and presents the attributes that have high values (above a specified threshold) and that more significantly contributed to the computed level of risk. The explanations use the following generic format:

"*The risk of [descriptor of risk] is [qualifier] because*:
The [$attribute_1$] is [*qualifier*] (fuzzy value)
The [$attribute_2$] is [*qualifier*] (fuzzy value)
...
The [$attribute_n$] is [*qualifier*] (fuzzy value)"

Where the detailed explanations are sorted in decreasing order of the respective attributes fuzzy value.

3.3.5 Advice phase

The advice phase is performed after the conclusion of the risk assessment, and offers recommendations about safety measures adequate to control the risk for situations where the risk level is Medium or higher. The recommendations can be generic and specific. Generic recommendations refer to advice (i.e., legislation, guidelines, best practice) relating to a type of risk in general (e.g., risk of falls from height); while specific recommendations refer to advice that addresses a specific type of attribute that contributes to the risk (e.g., collective protection installed in site).

The generic recommendations use the following format:

"Regarding the risk of [descriptor of risk] consider the following advice
Generic $Recommendation_1$
...
Generic $Recommendation_n$"

The selection of the specific recommendations is performed using a backward chaining inference process based on the risk assessment fuzzy rules. This process identifies and ranks the key attributes that contributed to the risk assessment result (i.e., the attributes with high membership values), and provides recommendations in this order.

The specific recommendations use the following format:

"Regarding the [attribute1] of the risk of [descriptor of risk] consider the following advice
Specific Recommendation1
...
Specific Recommendationn"

4. Application example

In this section it will be demonstrated the use of the RA_X fuzzy model in support of risk management. The example presented analyzes a construction work activity, which is pouring concrete into the forms of the structure of a building. Since the activity is performed on a platform located several meters in the air, the risk analysis presented regards the risk of "falls from height".

Risk	Hazard	Attributes	
Falls from height	• Work at height	• Height	
	Safety Control Factors	**Attributes**	
	• Collective Protection (Physical)	• Safety barriers	• Safe Access
	• Collective Protection (Organizational)	• Supervision • Security Signs/ Warnings	• Techniques and Procedures
	• Personnel Protection	• Harness/Lifeline	
	Potentiating Factors	**Attributes**	
	• Work Activity	• Type of floor/Tidiness • Manual materials handling • Use of power/heavy tools • Handling suspended loads	• Interaction with other work activities
	• Environmental Factors	• Wind • Rain • Cold • Noise	• Vibration • Illumination • Dust
	• Psychosocial Factors	• Work pace • Extra Work	• Stress
	• Individual Factors	• Hearing • Vision • Alcohol consumption	• Safety behaviour • Type of footwear • Safety training

Table 2. Example of main factors and attributes considered in the assessment of the risk "falls from height"

As explained before, the risk assessment is based on attributes related with three categories of main factors (hazard, safety control factors and potentiating factors). Table 2 illustrates the main factors and examples of corresponding attributes for assessing the risk of "falls from height". For example, "Work at height" is the Hazard and "Height" is the attribute required for this analysis. The list of attributes is used during the data collection phase to ask for the relevant input data for the risk analysis. If the user doesn't provide data to some attribute the model considers that this attribute is in such a state that is not contributing to the risk.

Table 3 synthesizes the application of the RA_X model. The collected input data is shown in column "Raw Data".

	Attribute	Raw Data	Fuzzy Attribute Value	Aggregated Values		Fuzzy Risk Level (Crisp Risk Level)
Hazard						
Work at height	Height	4 m	1	1		
Safety Control						
Individual	Harness/Life line	Inadequate	0.75	0.75		
Collective	Barrier	Inexistent	1			
Potentiating Factors						
Work Activity	Type of floor/Tidiness	Inadequate	0.75	0.75	0.95	0.72 (High)
	Use of power/heavy tools	Very adequate	0			
Environmental Factors	Illumination	Adequate	0.25	0.25		
Individual	Safety behaviour	Little adequate	0.5	0.83		
	Type of footwear	Very adequate	0			
	Safety training	Inadequate	0.75			

Table 3. RA_X application example in the assessment of the risk "falls from height" for an activity of pouring concrete

In this case the Height was obtained by measurement and the other data are opinions. The fuzzification of the data was done using the membership function presented in Figure 4 for the Height, and the Linguistic Variable "inadequacy" (Figure 5) for the remaining subjective data (refer to subsection 3.2), and the results of the fuzzification process are presented in column "Fuzzy Attribute Value". The results of the partial fuzzy inference processes are shown in column "Aggregated Values" (refer to subsection 3.3). Finally, the fuzzy risk level and the corresponding crisp level, obtained by defuzzification (see Figure 6) are presented in column "Fuzzy Risk Level (Crisp Risk Level)" (refer to subsection 3.3.3).

In short, the risk assessment based on the RA_X model is that there is a high risk of falls from height for an activity where the workers operate at a height of 4 m, the best protection offered is deemed as inadequate and the more relevant potentiating factors are the inadequate type of floor and safety training. The output of this assessment is done using a sentence in natural language, such as:

"The risk of falls from height is High"

As mentioned before the system can offer explanations about the results presented. The explanation regarding this risk assessment would adopt the following format:

"The risk of falls from height is High because:

The Height is very inadequate (1)
The Harness/Life line is inadequate (0.75)
The Type of floor/Tidiness is inadequate (0.75)
The Safety training is inadequate (0.75)"

Regarding advice the RA_X can offer generic and specific recommendations that can be customized to the regional specificity of the users. Generic recommendations to the risk of falls from height include multimedia documents or internet links to, for instance, regulations, guidelines, best practices or software tools (e.g., European Directive 2001/45/EC (EU, 2001), European norms for protection against falls from heights (CEN, 2008), OSHA's Guidelines for the Prevention of Falls (OSHA, 1998), (OSHA, 2010c), OSHA Construction eTool (OSHA, 2010a), HSE's Interactive Guide (HSE, 2010)). Specific recommendations include the same type of references, but addressing the individual issues that emerged as contributing significantly to the risk. In the present example, the recommendations would address themes like improving personnel protection (e.g., (BSI, 2005)), collective protection (e.g. (NASC, 2008)), type of working floor (e.g. (OSHA, 2010b)) or safety training (e.g. (HSE, 2008)).

5. Conclusion

Fuzzy Logics has been used to handle uncertainty in human-centred systems (e.g., ergonomics, safety, occupational stress) analysis, as a way to deal with complex, imprecise, uncertain and vague data.

This chapter presented the main features of the RA_X FMADM model, which was developed to implement a fuzzy expert system for supporting risk management activities. In the current stage a prototype was implemented for test and validation purposes. The support of a proactive risk management is achieved by assessing potential factors that contribute for occupational accident occurrence and by guiding on the adoption of safety measures.

The RA_X is meant to be a flexible and easy to use system, which can process both objective and subjective input data and provide risk assessment and advice for a broad variety of occupational activities. The results are offered using natural language. The system also provides means to perform trend analysis supporting the follow-up and monitoring of risks in work situations.

Following a quite simple Knowledge Engineering process, the Knowledge Base of the RA_X expert system can be updated to incorporate new risks, broadening the scope of application, and can be customized to different national realities accommodating, for instance, to different legal frameworks or level of action requirements, which affect the assessment process and/or the advice offered.

The advantages of this fuzzy system compared with traditional methodologies based on the estimation of two parameters (probability and severity) are obvious. First, the system is more thorough on the risk assessment, considering a wider range of factors, contributing to the implementation of a holistic approach to the assessment of risks, namely by including organizational and individual factors. Another important advantage is the fact that the methodology used allows the combination of objective and subjective data in a coherent way. Finally, it supports the full cycle of the risk management process (including hazard identification, risk assessment, advice on risk control and monitoring support), which is key for the promotion of safety and health at work.

The RA_X system is ongoing tests and evaluations by experts that are representative of the expected typical users of this new approach.

A future step is the web implementation of the RA_X system so that the most updated set of knowledge can be remotely accessed, which allows also exploiting the benefits offered by mobile devices, such as Tablets or iPads.

6. References

BSI (2005). BS 8437:2005. Code of practice for selection, use and maintenance of personal fall protection systems and equipment for use in the workplace, British Standard Institutions.

BSI (2007). Occupational health and safety management systems - Requirements, BS OHSAS 18001: 2007, British Standard Institutions.

CEN (2008). EN 363: Personal fall protection equipment. Personal fall protection systems. European Committee for Standardization - CEN.

EASHW (2002). New trends in accident prevention due to the changing world of work European Agency for Safety and Health at Work. (http://osha.europa.eu/en/publications/reports/208).

EASHW (2010). Statistics European Agency for Safety and Health at Work. http://osha.europa.eu/en/statistics/index.stm .

EC (2009). Occupational Health and Safety Risks in the Healtcare Sector European Commision http://www.eurogip.fr/docs/Commission_europeenne_guide_secteur_sante_2009_EN.pdf .

EU (2001). Directive 2001/45/EC of 27June 2001 concerning the minimum safety and health requirements for the use of work equipment by workers at work. Official Journal L 195 , 19/07/2001 P. 0046 - 0049 http://eur-lex.europa.eu/LexUriServ/LexUriServ.do?uri=CELEX:32001L0045:EN:HTML.

Eurostat (2009). Population and social conditions (http://epp.eurostat.ec.europa.eu/cache/ITY_OFFPUB/KS-SF-09-063/EN/KS-SF-09-063-EN.PDF). Eurostat. Statistics in focus 63.

Gupta, J. N. D., Forgionne, G. A.& M.T., M., Eds., 2006. Intelligent Decision-making Support Systems: Foundations, Applications and Challenges (Decision Engineering), Springer.

Harms-Ringdahl, L. (2001). Safety Analysis: Principles And Practice In Occupational Safety, Taylor & Francis.

HSE (2008). Health and safety training. What you need to know (INDG345). Available at http://www.hse.gov.uk/pubns/indg345.pdf Health and Safety Executive.

HSE (2010). Fallington (Interactive guide). Available at http://www.hse.gov.uk/falls/heightaware/flashindex.htm. Health and Safety Executive.

Monteiro, T. (2006). Análise de Riscos na Construção Civil. Construção e Validação de Base de Conhecimento de um Sistema Pericial. Lisboa. Lisboa-Portugal.

NASC (2008). SG4:05 Appendix A. Interim Guidance on Collective Fall Prevention Systems in Scaffolding. National Access & Scaffolding Confederation. http://v35.up1.universalpixel.com/ams/assets/NASC532147/SG4_05%20Appendix%20A_web.pdf. National Access & Scaffolding Confederation.

NSW. 2011. "Six steps to Occupational Health and Safety. Available at http://www.une.edu.au/od/files/OHSSixsteps.pdf."

Nunes, I. L. (2005). Fuzzy Multicriteria Model for Ergonomic workplace analysis and Risk analysis. Information Technology, Knowledge Management and Engineering for Enterprise Productivity and Quality of Working Life (International Conference: Computer-Aided Ergonomics and Safety - CAES'05), Kosice-Slovak Republic.

Nunes, I. L. (2006a). ERGO_X - The Model of a Fuzzy Expert System for Workstation Ergonomic Analysis. International Encyclopedia of Ergonomics and Human Factors. Karwowski, CRC Press: 3114-3121.

Nunes, I. L. (2006b). Quantitative Method for Processing Objective Data from Posture Analysis. International Encyclopedia of Ergonomics and Human Factors. Karwowski, CRC Press: 3306-3309.

Nunes, I. L. (2007). Knowledge Acquisition for the Development of an Upper- Body Work-Related Musculoskeletal Disorders Analysis Tool. Human Factors and Ergonomics in Manufacturing 17(2): 149-162.

Nunes, I. L. (2009). FAST ERGO_X – a tool for ergonomic auditing and work-related musculoskeletal disorders prevention. WORK: A Journal of Prevention, Assessment, & Rehabilitation 34(2): 133-148.

Nunes, I. L. (2010a). Handling Human-Centered Systems Uncertainty Using Fuzzy Logics – A Review. The Ergonomics Open Journal 3: 38-48.

Nunes, I. L. (2010b). Risk Analysis for Work Accidents based on a Fuzzy Logics Model. 5th International Conference of Working on Safety - On the road to vision zero?, Roros. Norway.

OSHA (1998). OSHA 3146 (Revised): Fall Protection in Construction. http://www.osha.gov/Publications/osha3146.pdf, U.S. Department of Labor. Occupational Safety and Health Administration.

OSHA (2010a). OSHA Construction eTool. http://63.234.227.130/SLTC/etools/construction/falls/mainpage.html (accessed in November 2010), U.S. Department of Labor. Occupational Safety and Health Administration.

OSHA (2010b). Standard 1910.23: Guarding floor and wall openings and holes. http://www.osha.gov/pls/oshaweb/owadisp.show_document?p_table=STAND

ARDS&p_id=9715. U.S. Department of Labor. Occupational Safety and Health Administration.

OSHA (2010c). Standard 1926.501: Duty to have fall protection. http://63.234.227.130/pls/oshaweb/owadisp.show_document?p_table=STANDARDS&p_id=10757 (accessed in November 2010). U.S. Department of Labor. Occupational Safety and Health Administration.

Reason, J. (1997). Managing the risks of organizational accidents, Ashgate Publishing Ltd,Aldershot Hants

Turban, E., Aronson, J.& Liang, T.-P. (2004). Decision Support Systems and Intelligent Systems.

Turban, E., Sharda, R.& Delen, D. (2010). Decision Support and Business Intelligence Systems, Prentice Hall.

Yager, R. R. (1988). On Ordered Weighted Averaging Aggregation Operators in Multicriteria Decison Making. IEEE Transactions on Systems, Man, and Cybernetics 18(1): 183-190.

Zimmermann, H.-J. (2001). Fuzzy Set Theory and Its Applications, Kluwer Academic Publishers.

3

A Fuzzy Approach for Risk Analysis with Application in Project Management

Sina Khanmohammadi[1] and Javad Jassbi[2]
[1]Faculty of Science, Technology and Creative Arts, School of Engineering and Technology, University of Hertfordshire, Hertfordshire,
[2]Department of Industrial Management, Islamic Azad University, Science and Research Branch, Tehran,
[1]UK
[2]Iran

1. Introduction

The Critical Path Method (CPM) and its development to probabilistic environment, the Program Evaluation and Review Technique (PERT), are the most common tools for predicting and managing different short time or long time projects. However, one of the main difficulties in using mathematical models in real world applications is the vagueness and uncertainty of data and parameters such as activity durations and risky conditions. The constructed network for project management (as a mathematical model) is an aid for control of project implementation with deterministic time durations. However, realization of this approach is difficult in the situation where most of activities will be executed for the first time. One solution offered for this difficulty is the assignment of probabilistic values for estimated durations of activities. In PERT, three estimations called pessimistic, most likely and optimistic values are assigned for each activity. Then the mean duration and its standard deviation are calculated by

$$D = \frac{a + 4m + b}{6} \tag{1}$$

and

$$\sigma = \frac{b - a}{6} \tag{2}$$

Where a, m and b are the optimistic, most likely and pessimistic values respectively. D is the expected (weighted mean) duration of activity and σ is the standard deviation of the three values (Kerzner, 2009). The project duration (sum of durations of critical path) is estimated by using the estimated durations of activities. Also, the probability of finishing the project before a predicted time (by using PERT) is calculated based on the standard deviations without considering other real world factors such as probability of impacts on project (such as inflation or stagnation) , impact threat and ability to retaliate. Hence a new approach based on fuzzy inference system and fuzzy decision making is introduced to have more realistic procedure for project management in real world applications. Fuzzy set is introduced by Zadeh in 1965 (Zadeh, 1965). Different applications of fuzzy sets are studied by researches in different fields (Jamshidi et al., 1993). T. J. Ross has published an interesting book on fuzzy sets theory and its applications in engineering (Ross, 2010). Several papers are also published on applications of fuzzy sets in project management (Chanas et al., 2002; Shipley et al, 1997). M. F. Shipley et al. have used the fuzzy logic approach for determining probabilistic fuzzy expected values in a project management application (Shipley et al, 1996). An extension of their method is introduced and used for determination of expected values for estimated delays of activities in (Khanmohammadi et al., 2001). The procedure introduced here deals with defining multi-purpose criticalities for activities where some other features such as probability of impact, impact threat and ability to retaliate are considered as criticality factors of activities in project management process. In this way the risky situations (vulnerabilities) of activities are calculated using a fuzzy inference system which will be used for calculating the risky situation for each activity as a main criticality factor.

Considerable quantitative models have been introduced in literature to calculate the level of risk; which is simply defined as the rate of threat or future deficit of any system imposed by controllable or uncontrollable variables (Chavas, 2004; Doherty, 2000). Several factors such as probability of occurrence, impact threat and ability to retaliate are introduced as affecting factors on the risk. Then it is tried to find the mathematical relation between affecting factors and the value (level) of the risk (Li & Liao, 2007; McNeil et al., 2005). The concept of risk is considerably wide. It can contain strategic, financial, operational or any other type of risk.

The concept of fuzzy risky conditions for activities is introduced in sections 2 and 3. In section 4 the concept of Multi-Critical PERT by considering risky levels for activities is introduced and a typical project network is considered as a case study for analyzing the effect of imposing the risky level of activities to criticality. The results are compared to classic PERT by means of Mont Carlo simulation using random variables. Another typical example, project management of rescue robot that provides preliminary processes for helping injured people before the arrival of rescue teams, is studied in section 5. Analysis of obtained results and conclusions are presented in section 6.

2. Classic and fuzzy risk analysis

Fig. 1 shows a classic and simple model of risk analysis. It consists of two factors: Impact threat and ability to retaliate. In this model the risk value is classified in four groups. Each group represents a risky condition for the system (organization, project, activity …). Fig. 2 shows the points (situations) with identical risky levels. The distributions of points with the identical risks (contours of different levels) are also presented in Fig. 2. Points O and + represent the risky situations for two systems with ability to retaliate and impact threats of (1,8) and (4.9,5.1) respectively.

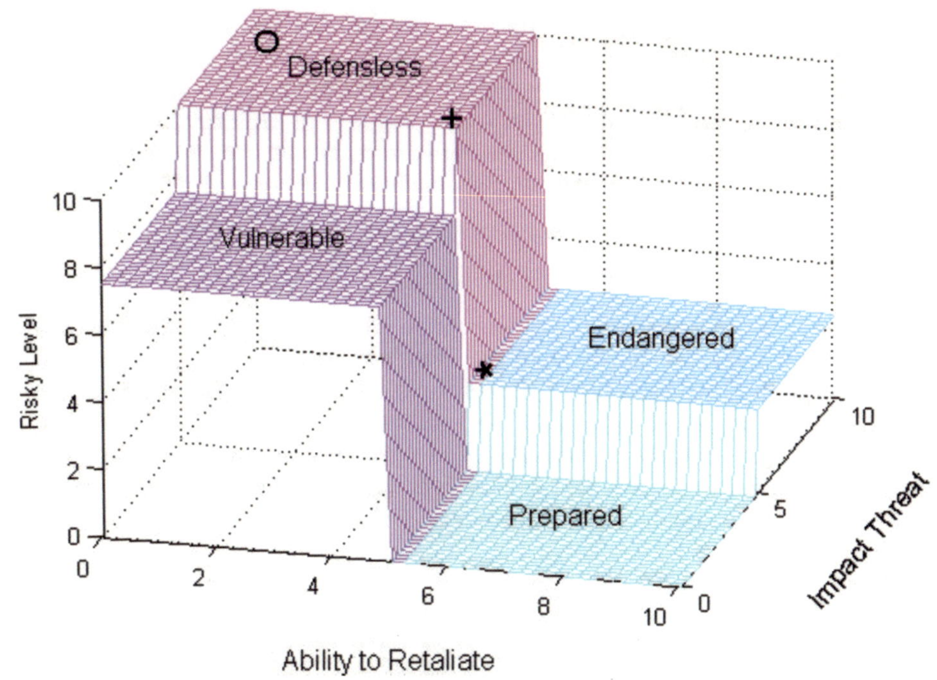

Fig. 1. Risky situations classified in 4 levels

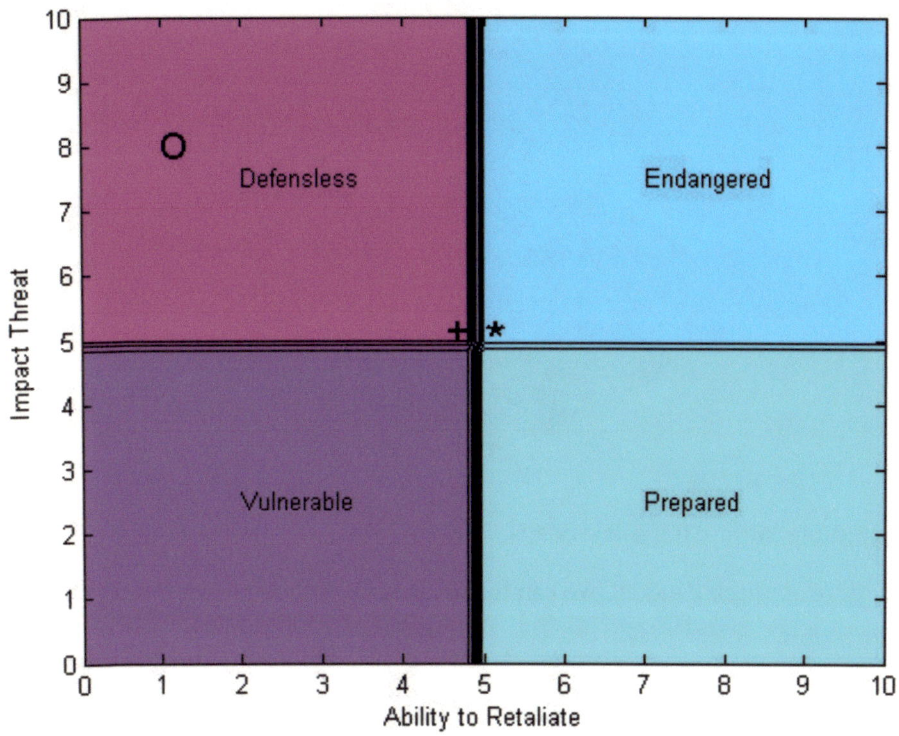

Fig. 2. Different levels of situations (contours of Fig. 1.)

This model is very simple, but it has some structural drawbacks. For example the system + which is in Defenseless situation will change to entirely different condition (Endangered), point (*), with infinity small deviation in ability to retaliate. Also because of its geometrical structure, this model suffers from the lack of considering additional parameters for risk analysis. Another method which has gained more attraction in the risk analysis literature is the model presented by Eq. (3), based on the linear combination of ability to retaliate and impact threat.

$$\text{Risk} = (\text{ability to retaliate}) \times (\text{impact threat}) \quad (3)$$

Fig. 3 represents the continuous increasing surface (risk levels) generated by means of Eq. (3). Two particular levels are shown by the cutting planes K1 and K2. Positions O, + and * are also presented in this figure. Fig. 4 shows some contours of risky surface. As it is seen, by using this model any small change in the values of impact threat and ability to retaliate will cause a very small deviation on the risky level of system. This model is more realistic than the one presented by Figs. 1 and 2. However, it also has its limitations for real world applications because it simplifies the complicated relation between different factors to a linear relation.

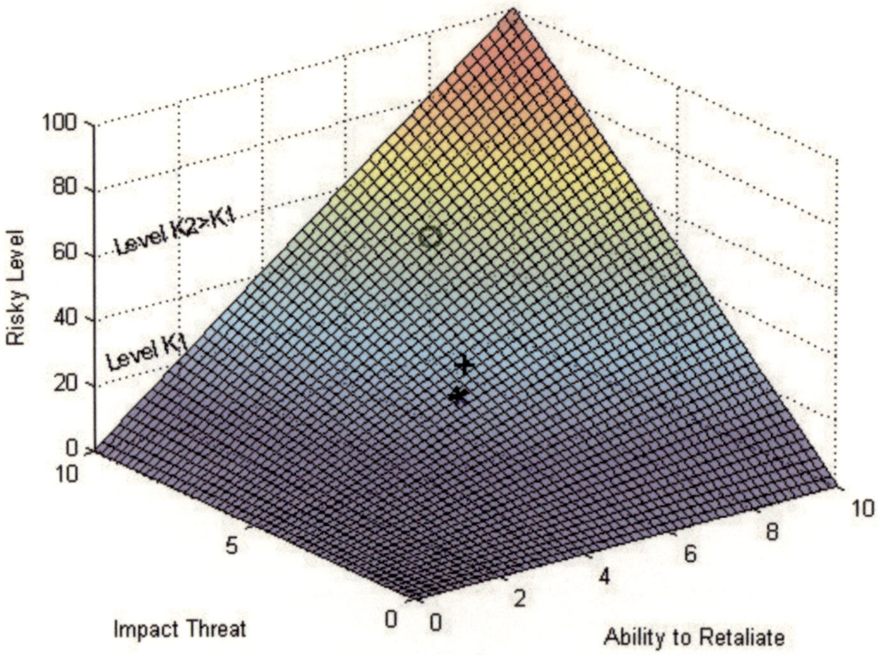

Fig. 3. Continuous surface for risk levels

To have a more applicable model, we can formulate our problem as an input output system by:

$$R = F(X) \quad (4)$$

Where X is the set of input variables which affect the level of the risk, R is the level of the risk and F(.) is a nonlinear function (Kreinovich et al., 2000).

The problem here is to find an appropriate model by which the level of risk of the system can be determined in complex situations where there is no access to all data, or the historical data is useless. This problem may be solved by using Fuzzy inference system.

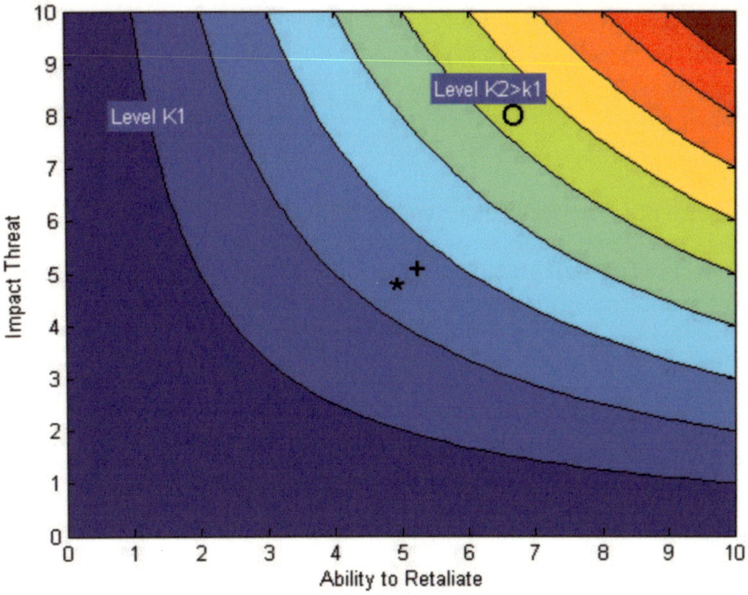

Fig. 4. Some contours of Fig. 3.

3. Fuzzy model

Fuzzy inference systems (FIS) are rule-based systems with concepts and operations associated with fuzzy set theory and fuzzy logic (Mendel, 2001; Ross, 2010). These systems map an input space to an output state; therefore, they allow constructing structures that can be used to generate responses (outputs) to certain stimulations (inputs), based on stored knowledge on how the responses and stimulations are related. The knowledge is stored in the form of a rule base, i.e. a set of rules that express the relations between inputs and the expected outputs of the system. Sometimes this knowledge is obtained by eliciting information from specialists. These systems are known as fuzzy expert systems (Takács, 2004). Another common denomination for FIS is fuzzy control systems (see for example (Mendel, 2001)).

FIS are usually divided in two categories (Mendel, 2001; Takagi & Sugeno, 1985): multiple input, multiple output (MIMO) systems, where the system returns several outputs based on the inputs it receives; and multiple input, single output (MISO) systems, where only one output is returned from multiple inputs. Since MIMO systems can be decomposed into a set of MISO systems working in parallel, all that follows will be exposed from a MISO point of view (Mamdani & Assilian, 1999). In our risk analysis model a fuzzy inference system is introduced for calculating the risky situations of systems by considering different factors such as probability, impact threat and ability to retaliate (Cho et al., 2002; Nguene & Finger, 2007). Fig. 5 shows the block diagram of a multi input single output fuzzy risk analysis system for the mentioned factors (Carr & Tah, 2001).

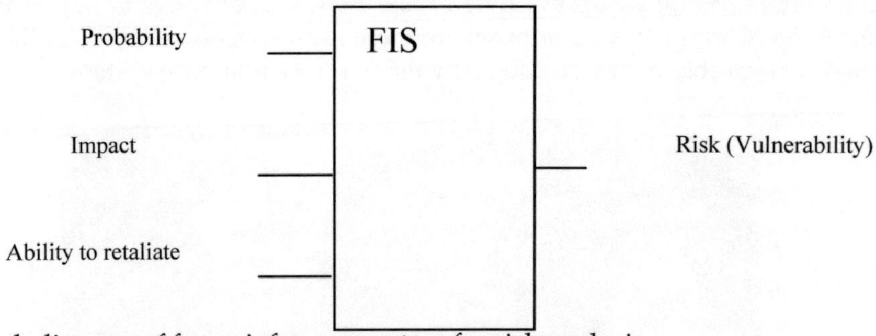

Fig. 5. Block diagram of fuzzy inference system for risk analysis

In this work the following Bell shape membership function is used to determine the fuzzy values of inputs for determining the risky levels of activities by FIS.

$$\mu_A(x) = \frac{1}{1 + d(x-c)^2} \tag{5}$$

Where $\mu_A(x)$ is the membership of variable x in fuzzy value A, c is the median of the fuzzy value and d is the shape parameter. Fig. 6 shows the bell shape membership functions for different fuzzy verbal values.

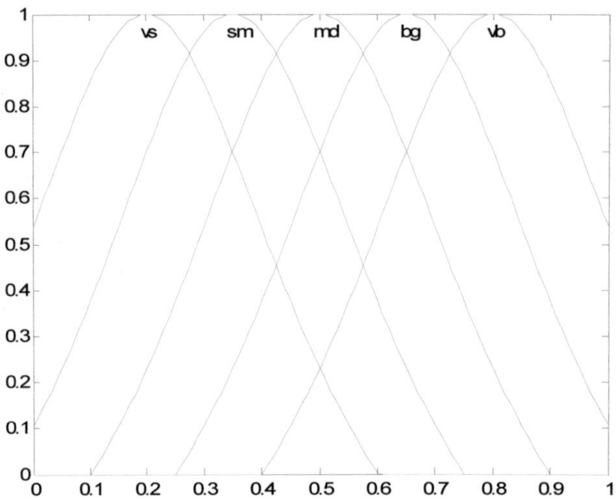

Fig. 6. Membership functions of different fuzzy verbal values vs: Very Small, sm: Small, md: Medium, bg: Big, vb: Very Big

The reason for implementing bell shape membership function is that because of its smoothness (comparing Triangular memberships), and simple formula (comparing Gaussian memberships) it is more appropriate for getting qualitative data from experts.

This model is implemented to the simple model of risk analysis, presented in section 2, to have an idea on the main difference between the classic and fuzzy risky levels. Fig. 7 shows the surface and counters of risky levels of organizations +, and O for 50% probability of impact.

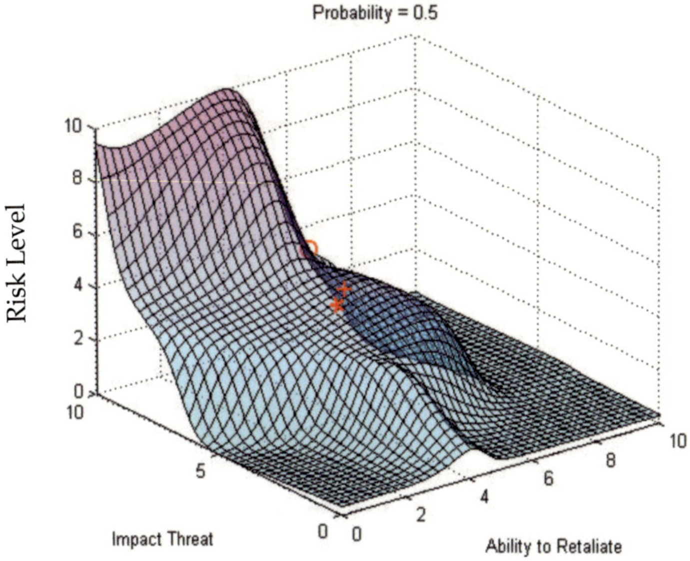

(a)

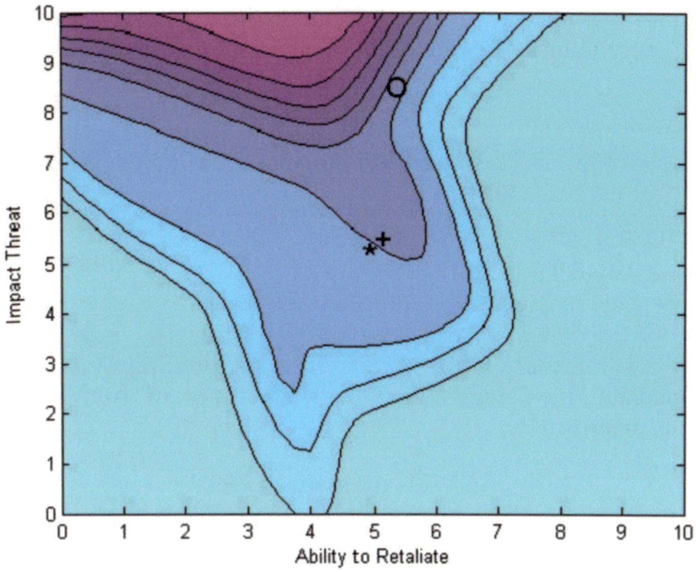

(b)

Fig. 7. (a) Risky surface and (b) Counters of the simple example by using fuzzy inference system

As it is seen in Fig. 7, organization + which is in appropriately Defenseless situation will change to appropriately Endangered situation, point **(*)**, with infinity small deviations in ability to retaliate and in impact threat, which is more realistic comparing to the classic one. To have an idea on utilization of risk management on criticality of activities besides other criticality criteria, the multi critical PERT is introduced in section 4.

4. Multi critical PERT by considering risky levels

The multi critical PERT uses the data presented by table 1 to define the multi-purpose criticality of activities.

Activity	a	m	b	V	PFA	RLA	SFA	SCA	COR	MPC

Table 1. Data used by Multi-Critical PERT

The procedure for using these data to calculate the multi-purpose criticalities of activities is as follows:

Algorithm

Step 1. Perform classic PERT to calculate Durations of activities D, variances V, Earliest Start Times ES, Latest Finish times LF, Free slack times FS and Total slack times TS, where scheduled times ST may be imposed to different events.

Step 2. Calculate the Duration Range of activities DR=LF-ES.

Step 3. Calculate the Probability of Finishing each Activity PFA in duration range DR, by considering duration D and standard deviation $\sigma = \sqrt{V}$.

$$PFA = p(D \leq DR) \tag{6}$$

Step 4. Use the fuzzy inference system to calculate the Risky Level of each Activity RLA by using the fuzzy values of probability of impact pr, impact treat im, and ability to retaliate ar.

The following experimental data gathered from experts are fed to ANFIS (Artificial Neural Fuzzy Inference System) in MATLAB and 14 appropriate FIS rules (Fig. 8) are generated by means of "genfis3" for the case study.

Probability = [1 .5 1.2 .8 .4 1.7 .8 .2 .2 .7 .5 .5 1 1 .6 .1 .3 .4]
Impact = [10 0 5 5 5 2 7 0 8 8 9 3 10 10 10 8 2 10 2 6 .8]
Ability to retaliate = [4 10 5 5 2 3 3 5 2 7 5 5 3 2 10 0 8 4 6 8 1]
Risky level = [7.5 0 1 3 0 5 1 0 4 2 .5 0 4.5 2.5 0 10 .5 3 0 0 0]

Step 5. Normalize the free slack times of activities by dividing them to their maximum value. Calculate the Severity of Free slack times of Activities SFA based on durations of activities by:

$$\text{SFA} = 1\text{- normalized FS} \tag{7}$$

Step 6. Normalize the total slack times of activities by dividing them to their maximum value. Calculate the Severity of Criticalities of Activities SCA based on durations of activities by:

$$\text{SCA} = 1\text{- normalized TS} \tag{8}$$

Step 7. Perform CPM to calculate total slacks of activities where RLAs are used instead of durations for activities to calculate the criticalities based on risky levels (COR). Normalize CORs by dividing them to their maximum value.

Step 8. Use V, SFA, SCA, PFA, RLA and COR as criteria with corresponding weighs W_i (defined by experts), to calculate Multi-Purpose Criticalities (MPC) of activities, where for each activity:

$$MPC = w_1 \times V + w_2 \times PFA + w_3 \times RLA + w_4 \times SFA + w_5 \times SCA + w_6 \times COR \quad (9)$$

Step 9. Classify activities based on MPCs.

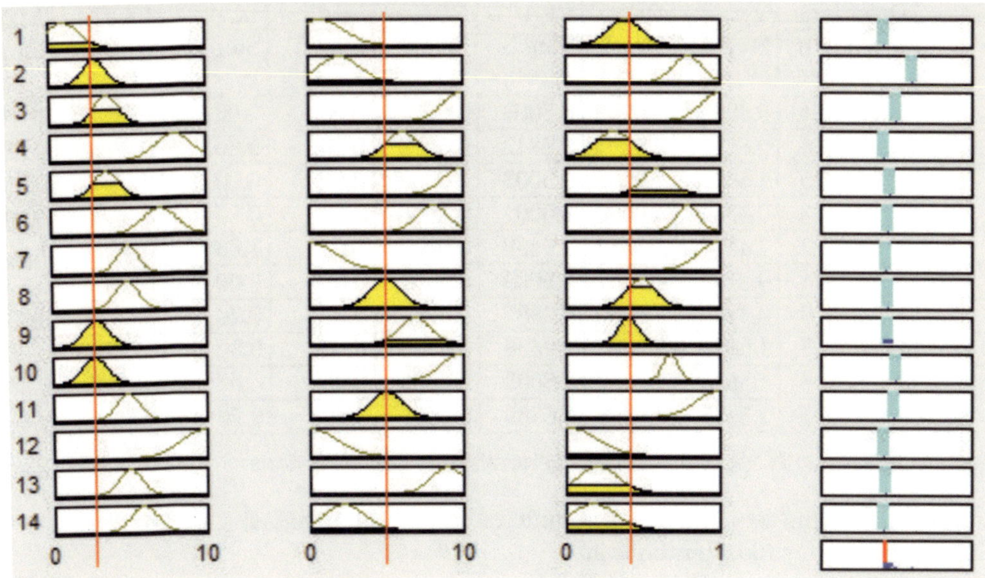

Fig. 8. Rule base generated by ANFIS

Fig. 9 shows the network representation of a typical project. The data for activities is represented in table 2.

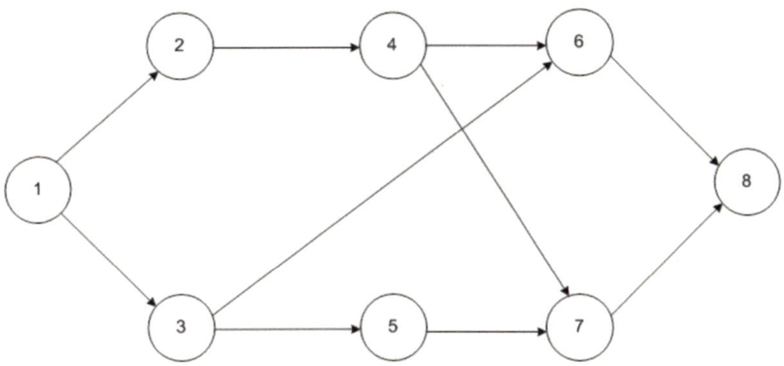

Fig. 9. Network representation of typical project

To compare the efficiency of multi critical PERT with the classic one, 1000 tests are performed using Mont Carlo simulation by generating uniform distributed random numbers r to be used in Equations (10) and (11). For each activity, two costs of impact are calculated where:

a. SCA is considered as a factor of criticality (Expense_on_SCA), by using Eq. (10)

$$\text{Expense\_on\_SCA} = \max\{0, r - SCA\} \quad (10)$$

b. MPC is considered as a factor of criticality (Expense_on_MPC), by using Eq. (11)

$$\text{Expense\_on\_MPC} = \max\{0, r - \text{MPC}\} \tag{11}$$

Activity	Durations			V	DR	PFA	RLA	SFA	SCA	COR	MPC
	a	m	b	Step 1 W_1=0.3	Step 2	Step 3 W_2=0.7	Step 4 W_3=0.9	Step 5 W_4=0.5	Step 6 W_5=0.9	Step 7 W_6=0.7	Step 8
1-2	2	3	4	0.3906	3.0000	0.5003	0.0071	0.00	0.00	0.0000	0.1503
1-3	1	3	4	0.8789	4.8333	0.9842	0.5840	0.00	0.80	0.4691	0.8806
2-4	1	3	5	1.5625	3.0000	0.5003	1.0000	0.00	0.00	0.0000	0.5356
3-5	1	2	3	0.3906	4.0000	1.000	0.0006	0.00	0.80	1.0000	0.8054
3-6	2	5	7	2.4414	7.3333	0.9458	0.0024	1.00	1.00	0.4691	1.0000
4-6	3	4	6	0.8789	4.1667	0.5003	0.0008	0.00	0.00	0.0000	0.1704
4-7	3	4	5	0.3906	4.5000	0.7887	0.0787	0.00	0.20	0.4421	0.4310
5-7	1	4	5	1.5625	5.6667	0.9458	0.0000	0.60	0.80	1.0000	0.9560
6-8	2	5	6	1.5625	4.6667	0.5003	0.4829	0.00	0.00	0.0000	0.3628
7-8	3	4	7	1.5625	4.8333	0.6559	0.0077	0.40	0.20	0.4421	0.4633

Table 2. Activities with appropriate data generated in different steps

Considering that the expense of each unit of impact is 1000$, the mean values of the obtained expenses for 1000 iterations are
Mean value of Expense_on_SCA = 2720.3 $
Mean value of Expense_on_MPC = 1356.3 $

It means that in real world applications, with probabilistic and non precise situations for finishing activities, if we consider MPC as the criticality of activities our project managements will be more realistic causing less expenses.

Fig. 10 represents the two Expenses, for 1000 tests.

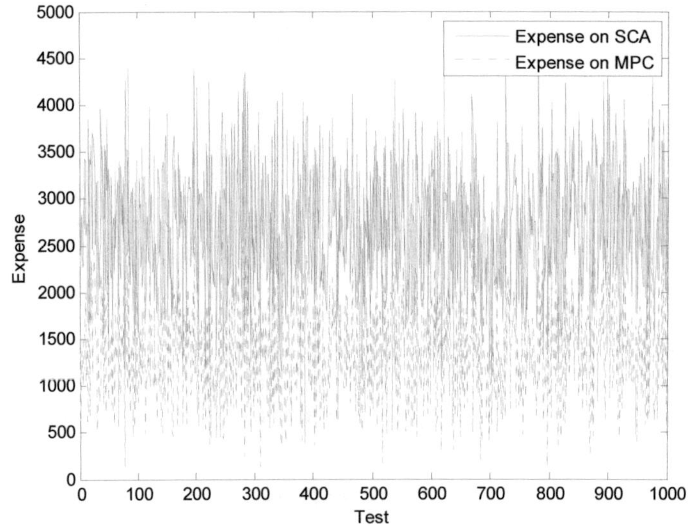

Fig. 10. Two Expenses, for 1000 tests

As another interesting application, a heuristic method for simultaneous rescue robot path-planning and mission scheduling is introduced based on Graphic Evaluation and Review Technique (GERT) (Alan & Pritsker, 1966), along with multi criteria decision making and artificial potential fields path-planning.

5. Rescue robot path planning

Consider some groups of injured people who are trapped in a disastrous situation. These people are categorized into several groups based on the severity of their situation. A rescue robot, whose ultimate objective is to reach injured groups and provide preliminary aid for them through a path with minimum risk, has to perform certain tasks on its way towards targets before the arrival of rescue team. A decision value is assigned to each target based on the whole degree of satisfaction of the criteria and duties of the robot in the way toward the target, and the importance of rescuing each group based on their category and the number of injured people. The resulted decision value defines the strength of the attractive potential field of each target. Dangerous environmental parameters are defined as obstacles whose risk determines the strength of the repulsive potential field of each obstacle. Moreover, negative and positive energies are assigned to the targets and obstacles respectively. These energies vary with respect to different environmental factors.

5.1 Potential feld path planning

The potential field method has been studied extensively for mobile robot path planning (Latombe, 1990). The basic idea behind the potential field method is to define an artificial potential field (energy) in the robot's workspace in which the robot is attracted to its goal position and is repulsed away from the obstacles (Alsultan & Aliyu, 1996; Khanmohammadi & Soltani, 2011). Despite the problems in architecture of potential field such as local minima and oscillation in narrow passages, this method is particularly attractive because of its mathematical elegance and simplicity (Casper & Yanco, 2002; Chadwick, 2005; Tadokoro et al, 2000). For simplicity, we assume that the robot is of point mass and moves in a two-dimensional (2-D) workspace. Its position in the workspace is denoted by $q = [x\ y]^T$. The most commonly used attractive potential U_{att} and the corresponding attractive force F_{att} takes the form:

$$U_{att}(q) = \frac{1}{2}\xi\rho^{m}(q_{goal}, q) \tag{12}$$

$$F_{att} = -\nabla U_{att} = \xi(q_{goal} - q)$$

Where ξ is a positive scaling factor, $\rho(q_{goal}, q) = \|q_{goal} - q\|$ is the distance between the robot q and the goal q_{goal}, and $m = 1$ or 2. For $m = 1$, the attractive potential is conic in shape and the resulting attractive force has constant amplitude except at the goal, where U_{att} is singular. For $m = 2$, the attractive potential is parabolic in shape. Also, the attractive force converges linearly toward zero as the robot approaches the goal.

One commonly used repulsive potential function and the corresponding repulsive force is given by:

$$U_{rep} = \begin{cases} \frac{1}{2}\eta\left(\frac{1}{\rho(q,q_{obs})} - \frac{1}{\rho_0}\right)^2, & if\, \rho(q,q_{obs}) \le \rho_0 \\ 0 \quad , & if\, \rho(q,q_{obs}) > \rho_0 \end{cases} \tag{13}$$

$$F_{rep} = -\nabla U_{rep} = \begin{cases} \eta\left(\frac{1}{\rho(q,q_{obs})} - \frac{1}{\rho_0}\right)\frac{1}{\rho^2(q,q_{obs})}\nabla\rho(q,q_{obs}), & if\, \rho(q,q_{obs}) \le \rho_0 \\ 0 \quad , & if\, \rho(q,q_{obs}) > \rho_0 \end{cases}$$

Where η is a positive scaling factor, $\rho\ (q,q_{obs})$ denotes the minimal distance from the robot q to the obstacle, q_{obs} denotes the point on the obstacle such that the distance between this point and the robot is minimal between the obstacle and the robot, and ρ_0 is a positive constant denoting the distance of influence of the obstacle. The total force applied to the robot is the sum of the attractive force and the repulsive force which determines the motion of the robot (Jacoff et al., 2000).

$$F_{total} = F_{att} + F_{rep} \tag{14}$$

5.2 Graphic evaluation and review technique

In fact GERT is a generalized form of PERT, where the probability of occurrence of activities of the project is taken into consideration. In other words in PERT, either an activity occurs (probability=1) or it does not occur (probability=0); however, in GERT the probability of occurrence of each activity can be a real number between zero and one. GERT approach addresses the majority of the limitations associated with PERT/CPM technique and allows loops between tasks. The fundamental drawback associated with the GERT technique is that a complex program (such as Monte Carlo simulation) is required to model the GERT system.

5.3 Proposed methodology

Given the graph representing the sequence of activities in a disastrous situation, the first step is to obtain necessary information for making decision. The mentioned information consists of: a) parameters affecting the decision making, which are mostly predefined and weighted, and b) estimating approximate durations of activities which may occur during the mission. The mentioned parameters are categorized in two main classes; one of them deals with the degree of satisfaction of the criteria defined in tasks of the robot, and the other one is concerned with importance of targets. These parameters are listed in table 3.

Having gained the necessary data via a questionnaire of experts, PERT algorithm is used for the process of durations of activities. The resulted output is a part of the data needed for Multiple Criteria Decision Making (MCDM) analysis which consists of: standard deviation, free slack and total slack for activities, and the probability of occurrence of activities before a certain time.

The outputs of PERT and the degree of satisfaction of criteria defined for intermediate actions of robot, along with the importance of each criterion are given to MCDM algorithm as inputs. MCDM makes a decision and assigns a decision value for each activity. These values are treated as the virtual durations of activities and are given to CPM. It is obvious that output E_s (Earliest starts representing the decision indexes of missions) of CPM can be interpreted as the degree of fulfillment of the activities leading to a certain event. By comparing the E_s of the last events of several missions, we can deduce which mission fulfills our criteria better than the other ones.

Human factors		Environmental parameters		Parameters Concerning the robot	
H1	Capacity for reducing the life risk of the rescue team	E1	Prevention of air positioning in the surroundings	R1	Destruction of accessories
H2	Rescuing and preventing personal damage to the injured person	E2	Prevention destruction of path for the rescue team	R2	Annihilation of the robot
		E3	Prevention of fire danger in the peripheries	R3	Repairable damage to the robot
				R4	Damage negligible for the robot to be able to continue its task

Table 3. Main criteria for choosing the path

The ultimate objective of rescue mission is to help the injured people. The injured situations are divided into four groups: endangered, vulnerable, defenseless and prepared. To compare different groups of injured people four criteria are considered (refer to Table 6). The weights of criteria along with the degree of satisfaction of different criteria are given to MCDM algorithm and a decision value is calculated for each group of injured people as targets. In fact ξ (the positive scaling factor for attractive force) for each target is calculated as follows:

$$\xi_i = \text{norm}\,(E_{si}) + \text{norm}\,(ADV_i) \tag{15}$$

Where *norm* is normalization operator and ADV_i is the Attraction Decision Value of the ith target.

Considering environmental situation and defining certain criteria for degree of danger of each obstacle, a similar approach is possible for determining the scaling factor η of the repulsive force. The degree of satisfaction of each criterion is fed into MCDM and the resulting decision value equals the positive scaling factor of repulsive force:

$$\eta_i = \text{norm}\,(RDV_i) \tag{16}$$

Where RDV_i is the Repulsive Decision Value of the ith obstacle.

Having obtained the corresponding strength of the attractive and repulsive potential field, the path planning algorithm is established and the optimal path with respect to least time, least risk and most help to injured people is achieved.

5.4 Case study and simulation

Assume that two groups of injured people with different number of people and different categories of injuring are identified. One of the groups is located near a gas station, where people are endangered by the threat of explosion and the other group is next to a building and is threatened by the collision risk of the building. The rescue robot must choose one of the groups as the priority of its mission. Also it is expected that the rescue robot accomplishes several intermediate tasks such as searching for any injured person isolated from other members of identified group, taking picture of the surroundings and sending it to the rescue team, sensing the environmental factors that can signify explosion, etc. Fig. 11 demonstrates the GERT network for rescue mission.

The list of activities for the network represented in Fig. 11, are listed in table 4. The criteria for intermediate actions of robot in choosing the path are listed in Table 5.

The three optimistic, most likely and pessimistic values for the duration of each activity and the fulfillment of the main criteria (by performing each activity) which are listed in Table 5 are estimated based on the experts' opinions. In this table H, E and R indicate parameters concerning human, environment and the robot, respectively (Khanmohammadi & Soltani, 2011).

Durations of activities (first column of Table 5) are given to the PERT algorithm and standard deviation, free slack and total slack for activities, and the probability of performing activities in the range DR are obtained as the outputs of PERT. The output of the PERT and the degree of the satisfaction of the criteria by intermediate actions (H_1, H_2, E_1, E_2, E_3, R_1, R_2, R_3 and R_4 columns) are fed to MCDM algorithm which yields a decision value for each activity. These decision values are treated as the virtual durations of activities and comprise the inputs of the CPM algorithm. Since there is the possibility of obtaining negative decision values, to avoid assigning negative inputs to CPM, the values are normalized in the range [1,10]. E_s in the output of the CPM represents the degree of satisfaction of each activity in each network (mission index). The following values are obtained for the networks of the gas station (target 1) and building (target 2), respectively.

$$E_{s1}= 52.9434,\ E_{s2}= 27.0122.$$

As defined in the previous section, a set of criteria is defined for the injured people to be able to distinguish which group of injured people are more at risk. These criteria are described in Table 6.

The degree of satisfaction of these criteria along with the weight (importance) related to each criterions are the inputs of MCDM and the decision value for each target is the value assigned to ADV_i.

Similar to the procedure above, a set of criteria is defined for the degree of danger of the obstacles based on the environmental situation. Consider three kinds of obstacles consisting: Risk of fire, Risk of electric shock and Risk of building collision. Table 7 summarizes the factors involved.

Similar to obtaining ADVs, RDVs (Repulsive Decision Values) are simply obtained by using MCDM algorithm on the importance of each criterion and the degree of satisfaction of them for each obstacle. For comparison purpose, consider two scenarios with different environmental situations and different groups of troubled people.

Activity	Description	Activity	Description
0-2	Building	2-4	Applying the sensor to detect poisonous gas
4-6	Gas detected	6-8	Evaluating the probability of explosion by means of thermal sensors
8-10	Possibility of explosion present	10-26	Signaling warning to the rescue team for possibility of explosion
8-12	No Possibility for explosion	12-14	Considering the data of the sensor for CO2 and respiration
14-18	Human life detected	18-20	Providing the living person with oxygen
20-24	Dummy activity	18-24	Signaling assistance message to the rescue team
18-22	Signaling warning to the rescue team to wear gas masks	22-24	Dummy activity
24-26	Aggregated tasks	14-16	No Human life detected
16-26	Signaling warning to the rescue team to wear gas masks	4-26	No dangerous gas detected
26-80	----------	2-28	Applying the sensor to detect CO2
28-36	No CO2 detected	28-30	CO2 detected
30-32	Signaling assistance message to the rescue team	32-34	Dummy activity
30-34	Providing the living person with oxygen	34-36	----------
36-80	----------	2-38	Noise detection
38-46	No Noise detected	38-40	Noise detected
40-42	Providing the living person with oxygen	42-44	Dummy activity
40-44	Signaling assistance message to the rescue team	44-46	----------
46-80	----------	2-48	Applying the sensor to measure temperature
48-60	Low temperature	60-62	Signaling message to the rescue team to evaluate the place for possible conflagration
48-50	High temperature	50-54	Signaling assistance message to the rescue team

Activity	Description	Activity	Description
50-52	Applying the extinguisher	52-54	Dummy activity
54-62	----------	48-56	Extremely high temperature
56-62	Applying the extinguisher	62-80	----------
2-64	Detecting bumpy plains	64-76	No Roughness detected
64-66	Roughness detected	66-68	Considering the data of the sensor of CO2 and Respiration
68-70	No alive Human detected	70-72	Leveling the path
72-74	Dummy activity	70-74	Signaling message to the rescue team responsible for leveling the path
74-76	----------	68-76	Human life detected
76-80	----------	2-78	Taking photos of the surroundings
78-80	Sending the photos		
0-1	Gas Station	1-3	Taking photos of the surroundings
1-5	Detecting the temperature of the surroundings with sensor	5-7	Moving to the point with highest temperature
7-33	Using nitrogen to cool down the surroundings	7-13	Applying the extinguisher
13-33	Dummy activity	7-9	Applying the sensor to detect gas leakage
9-11	gas leakage detected	11-15	Signaling warning to the rescue team
15-29	Dummy activity	11-17	Using nitrogen to cool down the surroundings
17-29	Dummy activity	11-29	Applying the extinguisher
11-19	Applying the sensor to detect CO2	19-27	No CO2 detected
19-21	CO2 detected	21-23	Providing the living person with oxygen
23-25	Dummy activity	21-25	Signaling assistance message to the rescue team
25-27	----------	27-29	----------
29-31	----------	31-33	----------
9-31	----------	3-33	Sending photos

* Activities with the dashed lines in the description do not signify any specific activity. They represent the priority considered in making decision

Table 4. List of activities for Network of Fig. 11.

Activity Numbers	Duration(sec)			H1			H2			E1			E2			E3			R1			R2			R3			R4		
	a	m	b	a	m	b	a	m	b	a	m	b	a	m	b	a	m	b	a	m	b	a	m	b	a	m	b	a	m	b
0-2	0	0	0	0.75	0.8	0.95	0.75	0.8	0.95	0	0	0	0	0	0	0	0	0	0	0	0	0	0	0	0	0	0	0	0	0
2-4	2	5	8	0	0	0	0.75	0.8	0.95	0.5	0.6	0.7	0	0	0	0.5	0.6	0.7	0	0	0	0	0	0	0	0	0	0	0	0
2-28	2	6	10	0	0	0	0.75	0.9	0.95	0	0	0	0	0	0	0	0	0	0	0	0	0	0	0	0	0	0	0	0	0
2-38	2	6	10	0	0	0	0.8	0.9	0.95	0	0	0	0	0	0	0	0	0	0	0	0	0	0	0	0	0	0	0	0	0
2-48	2	6	8	0.65	0.8	0.85	0.65	0.8	0.85	0.3	0.5	0.6	0.2	0.4	0.5	0.5	0.6	0.8	0	0	0	0	0	0	0.4	0.25	0.1	0.5	0.3	0.2
2-64	3	7	10	0	0	0	0	0	0	0	0	0	0	0	0	0	0	0	0	0	0	0	0	0	0	0	0	0	0	0
2-78	3	6	10	0	0	0	0.25	0.35	0.5	0	0	0	0	0	0	0	0	0	0	0	0	0	0	0	0	0	0	0	0	0
4-6	0	0	0	0	0	0	0	0	0	0	0	0	0	0	0	0	0	0	0	0	0	0	0	0	0	0	0	0	0	0
6-8	6	9	15	0.75	0.9	0.95	0.35	0.5	0.6	0	0	0	0	0	0	0	0	0	0.6	0.5	0.3	0.6	0.4	0.3	0.7	0.5	0.3	0.7	0.6	0.4
8-12	0	0	0	0	0	0	0	0	0	0	0	0	0	0	0	0	0	0	0	0	0	0	0	0	0	0	0	0	0	0
12-14	3	4	7	0	0	0	0.5	0.7	0.85	0	0	0	0	0	0	0	0	0	0	0	0	0	0	0	0	0	0	0	0	0
14-18	0	0	0	0	0	0	0	0	0	0	0	0	0	0	0	0	0	0	0	0	0	0	0	0	0	0	0	0	0	0
18-20	20	35	45	0	0	0	0.65	0.8	0.9	0	0	0	0	0	0	0	0	0	0	0	0	0	0	0	0	0	0	0	0	0
18-22	2	4	8	0.65	0.8	0.9	0	0	0	0	0	0	0	0	0	0	0	0	0	0	0	0	0	0	0	0	0	0	0	0
18-24	2	4	8	0	0	0	0.65	0.8	0.9	0	0	0	0	0	0	0	0	0	0	0	0	0	0	0	0	0	0	0	0	0
20-24	0	0	0	0	0	0	0	0	0	0	0	0	0	0	0	0	0	0	0	0	0	0	0	0	0	0	0	0	0	0
22-24	0	0	0	0	0	0	0	0	0	0	0	0	0	0	0	0	0	0	0	0	0	0	0	0	0	0	0	0	0	0
24-26	0	0	0	0	0	0	0	0	0	0	0	0	0	0	0	0	0	0	0	0	0	0	0	0	0	0	0	0	0	0
26-80	0	0	0	0	0	0	0	0	0	0	0	0	0	0	0	0	0	0	0	0	0	0	0	0	0	0	0	0	0	0
28-30	0	0	0	0	0	0	0	0	0	0	0	0	0	0	0	0	0	0	0	0	0	0	0	0	0	0	0	0	0	0
30-32	2	3	7	0	0	0	0.75	0.9	0.95	0	0	0	0	0	0	0	0	0	0	0	0	0	0	0	0	0	0	0	0	0
30-34	15	25	40	0	0	0	0.75	0.85	0.9	0	0	0	0	0	0	0	0	0	0	0	0	0	0	0	0	0	0	0	0	0
32-34	0	0	0	0	0	0	0	0	0	0	0	0	0	0	0	0	0	0	0	0	0	0	0	0	0	0	0	0	0	0
34-36	0	0	0	0	0	0	0	0	0	0	0	0	0	0	0	0	0	0	0	0	0	0	0	0	0	0	0	0	0	0
36-80	0	0	0	0	0	0	0	0	0	0	0	0	0	0	0	0	0	0	0	0	0	0	0	0	0	0	0	0	0	0
38-46	0	0	0	0	0	0	0	0	0	0	0	0	0	0	0	0	0	0	0	0	0	0	0	0	0	0	0	0	0	0
46-80	0	0	0	0	0	0	0	0	0	0	0	0	0	0	0	0	0	0	0	0	0	0	0	0	0	0	0	0	0	0
48-60	0	0	0	0	0	0	0	0	0	0	0	0	0	0	0	0	0	0	0	0	0	0	0	0	0	0	0	0	0	0
60-62	2	4	7	0	0	0	0.65	0.8	0.9	0.6	0.8	0.95	0.6	0.8	0.9	0.8	0.9	0.95	0	0	0	0	0	0	0	0	0	0	0	0
62-80	0	0	0	0	0	0	0	0	0	0	0	0	0	0	0	0	0	0	0	0	0	0	0	0	0	0	0	0	0	0
64-66	0	0	0	0	0	0	0	0	0	0	0	0	0	0	0	0	0	0	0	0	0	0	0	0	0	0	0	0	0	0
66-68	3	4	7	0	0	0	0.5	0.6	0.75	0	0	0	0	0	0	0	0	0	0	0	0	0	0	0	0	0	0	0	0	0
68-76	0	0	0	0	0	0	0	0	0	0	0	0	0	0	0	0	0	0	0	0	0	0	0	0	0	0	0	0	0	0
76-80	0	0	0	0	0	0	0	0	0	0	0	0	0	0	0	0	0	0	0	0	0	0	0	0	0	0	0	0	0	0
78-80	2	4	7	0	0	0	0	0	0	0	0	0	0	0	0	0	0	0	0	0	0	0	0	0	0	0	0	0	0	0

Activity Numbers	Duration(sec)			H1			H2			E1			E2			E3			R1			R2			R3			R4		
	a	m	b	a	m	b	a	m	b	a	m	b	a	m	b	a	m	b	a	m	b	a	m	b	a	m	b	a	m	b
0-1	0	0	0	0.6	0.8	0.9	0.65	0.8	0.9	0.7	0.85	0.95	0.5	0.6	0.8	0.7	0.85	0.95	0.9	0.85	0.75	0.95	0.9	0.75	0.95	0.9	0.75	0.65	0.5	0.4
1-3	6	15	25	0.1	0.15	0.4	0.1	0.15	0.25	0	0.05	0.15	0	0.05	0.15	0	0	0	0	0	0	0	0	0	0	0	0	0	0	0
1-5	5	6	10	0	0.05	0.2	0.1	0.15	0.25	0.15	0.25	0.3	0.1	0.15	0.3	0.15	0.25	0.3	0	0	0	0	0	0	0	0	0	0	0	0
3-33	1	3	6	0	0	0	0	0	0	0	0	0	0	0	0	0	0	0	0	0	0	0	0	0	0	0	0	0	0	0
5-7	3	10	20	0.05	0.1	0.25	0.1	0.25	0.4	0.15	0.25	0.3	0.05	0.15	0.2	0.2	0.25	0.35	0.95	0.8	0.7	0.9	0.8	0.75	0.95	0.9	0.8	0.9	0.8	0.75
7-9	3	8	12	0.6	0.8	0.95	0.75	0.9	0.95	0.65	0.8	0.85	0.6	0.75	0.85	0.6	0.75	0.85	0.4	0.3	0.1	0.4	0.2	0.1	0.4	0.3	0.25	0.6	0.5	0.3
7-13	18	24	40	0.25	0.4	0.6	0.6	0.8	0.9	0.65	0.8	0.9	0.7	0.75	0.85	0.65	0.8	0.9	0.8	0.6	0.5	0.8	0.6	0.5	0.9	0.7	0.6	0.95	0.9	0.75
7-33	20	28	40	0.4	0.6	0.75	0.75	0.9	0.95	0.75	0.9	0.95	0.75	0.9	0.95	0.75	0.9	0.95	0.6	0.4	0.3	0.7	0.5	0.4	0.95	0.8	0.65	0.95	0.9	0.75
9-11	0	0	0	0	0	0	0	0	0	0	0	0	0	0	0	0	0	0	0	0	0	0	0	0	0	0	0	0	0	0
11-15	2	3	6	0.75	0.9	0.95	0	0	0	0	0	0	0	0	0	0	0	0	0	0	0	0	0	0	0	0	0	0	0	0
11-17	20	25	35	0.65	0.8	0.9	0.65	0.8	0.9	0.7	0.85	0.95	0.7	0.85	0.95	0.6	0.75	0.8	0.5	0.3	0.15	0.5	0.3	0.25	0.6	0.5	0.3	0.65	0.5	0.3
11-19	3	8	12	0	0	0	0.75	0.9	0.95	0	0	0	0	0	0	0	0	0	0	0	0	0	0	0	0	0	0	0	0	0
11-29	14	20	30	0.4	0.6	0.75	0.6	0.75	0.8	0.65	0.8	0.9	0.1	0.25	0.4	0.6	0.7	0.85	0.5	0.4	0.25	0.4	0.25	0.1	0.65	0.5	0.35	0.8	0.75	0.55
13-33	0	0	0	0	0	0	0	0	0	0	0	0	0	0	0	0	0	0	0	0	0	0	0	0	0	0	0	0	0	0
15-29	0	0	0	0	0	0	0	0	0	0	0	0	0	0	0	0	0	0	0	0	0	0	0	0	0	0	0	0	0	0
17-29	0	0	0	0	0	0	0	0	0	0	0	0	0	0	0	0	0	0	0	0	0	0	0	0	0	0	0	0	0	0
19-27	0	0	0	0	0	0	0	0	0	0	0	0	0	0	0	0	0	0	0	0	0	0	0	0	0	0	0	0	0	0
27-29	0	0	0	0	0	0	0	0	0	0	0	0	0	0	0	0	0	0	0	0	0	0	0	0	0	0	0	0	0	0
29-31	0	0	0	0	0	0	0	0	0	0	0	0	0	0	0	0	0	0	0	0	0	0	0	0	0	0	0	0	0	0
31-33	0	0	0	0	0	0	0	0	0	0	0	0	0	0	0	0	0	0	0	0	0	0	0	0	0	0	0	0	0	0

* Values other than durations of activities are normalized in the range [0,1]

Table 5. Durations of activities and satisfaction levels of criteria by performing each activity

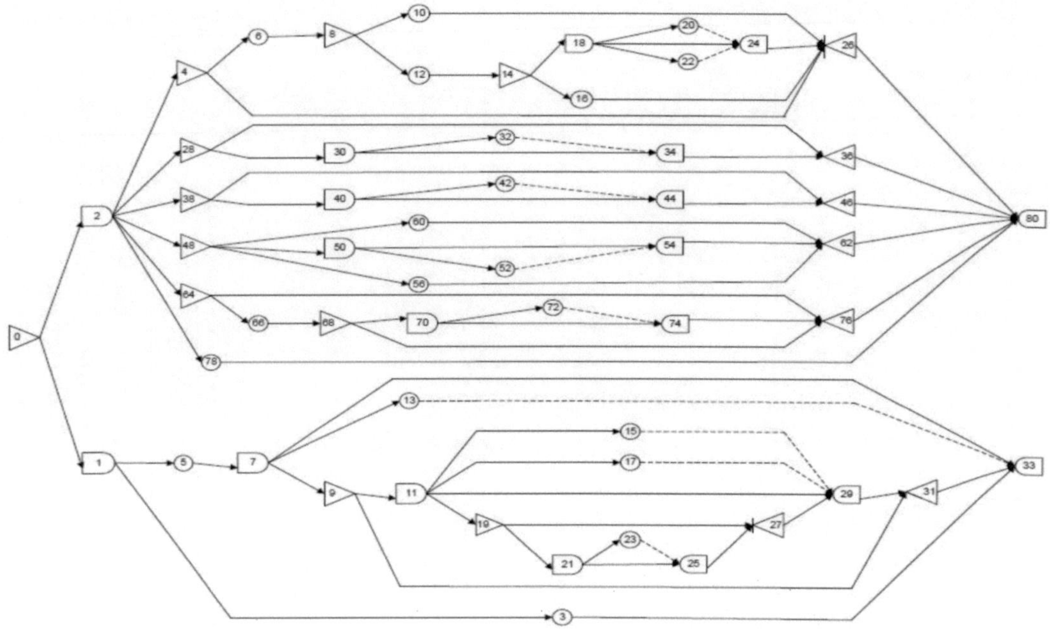

Fig. 11. Network of project activities

Category and Number of the troubled people	Exposure to dangerous situation
• Category of the troubled people: endangered, defenseless, vulnerable, prepared • Number of the people in each category Health status of the injured people	• Adjacency of the danger

Table 6. Criteria for calculating the priority values of injured groups

Type of the obstacle	Criteria and factors involved
• Fire • Building collision • Electric shock	- Temperature – existence of flammable material in the vicinity – rainy/dry weather - Humidity – fundamental robustness of building – possibility of building collision - Humidity – rainy/dry weather

Table 7. Criteria for measuring the danger level of obstacles

Scenario 1

group1: 25 people near gas station comprised of 15 endangered (injured) 5 vulnerable, 5 defenseless

group2: 15 people near a building with possibility of collision comprised of 4 injured and 11 defenseless.

The introduced procedure has been run twice, once for hot and dry and once for cold and rainy weather. Results are illustrated in Fig. 12. Priority is given to the first target (group1 near gas station) by robot. As it is seen in Fig. 12(a), the rescue robot tries to get as far as possible from the power electric station when it is rainy and it gets a shorter path (near electric power station) in dry conditions, Fig. 12(b).

Scenario 2

group1: 15 people near gas station comprised of 15 endangered (injured), 5 vulnerable, 5 defenseless

group2: 25 people near a damaged building with possibility of collision comprised of 4 injured and 11 defenseless.

We have considered the mentioned environmental conditions and the results are illustrated in Fig. 12.

The priority is given to the second target (group2 near damaged building) by rescue robot. In case one, when it is cold and rainy, the possibility of explosion is low, so the robot gets closer to the gas station, Fig. 13(a). But when it is hot, robot tries to be far from the gas

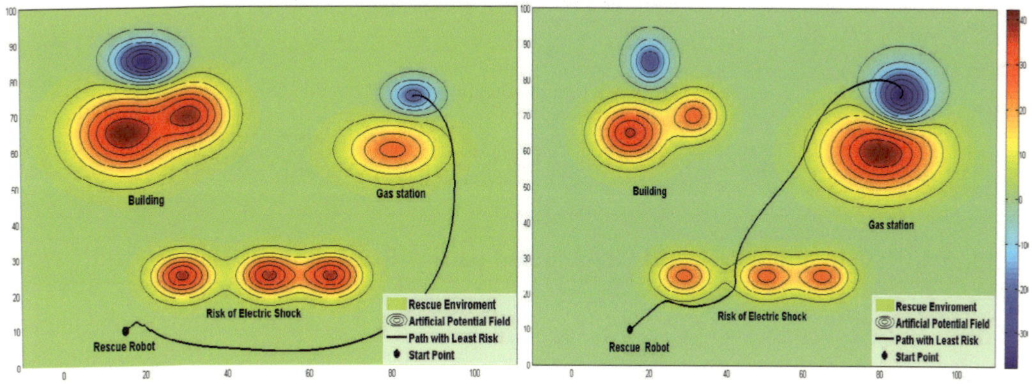

Fig. 12. Generated path for the first scenario: (a) cold and rainy condition, (b) hot and dry condition

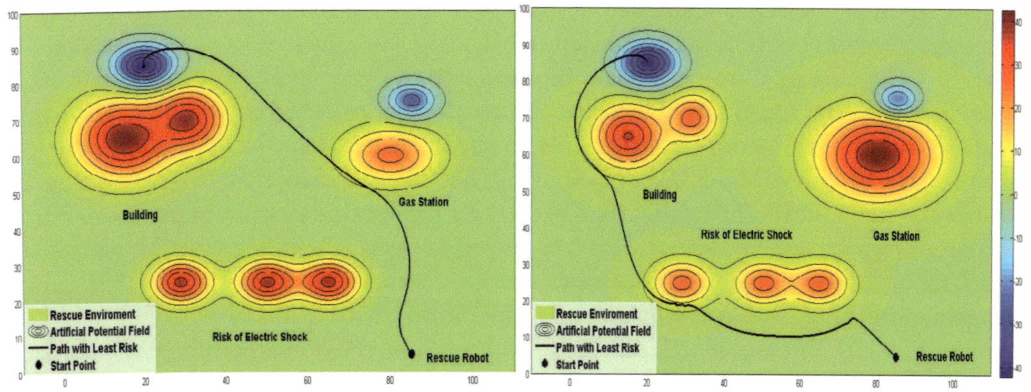

Fig. 13. Generated path for second scenario: (a) cold and rainy condition, (b) hot and dry condition

station where there is the risk of explosion, Fig. 13(b). The simulation results show the fact that the introduced algorithm is flexible in terms of the environmental conditions and the factors involved in targets.

To further illustrate the conceptual basis of the utilized potential field, a 3D representation of the risk potential function and the corresponding optimal path are represented in Fig. 14.

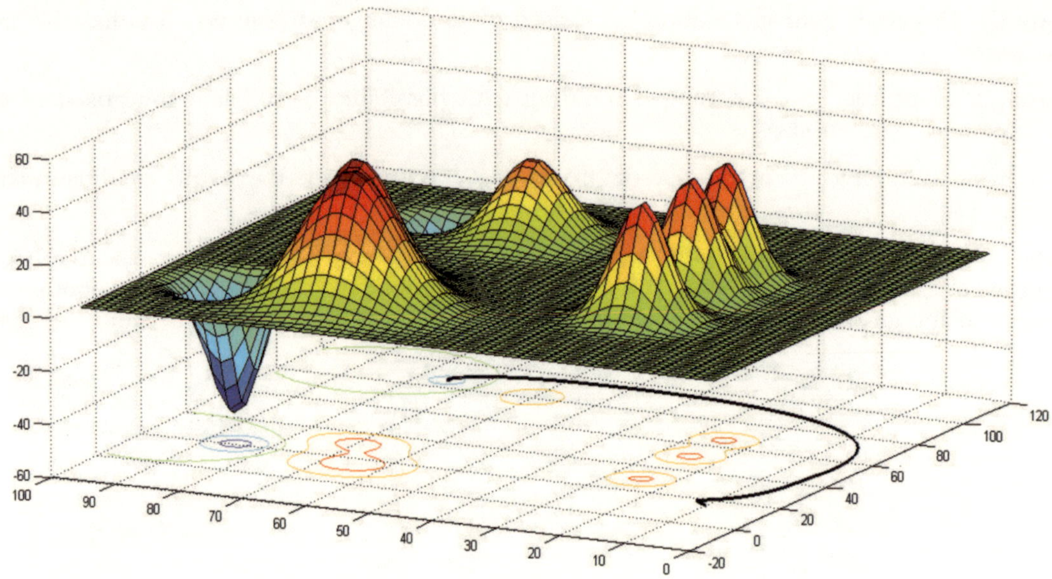

Fig. 14. Artificial potential field and the obtained path with minimum risk

6. Conclusion

A new fuzzy approach is introduced to perform a more applicable risk analysis in real world applications. This procedure is used to determine the multi-purpose criticalities of activities where six main factors V, SFA, SCA, PFA, RLA and COR are considered as criticality indexes. A fuzzy inference system with three inputs: probability of impact, impact treat, and ability to retaliate is used to calculate the values of RLA for activities. The output of FIS represents the risky level of each activity. The decision values obtained by classic multi criteria decision making problem are then considered as criticality indexes of activities. The obtained results are compared to classic PERT, from the view point of impact expenses, by using the Mont Carlo method. It has been shown that by considering the multipurpose criticalities (instead of total slacks) a considerable amount of expenses caused by different impacts may be saved. The introduced method is applied to simultaneous task scheduling and path planning of rescue robots. Simulation results show that project management technique along with risk analysis by means of artificial potential field path planning is an efficient tool which may be used for rescue mission scheduling by intelligent robots. The algorithm is flexible in terms of environmental situation and the effective factors in risk analysis. In fact the proposed method merges the path planning methods with rescue mission scheduling.

7. References

Alan, A., & Pritsker, B. (1966). GERT: *Graphical Evaluation and Review Technique,* Rand Corp

Alsultan, K. S., & Aliyu, M. D. S. (1996). A new potential field-based algorithm for path planning. *Journal of intelligent and robotic systems,* Vol. 17, No. 3, (November 1996), pp. (265–282)

Carr, V., & Tah, J. H. M. (2001). A Fuzzy approach to construction project risk assessment and analysis: construction project risk management system. *Advances in Engineering Software,* Vol. 32, No. 10-11, (October-November 2001), pp. (847-857)

Casper, J., & Yanco, H. (2002). AAAI/RoboCup-2001 Robot Rescue. *AI Magazine,* Vol. 23, No. 1, (Spring 2002)

Chadwick, R. A. (2005). The Impacts of Multiple Robots and Display Views: An Urban Search and Rescue Simulation. *Human Factors and Ergonomics Society, Annual Meeting Proceeding Cognitive Engineering and Decision Making,* (January 2005), pp. (387-391)

Chanas, S., Dubois, D., & Zielinski, P. (2002). On the Sure Criticality of Tasks in Activity Networks with Imprecise Durations. *IEEE Transactions on systems, man, and cybernetics part B,* Vol. 32, No. 4, (August 2002), pp. (393-407)

Chavas, J. P. (2004). *Risk Analysis in Theory and Practice,* Elsevier, ISBN – 10: 0121706214

Cho, H. N., Choi, H. H., & Kim, Y. B. (2002). A risk assessment methodology for incorporating uncertainties using fuzzy concepts. *Reliability Engineering & System Safety,* Vol. 78, No. 2, (November 2002), pp. (173-183)

Doherty, N. A. (2000). *Integrated Risk Management: Techniques and Strategies for Managing Corporate Risk,* McGraw-Hill Professional

Jacoff, A., Messina, E., & Evans, J. (2000). A Standard Test Course for Urban Search and Rescue Robots, *Proceeding of performance metrics for intelligent systems workshop,* August - 2000

Jamshidi M., Vadiee N., & Ross T. J. (1993). *Fuzzy Logic and Control,* Prentice Hall

Kerzner, H. (2009). *Project Management: A System Approach to Planning, Scheduling and Controlling,* Wiley

Khanmohammadi, S., Charmi, M., & Nasiri, F. (2001). Delay Time Estimating in Project Management Using Fuzzy Delays and Fuzzy Probabilities, *Proceeding of International ICSC Congress on Computational Intelligence: Methods and Applications,* Bangore - UK, June - 2001

Khanmohammadi, S., & Soltani, R. (2011). Intelligent path planning for rescue robot. *World Academy of Science, Engineering and Technology,* No. 79, (April 2011), pp. (764-769)

Kreinovich, V., Nguyen H. T., & Yam Y. (2000). Fuzzy Systems are Universal Approximators for a Smooth Function and its Derivatives. *International Journal of Intelligent Systems,* Vol. 15, No. 6, (June 2000), pp. (565-574)

Latombe, J. C. (1990). *Robot Motion Planning,* Springer

Li, Y., & Liao, X. (2007). Decision support for risk analysis on dynamic alliance. *Decision Support Systems,* Vol. 42, No. 4, (January 2007), pp. (2043-2059)

Mamdani, E. H., & Assilian, S. (1999). An Experiment in Linguistic Synthesis with a Fuzzy Logic Controller. *International Journal of Human-Computer Studies,* Vol. 51, No. 2, (August 1999), pp. (135-147)

McNeil, A. J., Frey, R., & Embrechts, P. (2005). *Quantitative Risk Management: Concepts, Techniques and Tools,* Princeton University Press

Mendel, J. (2001). *Uncertain rule-based fuzzy inference systems: Introduction and new directions*, Prentice-Hall

Nguene, G. N., & Finger, M. (2007). A fuzzy–based approach for strategic choices in electric energy supply. The case of a swiss power provider on the eve of electricity market opening. *Engineering applications of Artificial Intelligence,* Vol. 20, No. 1, (February 2007), pp. (37-48)

Ross, T. J. (2010). *Fuzzy Logic with Engineering Applications*, Wiley

Shipley, M. F., De Korvin, A., & Omer, K. (1996). A fuzzy Logic Approach for Determining Expected values: A Project Management Application. *Journal of Operations Research Society,* Vol. 47, No. 4, (April 1996), pp. (562-569)

Shipley, M. F., De Korvin, A., & Omer, K. (1997). BIFPET methodology versus PERT in project management: fuzzy probability instead of the beta distribution. *Journal of Engineering and Technology Management,* Vol. 14, No. 1, (March 1997), pp. (49-65)

Tadokoro, S., Kitano, H., Takahashi, T., Noda, I., Matsubara, H., Shinjoh, A., Koto, T., Takeuchi, I., Takahashi, H., Matsuno, F., Hatayama, M., Nobe, J., & Shimada, S. (2000). The RoboCup-Rescue Project: A Robotic Approach to the Disaster Mitigation Problem, *Proceedings of IEEE international Conference on Robotics and Automation,* San Francisco - USA, April 2000

Takács, M. (2004). Critical Analysis of Various Known Methods for Approximate Reasoning in Fuzzy Logic Control, *Proceedings of 5th International Symposium of Hungarian Researchers on Computational Intelligence,* Budapest - Hungary, November 2004.

Takagi, T., & Sugeno, M. (1985). Fuzzy identification of systems and its applications to modelling and control, *IEEE Transactions on systems, man, and cybernetics,* Vol. SMC-15, No. 1, (January 1985), pp. (116-132)

Zadeh, L. A. (1965). Fuzzy Sets, *Information and Control,* Vol. 8, No.3, (June 1965), pp. (338-353)

4

A Concise Fuzzy Rule Base to Reason Student Performance Based on Rough-Fuzzy Approach

Norazah Yusof, Nor Bahiah Ahmad,
Mohd. Shahizan Othman and Yeap Chun Nyen
Faculty of Computer Science and Information System,
Universiti Teknologi Malaysia, Skudai, Johor
Malaysia

1. Introduction

A fuzzy inference system employing fuzzy if then rules able to model the qualitative aspects of human expertise and reasoning processes without employing precise quantitative analyses. This is due to the fact that the problem in acquiring knowledge from human experts is that much of the information is uncertain, inconsistent, vague and incomplete (Khoo and Zhai, 2001; Tsaganou et al., 2002; San Pedro and Burstein, 2003; Yang et al., 2005). The drawbacks of FIS are that a lot of trial and error effort need to be taken into account in order to define the best fitted membership functions (Taylan and Karagözoğlu, 2009) and no standard methods exist for transforming human knowledge or experience into the rule base (Jang, 1993).

Evaluation and reasoning of student's learning achievement is the process of determining the performance levels of individual students in relation to educational objectives (Saleh and Kim, 2009). Although Fuzzy inference system is a potential technique to reason the student's performance, as well as to present his/her knowledge status (Nedic et al., 2002; Xu et al., 2002; Kosba et al. 2003), it is a challenge when more than one factor involve in determining the student's performance or knowledge status (Yusof et. al, 2009). Hence, the reasoning of the student's performance for multiple factors is difficult. This issue is critical considering that the human experts' knowledge is insufficient to analyze all possible conditions as the information gained is always incomplete, inconsistent, and vague.

Addressing these matters, this work proposes a Neuro-Fuzzy Inference System (ANFIS), which combines fuzzy inference system and neural network, in order to produce a complete fuzzy rule base system (Jang, 1993). The fuzzy system represents knowledge in an interpretable manner, while the neural networks have the learning ability platform to optimize its parameters. Hence, ANFIS has the capability to perform parameter-learning rather than structural learning (Lin and Lu, 1996). ANFIS is expected to recognize other decisions that are previously not complete, in both the antecedents and consequent parts of the fuzzy rules. Unfortunately, too many fuzzy rules will result in a large computation time and space (Jamshidi, 2001). Therefore, reduction of knowledge is possible to be applied to determine the selection of important attributes that can be used to represent the decision system (Chen, 1999) based on the theory of rough sets. Fig. 1 shows the proposed fuzzy inference system.

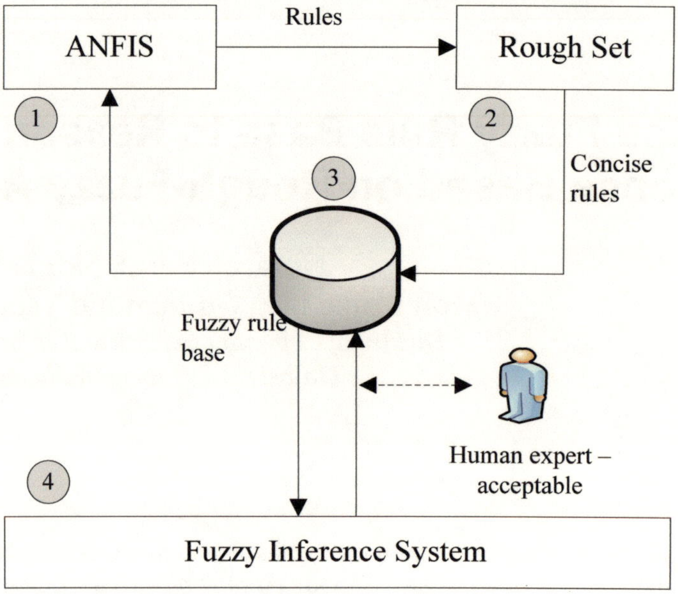

Fig. 1. The proposed Fuzzy Inference System

This chapter is divided into six sections. Section 1 is the introduction and the problem statements. Section 2 discusses about the student modeling and learning criteria. Section 3 presents the Human Expert Fuzzy Inference System model that defines the data representation and the rule base acquired from the human experts. Section 4 describes the ANFIS approach to form a complete fuzzy rule base to solve the problem of incomplete and vague decisions made by human. Section 5 presents the proposed Rough-Fuzzy approach to determine important attributes and refine the fuzzy rule base into a concise fuzzy rule base. Finally, section 6 presents the conclusions of the work.

2. Student modeling and the learning criteria

Student model represents the knowledge about the student's behavior and learning performance. In this work, student's performance are classified into three categories, named as Has Mastered (HM), Moderately Mastered (MM), and Not Mastered (NM). The conditions that determine the decision made about the student's performance is also depend on the criteria set by the human expert. There are four input conditions namely, the *score* (*S*), *time* (*T*), *attempts* (*A*), and *helps* (*H*) in which each of the input condition is represented by three term sets with values (Norazah, 2005).

a. Score (S) is the average scoring, x_1, which gains from each question of a learning unit and the term sets is represented by *low* (S_1), *moderate* (S_2), and *high* (S_3). It can be found by dividing the total marks for a set of given questions by the total number of questions (Q) in the set, as shown in equation (1).

$$x_1 = \frac{\sum_{i=1}^{Q} m_i}{Q} \tag{1}$$

Where :
m_i is marks from each question
Q is total number the question in the set

b. Time (T) is the average duration, x_2, taken by a student to answer the each question of a learning unit and with three term sets: *fast* (T_1), *average* (T_2), and *slow* (T_3). The average of time (x_2) is obtained by dividing the total time to answer a set of given questions by the total number of questions, see equation (2).

$$x_2 = \frac{\sum_{i=1}^{Q} T_i}{Q} \quad (2)$$

Where :
Q is total number of questions
T_i is the time spent to answer the i-th question

Measurement of time can be done by using the distribution method. Fig. 2 shows the T-score distribution, in which the mean is 50 and the standard deviation is 10.

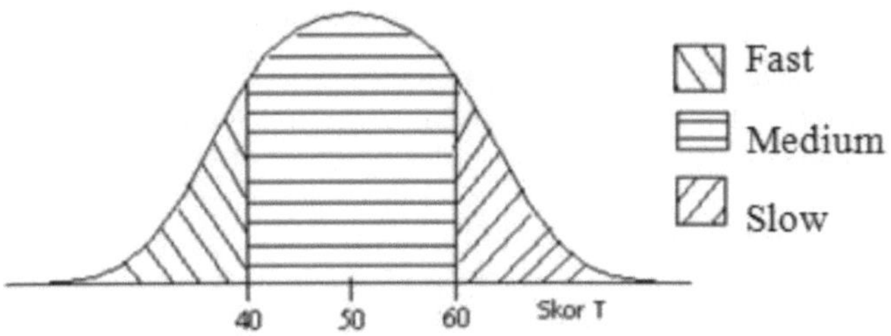

Fig. 2. T-score distribution for time taken to answer question

The time taken to answer each question (T_i) can be calculated by using the equation (3).

$$T_i = \frac{\frac{10(X_i - \bar{X}_i)}{\sigma_i} + 50}{100} \quad (3)$$

Where :
T_i is the time spent to answer the i-th question
X_i is the time spent by the student
$\bar{X}_i$ is mean score for the time spent distribution
σ_i is the standard deviation for the i-th question

The numbered "10" is distance value of standard deviation from mean, while numbered "50" is value of mean. T-score is divided by 100 so that able to get the value in the range 0 to 1.

c. Attempt (A) is the average number of tries , x_3, for a given learning unit, in which it is counted after student give a wrong answer for the first attempt and the question will repeat again for student to answer until correct. The term sets involve: *a few* (A_1), *average* (A_2), and *many* (A_3). The average of attempt (x_3) is calculated as equation (4). Dividing the total number of tries to answer a set of given questions by the total number of questions in the set.

$$x_3 = \frac{\sum_{i=1}^{Q} t_i}{Q} \tag{4}$$

Where :
Q is total number of questions

The number of attempt (t_i) is determined by calculating the number of attempts made (a_i) to answer a given question and dividing it by the maximum number of attempts (P_i) allowed for the question.

$$t_i = \frac{a_i}{P_i} \tag{5}$$

Where :
a_i is the number of attempts made to answer a given question
P_i is the maximum number of attempts allowed for the question

d. Help (H) is the average amount of help, x_4, of a learning unit where it able to help student by giving some hints or notes to answer the question. The term sets involve: *little* (H_1), *average* (H_2),and *needed* (H_3).

The average amount of help (x_4) is calculated as equation (6), by dividing the total amount of help accessed by a student in answering a set of given questions by the total number of questions in the set.

$$x_4 = \frac{\sum_{i=1}^{Q} h_i}{Q} \tag{6}$$

Where :
Q is the total number of questions
h_i is the total amount of help accessed by a student

The amount of help (h_i) is found by calculating the number of help (l_i) links that a student accessed while answering a given question and dividing it by the maximum number of help links (H_{max}) provided for a given question.

$$h_i = \frac{l_i}{H_{max}} \tag{7}$$

The output consequent of the student model is the student's performance and can be represented as *has mastered* (P_1), *moderately mastered* (P_2) and *not mastered* (P_3) for the output. A student is classified as *has mastered* in a particular learning unit, when the student earns high scores (i.e. greater than 75%) with below 40% of time spent, not exceeding 25% of number of tries needed and number of helps. Besides that, a student is classified as *moderately mastered* when the student earns a moderate score, with moderate time spent, tries more than once, and number of help needed. For example, a moderate score would be rated in between 35% and 75%, time spent between 40% and 60%, tries between 25% and 75%, and help between 25% and 75%. Furthermore, a student is classified as *not mastered* when the student has a low score with a lot of time, many tries and many help needed. However, in acquiring knowledge from the human experts is that, they cannot decide on all possible students learning performance. Bases on a survey done by Norazah (2005), there are only 18 decisions about the student's behavior are formed with certainty from seven subject matter experts; and these decisions are considered as the acceptable rules. All other decisions that are not certain and have conflicts are being discarded from the rules.

Criteria item	Has Mastered $y > 75$		Moderately Mastered $75 \geq y \geq 25$		Not Mastered $y < 25$	
	Value	Label	Value	Label	Value	Label
Scores (S)	$x_1 \geq 75\%$	High	$75\% \geq x_1 \geq 35\%$	Md	$x_1 < 35\%$	Low
Time (T)	$x_2 < 40$	Fast	$60 \geq x_2 \geq 40$	Avg	$x_2 > 60$	Slow
Attempt (A)	$x_3 < 25\%$	A Few	$75\% \geq x_3 \geq 25\%$	Avg	$x_3 > 75\%$	Many
Help (H)	$x_4 < 25\%$	Little	$75\% \geq x_4 \geq 25\%$	Avg	$x_4 > 75\%$	Needed

Table 1. The criteria for the student's performance

3. Human expert Fuzzy Inference System

Human expert's FIS uses a collection of fuzzy membership functions and rules to reason about student's performance. FIS consists of a fuzzification interface, a rule base, a database, a decision-making unit, and finally a defuzzification interface.

To compute the output of this fuzzy inference system given the inputs, four steps has to be followed (Norazah, 2005):

a. Compare the input variables with the membership functions on the antecedent part to obtain the membership values of each linguistic label. This step is called fuzzification.
b. Combine the membership values on the premise part to get firing strength of each rule.
c. Generate the qualified consequents or each rule depending on the firing strength.
d. Aggregate the qualified consequents to produce a crisp output. This step is called defuzzification.

3.1 Fuzzification

In the fuzzification stage, the input and output of the fuzzy inference system are determined. Table 2 and Table 3 exhibit examples of the four input and one output

Fuzzy input variable	Fuzzy linguistic terms	Numerical range (normalized)
Score (S)	{Low,	[0.14, 0.0]
	Moderate,	[0.12, 0.55]
	High}	[0.14, 1.0]
Time (T)	{Fast,	[0.15, 0.0]
	Average,	[0.08, 0.5]
	Slow}	[0.15, 1.0]
Attempt (A)	{A few,	[0.12, 0.0]
	Average,	[0.12, 0.5]
	Many}	[0.12, 1.0]
Help (H)	{Little,	[0.12, 0.0]
	Average,	[0.12, 0.5]
	Needed}	[0.12, 1.0]

Table 2. The input variables of the Fuzzy Inference System

variables, in which each of the variables consists of three term values and labels as discussed in Section 2. The fuzzy output follows the zero-order Sugeno style inference, in which the output value of each fuzzy rule is a constant (Sivanandam et al., 2007). Fig. 3 shows the four inputs and one single output for the Human Expert FIS.

Fuzzy output variable	Fuzzy linguistic terms	Numerical range(normalized)
Performance (P)	{Not Mastered,	0.0
	Moderately Mastered,	0.5
	Has Mastered}	1.0

Table 3. The output variables of the Fuzzy Inference System

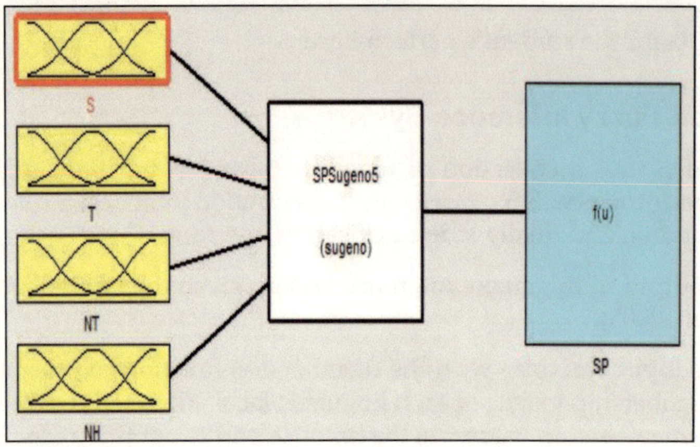

Fig. 3. Four inputs and single output for the Human Expert FIS

The membership function of the input is expressed by a Gaussian function specified by two parameters $\{\sigma, c\}$, and the membership value is derived by the formula in Fig. 4.

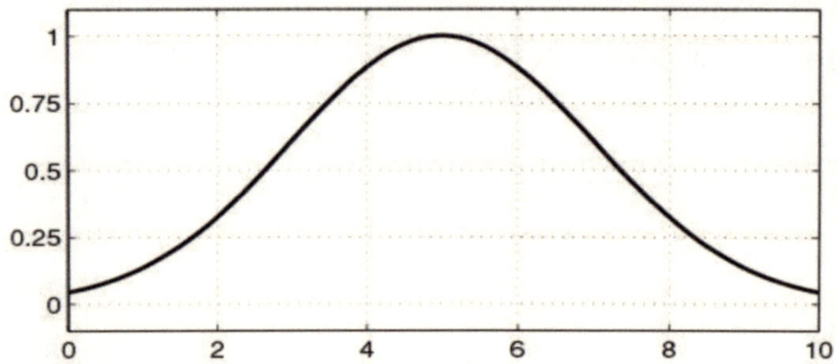

Fig. 4. Gaussian shape function $gaussian(x;\ 2{,}5)$

$$gaussian(x;\ \sigma, c) = \exp\left(-\left[\frac{x-c}{2\sigma}\right]^2\right) \tag{8}$$

Where :
c represents the membership function's center
σ determines the membership function's width

3.2 Creating fuzzy rules

Fuzzy rules are a collection of linguistic statements that describe how the fuzzy inference system should make a decision regarding classifying an input or controlling an output. Fig. 5 presents the four inputs and one output reasoning of the student's performance procedure for zero order Sugeno fuzzy model. Each input has its own membership function.

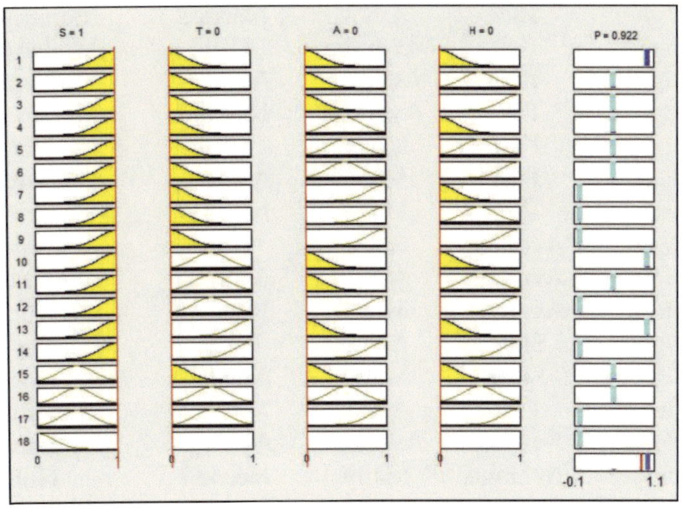

Fig. 5. Fuzzy reasoning procedures for Human Expert FIS model of Student's Performance

R_i have four input variables and one output variable as shown below:

R_i: IF S is μ_{i1} AND T is μ_{i2} AND A is μ_{i3} AND H is μ_{i4} THEN P is w_i

The rule R_i is the *i*-th rule in the fuzzy rule base system, the μ_i is the membership function of the antecedent part of the *i*-th rule for each input variable and w_i is the weight of the consequent of each rule. For example, for input1 is score and the membership function can classified as low, moderate or high. If *score* is *high* and *time* is *fast* and *attempt* is *a few* and *help* is *little* then *student performance* is *has mastered*. This process of taking input such as *score* and processing it through membership functions to determine the "high" score is called fuzzification. Based on the human experts' experience and knowledge about the students' performance, 18 initial rules that are certain have been constructed as shown in Table 4.

3.3 Combining outputs into an output distribution

The outputs of all of the fuzzy rules must now be combined to obtain one fuzzy output distribution. The output membership functions on the right-hand side of the figure are combined using the fuzzy operator AND to obtain the output distribution shown on the lower right corner of the Fig. 5. For a zero-order Sugeno model, the output level z is a constant. The output level z_i of each rule is weighted by the firing strength w_i of the rule (Lin and Lu, 1996). For example, for an ∩ rule with input 1 = x and input 2 = y, the firing strength is as shown in equation (9).

$$w_i = F_1(x) \cap F_2(y) \tag{9}$$

Where:
F_1 and F_2 are the membership functions for input 1 and 2, respectively

Rule	S	T	A	H	P
1	High	Fast	A few	Little	Has Mastered
2	High	Fast	A few	Average	Moderately Mastered
3	High	Fast	A few	Needed	Moderately Mastered
4	High	Fast	Average	Little	Moderately Mastered
5	High	Fast	Average	Average	Moderately Mastered
6	High	Fast	Average	Needed	Moderately Mastered
7	High	Fast	Many	Little	Not Mastered
8	High	Fast	Many	Average	Not Mastered
9	High	Fast	Many	Needed	Not Mastered
10	High	Average	A few	Little	Has Mastered
11	High	Average	A few	Average	Moderately Mastered
12	High	Average	Many	Needed	Not Mastered
13	High	Slow	A few	Little	Has Mastered
14	High	Slow	Many	Needed	Not Mastered
15	Moderate	Fast	A few	Little	Moderately Mastered
16	Moderate	Average	Average	Average	Moderately Mastered
17	Moderate	Average	Many	Needed	Not Mastered
18	Low	x	x	x	Not Mastered

Table 4. Initial fuzzy rules determine by human experts

3.4 Defuzzification of output distribution

The input for the defuzzification process is a fuzzy set and the output is a single number crispness recovered from fuzziness. Given a fuzzy set that encompasses a range of output values, we need to return one number, thereby moving from a fuzzy set to a crisp output. The final output of the system is the weighted average of all rule outputs, computed as in equation (10).

$$Final\ Output = \frac{\sum_{i=1}^{N} w_i z_i}{\sum_{i=1}^{N} w_i} \tag{10}$$

Finally, all the outputs of datasets for reasoning of the student's performance in the human expert FIS have been recorded.

Next section describes the ANFIS approach to form a complete fuzzy rule base to solve the problem of incomplete and vague decisions made by human.

4. Development of Adaptive Neuro-Fuzzy Inference System (ANFIS)

Basically, fuzzy rules and fuzzy reasoning are the backbone of fuzzy inference systems, which are the most important modeling tools based on fuzzy sets (Jang et al., 1997). Fuzzy reasoning is an inference procedure that derives conclusions from the set of fuzzy *If-Then* rules and known facts. The ANFIS model is proposed to form a complete fuzzy rule bases so that all possible input conditions of the fuzzy rules are being generated.

It is necessary to take into consideration the scarcity of data and the style of input space partitions. For example, for a single input problem, usually 10 data points are necessary to come up with a good model (Jang et al., 1997). Details on ANFIS model structure will be described in section 4.1.

4.1 ANFIS model structure

The ANFIS model structure consists of four nodes for input layer, the nodes of hidden layer and one node for output layer as presented in Fig. 6. The input layer represents the antecedent part of the fuzzy rule, which is the student's learning behavior such as the scores (*S*) earned, the time (*T*) spent, the attempts (*A*), and helps (*H*); the output layer represents the consequent part of the rule, i.e. the student's performance (*P*). The size of the hidden layer is determined experimentally.

In this work, the ANFIS model is trained with 18 fuzzy rules obtained from the human expert. These rules are considered as the rules that are certain. After that, 81 potential fuzzy rules are used for testing the network that represent the $3 \times 3 \times 3 \times 3$ rule antecedents.

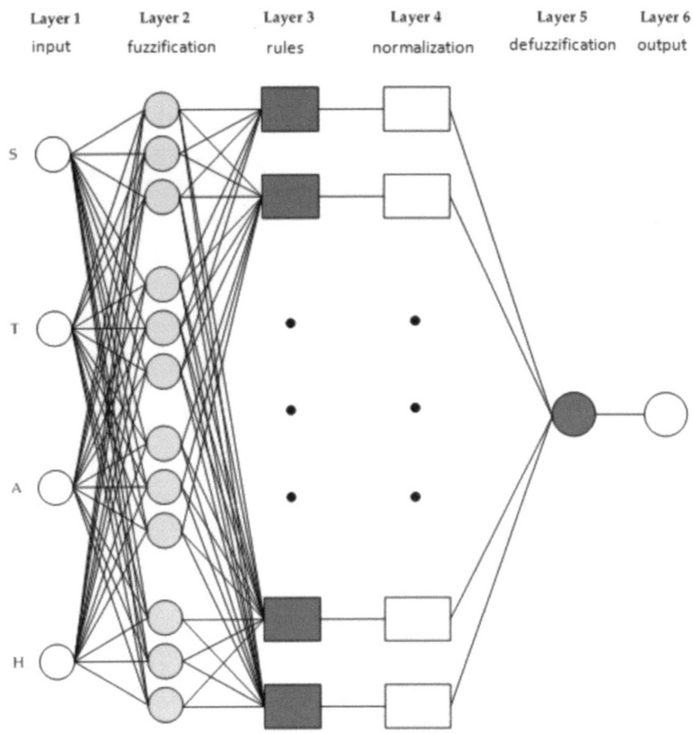

Fig. 6. ANFIS model structure

From the Fig. 6, every nodes of the same layer have similar functions. Layer 1 is the input layer and the neurons in this layer simply pass external crisp signals to Layer 2.

$$y_i^{(1)} = \mu_{Si}(S)$$
$$y_i^{(1)} = \mu_{Ti}(T)$$
$$y_i^{(1)} = \mu_{Ai}(A) \qquad (11)$$
$$y_i^{(1)} = \mu_{Hi}(H)$$

Where:
$\mu_{Si}(S), \mu_{Ti}(T), \mu_{Ai}(A), \mu_{Hi}(H)$ are the input
S_i, T_i, A_i, H_i are the linguistic value
$y_i^{(1)}$ is the output of input neuron *i* in Layer 1

Layer 2 is the fuzzification layer. Neurons in this layer perform fuzzification. In this student model, fuzzification neurons have a Gaussian function. A Gaussian function, which has a Gaussian shape, is specified as:

$$y_i^{(2)} = e^{-(\frac{x_i^{(2)} - c_i}{2\sigma})^2} \qquad (12)$$

Where:
$x_i^{(2)}$ is the input
$y_i^{(2)}$ is the output of neuron *i* in Layer 2
c represents the membership function's center
σ determines the membership function's width

Layer 3 is the rule layer. Each neuron in this layer corresponds to a single to a single Sugeno type fuzzy rule. A rule neuron receives inputs from the respective fuzzification neurons and calculates the firing strength of the rule it represents. In an ANFIS, the conjunction of the rule antecedents is evaluated by the operator product (Negnevitsky, 2005). Each node output represents the firing strength of a rule. Thus, the output of neuron *i* in Layer 3 is obtain as,

$$y_i^{(3)} = \overline{w_i} = \mu_{Si}(S) \times \mu_{Ti}(T) \times \mu_{Ai}(A) \times \mu_{Hi}(H) \quad i = 1,2 \qquad (13)$$

Layer 4 is the normalization layer. Each neuron in this layer receives inputs from all neurons in the rule layer and calculates the normalized firing strength of a given rule. The normalized firing strength is the ratio of the firing strength of a given rule to the sum of firing strengths of all rules. It represents the contribution of a given rule to the final result.

$$y_i^{(4)} = \overline{w_i} = \frac{w_i}{w_1 + w_2 + w_3 + w_4} \qquad (14)$$

Layer 5 is the defuzzification layer. Each neuron in this layer is connected to the respective normalization neuron and also receives initial input S, T, A, and H. A defuzzification neuron calculates the weighted consequent value of a given rule as,

$$y_i^{(5)} = \overline{w_i} f_i = \overline{w_i}(a_i S + b_i T + c_i NT + d_i NH + e_i) \qquad (15)$$

Where:
$\overline{w_i}$ is the output of the Layer 4
$y_i^{(5)}$ is the output of defuzzification neuron i in Layer 5
$\{a_i, b_i, c_i, d_i, e_i\}$ is a set of consequent parameter of rule i

Layer 6 is represented by a single summation neuron. This neuron calculates the sum of outputs of all defuzzification neurons and produces the overall ANFIS output (y).

$$y_i^{(6)} = overall\ output = \sum_i \overline{w_i} f_i = \frac{\sum_i w_i f_i}{\sum_i w_i} \tag{16}$$

4.2 Training with different training datasets

The preparation of the input patterns for training the ANFIS involves the conversion of the linguistic terms of the fuzzy rules into numeric values. Initially, there are 44 rules that are the certain and consistent rules, which are obtained from the human experts. The total number of input patterns for the training datasets is 44 rather than 18, because the 'x' symbol used in rule-18 in Table 4 should be represented by all possible linguistic terms for the respective antecedents.

The increments of the training datasets are very important until the ANFIS model had provided the best result and reasonably able to classify all of the student performance. Due to insufficient training data problem, the increments of 10 training patterns were proposed. Therefore, besides the 44 input patterns for training, this research also proposes 54, 64 and 69 trained ANFIS model.

In order to determine the best ANFIS model, ten tests had been carried out for each model and calculate their mean square errors (MSE). The error is the difference between the training data output value, and the output of the ANFIS corresponding to the same training data input value. The ANFIS model with the lowest mean square errors is being chosen for the next experiment.

4.3 Results and discussion on ANFIS

This section explains the testing results of the three ANFIS model selected from the trained fuzzy inference system. All the results had been tabulated in a line graphs to compare between ANFIS output based on 44, 54, 64 and 69 training datasets, respectively and the testing data.

In this section, four ANFIS model selected from the previous experiment are selected to test the 81 input data patterns. All the results had been tabulated into a line graphs to compare between the ANFIS output. Fig. 7 shows the comparison between ANFIS outputs based on 44 training datasets and testing data. There are 69.14% of the input patterns which are classified successfully and 30.86% which are misclassified.

Besides that, Fig. 8 shows the comparison between ANFIS outputs based on 54 training datasets and testing data. From the graph, there are 85.19% were classified successfully and 14.81% were misclassified. Therefore, the increment of the training datasets need to be executed, so that able to achieve better result.

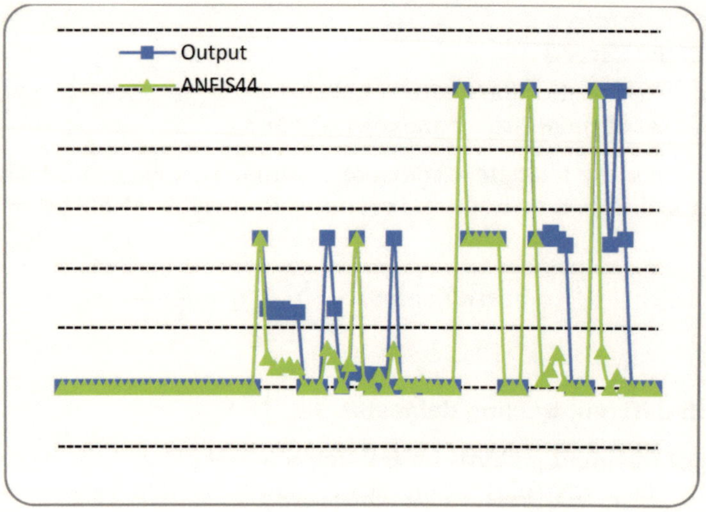

Fig. 7. Comparison between ANFIS outputs based on 44 training datasets and testing data

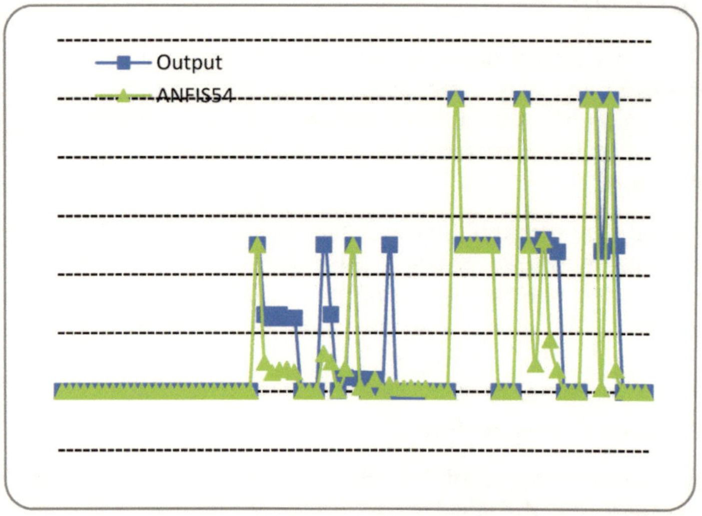

Fig. 8. Comparison between ANFIS outputs based on 54 training datasets and testing data

After incrementing the training data from 54 to 64, the results seem becomes better. Fig. 9 shows the comparison between outputs of ANFIS model based on 64 training datasets and outputs of the checking data. The outcomes of the trained ANFIS able to achieved up to 96.3% which are classified successfully. However, still have some of outputs are illogical decisions. There are 3.7% of the decisions are illogically.

Thus, another experiment carried out by using the 69 training datasets and finally the all the outputs of the ANFIS are able to classify all the 81 input patterns successfully. We can see it clearly in the Fig. 10. From the graph, both of the outputs are same and the ANFIS model can classify the student performance correctly in all possible conditions.

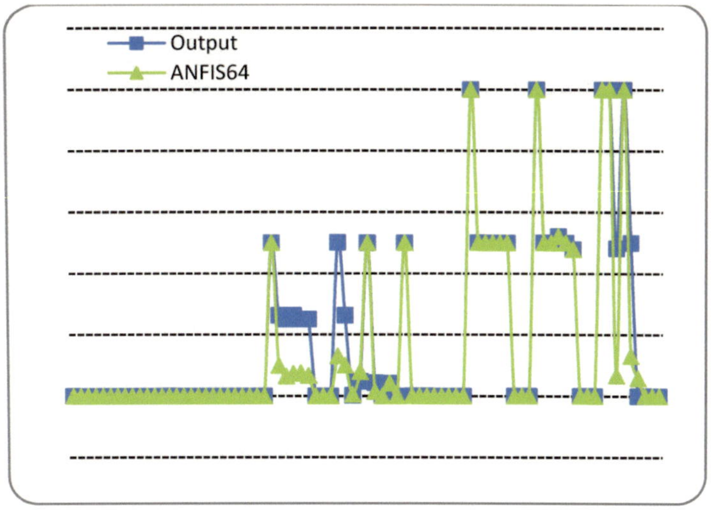

Fig. 9. Comparison between ANFIS outputs based on 64 training datasets and testing data

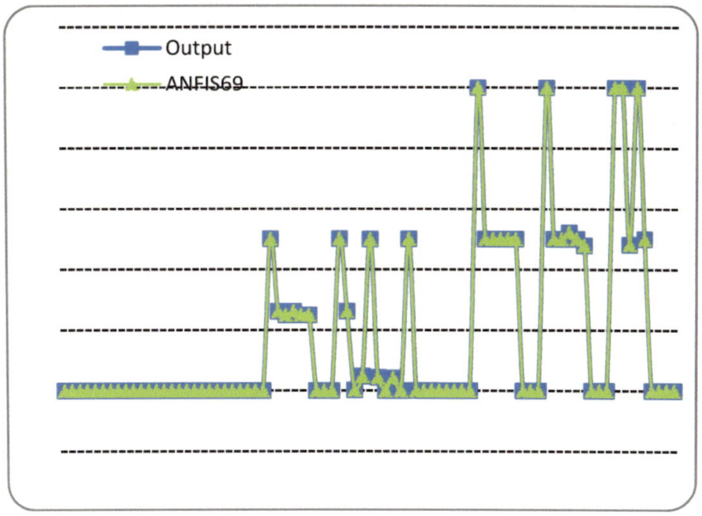

Fig. 10. Comparison between ANFIS outputs based on 69 training datasets and testing data

Moreover, the percentage of successful classification for each input data pattern have been calculated and shown in the Table 4 and Fig. 10. The table below indicates that the human experts' fuzzy rule base consisting of only 18 rules has the possibility of not giving all classification result. For 81 input datasets have been tested only 62% successfully classified; 1500 random input datasets, 66% successfully give the desired result. Meanwhile ANFIS based on 69 training datasets yield encouraging results than human experts' fuzzy rule base, they have successfully classified all the given input.

By analyzing and comparing the experimental results for the five fuzzy rule bases, it can be concluded that the human experts' fuzzy rule base is consistent but incomplete. This is because the 18 rules in this rule base were carefully selected to give full certainty for decisions. However, we found that not all situations covered by this 18 fuzzy rules and still have some rules are not stated. On the contrary, the complete fuzzy rule base in ANFIS is complete but still got some rules are inconsistent and the decision output is not logically. Although all situations for all four attributes are covered by the set of 81 rules, some of the rules have been found to have unnecessary conditions. Thus, the increment of the training data need to done, so that the ANFIS based on 69 training datasets able to eliminate the unnecessary conditions and the illogical decisions. Finally, the ANFIS model is consistent and complete; all situations for all four attributes are covered by the set of 69 training data, and there are no missing rules.

Fuzzy Rule Base	**Input data patterns**	
	81	**1500**
Human Experts	62.00%	66.00%
ANFIS (44)	69.14%	89.60%
ANFIS (54)	85.19%	99.47%
ANFIS (64)	96.30%	99.73%
ANFIS (69)	100.00%	100.00%

Table 5. Percentage of successful classifications correctly

5. Rough-fuzzy approach

ANFIS approach described in Section 4 has successfully formed a complete fuzzy rule that able to solve the problem of incomplete and vague decisions made by human. However, not all rules generated are significant and thus it is important to extract only the most significant rules in order to improve the classification accuracy. In this work, we propose Rough-Fuzzy approach to refine the fuzzy rule base into a concise fuzzy rule base (refer Fig. 11).

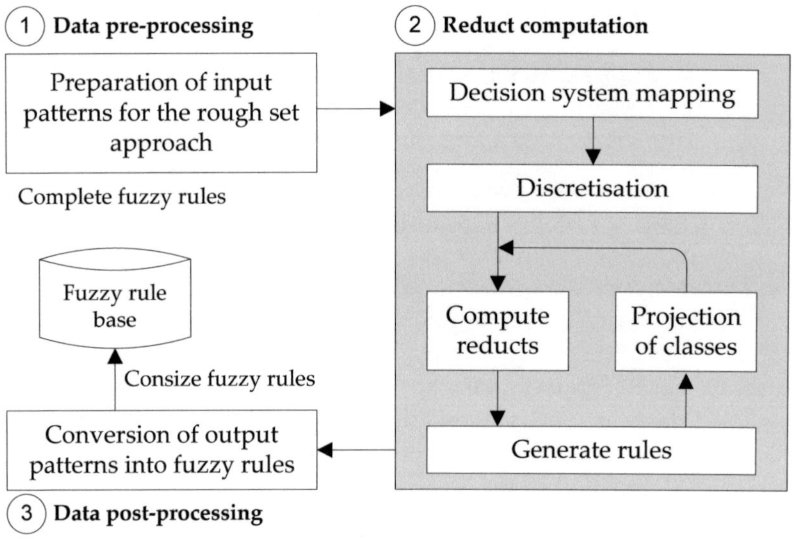

Fig. 11. The rough–fuzzy approach to constructing concise fuzzy rules

5.1 Rough fuzzy phases

The three main phases in the rough-fuzzy approach are data pre-processing, reduct computation and data post-processing as shown in Fig. 11 and described as follows:

Phase 1. Data pre-processing.

In this phase, the complete fuzzy rules are converts from linguistic terms into numeric values that correspond to the rough set format.

Phase 2. Reduct computation.

The fuzzy rules are mapped into a decision system format, discretisation of data, computation of reducts from data and derivation of rules from reducts.

a. In this problem, the fuzzy rules are mapped as rows; while the antecedents and the consequents of the rules are mapped into columns. In the rough set decision table, the antecedents and consequents of the fuzzy rules are labelled as condition and decision attributes, respectively.
b. Discretisation refers to the process of arranging the attribute values into groups of similar values. It involves the transformation of the fuzzy linguistic descriptions of the conditions and the decision attributes into numerical values. In this study, a conversion scheme is formulated to transform the conditions and decisions of fuzzy linguistic values into numerical representations.
c. Computation of reduct
   The reduct computation stage determines the selection of an important attribute that can be used to represent the decision system (Carlin et al., 1998). It is used to reduce the decision system, thus generating more concise rules. The rough set approach employs two important concepts related to reduction: one is related to reduction of rows, and the other one is related to reduction of columns (Chen, 1999). With the notion of an indiscernibility class, the rows with certain properties are grouped together, while with the notion of dispensable attributes, the columns with less important attributes are removed. Another essential concept in reduct computation is the lower and upper approximations, in which the computation involved in the lower approximation produces rules that are certain, while the computation involved in the upper approximation produces possible rules (Øhrn, 2001).
d. Rule Generation. A reduct is converted into a rule by binding the condition attribute values of the object class from which the reduct is originated to the corresponding attribute.

Phase 3. Data post-processing

The rules in rough set format are converted into linguistic terms of the concise fuzzy rule base.

5.2 Rough fuzzy experiment

In Section 4, there are 81 datasets that represent every possible value of the fuzzy rules with full certainty. This dataset is used for the development of the ANFIS model. Using Rosetta as rough set tool, the genetic algorithm with object reduct is the method used for computing reducts (Øhrn, 2001). This method implements a genetic algorithm for computing minimal hitting sets as described by Vinterbo and Øhrn (2000). Using rough set, we trained the fuzzy rules incrementally with different training data set that consist of 44, 54, 64 and 69 input data patterns as described in Section 4. The purpose of the iteration with different input patterns of ANFIS is to ensure that the decision is agreed by human expert.

Table 6 shows the number of reducts, the number of rules and the rule percentage of rough set experiment with different input patterns. The result shows that ANFIS with 69 input patterns generates more concise rule with less number of reducts and less number of rules extracted compared to ANFIS with other pattern.

Model	No of Reducts	No of Rules	Percentage of Rules
1. Human expert	6	13	16%
2. ANFIS with 44 input patterns	11	23	28%
3. ANFIS with 54 input patterns	9	16	20%
4. ANFIS with 64 input patterns	7	13	16%
5. ANFIS with 69 input patterns	4	8	10%

Table 6. Number of reducts and rules based on different input patterns

To determine whether the performance of the concise fuzzy rule base is consistent with the performance of the complete fuzzy rule base, each rule bases of input patterns is compared.

Table 7 shows that the decision output given by both the rule bases of each input patterns has very small differences (in terms of its mean square error). This result confirms that the concise fuzzy rule base does not degrade the performance of the complete fuzzy rule base.

It can be seen from Table 7 that ANFIS with 69 input patterns matched exactly as predicted by experts with MSE value equal to zero. The reducts and rules generated by rough set for ANFIS with 69 input patterns is chosen for further discussion.

Complete Rule Base (81 Rules)	Concise Rule Base	MSE
ANFIS with 44 input patterns	23 Rules	4.76E07
ANFIS with 54 input patterns	16 Rules	1.02E07
ANFIS with 64 input patterns	13 Rules	3.70E10
ANFIS with 69 input patterns	8 Rules	0.00

Table 7. MSE result of Complete vs Concise Rule Base

Furthermore, Table 8 shows four object-related reduct generated by Rosetta for ANFIS with 69 input patterns. All reducts has 100% support, which mean that all objects are mapped deterministically into a decision class. In other words, the support for the decision rule is the probability of an object to be covered by the description that belongs to the class (Grzymala-Busse, 1991).

Class	Reduct	Support
C_1	{Score}	100
C_2	{Attempt}	100
C_3	{Score , Attempt}	100
C_4	{Score , Attempt, Help}	100

Table 8. Object-related reduct based on ANFIS 69 model

Rules generated from reduct are representative rules extracted from the data set. Since a reduct is not unique, rule sets generated from different reducts contain different sets of rules as shown in Table 9.

Rule set	Rules
R_1	Score = low => Performance = not mastered
R_2	Attempt = many => Performance = not mastered
R_3	Score = moderate AND Attempt = a few => Performance = moderately mastered
R_4	Score= moderate AND Attempt = average => Performance = moderately mastered
R_5	Score= high AND Attempt = average => Performance = moderately mastered
R_6	Score= high AND Attempt = a few AND Help = little => Performance = has mastered
R_7	Score= high AND Attempt = a few AND Help = average => Performance = moderately mastered
R_8	Score= high AND Attempt = a few AND Help = needed => Performance = moderately mastered

Table 9. Rule Generation

For example, the given reduct from Table 8 i.e. reduct {Score, Attempt}, is presented by three rules as shown in Table 9 namely R_3, R_4, and R_5.

R_3 : IF Score = moderate AND Attempt = a few THEN Performance = moderately mastered

R_4 : IF Score= moderate AND Attempt = average THEN Performance = moderately mastered

R_5 : IF Score= high AND Attempt = average THEN Performance = moderately mastered

A unique feature of the rough set method is its generation of rules that played an important role in predicting the output. Table 10 listed the rule generation analysis by Rosetta and provides some statistics for the rules which are support, accuracy, coverage and length. The rule coverage and accuracy are measured to determine the reliability of the rules. Below is the definition of the rule statistics (Bose, 2006).

a. The rule support is defined as the number of records in the training data that fully exhibit property described by the IF condition.
b. The rule accuracy is defined as the number of RHS support divided by the number of LHS support.
c. The conditional coverage is the fraction of the records that satisfied the IF conditions of the rule. It is obtained by dividing the support of the rule by the total number of records in the training sample.
d. The decision coverage is the fraction of the training records that satisfied the THEN conditions. It is obtained by dividing the support of the rule by the number of records in the training that satisfied the THEN condition.
e. The rule length is defined as the number of conditional elements in the IF part.

RS	RSupp	RA	CA	DC	RL
R_1	27	1	27/81= 0.333333	27/45= 0.6	1
R_2	27	1	27/81= 0.333333	27/45= 0.6	1
R_3	9	1	9/81= 0.111111	9/33= 0.272727	2
R_4	9	1	9/81= 0.111111	9/33= 0.272727	2
R_5	9	1	9/81= 0.111111	9/33= 0.272727	2
R_6	3	1	3/81= 0.037037	3/3=1	3
R_7	3	1	3/81= 0.037037	3/33= 0.090909	3
R_8	3	1	3/81= 0.037037	3/33= 0.090909	3

Legend:
RS – Rule Sets, RSupp – Rule Support, RA – Rule Accuracy, CA – Conditional Coverage, DC – Decision Coverage, RL – Rule Length

Table 10. Rule Generation Analysis

Coverage gives a measure of how well the objects describe the decision class. The conditional coverage is measured by the ratio of the number of rules that fulfil the conditional part of the rules to the overall number of rules in the sample. Meanwhile, the decision coverage is measured by the ratio of the number of rules that give decision rules to the overall number of rules in the sample. Accuracy gives a measure of how trustworthy the rule is in the condition. It is the probability that an arbitrary object belonging to Class C is covered by the description of the reduct (Grzymala-Busse, 1991). According to Pawlak (1998), an accuracy value of 1 indicates that the classes have been classified into decision classes with full certainty and consistency.

For example, there are 27 objects that fulfil the conditional part of the rule R_1, compared with the overall 81 rules in the sample. Therefore, the conditional coverage of this rule is about 0.3333. In addition, the decision for the performance and learning efficiency with the value of not mastered is used once in the fuzzy rule base and it is only given to rule R_1. Therefore, the decision coverage for this rule is 1. Finally, the accuracy value of this rule is 1, which means that this rule belongs to Class C_1 and is covered. Thus, it is said to have full certainty and is consistent. In conclusion, because all of the rules in Table 10 have accuracy values of 1, the concise fuzzy rules are reliable because they are covered, have full certainty, and are consistent.

6. Conclusion

In this study, fuzzy inference models provide an efficient way to reason about a student's learning achievement in quantitative way. In this work, a complete fuzzy rule base are formed using ANFIS approach, where all possible input conditions of the fuzzy rules are being generated apart from the 18 human experts' rules that are considered certain. By training the neural network with selected 18 conditions that are certain, the ANFIS is able to recognize other decisions that are previously not complete, in both the antecedents and consequent parts of the fuzzy rules. However, some of the decisions are found misclassified and inconsistent. In addition, it is realized that the number of fuzzy rules formed is directly related to the number of fuzzy term sets defined at the antecedents. As the number of fuzzy term sets increases, the fuzzy rules will also increases and will affect the computation time and space. Besides that, when there are too many rules, some of the rules may be found not significant. Therefore, this work proposes the Rough-Fuzzy approach that able to reduce the complete fuzzy rule base into a concise fuzzy rule base. This approach able to determine the selection of important attributes that can be used to represent the fuzzy rule base system. Therefore, the condition space is reduced by taking only a few conditions to achieve a reasonable size of the condition subspace. Moreover, the proposed concise fuzzy rule base is said to be reliable, due to the fact that it is covered, consistent and have full certainty.

7. Acknowledgment

The authors are especially grateful to the members of the Soft Computing Research Group (SCRG), Faculty of Computer Science and Information Systems, University of Technology Malaysia, for their encouraging support to this work. The authors would also like to thank Universiti Teknologi Malaysia (UTM) for their financial support under Research University Grant Vot. No. Q.J130000.7128.01H82 and Q.J130000.7128.02J57 as well as the FRGS Grant - Vot No. 4F026(NT:2000957).

8. References

Bose, I. (2006). Deciding the Financial Health of Dotcoms using Rough Sets, *Information & Management*, Vol. 43, No. 7, pp. 835-846, October, ISSN 0378-7206.

Carlin, U.S.; Komorowski, J. & Ohrn, A. (1998). Rough set analysis of patients with suspected acute appendicitis, *Proceedings of Information Processing and Management of Uncertainty in Knowledge-based Systems*, pp. 1528–1533.

Chen, Z. (1999). *Computational Intelligence for Decision Support.* CRC Press, ISBN 0849317991.

Grzymala-Busse, J.W. (1991). *Managing Uncertainty in Expert Systems*, Kluwer Academic Publishers, Boston, ISBN 0792391691.

Jamshidi, M. (2001). Autonomous control of complex systems: robotic applications, *Applied Mathematics and Computation*, Vol. 120, No. 1–3, pp. 15–29, ISSN 0096-3003.

Jang, J., -S. (1993). ANFIS:Adaptive-Network-Based Fuzzy Inference. *IEEE Trans. on Systems, Man and Cybernetics* 23: 665-685, ISSN 0018-9472.

Jang, J.-S. R.; Sun, C. -T., Mizutani, E. (1997). *Neuro-Fuzzy And Soft Computing: A Computational Approach to Learning and Machine Intelligence.* (1st ed.), United States of America: Prentice Hall, ISBN 0132610663.

Khoo, L.P. & Zhai, L.Y. (2001). Rclass*: *A Prototype Rough-set and Genetic Algorithms Enhanced Multi-concept Classification System for Manufacturing Diagnosis*, CRC Press.

Kosba, E.; Dimitrova, V. & Boyle, R., (2003) Using fuzzy techniques to model students in Web-based learning environment, in Palade, V., Howlett, R.J. & Jain, L. (Eds.): *Knowledge-based Intelligent Information and Engineering Systems*, 7th International Conference, KES 2003, Oxford, United Kingdom, September 2003, Proceedings Part II, pp. 222–229.

Lin, C. & Lu, Y. (1996). A neural fuzzy system with fuzzy supervised learning, *IEEE Transactions on Systems Man and Cybernetics, Part B* 26, pp. 744–763, ISSN 1083-4419.

Nedic, Z.; Nedic, V. & Machotka, J. (2002). Intelligent tutoring system for teaching 1st year engineering, *World Transactions on Engineering and Technology Education 2002, UICEE*, Vol. 1, No. 2, pp. 241–244.

Negnevitsky, M. (2005). Artificial Intelligence – A Guide to Intelligent Systems, Addison Wesley, ISBN 0-321-20466-2.

Norazah, Y. (2005). *Student Learning Assessment Model Using Hybrid Method*. Phd thesis. Universiti Kebangsaan Malaysia, Malaysia.

Øhrn, A. (2001). Rosetta Technical Reference Manual, Department of Computer and Information Science, Norwegian University of Science and Technology, Trondheim, Norway.

Pawlak, Z. (1998). Reasoning about data - A rough set perspective, *In*: Polkowski, L. and Skowron, A. (eds.), *Rough Sets and Current Trends in Computing '98*, (pp. 25–34), Berlin: Springer-Verlag, ISBN 3-540-64655-8.

Saleh. I., & Kim, S.I. (2009). A fuzzy system for evaluating student's learning achievement. *Expert systems with Applications*. 36(2009), pp. 6236-6243, ISSN 0957-4174.

San Pedro, J. & Burstein, F. (2003). Intelligent assistance, retrieval, reminder and advice for fuzzy multicriteria decision-making, in Palade, V., Howlett, R.J. & Jain, L.C. (Eds.): KES 2003, pp. 37–44, Springer-Verlag, Berlin, Heidelberg.

Sivanandam, S.N.; Sumathi, S., & Deepa, S.N. (2007). *Introduction to Fuzzy Logic using Matlab*. (1st ed.) Berlin Heidelberg, New York: Springer, ISBN 3540357807.

Taylan, O. & Karagözoğlu, B. (2009). An adaptive neurofuzzy model for prediction of student's academic performance. *Computers & Industrial Engineering*. pp. 1-10.

Tsaganou, G.; Grigoriadou, M. & Cavoura, T. (2002). Modelling student's comprehension of historical text using fuzzy casebased reasoning, *Proceedings of the 6th European Workshop on Case-based Reasoning for Education and Training*, Aberdeen, Scotland.

Vinterbo, S. & Øhrn A. (2000). Minimal approximate hitting sets and rule templates, *International Journal of Approximate Reasoning*, Vol. 25, No. 2, pp. 123–143, ISSN: 0888-613X.

Xu, D.; Wang, H. & Su, K. (2002). Intelligent student profiling with fuzzy models, *Proceeding of the 35th International Conference on System Sciences*, pp. 1–8, ISBN:0-7695-1435-9.

Yang, Y.; Hinde, C. & Gillingwater, D. (2005). A conceptual framework for society-oriented decision support, *AI and Society*, Vol. 19, pp.279–291, Springer-Verlag, ISSN 978-1-4244-5330-6.

Yusof, N.; Mohd. Zin, N. A., Mohd. Yassin, N., & Samsuri P. (2009). Evaluation of Student's Performance and Learning Efficiency based on ANFIS, *SocPar* pp. 460 - 465, ISBN 978-1-4244-5330-6.

Section 3

Application to Mechanical and Industrial Engineering Problems

Control of Efficient Intelligent Robotic Gripper Using Fuzzy Inference System

A.M. Zaki[1], O.A. Mahgoub[2], A.M. El-Shafei[2] and A.M. Soliman[1]
[1]*Power Electronics and Energy Conversion Department*
Electronics Research Institute, Cairo
[2]*Electric Power and Machines Department*
Faculty of Engineering, Cairo University, Cairo
Egypt

1. Introduction

In the last few years the applications of artificial intelligence techniques have been used to convert human experience into a form understandable by computers. Advanced control based on artificial intelligence techniques is called intelligent control. Intelligent systems are usually described by analogies with biological systems by, for example, looking at how human beings perform control tasks, recognize patterns, or make decisions. Fuzzy logic is a way to make machines more intelligent enabling them to reason in a fuzzy manner like humans. Fuzzy logic, proposed by Lotfy Zadeh in 1965, emerged as a tool to deal with uncertain, imprecise, or qualitative decision-making problems (Zadeh, 1965).

Controllers that combine intelligent and conventional techniques are commonly used in the intelligent control of complex dynamic systems. Therefore, embedded fuzzy controllers automate what has traditionally been a human control activity.

Traditional control approach requires modeling of the physical reality. Three methods may be used in the description of a system (Passino & Yurkovich, 1998) :

1. By experimenting and determining how the process reacts to various inputs, one can characterize an input-output table.
2. Control engineering requires an idealized mathematical model of the controlled process, usually in the form of differential or difference equations. But problems arise in developing a meaningful and realistic mathematical description of an industrial process: i- Poorly understood phenomena, ii- Inaccurate values of various parameters, iii-Model complexity.
3. Heuristic Methods: The heuristic method consists of modeling and understanding in accordance with previous experience, rules-of-thumb and often-used strategies. A heuristic rule is a logical implication of the form: If <condition> Then <consequence>, or in a typical control situation: If <condition> Then <action>. Rules associate conclusions with conditions. Therefore, the heuristic method is actually similar to the experimental method of constructing a table of inputs and corresponding output values where instead of having crisp numeric values of input and output variables, one use fuzzy values: IF input_voltage = Large THEN output_voltage = Medium.

Fuzzy control strategies come from experience and experiments rather than from mathematical models and, therefore, linguistic implementations are much faster accomplished. Fuzzy control strategies involve a large number of inputs, most of which are relevant only for some special conditions. Such inputs are activated only when the related condition prevails. In this way, little additional computational overhead is required for adding extra rules. As a result, the rule base structure remains understandable, leading to efficient coding and system documentation.

2. Logical inference

A connection between cause and effect, or a condition and a consequence is made by reasoning. Reasoning can be expressed by a logical inference or by the evaluation of inputs in order to draw a conclusion. We usually follow rules of inference which have the form: IF cause1 = A and cause2 = B THEN effect = C. Where A, B and C are linguistic variables.

2.1 Fuzzy sets

A fuzzy set is represented by a membership function defined on the universe of discourse. The universe of discourse is the space where the fuzzy variables are defined. The membership function gives the grade, or degree, of membership within the set of any element of the universe of discourse. The membership function maps the elements of the universe onto numerical values in the interval [0, 1]. A membership function value of zero implies that the corresponding element is definitely not an element of the fuzzy set, while a value of unity means that the element fully belongs to the set. A grade of membership in between corresponds to the fuzzy membership to the set. In practical situations there is always a natural **fuzzification** when someone analysis statements and a smooth membership curve usually better describes the grade that an element belongs to a set (Erdirencelebi et al., 2011).

Fuzzification: is the process of decomposing a system input and/or output into one or more fuzzy sets. Many types of curves can be used, but triangular or trapezoidal shaped membership functions are the most common because they are easier to represent in embedded controllers.

Fig. 1 shows a system of fuzzy sets for an input with trapezoidal and triangular membership functions.

The figure illustrates the process of fuzzification of the air temperature in order to control the operation of an air-conditioning system. There are five fuzzy sets for temperature: COLD, COOL, GOOD, WARM, and HOT.

Defuzzification: After fuzzy reasoning, we have a linguistic output variable that needs to be translated into a crisp value. The objective is to derive a single crisp numeric value that best represents the inferred fuzzy values of the linguistic output variable. Defuzzification is such inverse transformation which maps the output from the fuzzy domain back into the crisp domain.

Most commercial fuzzy products are rule-based systems that receive current information in the feedback loop from the device as it operates and control the operation of a mechanical or other device (Simoes & Friedhofer, 1997; Simoes & Franceschetti, 1999). A fuzzy logic system has four blocks as shown in figure 2. Crisp input information from the device is converted into fuzzy values for each input fuzzy set with the fuzzification block. The universe of discourse of the input variables determines the required scaling for correct per-unit operation. The scaling is very important because the fuzzy system can be retrofitted with other devices or ranges of operation by just changing the scaling of the input and output. The decision-making-logic determines how the fuzzy logic operations are performed, and together with the knowledge base determine the outputs of each fuzzy IF-THEN rule. Those are combined and converted to crispy values with the defuzzification block. The output crisp value can be calculated by the center of gravity.

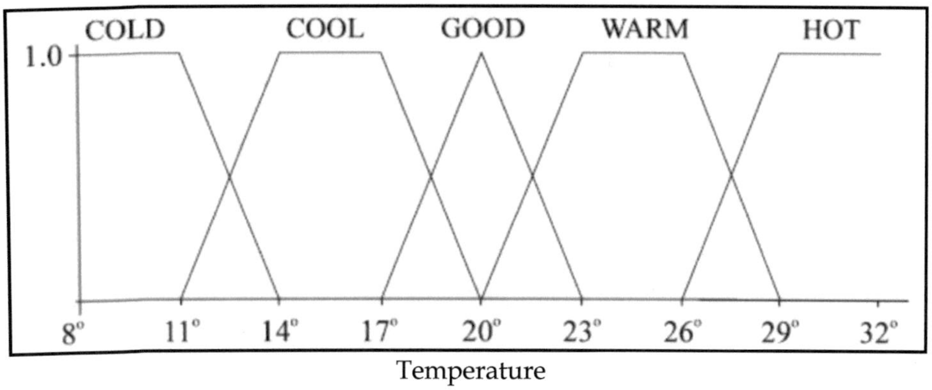

Fig. 1. Fuzzy sets defining temperature.

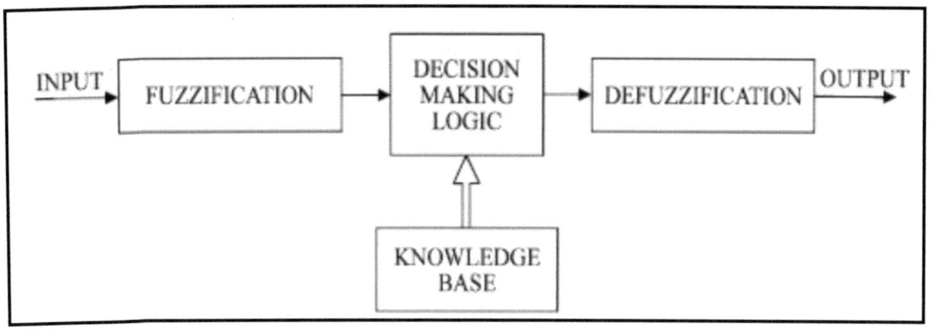

Fig. 2. Fuzzy Controller Block Diagram.

In order to process the input output reasoning, there are six steps involved in the creation of a rule based fuzzy system:

1. Identify the inputs and their ranges and name them.
2. Identify the outputs and their ranges and name them.
3. Create the degree of fuzzy membership function for each input and output.
4. Construct the rule base that the system will operate under.
5. Decide how the action will be executed by assigning strengths to the rules.
6. Combine the rules and defuzzify the output.

3. Adaptive Neuro-Fuzzy Inference System (ANFIS)

In spite of some non-linear control problems can be handled using neural control schemes, in situations where there is precise tracking of fast trajectories for non-linear systems with high nonlinearities and large uncertainties, neural control schemes are severely inadequate (Denai et al., 2004). Adaptive Neuro-Fuzzy Inference Systems are realized by an appropriate combination of neural and fuzzy systems and provide a valuable modeling approach of complex systems (Denai et al., 2004; Rezaeeian et al., 2008; Hanafy, 2010).

The proper selection of the number, the type and the parameter of the fuzzy membership functions and rules is crucial for achieving the desired performance and in most situations, it is difficult. Yet, it has been done in many applications through trial and error. This fact highlights the significance of tuning fuzzy system. Adaptive Neuro-Fuzzy Inference Systems are Fuzzy Sugeno models put in the framework of adaptive systems to facilitate learning and adaptation. Such framework makes FLC more systematic and less relying on expert knowledge. To present the ANFIS architecture, let us consider two-fuzzy rules based on a first order Sugeno model:

Rule 1: if (x is A_1) and (y is B_1) then

$$(f_1 = p_1x + q_1y + r_1)$$

Rule 2: if (x is A_2) and (y is B_2) then

$$(f_2 = p_2x + q_2y + r_2)\text{j}$$

ANFIS architecture to implement these two rules is shown in figure 3. Note that a circle indicates a fixed node whereas a square indicates an adaptive node (the parameters are changed during training). In the following presentation O_L denotes the output of node i in layer L.a

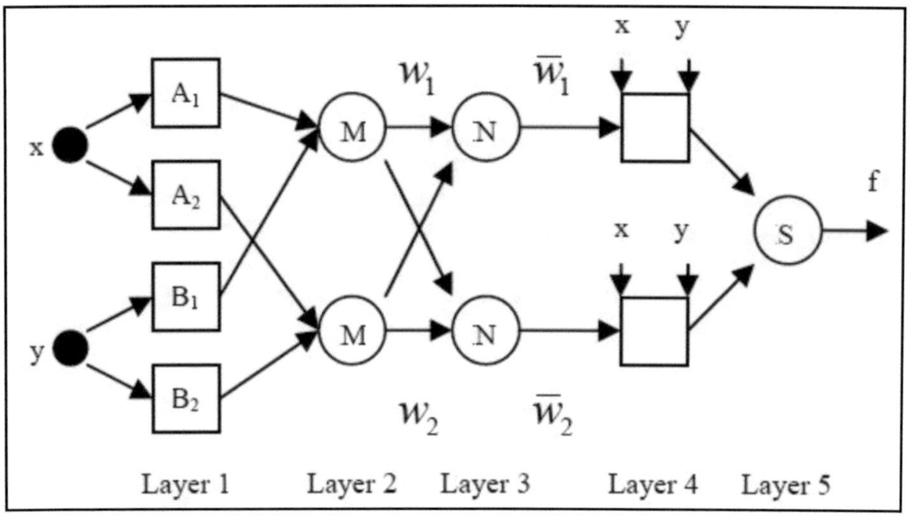

Fig. 3. Construct of ANFIS.

Layer 1: the fuzzy membership function (MF) represented by the node: All the nodes in this layer are adaptive nodes, i is the degree of the membership of the input to

$$O_{1,i} = \mu_{Ai}(x) \qquad i=1,2$$

Where a_i, b_i, and c_i are the parameters for the MF

$$O_{1,i} = \mu_{Bi-2}(y) \qquad i=3,4 \tag{1}$$

A_i and B_i can be any appropriate fuzzy sets in parameter form. For example, if bell MF is used then

$$\mu_{Ai}(x) = \frac{1}{1+[(\frac{x-c_i}{a_i})^2]^{b_i}} \qquad i=1,2 \tag{2}$$

Layer 2: The nodes in this layer are fixed (not adaptive). These are labeled M to indicate that they play the role of a simple multiplier. The outputs of these nodes are given by:

$$O_{2,i} = w_i = \mu_{Ai}(x)\mu_{Bi}(y) \qquad i=1,2 \tag{3}$$

The output of each node in this layer represents the firing strength of the rule.

Layer 3: Nodes in this layer are also fixed nodes. These are labeled N to indicate that these perform a normalization of the firing strength from previous layer. The output of each node in this layer is given by:

$$O_{3,i} = \overline{w}_i = \frac{w_i}{w_1 + w_2} \qquad i=1,2 \tag{4}$$

Layer 4: All the nodes in this layer are adaptive nodes. The output of each node is simply the product of the normalized firing strength and a first order polynomial:

$$O_{4,i} = \overline{w}_i f_i = \overline{w}_i(p_i x + q_i y + r_i) \qquad i=1,2 \tag{5}$$

Where: p_i, q_i, and r_i are design parameters (consequent parameter since they deal with the then-part of the fuzzy rule).

Layer 5: This layer has only one node labeled S to indicate that it performs the function of a simple summer. The output of this single node is given by:

$$O_{5,i} = f = \sum_{i=1}^{2} \overline{w}_i f_i = \frac{\sum_{i=1}^{2} w_i f_i}{\sum_{i=1}^{2} w_i} \tag{6}$$

In this ANFIS architecture, there are two adaptive layers (1, 4). Layer 1 has three modifiable parameters (a_i, b_i, and c_i) pertaining to the input MFs. These parameters are called premise parameters. Layer 4 has also three modifiable parameters polynomial. These parameters are called consequent parameters (p_i, q_i, r_i) pertaining to the first order.

In order to improve the training efficiency, a hybrid learning algorithm is applied to justify the parameters of input and output membership functions. The antecedent parameters (the parameters related to input membership functions) and the consequent parameters (the parameters related to output membership functions) are two parameter sets in the architecture which should be tuned. When we suppose that premise parameters are fixed, then the output of ANFIS will be a linear combination of the consequent parameters. So, the output can be written as:

$$f = \overline{w}_1 f_1 + \overline{w}_2 f_2 \tag{7}$$

With substituting Equation (5) in Equation (7), the output can be rearranged as:

$$f = (\overline{w}_1 x)p_1 + (\overline{w}_1 y)q_1 + (\overline{w}_1)r_1 + (\overline{w}_2 x)p_2 + (\overline{w}_2 y)q_2 + (\overline{w}_2)r_2 \tag{8}$$

So, the consequent parameters can be tuned by the least square method. On the other hand, if consequent parameters are fixed, the premise parameters can be adjusted by the gradient descent method. ANFIS utilizes hybrid learning algorithm in which the least square method is used to identify the consequent parameters in forward pass and the gradient descent method is applied to determine the premise parameters in backward pass.

Not yet, many recent developments in evolutionary algorithms have provided several strategies for NFIS design. Three main strategies, including Pittsburg-type, Michigan-type, and iterative rule learning genetic fuzzy systems, focus on generating and learning fuzzy rules in genetic fuzzy systems (Lin et al.;2008)

4. Fuzzy controllers using susbtractive clustering

A common way of developing Fuzzy Controller is by determining the rule base and some appropriate fuzzy sets over the controller's input and output ranges. An efficient approach, namely, Fuzzy Subtractive Clustering is used here, which minimizes the number of rules of Fuzzy Logic Controllers. This technique provides a mechanism to obtain the reduced rule set covering the whole input/ output space as well as membership functions for each input variable. In (Chopra et al., 2006), Fuzzy subtractive clustering approach is shown to reduce 49 rules to 8 rules where simulation of a wide range of linear and nonlinear processes is carried out and results are compared with existing Fuzzy Logic Controller with 49 rules.

4.1 Introduction to cluster analysis

By definition, cluster analysis is grouping of objects into homogenous groups based on same object features. Clustering of numerical data forms the basis of many classification and system-modeling algorithms. The purpose of clustering is to identify natural grouping of data from a large data set to produce a concise representation of a system's behavior. Clustering algorithms typically requires the user to pre-specify the number of cluster centers and their initial locations. The locations of the cluster centers are then adapted in a way such that these can better represent a set of data points covering the range of data behavior. The Fuzzy Clustering Means (FCM) algorithm (Bezdek, 1990) method is well-known example of such clustering algorithm. For these algorithms, the quality of the solution depends strongly on the choice of initial values i.e., the number of cluster centers and their initial locations (Nikhil et al., 1997) .

In (Yager & Filev, 1994), the authors proposed a simple and effective algorithm, called the mountain method, for estimating the number and initial location of cluster centers. Their method is based on girding the data space and computing a potential value for each grid point based on its distances to the actual data points; a grid point with the highest potential value is chosen as the first cluster center and the potential of all grid points are reduced according to their distance from the cluster center. The next cluster center is then placed at the grid point with the highest remaining potential value. This procedure of acquiring new cluster center and reducing the potential of surrounding grid points is repeated until the potential of all grid points falls below a threshold. Although this method is simple and effective, the computation grows exponentially with the dimension of the problem. The author in (Chiu, 1994) proposed an extension of this mountain method, called subtractive clustering, in which each data point, rather than the grid point, is considered as a potential cluster center. Using this method, the number of effective "grid points" to be evaluated is simply equal to the number of data points, independent of the dimension of the problem. Another advantage of this method is that it eliminates the need to specify a grid resolution, in which tradeoffs between accuracy and computational complexity must be considered.

4.2 The subtractive clustering method

To extract rules from data, we first separate the training data into groups according to their respective class. Consider a group of n data points {X1, X2,…, Xn} for a specific class, where Xi is a vector in the input feature space. Assume that the feature space is normalized so that all data are bounded by a unit hypercube. We consider each data point as a potential cluster center for the group and define a measure of the potential of data point Xi to serve as a cluster center as

$$P_i = \sum_{j=1}^{n} e^{-\alpha \left\| x_i - x_j \right\|^2} \quad (9)$$

Where

$$\alpha = \frac{4}{r_a^2} \quad (10)$$

$\|.\|$ denotes the Euclidean distance, and r_a is a positive constant. Thus, the measure of the potential of a data point is a function of its distances to all other data points in its group. A data point with many neighboring data points will have a high potential value. The constant r_a is effectively a normalized radius defining a neighborhood; data points outside this radius have a little influence on the potential. Note that because the data space is normalized, r_a =1.0 is equal to the length of one side of the data space. After the potential of every data point in the group has been computed, we select the data point with the highest potential as the first cluster center. Let x_1^* be the location of the first cluster center and P_1^* be its potential value. We then revise the potential of each data point x_i in the group by the formula

$$P_i \Leftarrow P_i - P_1^* e^{-\beta\left\|x_i - x_1^*\right\|^2} \tag{11}$$

Where

$$\beta = \frac{4}{r_b^2} \tag{12}$$

and r_b is a positive constant. Thus, we subtract an amount of potential from each data point as a function of its distance from the first cluster center. The data points near the first cluster center will have greatly reduced potential, and therefore will unlikely be selected as the next cluster center for the group. The constant r_b is effectively the radius defining the neighborhood which will have measurable reductions in potential. To avoid obtaining closly spaced cluster centers, we typically choose $r_b = 1.25\ r_a$ (Chopra et al. , 2006).

When the potential of all data points in the group has been reduced according to Equation 11, we select the data point with the highest remaining potential as the second cluster center. We then further reduce the potential of each data point according to their distance potential as the second cluster center. In general, after the K' th cluster center has been obtained, we revise the potential of each data point by the formula

$$P_i \Leftarrow P_i - P_k^* e^{-\beta\left\|x_i - x_k^*\right\|^2} \tag{13}$$

Where x_k^* is the location of the K' th cluster center and p_k^* is its potential value. The process of acquiring new cluster center and reducing potential repeats until the remaining potential of all data points in the group is below some fractions of the potential of the first cluster center P_1^*. Typically, one can use $p_k^* < 0.15P_1^*$ as the stopping criterion (Chiu, 1997).

Each cluster center found in the training data of a given class identifies a region in the feature space that is well populated by members of that class. Thus, we can translate each cluster center into a fuzzy rule for identifying the class.

Suppose cluster center x_i^* was found in the group of data for class c1; this cluster center provides the rule:

Rule i : If {x is near x_i^* } then class is c1.

The degree of fulfillment of {x is near x_i^* } is defined as

$$\mu_i = e^{-\alpha\left\|x - x_i^*\right\|^2} \tag{14}$$

Where α is a constant defined by Equation 10 .

By applying subtractive clustering to each class of data individually, we thus obtain a set of rules for identifying each class. The individual sets of rules can then be combined to form the rule base of the classifier. For example, suppose we found 2 clusters centers in class c1 data, and 5 cluster centers in class c2 data, then the rule base will contain 2 rules that identify class c1 members and 5 rules that identify class c2 members. When performing classification, the output class of the classifier is simply determined by the rule with the highest degree of fulfillment.

5. ANFIS control of an intelligent robotic gripper

The effectiveness of the Fuzzy Inference control will be illustrated here by applying the method to control the operation of a robotic gripper. The robotic gripper will be first described, its operation principle will be illustrated, then the application of the Adaptive Network Fuzzy Inference System control to the gripper system will be presented.

Generally, the main goal of robotic gripper during object grasping and object lifting process is applying sufficient force to avoid the risk of a difficult task or sometimes a task that could not be achieved. The problem can be posed as an optimization problem (Ottaviano et al.,2000; Bicchi & Kumar,2000). Sensory systems are very important in this field. Two types of sensing are most actively being investigated to increase robot awareness: contact and non-contact sensing. The main type of non-contact sensing is vision sensing where video camera is processed to give the robot the object information. However, it is costly and gives no data concerning forces (Lorenz et al.,1990). Tactile sensing, on the other hand, has the capability to do proximity sensing as well as force sensing, it is less expensive, faster and needs less complex equipment (Choi et al.,2005). The basic principle of the Slip-Sensitive Reaction used in this work is that, the gripper should be able to automatically react to object slipping during grasp with the application of greater force. A lot of researches have been focusing on fingertip sensors development to detect slippage and applied force (Dario & De Rossi ,1985; Friedrich et al., 2000), which requires complicated drive circuit and suffers from difficult data processing and calibration. Polyvinylidene fluoride (PVDF) piezoelectric sensors are presented in (Barsky et al.,1989) to detect contact normal force as well as slip. Also, an array 8x8 matrix photo resistor is introduced in (Ren et al.,2000) to detect slippage. A slip sensor based on the operation of optical encoder used to monitor the slip rate resulting from insufficient force is presented in (Salami et al, 2000). However, it is expensive and have some constrains on the object to be lifted. Several researchers handle finger adaptation using more than one link in one finger to verify stable grasping (Seguna & Saliba, 2001; Dubey & Crowder, 2004). This results in complicated mechanical system leading to difficulty in control and slow response. Fuzzy controllers have been very successful in solving the grasping problem, as they do not need mathematical model of the system (Dominguez-Lopez & Vila-Rosado, 2006). In this study, a new design and implementation of robotic gripper with electric actuation using brushless dc servo motor is presented. Standard sensors adaptation in this work leads to maintaining the simplicity of the mechanical design and gripper operation keeping a reasonable cost. The gripper control was achieved through two control schemes. System modeling had been introduced using ANFIS approach. A new grasping scenario is used in which we collect information about the masses of the grasped objects before starting the grasping process without any additional sensors. This is achieved through knowledge of object pushing force that allows applying an appropriate force and minimizing object displacement slip through implementation of the proposed fuzzy control.

5.1 Gripper design and configuration

A proper gripper design can simplify the overall robot system assembly, increase the overall system reliability, and decrease the cost of implementing the system. Hence, the design of the gripping system is very important for the successful operation.

5.1.1 Gripper design guidelines

It may not be possible to apply all the guidelines to any one design. Sometimes, one guideline may suggest one design direction while another may suggest the opposite. Each particular situation must be examined and a decision must be made to favor the more relevant guidelines (Monkman et al,2007). The design guidelines may be as follows: -

1. Minimize the gripper weight: This allows the robot to accelerate more quickly.
2. Grasp objects securely: This allows the robot to run at higher speeds thereby reducing the cycle time.
3. Grip multiple objects with a single gripper: This helps to avoid tool changes.
4. Fully encompass the object with the gripper: This is to help hold the part securely.
5. Do not deform the object during grasping: Some objects are easily deformed and care should be taken when grasping these objects.
6. Minimize finger length: Obviously, the longer the fingers of the gripper the more they are going to deflect when grasping an object.
7. Design for proper gripper-object interaction: If, however, a flat surface is being used, then a high friction interface is desired since the part would not be aligned anyway and the higher friction increases the security of the grasp.

5.1.2 Two fingers gripper selection

The objects may vary in size and shape. Thus the gripper should be able to handle objects of different shapes and sizes in a particular range. Gripper should be compact so that it does not interfere with other equipment. The use of conical fingers "three fingers or more" will help holding the parts securely. But if we have an object larger than these conical fingers, the object could not be gripped properly. Parallel moving fingers are a good solution in this case. This parallel movement also helps in gripping objects internally. Since the force is acting at a point or line in conical form of gripping it may lead to wear and tear of both the object and the finger. But in the parallel finger arrangement, the force will be distributed over an area. The two-fingers grasp may be considered the simplest efficient grasping configuration.

5.1.3 Gripper configuration

The developed gripper device was configured with a two parallel finger design for its wide applications in spite of its precise control need. One finger is fixed and the other is movable to ease the control and minimize the cost as shown in figure 4. The fingers are flat and rectangular in shape. The housing of the gripper and fingers were made of aluminum sheet for light weight consideration with proper thickness to ease the machining and holes puncture through edges. This gives simple assembly and ease in maintenance. The movable finger is driven on a lead screw and guided by a linear bearing system with the advantage of self-locking capability, low cost and ease of manufacture.

To control the gripping of the object, we need to measure both the force applied to the object and the object slip. A standard commercial force sensor resistor FSR (Flexiforce A201 working in the range of 0-1 lb (4.4N)) is used to measure the applied force. Also Phidget vibrator sensor is adapted as slip sensor to give information about object slip rate in m/sec. These two sensors are tactile sensors. The actuator used to drive the movable finger is a permanent magnet brushless dc motor (BLDC). It has the advantage of high power density, ease of control, high efficiency, low maintenance and low rotor inertia. BLDC servo motor used is an internal rotor motor "BLD3564B" from Minimotor inc. with its drive circuit "BLD5604-SH2P" .

The design of the gripper fingers must take some restrictions into consideration. Long fingers require high developed torque and short fingers impose restrictions on object dimensions. Hence fingers are selected to be 15 cm long. Also, a contact rubber material area between the fingers and the object of 25 mm by 25 mm is used to decrease the pressure on the object, increase the friction, and avoid deformation from centric concentrated force. With this gripper configuration, we succeeded to verify all previous design guidelines except guideline no.4 as our proposed gripper doesn't fully encompass the object in order to be able to grasp a greater variety of objects, although this imposes more difficulty in the control during gripping.

6. Robotic gripper modeling

To build the proposed controller, we need to get information about the system characteristics for use in simulation and experimental work. Hence, input/output variables of the system are measured and processed. The input variable to the system is the speed control command to the servo motor drive expressed as reference voltage V_{ref} . The applied force on the object is the output variable F_{app}. The deformable compliant rubber material covering the contact area of the fingers, as shown in figure 4, is important to allow a wide range of force control for solid objects as well as decreasing the pressure on the object and increasing the friction. Hence, we need to model the variation of the applied force F_{app} by the gripper finger with time at different reference voltage control commands V_{ref} .

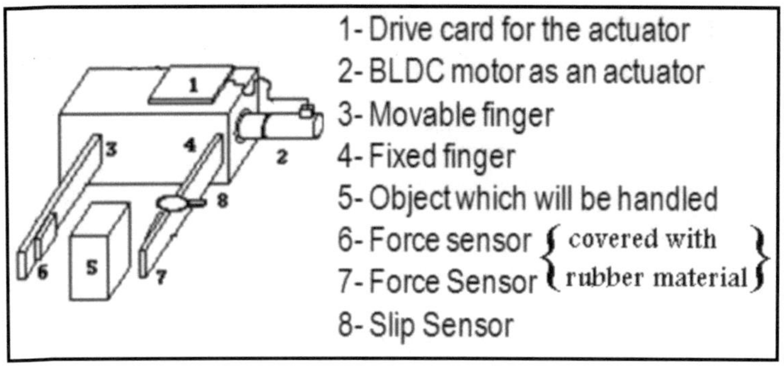

Fig. 4. Gripper configuration.

Experimentally, and due to the mechanism constraint according to the gripper design, the applied force by the gripper fingers F_{app} on the objects could not decrease if the reference voltage control command V_{ref} is decreased. To verify the proposed controller, a model was built using MATLAB software package considering the mechanical constraints, which in turn lead to the accumulation of the applied force when V_{ref} is changed. For practical control, a maximum limit was set to the applied force $F_{max.app}$, figures 5 & 6. From this simulation model, the set of training data, checking data and testing data to be used for ANFIS model training were prepared.

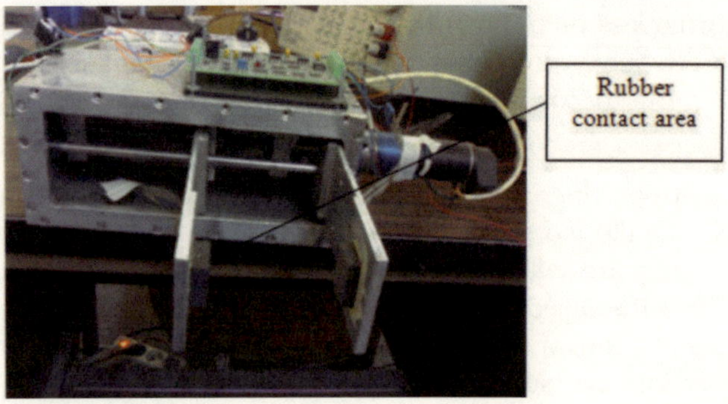

Fig. 5. Gripper prototype.

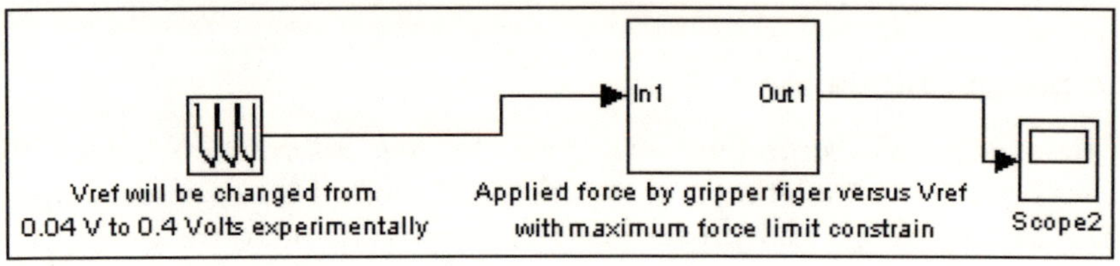

Fig. 6. Gripper simulation using MATLAB considering the maximum applied force.

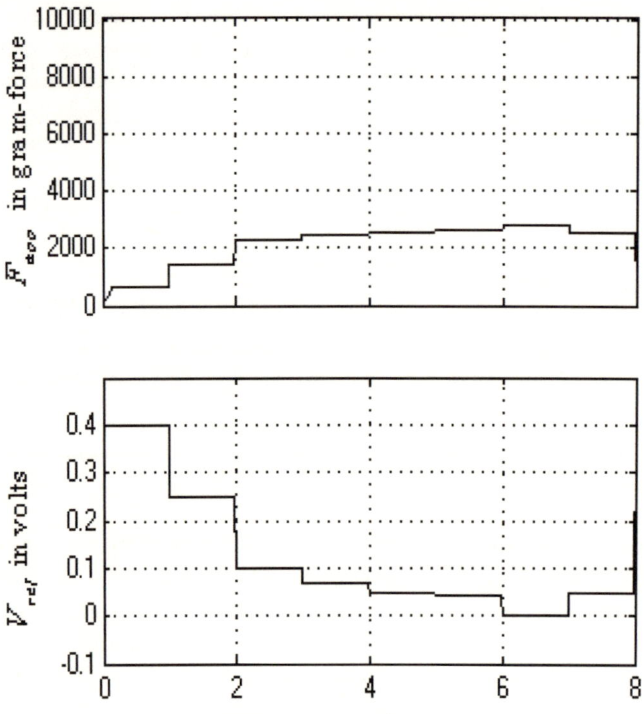

Fig. 7. Gripper simulation results considering the maximum applied force.

6.1 Force sensor calibration and modeling

The experiment was set up as shown in figure 8. Different masses were used for calibration considering the maximum force that can be applied to the sensor according to its data sheet. The whole sensitive area should be subjected to the applied force. Using the nonlinear least squares fitter we can fit a function to our recorded measurements as shown in figure.9. From the force sensor data sheet, the sensitive area is 0.7136 cm2, whereas the contact area between the object and any finger is 6.25 cm2 "the rubber material has a contact surface

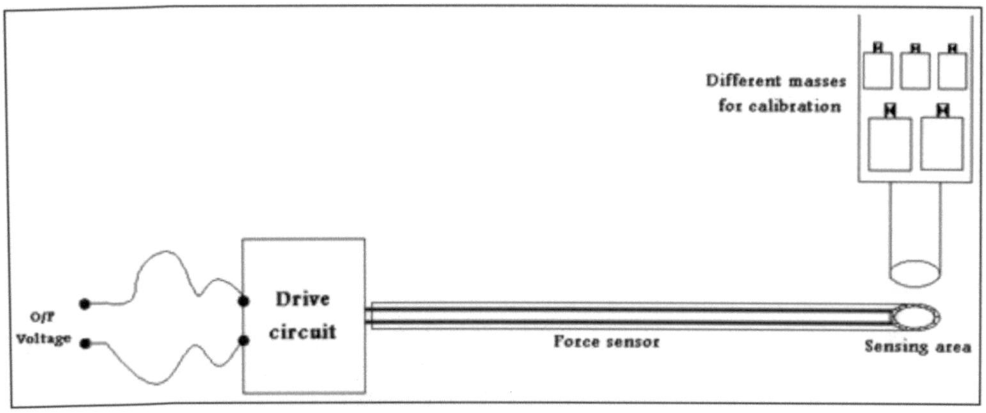

Fig. 8. Experimental test for force sensor calibration

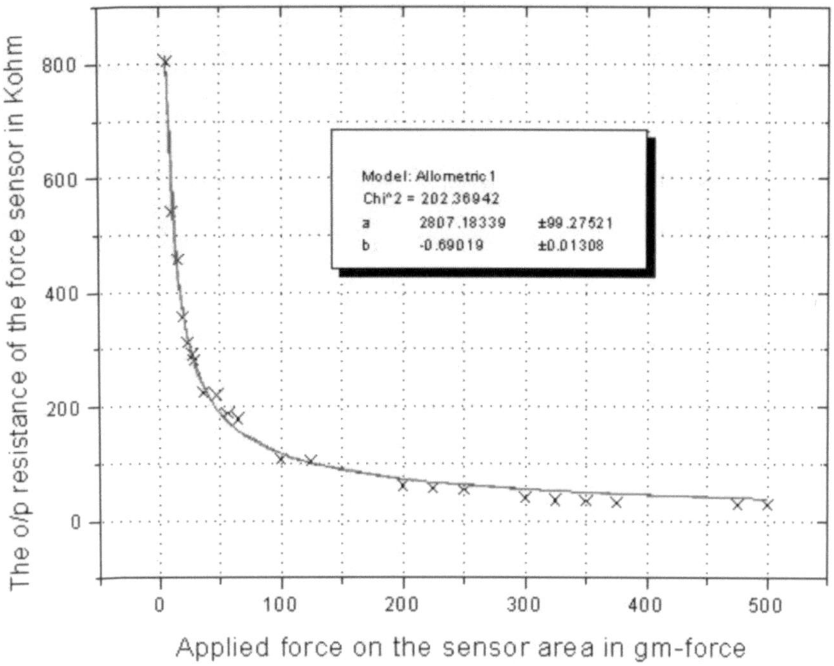

Fig. 9. Allometric function curve fitting.

dimensions 2.5cm x 2.5cm". Hence, there is a conversion factor, which converts the applied force by the finger on the object to the applied force on the sensor area as follows: -

$$F_{app} = 8.76 \ F_{sens} \tag{15}$$

Using the proposed drive circuit shown in figure 10, we can deduce a formula that describes the relation between the analog output voltage from the force sensor and the applied force by the gripper finger as follows: -

$$V_{out} = 5 * R_f \ / \ a * ((F_{app} / 8.76) \wedge b) \tag{16}$$

Where: a = 2807.18, b = -0.69019 and R_f = 65 Kohm

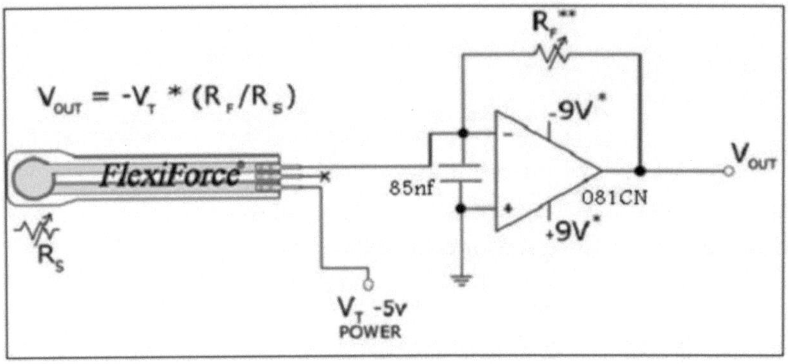

Fig. 10. Proposed drive circuit.

6.2 ANFIS modeling for input/output gripper variables

Adaptive Neuro-Fuzzy Inference Systems, ANFIS, are realized by an appropriate combination of neural and fuzzy systems and provide a valuable modeling approach of complex systems (Rezaeeian et al.,2008). The ANFIS structure is applied on our proposed robotic gripper, figure 11, based on the measured data which are simulated using MATLAB software package as shown in figure 6 and figure 7. We use 161 training data, 46 checking data, and 46 testing data. The training data are shown in figure 12. The surface rules viewer for the developed FIS model using ANFIS is shown in figure 13. Simulation results of the gripper using ANFIS modeling is shown in figure 14.

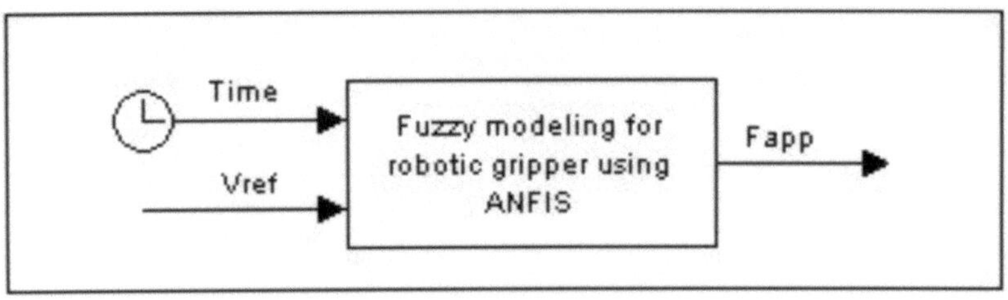

Fig. 11. Robotic gripper using ANFI.S

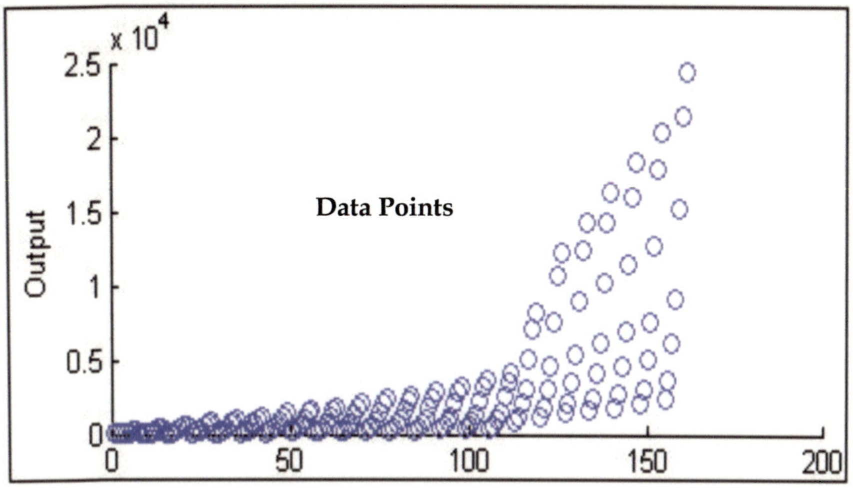

Fig. 12. Training data.

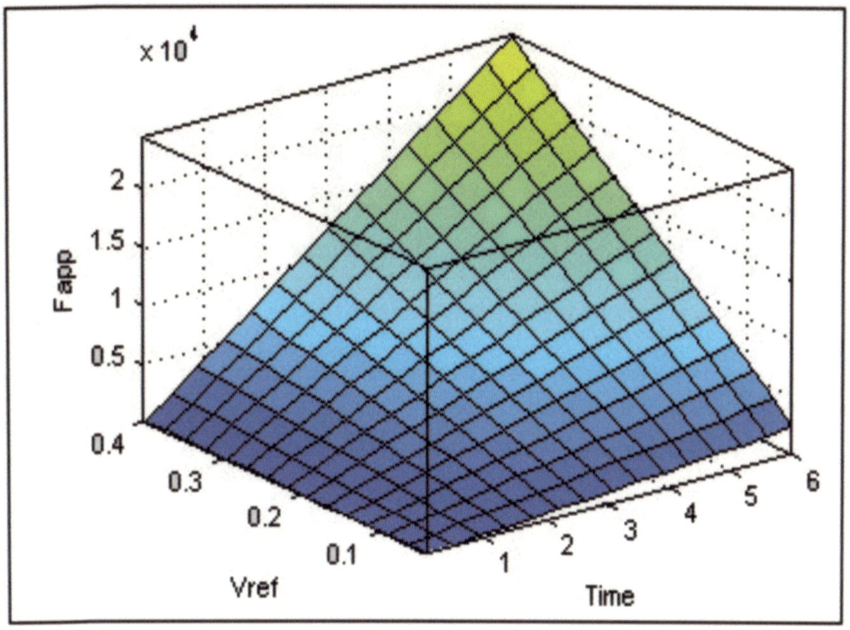

Fig. 13. Surface rules viewer for the developed FIS model using ANFIS.

6.3 Object modeling

It is known that the occurrence of slip for a solid object during grasping and lifting mainly depends on its mass, its coefficient of friction and also on the applied forces. If the applied force is not enough, acceleration is generated which leads to increased rate of slip and object dropping after certain time. This time depends on the applied force, the object mass and the coefficient of friction. Equation 3 determines the object acceleration as a function of the normal applied forces by the gripper fingers and the coefficient of friction as shown in figure.14. Object simulation result is shown in figure.15, which indicates that the slippage is stopped after a period of time depending on the rate of force increase.

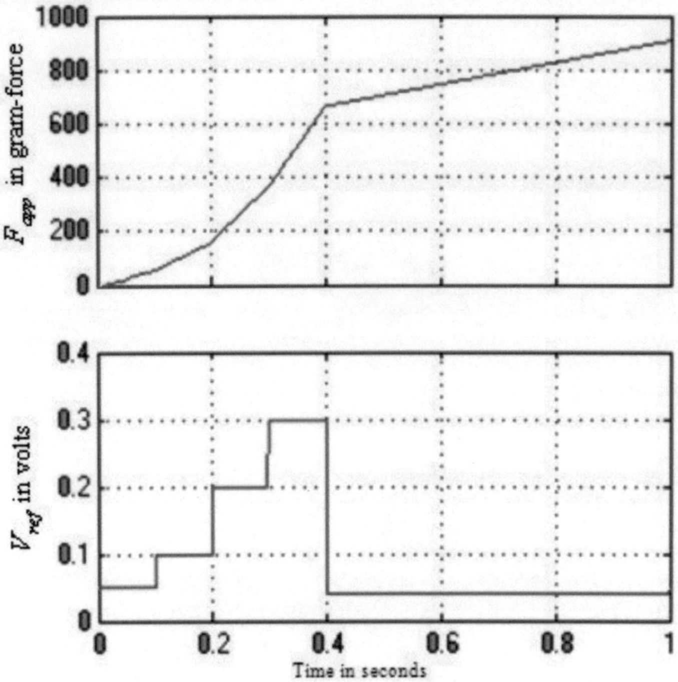

Fig. 14. Gripper simulation results using ANFIS modeling.

$$m \times a = m \times g - 2 \times \mu \times F_{app} \tag{17}$$

Where m is the object mass in kg, μ is the coefficient of friction, g is the earth gravity equal to 9.8 m/s2, and finally α is the object acceleration in m/s2

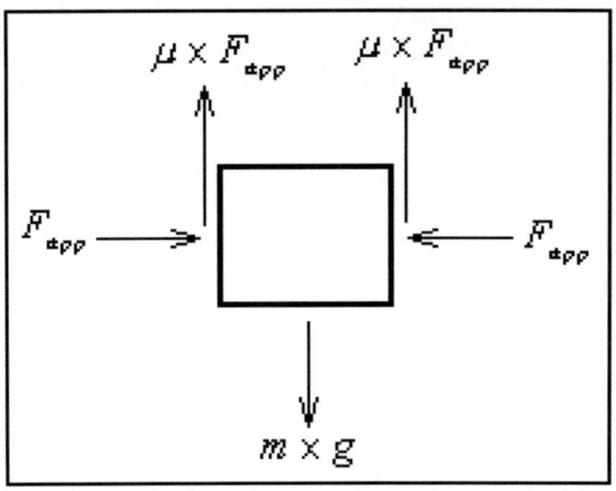

Fig. 15. Applied forces on the object.

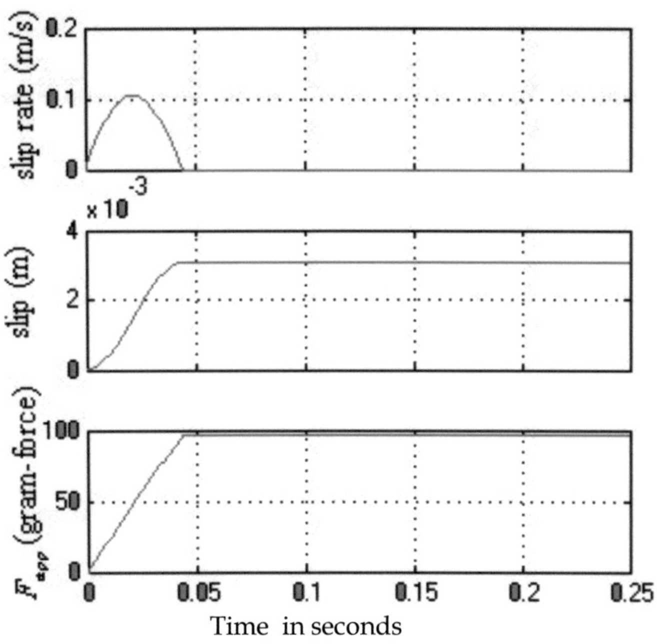

Fig. 16. Object simulation results when Mass=100 gm and μ=0.5.

6.4 Slip sensor calibration and modeling

To measure the slip amount for an object subjected to grasping, lifting and handling, a piezoelectric vibration sensor was used. A piezoelectric transducer is displaced from the

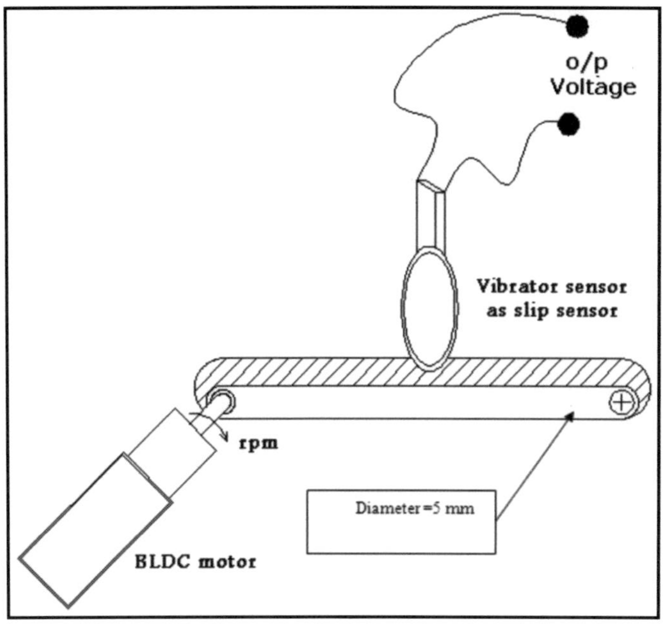

Fig. 17. Experimental tests for slip sensor calibration.

mechanical neutral axis, bending creates strain within the piezoelectric element and generates voltage signal. Experimentally, if the edge of this sensor is subjected to different speeds, it can generate different values of analog voltage that depend on those speed values. The experiment was set up as shown in figure 17. The motor was run at different speeds and the output of the sensor was recorded. The speed to which the sensor is subjected equals to (Pi * 5 * rpm/60) mm/sec. Linear curve fitting had been applied to get the optimum modeling for the assigned slip sensor as shown in figure 18.

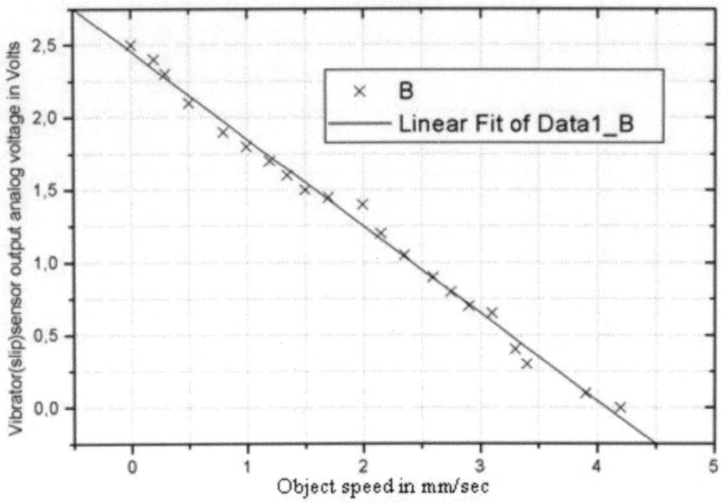

Fig. 18. Linear fit for slip sensor based on measured values.

The fitting parameters are recorded as follows:-

$$Y = A + B * X \tag{18}$$

Where: A = 2, 45319, and B = -0, 60114

X is an independent variable that represents the object slip rate "object speed" in mm/sec. Y is a dependent variable that represents the slip sensor analog output voltage in volts.

7. Gripper system controller

Our proposed controller was developed by emulating the action of the human to handle any, object during lifting it. First, he touches the object to examine its temperature and stiffness. Then, he tries to lift it by applying small force to move it or lift it in order to acquire some information about its weight and stiffness. Then he estimates the force needed to lift this object and takes the decision if he can lift it or not. Based on these observations, two control schemes were developed with different feedback variables.

7.1 First scheme controller

During object grasping and lifting process, it is not guaranteed that the two fingers will be in contact with the object at the beginning. Hence, a pushing force will be applied by one finger (the movable finger) until complete contact. Normally, this pushing force is less than the force needed to lift the object, but is a function of the object mass and its coefficient of friction. Figure 19 shows the block diagram of the first proposed controller scheme. Two integrated fuzzy controllers were built in this scheme as follows:

1. The first fuzzy controller is a reference voltage controller with two input variables, the slip-rate and its derivative.
2. The second fuzzy controller is a gain controller for the output of the first controller with one input variable, the pushing force.

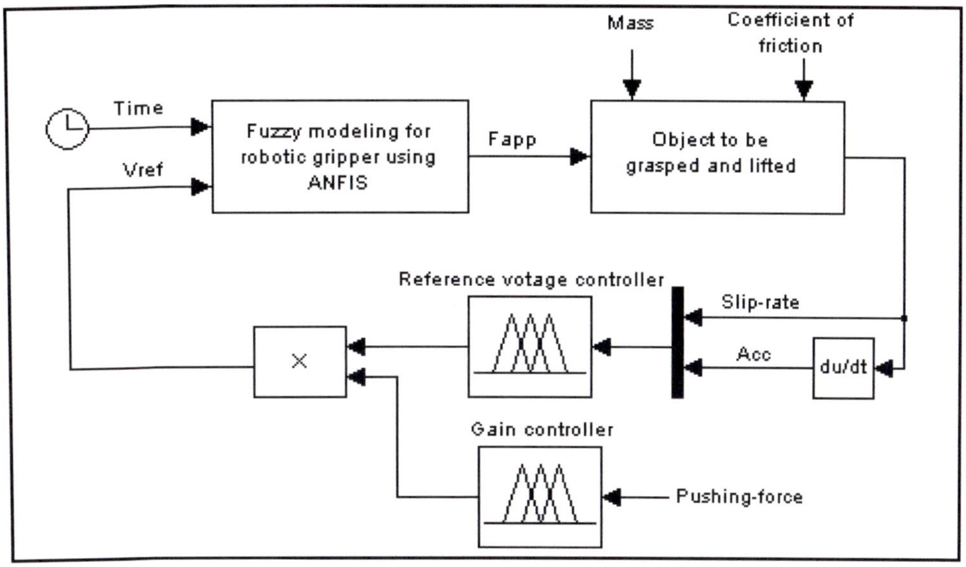

Fig. 19. Block diagram of the first scheme controller

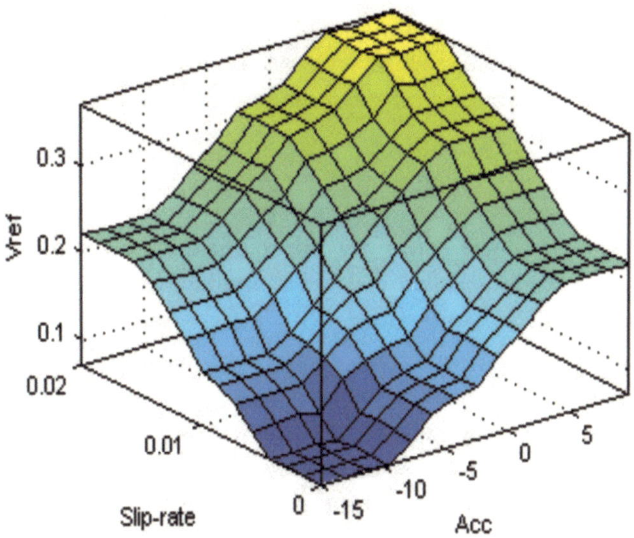

Fig. 20. Surface viewer of the reference voltage controller.

The function of the second controller is to decrease or increase the reference voltage command. The output of this controller is based on the pushing force applied on the object before grasping and lifting process. Figures 20 and 21 show the surface viewers for the two controllers in this scheme. Simulation results show the response of this scheme as shown in Figure 22.

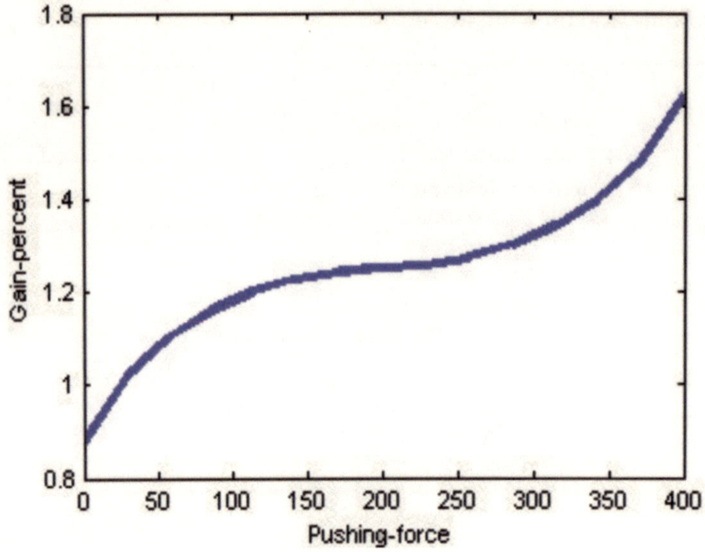

Fig. 21. Surface viewer of the gain controller.

7.2 Second scheme controller

Three integrated fuzzy controllers were built in this scheme as shown in figure 23:-

1. Guess starter reference voltage controller
2. Increased percent controller for starter reference voltage command.
3. Enhancement controller for the starter reference voltage command.

The first controller function is to guess the acceleration of the object resulting from small applied force and to give the suitable value of reference voltage command, the second controller function is to sense the pushing force to the object before the grasping process and its output is multiplied by the first controller output, the function of the third controller is to enhance the response of the two previous controllers based on the object acceleration and the applied force feed-back.

The controllers receive the object acceleration, object acceleration rate, pushing force and the applied force as feedback variables and adjust the finger motion. The response of this scheme is shown in figure 24 which indicates a faster response and lower slippage than the first scheme controller. Also figures 25 and 26 show the effect of pushing force variation on the system response. In the case shown in figure 26, F_{push} is higher than in the case shown in figure 25. So the higher value of F_{push} used as feed-back to the control system leads to lower slip amount.

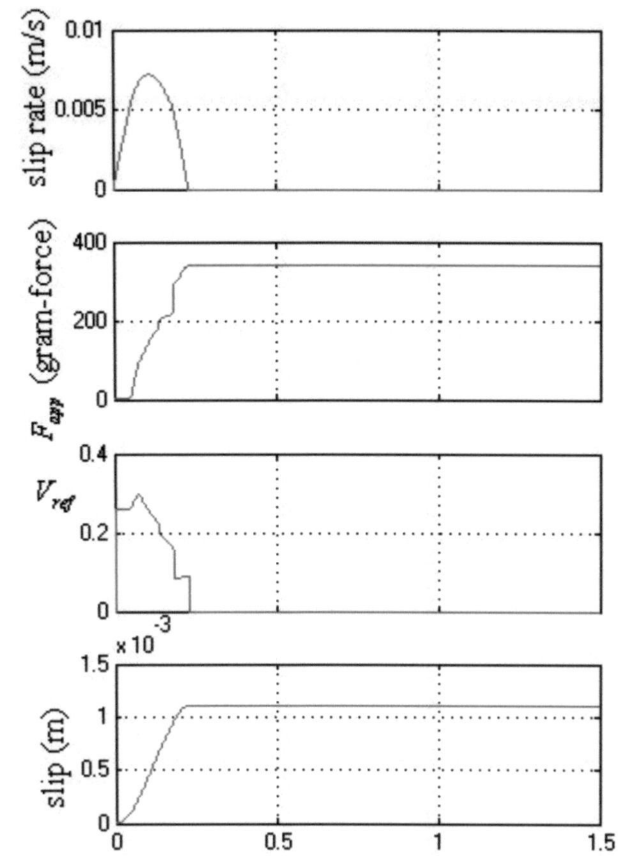

Fig. 22. System response for the first scheme controller: Mass=300 gm and F_{push} =150 g

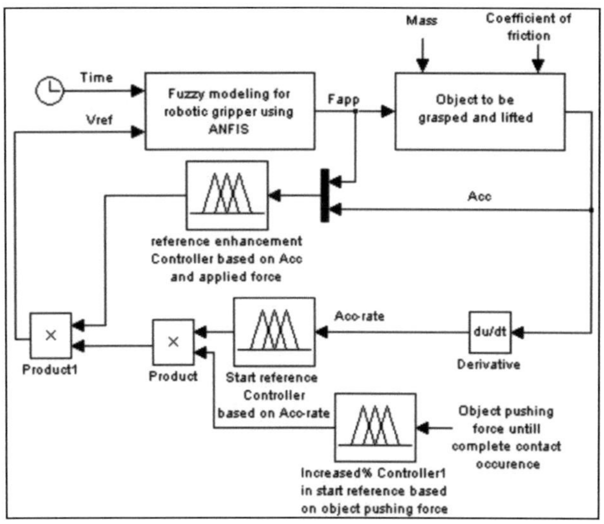

Fig. 23. Block diagram of the second scheme controller.

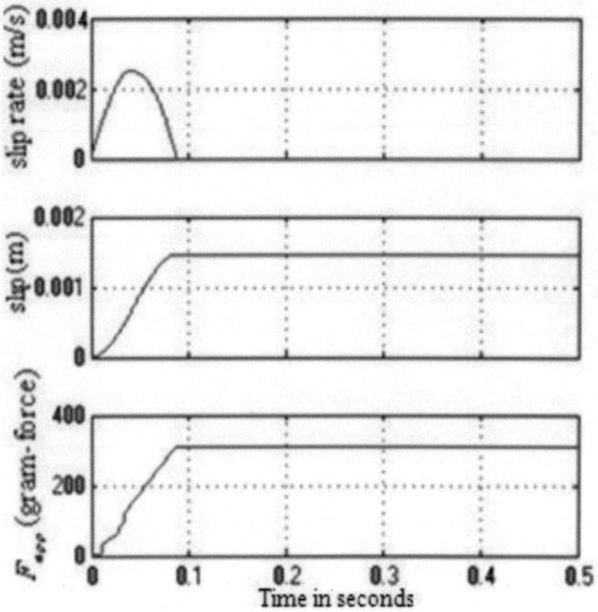

Fig. 24. System response for the second scheme controller Mass = 300 gm and F_{push} =150 g

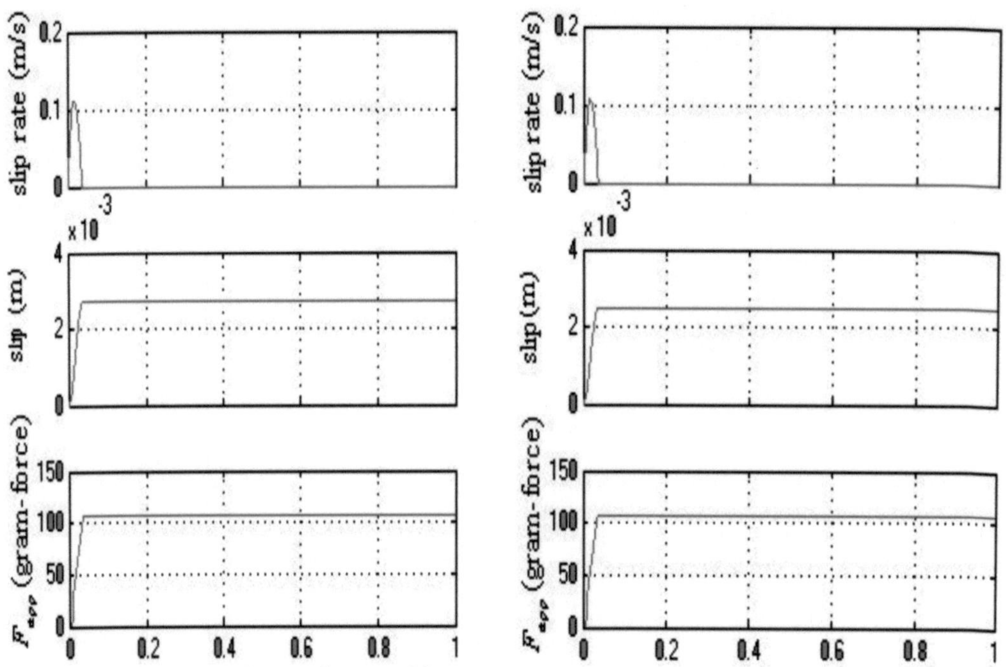

(a) Mass=100 gm, μ =0.5, and F_{push} =20 gm-force

(b) Mass=100 gm, μ =0.5, and F_{push} =40 gm-force

Fig. 25. Slippage parameters and applied force.

8. Experimental results

Experimental work was established to verify the gripper system performance. Every part of the system was verified from the design concept, the manufacturing and control aspects. The mechanical system performance was tested and suitable refinements were performed. Sensors were calibrated and their necessary drive circuits were built. The actuator characteristics were studied in order to be taken into consideration during grasping process. Figure 26 shows the flowchart that describes the experimental scenario and proposed algorithm. Figures 27 and 28 show the system response during grasping and lifting for 1000gm object mass. Figures 27(a) and 28(a) show good performance although the start reference controller based on pushing

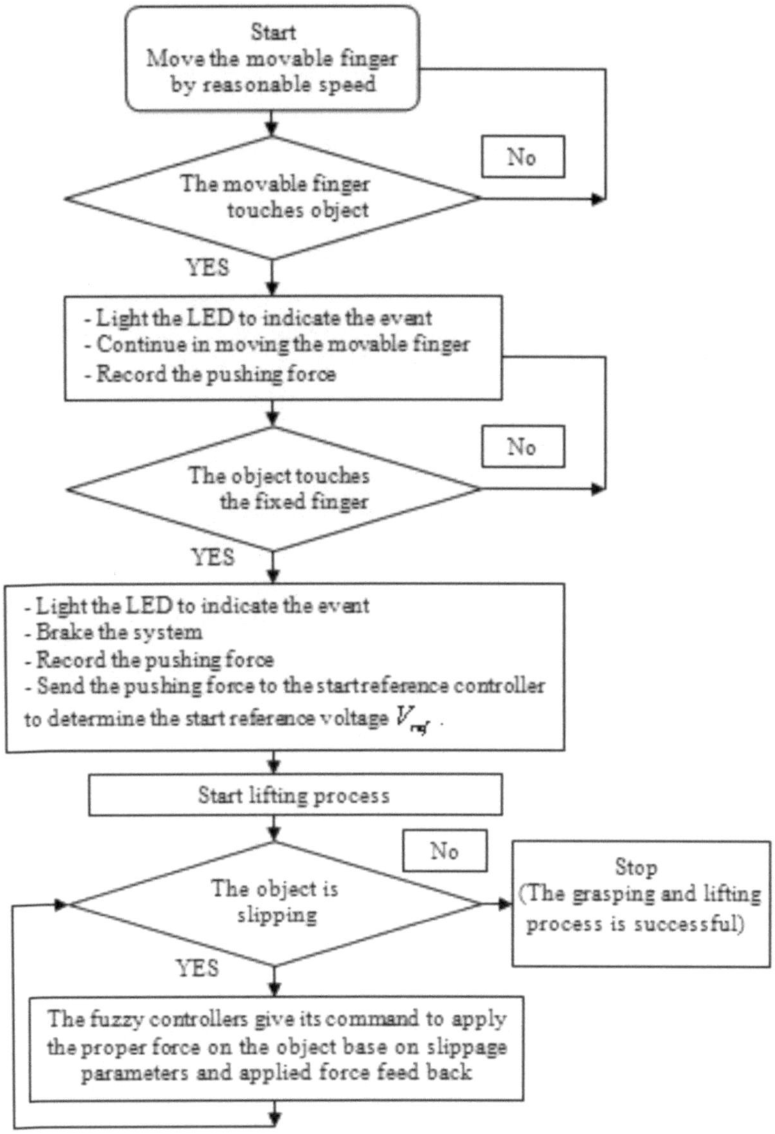

Fig. 26. Flow chart of the proposed scenario.

Considering the start reference controller based on pushing force as shown in Figure.27 (b) and in Figure. 28 (b), we can minimize the time of the grasping and lifting process. Moreover, a slip displacement reduction was achieved. To confirm and verify the robustness

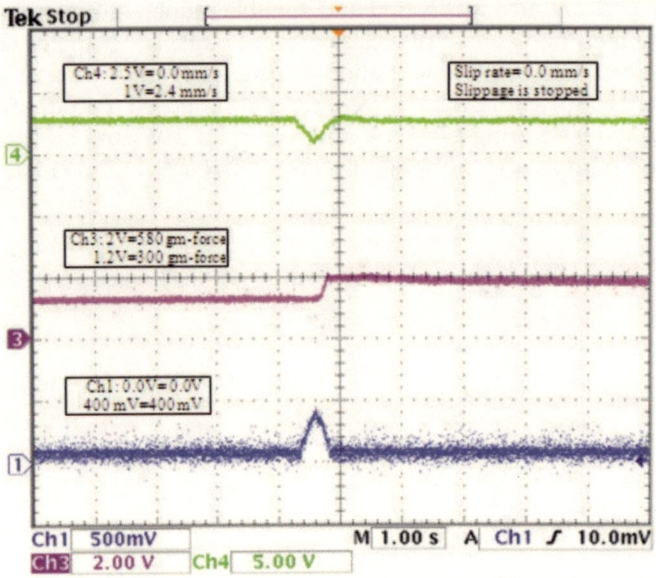

Ch4: Slip-rate (mm/s) – Ch3: Fapp (gm-force) – Ch1: Vref (V)

(a) Pushing force is not considered

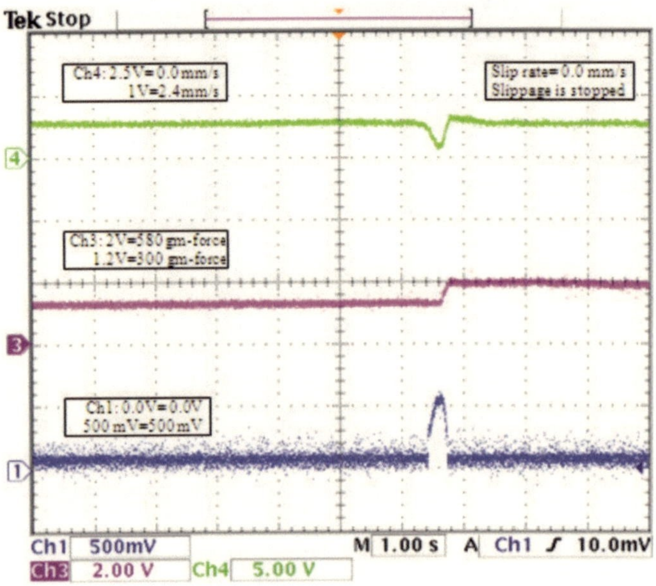

Ch4: Slip-rate (mm/s) – Ch3: Fapp (gm-force) – Ch1: Vref (V)

(b)Pushing force is considered

Fig. 27. System response when mass=550gm

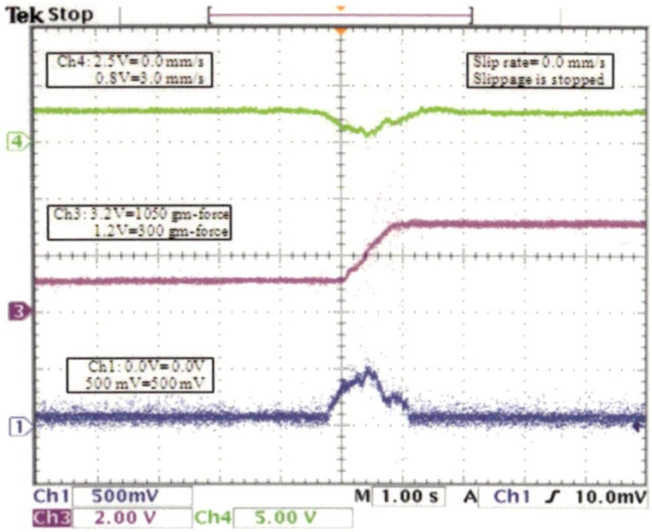

Ch4: Slip-rate (mm/s) – Ch3: Fapp (gm-force) – Ch1: Vref (V)

(a) Pushing force is not considered

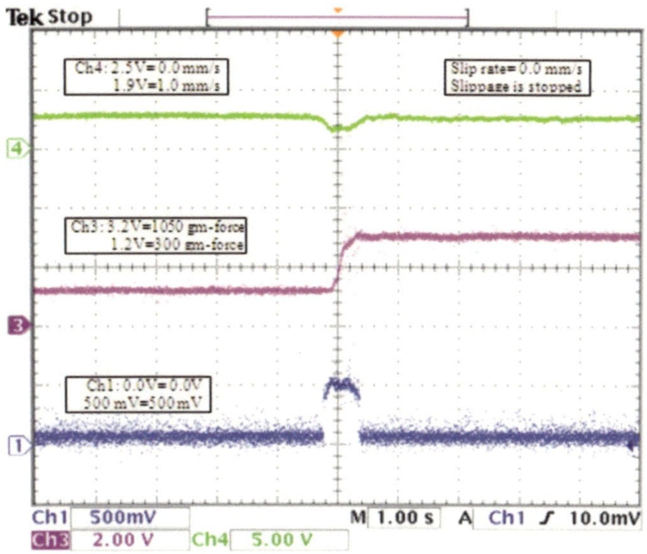

Ch4: Slip-rate (m/s) – Ch3: Fapp (gm-force) – Ch1: Vref (V)

(b) Pushing force is considered

Fig. 28. System response when mass=1000gm

force is not considered. The duration of the grasping and lifting process was in the range of 1 second and the slip displacement is in the range of 2 millimeters.

of the developed gripper set-up and its control, we disturb the assigned system by a sudden increase in object mass. The gripper system response was found as shown in Fig.29, which keeps the time of slippage and slip displacement in the range of 1 second and 2 millimeters respectively. In the mean time Table 1 shows a comparison between the two proposed schemes. The enhancement in the response when the pushing force is considered gives us the opportunity to grasp safely objects with higher mass than in the first scheme where F_{push}

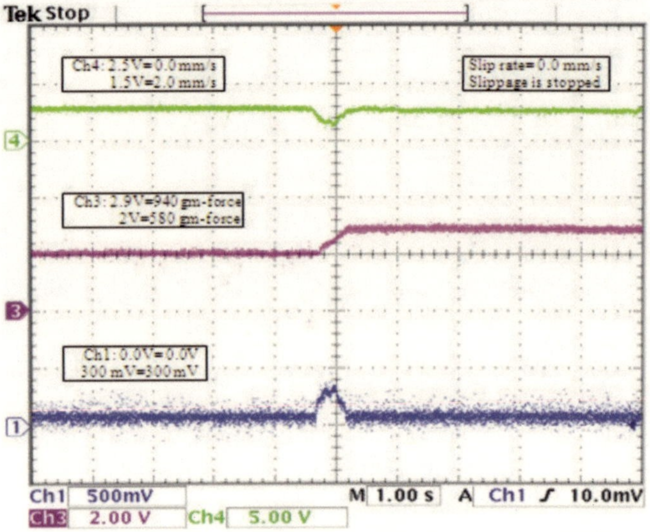

Ch 4:slip rate(mm/s) – Ch 3: Fapp(gm-force) – Ch1: Vref(V)

Fig. 29. System response when mass is suddenly increased from 550 to 900gm

		First scheme controller response		Second scheme controller response	
Mass (gram)	Pushing force (gram-force)	Time of process (sec)	Slip (mm)	Time of process (sec)	Slip (mm)
1000	Considered	0.73	4.15	0.502	3
1000	Not considered	1.35	5.56	1.05	3.9
550	Considered	0.441	2.73	0.312	1.85
550	Not considered	0.872	3.51	0.582	2.42
300	Considered	0.395	2.01	0.285	1.41
300	Not considered	0.623	2.88	0.533	1.95
100	Considered	0.201	1.45	0.19	1.11
100	Not considered	0.291	2.09	0.21	1.62

Table 1.

is not considered. It is clear from the table that the performance of the system in the case of the second controller scheme is better than in the case of the first controller. The duration of the process is lower in the second scheme and also the amount of the slip is reduced for all test cases where the mass of the object is varying between 100g and 1000g. This proves that the feedback variables choice is very important and has a great effect on the system performance.

9. References

Barsky M. F., Lindner D. K., and Claus R. O.(1989), "Robot gripper control system using PVDF piezoelectric sensors", *IEEE Transaction on Ultrasonic, Ferroelectrics, and Frequency Control*, Vol. 36(No. 1), pp.129-134.

Bicchi A. and Kumar V. (2000), "Robotic grasping and contact: A review", *Proceedings of the 2000 IEEE International Conference on Robotics and Automation*, San Francisco, CA, Vol.1, pp. 348–353.

Chiu S.L. (1994), Fuzzy model identification based on cluster estimation, Journal of Intelligent and Fuzzy System, Vol.2, 267-278.

Chiu S. L. (1997), An efficient method for extracting fuzzy classification rules from high dimensional data, Journal of Advanced Computational Intelligence, Vol.1(No.1), 31-35.

Choi B., H. Choi H., and Kang S.(2005) ," Development of tactile sensor for detecting contact force and slip", *IEEE/RSJ International Conference on Intelligent Robots and Systems* (IROS 2005), 2005, pp. 2638- 2643.

Chopra S., Mitra R. & Kumar V. (2006), Analysis of fuzzy PI and PD type controllers using subtractive clustering, International Journal of Computational Cognition , Vol. 4(No. 2), 30-34.

Chopra S., Mitra R., & Kumar V. (2006), Reduction of fuzzy rules and membership functions and its application to fuzzy PI and PD type controllers, International Journal of Control, Automation, and Systems, Vol. 4(No. 4), 438-447.

Dario P. and De Rossi D. (1985), "Tactile sensors and the gripping challenge", *IEEE Spectrum*, Vol.5(No.22), pp.46-52.

Denai M. A., Palis F. & Zeghbib A. (2004), ANFIS based modeling and control of non-linear systems: A tutorial, IEEE International Conference on Systems, Man and Cybernetics, 3433-3438

Dominguez-Lopez J. A., and Vila-Rosado D. N.," Hierarchical Fuzzy Control to Ensure Stable Grasping", *Seventh Mexican International Conference on Computer Science (ENC'06)*, Sept. 2006, pp. 37 – 43.

Dubey V., and Crowder R. (2004), "Grasping and control issues in adaptive end effectors", in *ASME Design Engineering Technical Conferences*, Salt Lake City, Utah.

Erdirencelebi D., Yalpir S. (2011), "Adaptive network fuzzy inference system modeling for the input selection and prediction of anaerobic digestion effluent quality", Journal of Applied Mathematical Modelling, Vol.35, pp 3821-3832.

Friedrich W., Lim P., and Nicholls H. (2000), "Sensory gripping system for variable products", *Proceedings of the 2000 IEEE International Conference on Robotics and Automation*, San Francisco, California, USA, pp. 1982-1987.

Hanafy O. Th. (2010), "A modified algorithm to model highly nonlinear system",Journal of American Science, Vol.6(No 12), pp747-759.

Lin C. J., Chen C. H., & Lin C. T. (2008), "Efficient self-evolving evolutionary learning for neurofuzzy inference system" IEEE Transactions On Fuzzy Systems, Vol. 16(No. 6), 1476-1490.

Lorenz R.D., Meyer K. M., and Van de Riet D.M.(1990), "A novel, compliant, four degree-of-freedom, robotic fingertip sensor", *IEEE Transaction on Industry Applications*, Vol. 26 (No. 4,) , pp. 613-619.

Luo R.C., Su K.L. and Henry S.H.(2000), "An Implementation of Gripper Control Using the New Slipping Detector by Multi-sensor Fusion Method", , *IECON 2000, 26th Annual Conference of the IEEE Industrial Electronics Society*, Vol.2, pp. 888 - 893.

Monkman G. J., Hesse S., Steinmann R., and Schunk H. (2007), "*Robot Grippers*", Wiley-VCH.

Nikhil R., Pal K., Bezdek J. C. & Runkler T. A. (1997), Some issues in system identification using clustering, Proc. of International Conference on Neural Networks, Vol. 4, 2524-2529

Ottaviano E., Toti M., and Ceccarelli M.(2000), "Grasp force control in two-finger grippers with pneumatic actuation", *Proceedings of the 2000 IEEE International Conference on Robotics and Automation*, San Francisco, USA, Vol.2, pp. 1976 – 1981.

Passino, K. M. & Yurkovich S. (1998), Fuzzy Control, Addison Wesley Longman Inc., Menlo Park, California.

Rezaeeian A., Koma A. Y, Shasti B. & Doosthoseini A. (2008), ANFIS modeling and feed forward control of shape memory alloy actuators, International Journal of Mathematical Models and Methods in Applied Sciences, Vol.2 (No 2), 228-235.

Salami M-J. E., N. Mir-Nassiri N. and Sidek S. N. (2000)," Design of intelligent multi-finger gripper for a robotic arm using a DSP-based fuzzy controller", *Proceedings of TENCON 2000*, Kuala Lumpur, Malaysia, Vol. 3, 24-27 Sept. 2000, pp. 348-353.

Seguna C.M. and Saliba M.A.(2001), "The mechanical and control system design of a dexterous robotic gripper", *the 8th IEEE International Conference on Electronics, Circuits and Systems, ICECS 2001*, Vol. 3, pp. 1195 - 1201.

Simoes M. G. & Friedhofer M. (1997), "An implementation methodology of a fuzzy based decision support algorithm", International Journal of Knowledge-Based Intelligent Engineering Systems, Vol.1 (No. 4), 267-275.

Simoes M. G. & Franceschetti N. N. (1999), Fuzzy optimization based control of a solar array system, IEE Proceedings-Electric Power Applications, Vol. 14 (No.5), September 1999, 552-558.

Yager R.R. & Filev D.P. (1994), Generation of fuzzy rules by mountain clustering, Journal of Intelligent and Fuzzy System, Vol.2, 209-219.

Zadeh, L. A. (1965), Fuzzy set, Information and Control, Vol. 8, 338-353.

6

Fuzzy Logic Controller for Mechatronics and Automation

Muhammad Mahbubur Rashid[1] and Mohamed Azlan Hussain[2]
[1]*Dept. of Mechatronics Engineering International Islamic University Malaysia,*
[2]*Dept. of Chemical Engineering, University Malaya a*
Malaysia

1. Introduction

Conventional car suspensions systems are usually passive, i.e have limitation in suspension control due to their fixed damping force. Semi-active suspension system which is a modification of active and passive suspension system has been found to be more reliable and robust but yet easier and cheaper than the active suspension system.

1.1 Vehicle primary suspensions

Primary suspension is the term used for suspension components connecting the wheel assemblies of a vehicle to the frame of the vehicle (Fig.1). This is in contrast to the suspension components connecting the frame and body of the vehicle, or those components located directly at the vehicle's seat, commonly called the secondary suspension. Usually a vehicle contains both primary and secondary suspension system but primary suspension is chosen for control. There are two basic types of elements in conventional suspension systems. These elements are springs and dampers. The role of the spring in a vehicle's suspension system is to support the static weight of the vehicle. The role of the damper is to dissipate vibrational energy and control the input from the road that is transmitted to the vehicle. Primary suspensions are divided into passive, active and semi active systems [Miller 1990], as will be discussed next, within the context of this study.

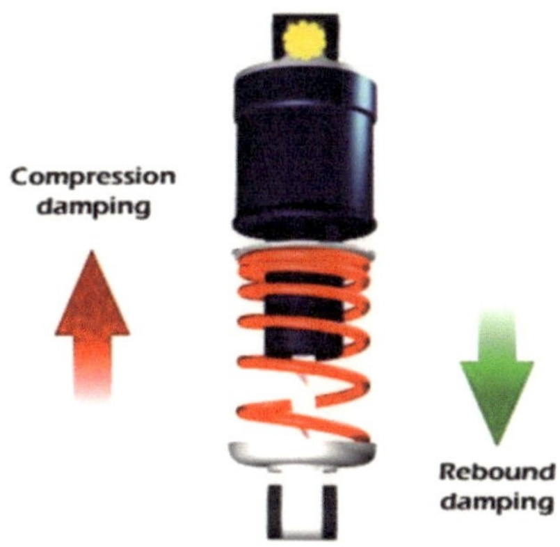

Fig. 1. Primary suspension system

1.2 Passive damping

A passive suspension system is one in which the characteristics of the components (springs and dampers) are fixed. A passive control system does not require an external power source. Passive control devices impart forces that are developed in response to the motion of the wheel hop.

1.3 Active damping

An active control system is one in which an external source of energy to control actuator(s) that apply forces to the suspension system and the schematic diagram of typical active suspension systems arrangement are shown in Fig 2. The force actuator is able to both add and dissipate energy from the system, unlike a passive damper, which can only dissipate energy.

Fig. 2. Active suspension system's oil/air connection diagram

1.4 Semi active damping

In semi active damping, the damper is adjustable and may be set to any value between the damper-allowable maximum and minimum values. Semi active control systems are a class of active control systems for which no external energy is needed like active control systems.

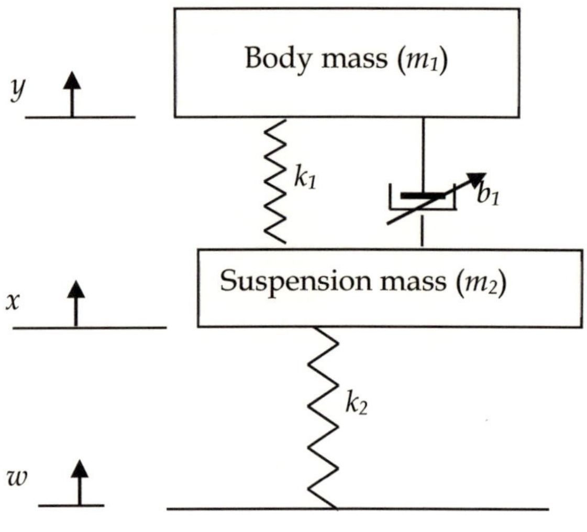

Fig. 3. Quarter-Car Model

In Fig 3, the model for one-quarter of a car is represented. The mass of this portion of the vehicle body (sprung mass) and one tire (unsprung mass) is defined respectively by m_1 and m_2 , with their corresponding displacements defined by Y and X. The suspension spring, k_1 , and damper, b_1 , are attached between the vehicle body and tire, and the stiffness of the tire is represented by k_2 . The relative velocity across the suspension damper of this model is defined by

$$v_{rel} = \dot{y} - \dot{x} \tag{1}$$

1.5 Modeling of quarter car model

Before modeling an automatic suspension system, a quarter car model (i.e. model for one of the four wheels) is used to simplify the problem to a one-dimensional (only vertical displacement of the car is considered) spring-damper system. The reason for choosing the quarter car model is to analyze and control the suspension for each wheel separately and accurately. The schematic diagram of a quarter car system is shown in Figure 4

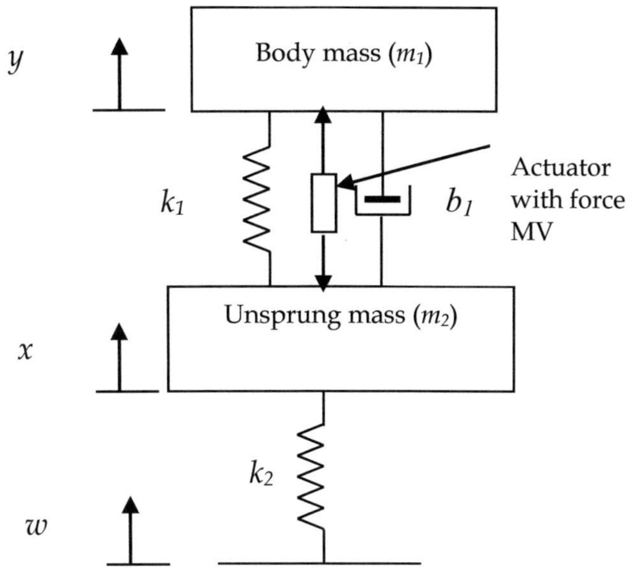

Fig. 4. Modeling of quarter-car suspension system

The parameters used for the system are shown in Table 1.

Parameters	Amount
m_1 (Body Mass or sprung mass)	315 kg
m_2 (Suspension Mass or unsprung mass)	45 kg
k_2 (Tyre Stiffness)	190000N/m
k_1 (Suspension spring constant)	40000N/m
b_1 (Damping Constant of Suspension)	290N/m

Table 1. Parameters of the active suspension system

In this system, k_1 represents the spring constant of the suspension system, w represents the road disturbances, and x represents the unsprung mass displacement. b_1, k_2 and y represent damping constant of suspension, value of tyre stiffness and the sprung mass displacement respectively. Control force (MV) is the force from the controller which will be applied to the suspension system.

From Figure 5, applying Newton's law, the following differential equations are obtained

$$m_1\ddot{y} = -b_1(\dot{y} - \dot{x}) - k_1(y - x) + MV \tag{2}$$

$$m_2\ddot{x} = b_1(\dot{y} - \dot{x}) + k_1(y - x) - k_2(x - w) - MV \tag{3}$$

1.6 Fuzzy logic controller for the suspension system

Typically a fuzzy logic controller is composed of three basic parts; (i) input signal fuzzy-fication, (ii) a fuzzy engine that handles rule inference and (iii) defuzzification that generates a continuous signal for actuators such as control valves. The schematic diagram is shown in Figure 6.

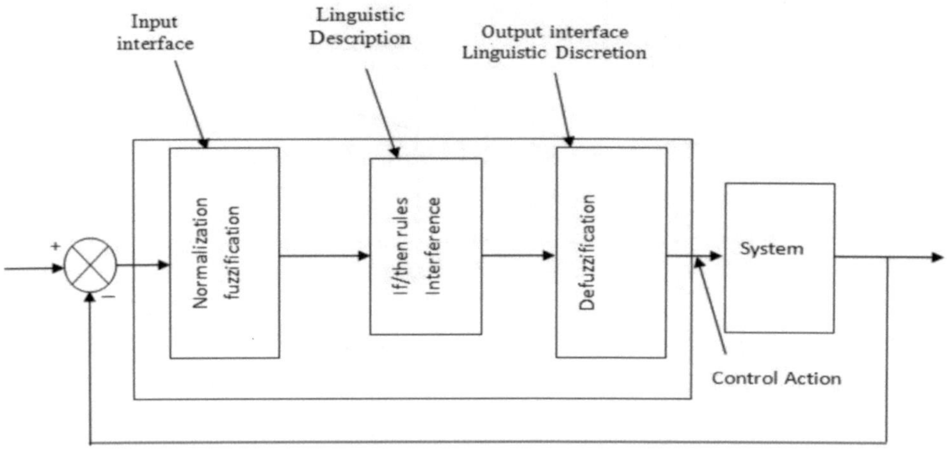

Fig. 5. Schematic diagrams for a typical fuzzy logic controller

The fuzzification block transforms the continuous input signal into linguistic fuzzy variables such as small, medium, and large. The fuzzy engine carries out rule inference where human experience can easily be injected through linguistic rules. The defuzzification block converts the inferred control action back to a continuous signal that interpolates between simultaneously fired rules.

1.7 Design of fuzzy controller for the suspension system

The basic process of designing a fuzzy logic controller for the suspension systems involves 5 steps:

a. Formulating the problem and selecting the input and output variables state. For this suspension system, the inputs to the fuzzy controller are the velocity of sprung mass (car body) at any time, and the velocity of unsprung-mass. The manipulated variable is produced and sent to the actuating valve for controlling the suspension.

b. Selecting the fuzzy inference rules. This generally depends on human experience and trial-and error. The interference rule is selected based on the open loop response of the suspension system.Typically; trial-and-error approach is done to obtain better result.
c. Designing fuzzy membership functions for each variable. This involves determining the position, shape as well as overlap between the adjacent membership function, as these are major factors in determining the performance of the fuzzy controller.
d. Performing fuzzy inference based on the inference method. Smoothness of the final control surface is determined by the inference and defuzzification methods. The use of a universe of discourse requires a scale transformation, which maps the physical values of the process state variables into a universe of discourse. This is called normalization. Furthermore, output de-normalization maps the normalized value of the control output variables into their respective physical universe of discourse. In other words, scaling is the multiplication of the physical input value with a normalization factor so that it is mapped onto the normalized input domain. De-normalization is the multiplication of the normalized output value with a de-normalization factor so that it maps onto the physical output domain. Such scale transformation is required both for discrete and continuous universe of discourse. The scaling factors which describe a particular input normalization and output denormalization play a role similar to those of the gain coefficients in a conventional controller. In other words, they are of utmost importance with respect to controller performance and stability related issues, i.e., they are a source of possible instability, oscillation problems and deteriorated damping effects.
e. Selecting a defuzzification method to derive the actual control action. The choice of the defuzzification method determines to a large extent the "quality" of control as well as the computational cost of the controller and hence must be chosen carefully. In this case defuzzification is done by using gain block to minimize the disturbance.

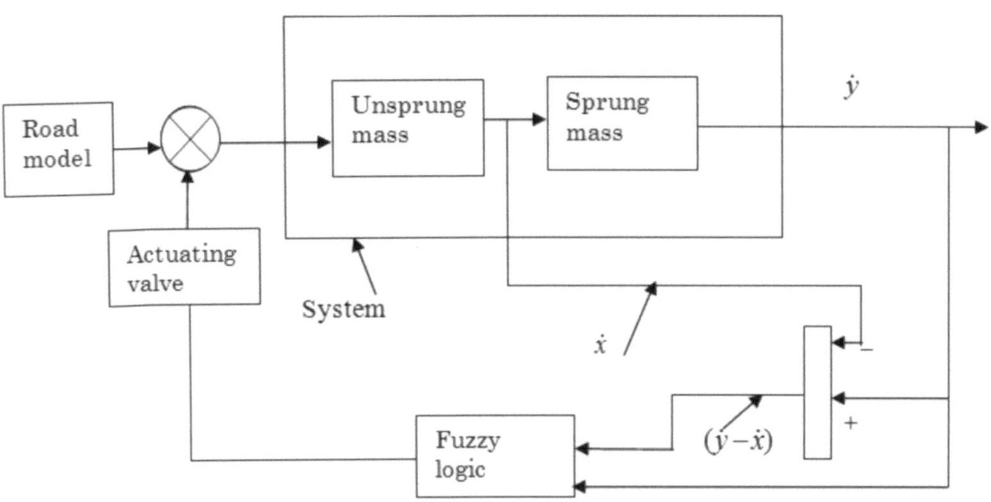

Fig. 6. Block diagram representation of the control system

In this case, velocity of sprung mass (car body) and difference between sprung mass velocity and unsprung mass velocity are used as fuzzy controller inputs and the output is the actuator force. The universe of discourse of the input and output variables are selected based on the results of simulation under different conditions. Triangle membership for the input and output variables with seven values is used for each variable. The triangular membership function are Negative Big [NB], Negative medium [NM], Negative small [NS], Zero [ZE], Positive Small [PS], Positive Medium [PM], Positive Big [PB] respectively. The block diagram of the suspension system control by fuzzy-logic is shown in Figure 8 and 9

1.8 Quantization levels of a universe of discourse (range of membership function)

Fuzzy quantization level basically determines the number of primary fuzzy sets. The number of primary fuzzy sets determines the smoothness of the control action and thus, can vary depending on the resolution required for the variable. The choice of quantization level has an essential influence on how fine a control can be obtained (Lee, 1990a). A coarse quantization for large errors and finer quantization for small errors are the usual choice in the case of quantized continuous domains.

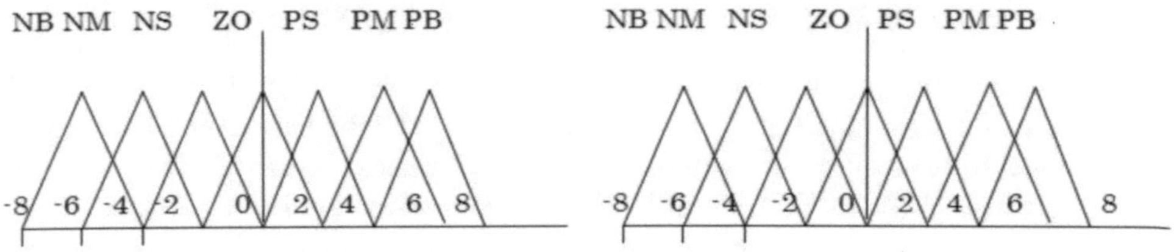

Fig. 7. Fuzzy input membership function

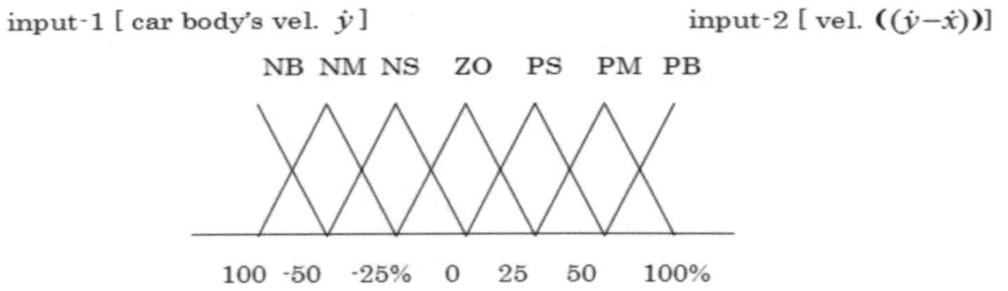

Fig. 8. Fuzzy output membership function

According to different input conditions, the actuating valve will open from –100% to +100% for smooth control of suspension. In this work, scaling for both two inputs is set from -8 to +8 with an increment of 2 from the lowest value and that for output is set from -100 to 100% with increment of 25% is the from lowest value.

1.9 Fuzzy controller performance for suspension control

The performance of the controller is investigated through various studies involving nominal operating condition and also when the set point is fixed to zero and the input disturbance are changes in different modes. However to be more realistic, various types input disturbances are applied into the system, such as sinusoidal, square wave, saw-tooth input disturbances in order to observe the performances of the Fuzzy controller. Since road disturbances do not have a particular pattern, different types input disturbances such as sinusoidal and random signals are used so that the controller can control all type road disturbances.

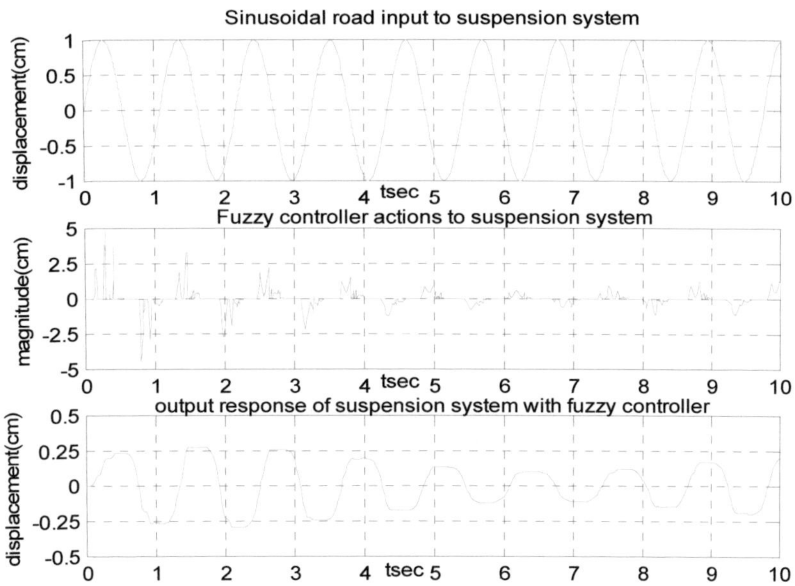

Fig. 9. Suspension controller responses with sinusoidal input

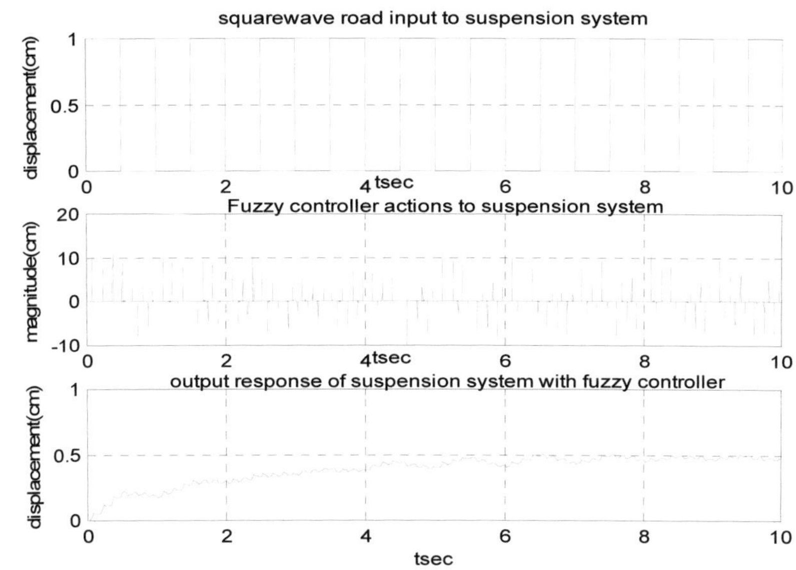

Fig. 10. Suspension controller responses with square-wave input

The responses of suspension system using fuzzy controller for square wave, sinusoidal, and saw-tooth input disturbances are shown in Figure 10 to 13 respectively. In Figure 10, sine wave input disturbance with amplitude of 1(cm) and frequency of 1 Hz is used, the controller action and output response are also shown. In Figure 11, square wave input disturbance with amplitude of 1 (cm) and frequency of 1 Hz is used, the controller action

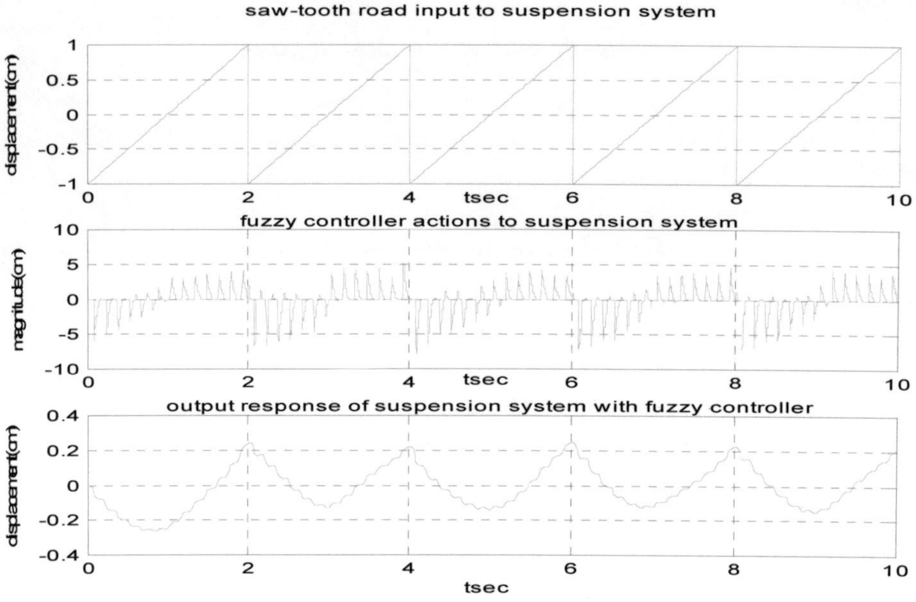

Fig. 11. Suspension controller responses with saw tooth wave input

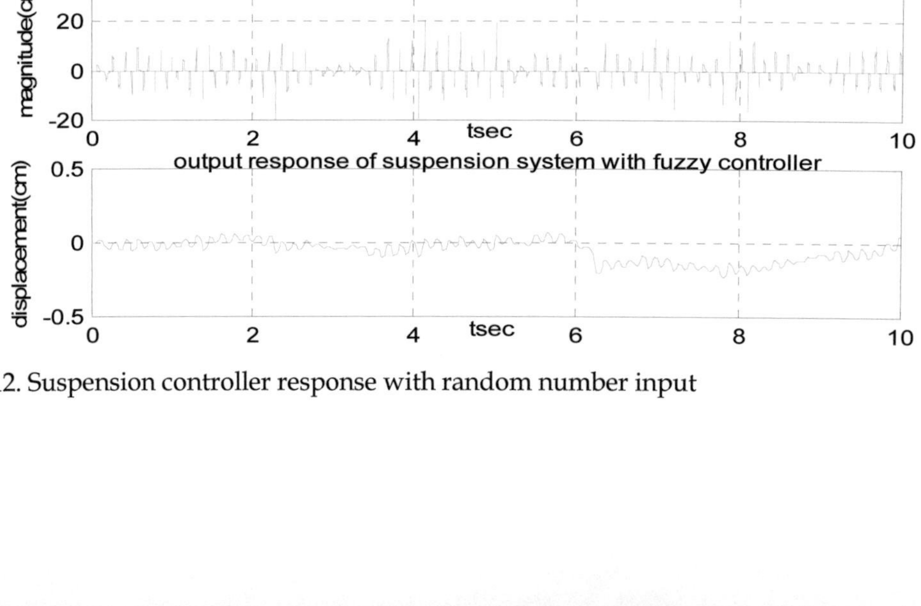

Fig. 12. Suspension controller response with random number input

and output response are also shown. In Figure 12, sawtooth input disturbance with output values [0 2] (disturbance changing from 0 to 1) and frequency of 0.5 Hz is used, the controller action and output response are also shown. In Figure 13, random number input disturbance with variance of 1, mean value of 0, initial speed of 0 and sampling time 0 is used, the controller action and output response are also shown.

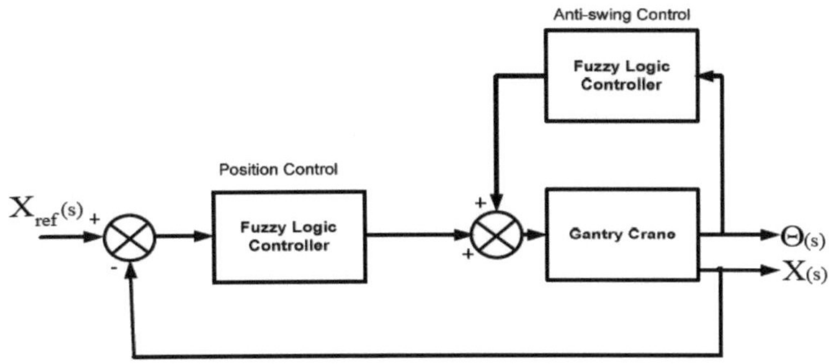

Fig. 13. Block diagram of FLC rotary crane system with position control and anti swing control.

Four types of input disturbances are used to observe the controller action with respect to input and the responses of the suspension output. Both controller action and output response seemed to be satisfactory, since more than 85% disturbances are rejected in all cases.

1.10 Summary

The designed fuzzy logic controller and hybrid controller were applied to a car Active suspension system. Since the road model is almost irregular therefore different type disturbances are applied to the system. Fuzzy logic controller was applied to car suspension system with different type disturbances. While the sinusoidal input is applied to the suspension system, fuzzy controller eliminates 75% of the disturbances during first 4 sec. and about 90% for the rest period. In the case of square wave disturbances, average 50% disturbances were rejected from the system during whole period. For the saw-tooth wave disturbances, 15-20% disturbances are present during all over the period. For random disturbances, fuzzy controller is able to eliminate the disturbances entirely.

2. Fuzzy logic controller for rotary crane system automation

2.1 Introduction

The main purpose of controlling a Rotary crane is transporting the load as fast as possible without causing any excessive sway at the final position. Active sway angle control of Rotary crane consists of artificially generating sources that absorb the energy caused by the unwanted sway angle of the rope in order to cancel or reduce their effect on the overall system.

In Rotary Crane System, two main objectives are to be achieved that is the positioning and at the same time avoiding the swinging of the hooked object. These two functions are depending on the speed of the crane motion. Usually the crane is handled manually by human operator and the balancing control is also done by him/her. The balancing control is depending on the skills/experiences of the human operator to move the payload safely and accurately. However, human skills are not always accurate at all time. This may due to the fatigue error that the human faces during the time of operation. Thus, new controller for this application is required for controlling the positioning and anti swing process. Fuzzy logic has the capability to provide the human like control and suitable in designing the new controller for both processes.

Wahyudi et.al [2] designed the adaptive fuzzy-based feedback controllers for gantry crane system.

2.2 Modeling of the rotary crane

The modeling of the rotary crane system is done based on the Euler-Lagrange formulae. Considering the motion of the rotary crane system on a two-dimensional plane, the kinetic energy of the system can thus be formulated as

$$T = \frac{1}{2}M\dot{x}^2 + \frac{1}{2}m(\dot{x}^2 + \dot{l}^2 + l^2\dot{\theta}^2 + 2\dot{x}\dot{l}\sin\theta + 2\,\dot{x}l\dot{\theta}\cos\theta) \tag{4}$$

The potential energy of the beam can be formulated as

$$U = -mgl\cos\theta \tag{5}$$

To obtain a closed-form dynamic model of the rotary crane, the energy expressions in (4) and (5) are used to formulate the Lagrangian $L=T-U$. Let the generalized forces corresponding to the generalized displacements $q = \{x,\theta\}$ be $F = \{Fx, 0\}$. Using Lagrangian's equation

$$\frac{d}{dx}\frac{\partial L}{\partial q_j} - \frac{\partial L}{\partial q_j} = F_j \tag{6}$$

the equation of motion is obtained as below,

$$F_x = (M+m)\ddot{x} + ml(\ddot{\theta}\cos\theta - \dot{\theta}^2\sin\theta) + 2m\dot{l}\,\dot{\theta}\cos\theta + m\ddot{\theta}\sin\theta$$

$$l\ddot{\theta} + 2\dot{l}\dot{\theta} + \ddot{x}cos\theta + gsin\theta = 0 \tag{7}$$

In order to eliminate the nonlinearity equation in the system, a linear model of rotary crane system is obtained. The linear model of the uncontrolled system can be represented in a state-space form as shown in equation (6) by assuming the change of rope and sway angle are very small.

$$\dot{x} = Ax + Bu \tag{8}$$

$$y = Cx \tag{9}$$

$$x = [x\ \theta\ \dot{x}\ \dot{\theta}]^T$$

$$\mathbf{A} = \begin{bmatrix} 0 & 0 & 1 & 0 \\ 0 & 0 & 0 & 1 \\ 0 & \frac{mg}{M} & 0 & 0 \\ 0 & \frac{(M+m)g}{Ml} & 0 & 0 \end{bmatrix} \quad \mathbf{B} = \begin{bmatrix} 0 \\ 0 \\ \frac{1}{M} \\ \frac{1}{Ml} \end{bmatrix} \quad \mathbf{C} = [1\ \ 0\ \ 0\ \ 0],\ \mathbf{D} = [0]$$

\

2.3 Controller design

The controller is designed based on the information of the skillful operators and analyzed experimentally with the lab-scale gantry crane. The proposed controller consists of two fuzzy logic controllers. Both FLCs are designed to control the position and anti swing respectively. Error and error rate are considered to be the inputs of the each FLC as shown in Fig 13

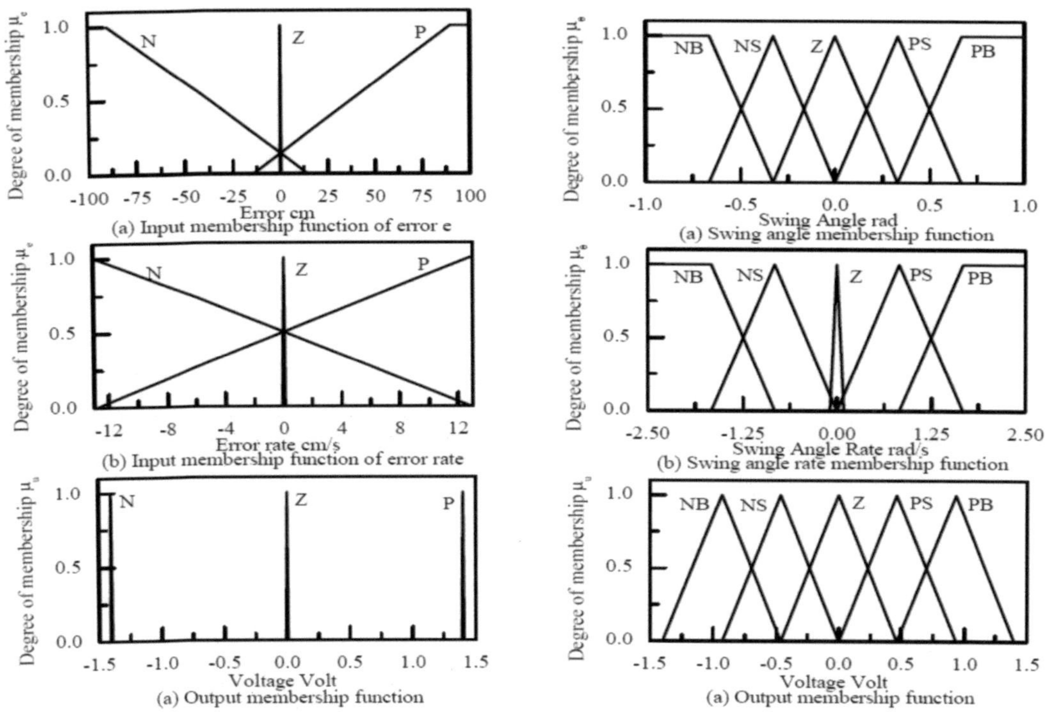

Fig. 14. Membership functions for both FLCs for position and anti-swing control. The following tables show how the rules are constructed based on the knowledge of the skillful operators.

Error Rate/Error		Error rate $\dot{e}(t)$		
		P	Z	N
Error e(t)	P	P	P	P
	Z	N	Z	P
	N	N	N	N

Table 2. Fuzzy rule base of position control

Swing angle rate/ Swing angle		Swing angle rate $\dot{\theta}(t)$				
		PB	PS	Z	NS	NB
Swing angle	PB	PB	PB	PB	PB	PB
	PS	PB	PS	PS	PS	PS
	Z	PB	PS	Z	NS	NB
	NS	NS	NS	NS	NS	NB
	NB	NB	NB	NB	NB	NB

Table 3. Fuzzy rule base of anti-swing control

Where
P = Positive, Z = Zero, N = Negative, PB = Positive Big, PS = Positive Small, NB = Negative Big, NS = Negative Small

For fuzzy inference, Mamdani's Min-Max method is used in both position and anti-swing control. As for defuzzification, centre of area or COA method is used to calculate the crisp value where the final outputs for both controllers are in Voltage. The results of the fuzzy controllers were obtained experimentally and the comparison between classical PID controller and FLC is compared as in following table.

Controller	Reference (cm)	Overshoot (%)	Settling time (s)	Rise Time (s)	Steady-State Error (cm)
PID/PD	40	5.33	50	2.92	-0.803
	70	7.92	50	4.59	-2.19
Fuzzy/Fuzzy	40	2.62	5.44	3.00	0.465
	70	1.71	6.73	4.96	0.158

Table 4. Positioning perfomances

Controller	Reference (cm)	Maximum Amplitude (rad	Settling time (s)
PID/PD	40	0.04	10.9
	70	0.04	12.7
Fuzzy/Fuzzy	40	0.06	5.4
	70	0.06	6.7

Table 5. Anti-swing performances

Fuzzy Controllers show more satisfied result as compared to PID controller where the percentage overshoot and Settling Time were greatly improved. With lower settling time obtained by using the FLC, the performance of the rotary crane system is more stable than with the PID controller.

3. Fuzzy lozic controller for point to point position control

3.1 Introduction

Point-to-point position control is one of the motion control systems that concern much the precision and speed in its performance. Nevertheless, to develop such a high precision and speed controller is quite complicated because of the nonlinearity function in the system such as friction and saturation. Both conditions cannot be compensated or modeled simply by using the linear control theory. Thus, an alternative controller should be developed to overcome this nonlinearity system.

In the motion control system, two main sources are identified to be the parameters variations that cause the nonlinearity condition. There are frictions and inertia variations. The variations of the inertia occur because of numbers of different payload. The different payload at the same time would also cause the different Coulomb friction variations. Both variations are the main parts that need to be solved to improve the performance of the system.

PID controller is one of the most used techniques in motion control system due to its simplicity and performances. However, PID controller could only be used effectively in linear system and does not work well with the nonlinearity system. Even if the model of the system is to be developed with PID controller, it would be complicated and this may affect the performance speed of the hardware.

Again, fuzzy approach is the most suitable technique in developing the control algorithm that relates with the nonlinearity function. With its capability in simplifying the model of the system, it can realize the high speed high precision of the system. M. M. Rashid et.al [5] in his article proposed a design of PID controller with added fuzzy logic controller (FLC) of fuzzy-tuned PID controller. With the addition of the FLC, the PID controller can adapt, learn or change its parameters based on the conditions and desired performance.

In this design, fuzzy logic is used to determine the PID controller gains, Kp, Ki, Kd as the function of error and error rate as illustrated in the following block diagram

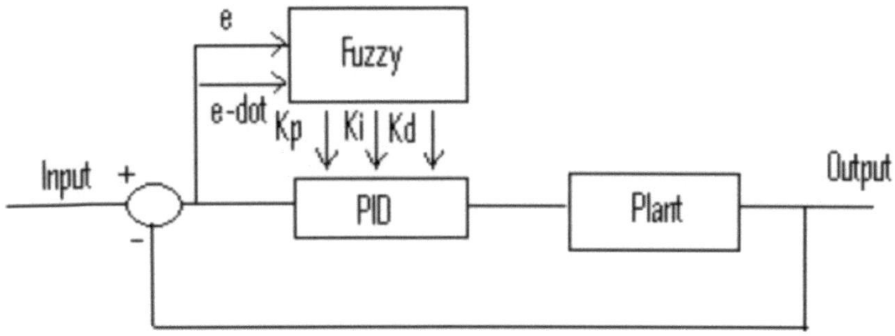

Fig. 15. Structure of the Fuzzy-tuned PID controller

In developing the fuzzy-tuned PID controller, two design stages are used as follows:

1. Nominal values for PID controller gains are designed based on the linear model
2. Based on the current PID controller gains, the fuzzy tuner is designed to produce Kp, Ki and Kd.

Since there are three gains to be produced, there would be 3 fuzzy tuners to be designed. Each of them has two inputs (error and error rate) and one output (gain). Different membership functions and rules are constructed in each fuzzy tuner.

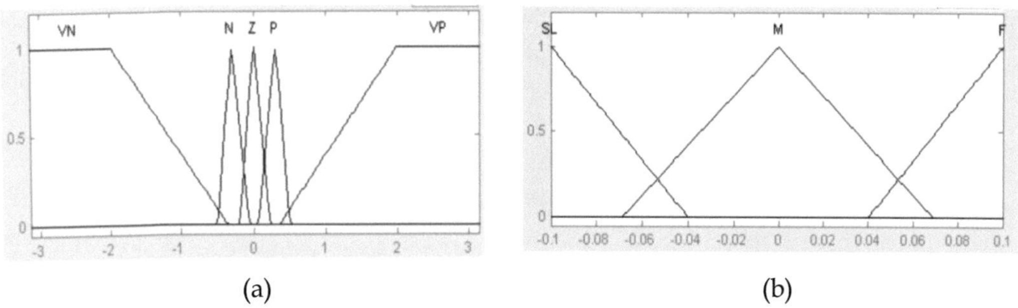

Fig. 16. Membership function of a) the error and b) error rate for Kp fuzzy tuner

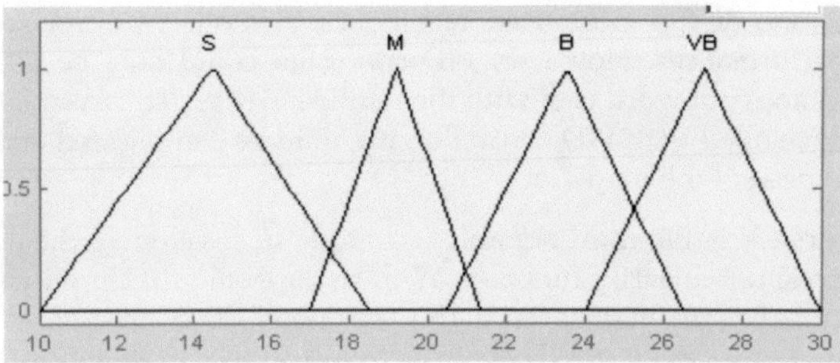

Fig. 17. Membership function of output, Kp

		Error				
Error Rate		**VN**	**N**	**Z**	**P**	**VP**
	SL	S	B	S	M	
	M	VB	B	VB	B	
	F	VB	VB	VB	VB	

Table 6. Rules base for Kp

In defuzzification, the output of crisp value is then obtained by using the Centre of Area (COA) method for gain Kp.

The following figures show the membership function of error, error rate, output and rule base for deriving the gain Kd

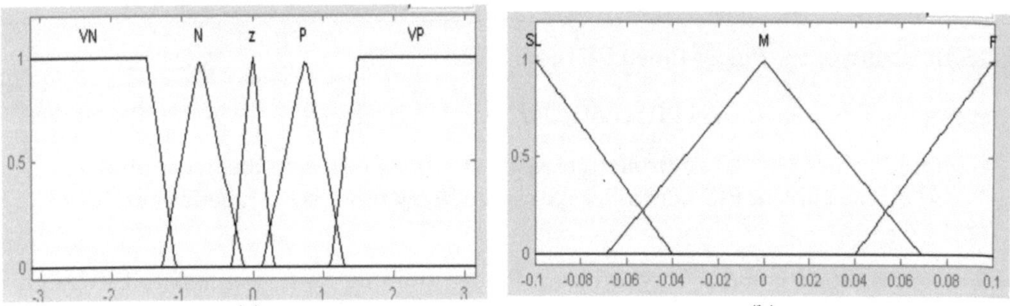

(a) (b)

Fig. 18. Membership function of a) the error and b) error rate for Kd fuzzy tuner

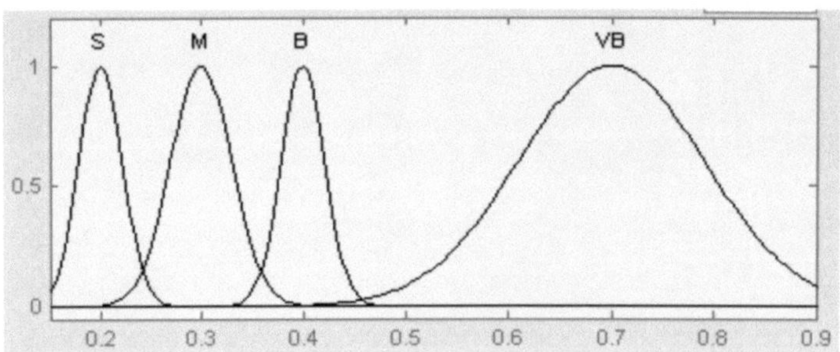

Fig. 19. Membership function for output gain Kd

	Error					
Error Rate		VN	N	Z	P	VP
	SL	VB	M	B	M	VB
	M	M	M	S	M	M
	F	S	S	M	S	S

Table 7. Rules constructed for Kd fuzzy tuner

To defuzzyfy the output Kd, COA is also used to produce the crisp value. Different membership functions are used for obtaining the gain Ki as shown in the following figures.

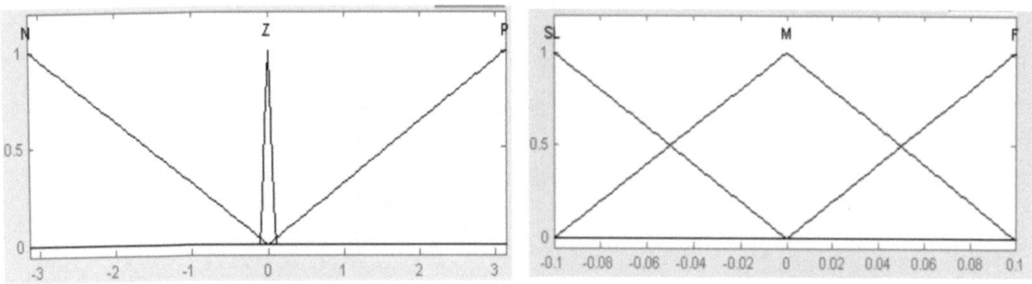

(a) (b)

Fig. 20. Membership function of a) the error and b) error rate for Ki fuzzy tuner

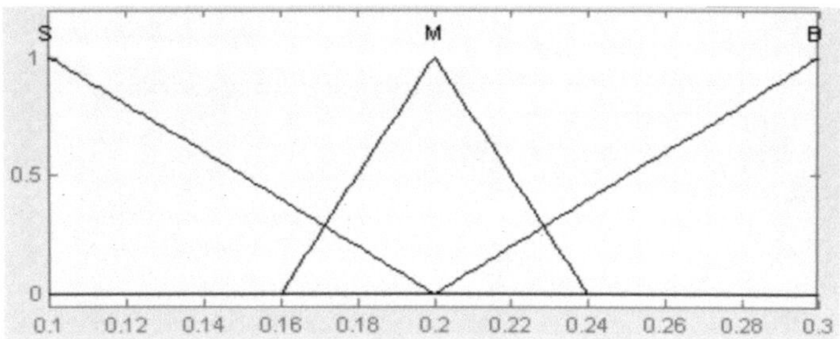

Fig. 21. Membership function for output gain Ki

	Error			
Error Rate		N	Z	P
	SL	S	S	S
	M	M	S	M
	F	B	M	S

Table 8. Rules constructed for gain Ki.

Finally, the gain Ki is defuzzified by using the COA as well to obtain the crisp value of integral gain Ki. The fuzzy-tuned PID controller is tested with rotary positioning system for nominal object and increased inertia as visualized in the following figures.

As listed in the table above, F-PID controller shows better performance with the improvement of the settling time and accuracy. Less error in F-PID controller indicates the high robustness of the controller and thus proving the capability of the fuzzy approach in this system.

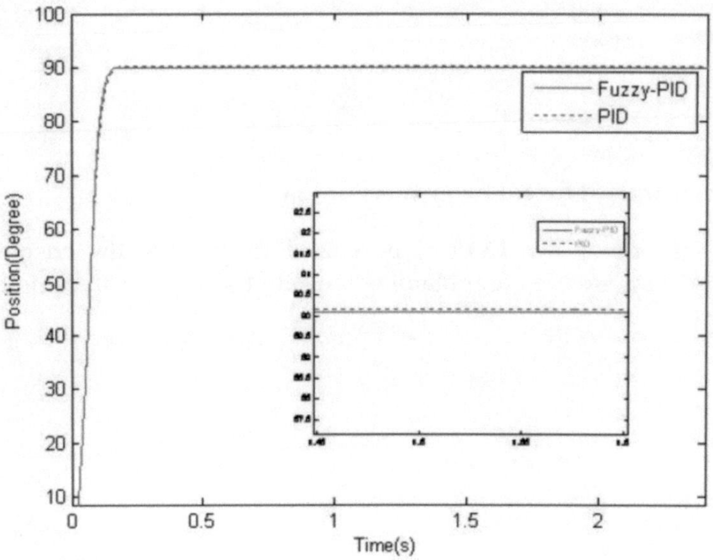

(a)

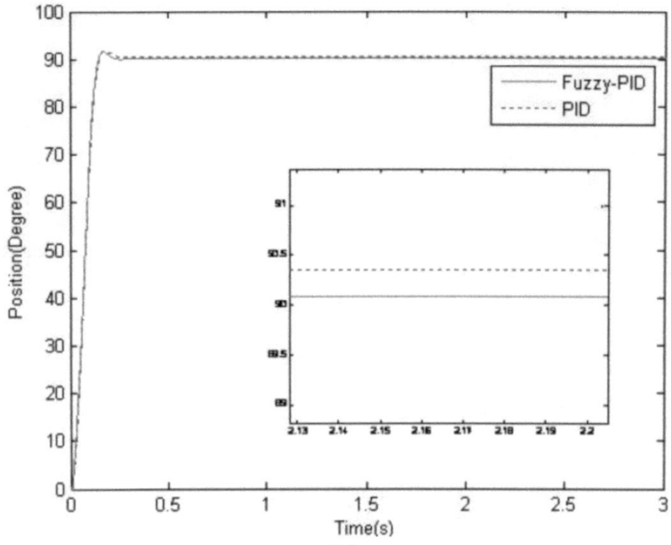

(b)

Fig. 22. System responses of a) nominal object and b) increased inertia

Plant	Controller	PO	Ts	Accuracy (Error)
Nominal	PID	0	0.18	0.176
	F-PID	0	0.17	0.088
Increased Inertia	PID	1.6	0.28	0.356
	F-PID	1.6	0.24	0.088

Table 9. Comparison of the performances of PID and F-PID controllers.

4. Mobile autonomous robot system

4.1 Introduction

Mobile robots are generally those robots which can move from place to place across the ground. Mobility give a robot a much greater flexibility to perform new, complex, exciting tasks. The world does not have to be modified to bring all needed items within reach of the robot. The robots can move where needed. Fewer robots can be used. Robots with mobility can perform more natural tasks in which the environment is not designed specially for them. These robots can work in a human centred space and cooperate with men by sharing a workspace together [9].

4.2 Mechanism

A mobile robot needs locomotion mechanisms that enable it to move unbounded throughout its environment. There is a large variety of possible ways to move which makes the selection of a robot's approach to locomotion an important aspect of mobile robot design. Most of these locomotion mechanisms have been inspired by their biological counterparts which are adapted to different environments and purposes.[9],[10] Many biologically inspired robots walk, crawl, slither, and hop.

In mobile robotics the terms omnidirectional, holonomic and non holonomic are often used, a discussion of their use will be helpful.[9]

The terms holonomic and omnidirectional are sometimes used redundantly, often to the confusion of both. Omnidirectional is a poorly defined term which simply means the ability to move in any direction. Because of the planar nature of mobile robots, the operational space they occupy contains only three dimensions which are most commonly thought of as the x, y global position of a point on the robot and the global orientation, θ, of the robot. Whether a robot is omnidirectional is not generally agreed upon whether this is a two-dimensional direction, x, y or a three-dimensional direction, x, y, θ. In this context a non holonomic mobile robot has the following properties:

- The robot configuration is described by more than three coordinates. Three values are needed to describe the location and orientation of the robot, while others are needed to describe the internal geometry.
- The robot has two DOF, or three DOF with singularities. (One DOF is kinematically possible but is it a robot then?)
- In this context a holonomic mobile robot has the following properties:
- The robot configuration is described by three coordinates. The internal geometry does not appear in the kinematic equations of the abstract mobile robot, so it can be ignored.
- The robot has three DOF without singularities.
- The robot can instantly develop a wrench in an arbitrary combination of directions x, y, θ.
- Non holonomic robots are most prevalent because of their simple design and ease of control. By their nature, non holonomic mobile robots have fewer degrees of freedom than holonomic mobile robots. These few actuated degrees of freedom in non holonomic mobile robots are often either independently controllable or mechanically decoupled, further simplifying the low-level control of the robot. Since they have fewer

degrees of freedom, there are certain motions they cannot perform. This creates difficult problems for motion planning and implementation of reactive behaviours.

- Holonomic however, offer full mobility with the same number of degrees of freedom as the environment. This makes path planning easier because there aren't constraints that need to be integrated. Implementing reactive behaviours is easy because there are no constraints which limit the directions in which the robot can accelerate.

In general, the mobile robot deals with the environment that is not certain and unknown. The environment may consist of several obstacles and paths which the robot has to go through. At the same time, the robot has to maintain its stability when changing direction if it faces the obstacles. This would definitely require the good control of the robot to make it reach to the desired points. With the limited information obtained during its operational, the fuzzy control is the best method to optimize its time consuming and energy consumption while reaching its goal. Harmeet Singh [4] in his work mentioned that the fuzzy control technique is the most suitable method to deal with the variability and unknown parameters in the given system. He also listed the constraints of the mobile robots that can be fulfilled with the fuzzy control techniques. There are:-

1. Difficulty in deriving the mathematical model of the environment. Even if it is simplified, the model could be very complex to be implemented with the hardware.
2. Sensors that are equipped on the mobile robot could be different and varies. The model of the conventional controller may not considering certain data obtained from the sensors which might lead to the instability of the robot.
3. Need of the real-time operation. Thus, the robot requires fast responds and operations. Complicated robot controller will lead to slow and undesired performance.

Generally, a mobile robot is built with wheels, motors and controller. The controller is designed in two types of control method. The open loop control and closed loop feedback control types [5]. In open loop control, the inputs are provided beforehand to make the robot reach the goal. This involves certain known parameters such as the acceleration or torque of the motor, the turning point and stop point, and time operation where the robot needs to stop or make a turning, and the angle of turning. This type of methods would only suitable for the known environment and paths. For the closed loop strategies, the sensors are equipped with the robots and the robot will respond to the certain data obtained through sensors. The robot will act in a way that the controller was designed beforehand. For instant, the robot is programmed to move to the right direction if it faces any obstacle in front.

4.3 Controller design

In the real system, the obstacles or paths are not the ideal and vary in shapes and locations. If the robot is set to turn right when facing the obstacles, it does not mean the robot must turn 90 degree to the right. The controller should be designed in a way that it still approaching the desired target. Otherwise, it may turn back to its original point and that would not only consume time but waste energy as well. Thus, a good control must have very details conditions and settings to optimize the performance of the robot. The conventional type of control that is already designed is P, PI and PID control. However, the model becomes more complicated and difficult to implement with. Another alternative is by using the fuzzy algorithm. Fuzzy logic is becoming more popular among the control method in designing the complex system as it is approved in many researches that it can simplify a complex model. Furthermore, fuzzy logic drives the controller to think like human in optimizing the performance. In this application where the robot needs details output such as how right it should turn or how fast it should accelerate, fuzzy approach could overcome these constraints.

Hairol Nizam[6] in his work explained the design of fuzzy algorithm for robot in approaching the desired destination.

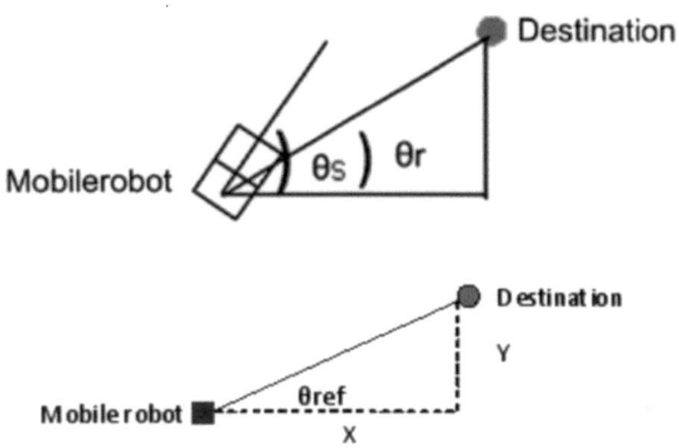

Fig. 23. Autonomous Robot with parameters defined

The figure shows two angles assigned as linguistic variables. The θ_s and θ_r will be compared with θ_{ref} to obtain the linguistic values. The following table shows how the rules are constructed.

			θ_s	
		Large	Equal	Small
θ_r	Large	Right	Right	Left
	Equal	Right	Forward	Left
	Small	Right	Left	Left

Table 10. Fuzzy Rules for Autonomous Robot

From the table, the rules can be constructed as listed below

Rule 1; IF θs is Large and θr is Large, Then direction is *Right*
Rule 2; IF θs is Large and θr is Equal, Then direction is *Right*
Rule 3; IF θs is Large and θr is Small, Then direction is *Right*
Rule 4; IF θs is Equal and θr is Large, Then direction is *Right*
Rule 5; IF θs is Equal and θr is Equal, Then direction is *forward*
Rule 6; IF θs is Equal and θr is Small, Then direction is *Right*
Rule 7; IF θs is Small and θr is Large, Then direction is *Left*
Rule 8; IF θs is Small and θr is Equal, Then direction is *Left*
Rule 9; IF θs is Small and θr is Small, Then direction is *Left*

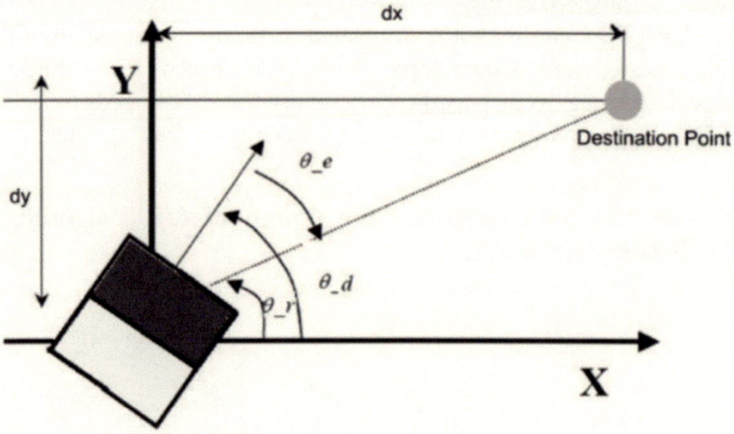

Fig. 24. Parameter defined for mobile robot

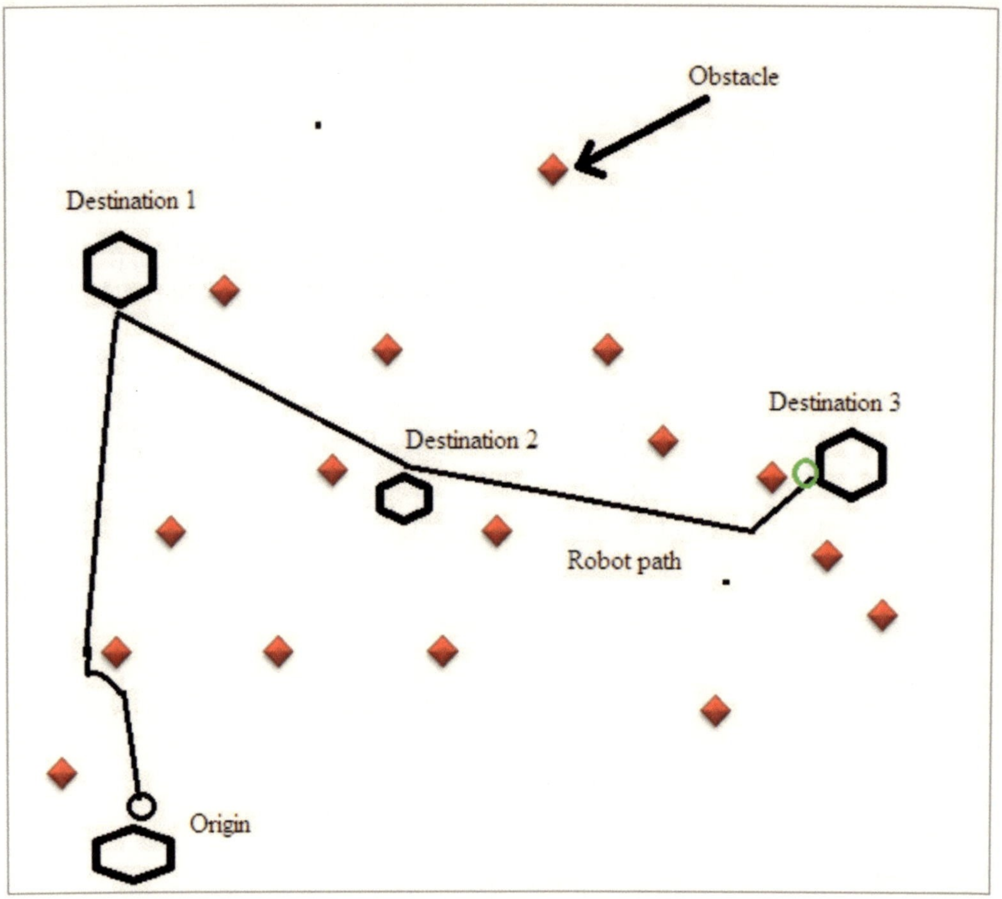

Fig. 25. Robot following path with obstacle avoidance criteria

In this case, the distance between the destination point and the robot is determined with the destination position, $d_e = \sqrt{{d_x}^2 + {d_y}^2}$, and destination angle, $\theta_e = \theta_d - \theta_r$.

With the rules constructed, the mobile robot could be guided to the direction of the destination point with minimum movement.

5. References

[1] Ismail, H., Akyüz, Selcuk Kizir, Zafer Bingül, (2011). *"Fuzzy Logic Control of Single Link Flexible Joint Manipulator"*, Department of Mechatronics Engineering, Kocaeli University, Turkey.

[2] Kelly Cohen, Tanchum Weller, Joseph Z, Ben-Esher, (2000). *"Active Control of Flexible Structures Based on Fuzzy Controllers"*, Department of Aerospace Engineering, I.I.T., Technion City, ICAS Congress.

[3] Lynch P.J. and Banda S.S., (1988). *"Active Control for Vibration Damping, Large Space Structures: Dynamics and Control"*, Ed. Atluri S.N and Amos A.K., Springer-Verlag Berlin Heidelberg, pp. 239-262.

[4] Harmeet Singh, Sanchit Arora, Aparna Mehra, (2008).*"Using Fuzzy Logic for Mobile Robot Control"*, Mathematics Department, Indian Institute of Technology Delhi.

[5] Vamsi Mohan Peri, Dan Simon, *"Fuzzy Logic Control For an Autonomous Robot"*, Department of Electrical and Computer Engineering, Cleveland State University.

[6] Razif Rashid, I. Elamvazuthi, Mumtaj Begam, M. Arrofiq "Fuzzy-based Navigation and Control of a Non-Holonomic Mobile Robot Journal of computing", volume 2, issue 3, march 2010, issn 2151-9617

[7] Hairol Nizam Mohd Shah, Marizan Sulaiman, Syed Najib Syed Salim, (2007).*"Fuzzy Logic Approach for Mobile Robot In Intelligent Space"*, Journal of Institute of Engineers Malaysia, Vol. 68, No. 4.

[8] V. K. Banga, R. Kumar, Y. Singh, (2009). *"Fuzzy-Genetic Optimal Control for Four Degree"*, World Academy of Science, Engineering and Technology 60.

[9] H. Eskandar, Pouya Salehi, M.H.Sabour (2010). *"Fuzzy Logic Tracking Control for a Three Wheel Circular Robot in Unknown Environment"*, World Applied Science Journal, Vol. 11(3), pp. 321-326.

[10] Robert Holmberg, "Design and Development of Powered-Castor Holonomic Mobile Robots", Stanford University, 2000

[11] Roland Siegwart, Illah R. Nourbakhsh "Introduction to Autonomous Mobile Robots", The MIT Press, Massachusetts Institute of Technology, Cambridge, Massachusetts, 2004

[12] Mohd Ashraf Ahmad "European Journal of Scientific Research" Vol.27 No.3 (2009), pp.322-333 EuroJournals Publishing, Inc. 2009

[13] Wahyudi and J. Jalani "Intelligent Gantry Crane System" Proceedings of the 2nd International Conference on Mechatronics, ICOM'05 10-12 May *2005, Kuala Lumpur, Malaysia*

[14] Jamaludin J., Wahyudi, Iswaini and Suhaimi A, "Development of Automatic Gantry Crane Part2:Controller Design and Implementation", in Proc. The 5_{th} Industrial Electronics Seminar 2004, Surabaya, 11 October 2004.

7

Fuzzy Inference Systems Applied to the Analysis of Vibrations in Electrical Machines

Fredy Sanz, Juan Ramírez and Rosa Correa
Cinvestav
Mexico

1. Introduction

Within industry, the concept of maintenance can be handled in different ways. It can be done periodically at predefined times, according to the type of machine, and according to the manufacturers' recommendations. In this case, it is referred to as scheduled preventive maintenance. Maintenance done when there is faulty equipment is commonly called corrective maintenance. Employing electrical machines' operating signals may be useful for diagnosis purposes.

Three-phase electrical machines such as induction motors or generators are used in a wide variety of applications. In order to increase the productivity and to reduce maintenance costs, condition monitoring and diagnosis is often desired. A wide variety of conditioning monitoring techniques has been introduced over the last decade. These include the electric current signature and stator vibrations analysis (Cusido & Romeral & Ortega & Espinoza, 2008; Blodt & Granjon & Raison & Rostaing, 2008; Blodt & Regnier & Faucher, 2009; Riera & Daviu & Fulch, 2008).

Nowadays, industry demands solutions to provide more flexible alternatives for maintenance, avoiding waste of time in case of major requirements to unforeseen failures, as well as time of scheduled maintenance. This creates the necessity to propose and implement predictive technologies, which ensure that machinery receive attention only when they present some evidence of their mechanical properties deterioration (Taylor, 2003). Vibrations have been one of the usual machinery's physical state indicators.

Some issues related to failures in machinery are as follows:

1. Different problems can be apparent with the same frequency. For example, the unbalance, the one-axis flexion, the misalignment or some resonances, all can be apparent within the same frequency interval. Likewise, a machine may vibrate due to problems related with another machine to which it is coupled.
2. Models do not precisely represent the machine's behavior, since frequently studies assume that the constituent parts and load mechanics are perfectly symmetric. Likewise, in the electrical motor's case, normally it is assumed that electrical sources are balanced.

3. The precise analysis of a problem at a given frequency depends on the presence of one or more related frequencies. In the current methods, an important difficulty is the need to monitor through sophisticated sensors. Additionally, failures detection depends on the load's inertia.

Different detection techniques for machines' state monitoring have been studied. Some techniques are based on analyzing electrical signals, some others are based on vibration measurements, and some combine them. In this paper, vibration measurements are used for monitoring purposes.

Vibrations must be properly evaluated, especially those associated to rotating machinery. Capturing vibration patterns, using identification techniques and signal processing, distinctive signatures for failures detection can be set. This could help to anticipate the occurrence of equipment damage, and therefore, corrective actions can be taken to avoid the high cost of a partial or total machinery replacement, as well as economic expenses caused by their unavailability.

2. Preliminaries

In this research, historical developments around the vibration analysis have been reviewed, while the use of emerging technologies are proposed to identify failures in rotating electrical machines. Through a wavelet decomposition, it is possible to extract information that enables the detection of signal changes under significant vibrations, affecting the equipments' useful life. The vibration signals have been utilized to detect failures in rotating electrical machines. However, the use of Fourier-based techniques is not practical, because such techniques need stable and long-term records.

No given rules exist to allow characterization of the type of machine, size, or even some specific operating characteristics through vibration patterns. It is relevant to establish strategies able to identify a failure, and even to differentiate among the types of failures. Thus, the neural networks may be quite useful. Through learning elements, neural networks are able to infer the actual conditions of the system under analysis. In this application, the Adaptive Network Based Fuzzy Inference System (ANFIS) has been selected for such purposes.

ANFIS is an Artificial Neuro-Fuzzy Inference System, which is functionally equivalent to fuzzy inference systems. It represents a Sugeno-Tsukamoto fuzzy model, that uses a hybrid learning algorithm (Omar, 2010; Jang, 1993; Jang & Sun, 1996; Bonissone & Badami & Chiang & Knedkar & Schutter, 1996; Jang & Gulley, 1995; Michie & Spregelhart & Taylor, 1994).

2.1 Fuzzy inference systems

It is necessary to study other alternatives because the system models based on conventional mathematical tools, like differential equations, is not well suited for dealing with ill-defined and uncertain systems (Proakis, 2001). Through the use of vibration signals, it is possible to implement tools able to differentiate characteristics to establish the electrical machine's conditions. A fuzzy inference system employing fuzzy *if-then* rules can model the qualitative aspects of human knowledge and reasoning processes without employing precise quantitative analyses. The fuzzy modeling or fuzzy identification, was first explored systematically by Takagi and Sugeno (Takagi & Sugeno, 1985). There are some basic aspects of this approach that require some comments. In particular:

1. Vibration signals in electrical machines have information, which can be used to predict the machine's state. Figure 1, shows the basic inference composition.
2. Patterns captured under different conditions may be similar, therefore it is necessary an inference system that facilitates the identification process.

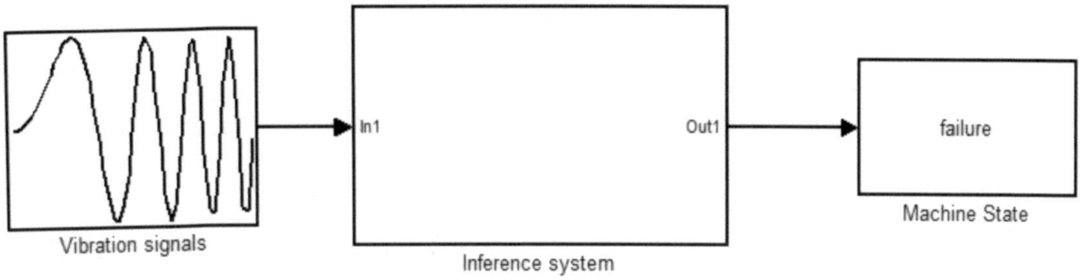

Fig. 1. Basic inference system

2.2 Fuzzy *if-then* rules

Fuzzy *if-then* rules or fuzzy conditional statements are expressions of the form *IF* A *THEN* B, where A and B are labels of fuzzy sets (Zadeh, 1965) characterized by appropriate membership functions. Due to their concise form, fuzzy *if-then* rules are often employed to capture the imprecise modes of reasoning that play an essential role in the human ability to make decisions in an environment of uncertainty and imprecision. An example that describes a simple fact is:

If vibration is high, it is possible the bars' failure

where *vibration* and *failure* are linguistic variables (Jang, 1994); *high* (*small*) are linguistic values or labels that are characterized by membership functions.

A different form of fuzzy *if-then* rules, proposed by (Omar, 2010; Takagi & Sugeno, 1985, as cited in Jang, 1993), have fuzzy sets involved only in the premise part. Both types of fuzzy *if-then* rules have been used extensively in both modeling and control. Through the use of linguistic labels and membership functions, a fuzzy *if-then* rule can easily capture the spirit of a "*rule of thumb*" used by humans. From another point of view, due to the qualifiers on the premise parts, each fuzzy *if-then* rule can be viewed as a local description of the system under consideration. Fuzzy *if-then* rules form a core part of the fuzzy inference system described in the following.

2.3 Fuzzy inference system structure for vibration analysis

Fuzzy inference systems are also known as fuzzy-rule-based systems, fuzzy models, fuzzy associative memories (FAM), or fuzzy controllers when used as controllers. Basically, a fuzzy inference system is composed by five functional blocks (Jang, 1993), Fig. 2.

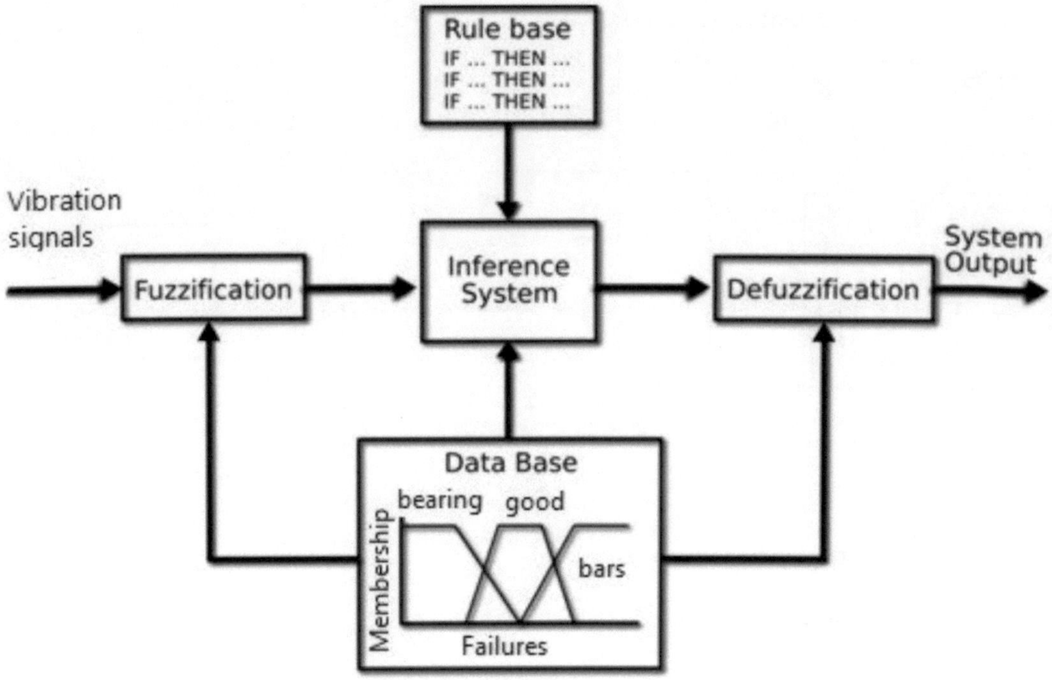

Fig. 2. Fuzzy inference system structure

- i. A rule base containing a number of fuzzy *if-then* rules.
- ii. A database which defines the membership functions of the fuzzy sets used in the fuzzy rules.
- iii. A decision-making unit which performs the inference operations on the rules.
- iv. A fuzzification interface which transforms the crisp inputs into degrees of match with linguistic values.
- v. A defuzzification interface which transforms the fuzzy results of the inference into a crisp output.

Frequently, the rule base and the database (e.g. vibrations data in different conditions) are jointly referred to as the *knowledge base.*

The steps of fuzzy logic (inference operations upon fuzzy *if-then* rules) performed by fuzzy inference systems for machine's diagnoses are shown in Figure 3.

Several types of fuzzy logic have been proposed in the open research. Depending on the types of fuzzy reasoning and fuzzy *if-then* rules employed, most fuzzy inference strategies may be classified as follows (Jang, 1993).

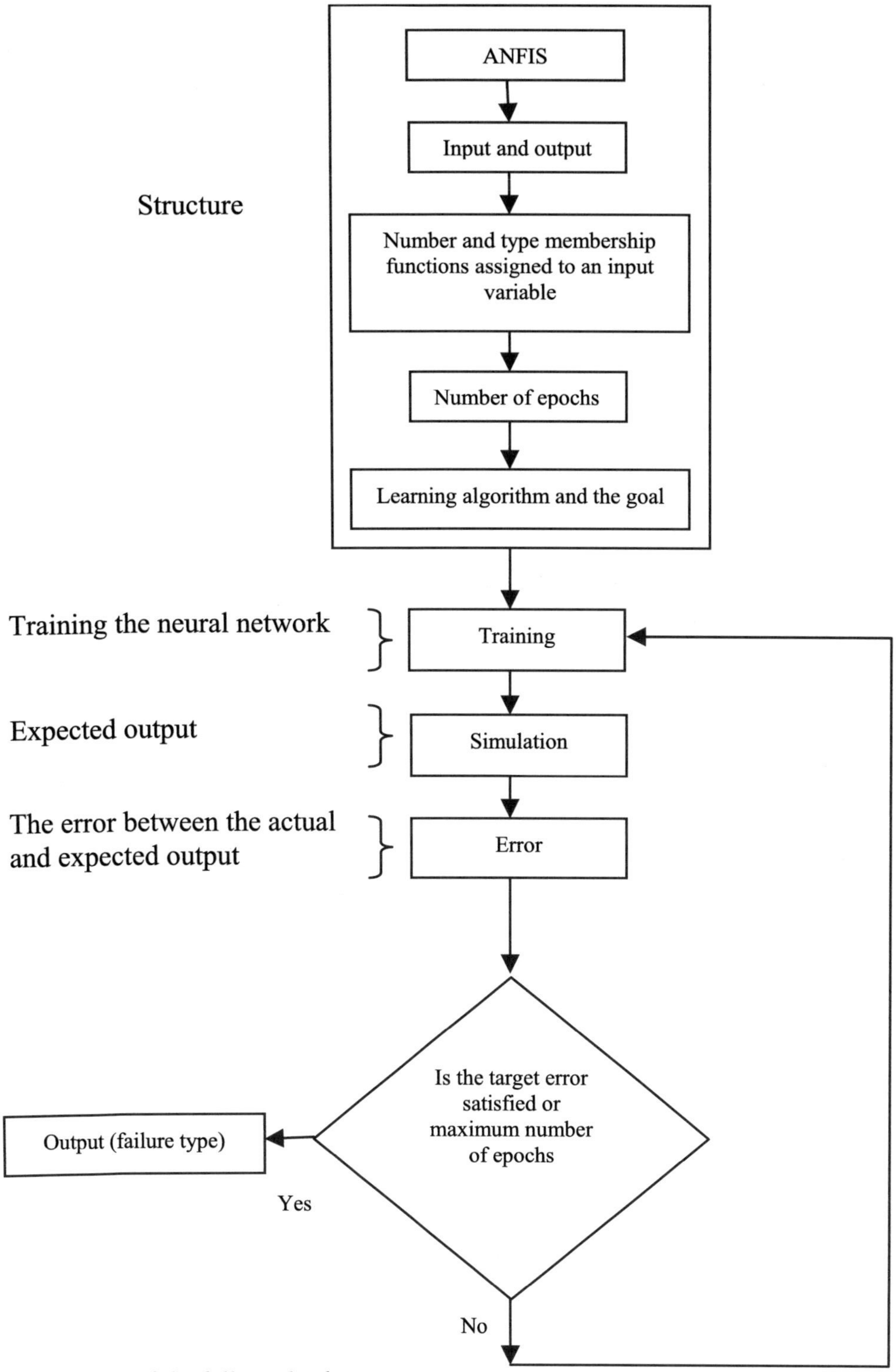

Fig. 3. Flowchart of the followed inference strategy

Type 1: The overall output is the weighted average of each rule's crisp output induced by the rule's firing strength and output membership functions. The output membership functions used in this scheme must be monotonic functions (lee, 1990).

Type 2: The overall fuzzy output is derived by applying maximization operation to the qualified fuzzy outputs, each of which is equal to the minimum of firing strength and the output membership function of each rule. Various schemes have been proposed to choose the final crisp output based on the overall fuzzy output; some of them are the centroid of area, mean of maxima, maximum criterion, etc., (Lee, 1990).

Type 3: In (Lee, 1990, as cited in Takagi & Sugeno, 1985) fuzzy *if-then* rules are used. The output of each rule is a linear combination of input variables plus a constant term, and the final output is the weighted average of each rule's output.

2.4 ANFIS basics

In ANFIS, the adaptive network structure is a multilayer feed-forward network where each node performs a particular function (node function) on incoming signals as well as a set of parameters pertaining to this node. The node functions may vary from node to node, and the choice of each node function depends on the overall input-output function that the adaptive network is required to carry out. Notice that links in an adaptive network indicate the flow direction of signals between nodes; no weights are associated with the links.

Functionally, there are almost no constraints on the node functions of an adaptive network, except piecewise differentiability. Structurally, the only restriction of the network configuration is that it should be of feed-forward type. Due to these minimal restrictions, the adaptive network's applications are immediate and immense in various areas. (Jang, 1993) proposed a class of adaptive networks that are functionally equivalent to fuzzy inference systems. The proposed architecture is referred to as ANFIS, standing for adaptive-network-based fuzzy inference system.

An adaptive network is a structured network composed by nodes and directional links, which connect nodes, Fig. 4. All or some nodes are adaptive. It means that results depend on nodes' parameters, and the learning rules specify how these parameters must change in order to minimize an error. The adaptive network is constituted by a multilayer feedback network, where each node performs a particular task (node function) on the incoming signals, as well as a set of node parameters.

The ANFIS can be trained by a hybrid learning algorithm (Jang, 1993; Jang & Sun, 1996; Jang & Gulley, 1995). It uses a two-pass learning cycle. In the forward pass, the algorithm uses the least-squares method to identify the consequent parameters on the layer 4. In the backward pass, the errors are propagated backward and the premise parameters are updated by gradient descent.

ANFIS is a tradeoff between neural and fuzzy systems, providing: (*i*) smoothness, due to the Fuzzy interpolation; (*ii*) adaptability, due to the neural net backpropagation; (*iii*) ANFIS however has a strong computational complexity restriction.

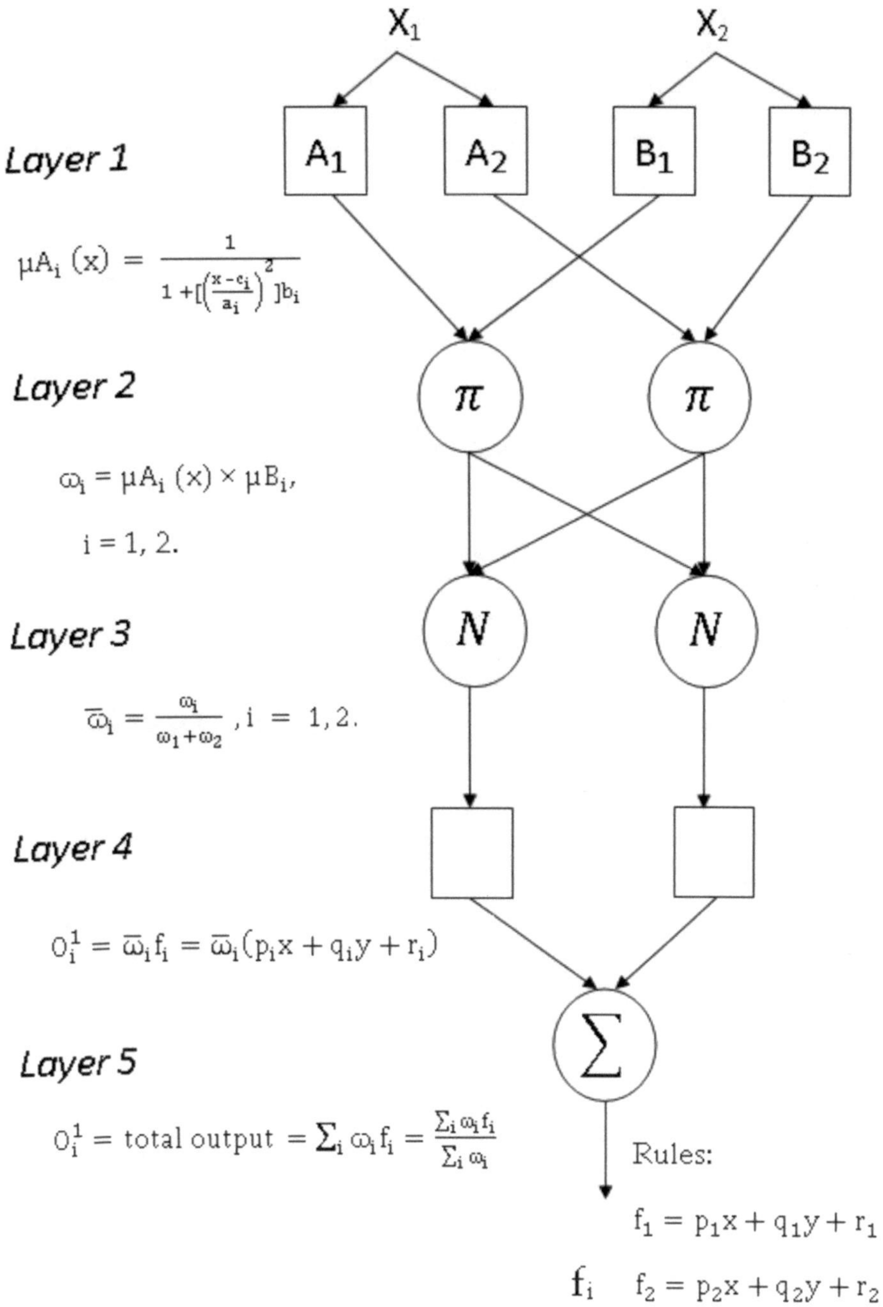

Fig. 4. Set of calculations in ANFIS

where:
x_i is the input into node i
A_i is the linguistic label
μA_i is the A_i's membership function.

$\{a_i, b_i, c_i\}$ is the set of parameters. Modifying these parameters, the shape of the bell functions change, so that exhibit different forms of membership functions for the linguistic label A_i.
ϖ is the level-3 output.
$\{p_i, q_i, r_i\}$: is the set of parameters, which at this level may be referred to as consequent parameters.

2.5 Vibration analysis by wavelets

The raw material to make any inference about the machinery's condition is the information captured from vibration signals. The proposition is to utilize the vibration's raw signals to infer about the engine's state. A structured analysis may characterize the nature of the vibration, figure 5.

Wavelets transformation is the disintegration of a signal which becomes represented by means of function approximations and differences, which are divided by levels, figure 6, each of which have different resolutions, being equivalent to filtering the signal through a filter bank. The initial filtering takes the signal and passes it through the first bank, resulting in two signals with different frequency bands (high and low bands).

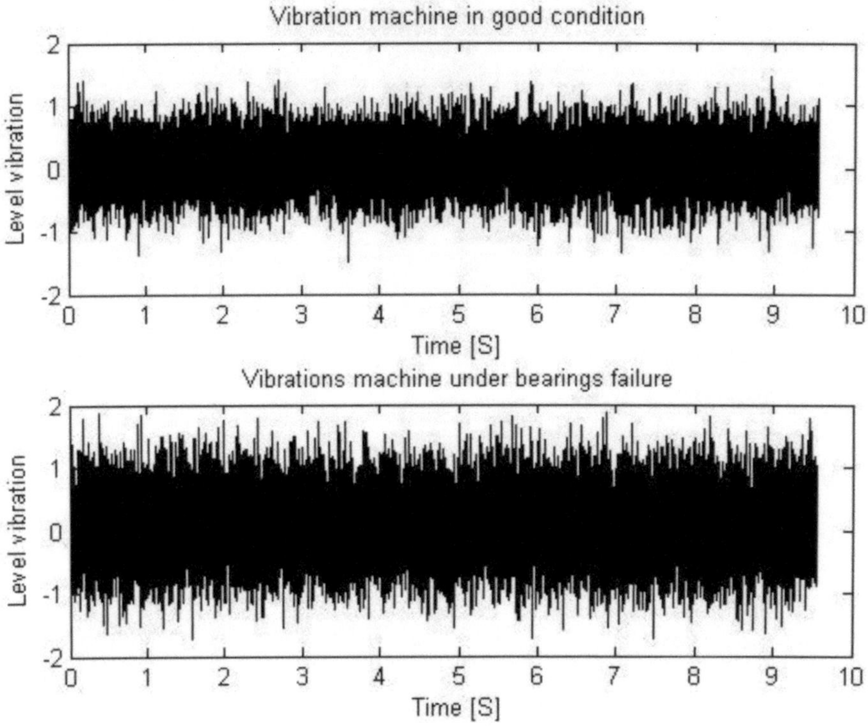

Fig. 5. Vibration patterns under failure and normal conditions.

The time-frequency resolution of the transformed wavelet satisfies the Nyquist sampling theorem. That is, the maximum frequency component embedded into a signal can be uniquely determined if the signal is sampled at a frequency F_s, which exceeds or equals the double of the signal's maximum frequency F_{max}. At the limit, if $F_s = 2F_{max}$ then:

$$F_{max} = F_s/2 = 1/(2T) \tag{1}$$

where T is the sampling interval. That is, if the frequency F_{max} of the original signal is divided into two sub-frequency bands, where p / 2 is the highest frequency band, it leads to F_s= p and T = 1 / p. To clarify the concept, consider the scheme of underlying filters, which perform the discrete wavelet transformation. Under this concept, for each filtering level the incoming signal is split into low and high frequencies. Since the output from low frequencies is subjected to additional filters, the resolution increases as the spectrum is divided again into two sub-bands.

The resolution time is reduced because of the decimation that takes place. The above-mentioned strategy has been employed to make an inference about the engine's state, using vibration measurements as input

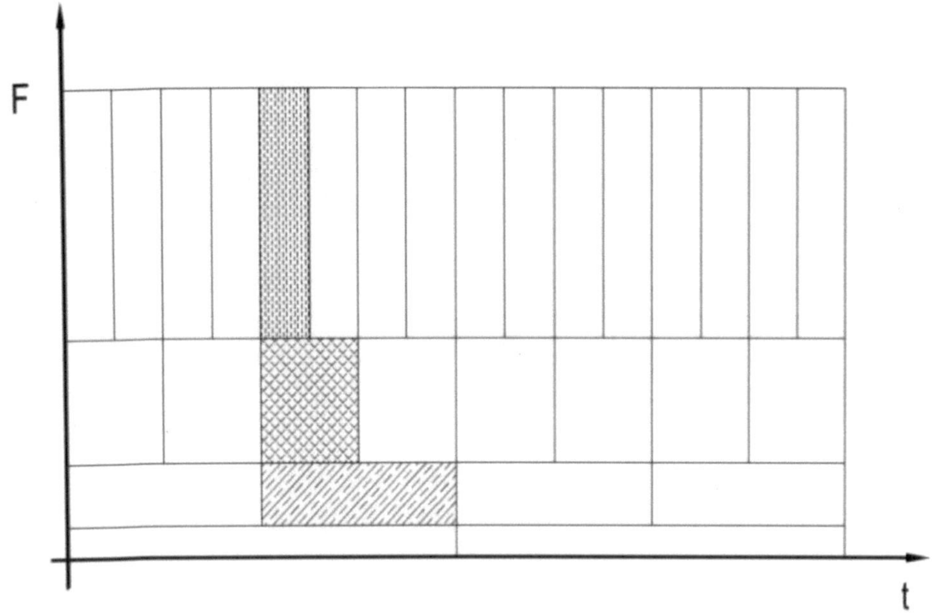

Fig. 6. Time-Frequency resolution of a transformed wavelet

3. Proposition

It is important to emphasize that the main aim of this chapter is the inference system, and to present the structured method for signal processing. The necessary requirements to establish the machine's operating conditions are presented below, and consist in a hybrid method decomposed in two phases. Phase I is the adequacy of the signal, while phase II is the inference or identification procedure, figure 7. Both phases I and II may be represented by two functional blocks that perform different treatments to the vibration signals.

The process of the adequacy signal is necessary because the exclusive ANFIS application to minimally invasive faults does not generate a successful inference process

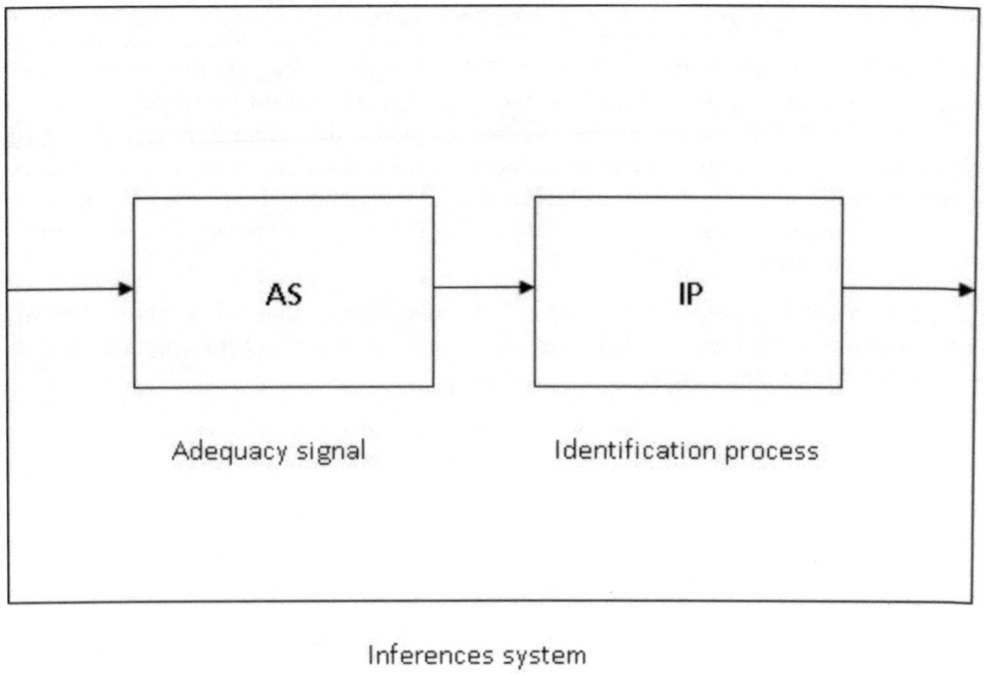

Fig. 7. Stages of the inference system

In this application, measurements are taken by a 12-bit LIS3L02ASA vibration sensor (accelerometer based on MEMS - Microelectromechanical system), which provides measurement of displacement in three axes. Additionally, to reduce the noise/signal proportion, filtering is added.

Thus, the triaxial accelerometer, is one of the most important parts of the instrumentation system, being located in the engine body, which measures vibrations based on three axes (x, y, z) using a sampling rate of 1500Hz. The ADS7841 is a converter equipped with serial synchronous communication interface with 200KHz conversion rate. After the digitalized data is sent via the RS232 card to capture, the system data acquisition uses a MAX3243 circuit.

The sensor provides vibration measurements in three axes. In this research, it was noticed that the perpendicular axes to the axis of rotation have more useful information to identify a failure occurrence. Thus, in order to optimize the computational load, data from the x-axis were used.

4. Case study

The machine used in this study is a 1 HP induction motor, where the load is represented by an alternator coupled to the motor through a band. The alternator feeds a bank of resistors, Fig. 8. Vibration measurements of machines in good condition and under fault conditions are captured and processed in ANFIS to simulate an inference process to identify the occurrence of a specific failure.

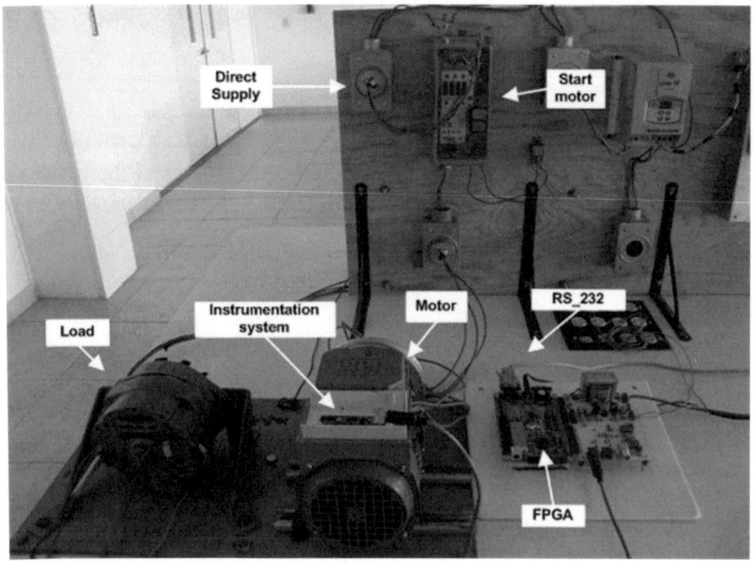

Fig. 8. Induction motor's arrangement

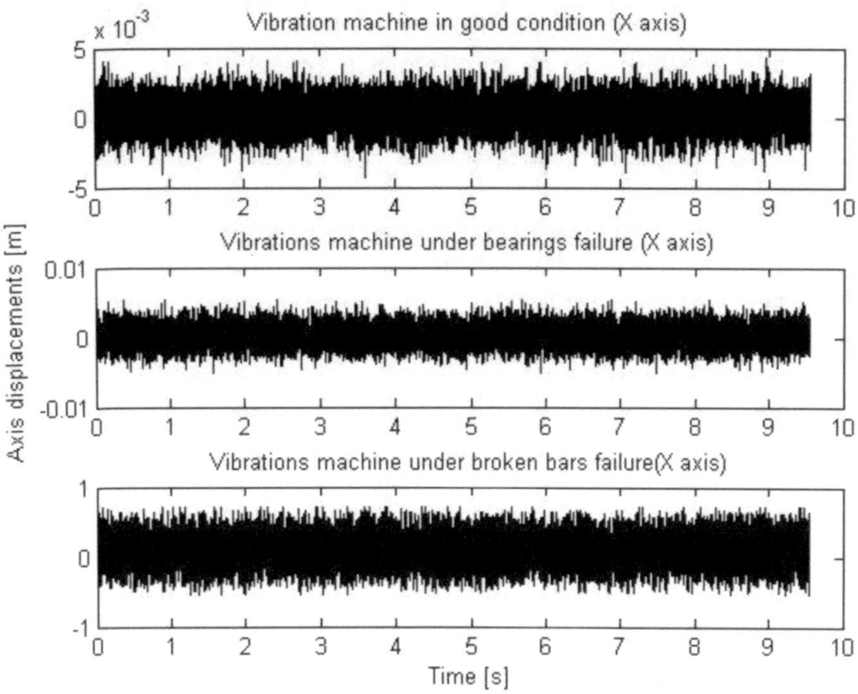

Fig. 9. Vibrations under different conditions

The proposed hybrid method aims to identify the fault states in rotating machines, distinguishing the smooth operation from failure conditions by measuring vibration signals. Vibration measurements have been monitored in three axes: x, y, and z under the following operating conditions:

1. A motor in good condition
2. A motor with bearing fault
3. A motor with broken bars

In the case of bearing failure, there is a minimally invasive phenomenon in the machine's vibration, contrary to a broken bars failure, which gives rise to notorious vibration, Fig 9. The preliminary coarse filtering process is performed by the assembled sensor.

Likewise, at a first glance, the vibrations in the axial direction are more noticeable. Thus, their measurements are employed in the following analysis.

5. Results and discussion

As above mentioned, some minor failures such as bearing failures are not distinguishable by exclusive use of ANFIS, figure 10. This is why the use of wavelets provides an effective tool for the identification of different types of failures in electric machines.

The results presented in the following are attained through simulations using real data, when the induction motor is under normal operating conditions and failure.

Phase I:

To exemplify the proposed strategy, the following results are obtained by using the x-axis measurement only. Firstly, the wavelet decomposition requires that n levels be selected, so that the inference process has sufficient information to identify the faulted condition. That is, the quantity of levels is proportional to the filtering quality. In this application, due to the good performance obtained when a correlation test to verify the data stability is carried out, n = 2 will be used.

That is, the number of levels affects the number of sets resulting from the wavelet decomposition, leading to four functions: two for high frequency, and two for low frequency. Figure 11 shows the wavelet decomposition corresponding to the motor in good condition.

In this study the Meyer wavelet family is used (which properties are symmetry, orthogonality, biortogonality) and the Shannon Entropy decomposition was used (Zadeh, 1965; Proakis, 2001; Anderson, 1984; Oppemheim & Schafer 2009)

Phase II:

Once the wavelet decomposition is evaluated, data must be structured and handled by the software, with the proper procedure.

Training data: the historical data set representing each particular state of the machine requires the corresponding wavelet decomposition.

Checking data: data used to test and infer. From a practical standpoint, they are the vibration measurements under the studied condition.

Tags: correspond to that feature that allows the user to differentiate one condition from another. For the studied case, numerical levels will be used for each engine's state.

Applying the proposed method to failures on bearings and broken bars, Figures 12-13 depict a typical result. It is noteworthy that the checking and training data are perfectly differentiable through level changes observed in the data. Labels are selected by the user to have a reference, which is the state that the machine is undergoing.

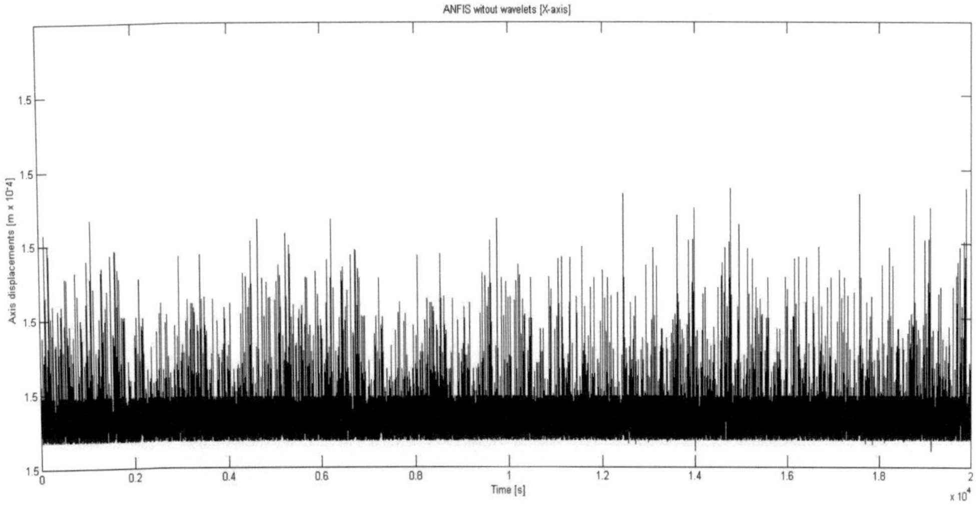

Fig. 10. Bearing failure ANFIS without wavelet decomposition

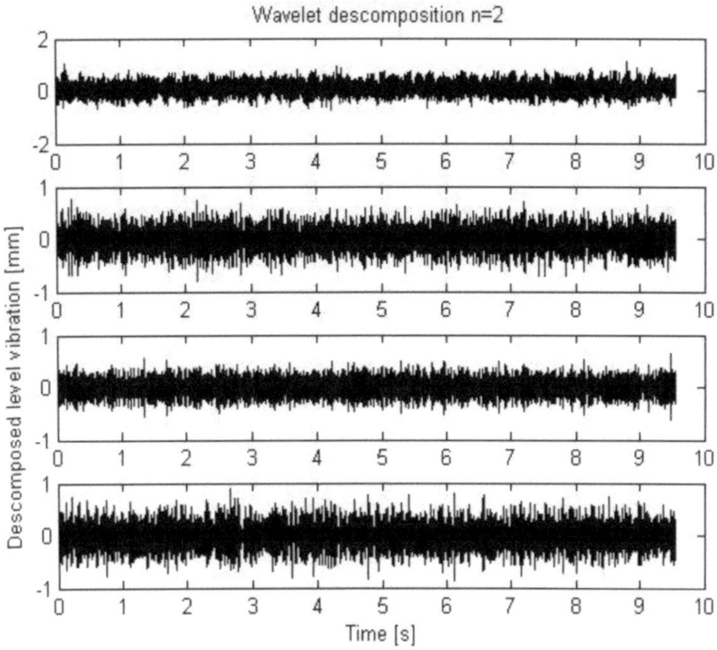

Fig. 11. A machine in good condition: wavelet decomposition, n=2.

Additionally, Figures 14-15 display the Root Mean Squared Error (RMSE) between the checking and training curves, for both failures, where the RMSE is a quadratic scoring rule, which measures the average magnitude of the error. Expressing the expression in words, the difference between the forecasted and the corresponding observed values are each squared and then averaged over the sample. Finally, the square root of the average is calculated, since the errors are squared before they are averaged.

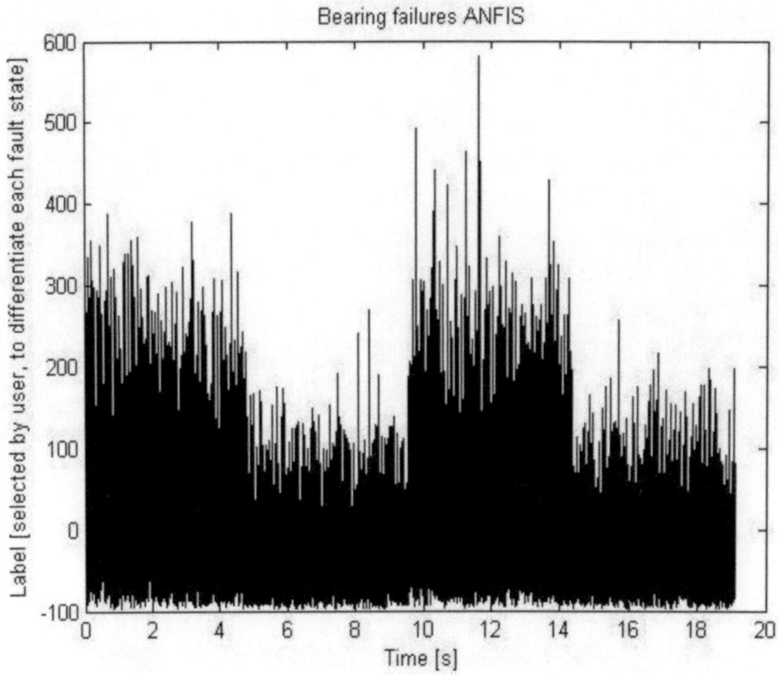

Fig. 12. Bearing failure

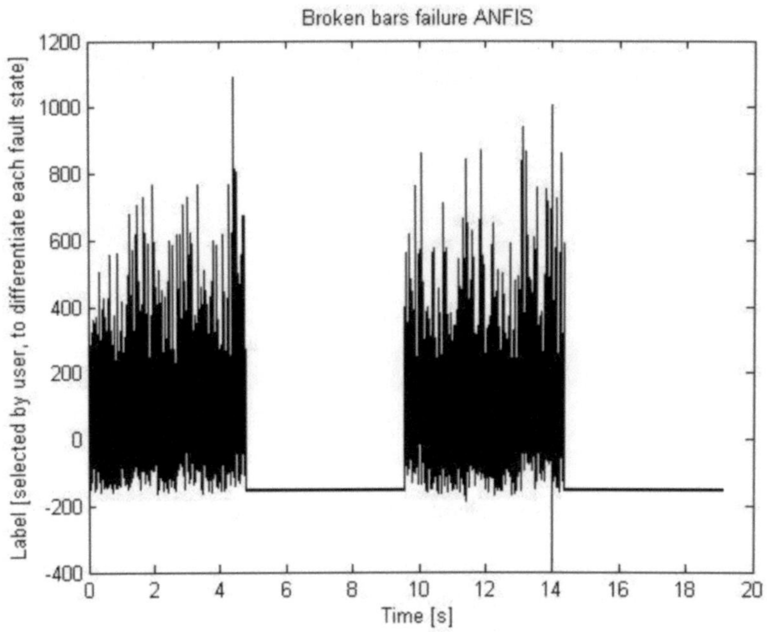

Fig. 13. Broken bars failure

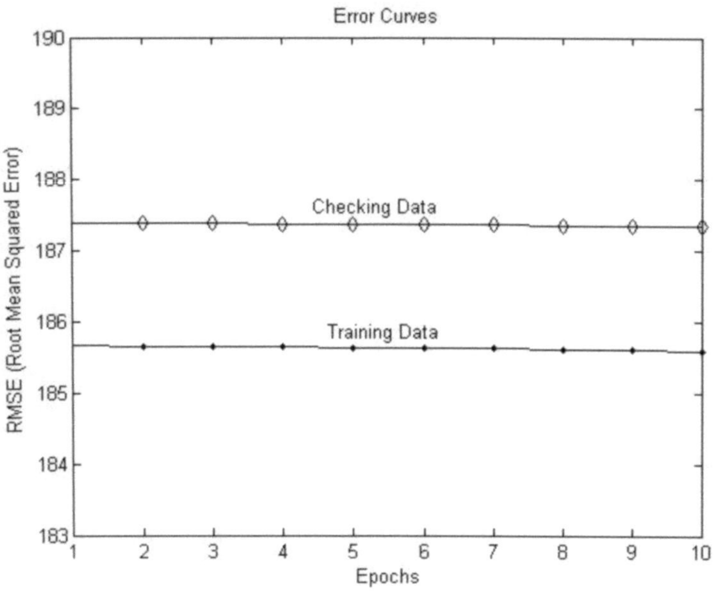

Fig. 14. Error between checking and training curves for bearing failures

It is important to clarify that, for the training-optimization process, ANFIS uses a combination of the method by least squares and gradient descent.

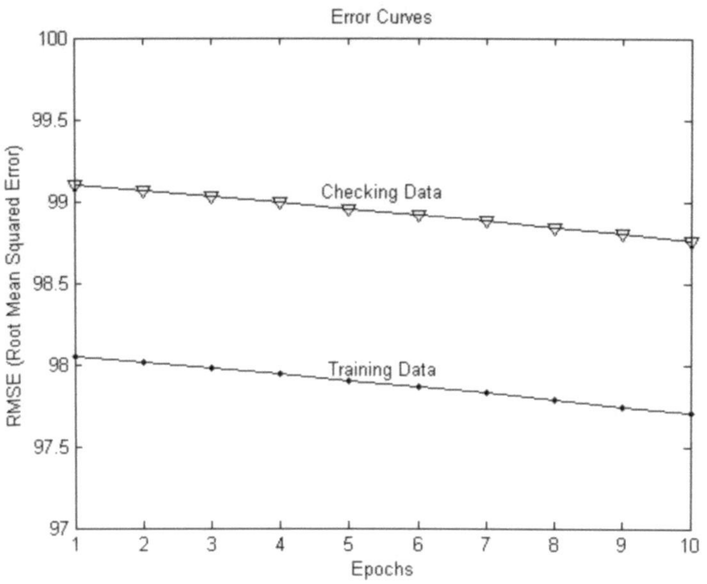

Fig. 15. Error between checking and training curves for broken bars

In Figures 16-17 the mean for both failures are exhibited, which have been calculated as an average data set for each level, where it is clear that inference process has been successful, because the labels are clearly differentiable, where positive and negative values are the result of a previous selection of tags formed by numerical extremes to differentiate the states where the motor is.

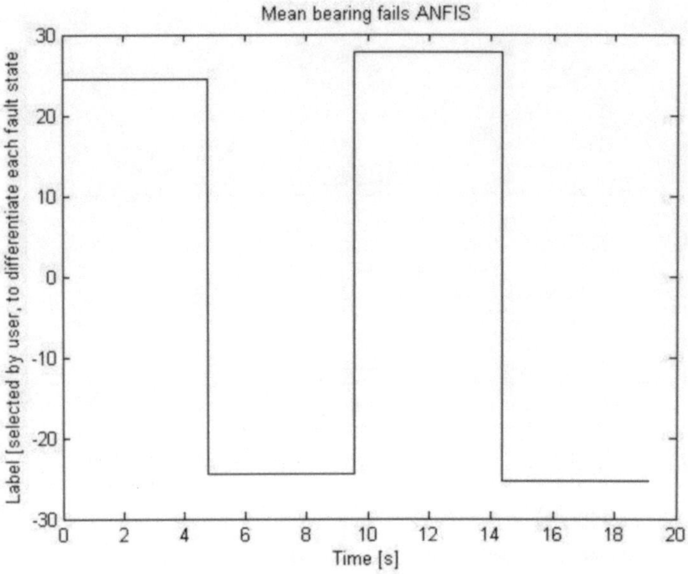

Fig. 16. Mean under bearing failure

Fig. 17. Mean under broken bars failure

6. Conclusions

The study of vibration in rotating electrical machines through ANFIS requires the use of signal conditioning tools, which are introduced through the training and test arrays. Special care should be taken with some overlapping modes, especially in those failures that, due to their nature, do not generate large perturbations in oscillations, but represent an imminent risk to the engine's life.

The failures considered in the electrical machines studied, reflected changes in the three axes x, y and z. However, they are most noticeable in those that are axial to the axis of rotation, allowing the detection of failures through the analysis on a single axis, instead opening the way for the use of less sophisticated sensors, reducing the implementation costs.

In the inference process it is quite attractive to use pragmatic strategies to handle large amount of measured information, and able to identify the machinery's operating condition.

The errors between the check and learning curves for the two types of studied failures are satisfactory for identification purposes in both cases. Thus, ANFIS has been successfully applied to distinguish between such failures.

7. Acknowledgment

Our gratitude to Universidad de Guanajuato for providing data for this research.

8. References

Anderson, T. (1984). *An introduction to Multivariate Statistical Analysis*, Wiley, ISBN 978-0471889878, Stanford, California, United States of America

Blodt, M.; Granjon, P.; Raison, B.; & Rostaing, G. (2008) Models for Bearing Damage Detection in Induction Motors Using Stator Current Monitoring. *IEEE Transactions on Industrial Electronics*, Vol. 55, No. 4, pp. 1813-1822. ISSN 0278-0046

Blodt, M.; Regnier, J.; & Faucher, J. (2009). Distinguishing Load Torque Oscillations and Eccentricity Faults in Induction Motors Using Stator Current Wigner Distributions. *IEEE Transactions on Industry Applications*, Vol. 45, No. 6. pp. 1991-2000, ISBN: 1-4244-0364-2

Bonissone, P.; Badami, V.; Chiang, K.; Khedkar, P.; Marcelle, K. & Schutten, M. (1995). Industrial applications of fuzzy logic at General Electric. *Proceedings of the IEEE*, Vol. 83, No.3, pp 450-465, ISSN 0018-9219

Cusido, J.; Romeral, L.; Ortega, J.; Rosro, J., & Espinosa, A. (2008). Fault Detection in Induction Machines Using Power Spectral Density in Wavelet Decomposition. *IEEE Transactions on Industrial Electronics*, Vol. 55, No. 2, pp. 633-643, ISSN 0278-0046

Jang, J. (1993). ANFIS: adaptive-network-based fuzzy inference system. *IEEE Transaction Systems, Man, Cybernetics*, Vol. 23, No. 3, pp. 665-685, ISSN 018-9472

Jang, J. & Sun, C. (1995). Neuro-fuzzy modeling and control. *Proceedings of the IEEE*, Vol. 83, No. 3, pp 378-406. ISSN 0018-9219

Jang, J. & Gulley, N. (1995). *The Fuzzy Logic Toolbox for use with MATLAB*, The MathWorks, Inc., Natick, Massachusetts

Lee, C. (1990). Fuzzy logic in control systems: fuzzy logic controller. *Systems, Man and Cybernetics, IEEE Transactions on*, Vol.20, No. 2, pp. 404 - 418, ISSN 0018-9472

Michie, D.; Spiegelhart, D. & Taylor, C. (1994) *Machine Learning, Neural and Statistical Classification*, Ellis Horwood, ISBN 978-8188689736, New York

Omar, M.; Zaidan, M .; & Tokhi, M. (2010). Modelling of a Flexible Manoeuvring System Using ANFIS Techniques. *Computer Modelling and Simulation (UKSim) 12th International Conference on*, pp. 33-38, ISBN 978-1-4244-6614-6

Oppenheim, A.; Schafer, R. & Padgett, W. (2009). *Discrete-Time Signal Processing*, Prentice Hall, ISBN 978-0131988422

Proakis, J. (2001). *Digital Communications*. McGraw-Hill Science and Engineering, ISBN 978-0072321111. United States of America

Riera, M.; Antonio, J.; Roger, J.; & Palomares, M. (2008). The Use of the Wavelet Approximation Signal as a Tool for the Diagnosis of Rotor Bar Failures. *IEEE Transactions on Industry Applications*, Vol. 44, No. 3, ISSN 0093-9994

Tagaki, T. & Sugeno M. (1985). Fuzzy identification of systems and its applications to modeling and control, *IEEE Transaction Systems., Man, Cybernetics.*, Vol. 15, pp. 116-132, ISSN 018-9472

Taylor, J. (2003). *The Vibration Analysis Handbook*. Vibration Consultants. ISBN 978-0964051720

Zadeh, L. (1965). Fuzzy sets. *Information and Control Elservier Science,* Vol. 8, pp. 338-353, ISSN: 0019-9958

8

The Hybrid Intelligent Method Based on Fuzzy Inference System and Its Application to Fault Diagnosis

Yaguo Lei
State Key Laboratory for Manufacturing Systems Engineering,
Xi'an Jiaotong University,
Xi'an
China

1. Introduction

Large-scale and complex mechanical equipments usually operate under complicated and terrible conditions such as heavy duty, erosion, high temperature, etc. Therefore, it is inevitable for the key components (bearings, gears and shafts, etc.) of these equipments to suffer faults with various modes and different severity degrees. However, faults of large-scale and complex mechanical equipments are characterized by weak response, multi-fault coupling, etc., and it is hard to detect and diagnose incipient and compound faults for these equipments.

One of the principal tools for diagnosing mechanical faults is vibration-based analysis [1–3]. Through the use of processing techniques of vibration signals, it is possible to obtain vital diagnosis information from the signals [4, 5]. Traditional fault diagnosis techniques are performed by diagnosticians observing the vibration signals and the spectra using their expertise and special knowledge. However, for mechanical equipments having complex structures, many monitoring cells and high degrees of automation, there is lots of data to be analyzed in the process of fault diagnosis. Obviously, it is impossible for diagnosticians to manually analyze so many data. Thus, the degree of automation and intelligence of fault diagnosis should be enhanced [6]. Researchers have applied artificial intelligent techniques to fault diagnosis of mechanical equipments, such as expert systems, fuzzy logic, neural networks, genetic algorithms, etc [7–10]. Correspondingly, prominent achievements have been obtained in the field of intelligent fault diagnosis. With the advancement of studies and applications, however, researchers find that individual intelligent techniques have their advantages and shortcomings as well. For incipient and compound faults of mechanical equipments, the diagnosis accuracy using an individual intelligent technique is quite low and the generalization ability is considerably weak. Thus, it is urgent and necessary to develop novel techniques and methods to solve these problems.

The combination of multiple intelligent techniques has been intensively studied to overcome the limitations of individual intelligent techniques and achieve better performance [11–13]. Multiple intelligent classifiers input different feature sets usually exhibit complementary classification behaviors. Thus, if the classification results of multiple intelligent techniques are combined to yield the final classification result, the final performance may be superior to the best performance of individual classifiers [14–16].

Based on the above analysis, a hybrid intelligent fault diagnosis method is presented in this chapter to diagnose incipient and compound faults of complex equipments. The method is developed by combining multiple adaptive neuro-fuzzy inference systems (ANFISs), genetic algorithms (GAs) and vibration signal processing techniques. The method employs signal preprocessing techniques to mine fault information embedded in vibration signals. Statistical features reflecting machinery health conditions from various aspects are synthesized to construct multiple feature sets and to fully reveal fault characteristics. Using an improved distance evaluation technique, the sensitive features are selected from all feature sets. Based on the independency and the complementary in nature of multiple ANFISs with different input feature sets, a hybrid intelligent method is constructed using GAs. The hybrid intelligent method is applied to fault diagnosis of rolling element bearings. The experimental results show the method based on multiple fuzzy inference systems is able to reliably recognize both incipient faults and compound faults.

The rest of this chapter is organized as follows. Section 2 presents the hybrid intelligent method based on fuzzy inference system. Feature extraction and selection, and adaptive neuro-fuzzy inference system are also introduced in this section. Section 3 gives two cases of fault diagnosis for rolling element bearings. The hybrid intelligent method is applied to diagnosing bearing faults and the corresponding results are reported. Section 4 compares the proposed hybrid intelligent method with individual intelligent methods in the light of classification accuracy, and further discusses the causes of the improvement produced by the hybrid method. Finally, conclusions are given in Section 5.

2. The hybrid intelligent method based on fuzzy inference system

The hybrid intelligent method is shown in Fig. 1. It includes the following five steps. First, vibration signals are filtered, and at the same time they are decomposed by empirical mode decomposition (EMD) and intrinsic mode functions (IMFs) are produced. The filtered signals and IMFs are further demodulated to calculate their Hilbert envelope spectra. Second, six feature sets are extracted. They are respectively time- and frequency-domain statistical features of both the raw and preprocessed signals. Third, each feature set is evaluated and a few sensitive features are selected from it by applying the improved distance evaluation technique. Correspondingly, six sensitive feature sets are obtained. Forth, each sensitive feature set is input into one classifier based on ANFIS for training and testing. There are altogether six different classifiers corresponding to the six sensitive feature sets. Fifth, the weighted averaging technique based on GAs is employed to combine the outputs of the six ANFISs and come up with the final diagnosis results.

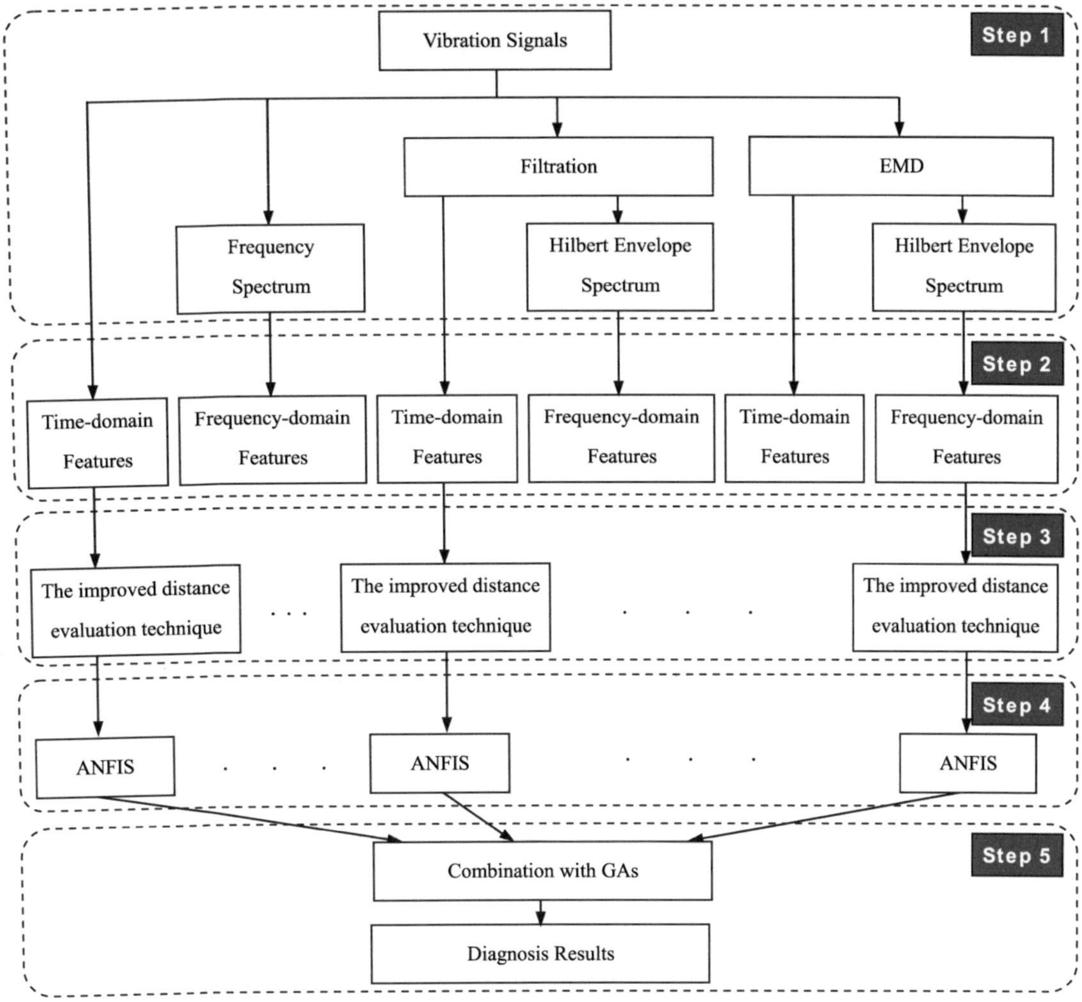

Fig. 1. Flow chart of the hybrid intelligent fault diagnosis method

2.1 Feature extraction

2.1.1 Statistical features of raw signals

Twenty-four feature parameters (p_1–p_{24}), presented in Table 1, are extracted [6] in this study. Eleven parameters (p_1–p_{11}) are time-domain statistical features and thirteen parameters (p_{12}–p_{24}) are frequency-domain ones. Once faults occur in mechanical equipments, the time-domain signal may change. Both its amplitude and distribution will be different from those of signals collected under healthy conditions. In addition, the frequency spectra and its distribution may change as well, which indicates that new frequency components appear and the convergence of frequency spectra varies. Parameter p_1 and p_3–p_5 reflect the vibration amplitude and energy in time domain. Parameter p_2 and p_6–p_{11} represent the time series distribution of the signal in time domain. Parameter p_{12} indicates the vibration energy in frequency domain. Parameter p_{13}–p_{15}, p_{17} and p_{21}–p_{24} describe the convergence of the spectrum power. Parameter p_{16} and p_{18}–p_{20} show the position change of major frequencies.

Time-domain feature parameters		Frequency-domain feature parameters	
$p_1 = \frac{\sum_{n=1}^{N} x(n)}{N}$	$p_7 = \frac{\sum_{n=1}^{N} (x(n) - p_1)^4}{(N-1)p_2^4}$	$p_{12} = \frac{\sum_{k=1}^{K} s(k)}{K}$	$p_{19} = \sqrt{\frac{\sum_{k=1}^{K} f_k^4 s(k)}{\sum_{k=1}^{K} f_k^2 s(k)}}$
$P_2 = \sqrt{\frac{\sum_{n=1}^{N} (x(n) - p_1)^2}{N-1}}$	$p_8 = \frac{p_5}{p_4}$	$p_{13} = \frac{\sum_{k=1}^{K} (s(k) - p_{12})^2}{K-1}$	$p_{20} = \frac{\sum_{k=1}^{K} f_k^2 s(k)}{\sqrt{\sum_{k=1}^{K} s(k) \sum_{k=1}^{K} f_k^4 s(k)}}$
$p_3 = (\frac{\sum_{n=1}^{N} \sqrt{\lvert x(n) \rvert}}{N})^2$	$p_9 = \frac{p_5}{p_3}$	$p_{14} = \frac{\sum_{k=1}^{K} (s(k) - p_{12})^3}{K(\sqrt{p_{13}})^3}$	$p_{21} = \frac{p_{17}}{p_{16}}$
$p_4 = \sqrt{\frac{\sum_{n=1}^{N} (x(n))^2}{N}}$	$p_{10} = \frac{p_4}{\frac{1}{N}\sum_{n=1}^{N} \lvert x(n) \rvert}$	$p_{15} = \frac{\sum_{k=1}^{K} (s(k) - p_{12})^4}{K p_{13}^2}$	$p_{22} = \frac{\sum_{k=1}^{K} (f_k - p_{16})^3 s(k)}{K p_{17}^3}$
$p_5 = \max \lvert x(n) \rvert$	$p_{11} = \frac{p_5}{\frac{1}{N}\sum_{n=1}^{N} \lvert x(n) \rvert}$	$p_{16} = \frac{\sum_{k=1}^{K} f_k s(k)}{\sum_{k=1}^{K} s(k)}$	$p_{23} = \frac{\sum_{k=1}^{K} (f_k - p_{16})^4 s(k)}{K p_{17}^4}$
$p_6 = \frac{\sum_{n=1}^{N} (x(n) - p_1)^3}{(N-1)p_2^3}$		$p_{17} = \sqrt{\frac{\sum_{k=1}^{K} (f_k - P_{16})^2 s(k)}{K}}$	$p_{24} = \frac{\sum_{k=1}^{K} (f_k - p_{16})^{1/2} s(k)}{K\sqrt{p_{17}}}$
		$p_{18} = \sqrt{\frac{\sum_{k=1}^{K} f_k^2 s(k)}{\sum_{k=1}^{K} s(k)}}$	
where $x(n)$ is a signal series for $n = 1,2,\ldots,N$, N is the number of data points.		where $s(k)$ is a spectrum for $k = 1,2,\ldots,K$, K is the number of spectrum lines; f_k is the frequency value of the kth spectrum line.	

Table 1. The feature parameters

Each vibration signal is processed to extract eleven time-domain features and thirteen frequency-domain features from its spectrum. The time- and frequency-domain features extracted here are hereafter referred as **feature set 1** and **feature set 2**, respectively. Therefore, feature sets 1 and 2 contain 11 and 13 feature values, respectively.

2.1.2 Statistical features of filtered signals

The examination of vibration signals indicates the presence of low-frequency interference. The signals are subjected to either high-pass or band-pass filtration to remove the low-frequency interference components. F filters are adopted and the selected filtration frequencies should completely cover the frequency components characterizing faults of mechanical equipments. The eleven time-domain features are extracted from each of the filtered signals. Therefore $11\times F$ time-domain features are obtained and defined as **feature set 3**.

In addition, the interference within the selected frequency band can be minimized by demodulation. Demodulation detection makes the diagnosis process a little more independent of a particular machine since it focuses on the low-amplitude high-frequency broadband signals characterizing machine conditions [17]. By performing demodulation and Fourier transform on the F filtered signals, we can obtain F envelope spectra. The envelope spectra are further processed to extract another set of $13\times F$ frequency-domain features. This feature set is referred as **feature set 4**.

2.1.3 Statistical features of IMFs

To extract more information, each of these raw signals is decomposed using the EMD method. EMD is able to decompose a signal into IMFs with the simple assumption that any signal consists of different simple IMFs [18]. For signal $x(t)$, we can decompose it into I IMFs $c_1, c_2, \ldots, c_I$ and a residue r_I, which is the mean trend of $x(t)$. The IMFs include different frequency bands ranging from high to low. The frequency components contained in each IMF are different and they change with the variation of signal $x(t)$, while r_I represents the central tendency of signal $x(t)$. A more detailed explanation of EMD can be found in Ref. [18].

Generally, first S IMFs containing valid information are selected to further analysis. Similar to the feature extraction method of the raw signals, the eleven features in time domain are extracted from each IMF. Then, we get an additional set of $11\times S$ time-domain features referred as **feature set 5**.

Each IMF is demodulated and its envelope spectrum is produced. We extract the thirteen frequency-domain features from the envelope spectrum and finally derive another set of $13\times S$ frequency-domain features defined as **feature set 6**.

2.2 Feature selection

Although the above features may detect faults occurring in mechanical equipments from different aspects, they have different importance degrees to identify different faults. Some features are sensitive and closely related to the faults, but others are not. Thus, before a feature set is fed into a classifier, sensitive features providing mechanical fault-related information need be selected to enhance the classification accuracy and avoid the curse of dimensionality as well. Here, an improved distance evaluation technique is presented and it is used to select the sensitive features from the whole feature set [6].

Suppose that a feature set of C machinery health conditions is

$$\{q_{m,c,j}, m = 1,2,\ldots,M_c; c = 1,2,\ldots,C; j = 1,2,\ldots,J\}, \tag{1}$$

where $q_{m,c,j}$ is the jth eigenvalue of the mth sample under the cth condition, M_c is the sample number of the cth condition, and J is the feature number of each sample. We collect M_c samples under the cth condition. Therefore, for C conditions, we get $M_c \times C$ samples. For each sample, J features are extracted to represent the sample. Thus, $M_c \times C \times J$ features are obtained, which are defined as a feature set $\{q_{m,c,j}\}$.

Then the feature selection method based on the improved distance evaluation technique can be given as follows.

Step 1. Calculating the average distance of the same condition samples

$$d_{c,j} = \frac{1}{M_c \times (M_c - 1)} \sum_{l,m=1}^{M_c} \left| q_{m,c,j} - q_{l,c,j} \right|, \quad l,m = 1,2,\ldots,M_c, l \neq m; \tag{2}$$

then getting the average distance of C conditions

$$d_j^{(w)} = \frac{1}{C} \sum_{c=1}^{C} d_{c,j}. \tag{3}$$

Step 2. Defining and calculating the variance factor of $d_j^{(w)}$ as

$$v_j^{(w)} = \frac{\max(d_{c,j})}{\min(d_{c,j})}. \tag{4}$$

Step 3. Calculating the average eigenvalue of all samples under the same condition

$$u_{c,j} = \frac{1}{M_c} \sum_{m=1}^{M_c} q_{m,c,j}; \tag{5}$$

then obtaining the average distance between different condition samples

$$d_j^{(b)} = \frac{1}{C \times (C-1)} \sum_{c,e=1}^{C} \left| u_{e,j} - u_{c,j} \right|, \quad c,e = 1,2,\ldots,C, c \neq e. \tag{6}$$

Step 4. Defining and calculating the variance factor of $d_j^{(b)}$ as

$$v_j^{(b)} = \frac{\max(\left| u_{e,j} - u_{c,j} \right|)}{\min(\left| u_{e,j} - u_{c,j} \right|)}, \quad c,e = 1,2,\ldots,C, c \neq e. \tag{7}$$

Step 5. Defining and calculating the compensation factor as

$$\lambda_j = \frac{1}{\dfrac{v_j^{(w)}}{\max(v_j^{(w)})} + \dfrac{v_j^{(b)}}{\max(v_j^{(b)})}}. \tag{8}$$

Step 6. Calculating the ratio of $d_j^{(b)}$ to $d_j^{(w)}$ and assigning the compensation factor

$$\alpha_j = \lambda_j \frac{d_j^{(b)}}{d_j^{(w)}}; \tag{9}$$

then normalizing α_j by its maximum value and getting the distance evaluation criteria

$$\bar{\alpha}_j = \frac{\alpha_j}{\max(\alpha_j)}. \tag{10}$$

Clearly, larger $\bar{\alpha}_j$ ($j = 1,2,\ldots,J$) indicates that the corresponding feature is better to distinguish the C conditions. Thus, the sensitive features can be selected from the feature set $q_{m,c,j}$ according to the distance evaluation criteria $\bar{\alpha}_j$ from large to small.

2.3 Review of ANFIS

The adaptive neuro-fuzzy inference system (ANFIS) is a fuzzy Sugeno model of integration where the final fuzzy inference system is optimized using the training of artificial neural networks. It maps inputs through input membership functions and associated parameters, and then through output membership functions to outputs. The initial membership functions and rules for the fuzzy inference system can be designed by employing human expertise about the target system to be modeled. Then ANFIS can refine the fuzzy if-then rules and membership functions to describe the input/output behavior of a complex system. Jang [19] found that even if human expertise is not available it is possible to intuitively set up reasonable membership functions and then employ the training process of artificial neural networks to generate a set of fuzzy if-then rules that approximate a desired data set.

In order to improve the training efficiency and eliminate the possible trapping due to local minima, a hybrid learning algorithm is employed to tune the parameters of the membership functions. It is a combination of the gradient descent approach and least-squares estimate. During the forward pass, the node outputs advance until the output membership function layer, where the consequent parameters are identified by the least-squares estimate. The backward pass uses the back propagation gradient descent method to update the premise parameters, based on the error signals that propagate backward. More detailed description regarding ANFIS can be referred to Ref. [19].

2.4 The combination of multiple ANFISs

The hybrid intelligent method is implemented by combining multiple ANFISs using GAs. The idea of combining multiple classifiers into a committee is based on the expectation that the committee can outperform its members. The classifiers exhibiting different behaviors will provide complementary information each other. When they are combined, performance improvement will be obtained. Thus, diversity between classifiers is considered as one of the desired characteristics required to achieve this improvement. This diversity between classifiers can be obtained through using different input feature sets.

In this study, the six different feature sets have been extracted and the relevant six sensitive feature sets have been selected. ANFIS is used as the committee member. The weighted averaging technique is utilized to combine the six classifiers based on ANFIS, and the final classification result of the hybrid intelligent method is given as follows:

$$\hat{y}_n = \sum_{k=1}^{6} w_k \hat{y}_{n,k}\,, \quad n = 1,2,\ldots,N'\,, \quad k = 1,2,\ldots,6\,, \tag{11}$$

subject to

$$\begin{cases} \sum_{k=1}^{6} w_k = 1, \\ w_k \geq 0, \end{cases} \tag{12}$$

where $\hat{y}_n$ and $\hat{y}_{n,k}$ represent the classification results of the nth sample using the hybrid intelligent method and the kth individual classifier respectively, w_k is the weight associated with the kth individual classifier, and N' is the number of all samples.

Here, the weights are estimated by using GAs to optimize the fitness function defined by Equation (13). Real-coded genomes are adopted and a population size of ten individuals is used starting with randomly generated genomes. The maximum number of generations 100 is chosen as the termination criterion for the solution process. Non-uniform-mutation function and arithmetic crossover operator [20] are used with the mutation probability of 0.01 and the crossover probability of 0.8, respectively.

$$f = \frac{1}{1+E}, \tag{13}$$

where E is root mean square training errors expressed as

$$E = [\frac{1}{N''} \sum_{n=1}^{N''} (y_n - \hat{y}_n)^2]^{\frac{1}{2}}\,, \quad n = 1,2,\ldots,N''\,, \tag{14}$$

where y_n is the real result of the nth training sample, and N'' is the number of the training samples.

3. Applications to fault diagnosis of rolling element bearings

Rolling element bearings are core components of large-scale and complex mechanical equipments. Faults occurring in the bearings may lead to fatal breakdowns of mechanical equipments. Therefore, it is significant to be able to accurately and automatically detect and diagnosis the existence of faults occurring in the bearings. In this section, two cases of rolling element bearing fault diagnosis are utilized to evaluate the effectiveness of the hybrid intelligent method. One is fault diagnosis of bearing test rig from Case Western Reserve University (CWRU), which involves bearing faults with different defect sizes [21]. The other is fault diagnosis of locomotive rolling bearings having incipient and compound faults. The vibration signals were measured under various operating loads and different bearing conditions including different fault modes and severity degrees in both cases.

3.1 Case 1: Fault diagnosis of bearings of CWRU test rig

Faults were introduced into the tested bearings using the electron discharge machining method. The defect sizes (diameter, depth) of the three faults (outer race fault, inner race fault and ball fault) are the same: 0.007, 0.014 or 0.021 inches. Each bearing was tested under four different loads (0, 1, 2 and 3 hp). The bearing data set was obtained from the experimental system under four different health conditions: (1) normal condition; (2) with outer race fault; (3) with inner race fault; (4) with ball fault. Thus, the vibration data was collected from rolling element bearings under different operating loads and health conditions. More information regarding the experimental test rig and the data can be found in Ref. [21].

We conduct three investigations over three different data subsets (A–C) of the rolling element bearings. The detailed descriptions of the three data subsets are shown in Table 2. Data set A consists of 240 data samples of four health conditions (normal condition, outer race fault, inner race fault and ball fault) with the defect size of 0.007 inches under four various loads (0, 1, 2 and 3 hp). Each of the four health conditions includes 60 data samples. Data set A is split into two sets: 120 samples for training and 120 for testing. It is a four-class classification task corresponding to the four different health conditions.

Data set B also contains 240 data samples. 120 samples with the detect size of 0.021 inches are used as the training set. The remaining 120 samples with the detect size of 0.007 inches are identical with the 120 training samples of data set A and form the testing samples of data set B. The purpose of using this data set is to test the classification performance of the proposed method to incipient faults when it is trained by the serious fault samples.

Data set C comprises 600 data samples covering four health conditions and four different loads. Each fault condition includes three different defect sizes of 0.007, 0.014 and 0.021 inches, respectively. The 600 data samples are divided into 300 training and 300 testing instances. For data set C, in order to identify the severity degrees of faults, we solve the ten-class classification problem.

As mentioned in Section 2, the statistical features are extracted from the raw signal, filtered signal and IMF of each data sample. Three band-pass (BP1–BP3) and one high-pass (HP) filters are adopted for this bearing data. The band-pass frequencies (in kHz) of the BP1–BP3 filters are chosen as: BP1 (2.2–3.8), BP2 (3.0–3.8), and BP3 (3.0–4.5), respectively. The cut-off frequency of the HP filter is chosen as 2.2 kHz. These frequencies are selected to cover the frequency components representing bearing faults.

Data set	The number of training samples	The number of testing samples	Defect size of training/testing samples (inches)	Health conditions	Label of classification
A	30	30	0/0	Normal	1
	30	30	0.007/0.007	Outer race	2
	30	30	0.007/0.007	Inner race	3
	30	30	0.007/0.007	Ball	4
B	30	30	0/0	Normal	1
	30	30	0.021/0.007	Outer race	2
	30	30	0.021/0.007	Inner race	3
	30	30	0.021/0.007	Ball	4
C	30	30	0/0	Normal	1
	30	30	0.007/0.007	Outer race	2
	30	30	0.007/0.007	Inner race	3
	30	30	0.007/0.007	Ball	4
	30	30	0.014/0.014	Outer race	5
	30	30	0.014/0.014	Inner race	6
	30	30	0.014/0.014	Ball	7
	30	30	0.021/0.021	Outer race	8
	30	30	0.021/0.021	Inner race	9
	30	30	0.021/0.021	Ball	10

Table 2. Description of three data subsets

In order to demonstrate the enhanced performance of the hybrid intelligent method based on fuzzy inference system, the method is compared with individual classifiers based on ANFIS. Considering the computational burden, in each investigation, only four sensitive features are selected from each of the six feature sets using the improved distance evaluation technique and then input into the corresponding classifier. For data set A, distance evaluation criteria $\overline{\alpha}_j$ of the six feature sets are shown in Fig. 2. The diagnosis results of the four data sets are shown in Table 3 and Fig. 3, respectively.

Observing the results in Table 3 and Fig. 3, we can get the following interesting things.

1. For data set A, since this classification problem is relatively simple, both the six individual classifiers and the hybrid intelligent method achieve the high training and testing accuracy (100%). However, comparing the classification error of the hybrid intelligent method with those of the individual classifiers plotted in Fig. 4, we can see that the classification error of the hybrid intelligent method is the least.

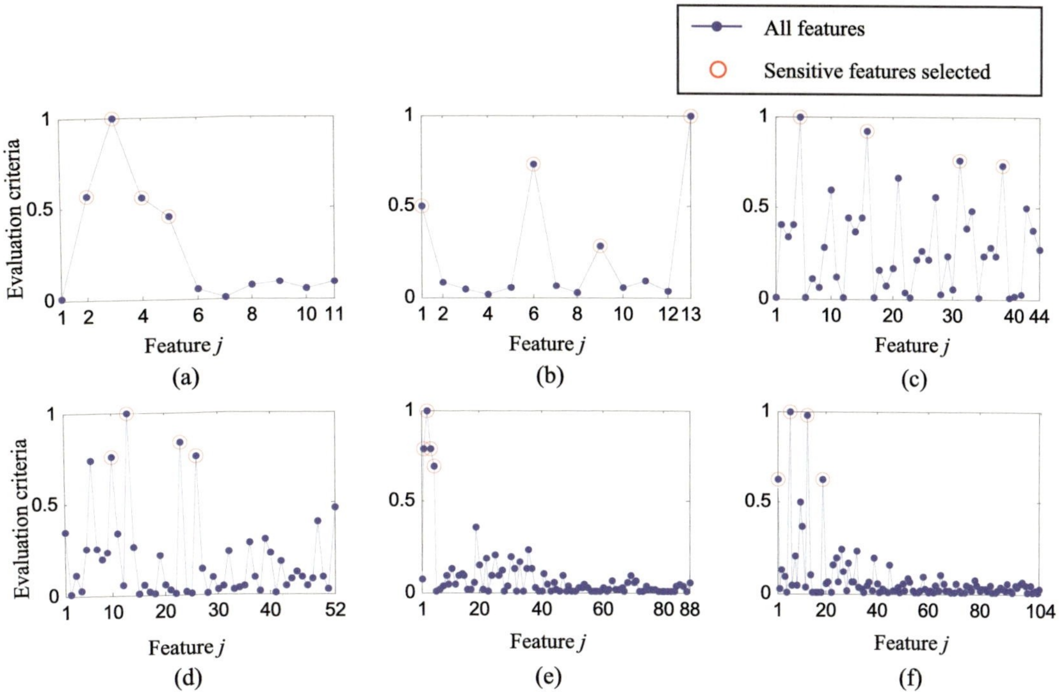

Fig. 2. Distance evaluation criteria of six feature sets of data set A: (a) feature set 1, (b) feature set 2, (c) feature set 3, (d) feature set 4, (e) feature set 5, and (f) feature set 6.

Data set	Classifier 1		Classifier 2		Classifier 3		Classifier 4	
	Training	Testing	Training	Testing	Training	Testing	Training	Testing
A	100	100	100	100	100	100	100	100
B	100	62.5	100	79.17	100	74.17	100	80
C	65.67	61	90	87.67	72.67	68	80.33	77

Data set	Classifier 5		Classifier 6		Average of six classifiers		Hybrid method	
	Training	Testing	Training	Testing	Training	Testing	Training	Testing
A	100	100	100	100	100	100	100	100
B	100	55.83	100	81.67	100	72.22	100	90.83
C	67.67	67	87.33	81	77.28	73.61	93.67	91.33

Table 3. Diagnosis results of the CWRU bearings using the hybrid intelligent classifier and individual classifiers

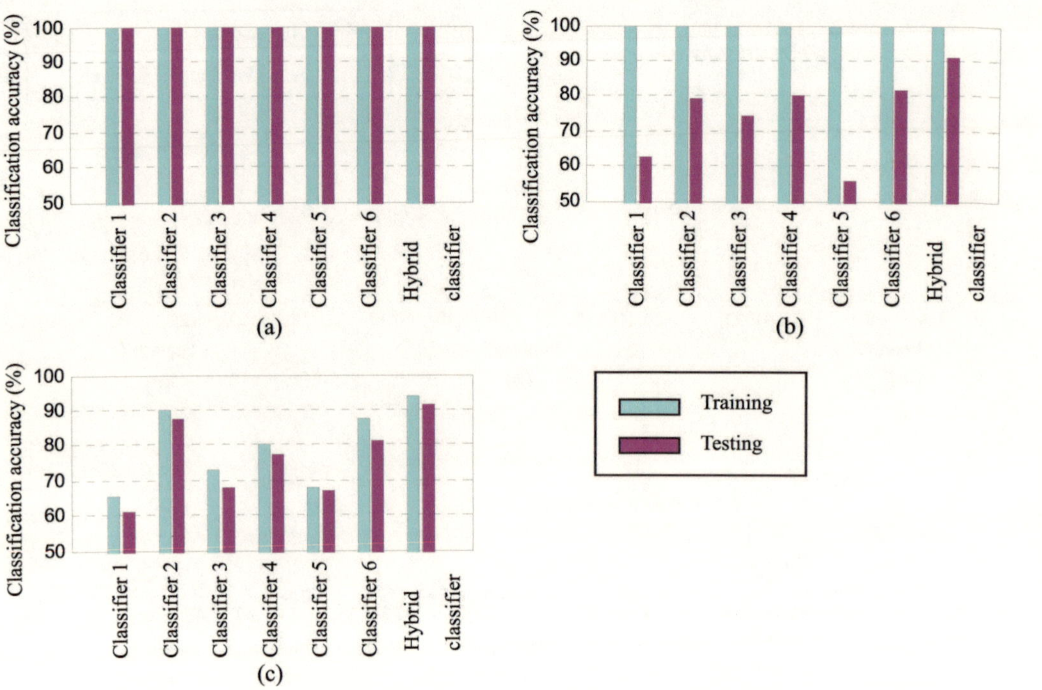

Fig. 3. Diagnosis results of the CWRU bearings: (a) data set A, (b) data set B, and (c) data set C.

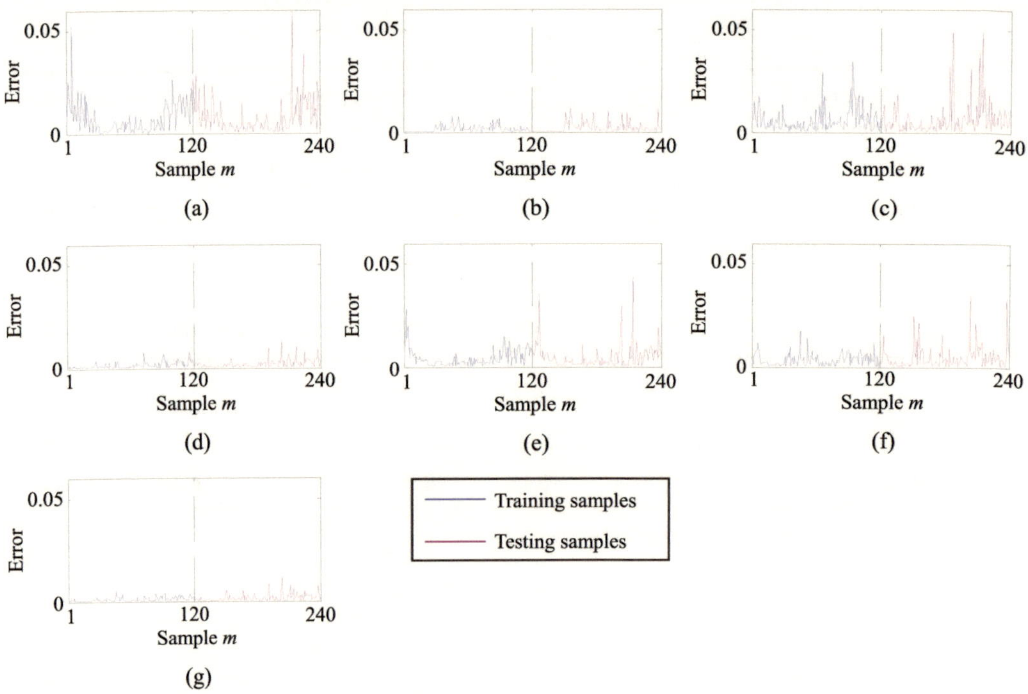

Fig. 4. Classification errors: (a) classifier 1, (b) classifier 2, (c) classifier 3, (d) classifier 4, (e) classifier 5, (f) classifier 6, and (g) the hybrid intelligent classifier.

2. For data set B, we can see that the training accuracies of all the classifiers are 100%. However, the hybrid intelligent method produces better testing performance (90.83%) than any of the individual classifiers ranging from 55.83% to 81.67% (average 72.22%). This result validates that the hybrid intelligent classifier trained by the serious fault data can diagnose the incipient faults with a higher accuracy in comparison with the individual classifiers.

3. For data set C, the training success rates of all the classifiers decrease and range from 65.67% to 93.67% because it is a ten-class classification problem and therefore relatively difficult. But the highest training accuracy (93.67%) is still generated by the hybrid intelligent method. For testing, the classification success of the six individual classifiers is in the range of 61–87.67% (average 73.61%), whereas the classification success of the hybrid method is much higher (91.33%). These imply that the hybrid method can identify both the different fault modes and the different fault severities better.

3.2 Case 2: Fault diagnosis of locomotive rolling bearings

The test bench of locomotive rolling bearings is shown in Fig. 5. The test bench consists of a hydraulic motor, two supporting pillow blocks (mounting with normal bearing), a tested bearing (52732QT) which is loaded on the outer race by a hydraulic cylinder, a hydraulic radial load application system, and a tachometer for shaft speed measurement. The bearing is installed in a hydraulic motor driven mechanical system. 608A11-type ICP accelerometers with a bandwidth up to 5 kHz are mounted on the load module adjacent to the outer race of the tested bearing for measuring its vibrations. The Advanced Data Acquisition and Analysis System by Sony EX is used to capture the vibration data. Parameters in the experiment are listed in Table 4.

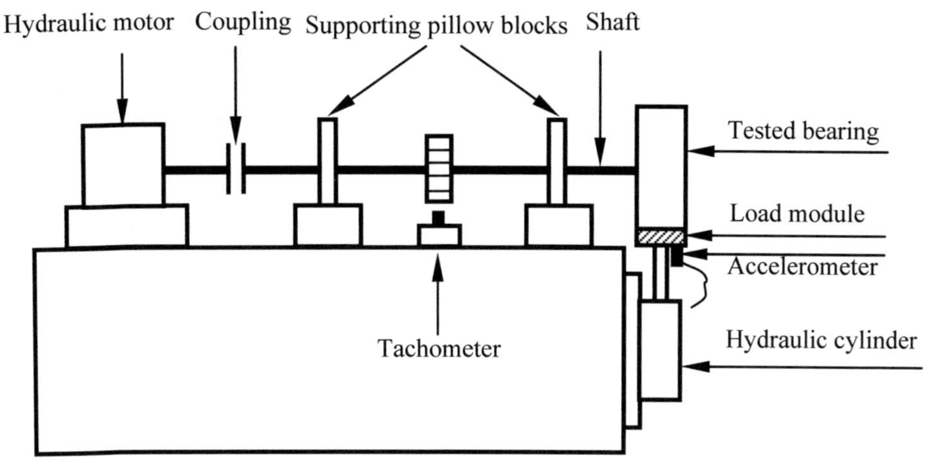

Fig. 5. Test bench of the locomotive rolling bearings.

A bearing data set containing nine subsets is obtained from the experimental system under the nine different health conditions. The nine conditions of bearings, shown in Table 5, involve not only incipient faults but also compound faults. The incipient faults are actually slight rub of outer races, inner races or rollers. These faulty bearings are shown in Fig. 6. Each data subset corresponds to one of the nine conditions and it consists of 50 samples.

Each sample is a vibration signal containing 8192 sampling points. Thus, the bearing data set includes altogether 450 data samples, which is divided into 225 training and 225 testing samples. This data is used to demonstrate the effectiveness of the proposed hybrid intelligent method in simultaneously identifying incipient faults and compound ones.

Parameter	Value
Bearing specs	52732QT
Load	9800N
Inner race diameter	160mm
Outer race diameter	290mm
Roller diameter	34mm
Roller number	17
Contact angle	0°
Sampling frequency	12.8 kHz

Table 4. Parameters in the experiment

Condition	Rotating speed	Label
Normal condition	About 490 rpm	1
Slight rub fault in the outer race	About 490 rpm	2
Serious flaking fault in the outer race	About 480 rpm	3
Slight rub fault in the inner race	About 500 rpm	4
Roller rub fault	About 530 rpm	5
Compound faults in the outer and inner races	About 520 rpm	6
Compound faults in the outer race and rollers	About 520 rpm	7
Compound faults in the inner race and rollers	About 640 rpm	8
Compound faults in the outer and inner races and rollers	About 550 rpm	9

Table 5. Health conditions of the locomotive rolling bearings

Two band-pass (BP1 and BP2) and one high-pass (HP) filters are used to filter the vibration signals of locomotive rolling bearings. The band-pass frequencies (in kHz) of the BP1 and BP2 filters are chosen as 1.5–2.7 and 1.5–4, respectively. The cut-off frequency of the HP filter is chosen as 3kHz. Similar to case 1, four sensitive features are selected from each of the six feature sets using the improved distance evaluation technique and then input into the corresponding classifier. The classification results of the hybrid intelligent method and six individual classifiers are shown in Fig. 7.

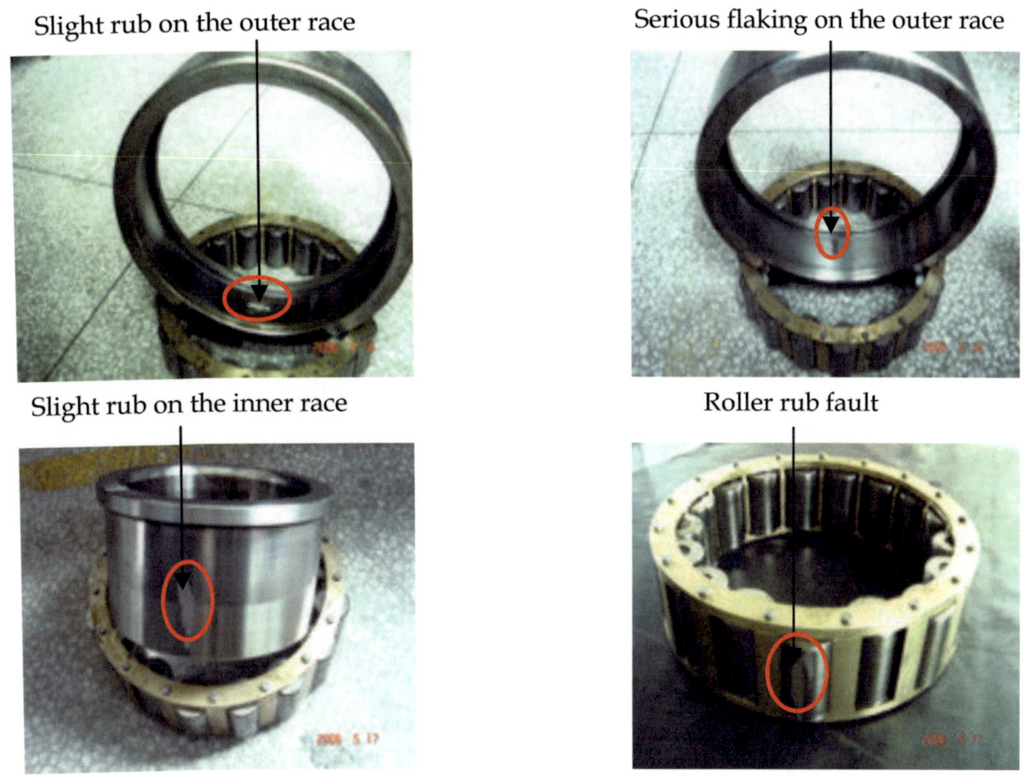

Fig. 6. Faults in the locomotive rolling bearings.

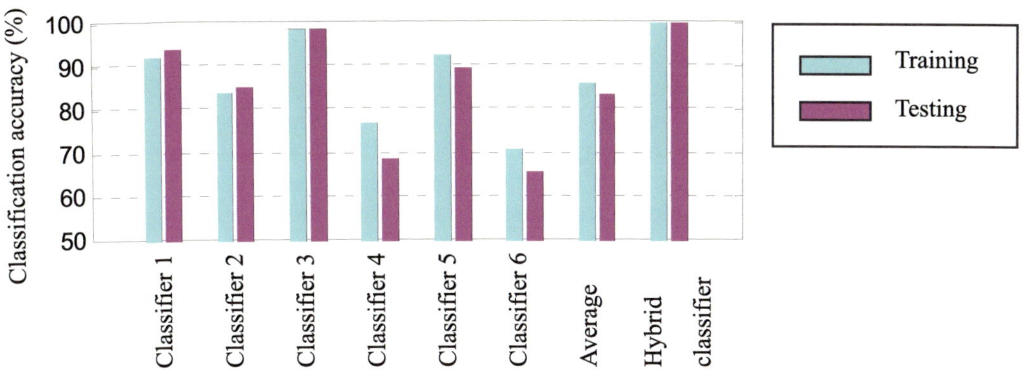

Fig. 7. Diagnosis results of the locomotive rolling bearings.

It is seen that the training accuracies of six individual classifiers are from 70.67% to 98.60% (average 85.69%) and the testing accuracies from 65.33% to 98.60% (average 83.39%). For the proposed hybrid intelligent method, however, both the training and testing accuracies are 100%. This result shows that the hybrid method achieves obvious improvements in recognition accuracy and provides a better generalization capability compared to the individual classifiers. Therefore, it is able to effectively identify not only incipient faults but also compound faults of locomotive rolling bearings.

4. Discussions

1. Comparing the diagnosis results of the proposed hybrid intelligent method with those of individual classifiers, we find that the testing accuracies of the hybrid intelligent method (100% for data set A, 90.83% for data set B and 91.33% for data set C in case 1; 100% in case 2) increase by 0, 18.61%, 17.72% and 16.61% compared with the average accuracies of the six individual classifiers. In addition, although the highest classification accuracy (100%) is obtained by all the classifiers for data set A in case 1, the classification error of the hybrid intelligent method is least among all classifiers. Thus, the proposed hybrid intelligent method is superior to the individual classifiers in the light of the classification accuracies.

2. All the above comparisons prove that the proposed hybrid intelligent method obtains significant improvements in fault diagnosis accuracy compared to the individual classifiers. It reliably recognizes both incipient faults and compound faults of rolling element bearings. The success obtained by the hybrid intelligent method may be attributed to the following three points. 1) Extracting both time- and frequency-domain features better reflects the machinery health conditions. 2) Selecting the sensitive features reflecting the fault characteristics avoids interference of other fault-unrelated features. 3) Combining multiple intelligent classifiers based on fuzzy inference system raises diagnosis accuracy.

3. The problems studied in this chapter cover single fault diagnosis, incipient fault diagnosis and compound fault diagnosis, and therefore they are typical cases of machinery fault diagnosis. The satisfactory experiment results demonstrate the effectiveness and generalization ability of the hybrid intelligent method. Although the proposed method is applied to fault diagnosis of the rolling element bearings successfully, it may also be employed to fault diagnosis of other rotating machinery.

5. Conclusions

In this chapter, a hybrid intelligent method based on fuzzy inference system is proposed for intelligent fault diagnosis of rotating machinery. In the method, several preprocessing methods, like empirical mode decomposition (EMD), filtration and demodulation, are utilized to mine fault information from vibration signals. In order to remove the redundant and irrelevant information, an improved distance evaluation technique is presented and used to select the sensitive features. Multiple fuzzy inference systems are combined using genetic algorithms (GAs) to enhance fault identification accuracy. The experimental results show that the hybrid intelligent method enables the identification of incipient faults and at the same time recognition of compound faults.

6. Acknowledgements

This research is supported by National Natural Science Foundation of China (51005172), the Fundamental Research Funds for the Central Universities and the Preferred Support Funds of the Scientific Research Project of the Ministry of Human Resources and Social Security of China for Returned Scholars.

7. References

[1] V. Indira, R. Vasanthakumari, V. Sugumaran, Minimum sample size determination of vibration signals in machine learning approach to fault diagnosis using power analysis, Expert Systems with Applications 37 (2010) 8650–8658.

[2] E. P. de Moura, C. R. Souto, A. A. Silva, et al., Evaluation of principal component analysis and neural network performance for bearing fault diagnosis from vibration signal processed by RS and DF analyses, Mechanical Systems and Signal Processing 25 (2011) 1765–1772.

[3] N. R. Sakthivel, V. Sugumaran, S. Babudevasenapati, Vibration based fault diagnosis of monoblock centrifugal pump using decision tree, Expert Systems with Applications 37 (2010) 4040–4049.

[4] Y. G. Lei, Z. J. He, Y. Y. Zi, et al., New clustering algorithm-based fault diagnosis using compensation distance evaluation technique, Mechanical Systems and Signal Processing 22 (2008) 419–435.

[5] S. J. Loutridis, Self-similarity in vibration time series: application to gear fault diagnostics, Transactions of the ASME, Journal of vibration and acoustics 130 (2008) 1–9.

[6] Y. G. Lei, Z. J. He, Y. Y. Zi, et al., Fault diagnosis of rotating machinery based on multiple ANFIS combination with GAs, Mechanical Systems and Signal Processing 21 (2007) 2280-2294.

[7] Y. G. Lei, Z. J. He, Y. Y. Zi, A new approach to intelligent fault diagnosis of rotating machinery, Expert Systems with Applications 35 (2008) 1593–1600.

[8] K. Mollazade, H. Ahmadi, M. Omid, et al., An intelligent model based on data mining and fuzzy logic for fault diagnosis of external gear hydraulic pumps, Insight 51 (2009) 594–600.

[9] Y. G. Lei, Z. J. He, Y. Y. Zi, Application of an intelligent classification method to mechanical fault diagnosis, Expert Systems with Applications 36 (2009) 9941-9948.

[10] B. Samanta, C. Nataraj, Use of particle swarm optimization for machinery fault detection, Engineering Applications of Artificial Intelligence, 22 (2009) 308–316.

[11] S. Rasheed, D. Stashuk, M. Kamel, Fusion of multiple classifiers for motor unit potential sorting, Biomedical Signal Processing and Control 3 (2008) 229–243.

[12] Y. Bi, J. Guan, D. Bell, The combination of multiple classifiers using an evidential reasoning approach, Artificial Intelligence 172 (2008) 1731–1751.

[13] F. Huenupán, N. B. Yoma, C. Molina, Confidence based multiple classifier fusion in speaker verification, Pattern Recognition Letters 29 (2008) 957–966.

[14] Y. G. Lei, Z. J. He, Y. Y. Zi, A combination of WKNN to fault diagnosis of rolling element bearings, Transactions of the ASME, Journal of Vibration and Acoustics 131 (2009) 1-6.

[15] A. K. J. Mohammad, R. Langari, A hybrid intelligent system for fault detection and sensor fusion, Applied Soft Computing, 9 (2009) 415–422.

[16] Y. G. Lei, M. J. Zuo, Z. J. He, et al., A multidimensional hybrid intelligent method for gear fault diagnosis, Expert Systems with Applications 37 (2010) 1419-1430.

[17] U. Benko, J. Petrovčič, D. Juričić, et al., An approach to fault diagnosis of vacuum cleaner motors based on sound analysis, Mechanical Systems and Signal Processing 19 (2005) 427–445.

[18] N. E. Huang, Z. Shen, S. R. Long, The Empirical mode decomposition and the Hilbert spectrum for nonlinear and non-stationary time series analysis, Proceedings of the Royal Society of London 454 (1998) 903–995.
[19] J. S. R. Jang, ANFIS: adaptive-network-based fuzzy inference system, IEEE Transactions on Systems, Man, Cybernetics 23 (1993) 665–685.
[20] Z. Michalewicz, Genetic Algorithms + Data Structures = Evolution Programs, 3rd Edition, Springer, NY, USA, 1999.
[21] X. S. Lou, K. A. Loparo, Bearing fault diagnosis based on wavelet transform and fuzzy inference, Mechanical Systems and Signal Processing 18 (2004) 1077–1095.

9

Some Studies on Noise and Its Effects on Industrial/Cognitive Task Performance and Modeling

Ahmed Hameed Kaleel[1] and Zulquernain Mallick[2]
[1]Baghdad University
[2]Jamia Millia Islamia,
[1]Iraq
[2]India

1. Introduction

Present industrial environment is quite different than past. Globalization and market driven forces has made the working environment quite competitive. It is quite obvious that these factors when combined with environmental factors, lead to poor operators/workers performance. Therefore, ergonomists has new challenges in terms of predicting workers efficiency as well as workers health protection and well being.

High noise level exposure leads to psychological as well physiological problems. It results in deteriorated cognitive task efficiency, although the exact nature of work performance is still unknown. To predict cognitive task efficiency deterioration, neuro-fuzzy tools were used. It has been established that a neuro-fuzzy computing system helps in identification and analysis of fuzzy models. The last decade has seen substantial growth in development of various neuro-fuzzy systems. Among them, adaptive neuro-fuzzy inference system provides a systematic and directed approach for model building and gives the best possible design parameters in minimum possible time.

Input variables were noise level, cognitive task type, and age of workers. Out-put variable was predicted in terms of reduction in cognitive task efficiency. The cause-effect relationships of these parameters are complex, uncertain, and non-linear in nature therefore, it is quite difficult to properly examine it by conventional methods. Hence, an attempt is made in present study to develop a neuro-fuzzy model to predict the effects of noise pollution on human work efficiency as a function of noise level, cognitive task type, and age of the workers practicing cognitive type of task at (I.T.O power plant station, centrifugal pump industry WPIL India Limited, and Shriram Piston & Rings limited) industries. Categorization of noise and its levels (high, medium, and low) was based on a survey conducted for this purpose.

A total of 155 questionnaires were distributed among the workers of industries under reference. Likert scale has been used to evaluate the answers densities which ranges between "strongly disagree" to "strongly agree". Cognitive workers performance was evaluated based on self administrated questionnaire survey, which consisted of 55-questions, covering all possible reported effects of cognitive task on cognitive task performance.

The model was implemented on neural Fuzzy Logic Toolbox of MATLAB using Sugeno technique. The modeling technique was based on the concept of neural Fuzzy Logic, which offers a convenient means of representing the relationship between the inputs and outputs of a system in the form of IF-THEN rules. Model has been built under The Recommended Exposure Limit (REL) for workers engaged in occupation such as engineering controls, administrative controls, and/or work practices is 90 dB(A) for 8 hr duration OSHA. In order to validate the model 20% data sets were used for testing purpose.

2. Literature review

Since the last one-decade or so extensive research work has been in progress in the field of affects of noise on the health, comfort and performance of people under the banner of the discipline environmental Ergonomics. The matter content available on the topic is found to be highly scattered in literature. An attempt has been made in this chapter to present the matter content in a systematic manner under different chapters as given below:

2.1 Studies on Industrial/cognitive task performance

Rasmussen (2000) [1] Society is becoming increasingly dynamic and integrated owing to the extensive use of information technology. This has several implications that pose new challenges to the human factors profession. In an integrated society, changes and disturbances propagate rapidly and widely and the increasing scale of operations requires also that rare events and circumstances are considered during systems design. In this situation, human factors contributions should be increasingly proactive, not only responding to observed problems, but also, they should be based on models of adaptive human behavior in complex, dynamic systems.

Murata, et al. (2000) [2] To clarify whether job stressors affecting injury due to labor accidents differ between Japanese male and female blue-collar workers, the Job Content Questionnaire (JCQ), assessing dimensions of job stressors based on the demand-control-support model, was applied to 139 blue collar workers in a manufacturing factory. Of them, 24 male and 15 female workers suffered from injuries at work. In the female workers with the experience of work injury, the job demand score and job strain index (i.e., the ratio of job demand to job control) of the JCQ were significantly higher and the score of coworker support was significantly lower, than those in the female workers without the experience. High job demand (or, high job strain and low coworker support) was significantly related to work injury in all the female workers. Between the male workers with and without work injury, however, there was no significant difference in any job stressors. This pilot study suggests that high job strain (specifically, high job demand), as well as low coworker support, are important factors affecting work injury in Japanese female blue-collar workers. Further research with a large number of male blue-collar workers will be required to seek other factors that may be associated with work injury.

Genaidy (2005) [3] Advances in human-based systems have progressed at a slower pace than those for technological systems. This is largely attributed to the complex web of variables that jointly influence work outcomes, making it more difficult to develop a quantitative methodology to solve this problem. Thus, the objective of this study was to develop and validate work compatibility as a diagnostic tool to evaluate musculoskeletal and stress outcomes. Work compatibility is defined as a latent variable integrating the positive and negative impact characteristics of work variables in the human-at-work system in the form of a prescribed relationship. The theoretical basis of work compatibility is described at length in terms of concepts and models. In addition, approximate reasoning solutions for the compatibility variables are presented in terms of three models, namely, linear, ratio, and expert. A test case of 55 service workers in a hospital setting has been used to validate work compatibility with respect to severe musculoskeletal and high stress outcomes. The results have demonstrated that the expert compatibility model provided the stronger and more significant associations with work outcomes in comparison to the linear and ratio compatibility models. In conclusion, although the work compatibility validation is limited by both the cross-sectional design and sample size, the promising findings of this exploratory investigation suggest that further studies are warranted to investigate work compatibility as a diagnostic tool to evaluate musculoskeletal and stress outcomes in the workplace.

Genaidy, et al. (2007) [4] Although researchers traditionally examined the 'risk' characteristics of work settings in health studies, few work models, such as the 'demand-control' and 'motivation-hygiene theory', advocated the study of the positive and the negative aspects of work for the ultimate improvement of work performance. The objectives of the current study were: (a) to examine the positive and negative characteristics of work in the machining department in a small manufacturing plant in the Midwest USA, and, (b) to report the prevalence of musculoskeletal and stress outcomes. A focus group consisting of worker experts from the different job categories in the machining department confirmed the management's concerns. Accordingly, 56 male and female workers, employed in three shifts, were surveyed on the demand/energizer profiles of work characteristics and self-reported musculoskeletal/stress symptoms. On average, one-fourth to one-third of the workers reported 'high' demand, and over 50% of the workers documented 'low' energizers for certain work domains/sub-domains, such as 'physical task content'/'organizational' work domains and 'upper body postural loading'/'time organization' work sub-domains. The prevalence of workers who reported 'high' musculoskeletal/stress disorder cases, was in the range of 25-35% and was consistent with the results of 'high' demands and 'low' energizers. The results of this case study confirm the importance of adopting a comprehensive view for work improvement and sustainable growth opportunities. It is paramount to consider the negative and positive aspects of work characteristics to ensure optimum organizational performance. The Work Compatibility Improvement Framework, proposed in the reported research, is an important endeavor toward the ultimate improvement and sustainable growth of human and organizational performance.

John, et al. (2009) [5]The main objective of this study was to test the research question that human performance in manufacturing environments depends on the cognitive demands of the operator and the perceived quality of work life attributes. The second research question was that this relationship is related to the operator's specific task and time exposure. Two manufacturing companies, with a combined population of seventy-four multi-skilled, cross-trained workers who fabricated and assembled mechanical and electrical equipment, participated in an eight month, four-wave pseudo panel study. Structural equation modeling and invariance analysis techniques were conducted on the data collected during cognitive task analysis and the administration of questionnaires. Human performance was indicated to be a causal result of the combined, and uncorrelated, effect of cognitive demands and quality of work attributes experienced by workers. This causal relationship was found to be dependent on the context of, but not necessarily the time exposed to, the particular task the operator was involved with.

2.2 Studies on age related noise effects

As age effects, sensitivity to the high frequencies is lost first and the loss is irreversible. In audiometry, such loss is described as a permanent threshold shift. Audiometric testing consists of determination of the minimum intensity (the threshold) at which a person can detect sound at a particular frequency. As sensitivity to particular frequencies is lost as a result of age or damage, the intensity at which a stimulus can be detected increases. It is in this sense that hearing loss can be described as a threshold shift. Studies have shown age decrements in performance of sustained attention tasks.

Parasuranam, et al. (1990) [6] Thirty-six young (19-27 years), middle-aged (40-55 years), and old (70-80 years) adults performed a 30-min vigilance task at low (15 per min) and high (40 per min) event rates for 20 sessions. Skill-acquisition curves modeled on power, hyperbolic, and exponential functions were predicted. With extensive practice, hit rates increased and false-alarm rates decreased to virtually asymptotic levels. Skill development was best described by the hyperbolic function. Practice reduced but did not eliminate the vigilance decrement in all subjects. The event-rate effect-the decrease in hit rate at high event rates-was reduced with practice and eliminated in young subjects. Hit rates decreased and false-alarm rates increased with age, but there was little attenuation of age differences with practice. Implications for theories of vigilance, skill development, and cognitive aging are discussed.

Hale (1990) [7] Children respond more slowly than young adults on a variety of information-processing tasks. The global trend hypothesis posits that processing speed changes as a function of age, and that all component processes change at the same rate. A unique prediction of this hypothesis is that the overall response latencies of children of a particular age should be predictable from the latencies of young adults performing the same tasks-without regard to the specific componential makeup of the task. The current effort tested this prediction by examining the performance of 4 age groups (10-, 12-, 15-, and 19-year-olds) on 4 different tasks (choice reaction time, letter matching, mental rotation, and abstract matching). An analysis that simultaneously examined performance on all 4 tasks provided strong support for the global trend hypothesis. By plotting each child group's performance on all 4 tasks as a function of the young adult group's performance in the corresponding task conditions, precise linear functions were revealed: 10-year-olds were approximately 1.8 times slower than young adults on all tasks, and 12-year-olds were approximately 1.5 times slower, whereas 15-year-olds appeared to process information as fast as young adults.

Madden (1992) [8] Examined in three experiments a revised version of the Eriksen and Yeh (C. W. Eriksen and Y.-Y. Yeh, 1985) model of attentional allocation during visual search. Results confirmed the assumption of the model that performance represents a weighted combination of focused-and distributed-attention trials, although they were relied on focused attention more than was predicted. Consistent with the model, predictions on the basis of the assumption of a terminating search fit the data better than predictions on the basis of an exhaustive search. The effects of varying cue validity favored an interpretation of focused attention in terms of a processing gradient rather than a zoom lens. Although the allocation of attention across trials was similar for young and older adults, there was an age-related increase in the time required to allocate attention within individual trials.

Carayon, et al. (2000) [9] There have been several recent reports on the potential risk to hearing from various types of social noise exposure. However, there are few population-based data to substantiate a case for concern. During the last 10-20 years use of personal cassette players (PCPs) has become very much more prevalent, and sound levels in public nightclubs and discotheques are reported to have increased. This study investigated the prevalence and types of significant social noise exposure in a representative population sample of 356 18-25 year olds in Nottingham. Subjects were interviewed in detail about all types of lifetime noise exposure. Noise measurements were also made for both nightclubs and PCPs. In the present sample, 18.8% of young adults had been exposed to significant noise from social activities, compared with 3.5% from occupational noise and 2.9% from gunfire noise. This indicates that social noise exposure has tripled since the early 1980s in the UK. Most of the present day exposure, measured in terms of sound energy, comes from nightclubs rather than PCPs. Moreover, 66% of subjects attending nightclubs or rock concerts reported temporary effects on their hearing or tinnitus. As will be reported in a later publication, any persistent effect of significant noise exposure on 18-25 year olds is difficult to show, however these data suggest that further work is indicated to study the possibility of sub-clinical damage, and also to consider the implications for employees of nightclubs.

Boman, et al. (2005) [10] The objectives in this paper were to analyze noise effects on episodic and semantic memory performance in different age groups, and to see whether age interacted with noise in their effects on memory. Data were taken from three separate previous experiments that were performed with the same design, procedure and dependent measures with participants from four age groups (13-14, 18-20, 35-45 and 55-65 years). Participants were randomly assigned to one of three conditions: (a) meaningful irrelevant speech, (b) road traffic noise, and (c) quiet. The results showed effects of both noise sources on a majority of the dependent measures, both when taken alone and aggregated according to the nature of the material to be memorized. However, the noise effects for episodic memory tasks were stronger than for semantic memory tasks. Further, in the reading comprehension task, cued recall and recognition were more impaired by meaningful irrelevant speech than by road traffic noise. Contrary to predictions, there was no interaction between noise and age group, indicating that the obtained noise effects were not related to the capacity to perform the task. The results from the three experiments taken together throw more light on the relative effects of road traffic noise and meaningful irrelevant speech on memory performance in different age groups.

2.3 Studies on noise effects related to task performance

Suter (1991) [11] The effects of noise are seldom catastrophic, and are often only transitory, but adverse effects can be cumulative with prolonged or repeated exposure. Although it often causes discomfort and sometimes pain, noise does not cause ears to bleed and noise-induced hearing loss usually takes years to develop. Noise-induced hearing loss can indeed impair the quality of life, through a reduction in the ability to hear important sounds and to communicate with family and friends. Some of the other effects of noise, such as sleep disruption, the masking of speech and television, and the inability to enjoy one's property or leisure time also impair the quality of life. In addition, noise can interfere with the teaching and learning process, disrupt the performance of certain tasks, and increase the incidence of antisocial behavior.

Evans, et al. (1993) [12] Large numbers of children both in the United States and throughout the economically developing world are chronically exposed to high levels of ambient noise. Although a great deal is known about chronic noise exposures and hearing damage, much less is known about the non-auditory effects of chronic ambient noise exposure on children, to estimate the risk of ambient noise exposure to healthy human development, more information. About and attention to non-auditory effects such as psycho-physiological functioning, motivation, and cognitive processes is needed. This article critically reviews existing research on the non-auditory effects of noise on children; develops several preliminary models of how noise may adversely affect children; and advocates an ecological perspective for a future research agenda.

Evans, et al. (1997) [13] In the short term, noise induced arousal, may produce better performance of simple tasks, but cognitive performance deteriorates substantially for more complex tasks (i.e. tasks that require sustained attention to details or to multiple cues; or tasks that demand a large capacity of working memory, such as complex analytical processes). Some of the effects are related to loss in auditory Comprehension and language acquisition, but others are not, among the cognitive effects, reading, attention, problem solving and memory are most strongly affected by noise. The observed effects on motivation, as measured by persistence with a difficult cognitive task, may either be independent or secondary to the aforementioned cognitive impairments. For aircraft noise, the most important effects are interference with rest, recreation and watching television. This is in contrast to road traffic noise, where sleep disturbance is the predominant effect. The primary sleep disturbance effects are: difficulty in falling asleep (increased sleep latency time); awakenings; and alterations of sleep stages or depth, especially a reduction in the proportion of REM-sleep (REM = rapid eye movement). Other primary physiological effects can also be induced by noise during sleep, including Noise sources 7 increased blood pressure; increased heart rate; increased finger pulse amplitude; vasoconstriction; changes in respiration; cardiac arrhythmia; and an increase in body movements.

Smith (1998) [14] This paper examines the operation of urban bus transport systems based upon exclusive bus roadways (bus ways) in three cities in Brazil. The historic, economic, political, regulatory and operating context for these services is discussed. The strengths and weaknesses of bus way systems in Curitiba, Porto Allegre and São Paulo are compared, with particular reference to the operating capacity of the bus ways. The paper concludes with an assessment of the importance of operations techniques, infrastructure development, land use planning, political stability and regulation to the success or failure of these systems.

Berglund, et al. (1999) [15] Two types of memory deficits have been identified under experimental noise exposure: incidental memory and memory for materials that the observer was not explicitly instructed to focus on during a learning phase. For example, when presenting semantic information to subjects in the presence of noise, recall of the information content was unaffected, but the subjects were significantly less able to recall, for example, in which corner of the slide a word had been located. There is also some evidence that the lack of "helping behavior" that was noted under experimental noise exposure may be related to inattention to incidental cues.

Birgitta, et al. (1999) [16] Exposure to night-time noise also induces secondary effects, or so-called after effects. These are effects that can be measured the day following the night-time exposure, while the individual is awake. The secondary effects include reduced perceived sleep quality; increased fatigue; depressed mood or well-being; and decreased performance.

Stansfeld (2000) [17] Noise, including noise from transport, industry, and neighbors, is a prominent feature of the urban environment. This paper reviews the effects of environmental noise on the non-auditory aspects of health in urban settings. Exposure to transport noise disturbs sleep in the laboratory, but generally not in field studies, where adaptation occurs. Noise interferes with complex task performance, modifies social behavior, and causes annoyance. Studies of occupational noise exposure suggest an association with hypertension, whereas community studies show only weak relations between noise and cardiovascular disease. Aircraft and road-traffic noise exposure are associated with psychological symptoms and with the use of psychotropic medication, but not with the onset of clinically defined psychiatric disorders. In carefully controlled studies, noise exposure does not seem to be related to low birth weight or to congenital birth defects. In both industrial studies and community studies, noise exposure is related to increased catecholamine secretion. In children, chronic aircraft noise exposure impairs reading comprehension and long-term memory and may be associated with increased blood pressure. Noise from neighbors causes annoyance and sleep and activity interference health effects have been little studied. Further research is needed for examining coping strategies and the possible health consequences of adaptation to noise.

WHO (2002) [18] It has been documented in both laboratory subjects and in workers exposed to occupational noise, that noise adversely affects cognitive task performance. In children, too, environmental noise impairs a number of cognitive and motivational parameters.

Harris, et al. (2005) [19] Studies from our lab show that noise exposure initiates cell death by multiple pathways, therefore, protection against noise may be most effective with a multifaceted approach. The Src protein tyrosine kinase (PTK) signaling cascade may be involved in both metabolic and mechanically induced initiation of apoptosis in sensory cells of the cochlea. The current study compares three Src-PTK inhibitors, KX1-004, KX1-005 and KX1-174 as potential protective drugs for NIHL. Chinchillas were used as subjects. A 30 microl drop of one of the Src inhibitors was placed on the round window membrane of the anesthetized chinchilla; the vehicle (DMSO and buffered saline) alone was placed on the other ear. After the drug application, the middle ear was sutured and the subjects were exposed to noise. Hearing was measured before and several times after the noise exposure and treatment using evoked responses. At 20 days post-exposure, the animals were anesthetized their cochleae extracted and cochleograms were constructed. All three Src inhibitors provided protection from a 4 h, 4 kHz octave band noise at 106 dB. The most effective drug, KX1-004 was further evaluated by repeating the exposure with different doses, as well as, substituting an impulse noise exposure. For all conditions, the results suggest a role for Src-PTK activation in noise-induced hearing loss (NIHL), and that therapeutic intervention with a Src-PTK inhibitor may offer a novel approach in the treatment of NIHL.

2.4 Studies on the fuzzy logic and their application

Lah, et al. (2005) [20] Developed an experimental model for found that the controlled dynamic thermal and illumination response of human-built environment in real-time conditions. He was designing an experimental test chamber for thermal and illumination response on a human performance. The time-dependent outside conditions as external system disturbances, the air temperatures and the solar radiation oscillation are also included as input data, this input data controlled by fuzzy logic toolbox. After the many experiments they were found that outside conditions as sun light & temperature was highly effects on human performance.

Zaheeruddin, et al. (2006) [21] Developed a model (system) for predicting the effects of sleep disturbance by noise on humans as a function of noise level, age, and duration of its occurrence. The modeling technique is based on the concept of fuzzy logic, which offers a convenient way of representing the relationships between the inputs and outputs of a system in the form of IF-THEN rules. They were taken the three input variables; such as noise level, duration of sleep and age of the person and one output variable is noise effect (sleep disturbance). In this model they was decided the range of the variables & fluctuated these ranges in fuzzy logic model. After fluctuation they were found the many output variables. They were concluded that the middle-aged people have more probability of sleep disruption than the young people at the same noise levels. However, very little difference is found in sleep disturbance due to noise between young and old people. In addition, the duration of occurrence of noise is an important factor in determining the sleep disturbance over the limited range from few seconds to few minutes. Finally, authors have compared our model results with some of the findings of researchers reported in International Journals.

Zaheeruddin (2006) [22] Studied that noise effects on industrial worker performance. From the literature survey, they observed that the three most important factors influencing human work efficiency are noise level, type of task, and exposure time. Therefore they was developed a model on neuro-fuzzy system. According his model they were taken three input variables (noise level, type of task & exposure time) and one output variables (reduction in work efficiency). All variables apply in neuro-fuzzy models and collect the results. He was concluded that the main thrust of the present work has been to develop a neuro-fuzzy model for the prediction of work efficiency as a function of noise level, type of tasks and exposure times. It is evident from the graph that the work efficiency, for the same exposure time, depends to a large extent upon the noise level and type of task. It has also been verified that simple tasks are not affected even at very high noise level while complex tasks get significantly affected at much lower noise level.

Aluclu, et al. (2008) [23] They described noise-human response and a fuzzy logic model developed by comprehensive field studies on noise measurements (including atmospheric parameters) and control measures. The model has two subsystems constructed on noise reduction quantity in dB. The first subsystem of the fuzzy model depending on 549 linguistic rules comprises acoustical features of all materials used in any workplace. Totally 984 patterns were used, 503 patterns for model development and the rest 481 patterns for testing the model. The second subsystem deals with atmospheric parameter interactions with noise and has 52 linguistic rules. Similarly, 94 field patterns were obtained; 68 patterns were used for training stage of the model and the rest 26 patterns for testing the model.

These rules were determined by taking into consideration formal standards, experiences of specialists and the measurements patterns. They were found that the model was compared with various statistics (correlation coefficients, max-min, standard deviation, average and coefficient of skewers) and error modes (root mean square Error and relative error). The correlation coefficients were significantly high, error modes were quite low and the other statistics were very close to the data.

Zaheeruddin, et al. (2008) [24] They developed an expert system using fuzzy approach to investigate the effects of noise pollution on speech interference. The speech interference measured in terms of speech intelligibility is considered to be a function of noise level, distance between speaker and listener, and the age of the listener. The main source of model development is the reports of World Health Organization (WHO) and field surveys conducted by various researchers. It is implemented on Fuzzy Logic Toolbox of MATLAB using both Mamdani and Sugeno techniques. They were found his result from fuzzy logic model & comparison of the results from World Health Organization (WHO) and U.S. Environmental Protection Agency (EPA). After comparison they were concluded that the model has been implemented on Fuzzy Logic Toolbox of MATLAB the results obtained from the proposed model are in good agreement with the findings of field surveys conducted in different parts of the world. The present effort also establishes the usefulness of the Fuzzy technique in studying the environmental problems where the cause-effect relationships are inherently fuzzy in nature.

Mamdani, et al. (1975) [25] Studied after an experiment on the "linguistic" synthesis of a controller for a model industrial plant (a steam engine). Fuzzy logic is used to convert heuristic control rules stated by a human operator into an automatic control strategy. They developed 24 rules for controlling stem engine. The experiment was initiated to investigate the possibility of human interaction with a learning controller. However, the control strategy set up linguistically proved to be far better than expected in its own right, and the basic experiment of linguistic control synthesis in a non-learning controller is reported here.

Ross (2009) [26] Presented their approach to introduce some applications of fuzzy logic, introduced the basic concept of fuzziness and distinguish uncertainty from other form of uncertainty. It also introduce the fundamental idea of set membership, thereby laying the foundation for all material that follows, and presents membership functions as the format used from expressing set membership. Chapters discussed the fuzzification of scalar and the deffuzification of membership functions & various forms of the implication operation and the composition operation provided.

2.5 Studies on the noise survey

Nanthavanij, et al. (1999) [27] Developed noise contours by two procedures: 1) Analytical and 2) Graphical. The graphical procedure requires input data: ambient noise level, noise levels generated by individual machines, and the (x, y) coordinates of the machine locations. When draw the noise contours in work shop floor, a set of mathematical formulae is also developed to estimate the combined noise levels at predetermined locations (or points) of the workplace floor. Contour lines are then drawn to connect points having an equal noise level. The analytical nature of the procedure also enables engineers to quickly construct the noise contour map and revise the map when changes occur in noise levels due to a workplace re-layout or an addition of a new noise source.

Kumar (2008) [28] Studied the case of high level of noise in rice mills and to examine the response of the workers towards noise. They was done a noise survey was conducted in eight renowned rice mills of the north-eastern region of India. They were following the guidelines of CCOHS for noise survey. Their model as same like above author model. But they was taking the size of grid is 1m X 1m.

3. Problem statement

Based on the literature surveyed as presented in the previous section, it was observed that noise as a pollutant produces contaminated environment, which affects adversely the health of a person and produces ill effects on living, as well as on non-living things. The prominent adverse effects of noise pollution on human beings include noise-induced hearing loss, work efficiency, annoyance responses, interference with communication, the effects on sleep, and social behavior. The effects on work efficiency may have serious implications for industrial workers and other occupations. The effects of noise on human performance have also been investigated by researchers based on sex, laterality, age and extrovert introvert characteristics. However, these factors do not affect human performance significantly. Therefore, depending on the nature of the task, human performance gets affected differently under the impact of different levels of noise and cognitive task type.

After the literature review, we are now much better able to understand why the benefits of low noise level at workplace, taking into account the nature of cognitive task performed, are also important. A part from the health and well-being advantages for the workers themselves, low noise level also leads to better work performance (speed), fewer errors and rejects, better safety, fewer accidents, and lower absenteeism. The overall effect of all this is better productivity. For an industrial environment (moderately type of cognitive task), total productivity increase as a result of reducing noise level, the indirect correlation between worker's age and the increase in production, improvement in attitude, the availability of workers, and working efficiency. There have been several studies to demonstrate the effect of either ages or noise on the performance of various tasks of industrial relevance. It was shown that increasing cognitive work difficulty was predisposed to increased reduction in cognitive work efficiency in industries. But second site we have already discussed that, when level of noise increase then this reduces the efficiency of the worker.

In the present study an attempt has been made to develop a neural fuzzy expert system to predict human cognitive task efficiency as a function of noise level, age of the worker and cognitive task type. We have observed that cognitive task type affects the efficiency of worker in various level of noise in industries. The model is implemented on Fuzzy Logic Toolbox @ MATLAB 2007.

4. Methodology

4.1 Introduction

Noise is one of the physical environmental factors affecting our health in today's world. Noise is generally defined as the unpleasant sounds, which disturb the human being physically and physiologically and cause environmental pollution by destroying environmental properties. The general effect of noise on the hearing of workers has been a topic of debate among scientists for a number of years. Regulations limiting noise exposure of industrial workers have been instituted in many places. For example, in the U.S., the Occupational Noise Exposure Regulation states that industrial employers must limit noise exposure of their employees to 85 dB (A) for 8 hr period.

Based on the literature surveyed as presented in previous section, it was observed that a great majority of people working in industry are exposed to noise with different cognitive task type. In this study, attempt has been made to find out the combined effects of noise level and cognitive task type on industrial worker's performance. Attempt has also been made in present study to identify the noisy industries located in Delhi and around Delhi. Different industries with or without noise were categorized based on measured sound pressure level.

Sound pressure level for industries clearly shown in Appendix-A. In this context, measurement the sound pressure level and cognitive task type, questionnaire studies have been conducted at automobile, power plant and steel textile industries in and around Delhi and also noise counters has been drawn for noisy industries. Assuming that the working environment (Temperature, Humidity, illumination level, other facilities), are same in the industries under reference; categorization has been made as presented in the Table 4.1(a) and 4.1(b).

S.No.	Industry	Noise level (dB (A))	Category	workers number
1.	Shriram Piston and Rings Limited, Ghaziabad	45 – 95	Low noise level	44
2.	WPIL India Limited, Ghaziabad	63 – 102	Medium noise level	38
3.	I.T.O power plant station New Delhi	75-116	High noise level	73

Table 4.1. (a) Industries name & their category with reference to noise level.

S.No.	Industry	Old age 46 up	Medium age 31-45	Young age 15-30
1.	Shriram Piston and Rings Limited, Ghaziabad	8	18	18
2.	WPIL India Limited, Ghaziabad	10	12	16
3.	I.T.O power plant station New Delhi	14	22	37

Table 4.1. (b) Industries name with reference to workers age groups.

In addition to this, the questionnaire data was segregated based on various sections of above-mentioned industries. Performance rating was obtained based on questionnaire survey for different noise levels and type of cognitive task (simple, moderate, and complex). On the collected performance rating data, we have implemented our model using Sugeno technique (Fuzzy Logic Tool box) of MATLAB. It is a three input-one output system. The input variables are noise level, Age of the worker or operator, and cognitive task type and the reduction in cognitive task efficiency is taken as the output variable. The whole methodology shown in Figure 4.1

4.2 Material and methods

In the present study industrial noise measurement technique carried out at three different industries (ITO power plant station, centrifugal pump industry WPIL India Limited, and Shriram Piston & Rings Limited). Selection of industry was based on requirement of study i.e., worker working under different noise levels as well as cognitive task type (simple, moderate, and complex). Questionnaire established with a group of questions refer to parameters will be effected by the noise levels as well as type of cognitive task. Questionnaire asked questions about the age, skill discretion, psychological job demands, etc. Likert scale is used to evaluate the answers density from strongly disagree to strongly agree. Operators and supervisor fulfils the questionnaire on the working day after 8 hrs continuous working, Questionnaire form contains 55 questions. Only workers doing cognitive task were taken in this study. To check the reliability of the survey, the cronbach's alpha value was calculated. Similar sets of items of the questionnaire were identified and cronbach's alpha was calculated [2]. If the value is more than 0.7, then the survey was considered to be reliable. Present model include three inputs and one output, first input is noise level measured by sound level meter, second and third inputs were age and cognitive task type, assessed by questionnaire, and one output was reduction on cognitive task efficiency assessed by using the questionnaire also.

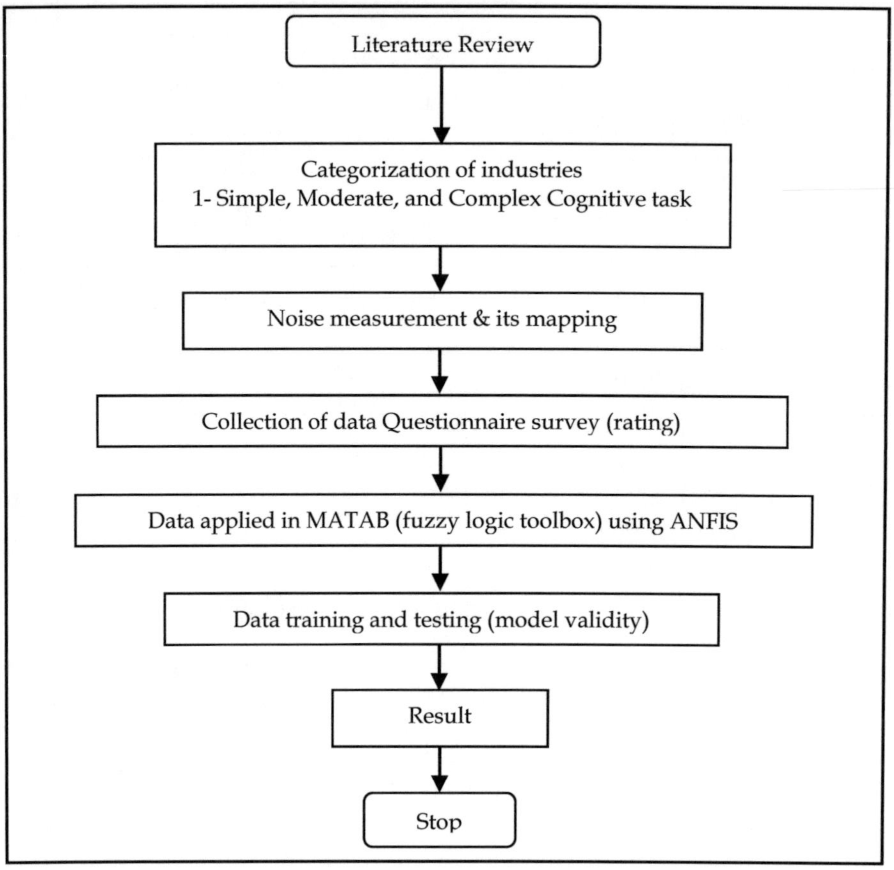

Fig. 4.1. Flow diagram for methodology

4.2.1 Description of study area

A 330 MW Pragati power station is located in New Delhi, latitude (28°37 ' -28°38 ') at longitude (77°14 ' -77°15 ') near (Income Tax Office) ITO beside the highway at 0.3 Km from World Health Organization (WHO) building as shown in Figure 4.2. A centrifugal pumps WPIL India Limited, located in Ghaziabad, latitude (28°40 '57) at longitude (77°25'41) as shown in Figure 4.3.

Fig. 4.2. Geographical location of I.T.O power plant (New Delhi).

Fig. 4.3. Geographical location of centrifugal pumps WPIL India Limited (Ghaziabad).

Fig. 4.4. Geographical location of Shriram Piston & Rings Ltd (Ghaziabad).

Shriram Piston & Rings Ltd. is located at Ghaziabad, latitude (28°41′07) at longitude (77°26′06) as shown in Figure 4.4.

4.2.2 Description of cognitive task factors

Cognitive task (CT) questionnaire is prepared to assess the cognitive task among the workers in (I.T.O power plant station, centrifugal pump industry WPIL India Limited ,and Shriram Piston & Rings Lt.) Industries. This is self-administered questionnaire consists of 55-items. The operators were asked to respond to each and every item of questionnaire by giving subjective opinions from strongly disagrees to strongly agree. The items of the questionnaire were classified into the following factors.

The first factor is skill discretion, described by (possibility of learning new things, repetitive nature of the work, creative thinking at work, and high level of skill, time span of activities and developmental nature of job). The second factor is decision authority, described by (lot of say on job, freedom to take own decisions while working, continual dependence on others). Third scale is organizational decision latitude, described by (influence over organizational changes, influence over work team's decisions, regular meeting's of work team, supervising people as a part of job, influence over policies of union). Fourth factor is psychological job demands described by (work hard, work fast, excessive work, enough time to finish the job, conflicting demands). Fifth factor is emotional demands described by (emotional demanding work, negotiation with others, suppressing genuine emotion, ability to take care, constant consultation with others).

Sixth factor is family/work stress, described by (responsibility for taking care of home, inference of family life and work). The seventh factor is perceived support which is the sum of three sub factors namely supervisor support, coworker support, organizational support and procedural justice, supervisor support is described by (concern of supervisor and helpful supervisor). Coworker support is described by (helpful coworkers and friendly coworkers). Organizational support is described by (organizational care about worker's opinions, care about well-being, consideration of goals and values, concern about workers). Procedural justice is described by (collecting accurate information for making decisions, providing opportunities to appeal the decisions, generating standards to take consistent decisions). Eighth factor is job insecurity (steady work, threat to job security, recent layoff, future layoff, valuable skills, hard to keep job for long duration). Ninth factor is physical job demands, described by (requires much physical effort, rapid physical activities, heavy load at work, awkward body positions and awkward upper body positions). The tenth factor is collective control, described by (sharing the hardships of t he job, possibility of helping the coworkers and unity among workers).

The eleventh factor is cognitive task type, described by (felt depressed, sleep was restless, enjoyed life, felt nervous while work, exceptionally tired in the morning and exhausted mentally and physically at the end of the day).

After data collections, data was analyzed and scores for each worker (noise level, age, cognitive task type and cognitive task efficiency), input/output parameters were categorized. The values of scores were used to establish the rules for optimum model. Neural fuzzy model under reference used three input and one output parameters. Questionnaire answers graded the cognitive task type into three categories (simple, moderate, and complex). Noise levels prevalent in the industries were graded as (low, medium, high), while workers were graded into three categories as (young, medium, and old age workers). Then noise levels and age are scaled from 40 dB(A) to 110 dB(A), and 15 to 65 years respectively, and Cognitive task type scaled from (1) strongly disagree to (5) strongly agree. While the output (cognitive task efficiency) classified as questionnaire answers weight (0%=strongly disagree, 25%=disagree, 50%=neutral, 75%=agree, and 100% =strongly agree). Model was constructed according to questionnaire form responses.

4.2.3 Questionnaire studies (surveys) in the industry

Data may be obtained either from the primary source or the secondary source. A primary source is one that itself collects the data; a secondary source is one that makes available data which were collected by some other agency. A primary source usually has more detailed information particularly on the procedures followed in collecting and compiling the data. Many methods for collecting the data such as direct personal interview, Mailed questionnaire method, indirect oral interviews schedule sent through enumerators, Information from correspondents etc.

So our data is direct personal interview method, under this method of collecting data , there is a face to face contact with the persons from whom the information is to be obtained (known as informants).

4.2.4 Purpose of the questionnaire

1. To determine the effects of noise on the workers under different cognitive task type.
2. To determine the effect of the noise level on workers age.
3. For specifying workers comments on protection from noise.
4. To determine what parameters have negative and positive affect to noise level.
5. To find the threshold level of noise on industries for this kind of task.
6. To feed back these data to neural fuzzy logic model.

4.2.5 Why we used the questionnaire survey?

This method suitable for this study, the explanations are following:

- The information obtained by this method is likely to be more accurate because the interviewer can clear up doubts of the informants about certain questions and thus obtain correct information.
- The language of communication can be adjustable to the status and education level of the worker or operator.
- Due to the direct interaction the correct and desired information collected.
- The answers of the questions arranged in ranking order (low, medium, high and very high etc.), because answers easily implemented in Fuzzy logic toolbox. Its detail can be seen in the section 4.6

To obtain occupants opinions on the industrial/cognitive task, questionnaire was administered. This questionnaire was consisting of 55 questions related to cognitive work effects on industrial worker performance in different noise level environment. The objective of the detailed survey was to confirm and clarify the results obtained from the short-form survey. Questions corresponding to the statements in the short-form questionnaire were used. A total 155 questionnaire were distributed among the workers of automobile industries. Responses were made using likert scale 5-point scales instead of simple choices.

- Along with the questionnaire the demographic data like age, noise level, gender etc. were also collected.
- The operators or workers were asked to respond to the self administered questionnaire by giving their objective opinions.
- These responses were transferred to a five point likert scale by assigning the rating from 1 to 5.
- Not to cause any work loss in the general industry, the questionnaire forms were distributed during the day shift and collected the next day while it has been done on a one-to-one basis during the night shift.
- Each choice filled through the worker or operator at the time of working.
- All responses were collected and calculated the performance rating of the workers.

An example of the procedure used to calculate the value required is shown below:-

Sample survey response shows the procedure adopted for response collection of workers, all responses rating adding and divided by the number of questions to find out the ratio of the performance.

- Addition the input response (answers) = 2+4+2+3+1+3+3+2+2+2+3+2+3+3+2+3+2+3+ 3+2+2+2+3+1+3+4+3+4+1+3+2+2+4+1+1+2+2+2+4+3+3+3+2+2+3+3+2= 116
- Input Performance ratio (x) = 116/ 47 = 2.4
- Addition the output response (answers) =25%+0%+0%+0%+25%=50%

Output Performance ratio (η) =50%/5=10%

Similarly we have found the output performance ratio at different noise levels. Respectively and see the corresponding value of "reduction in cognitive work efficiency (η)" from Table 4.2, the detailed procedure for calculation has been described in Appendix-B.

Ratio value (η)	Reduction in cognitive task efficiency
0.00%	Strongly disagree (None)
25%	Disagree (Low)
50%	Neutral (moderate)
75%	Agree (High)
100%	Strongly agree (Very high)

Table 4.2. Rating ratio for reduction in cognitive task efficiency.

For Linguistic rules in Fuzzy logic Toolbox @ MATLAB software require 27 rules. Questionnaires were selected randomly from the given set of questionnaire depicted as linguistic rule.

4.3 Noise measurement

No single method or process exists for measuring occupational noise. Hearing safety and health professionals can use a variety of instruments to measure noise and can choose from a variety of instruments and software to analyze their measurements. The choice of a particular instrument and approach for measuring and analyzing occupational noise depends on many factors, not the least of which will be the purpose for the measurement and the environment in which the measurement will be made. In general, measurement methods should conform to the American National Standard Measurement of Occupational Noise Exposure, ANSI S12.19-1997 [ANSI 1996a].

4.4 Noise mapping

A noise survey or mapping takes noise measurements throughout an entire plant or section to identify noisy areas. Noise surveys provide very useful information which enables us to identify:

- Areas where employees are likely to be exposed to harmful levels of noise and personal dosimeter may be needed,
- Machines and equipment which generate harmful levels of noise,
- Employees who might be exposed to unacceptable noise levels, and
- Noise control options to reduce noise exposure.

Noise survey is conducted in areas where noise exposure is likely to be hazardous. Noise level refers to the level of sound. A noise survey involves measuring noise level at selected locations throughout an entire plant or sections to identify noisy areas. This is usually done with a sound level meter (SLM). A reasonably accurate sketch showing the locations of workers and noisy machines is drawn. Noise level measurements are taken at a suitable number of positions around the area and are marked on the sketch. The more measurements taken were more accurate the survey. A noise map can be produced by drawing lines on the sketch between points of equal sound level. Noise survey maps; provide very useful information by clearly identifying areas where there are noise hazards.

The following sections briefly explain the theory of sound and the contours estimation procedure. Theory Two basic formulae play an important role in estimating the noise level. Herein, the terms 'sound' and 'noise' are used interchangeably. These formulae convert sound power to sound intensity, and sound intensity to sound pressure level respectively.

$$I = \frac{P}{4\Pi d^2} \tag{4.1}$$

$$L = 10\log\left[\frac{I}{I_0}\right] \tag{4.2}$$

Where:
P is the sound power (W) of the noise source
I the sound intensity (W/m^2),
d the distance (m) from the noise source,
L is the sound pressure level (dB (A)),
I_0 is the reference sound intensity.

By knowing the noise level (L), in dB (A), of a given noise source, its noise level can be estimated at any distance (d) from the source. This can be achieved by initially converting the noise level (dB (A)) of the noise source into its sound power (watt) using Eq. (4.1) and Eq. (4.2) and by assuming that the noise level is measured at 1 m from the source (i.e., d=1). From the inverse square law, the sound intensity at a distance d from the noise source is then attenuated by Eq. (4.1). In case there are n noise sources, the combined noise level ($\bar{L}$) at any given location can be estimated using the following formula:

$$\bar{L} = 10\sum_{i=1}^{n} \log \frac{I}{I_0} \tag{4.3}$$

For the ease of computation, Eq. (4.2) can be rewritten as follows:

$$I = 10^{(L-120)/10} \tag{4.4}$$

Then, the combined sound intensity (I) can be directly computed from

$$\bar{I} = \sum_{i=1}^{n} 10 \frac{(L_i - 120)}{10} \tag{4.5}$$

4.4.1 Construction of a noise contour map

The procedure for constructing a noise contour map of the workplace can be described as Follows:

Initialization steps:-

1. **Determining (x, y) coordinates of machine locations:**

The layout of the factory floor must be obtained and all machines (or noise sources) must be plotted on the layout map. Since the computation requires an assumption of a pointed noise source, the machine location must be represented by a point on the X-Y plane. By selecting one corner of the factory floor as the reference origin (usually the lower left corner), the machine location can be expressed as a pair of X and Y coordinates which are measured from that reference point. That is, the location of machine k is expressed as, (X_k, Y_k)

2. **Determining the ambient noise intensity:**

The ambient noise level (dB (A)) must be either measured or estimated. For a direct measurement, the ambient noise is measured when none of the machines are operating. To obtain reliable data, several measurements should be taken from different locations and different times. Then the average noise level is calculated and used as the ambient noise level of the factory floor. It must be converted to the ambient noise intensity, I_{ab}, using Eq. (4.4).

3. **Determining the sound power of the machine:**

The machine noise level may be difficult to determine since it is impossible to isolate the machine and measure its noise level without any noise interference from others. If applicable, each machine can be operated and measurement taken correspondingly. Otherwise, the machine manufacturer can be contacted to obtain information (specifications) about the noise level generated by the machine. Similarly, the noise level of machine (k) must be expressed as the sound power (P_k), using the following conversion.

From the noise level in dB (A) of machine k, L_k, convert it to its sound power, P_k, using Equations (4.1) and (4.2), and by assuming that d =1 m.

$$P_k = 4\prod 10^{(L_k - 120)/10} \tag{4.6}$$

Repeat Equitation (4.8) for k=1 to m; Where m denotes the number of machines

4. Determining the locations where the combined noise levels will be estimated:

Next, a set of locations (points of interest) on the floor must be identified where the combined noise levels will be estimated. These points are expressed as (X_i, Y_i), i =1 to n, where n is the number of points. Conventionally, the factory floor layout is divided into grids. The grid dimension depends on the size of the factory floor and the required degree of accuracy of the noise contours. If the size of the factory is large and/or high degree of accuracy is required, the number of grids will be large (i.e., the grid size will be small). However, the larger the number of grids implies the longer time to construct the noise contours.

4.4.2 Computation steps

1. Computing the machine noise intensity at the specified location:

The noise intensity of machine k at location i, $I_{i,k}$, can be estimated using the following steps. Initially, the Euclidean distance, d_{ik}, between points i and k must be determined.

$$d_{ik} = [(x_i - x_k)^2 + (y_i - y_k)^2]^2 \tag{4.7}$$

Then, the machine noise intensity at location i is computed using Equation (4.3).

$$I = P_k / 4\prod d^2{}_{ik} \tag{4.8}$$

2. Combining all machine noise intensities:

The combined machine noise intensity at location i, CDCZ can be determined by adding all machine noise intensities $I_{i,k}$, k=1 to m.

$$\overline{I} = \sum_{k=1}^{m} \frac{P_k}{4\prod d^2{}_{ik}} \tag{4.9}$$

3. Adding the ambient noise intensity:

The effect of the ambient noise level must be accounted for by adding I_{ab} to Equitation (4.9). The combined noise intensity at location i now become:

$$\overline{I}_i = I_{ab} + \sum_{k=1}^{m} \frac{P_k}{4\prod d^2{}_{ik}} \tag{4.10}$$

By substituting Equation (4.8) into Equation (4.12), both the terms P_k and 4п disappear. Thus, Equation (4.10) can be written as:

$$\overline{I}_i = I_{ab} + \sum_{k=1}^{m} \frac{(L_k - 120)/10}{d^2{}_{ik}} \tag{4.11}$$

4. Converting the combined noise intensity into its noise level (dB (A)):

Finally, the combined noise intensity at location i is converted into the combined Noise level in dB (A), Li, using Equation (4.2).

4.5 Industrial noise surveys

4.5.1 NoiseAtWorkV1.31

Software for mapping and analysis of noise at workplaces for health and safety representatives (NoiseAtWorkV1.31) [29] is software for mapping and analysis of noise levels at places where people work. Based on measured noise levels and working times of employees, noise contours and Leq. 8hr values are calculated by the software. The software is used by health and safety representatives for the management of occupational noise risks.

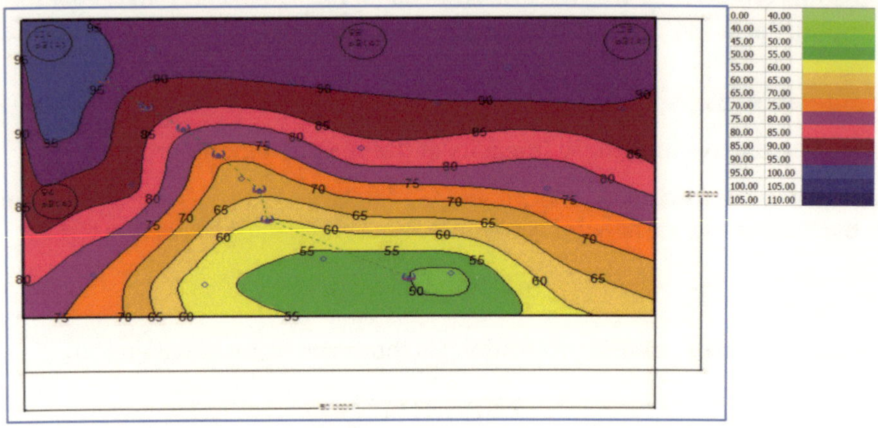

Fig. 4.5. Shriram Piston & Rings Lt. Ghaziabad Noise map (noiseatwork V1.31).

No.	X	Y	Leq
1	2.00	26.00	100.00
2	10.00	32.00	93.00
3	21.00	28.00	90.00
4	33.00	26.00	90.00
5	47.00	20.00	90.00
6	6.00	10.00	75.00
7	9.00	20.00	87.00
8	10.00	25.00	85.00
9	25.00	22.00	85.00
10	37.00	30.00	95.00
11	41.00	18.00	75.00
12	34.00	10.00	48.00
13	24.00	11.00	53.00
14	17.00	19.00	65.00
15	15.00	9.00	55.00

Table 4.3. (a) (X, Y) Coordinates of noise measurement and noise levels.

Loc	T [h]	Red [dB]	Leq [dB]	Dose [%]
1	8.00	–	95.47	213
2	8.00	–	84.33	46
3	8.00	–	78.69	21
4	8.00	–	71.63	8
5	8.00	–	64.20	3
6	8.00	–	59.60	1
7	8.00	–	49.92	–
Total	56.00		87.45	491

Table 4.3. (b) Employees location and dosage calculation.

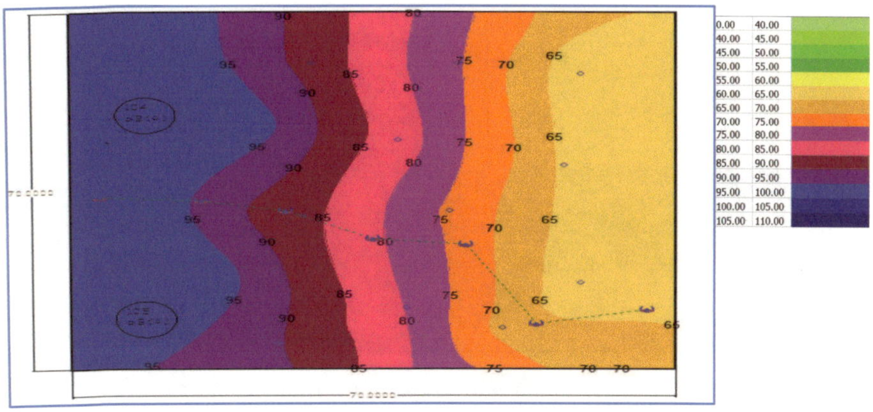

Fig. 4.6. WPIL India Limited, Ghaziabad Noise map (noiseatwork V1.31).

No.	X	Y	Leq
1	5.00	30.00	100.00
2	10.00	24.00	98.00
3	4.00	16.00	96.00
4	8.00	10.00	99.00
5	12.00	2.00	90.00
6	14.00	30.00	88.00
7	18.00	22.00	83.00
8	13.00	15.00	85.00
9	20.00	6.00	80.00
10	21.00	30.00	75.00
11	22.00	16.00	74.00
12	25.00	4.00	68.00
13	30.00	29.00	60.00
14	28.00	20.00	65.00
15	29.00	9.00	61.00

Table 4.4. (a) (X, Y) Coordinates of noise measurement and noise levels.

Loc	T [h]	Red [dB]	Leq [dB]	Dose [%]
1	8.00	–	97.69	290
2	8.00	–	92.81	148
3	8.00	–	86.68	63
4	8.00	–	80.51	27
5	8.00	–	72.80	9
6	8.00	–	66.32	4
7	8.00	–	64.03	3
Total	56.00		90.79	781

Table 4.4. (b) Employees location and dosage calculation.

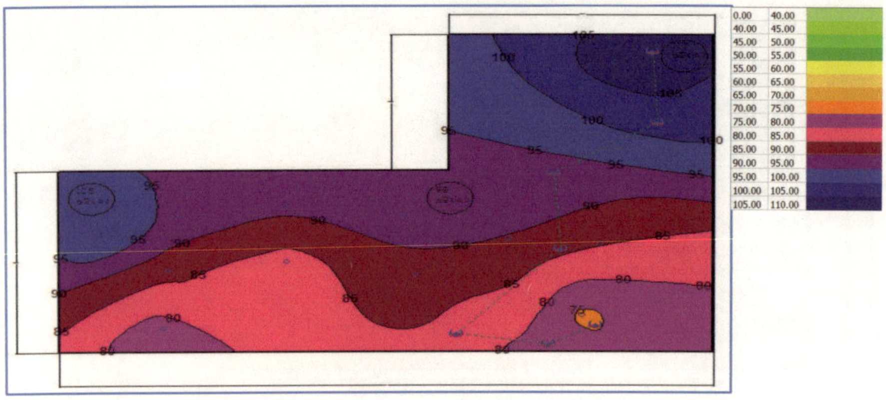

Fig. 4.7. (I.T.O) power plant station New Delhi Noise map (noiseatwork V1.31).

No.	X	Y	Leq
1	85.00	64.00	108.00
2	94.00	53.00	104.00
3	70.00	60.00	100.00
4	80.00	42.00	95.00
5	69.00	25.00	90.00
6	53.00	30.00	94.00
7	55.00	17.00	88.00
8	83.00	24.00	85.00
9	7.00	25.00	100.00
10	18.00	30.00	94.00
11	17.00	18.00	86.00
12	35.00	32.00	90.00
13	35.00	20.00	83.00
14	16.00	5.00	77.00
15	80.00	8.00	74.00

Table 4.5. (a) (X, Y) Coordinates of noise measurement and noise levels.

Loc	T [h]	Red [dB]	Leq [dB]	Dose [%]
1	8.00	–	107.50	1131
2	8.00	–	102.20	543
3	8.00	–	94.10	177
4	8.00	–	85.93	57
5	8.00	–	83.32	40
6	8.00	–	77.39	17
7	8.00	–	74.61	12
Total	56.00		100.36	2944

Table 4.5. (b) Employees location and dosage calculation.

4.6 Building systems with fuzzy logic toolbox

While fuzzy system are shown to be universal approximations to algebraic functions, it is not attribute that actually makes them valuable to us in understanding new or evolving problems. Rather, the primary benefit of fuzzy system theory is to approximate system behavior where analytical functions or numerical relations do not exist. Hence, fuzzy systems have a high potential to understand the very system that red void of analytic formulations: complex system. Complex system can be new systems that have not been tested, they can be system involved with the human condition such as biological or medical system, or they can be social, economic, or political systems, where the vast arrays of input and output could not all possibly be captured analytically or controlled in any conventional sense. Moreover the relationship between the cause and effects of these systems is generally not understood, but often can be observed.

Alternatively, fuzzy system theory can have utility in assessing some of our more conventional, less complex system. For example, for some problems exact solutions are not always necessary. An approximate but fast, solution can be useful in making preliminary design decisions or as an initial estimation in a more accurate numerical technique to save computational costs or in the myriad of situations where the inputs to a problem are vague, ambiguous, or not known at all.

Fuzzy models in a broad sense are of two types. The first category of the model proposed by Mamdani is based on the collections of IF-THEN rules with both fuzzy-antecedent and consequent predicates. The advantage of this model is that the rule base is generally provided by an expert, and hence, to a certain degree, it is transparent to interpretation and analysis. The second category of the fuzzy model is based on the Takagi-Sugeno-Kang (TSK) method of reasoning.

For this study we have establishment of the Sugeno type Fuzzy models under the recommendations of Occupational Safety and Health Administration (OSHA)[30], 90 dB (A) for 8 hr. duration, as shown in Figure 4.8, because of the adaptive data Surgeon's model is the proper method to build the model. Fuzzy Logic Toolbox is a collection of functions built on the MATLAB® numeric computing environment. Fuzzy logic has two different meanings. In a narrow sense, fuzzy logic is a logical system, which is an extension of multi valued logic. However, in a wider sense fuzzy logic (FL) is almost synonymous with the theory of fuzzy sets, a theory which relates to classes of objects with unsharp boundaries in which membership is a matter of degree.

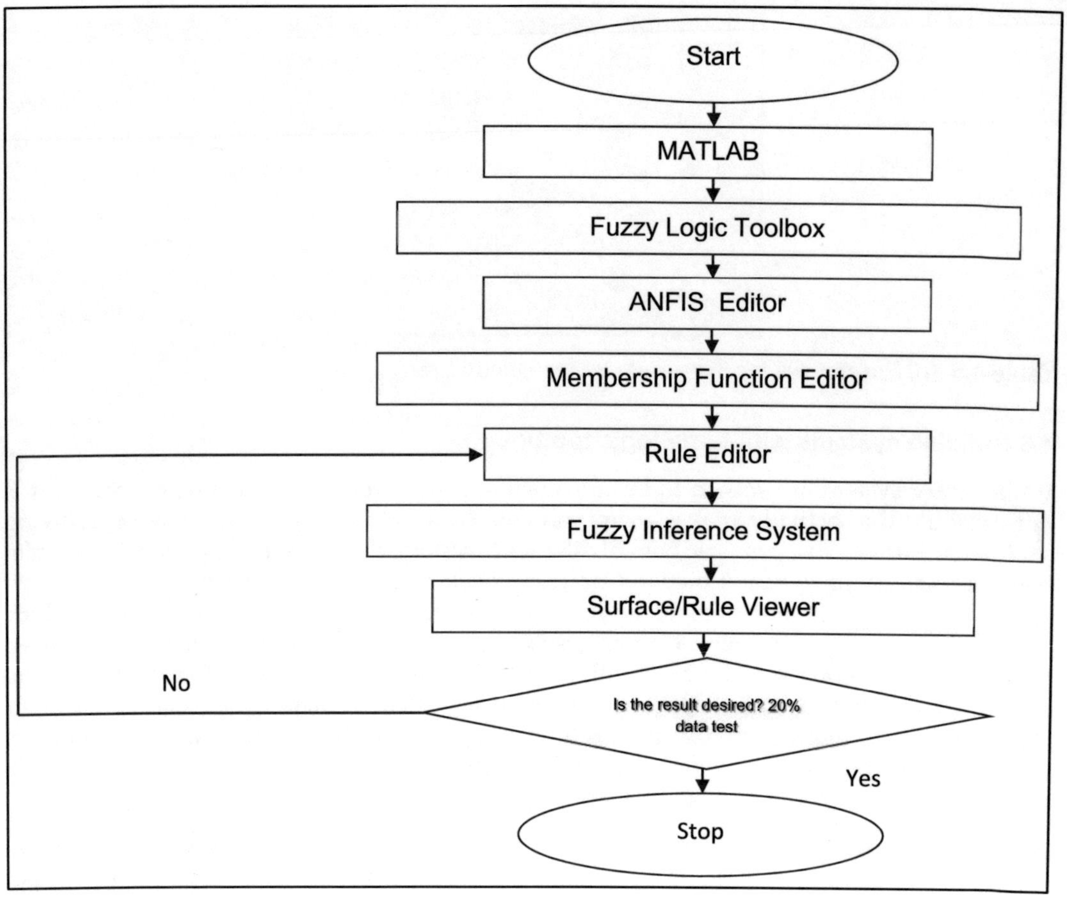

Fig. 4.8. Flow diagram for model structure.

4.6.1 Algorithm

1. Selection of the input and output variables.
2. Determination of the ranges of input and output variables.
3. Determination of the membership functions for various input and output variables.
4. Formation of the set of linguistic rules that represent the relationships between the system variables;
5. Selection of the appropriate reasoning mechanism for the formalization of the neural fuzzy model.
6. Check model validity by using 20% of input/output pairs.
7. Evaluation of the model adequacy;if the model does not produce the desired results, modify the rules in step 4.

4.6.2 Neuro-fuzzy computing

Neuro-fuzzy computing is a judicious integration of the merits of neural and fuzzy approaches. This incorporates the generic advantages of artificial neural networks like massive parallelism, robustness, and learning in data-rich environments into the system.

The modeling of imprecise and qualitative knowledge as well as the transmission of uncertainty is possible though the use of fuzzy logic. Besides these generic advantages, the neuro-fuzzy approach also provides the corresponding application specific merits [31-32] some of the neuro-fuzzy systems are popular by their shorts names. For example ANFIS [33], DENFIS [34], SANFIS [35] and FLEXNFIS [36], etc.

Our present model is based on adaptive neuro-fuzzy interface system (ANFS) an ANFIS is a fuzzy interface system implement in framework of adaptive neural networks. ANFIS either uses input/output data sets to construct a fuzzy interface system whose membership functions are tuned using a learning algorithm or an expert may be specify a fuzzy interface system and then the system is trained with the data pairs by an adaptive network . The conceptual diagram of ANFIS based on latter approach shown in figure 4.9. Is consists of two major components namely fuzzy interface system and adaptive neural network. A fuzzy interface system has five functional blocks. A fuzzifier converts real numbers of input into fuzzy sets. This functional unit essentially transforms the crisp inputs into a degree of match with linguistic values. The database (or dictionary) contains the Membership functions of fuzzy sets. The membership function provide flexibility to the fuzzy sets in modeling commonly used linguistic expressions such as "the noise level is low "or "person is young." A rule base consist of a set of linguistic statements of the form, if x is A then y is B, where A and B are labels of fuzzy sets on universes of discourse characterized by appropriate membership function of database . An interface engine perform s the interface operations on the rules to infer the output by a fuzzy reasoning method. Defuzzifier

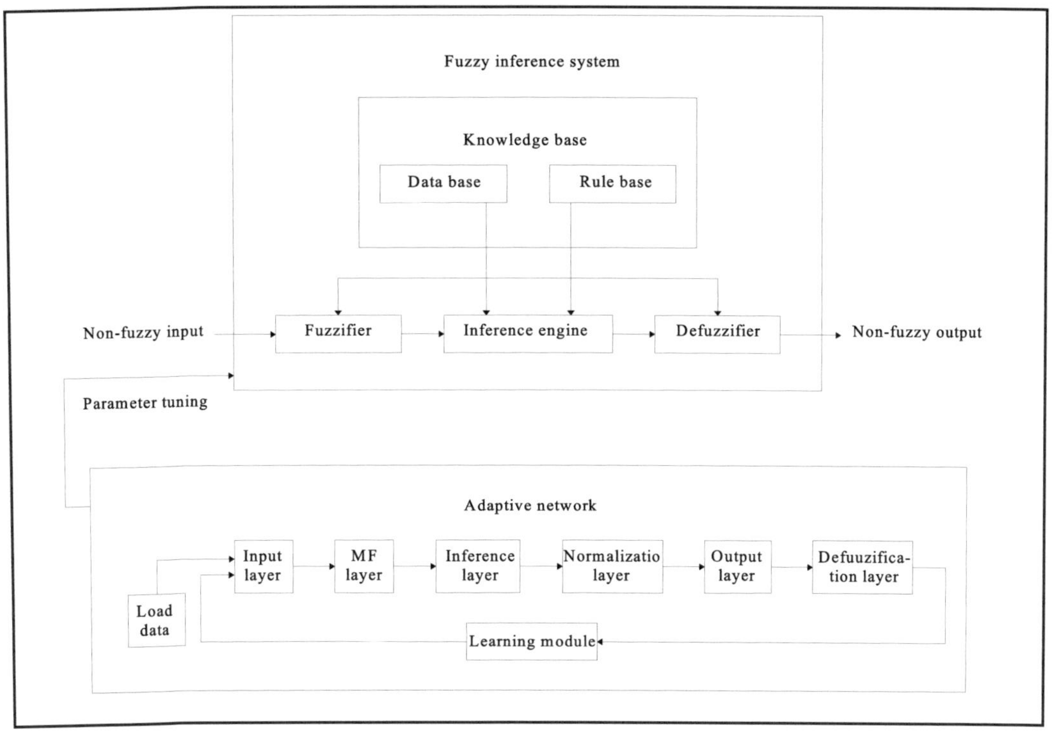

Fig. 4.9. Conceptual diagram of ANFIS.

converts the fuzzy outputs obtained by interface engine into a non-fuzzy output real number domain. In order to incorporate the capability of learning from input/output data sets in fuzzy interface systems, a corresponding adaptive neural network is generated. An adaptive network is a multi-layer feed-forward network consisting of nodes and directional links through which nodes are connected. As shown in Figure 4.10. Layer 1 is the input layer, layer 2 describes the membership functions of each fuzzy input, layer 3 is interface layer and normalizing is performed in layer 4. Layer 5 gives the output and layer 6 is the defuzzification layer. The layers consist of fixed and adaptive nodes, each adaptive node has asset of parameters and performs a particular function (node function) on incoming signals.

The learning model may consist of either back propagation or hybrid learning algorithm, the learning rules specifies how the parameter of adaptive node should be change to minimize a prescribed error measure [37]. The change in values of the parameters results in change in shape of membership functions associated with fuzzy interface system.

4.6.3 System modeling

The modeling process based on ANFIS can broadly be classified in three steps:

Step 1. System identification

The first step in system modeling is the identification inputs and outputs variables called the system's Takagi-Sugeno-Kang (TSK) model [33,34] are formed, where antecedent are defined be a set of non-linear parameters and consequents are either linear combination of input variables and constant terms or may be constants, generally called, singletons.

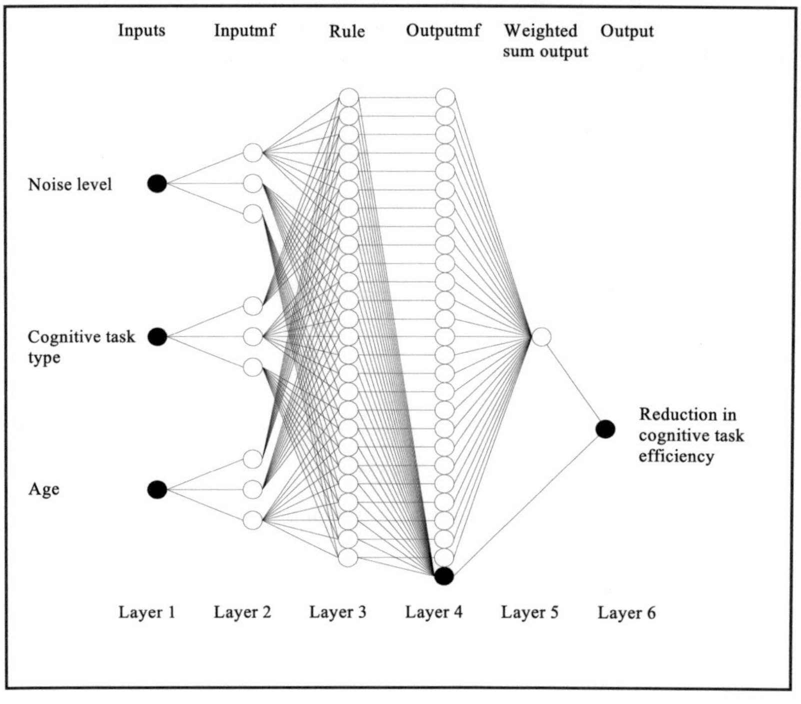

Fig. 4.10. ANFIS structure of the model.

Step 2. Determining the network structure

Once the input and output variables are identified, the neuro-fuzzy system is realized using a six-layered network as shown in Figure 4.10. The input, output and node functions of each layer are explained in the subsequent paragraphs

Layer 1: Input layer

Each node in layer 1 represents the input variables of the model identified in step 1 this layer simply transmits these input variables to the fuzzification layer.

Layer 2: Fuzzification layer

The fuzzification layer describes the membership function of each input fuzzy set, membership functions are used to characterize fuzziness in fuzzy sets, the output of each node i in this layer is given by $\mu_{A_i}(x_i)$ where the symbol $\mu_A(x)$ is the membership function. Its value on the unit interval (0, 1) measure the degree to which elements x belongs to the fuzzy set A, xi is the input to the node i and Ai is the linguistic label for each input variable associated with this node.

Each node in this layer is an adaptive node that is the output of each node depends on the parameters pertaining to these nodes. Thus the membership function for *A* can be any appropriate parameterized membership function. The most commonly used membership functions are triangular, trapezoidal, Gaussian, and bell shaped. Any of these choices may be used, the triangular and trapezoidal membership functions have been used extensively especially in real-time implementations due to their simple formulas and computational efficiency.

In our original fuzzy model [40] we have used triangular membership functions however since these membership functions are composed of straight line segments they are not smooth at corner points specified by the parameters though the parameters of these membership functions can be optimized using direct search methods but they are less efficient and more time consuming, also the derivatives of the functions are not continuous so the powerful and more efficient gradient methods cannot be used for optimizing their parameters Gaussian and bell shaped membership functions are becoming increasingly popular for specifying fuzzy sets as they are non-linear and smooth and their derivatives are continuous gradient methods can be used easily for optimizing their design parameters . Thus in this model, we have replaced the triangular fuzzy memberships with bell shapes functions (Table 4.7). The bell or generalized bell (or gbell) shaped membership function is specified by a set of three fitting parameters {*a*,*b*,*c*} as:

$$\mu_A(x) = \frac{1}{1 + \left[\left((x-c)/a\right)^2\right]^b} \tag{4.12}$$

The desired shape of gbell membership function can be obtained by proper selection of the parameters more specifically we can adjust *c* and *a* to vary the center and width of membership function, and *b* to control the slope at the crossover points. The parameter *b* gives gbell shaped membership function one more degree of freedom than the Gaussian membership function and allows adjusting the steepness at crossover points. The parameters in this layer are referred to as premise parameters.

Layer 3: inference layer

The third layer is inference layer. Each node in this layer is fixed node and represents the IF part of a fuzzy rule. This layer aggregates the membership grades using any fuzzy intersection operator which can perform fuzzy AND operation [35]. The intersection operator is commonly referred to as T-norm operators are min or product operators. For instance

IF x_1 is A_1 AND x_2 is A_2 AND x_3 is A_3 THEN y is $f(x_1, x_2, x_3)$

Where $f(x_1, x_2, x_3)$ is a linear functions of input variables or may be constant, the output of ith node is given as:

$$w_i = \mu_{A_1}(x_1) \times \mu_{A_2}(x_2) \times \mu_{A_3}(x_3) \tag{4.13}$$

Layer 4: normalization layer

The ith node of this layer is also a fixed node and calculates the ratio of the ith 'rules' firing strength in interference layer to the sum of all the rules firing strengths

$$\overline{w}_i = \frac{w_i}{w_1 + w_2 + \ldots + w_R} \tag{4.14}$$

Where i =1,2, , R and R is total number of rules. The outputs of this layer are called normalized firing strengths.

Layer 5: Output layer

This layer represents the THEN part (i.e., the consequent) of the fuzzy rule. The operation performed by the nodes in this layer is to generate the qualified consequent (either fuzzy or crisp) of each rule depending on firing strength. Every node i in this layer is an adaptive node. The output of the node is computed as:

$$O_i = \overline{w}_i f_i \tag{4.15}$$

Where $\overline{w}_i$ is normalized firing strength from layer 3 and f_i is a linear function of input variables of the form (pix1+qix2+ri)where {pi, qi, ri} is the parameter set of the node i, referred to as consequent parameters or f may be a constant if f_i is linear function of input variables then it is called first order Sugeno fuzzy model (as in our present model) and if f_i is a constant then it is called zero order Sugeno fuzzy model. This consequent can be linear function as long as it appropriately describes the output of the model within the fuzzy region specified by the antecedent of the rule. But in the present case, the relationship between input variables (noise level, cognitive task type, and age) and output (reduction in cognitive task efficiency) is highly non-linear. In Sugeno model, consequent can be taken as singleton, i.e. real numbers without losing the performance of the system.

Layer 6: Defuzzification layer

This layer aggregate the qualified consequent to produce a crisp output .the single node in this layer is a fixed node. It computes the weighted average of output signals of the output layer as:

$$O = \sum_i O_i = \sum_i \overline{w}_i f_i = \frac{\sum_i w_i f_i}{\sum_i w_i} \tag{4.16}$$

Step 3. Learning algorithm and parameter tuning

The ANFIS model fine-tunes the parameters of membership functions using either the back propagation learning algorithm is an error-based supervised learning algorithm. It employs an external reference signal, which acts like a teacher and generate an error signal by comparing the reference with the obtained response. Based on error signal, the network modifies the design parameters to improve the system performance. It uses gradient descent method to update the parameters. The input/output data pairs are often called as training data or learning patterns. They are clamped onto the network and functions are propagated to the output unit. The network output is compared with the desired output values. The error measure E^P, for P pattern at the output node in layer 6 may be given as:

$$E^P = \frac{1}{2}\left(T^P - O_6^P\right)^2 \tag{4.17}$$

Where T^P are the target or desired output and O_6^P the single node output of defuzzification layer in the network. Further the sum of squared errors for the entire training data set is:

$$E = \sum_P E^P = \frac{1}{2}\sum_P \left(T^P - O_6^P\right)^2 \tag{4.18}$$

The error measure with respect to node output in layer 6 is given by delta (δ):

$$\delta = \frac{\partial E}{\partial O_6} = -2\left(T - O_6\right) \tag{4.19}$$

This delta value gives the rate at which the output must be changed in order to minimize the error function, since the output of adaptive nodes of the given adaptive network depend on the design parameters so the design parameters must be updated accordingly. Now this delta value of the output unit must be propagated backward to the inner layers in order to distribute the error of output unit to all the layers connected to it and adjust the corresponding parameters the delta value for the layer 5 is given as:

$$\frac{\partial E}{\partial O_5} = \frac{\partial E}{\partial O_6}\frac{\partial O_6}{\partial O_5} \tag{4.20}$$

Similarly for any kth layer, the delta value may be calculated using the chain rule as:

$$\frac{\partial E}{\partial O_K} = \frac{\partial E}{\partial O_{K+1}}\frac{\partial O_{K+1}}{\partial O_K} \tag{4.21}$$

Now if α is a set of design parameters of the given adaptive network then

$$\frac{\partial E}{\partial \alpha} = \sum_{\alpha \in P} \frac{\partial E}{\partial O^I}\frac{\partial O^I}{\partial \alpha} \tag{4.22}$$

Where P is the set of adaptive nodes whose output depends on α thus update for the parameter α is given by:

$$\Delta\alpha = -\eta\frac{\partial E}{\partial \alpha} \tag{4.23}$$

Where η is the learning rate and may be calculated as:

$$\eta = \frac{K}{\sqrt{\sum_{\alpha}(\partial E / \partial \alpha)^2}} \tag{4.24}$$

Where 'k' is the step size. The value of k must be properly chosen as the change in value of k influences the rate of convergence.

Thus the design parameters are tuned according to the real input/output data pairs for the system .the change in value of parameter results in change in shape of membership functions initially defined by an expert .the new membership functions thus obtained after training gives a more realistic model of the system the back propagation algorithm though widely used for training neural networks may suffer from some problems. The back propagation algorithm is never assured of finding the global minimum. The error surface may have many local minima so it may get stuck during the learning process on flat or near flat regions of the error surface. This makes progress slow and uncertain.

Another efficient learning algorithm, which can be used for training the network, is hybrid-learning rule. Hybrid learning rule is a combination of least square estimator (LSE) and gradient descent method (used in back propagation algorithm). It is converges faster and gives more interpretable results. The training is done in two passes. In forward pass, when training data is supplied at the input layer, the functional signals go forward to calculate each node output. The non-linear or premise parameters in layer 2 remain fixed in this pass. Thus the overall output can be expressed as the linear combination of consequents parameters. These consequents parameters can be identified using least square estimator (LSE) method. The output of layer 6 is compared with the actual output and the error measure can be calculated as in eqs.(4-17 and 4-18). In backward pass, error rate prorogates backward from output end toward the input end and non-linear parameters in layer 2 are update using the gradient descent method (eqs.(4-19)-(4-24)) as discussed in back propagation algorithm . Since the conquest parameters are optimally identified using LSE under the condition that the premise parameters are fixed, the hybrid algorithm converges much faster as it reduces the search space dimensions of the original pure back propagation algorithm.

4.6.4 Implementation

We have implementation our model using ANFIS (fuzzy logic tool box) of MATLAB@ [39]. The system is first designed using Sugeno fuzzy interference system. It is the three inputs-one output system. The input variables are the noise level, cognitive task type, and age and the reduction in cognitive task efficiency is taken as the output variable. The input parameters are represented by fuzzy sets or linguistics variables Table 4.6. We have chosen gbell shaped membership functions (it is given the minimum error as shown it Table 4.7), to characterize these fuzzy sets. The membership functions for input variables are shown in Figure 4.11(a-c).

System's	Linguistic	Linguistic Values	Fuzzy Intervals
Input	Noise level	Low	40-90
		Medium	80-100
		High	90-110
	Cognitive task type	Simple	1-3
		Moderate	2-4
		Complex	3-5
	Age	Young age	15-35 years
		Medium age	30-50 years
		Old age	45-65 years
Output	Reduction In cognitive task Efficiency	None	0 %
		Low	25 %
		Moderate	50 %
		High	75 %
		Very high	100 %

Table 4.6. Inputs and outputs with their associated neural fuzzy values.

Mf type	Error(linear output)	Error(constant output)	Epoch (iteration)
Tri-mf	8.0327 e-007	2.5532 e-005	190
Trap-mf	1.0955 e-006	0.2886	190
Gbell-mf	6.0788 e-007	2.1502 e-005	190
Gauss-mf	6.1237 e-007	2.2678 e-005	190
Gauss2-mf	1.0014 e-006	2.1687 e-005	190
Pi-mf	1.7942 e-006	0.2886	190
Dsig-mf	2.4415 e-006	2.4847 e-005	190
Psig-mf	1.4882 e-006	2.4847 e-005	190

Table 4.7. Minimum error membership functions.

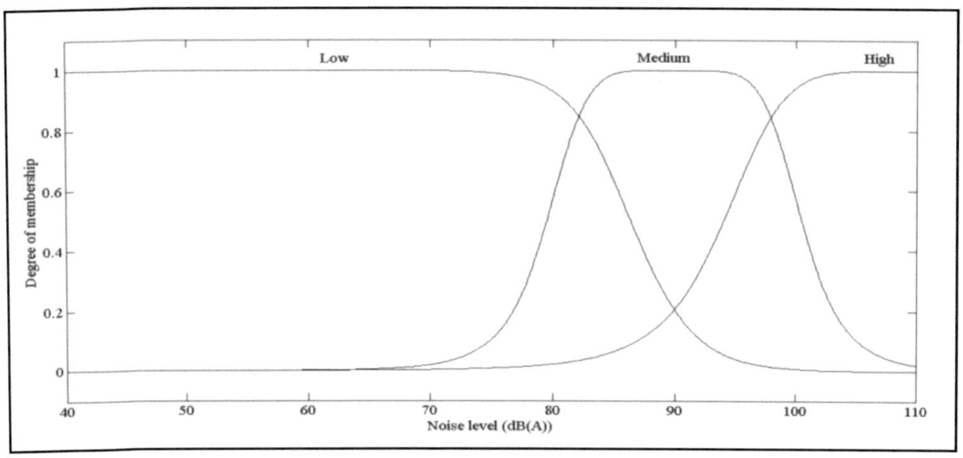

Fig. 4.11. (a) Membership functions of noise level.

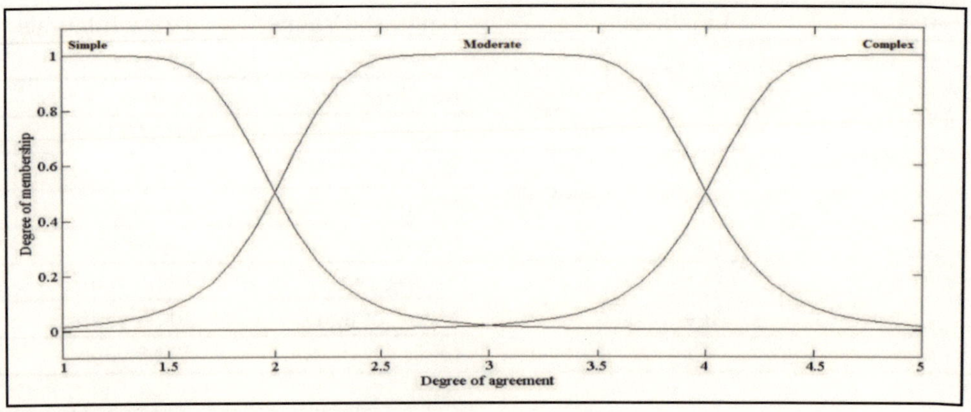

Fig. 4.11. (b) Membership functions of cognitive task type.

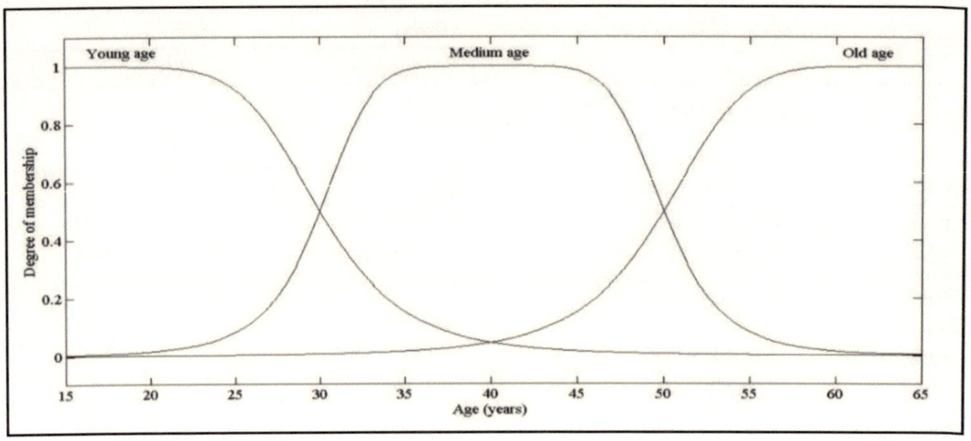

Fig. 4.11. (c) Membership functions of age group.

The membership functions are then aggregated using T-norm product to construct fuzzy IF-THEN rules that have a fuzzy antecedent part and constant consequent, The total number for rules is 27. Some of the rules are given below:

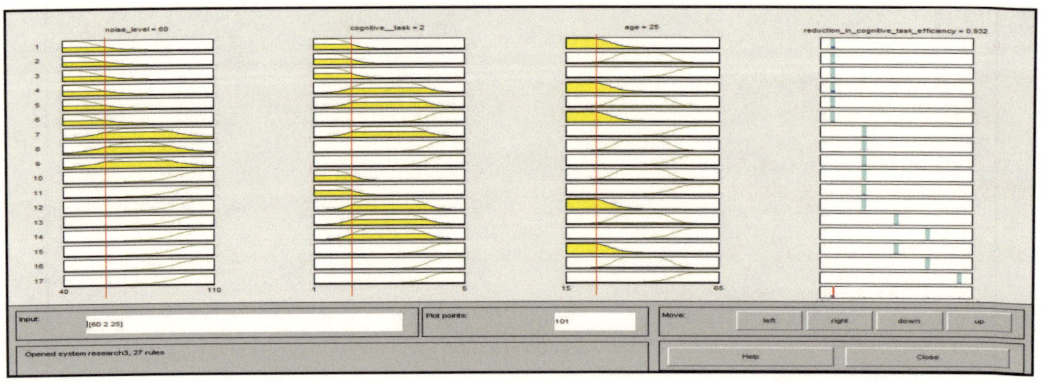

Fig. 4.12. Typical rules and their graphic representations in Sugeno approach.

R1, IF noise level is low AND cognitive task is simple AND age is young THEN reduction in cognitive task efficiency is approximately (none) 0%.

After constructions of fuzzy inference system, the model parameters are optimized using ANFIS. The network structure consists of 78 nodes. The total number of fitting parameters is 54, of which 27 are premise and 27 are consequent parameters. A hybrid learning rule is used to train the model according to input/output data pairs. The data pairs where obtained from questionnaire it was established for this purpose. We designed and developed our model based on conclusions of our studies [40, 41, and 42], out of the total 155 input/output data sets 124 (80%) data pairs were used for training the model. It was trained for 250 epochs with step size of 0.01 and error tolerance 0%. To validate the model 31 (20%) data sets were used testing purpose.

5. Result and discussion

The model was trained for 250 epochs and it was observed that the most of the learning was completed in the first 190 epochs as the root mean square error (RMSE) settles down to almost 0% at 190 th epoch. Figure 5.1(a) shows the training RMSE curve for the model after training the fuzzy inference system. It is found that the shape of membership functions is slightly modified.

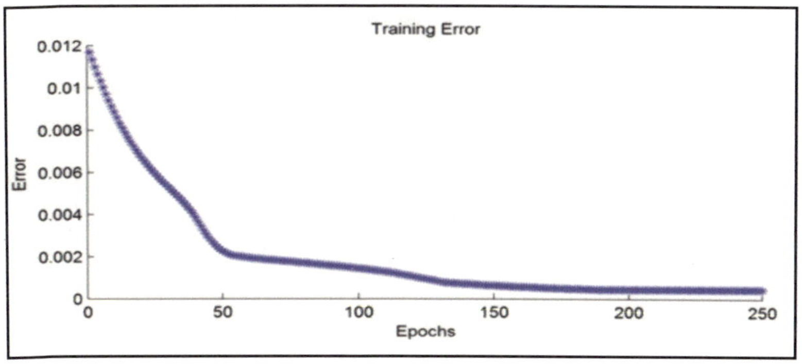

Fig. 5.1. (a) Training root means squared error.

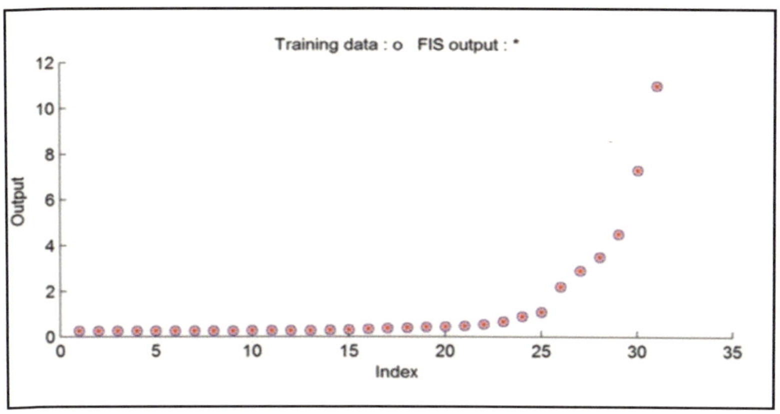

Fig. 5.1. (b) Data testing

This is because of the close agreement between the knowledge provided by the expert and input/output data pairs. While, Figure 5.1(b) shows data testing to check data validity. Hence, the impact of the noise level on cognitive human work efficiency is represented in the form of graphs in Figure 5.2, with the ages as parameters for different cognitive task type. The reduction in cognitive task efficiency up to the noise level of 75 dB (A) is almost negligible for all ages irrespective of cognitive task. Assuming effects of 25% reduction in cognitive work efficiency as low effect Figure 5.2(a) Show the reduction in cognitive task efficiency versus noise level with 'simple' cognitive task for 'young', 'medium', and 'old' ages. The cognitive work efficiency reduce to almost 29.6% at 90 dB (A) and above noise levels for 'old' ages but the 'young' and 'medium' age remain 'unaffected'.

It is to be observed from Figure 5.2(b) that the cognitive task efficiency is low (only 14.8%) at 85 dB (A) for 'young' age whereas for 'medium' and 'old' ages, the reduction in cognitive task efficiency is 26% and 45.9% respectively at the same noise levels for 'moderate' cognitive task . However the reduction in cognitive task efficiency is almost 21.5%, 38.9%, and 60.2% for 'young', 'medium' and 'old' ages, respectively at 90 dB (A) and above noise levels.

Figure 5.2(c) depicts the reduction in cognitive task efficiency with noise level at 'complex' cognitive task for 'young', 'medium', and 'old' ages. It is evident from this figure that the reduction in cognitive task efficiency is negligible up to the noise level of 80 dB (A) for 'young' age while it is about 26.4%, 34.1% for 'medium' and 'old' ages the cognitive task efficiency start reducing after 80 dB (A) even for 'young' and 'medium' ages. At 90 dB (A), cognitive task efficiency reduces to 36% , 56.7% and 75.1% for 'young', 'medium' and 'old' ages, respectively . There is significant reduction in cognitive task efficiency after 95 dB (A) for all ages. When noise level is in the interval of 100-105 dB (A), it is 45.6% for 'young', 68.3% for 'medium', and 91% for 'old' ages, respectively.

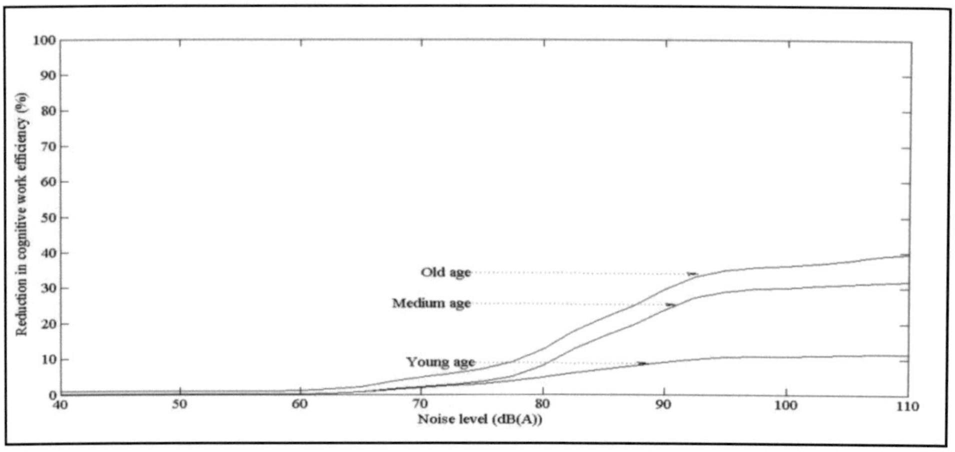

Fig. 5.2. (a) Reduction in cognitive task efficiency as a function of noise level at 'simple' cognitive task for various ages.

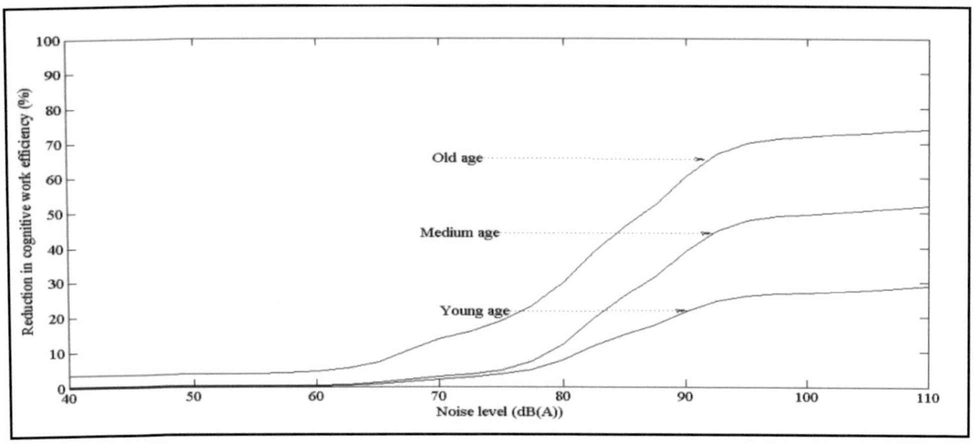

Fig. 5.2. (b) Reduction in cognitive task efficiency as a function of noise level at 'moderate' cognitive task for various ages.

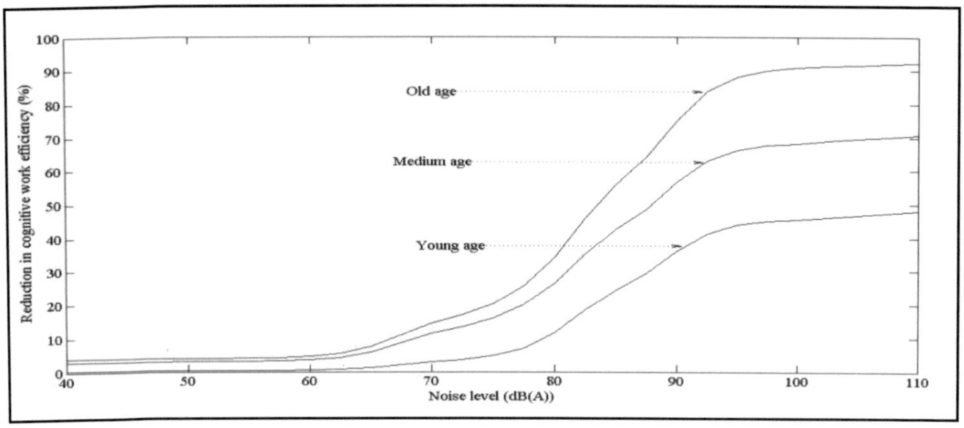

Fig. 5.2. (c) Reduction in cognitive task efficiency as a function of noise level at 'complex' cognitive task for various ages.

An alternative representation to Figure 5.2(a-c) discussed above is shown in Figure 5.3(a-c), in which the reduction in cognitive task efficiency with noise level for 'low', 'medium' and 'high' cognitive task at deferent ages is presented besides this following inference are readily down:

1. If age is 'young' as shown in Figure 5.3(a) the cognitive task efficiency reduces to 21.5% for 'moderate' and 36% for 'complex' cognitive tasks while it reduces 9.22% for 'simple' cognitive task at 90 dB (A) and above noise levels.
2. In case of 'medium' age, the cognitive task efficiency is reduced to 30.1%, 49.4%, and 68.3% at 100 dB (A) for 'simple', 'moderate' and 'complex' cognitive tasks, respectively as is evident from Figure 5.3(b).
3. For 'old' age, the reduction in cognitive task efficiency occurs even at much lower noise levels as can be observed from Figure 5.3(c). It is 36.2%, 71.9%, and 91% at 100 dB (A) for 'simple', 'moderate' and 'complex' cognitive tasks, respectively.

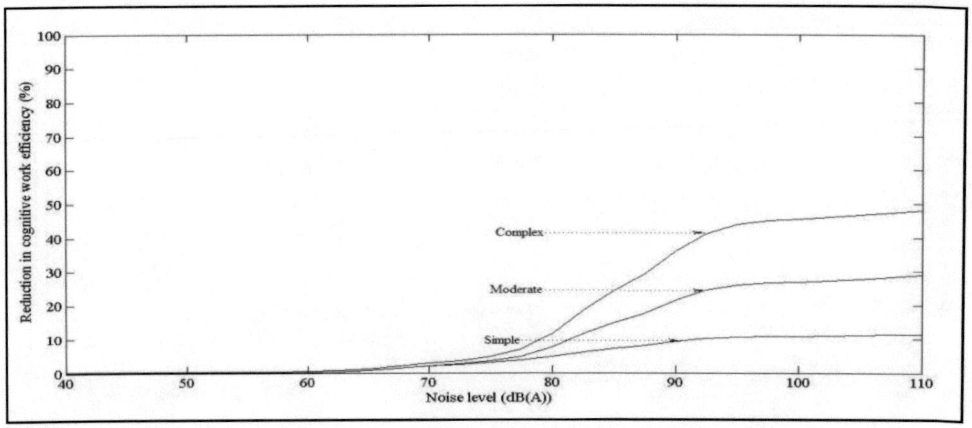

Fig. 5.3. (a) Reduction in cognitive task efficiency as a function of noise level for 'young' age for various cognitive tasks.

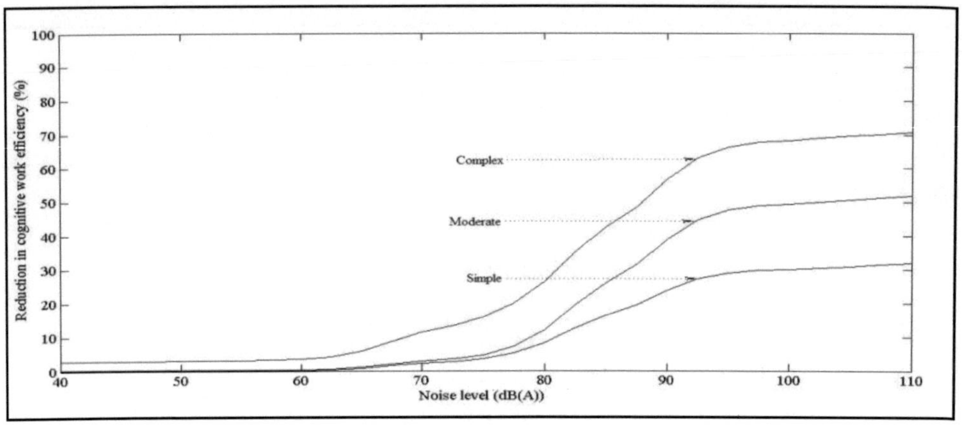

Fig. 5.3. (b) Reduction in cognitive task efficiency as a function of noise level for 'medium' age for various cognitive tasks.

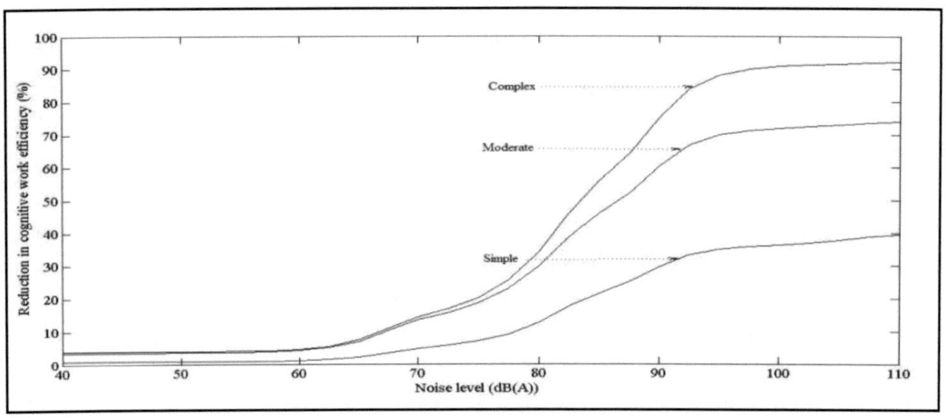

Fig. 5.3. (c) Reduction in cognitive task efficiency as a function of noise level for 'old' age for various cognitive tasks.

In order to observe the data behavior, we have compared some of our model results with deduction based on the criterion of Safe Exposure Limited recommended for industrial workers. The Recommended Exposure Limit (REL) for workers engaged in occupation such as engineering controls, administrative controls, and/or work practices is 85 dB (A) for 8 hr duration NIOSH (36), also recommended a ceiling limit of 115 dB(A). Exposures to noise levels greater than 115 dB (A) is not permitted regardless of the duration of the exposure time. There is almost no (0%) reduction in work efficiency when a person is exposed to the maximum permissible limit of 85 dB (A) for 8 hr and maximum (100%) reduction in work efficiency for a noise exposure of 105-115 dB (A) for 8 hr.

		NIOSH		OSHA	
S.No.	Noise levels dB(A)	Acoustic energy Dose(%)	Reduction in work efficiency(%)	model results	
				numerical value (%)	Fuzzy value
1	85	100	0	55.7	moderate
2	90	200	25	75.1	high
4	95	400	50	88.2	high
5	100	800	75	91	Very high
6	105	1600	100	91.6	Very high
7	110	3200	100	92.2	Very high
8	115	6400	100	92.2	Very high

Table 5.1. Data behavior comparison of the Results Based on Recommended Exposure Limit (REL) and the neural fuzzy model for moderate task.

6. Conclusion

The main thrust for the present work has been to develop a neuro-fuzzy model for the prediction of cognitive task efficiency as a function of noise level, cognitive task type and age. It is evident from the graph that the cognitive task efficiency, for the same cognitive task, depends to a large extent upon the noise level and age. It has also been verified that young age are slightly affected even at medium noise level while old ages get significantly affected at much lower noise level. It is to be appreciated that the training done using ANFIS is computationally very efficient as the desired RMSE value is obtained in very less number of epochs. Moreover, minor changes are observed in the shape of the membership functions after training the model. This is because of close agreement between the knowledge provided by expert and input/output data pairs.The present effort also establishes the usefulness of the fuzzy technique in studying the ergonomic environmental problems where the cause-effect relationships are inherently fuzzy in nature.

6.1 Scope for future research

1. The study may also be done by changing the input parameters such as: type of task, gender of the workers, environmental conditions (light, temperature, vibration, humidity) etc.
2. Data should collect from noisy environment for different ages for workers doing cognitive tasks, and the questionnaire form must be filled carefully to simulate high performance model.

3. The input & output variables range may also be converted into small ranges such as extremely low, very low, low, medium low, medium etc.
4. Input/output data must be categorized and scaled to set the optimum number and shape of membership functions, by increasing the probability (membership functions) model performance will be improved.
5. Workers subjected under high cognitive task must be working on low noise level environment to keep their performance.
6. This study proved the questionnaire studies it's easy to simulate and programming using neural-fuzzy model to give as approximately solution for several case steadies.
7. The problem of noise should be taken into consideration during their establishment phases (construction of the building, allocation of the machinery, etc.).
8. It's possible to modify the present model (FIS) to be a part of control system.

7. Appendix

7.1 Appendix-A

Department of labor occupational noise exposure standard

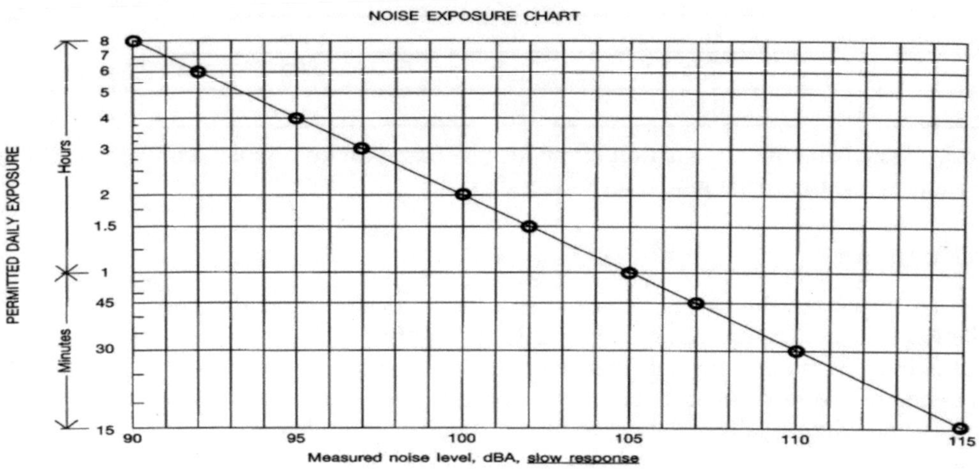

Fig. A.1. Permitted daily exposure time [30]

0	Duration per day (Hrs.)	Sound level dBA, slow response
1	8	90
2	6	92
3	4	95
4	3	97
5	2	100
6	1-1/2	102
7	1	105
8	½	110
9	1/4 or less	115

Table A.1. Permissible Noise Exposures

7.2 Appendix-B

1. Noise level	dB(A)				
2. age	years				
3. sex	M or F				
	STRONGLY DISAGREE	DISAGREE	NEUTRAL	AGREE	STRONGLY AGREE
4. Easy to learning new things	A	B	C	D	E
5. you like repetitive nature of work	A	B	C	D	E
6. You are creative thinking at work	A	B	C	D	E
7. Your skill is high	A	B	C	D	E
8. Care for time span of activities and development nature of job	A	B	C	D	E
9. Don't Have a lot of say on job	A	B	C	D	E
10. You are free to take own decision while working	A	B	C	D	E
11. You are not continual dependence on others	A	B	C	D	E
12. You are not affected by influence over organization change	A	B	C	D	E
13. You are not affected by influence of a policies of union	A	B	C	D	E
14. You are regular meeting of work team	A	B	C	D	E
15. Doesn't Supervising people at your job	A	B	C	D	E
16. You effected are not by influence over work team decision	A	B	C	D	E
17. Have a hard work	A	B	C	D	E
18. Don't Have a fast work	A	B	C	D	E

19.	Have excessive work	A	B	C	D	E
20.	Time is enough to finish your work	A	B	C	D	E
21.	There is conflicting demands on your job	A	B	C	D	E
22.	Have high emotional demands to work	A	B	C	D	E
23.	You are negotiation with others	A	B	C	D	E
24.	You suppressing genuine emotion	A	B	C	D	E
25.	Highly care for your job	A	B	C	D	E
26.	Your consultation is constant with others	A	B	C	D	E
27.	You don't have high responsibility to taking care for home	A	B	C	D	E
28.	You have high interference between family life and your job	A	B	C	D	E
29.	You get the concern and the help of your supervisor	A	B	C	D	E
30.	Have friendly and helpful coworkers	A	B	C	D	E
31.	Have organizational care about workers opinions	A	B	C	D	E
32.	You care about we-being	A	B	C	D	E
33.	Have high consideration of goals and values	A	B	C	D	E
34.	you concern about workers	A	B	C	D	E
35.	You need to collect accurate information to make decision	A	B	C	D	E
36.	You need providing opportunities to appeal the decision	A	B	C	D	E

37. You need generated standards to take consistent decision	A	B	C	D	E
38. Your work is steady	A	B	C	D	E
39. You are threat to job security	A	B	C	D	E
40. You are lay off recently	A	B	C	D	E
41. You have future lay off	A	B	C	D	E
42. You have valuable skills	A	B	C	D	E
43. Hard to keep job for long duration	A	B	C	D	E
44. Much physical effort is required	A	B	C	D	E
45. Have rapid physical activities	A	B	C	D	E
46. Have heavy loads at work	A	B	C	D	E
47. You feel awkward body position	A	B	C	D	E
48. You feel awkward upper body position	A	B	C	D	E
49. Sharing the hardship of the job	A	B	C	D	E
50 Have possibility to help the coworkers and a unity among workers	A	B	C	D	E
Feeling depressed	A	B	C	D	E
Sleep restless	A	B	C	D	E
Do not Enjoy life	A	B	C	D	E
Feel nervous while working	A	B	C	D	E
Exceptionally tired in the morning and exhausted mentally and physically at end of the day	A	B	C	D	E

Table B.1. Cognitive task (CT) questionnaire form for industrial applications [2]

8. References

[1] Rasmussen, J., 2000, Human factors in a dynamic information society: where are we heading? Ergonomics, vol. 43 (7), 869–879.

[2] Murata, K. , Kawakami, N. , and Amari, N. , 2000, Does job stress affect injury due to labor accident in Japanese male and female blue-collar workers?, Industrial Health, Vol. 38, 246-251.

[3] Genaidy, A., Karwowski, W., Shell, R.A., Khalil, S., Tuncel, S., Cronin, R., and Salem, O., 2005, Work compatibility, an integrated diagnostic tool for evaluating musculoskeletal responses to work and stress outcomes, International Journal of Industrial Ergonomics, vol. 35, 1109–1131.

[4] Genaidy, A.W., Karwowski, W., Salem, S., Jarrel, J., Paez, O., and Tuncel, S., 2007a, The work compatibility improvement framework: defining and measuring the human at-work system, Human Factors and Ergonomics in Manufacturing 17, vol.2, 1–64.

[5] John, K., Layer, Waldemar Karwowski , and Allen Furr, 2009 , The effect of cognitive demands and perceived quality of work life on human performance in manufacturing environments, International Journal of Industrial Ergonomics, vol. 39, 413–421.

[6] Parasuranam, R., and Giambra, L., 1990, Skill development in vigilance effects of event rate and age, Psychology and Ageing, vol. 6,155-169.

[7] Hale, S., 1990, A global developmental trend in cognitive processing speed, Child Development, vol. 61, 653-663.

[8] Madden, DJ. , 1992, Selective and visual Search: Revision of an allocation model and application to age differences. J Exp Psychol. Hum Percept Perform, vol.18 (3), 821-36.

[9] Carayon, P., and Smith, M.J., 2000, Work organization and ergonomics, Applied Ergonomics vol. 31 (6), 649-662.

[10] Boman, E., Enmarker, I., and Hygene, S., 2005, strength of noise effects on memory as a function of noise source and age, noise and health, vol. 15, 11-26.

[11] Suter, A., 1991, Noise and Its Effects, Administrative Conference of the United States, November.

[12] Evans, G.W., and Maxwell, L., 1997, Chronic noise exposure and reading deficits: the mediating effects of language acquisition, u.o.: Environment and Behaviour.

[13] Evans, GW., and Lepore, SJ., 1993, Nonauditory effects of noise on children: A critical review, Children's Environments, vol.10, 31-51.

[14] Smith, AW., 1998, The World Health Organization and the prevention of deafness and hearing impairment caused by noise, Noise and Health, vol.1(1),6-12.

[15] Berglund, B., Lindvall, T., Schwela, D., and Goh, KT., 1999, World Health Organization: Guidelines for Community Noise.

[16] Birgitta, Berglund, Thomas Lindvall, Dietrich, and Schwela. 1999, Extract from Guidelines for Community Noise: u.o.: World Health Organization.

[17] Stansfeld, S., Haines, M., and Brown, B., 2000, Noise and health in the urban environment, Rev Environ Health, vol.15, 43-82.

[18] WHO (2002). World Health Report: reducing risks, promoting healthy life. Geneva, World Health Organization.

[19] Harris, KC., Hangauer, D., and Henderson, D., 2005, Prevention of noise-induced hearing loss with Src-PTK inhibitors, Hear Res, vol. 208(1-2), 14-25.

[20] Lah, M. T., Zupancic, B., and Krainer, A., 2005, Fuzzy control for the illumination and temperature comfort in a test chamber, Building and Environment, vol. 40, 1626-1637.

[21] Zaheeruddin, and Jain, V.K., 2006, a fuzzy expert system for noise-induced sleep disturbance, Expert Systems with Applications, vol. 30, 761-771.

[22] Zaheeruddin, and Garima, 2006, a neuro-fuzzy approach for prediction of human work efficiency in noisy environment, Applied Soft Computing vol. 6, 283-294.

[23] Aluclu, I., Dalgic, A., and Toprak, Z.F., 2008, a fuzzy logic-based model for noise control at industrial workplaces, Applied Ergonomics, vol. 39, 368-378.

[24] Zaheeruddin, and Jain, V.K., 2008, An expert system for predicting the effects of speech interference due to noise pollution on humans using fuzzy approach, Expert Systems with Applications, vol. 35, 1978-1988.

[25] Mamdani, E. H., and Assilian, S., 1975, an experiment in linguistic synthesis with a fuzzy logic controller. International Journal of Man- Machine Studies, vol.7, 1-13.

[26] Ross, T.J., 2009, Fuzzy logic with engineering applications, John Wiley & sons inc., U.K.

[27] Nanthavanij, S., Boonyawat, T., and Wongwanthanee, S., 1999, Analytical procedure for constructing noise contours, International Journal of Industrial Ergonomics, vol. 23, 123-127.

[28] Kumar, G.V.P., Dewangan, K.N., sarkar, and kumari, A., 2008, occupation noise in rise mills, Noise & health journal, vol. 10, 55-67.

[29] NoiseAtWorkV1.31(http://www.softnoise.com)

[30] Occupational Safety and Health Administration (OSHA), 1989, Industrial hygiene field operation manual, Washington DC: US. Department of Labour, OSHA Instruction CPL 2.45B.

[31] Mitra, S., and Hayashi, Y., 2000, Neuro-fuzzy rule generation: survey in soft computing framework, IEEE Trans Neural Network, vol.11, 748-768.

[32] Kukolj, D., 2002, Design of adaptive Takagi-Sugeno-Kang fuzzy models, Applied Soft Computing, vol.2, 89-103.

[33] Sugeno, M., and Kang, G., 1988, Structure identification of fuzzy models, fuzzy sets system, vol.28, 15-33.

[34] Takagi, T., and Sugeno, M., 1985, Fuzzy identification of systems and its applications to modeling and control, IEEE Transactions on Systems, Man and Cybernetics, vol.15, 116-132.

[35] Klir, G., and Yuan, B., 1995, Fuzzy sets and fuzzy logic: theory and applications, Prentice Hall, NJ, Englewood Cliffs.

[36] National Institute for Occupational Safety and Health. DHEW (NIOSH). Criteria for a recommended standard: occupational noise exposure revised criteria 1996. (Online). Available from: http://www.nonoise. org/library/niosh/criteria.html. [Cited in 1996].

[37] Jang, J., 1993, ANFIS: adaptive-network based fuzzy. Inference system, IEEE Transactions on Systems, Man and Cybernetics, vol.23, 665-685.

[38] Zulquernain Mallick, Ahmed Hameed Kaleel and Arshad Noor Siddiqui,2009,An expert System for Predicting the Effects of Noise Pollution on Grass Trimming Task Using Fuzzy Modeling, International Journal of Applied Environmental Sciences ISSN 0973-6077 Vol. 4, Number 4,389-403.

[39] Fuzzy logic toolbox for use with MATLAB@, the math works Inc, USA, 2000.

[40] Hameed Kaleel Ahmed, Mallick Zulquernain, 2009, Expert system to predict effects of noise pollution on operators of power plant using neuro-fuzzy approach, Noise & Health An Inter-disciplinary International Journal, Vol.11 Issue 45 , 206-216.

[41] Ahmed Hameed Kaleel, Zulquernain Mallick , 2010, An expert System for Predicting Cognitive Performance in Reciprocating Pumps Industry Using Neuro-Fuzzy Approach, Proc. of the 3rd International Conference on Advances in Mechanical Engineering, January 4-6, 2010, S.V. National Institute of Technology, Surat -395 007, Gujarat, India, 647-651.

[42] Ahmed Hameed Kaleel, Abid Haleem and Zulquernain Mallick, 2009, Cognitive Task Assessment in steam Turbine Power Plant Station, All India Seminar Ergonomics for improved productivity EIP, 21-22 November, 10-15.

10

Fuzzy Inference System for Data Processing in Industrial Applications

Silvia Cateni and Valentina Colla
Scuola Superiore Sant'Anna, TeCIP Institute, PERCRO, Pisa
Italy

1. Introduction

In the last years Fuzzy Inference Systems (FIS) have been used in several industrial applications in the field of automatic control, data classification, decision analysis, expert systems, time series prediction, and pattern recognition.

The large use of FIS in the industrial field is mainly due to the nature of real data, that are often incomplete, noisy and inconsistent, and to the complexity of several processes, where the application of mathematical models can be impractical or even impossible, due to the lack of information on the mechanisms ruling the phenomena under consideration. Fuzzy theory is in fact essential and applicable to many complex systems and the linguistic formulation of its rule basis provides an optimal, very suitable and intuitive tool to formalise the relationships between input and output variables.

In real world database anomalous data (often called *outliers*) can be frequently found, which are due to several causes, such as erroneous measurements or anomalous process conditions. Outliers elimination is a necessary step, for instance, when building a training database for tuning a model of the process under consideration in standard operating conditions. On the other hand, in many applications, such as medical diagnosis, network intrusion or fraud detection, rare events are more interesting than the common samples. The rarity of certain patterns combined to their low separability from the rest of data makes difficult their identification. This is the case, for instance, of classification problems when the patterns are not equally distributed among the classes (the so-called *imbalanced dataset* (Vannucci et al., 2011)). In many real problems, such as document filtering and fraud detection, a binary classification problem must be faced, where the data belonging from the "most interesting" class are far less frequent than the data belonging to the second class, which corresponds to normal situations. The main problem with imbalanced dataset is that the standard learners are biased towards the common samples and tend to reduce the error rate without taking the data distribution into account.

In this chapter a preliminary brief review of traditional outlier detection techniques and classification algorithms suitable for imbalanced dataset is presented. Moreover some recent practical applications of FIS that are capable to outperform the widely adopted traditional methods for detection of rare data are presented and discussed.

2. Outlier detection

Outliers are measurements that are different from other values of the same dataset and can be due to measurement errors or to the variability of the phenomenon under consideration. Hawkins (Hawkins, 1980) defined an outlier as "*an observation that deviates so much from other observations as to arouse suspicion that it was generated by a different mechanism*".

The detection of outlier is an important step of data mining because it improves the quality of data and it represents a useful pre-processing phase in many applications, such as financial analysis, network intrusion detection and fraud detection (Hodge, 2004).

Classical outlier detection methods can be classified into four main groups: distance-based, density-based, clustering-based and statistical-based approaches. All these approaches have several advantages or limitations and in the last years a lot of contributions have been proposed on this subject. Artificial intelligence techniques have been widely applied to overcome the traditional methods and improve the cleanness of data; in particular some fuzzy logic-based approaches proved to outperform classical methodologies.

2.1 Distance-based methods

Distance-based method is based on the concept of the neighborhood of a sample and it was introduced by Knorr and Ng (Knorr & Ng, 1999). They gave the following definition: "*An object O in a dataset T is a DB(p,D)-outlier if at least fraction p of the objects in T lie at a distance greater than D from O*". The parameter p represents the minimum fraction of samples that is out of an outlier's D-neighborhood. This definition needs to fix a parameter and do not provide a degree of outlierness. Ramaswamy et al. (Ramaswamy et al., 2000) modified the definition of outlier: "*Outliers are the top n data points whose distance to the kth nearest neighbor is greatest*". Jimenez-Marquez et al. (Jimenez-Marquez et al., 2002) introduced the Mahalanobis Outlier Analysis (MOA) which uses Mahalnobis distance (Mahalanobis, 1936) as outlying degree of each point. Another outlier detection method based on Mahalanobis distance was proposed by Matsumoto et al. (Matsumoto et al., 2007). Mahalnobis distance is defined as the distance between each point and the center of mass. This approach considers outliers data points that are far away from their center of mass.

2.2 Density-based methods

Density-based methods calculate the density distribution of data and classify as outliers the points lying in low-density regions. Breunig et al. (Breunig et al., 2000) allocate a local outlier factor (LOF) to each point on the basis of the local density of its neighborhood. In order to understand the formula concerning the Local Outlier Factor is necessary introduce several definitions. The **k-distance** of a point x is the distance between two points x, y belonging to the dataset D such that for at least k points data $d(x,y')\leq d(x,y)$; where $y' \epsilon D\text{-}\{x\}$ and k an integer value. The **k distance neighborhood** of a data point x includes points whose distance from x is not greater than the *k distance*. Moreover the **reachability distance** of a data point x respect to the data point y is defined as the maximum between k-distance of y and distance between the two data points. The **Local reachability density** of the data point x is defined as the inverse of the mean reachability distance based on the *MinPts*-nearest neighbors of x. Finally the Local Outlier Factor is defined as the mean of the ratio of the local reachability density of x and the cardinality of the set including the *MinPts*-nearest neighbors of x. It is evident that *MinPts* is an important parameter of the proposed algorithm. Papadimitriou et al. (Papadimitriou et al., 2003) propose LOCI (Local Correlation Integral) which uses statistical values belonging to data to solve the problem of choosing values for *MinPts*.

2.3 Clustering-based methods

Clustering-based methods perform a preliminary clustering operation on the whole dataset and then classify as outliers the data which are not located in any cluster.

Fuzzy C-means algorithm (FCM) is a method of clustering developed by Dunn in 1973 (Dunn, 1973) and improved by Bezdek in 1981 (Bezdek, 1981). This approach is based on the notion of fuzzy c-partition introduced by Ruspini (Ruspini, 1969). Let us suppose $X=\{x_1, x_2, \dots x_n\}$ be a set of data where each *sample* x_h $(h=1, 2, \dots n)$ is a vector with dimensionality p. Let U_{cn} be a set of real $c \times n$ matrices where c is an integer value which can assume values between 2 and n. The fuzzy C-partition space for x is the following set:

$$M_{cn} = \{ U \in U_{cn};\ u_{ih} \in [0,1]\ ;\ \sum_{i=1}^{c} u_{ih} = 1,\ 0 < \sum_{h=1}^{n} u_{ih} < n \} \tag{1}$$

where u_{ih} is the degree of membership of x_n in cluster i $(1 \le i \le c)$. The objective of FCM approach is to provide an optimal fuzzy C-partition minimizing the following function:

$$J_m(U,V;X) = \sum_{h=1}^{n} \sum_{i=1}^{c} (u_{ih})^m \, \|x_k - v_i\|^2 \tag{2}$$

where $V=(v_1, v_2, \dots v_c)$ is a matrix of cluster centres, $\|.\|$ is the Euclidean norm and m is a weighting exponent $(m>1)$.

Many clustering-based outlier approaches have been recently developed. For instance, Jang et al. (Jang et al., 2001) proposed an outlier-finding process called OFP based on k-means algorithm. This approach considers small clusters as outliers. Yu et al. (Yu et al., 2002) proposed an outlier detection method called FindOut, which is based on removing of clusters from original data to identify outliers. Moreover He et al. (He et al., 2003) introduced the notion of cluster-based local outlier and outlier detection method (FindCBLOF), which exploits a cluster-based LOF in order to identify the outlierness of each sample. Finally Jang et al. (Jang et al., 2005) proposed a novel method in order to improve the efficiency of FindCBLOF approach.

2.4 Statistical-based methods

Statistical-based methods use standard distribution to fit the initial dataset. Outliers are defined considering the probability distribution and assuming that the data distribution is a priori known. The main limit of this approach lies in the fact that, for many applications, the prior knowledge is not always distinguishable and the cost for fitting data with standard distribution could be considerable. A widely used method belonging to distribution-based approaches has been proposed by Grubbs (Grubbs, 1969). This test is efficient if data can be approximated by a Gaussian distribution. The Grubbs test calculates the following statistics:

$$G_i = \frac{max_i\,(x_i - \mu)}{\sigma} \tag{3}$$

where μ is the mean value and σ the standard deviation of data. When G is greater than a fixed threshold the i-th data-point is classified as an outlier. The critical value depends on the required significance level of test; common values are 1% and 5%. Other similar tests that assume that data are normally distributed are Rosner's test (Gibbons, 1994) and Dixon's test (Dixon, 1993).

2.5 Fuzzy Inference System based method

In the last years novel interesting FIS-based outlier detection approaches have been proposed in order to outperform the classical approaches.

Yousri et al. (Yousri et al., 2007) proposes an approach which combine an outlier detection method with a clustering algorithm. The outlier detection method is used for two objectives: to give a hard membership for outliers to decide if the considered pattern is an outlier or not and to give a degree of outlierness. A clustering algorithm is then used to allocate patterns to clusters. Let P indicate the dataset and p its generic sample and let To be the outlier detection technique and Tc the adopted clustering algorithm. The combination of outlier detection and clustering algorithms is provided by the following formula, providing the degree of outlierness of a sample p:

$$O_p = \frac{w_o O_{To}(p) + w_c O_{Tc}(p)}{w_o + w_c} \tag{4}$$

where $O_{To}(p)$ is the degree of outlierness resulting from To for each sample p while $O_{Tc}(p)$ is the degree of outlierness resulting from Tc considering an outlier the patterns allocated to tiny clusters or not assigned to any cluster. Finally w_o and w_c represent the weights given to both algorithms to determine outliers. The two weights must be not negative ($w_o, w_c \geq 0$) and their sum must be positive ($w_o+w_c > 0$). Equation (4) can be rewritten as follows:

$$O_p = \frac{\frac{w_o}{w_c} O_{To}(p) + O_{Tc}(p)}{\frac{w_o}{w_c} + 1} \tag{5}$$

The parameter w_o/w_c should be accurately fixed considering a balance between the membership degree given to the outlier cluster and the clusters in the set of initial groups.

The main advantage of this approach is that it is general, i.e. it can combine any outlier detection method with any clustering algorithm, and it is effective with low and high dimensional dataset.

Another novel fuzzy approach is proposed by Xue et al. (Xue et al., 2010). The approach is called *Fuzzy Rough Semi-Supervised Outlier Detection* (FRSSOD) and combines two methods: the *Semi-Supervised Outlier Detection method* (SSOD) (Gao et al., 2006) and the clustering method called *Fuzzy Rough C-Means clustering* (FRCM) (Hu & Yu, 2005). The aim of this approach is to establish if samples on the boundary are outliers or not, by exploiting the advantages of both approaches. In order to understand FRSSOD a brief description of SSOD and FRCM is necessary.

SSOD is a semi-supervised outlier detection method (Li et al. 2007; Zhang et al. 2005; Gao et al., 2006; Xu & Liu, 2009) main that uses both unlabeled and labelled samples in order to improve the accuracy without the need for a high amount of data. Let us suppose that X is the dataset with n samples forming K clusters. The first l samples are labelled as binary values: the null samples are considered outliers while the unitary value are not outliers. If we consider that outliers are not included in any of the K clusters, an $n \times K$ matrix must be found whose elements t_{ih} ($i=1,2 \ldots ,n$; $h=1, 2, \ldots, K$) are unitary when x_i belongs to cluster C_h. Outliers are determined as points that do not belong to any clusters through the minimization of the following objective function:

$$Q = \sum_{i=1}^{n} \sum_{h=1}^{K} t_{ih} \; dist\,(c_h \,, x_i)^2 \; + \; \gamma_1 (n - \sum_{i=1}^{n} \sum_{h=1}^{K} t_{ih}) \; + \; \gamma_2 \sum_{i=1}^{l} \left| u_i - \sum_{h=1}^{K} t_{ih} \right| \quad (6)$$

where c_h represent the centroid of cluster C_h, $dist$ is the Euclidean distant and γ_1, γ_2 are adjusting parameters. The objective function is the sum of three parts. The first part come from k-means clustering and outliers are not considered, the second part is used to constrain the number of outliers below a certain threshold and finally the third part is used to maintain consistency of labelling introduced by authors with existing label.

FRCM is a combination between Fuzzy C-means algorithm and Rough C-means approach. Fuzzy C-means method was introduced by Dunn (Dunn, 1974) and it is an unsupervised clustering algorithm. The approach assigns a membership degree to each sample for each cluster by minimizing the following objective function:

$$J_m \,(U, V;\, X) = \sum_{k=1}^{n} \sum_{i=1}^{c} u_{ik}^{m} \, \|x_k - v_i\|^2 \quad (7)$$

where $V = (v_1, v_2, \ldots, v_c)$ is the vector representing the centres of the clusters, u_{ik} is the degree of membership of the sample x_k to the cluster i. The iteration stops when a stable condition is reached and the sample is allocated to the cluster for which the membership value is maximum. The centres initialization is an important step affecting the final result.

The RCM approach is based on the concept of C-means clustering and on the concept of rough set. Rough set was introduced by Pawlak (Pawlak, 1982; Pawlak, 1991). In the rough set concept each observation of the universe has a specified amount of information. The objects which have the same information are indistinguishable. A rough set, unlike a precise set, is characterized by lower approximation, upper approximation and boundary region. The lower approximation includes all objects belonging to the considered notion, while the upper approximation contains objects which possibly belong to the notion. The boundary region represents the difference between the two regions. In RCM method each cluster is considered as a rough set having the three regions. A sample, unlike in the classical clustering algorithm, can be member of more than one cluster. Also, it is possible to have overlaps between clustering. Lingras and West (Lingras & West, 2004) proposed a method based on the following four properties:

- A sample can belong only to one of lower approximation regions.
- The lower approximation region of a cluster must be a subset of its upper approximation region.
- If a sample do not belong to any lower approximation regions then it is member of at least two upper approximation regions.
- Samples belonging to boundary region are undecided data and are assigned to two or more upper approximation regions.

FRCM integrates the concept of rough set with the fuzzy set theory adding a fuzzy membership value of each point to the lower approximation and boundary region of a cluster. The approach divides data into two sets, a *lower approximation region* and a *boundary region*; then the points belonging to the boundary region are fuzzified. Let us suppose that $X=\{x_1, x_2, ..., x_n\}$ is the available dataset and $\underline{C_h}$ and $\overline{C_h}$ are respectively the lower and upper approximation of the cluster h. The boundary region is calculated as the difference between the two regions. If $u=\{u_{ih}\}$ are memberships of clusters the problem of FRCM become the optimization of the following function:

$$J_m(u,v) = \sum_{i=1}^{n}\sum_{h=1}^{H}(u_{ih})^m d_{ih}^2 \tag{8}$$

FRSSOD combines the two methods above described, i.e. FRCM and SSOD, in order to create a novel approach. Let X be the set of data with n samples and Y its subset formed by the first $l<n$ samples. The elements of Y are labelled as $y_i = \{1, 0\}$ where null value indicates that the considered point is an outlier. The normal points, i.e. points that are not considered outliers, form C clusters and each point normal point belong to each cluster with a membership value, while outliers do not belong to any cluster. The main aim of FRSSOD is to create a $n\times c$ matrix called u, whose generic entry u_{ik} represents the fuzzy membership degree of the i_{th} sample on the cluster. The optimization problem consists in the minimization of the following function:

$$J_m(u,v) = \sum_{i=1}^{n}\sum_{k=1}^{C}(u_{ik})^m d_{ik}^2 + \gamma_1\Big(n - \sum_{i=1}^{n}\big(\sum_{k=1}^{C}u_{ik}\big)^m\Big) + \gamma_2\sum_{i=1}^{l}\Big(y_i - \sum_{k=1}^{C}u_{ik}\Big)^2 \tag{9}$$

where γ_1 e γ_2 are adjusting positive parameters in order to make the three terms compete with each other and m is a fuzziness weighting exponent ($m>1$). As the idea of SSOD approach only normal points are divided in two clusters and also the points considered as outliers don't compare in the first term of the equation. Then the second term of the equation is used to maintain the number of outliers under a certain limit and finally the third term maintains consistency of user labelling with existing label punishing also the mislabelled samples. The proposed method is applied on a synthetic dataset and on real data and results show that FRSSOD can be used in many fields having fuzzy information granulation. The experimental results show also that the proposed method has many advantages over SSOD improving outlier detection accuracy and reducing false alarm rate thanks to the control on labelled samples. The main disadvantages of the FRSSOD method are that the result depends on the determination of number of cluster, initialization of the centres of clusters and adjustment parameters.

Another fuzzy based method to detect outliers is proposed by Cateni et al. (Cateni et al., 2009). The proposed approach combines different classical outlier detection techniques in order to overcome their limitations and to use their advantages. An important advantage of the proposed method lies in the fact that the system is automatic and no a priori assumptions are required. The method consists in calculating four features for each pattern by using the most popular outlier detection techniques:

1. **Distance-based.** The Mahalanobis distance is calculated and normalized with respect to its maximum value. Patterns which assume value near 1 are considered outliers.

2. **Clustering-based**. The clustering algorithm used for each method is the fuzzy C-means (FCM) that has already been described. The output of the clustering represents the membership degree of the selected samples to clusters and it lies in the range [0,1]. Samples for which such features is close to 0 have to be considered outliers. The FCM approach requires the number of clusters to be a priori known. If the distribution is unknown, it is not easy to find the optimal number of clusters. In this approach a validity measure based on intra-cluster and inter-cluster distance measures (Ray & Turi, 1999) is calculated in order to determine automatically the most suitable number of clusters. This step is fundamental because the result of clustering strongly depends on this parameter.
3. **Density-based.** For each pattern the Local Outlier Factor (LOF) is evaluated. This feature requires that the number of the samples of nearest neighbours K must be known a-priori. Here K corresponds to the number of elements in the less populated cluster that has been previously calculated by the Fuzzy C Means algorithm. The LOF parameter lies in the range [0;1] where the unitary value means that the considered sample is an outlier.
4. **Distribution-based.** The Grubbs test is performed and the result is a binary value: an unitary value indicates that the selected pattern is an outlier, is null otherwise.

This four features are fed as inputs to a FIS of the Mandani type (Mandani, 1974). The output of the system, called *outlier index*, represents the degree of outlierness of each pattern. Finally a threshold, set to 0.6, is used to point out the outliers.

The proposed method has been tested in a dataset provided by a steelmaking industry in the pre-processing phase. The extracted data represent the chemical analysis and process variables associated to the liquid steel fabrication. A dataset has been analyzed in order to find factors that affect the final steel quality. In this case outliers can be caused by sensor failures, human error during registration of data of off-line analysis or abnormal conditions; this kind of outliers are the most difficult to discover because they do not differ so much from some correct data. In the considered problem the variables which are mostly affected by outliers are tapping temperature, reheating temperature and the addition of aluminium. First of all each variable has been normalised in order to obtain values in the range [0,1]. Table 1 illustrates the results that have been obtained on 1000 measurements through 6 different approaches: a distance-based approach, a clustering-based approach a density-based approach, a distribution-based approach and two fuzzy-based approaches. The effective outliers are five and they have been pointed out by technical skilled personnel working on the plant and in the table are identified with alphabetic letters in order to understand how many and which outliers are correctly detected by several methods. In the second row the outliers are shown that are present for each considered variable and the other columns refer to outliers detected by each considered method. Finally, table 2 illustrates how many samples have been misclassified as outliers (the so-called *false alarms*) for each method.

Table 2 shows that fuzzy-base approach is able to detect all outliers present in the dataset without fall in false alarms errors. Therefore the obtained results confirm the effectiveness of the fuzzy-based approaches because they outperform traditional techniques and in particular the second fuzzy proposed approach (Cateni et al., 2009) obtains the best results.

	Tapping Temperature	Reheating Temperature	Aluminium addition
OUTLIERS	A -B - C	A - B - C	A - B - C - D –E
Mahalanobis distance	B	B	A - D – E
Fuzzy C-means	A – B	A - B	B – C
Local Outlier Factor	B	B	A - B - C – E
Grubbs Test	A	A	B - D – E
Fuzzy 1 (Yousri et al.,2007)	A – B	A - B	A - B - C – E
Fuzzy 2 (Cateni et al., 2009)	A - B –C	A - B -C	A - B - C - D –E

Table 1. Outlier Detection.

	Tapping Temperature	Reheating Temperature	Aluminium addition
OUTLIERS	A -B - C	A - B - C	A - B - C - D –E
Mahalanobis distance	0	0	1
Fuzzy C-means	0	0	1
Local Outlier Factor	1	0	0
Grubbs Test	0	0	2
Fuzzy 1 (Yousri et al.,2007)	0	0	0
Fuzzy 2 (Cateni et al., 2009)	0	0	0

Table 2. Number of false alarms.

3. Imbalanced datasets

In a classification task often there are more instances of a class than others. Class imbalance is mainly connected to the concept of *rarity.* There are two types of rarity, *rare cases* or *outliers* (as seen in the previous paragraph) and *rare class* where a class of interest includes few samples in comparison to the other classes present in the dataset. Outliers and rare classes are not related but there are empirical studies which demonstrate that the minority class contains more outliers than the majority class (Weiss and Provost, 2003). Imbalanced datasets are present in many real-world applications such as detecting cancerous cell (Chan and Stolfo, 1998), fraud detection (Phua et al., 2004), keyword extraction (Turney, 2000), oil-spill detection (Kubat et al., 1998), direct marketing (Ling and Li, 1998), and so on. Many approaches have been proposed in order to solve the imbalance problem (Visa and Ralescu, 2005) and they include resampling the training set, feature selection (Castillo and Serrano, 2004), one class learners (Raskutti and Kowalczyk, 2004) and finally cost-sensitive learners, that take into account the misclassification cost (Zadrozny et al., 2003). In this kind of data one class is significantly larger than other classes and often the targeted class (known as *positive* class) is the smallest one. In this cases classification is difficult because the conventional computational intelligence methods tend to classify all instances to the majority class (Hong et al., 2007). Moreover this methods (such as Multilayer Perceptron, Radial Basis Functions, Linear Discriminant Analysis...) cannot classify imbalanced dataset because they learn data based on minimization of accuracy without taking into account the error cost of classes (Visa & Ralescu, 2005; Alejo et al., 2006; Xie & Qiu, 2007).

The performance of machine learning is typically calculated by a confusion matrix. An example of the confusion matrix is illustrated in Tab.3 where columns represent the predicted class while the rows the actual class. Most of studies in imbalanced domain are referred to binary classification, as a multi-class problem can be simplified to a two-class problem. Conventionally the class label of the minority class is positive while the class label of the majority class is negative. In the table True Negative value (*TN*) represents the number of negative samples correctly classified, True Positive (*TP*) value is the number of positive samples correctly classified, False Positive (*FP*) is the number of negative samples classified as positive and finally the False Negative (*FN*) is the number of positive samples classified as negative. Other common evaluation measures are *Precision* (Prec) which is a measure of the accuracy providing that a specific class has been predicted and *Recall* (Rec) which is a measure of a prediction model to select instances of a certain class from a data set. In this case, Recall is also referred to as true positive rate and true negative rate is also called *Specificity* (Spec).

	Predicted Negative	Predicted Positive
Negative	TN	FP
Positive	FN	TP

Table 3. Confusion Matrix

Through this matrix the following widely adopted evaluation metrics can be calculated:

$$Accuracy = (TP+TN)/(TP+FN+FP+TN) \quad (10)$$

$$FP\ rate = Spec = FP/(TN+FP) \quad (11)$$

$$TP\ rate = Rec = TP/(TP+FN) \quad (12)$$

$$Prec = TP/(TP+FP) \quad (13)$$

$$F\text{ - }Measures = [(1+\beta^2)*Rec*Prec]/[(\beta^2*Prec)+Prec] \quad (14)$$

where β corresponds to the relative importance of *Precision* versus *Recall*. Typically $\beta=1$ when false alarms (false positive) and misses (false negative) can be considered equally costly.

3.1 Traditional approaches

In general approaches for imbalanced dataset can be divided in two categories: *external* and *internal* approaches. The external methods do not depend on the learning algorithm to be used: they mainly consist in a pre-processing phase aiming at balancing classes before training classifiers. Different re-sampling methods fall into this category. In contrast internal method develops variations of the learning algorithm in order to solve the imbalance problem.

3.1.1 External methods

Re-sampling strategies have several advantages. First of all re-sampling methods are competitive (McCharty, 2005) and often similar (Maloof, 2003) to the results obtained choosing the cost-sensitive learning. Moreover re-sampling methods are simple and do not require to modify the internal working of the classifier chosen (Elkan, 2001). Re-sampling methods are pre-processing techniques and they can be divided in two categories: oversampling techniques and undersampling techniques. Oversampling methods balance the classes by adding new points to the minority class while undersampling methods increase the number of samples belonging to the minority class.

The simplest re-sampling techniques are the random oversampling method and the random undersampling methods. The random oversampling method balances the distribution classes by randomly replicating some instances belonging to the minority class but random oversampling can lead to overfitting. The random undersampling technique randomly removes negative examples from the majority class encountering the problem to deleting some important information of the dataset. Both random techniques sample the dataset until the classes are approximately balanced. In order to solve the cited limitations improved re-sampling techniques have been proposed.

3.1.1.1 Oversampling techniques

Synthetic Minority Oversampling TEcnique (SMOTE) creates minority samples to over-sample the minority class avoiding the overfitting problem (Chawla et al., 2002). Instead of replicating existing data points SMOTE generates new samples as follow: for every minority example, its n nearest neighbours belonging to the same class are evaluated (in SMOTE n is set to 5); then new synthetic data points are randomly generated along the segment joining the original data point and its selected neighbour. Figure 1 shows an example concerning SMOTE algorithm: x represents the selected data point, n_i are the selected nearest neighbours and s_1, s_2 and s_3 are samples generated by the randomized interpolation.

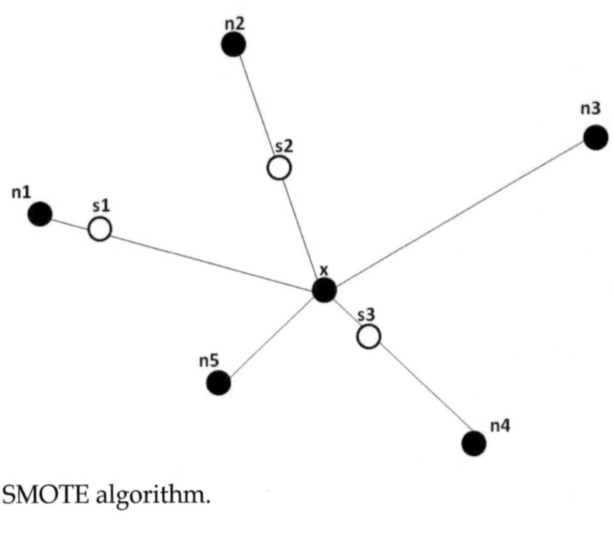

Fig. 1. Example of SMOTE algorithm.

As SMOTE over-generalizes the minority class but does not take into account the distribution of neighbours from the majority class another novel approach, called Borderline-SMOTE (Han et al., 2005), is proposed. This approach is a generalization of SMOTE approach, it focuses the attention on oversampling around samples located in the borderline between classes. This approach is based on the assumption that the positive instances are divided into three regions: *noise, borderline* and *safe* by considering the number of negative examples on k nearest neighbours. If n is the number of negative examples among the k nearest neighbours, the regions are defined as follow:

- Noise: $n=k$
- Borderline: $0.5k \leq n \leq k$
- Safe: $0 \leq n \leq 0.5k$

Borderline-SMOTE exploits the same oversampling technique as SMOTE but it oversamples only the instances belonging to the borderline region.

Bunkhumpornpat et al. proposed another approach called Safe-Level-SMOTE (Bunkhumpornpat et al., 2009). This method assigns for each positive data-points a *safe-level (sf)* which is defined as the number of positive data-points in the k nearest neighbours. If the safe level of an instance is close to k, then it considered safe. The safe level ratio is defined as the ratio between the safe level of a positive instance and the safe level of a nearest neighbours. Also each synthetic new point is generated in safe region by considering the safe level ratio of instances. This method is able to outperform both SMOTE and Borderline-SMOTE because they may generate instances in unsuitable positions such as overlapping or noise regions.

Wang et al. (Wang et al., 2006) propose a novel approach that improves the SMOTE algorithm by including the Locally Linear Embedding (LLE) algorithm (Sam & Lawrence, 2000). The SMOTE approach has an important limitation: it assumes that the local space between any positive samples is positive, i.e. belonging to the minority class. This fact could be not true if the training data is not linearly separable. This method maps the training data into a lower dimensional space through the Locally Linear Embedding technique, then SMOTE is applied in order to create the desirable number of synthetic data points and finally the new data points are mapped back to the initial input space. The so-called LLE-based SMOTE algorithm is evaluated on three datasets applying three different classifiers: Naive Bayesian, K-NN classifier and Support Vector Machine (SVM). Experimental results show that the LLE-based SMOTE algorithm outperforms the conventional SMOTE.

Liu and Ghosh (Liu & Ghosh, 2007) propose a novel oversampling method, called generative oversampling, which increases information to the training set by creating artificial minority class points on the basis of the probability distribution to model the minority class. Also, generative oversampling can be used if the data distribution can be approximated with an existing model. Firstly a probability distribution is chosen in order to model the minority class, then parameters for the probability distribution are studied on the basis of the training data and finally synthetic data points are created from the learned probability distribution until the necessary number of points belonging to the minority class has been reached. Authors demonstrate that this approach works well for a range of text classification datasets using as classifier a SVM classifier. This method is simple to develop and it is suitable for several data types by selecting appropriate generative models.

3.1.1.2 Undersampling techniques

A popular undersampling method is the Condensed Nearest Neighbour (CNN) rule (Hart, 1968). CNN is used in order to find a consistent subset of samples. A subset $\hat{S}$ is defined consistent with S if, using a one nearest neighbour, $\hat{S}$ correctly classifies the instances in S. Fawcett and Provost (Fawcet and provost, 1997) propose an algorithm to extract a subset $\hat{S}$ from S and using the approach as an undersampling method. Firstly one example belonging to the majority class is randomly extracted and put with all examples belonging to the minority class in $\hat{S}$. Then a 1-NN over the examples in $\hat{S}$ is used in order to classify the examples belonging to S. If an example in S is misclassified, it is moved to $\hat{S}$. The main aim of this method is to delete the examples belonging to the majority class which are distant from the decision border.

Another undersampling approach is the so-called *Tomek links* (Tomek, 1976). This method can be defined as follow: let us suppose that x_i and x_j are two examples belonging to different classes and $d(x_i, x_j)$ is their distance. A pair (x_i, x_j) is called a Tomek link if there is not an example x_k such that $d(x_i, x_l)< d(x_i, x_j)$ or $d(x_j, x_l)< d(x_i, x_j)$. If two examples are a Tomek link then either one of these is noise or both are borderline. If Tomek Link is used as underline sampling, only samples belonging to the majority class are removed. Kubat and Matwin (Kubat & Matwin, 1997) propose a method, called One-Side Selection (OSS) which uses both Tomek Link and CNN. Tomek Link is used as undersampling technique removing noisy and borderline samples belonging to the majority class. Borderline samples are considered as *unsafe* since noise can make them fall on the wrong side of the decision border. CNN is used to delete samples belonging to the majority class which are distant from the decision border. The remainder samples including *safe* samples of majority class and all samples belonging to the minority class, are used for learning.

3.1.2 Internal methods

Internal methods deal with variations of a learning algorithm in order to make it less sensitive for the class imbalance.

Two common methods Boosting and Cost-Sensitive learning are used in this area.

Boosting is a method used to improve the accuracy of weak classifiers. The most famous boosting algorithm is the so-called AdaBoost (Freund & Schapire, 1997). It is based on the fusion of a set of weak learners, i.e. classifiers which have better performance than random classifiers in a classification task. During the learning phase weak learners are trained and included in the strong learner. The contribution of the added learners is weighted on the basis of their performance. At the end all modified learners contribute to classify unlabelled samples. This approach is suitable to deal with imbalanced dataset because the samples, belonging to the minority class, are most likely to be misclassified and also have higher weights during iterations. In literature several approaches using boosting techniques for imbalanced dataset has been proposed (Guo & Viktor, 2004; Leskovec & Shawe-Taylor, 2003) and results confirm the effectiveness of the method.

Another effective approach is the cost-sensitive learning. In this approach cost is associated with misclassifying samples; the cost matrix is a numerical representation of the penalty of classifying samples from a class to another. A correct classification has not penalty and the cost of misclassifying minority examples is higher than the cost of misclassifying the majority examples. The aim of this approach is to minimize the overall cost on the training dataset. The cost matrix can balance the dataset by assigning the cost misclassifying a class with inverse proportion to its frequency. Another way is to set the cost matrix by considering the application driven criteria taking into account user requirements. Cost matrix is a general notion which can be exploited within common classifiers such as decision tree (Pazzali et al., 2004; Chawla, 2003) or neural networks (De Rouin et al., 1991).

Soler and Prim (Soler & Prim, 2007) propose a method based on the Rectangular Basis Function network (RecBF) in order to solve the imbalance problem. RecBF networks have been introduced by Berthold and Huber (Berthold & Huber, 1995) and are a particular type of Radial Basis Function (RBF) networks which exploit neurons with hyper-rectangular activation function in the hidden layer.

3.2 Fuzzy based approaches

In classification task with imbalanced dataset SVMs are widely used (Baser et al., 1992). In (Akbani et al., 2004; Japkowicz & Shayu, 2002) the capabilities of SVM and their effect on imbalance have been widely discussed. SVM is a widely used machine learning method which has been applied to many real world problems providing satisfactory results. SVM works effectively with balanced dataset but provides suboptimal classification models considering the imbalanced dataset; several examples demonstrate this conclusion (Veropoulus et al., 1999; Akbani et al., 2004; Wu & Chang, 2003; Wu & Chang, 2005; Raskutti & Kowalczyk, 2004; Imam et al., 2006; Zou et al., 2008; Lin et al., 2009; Kang & Cho, 2006; Liu et al., 2006; Haibo & Garcia, 2009). SVM is biased toward the majority class and provides poor results concerning the minority class.

A limit of the SVM approach is that it is sensitive to outliers and noise by considering all the training samples uniformly. In order to overcome this problem a Fuzzy SVM (FSVM) has been proposed (Lin & Wang, 2002) which is a variant of the traditional SVM algorithm. FSVM associates different fuzzy membership values (called weights) for different training samples in order to assign their importance degree of its class. Subsequently the proposed approach includes these weights inner the SVM learning algorithm in order to reduce the effect of outliers or noise when finding the separating hyperplane.

An extension of this approach is due to Wang et al. (Wang et al.,2005). They introduced two membership values for each training sample defining the membership degree of positive and negative classes. This approach has been proposed again by Hao et al. (Hao et al., 2007) based on the notion of *vague set*.

Spyrou et al. (Spyrou et al., 2005) propose another kind of fuzzy SVM approach which uses a particular kernel function built from fuzzy basis functions. There are also other works which combine fuzzy theory with SVM assigning a membership value to the outputs of the algorithm. For example Xie et al. (Xie et al., 2005) define a membership degree for the output class through the decision value generated by SVM algorithm, while Inoue and Abe (Inoue & Abe, 2001) use the fuzzy output decision for multiclass classification. Finally Mill and Inoue (Mill & Inoue, 2003) propose an approach which generates the fuzzy membership values for the output classes through the strengths support vectors.

Another typology of FSVM regards the extraction of fuzzy rules from the trained SVM model and a lot of works were been proposed (Chiang & Hao, 2004; Chen & Wang, 2003; Chaves et al., 2005; Castro et al., 2007).

The above approaches demonstrate that FSVM outperforms the traditional SVM algorithm avoiding the frequent problem of outliers and noise. However the FSVM technique, such as the SVM method, can be sensitive to the class imbalance problem. Batuwita and Palade (Batuwita & Palade, 2010) propose a novel method which uses the FSVM for class imbalance leraning (CIL). This approach, that is called FSVM-CIL, is able to classify with a satisfactory accuracy solving both the problems of class imbalance and outlier/noise. FSVM-CIL is been improved by Lakshmanan et al. (Lashmanan et al., 2011) extending the approach to multi-class classification problem instead of binary classification.

The general implementation scheme of the proposed approach is represented in figure 2.

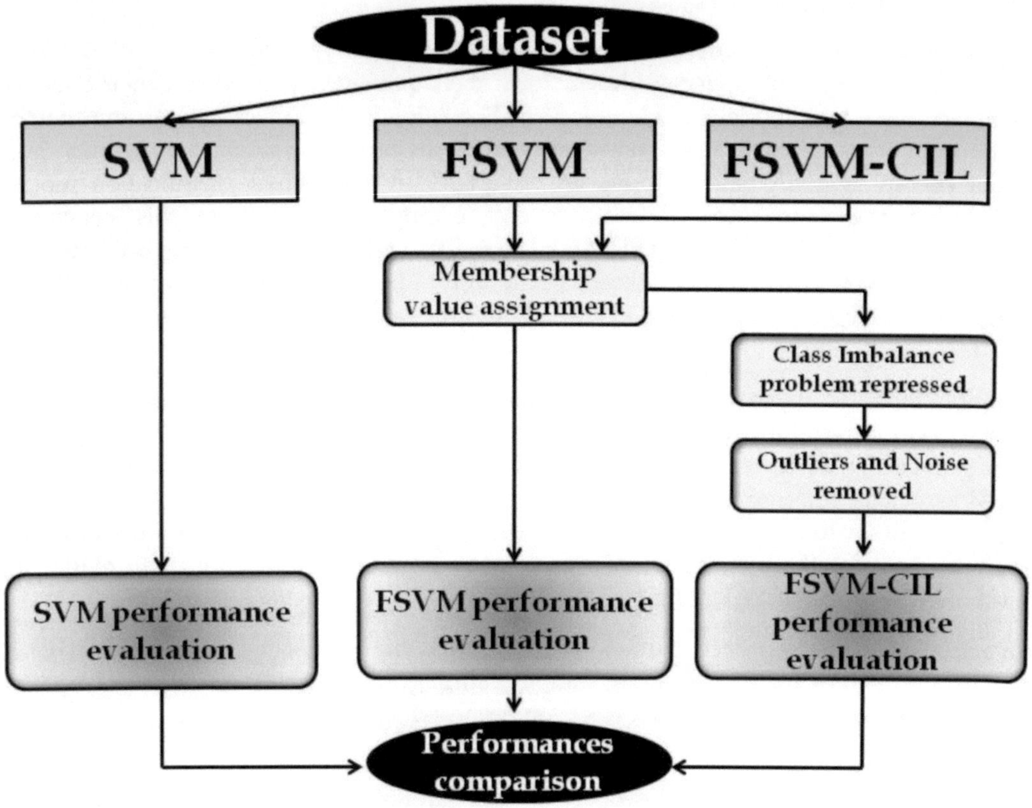

Fig. 2. Implementation diagram

FSVM-CIL method assigns a membership value for training examples in order to suppress the effect of class imbalance and to reflect the within-class importance of different training samples suppressing the effect of outliers and noise. Let us suppose that k_i^+ and k_i^- are the membership values of the positive class sample x_i^+ and negative class sample x_i^- in their own class respectively. They are calculated as follows:

$$k_i^+ = f(x_i^+)*k^+ \qquad k_i^- = f(x_i^-)*k \tag{15}$$

where k^+ and k^- are values which reflect the class imbalance such that $k^+ > k^-$ and $f(x_i)$ is defined considering the distance between x_i and its class centre d_i.

Samples near to the class centre are considered important samples because containing more information and also their $f(x_i)$ value is high. In contrast, samples which lie far away from centres are treated as outliers or noise and their $f(x_i)$ value is low. In FSVM-CIL approach authors use two separate decaying functions of distance to define $f(x_i)$: a linearly decaying function $f_{lin}(x_i)$ and $f_{exp}(x_i)$. The two functions are defined as follows:

$$f_{lin}(x_i) = 1-[d_i/(max\{d_i\}+a)] \tag{16}$$

where a is a small positive value which is introduced in order to avoid that $f_{lin}(x_i)$ could assume null value.

$$f_{exp}(x_i) = 2/(1+exp\{\beta d_i\}) \tag{17}$$

where β, which can assume values inner the range [0;1], determines the steepness decay and d_i is the Euclidean distance between x_i and its own centre.

The performance measure used in this approach is the geometric mean of sensitivity GM and it is represented in equation (18).

$$GM = \sqrt{SE * SP} \tag{18}$$

where SE and SP are the proportions of positive and negative samples among the correctly classified ones, respectively.

Three datasets (Blanke & Merz, 1988) have been exploited in order to demonstrate the effectiveness of the FSVM-CIL approach. Then a comparison between this method and SVM and FSVM has been evaluated considering both linear and exponential decaying function. Table 4 shows a description of the used datasets while Tab.5 illustrates the obtained results for the several approaches tested.

	# Positive Samples	# Negative Samples	IR
Ecoli	77	259	0.297
Pima Indians	268	500	0.536
Page Blocks	115	5358	0.021

Table 4. Datasets descriptions. IR represents the imbalance ratio, i.e. the ratio between the positive and the negative class.

As already mentioned, SVM classifier favours the majority class over the minority class obtaining an high value of SP and a low value of SE. This result confirms that SVM classifier is sensitive to the imbalance problem. Concerning FSVM results show that the best FSVM setting depends on the considered dataset. For Ecoli and Pima databases the choice of the type of decaying function is irrelevant while treating with page-blocks dataset the exponential decaying function provides better results than the linear one. Finally table shows that concerning FSVM-CIL approach, the use of exponential decaying function provides the best results independently from the considered dataset.

		SVM (%)	FSVM (lin) (%)	FSVM (exp) (%)	FSVM-CIL (lin) (%)	FSVM-CIL (exp) (%)
ECOLI	GM	88.59	88.53	85.50	89.08	90.64
	SE	78.67	78.18	78.64	90.02	92.45
	SP	93.12	93.60	92.97	86.52	88.19
PIMA	GM	70.18	69.78	71.33	71.56	72.74
	SE	55.04	54.55	55.60	66.94	69.10
	SP	89.50	87.5	82.50	76.14	76.35
PAGE	GM	76.47	79.15	81.62	94.51	95.05
	SE	58.26	61.74	67.06	93.81	93.14
	SP	99.54	91.48	99.01	95.21	95.36

Table 5. Classification results and comparison between several methods

Jesus et al. (Jesus et al., 2006) propose the study of the performance of Fuzzy Rule Based Classification System (FRBCS) in imbalanced datasets (Chi et al., 1996). The authors analyze the synergy of the linguistic FRBCS with some pre-processing techniques using several approaches such as undersampling, oversampling or hybrid models. A FRBCS is composed by a Knowledge Base (KB) and a Fuzzy Reasing Method (FRM). FRM uses the information of KB in order to determine the class for each sample which goes to the system. KB is composed of two elements: the Data Base (DB) which includes the notion of the fuzzy sets associated to the linguistic terms and the Rule Base (RB) which contains a set of classification rules.

The FRM, which is an inference procedure, utilizes the information of KB to predict a class from an unclassified sample. In a classification task the model of FRM includes four operations:

1. Compute the compatibility degree of data with the precedent of the rules.
2. Compute the association degree of data to the consequent class of each rule. This step consists in the generation of an aggregation function between the compatibility degree and the certainty degree of the rule with the class related.
3. Set the association degree of data with the several classes.
4. Classify by applying a decision function F on the association degree of data with classes.

FRBCS has been proposed in (Chi et al., 1996) and is an extension of the well known Wang & Mendel method (Wang & Mendel, 1992) to classification task. FRBCS finds the relationship between variables of the problem and establishes an association between the space of the features and the space of the classes. The main operations are as follows:

- Firstly a domain of variation of each feature Xi is determined, then fuzzy partitions are computed. This step is important in order to establish the linguistic partitions.
- For each example, a fuzzy rule is generated. Rules are created by considering several main steps.
  - Computing the matching degree of each example to the several fuzzy regions.
  - Assigning the selected example to the fuzzy region with the higher membership degree.

- Creating a rule for each example in this manner: the antecedent is determined by the selected Fuzzy region with the label of class of the sample in the subsequent.
- Compute the certainty degree.

In order to demonstrate the effectiveness of the proposed approach, authors considered several datasets belonging to the UCI repository with different degrees of imbalance.

The proposed method has been divided into three parts: an analysis of the use of pre-processing for imbalanced problems (such as SMOTE, random oversampling, random under-sampling ...), a study of the effect of the FRM and an analysis of the influence of the granularity applied to the linguistic partitions in combination with the inference method.

Results show that in all considered cases the presence of the pre-processing phase improves the behaviour of the learning algorithm.

The main conclusion of the proposed method is that the FRCM algorithm outperforms the other analyzed methods obtaining the best results adding a re-sampling operation before use the FRCM technique; moreover authors have found that FRBCSs perform well again the C4.5 decision tree in the context of very high imbalanced datasets.

An alternative to imbalance problem is the use of Complementary Learning Fuzzy Neural Network (CLFNN) which is proposed in (Tan et al., 2007). The use of fuzzy logic allows to tolerate uncertainty in the data reducing the effect of data imbalance. CLFNN has the main advantage that does not requires data pre-processing and hence, does not make any a prior assumption on data and does not alter the data distribution. This method exploits a neuro-fuzzy system which is based on complementary learning theory (Tan et al., 2005). Complementary learning is a system observed in human brain; with this theory different brain areas, which are segregated and mutually exclusive, are registered in order to recognize different objects (Gauthier, 2000). When an object is seen, registered areas are activated while the irrelevant areas are inhibited; this mechanism is called lateral inhibition. Generally complementary learning has the following characteristics:

- Features extraction of positive and negative examples.
- Separation of positive and negative information.
- Development of lateral inhibition.

According to this concepts, the different approaches that are present in the literature can be divided into three groups:

1. Positive/negative systems, where the system builds information on the basis only of the target class.
2. Neutral learning systems, where the notion of positive and negative does not exist.
3. Complementary learning systems, where the system creates knowledge on the basis of positive and negative classes considering the relation between positive and negative samples.

CLFNN is considered a 9-tuple $(X, Y, D, A, R, B, l, s, p)$. The definition of each element is as follows:

- $\boldsymbol{X}$ is the observation, belonging to the input space $\boldsymbol{U}$, which has a set of variables $\boldsymbol{x}=(x_1, x_2, \ldots, x_I)$.

- ***Y*** is the output associated to the input ***X***. If *M* is the number of possible outputs, ***Y***ϵ***V*** ($V=V_1$ x V_2 x ... x V_M) where ***V*** is the output space. Moreover ***Y*** is the union of Y^+ and Y^- which represent respectively the positive and negative output.
- ***D*** is a set of observation ***X*** and its relative output ***Y*** and represents the source knowledge data.
- ***A*** is a set of knowledge which explains the behaviour amongst samples ***X*** in ***D***.
- ***R*** represents the rules, i.e. the information learnt from ***D*** connecting the inputs to the relative outputs.
- ***B*** is a set of knowledge which explains the behaviour amongst samples ***Y*** in ***D***.
- ***l*** represents the learning function building the CLFNN based on ***D***. This function includes two complementary learning function: ***s*** and ***p***.
- ***s*** is the structure learning which builds the net. For instance a clustering algorithm can independently obtain the structures from data. Moreover it creates the fuzzy sets and memory elements that describe the underlying data. If the existing knowledge is not sufficient for data description, other nodes are added. The process ends when the structure of data is suitable to reflect the data *D*.
- ***p*** is the parameter learning which can be any supervised learning algorithm.

In CLFNN the behaviour is characterized by a linguistic term derived by fuzzy set ***A***. ***A*** is a mapping of ***X*** to the linguistic model of CLFNN; each set ***A*** identifies a set of locations in the input space characterizing by their membership functions. CLFNN is less subjected to data imbalance problem because it builds its knowledge from positive and negative classes separately and the influence of each class on the other one is minimized. Moreover in CLFNN the inference system uses the lateral inhibition which improves the system performance treating with imbalanced dataset.

In order to demonstrate the efficiency of CLFNN method, four imbalanced datasets are used: Single Photon Emission Computed Tomography (SPECT) (Blake & Merz, 1998), Wisconsin Breast Cancer diagnosis (WBCD) (Blake & Merz, 1998), Fine Needle Aspiration (FNA) (Cross & Harrison, 2006) and Thermogram (THERM).(Ng &Fok, 2003).

The dataset is divided in training set, testing set and validation set maintaining the class distribution. The averaged performance of CLFNN, which is calculated by the F-Measure over three cross-validation sets, is compared with other popular methods: Multilayer Perceptron (MLP)(Rosenblattx, 1958)., Radial Basis Function (RBF) (Powell, 1985), Linear Discriminant Analysis (LDA) (McLachlan, 2004), Decision tree C4.5 (Brodley & Utgoff,P.E.) and Support Vector Machine (SVM).

Table 6 illustrates the description of datasets and the averaged results obtained over the different cross validations with the several approaches. The acronym IR indicates the imbalanced ratio, i.e. the ratio between the number of positive samples and the number of negative samples.

Table 6 shows that CLFNN provides better results than the other approaches. In thermogram dataset none of the system can give satisfactory results because of its very high imbalance ratio but, also in this case, CLFNN outperforms the other approaches. This work confirms that CLFNN provides more consistent results over different data distributions coming a promising tool for handling imbalanced dataset.

	SPECT	WBCD	FNA	THERM
# Positive Samples	212	212	235	5
# Negative Samples	55	357	457	65
IR	3.85	0.59	0.51	0.07
MLP	0.762	0.925	0.917	0.2
RBF	0.8	0.912	0.912	0.2
C4.5	0.763	0.907	0.906	0.2
SVM	0.79	0.93	0.93	0.2
LDA	0.90	0.931	0.918	0.2
CLFNN	0.91	0.96	0.96	0.37

Table 6. Datasets description and averaged results.

4. Conclusions

Fuzzy Systems offer several advantages, among which the possibility to formalise and simulate the expertise of an operator in process control and tuning. Moreover the fuzzy approach provides a simple answer for processes which are not easily modelled. Finally they are flexible and nowadays they can be easily implemented and exploited also for real-time applications. This is the main reason why, in many industrial applications, dealing with processes that are difficult to model, fuzzy theory is widely adopted obtaining satisfactory results.

In particular, in this chapter, applications of FIS to industrial data processing have been presented and discussed, with a particular emphasis on the detection of rare patterns or events. Rare patterns are typically much difficult to identify with respect to common objects and often data mining algorithms have difficulty dealing with them. There are two kind of "rarity": rare case and rare classes. Rare cases, commonly known as outliers, refer to anomalous samples, i.e. observations that deviate significantly from the rest of data. Outliers may be due to sensor noise, process disturbances, human errors and instruments degradation. On the other hand, rare classes or more generally class imbalance, occur when, in a classification problem, there are more samples of some classes than others.

This chapter provides a preliminary review of classical outlier detection methods and then illustrates novel interesting detection methods based on Fuzzy Inference System. Moreover the class imbalance problem is described and traditional techniques are treated. Finally some actual Fuzzy based approaches are considered.

Results demonstrate how, in real world applications, fuzzy theory can effectively provide an optimal tool outperforming other traditional techniques.

5. References

Akbani, R., Kwek, S.& Japkowicz, N. (2004). Applying support vector machines to imbalanced datasets. *In Proceedings of 15th European Conference on Machine Learning*, Pisa, Italy, September 20-24, 2004.

Alejo, R., Garcia, V., Sotoca, J.M., Mollineda, R.A. & Sanchez, J.S. (2006). Improving the classification accuracy of RBF and MLP neural networks trained with imbalanced samples. *In E. Corchado et al. (Eds) IDEAL 2006*, pp.464-461.

Batuwita R. & Palade, V. (2010). FSVM-CIL: Fuzzy Suport Vector Machines for class Imbalance Learning. *IEEE Transactions on fuzzy system*, Vol. 3, N° 18, June 2010.

Berthold, M.R. & Huber, K.P. (1995). From radial to rectangular basis functions: a new approach for rule learning from large datasets. *Technical report*, University of Karlsruhe, 1995.

Bezdek, J.C. (1981). Pattern Recognition with Fuzzy Objective Function Algorithms, *Plenum Press*, New York.

Blake, C.L. (1998). UCI Repository of machine learning databases. *Irvine C.A.*, university of California, Department of Information and Computer science.

Boser, B. E., Guyon, I. M. & Vapnik, V. N. (1992). A training algorithm for optimal margin classifiers. *In D. Haussler, editor, 5th Annual ACM Workshop on COLT*, pages 144-152, Pittsburgh, PA, 1992. ACM Press

Breunig, N.M; kriegel, H.P. & Ng, R.T. (2000). LOF: Identifying density-based local outliers. *Proceedings of ACM Conference*, pp.93-104.

Brodley, C.E & Utgoff, P.E. (1995). Multivariate decision trees. *Machine Learning*, 19. pp. 45-77.

Bunkhumpornpat, C. Sinapiromsaran, K. & Lursinsap, C. (2009). Safe-Level-SMOTE: Safe Level Synthetic Oversampling technique fopr handling the class imbalanced problem. In *Proceedings PAKDD 2009*,Springer LNAI 5476, pp. 475-482.

Castillo, M.D. & Serrano, J.I. (2004) A multistrategy approach for digital text categorization from imbalanced documents. *SIGKDD Explor. Newsl.*, Vol. 6, N° 1, pp. 70-79.

Castro, J.; Hidalgo, L.; Mantas, C. & Puche, J. (2007). Extraction of fuzzy rules from Support vector machine. *Fuzzy Sets System*, Vol. 158, pp.2957-2077.

Cateni, S.; Colla, V. & Vannucci, M. (2009). A fuzzy system for combining different outliers detection methods, *Proceedings of the 25th conference on proceedings of the International conference: Artificial Intelligence and Applications*, , Innsbruck, Austria, 16-18 Febbraio 2009.

Chan, P.K. & Stolfo, S.J. (1998). Toward scalable learning with non-uniform class and cost distribution: a case study in credit fraud detection. *Kwowledge Discovery and data Mining*, pp.164-168.

Chaves, A.; Vellasco, M. & Tansheit, R. (2005). Fuzzy rule extraction from support vector machines, *5th inter. Conf. Hybrid Intell. System*, Rio de Janeiro, Brazil.

Chawla, N.V.; Hall, L.O., Bowyer, W. & Kegelmeyer, W.P. (2002) SMOTE: Synthetic Minoruty Oversampling TEcnique. *Journal of Artificial Intelligence Research*. 16, pp.321-327.

Chawla, N.V. (2003). C4.5 and imbalanced data sets: investigating the effect of sampling method, probabilistic estimate, and decision tree structure. *Workshop on learning from imbalanced dataset II, ICML*, Washington DC, 2003.

Chi, Z, Yan, H. & Pham,T. (1996). Fuzzy algorithms with applications to image processing and pattern recognition. *World Scientific.*

Chiang, J. & Hao, P. (2004). support Vector learning mechanism for fuzzy rule-based modeling: a new approach.*IEEE Trans. Fuzzy System*, vol 12, no 6, pp.1-12.

Chen, Y. & Wang, J. (2003). Support vector learning for fuzzy rule based classification systems, *IEEE Trans Fuzzy System*, Vol,11, no 6, pp.716-728.

Cross, S. & Harrison, R. F.(2006). Fine needle aspirated of breast lesions dataset. *Artificial Neural Networks in* Medicine World map.

De Rouin, E., Brown, J., Fausett, L. & Schneider, M., (1991). Neural network training on unequally represented classes. In Intelligent engineering systems through artificial neural networks, pp. 135-141, ASME press, NY. Dixon, W.J. (1953*). processing data for Outliers. Biometrics* 9, pp.74-89, 1953.

Dunn, J.C. (1973). A fuzzy relative of the ISODATA Process and its use in detecting compact well-separated clusters, *Journal of Cybernetics*,3, pp. 32-57, 1973.

Dunn, J.C. (1974). Some recent investigations of a new fuzzy partition algorithm and its application to pattern classification problems, *journal of Cibernetics* 4, pp.1-15, 1974.

Fawcett, T.& Provost, F.J. (1997). Adaptive fraud detection. *Data Mining Knowledge Discovery*, Vol. 1, N°3, pp.291-316.

Gao, J., Cheng, H. & Tan, P.N. (2006). Semi-supervised outlier detection. *Proceedings of the 2006 ACM Symposium on apllied Computing*, ACM Press, 2006, pp. 635-636.

Gauthier, I., Skuldlasky, P., Gore, J.C. & Andreson, A.W. (2000). Experise for cars and birds recruits brain areas involved in face recognition. *Nature Neuroscience*, Vol 3., (2), pp.191-197.

Gibbons, R.D. (1994). Statistical Methods for Groundwater Monitoring, *John Wiley & Sons*, New York.

Grubbs, F.E. (1969). Procedures for detecting outliyng observations in samples, *Technometric 11*, pp.1-21.

Guo, H. & Viktor, H. (2004) Learning from imbalanced data sets with boosting and data generation: the DataBoost-IM approach. *ACM SIGKDD Explorations Newsletter Special issue on learning from imbalanced datasets* Volume 6 , Issue 1 (June 2004).

Haibo, H & Garcia, E. (2009). Learning from Imbalanced Data. *IEEE Trans. Knowl. Data Eng.* Vol 21, no 9, pp.1263-1284.

Han, H. Wang, W & Mao,B. (2005). Borderline-SMOTE: A New Oversampling Method in Imbalanced Data sets Learning. *Proceeding of ICIC* Springer LNCS 3644, pp.878-887.

Hao, Y., Chi, X. & Yan, D. (2007) Fuzzy Support Vector Machinre based on vague sets for credit assessment. *Proc. 4th Int. Conf. Fuzzy System Knowl. Discov.* Changsha, China, vol.1 , pp. 603-607.

Hart, P. (1968). The condensed nearest neighbor rule. *IEEE Trans. Inform. Theory*, 14. pp.515-516.

Hawkin, D. (1980). Identification of outliers, Chapman and Hall, London 1980.

He,Z., Xu,X. & Deng, S. (2003) Discovering cluster-based local outliers, *Pattern recognition Letters*, pp.1651-1660.

Hodge, V.J. (2004). A survey of outlier detection methodologies, *Kluver Academic Publishers*, Netherlands, January, 2004.

Hong, X.; Chen, S. & Harris, C.J. (2007). A kernel based two class classifier for imbalanced datasets. *IEEE Transactions on Neural Networks,* vol 18 (1), pp.28-41.

Hu, Q. & Yu, D. (2005) An improved clustering algorithm for information granulation, *Proceedings of 2nd International Conference on Fuzzy Systems and Knowledge Discovery* (FSKD'05), vol 3613, LNCS, Springer-Verlag, Berlin Heidelberg Changsha, China, 2005, pp.494-504.

Imam, T., Ting, K. & Kamruzzaman, J. (2006). z-SVM: An SVM for improved classification of imbalanced data. In *Proceeding of Aust. Joint Conf.* AI, Hobart, Australia, pp. 264-273.

Inoue, T. & Abe, S. (2001). Support Vector machine for pattern classification. *Proc. Int. Conf. Neural Network,* Washington , D.C. pp.1449-1457.

Jang, M.F., Tseng, S.S, & Su, C.M. (2001). Two-phase clustering process for outliers detection. *Pattern Recognition Letters,* pp.691-700.

Jang, S., Li, Q., Wang, H. & Zhao, Y. (2005). A two-stage outlier detection method. *MINI-MICRO SYSTEMS,* pp.1237-1240.

Japkowicz, N. & Shaju, S. (2002). The class imbalance problem: a systematic study. *Intelligent Data Analysis,* Volume 6, Issue 5 (October 2002), Pages: 429 – 449.

Jesus, M.J., Fernandèz, A., Garcia, S. & Herrera, F. (2006) A first study of the use of fuzzy rule based classification systems for Problems with Imbalanced Data Sets. *Symposium on Fuzzy Systems in Computer Science (FSCS06).* Magdeburg, Germany, pp. 63-72 (2006).

Jimenez-Marquez, S.A., Lacroix, L. & Thibault, J. (2002) Statistical data validation methods for large cheese plant database. *J.Dairy Sci.,* 85(9), Sep 2002, pp. 2081-2097.

Kang, P. & Cho, S. (2006). EUS SVMs: Ensemble of under sampled SVMs for data imbalance problems. *Proc. of 13th International Conference Neural Inf. Process.,* Hong Kong, pp. 837-846.

Knorr, E.M., Ng, R. (2003). algorithms for Mining Distance-based Outliers in Large datasets, *Proceedings of VLDB,* pp.392-403, 2003.

Kubat, M. & Matwin, S. (1997). Addressing the curse of imbalanced training sets: one sided selection. *Proceedings of the Fourteenth International Conference on Machine Learning.* pp.179-186. Nashville Tennesse, Morgan, Kaufmann.

Kubat, M., Holte, R.C. and Matwin, S. (1998). Machine learning for the detection of oil spill in satelite radar images, *Machine Learning,* Vol. 30, N°2-3, pp.195-215.

Leskovec, J. & Shawe-Taylor, J. (2003). Linear programming boosting for uneven datasets. In *Proc. Of the 20th International conference on Machine learning (ICML-2003),* Washington DC, 2003.

Li, P., Chan, K.L. & Fang, W. (2006) Hybrid kernel machine ensemble for imbalanced data sets. *In Proc. Of the 18th Int. Conference on pattern recognition, (ICPR'06),* 2006.

Li, B.; Fang, L. & Guo, L. (2007) A novel data mining method for network anomaly detection based on transductive Scheme, *Advances in Neural Networks,* LNCS, VOL.4491, Springer Berlin, 2007, pp. 1286-1292.

Lin, C.F. & Wang, D. (2002) Fuzzy support Vector machine, *IEEE Trans. Neural Network,* vol 13, n 2, pp.464-471.

Lin, Z., Hao, Z. & Yang, X. Lium, X. (2009). Several SVM ensemble methods integrated with under-sampling for imbalanced data learning. *In Advanced Data Mining and Application,*Berlin, Germany Springer Verlag, pp.536-544.

Ling, C.X. & Li, C. (1998). Data Mining for direct marketing: problems and solutions. *Knowledge Discovery and data Mining,* pp.73-79.

Lingras, P. & West, C. (2004). Interval set clustering of web users with rough k-means, *Journal of Intelligent Information System,* Vol. 23, N°1, July 2004, pp. 5-16.

Liu, Y., An, A. & Huang, X. (2006). Boosting prediction accuracy of imbalanced dataset with SVM ensembles. *Proc. 10th Pac.-Asia Conf. Adv. Knowl. Discov. Data Mining,* Singapore pp.107-118.

Liu, A. & Ghosh, J. (2007). Generative Oversampling for Mining Imbalanced Datasets. *In DMIN* pp. 66-72.

Mahalanobis, P.C. (1936). On the generalized distance in statistics. *Proceedings of the National Institute of science of india,* pp.49-55.

Maloof, M. (2003). Learning when data sets are imbalanced and when costs are unequal and unknown. *ICML,* 2003.

Mandani, E.H. (1974). Application of fuzzy algorithms for control of simple dynamic plant. *Proceedings of the IEEE Control and Science,* 121, pp. 298-313, 1974.

Matsumoto, S., Kamei, Y., Monden, A. & Matsumoto, K. (2007). Comparison of outlier Detection methods in Fault-proneness Models. *Proceedings of the 1st International symposium on Emperical Software Engineering and measurements* (ESEM2007), pp. 461-463.

McCarthy, K., Zabar, B. & Weiss, G. (2005). Does cost sensitive learning beat sampling for classifying rare classes?. *UBDM'05* New York, NY, USA, ACM Press, pp.69-77.

McLachlan (2004). Discriminant Analysis and Statistical pattern recognition.*Wiley interscience.*

Mill, J. & Inoue, A. (2003). An application of fuzzy support vector. *Proc. 22nd Int. Conf. Neural Amer. fuzzy Inf. Process Soc.* Chicago, IL pp.302-306.

Ng, E.Y.K & Fok, S.C. (2003). A framework foe early discovery of breast tumor using thermography with artificial neural network. *The Breast Journal,* Vol. 9, 4, 2003, pp.341-343.

Papadimitriou, S. Kitawaga, H. Gibbons, P. & Faloutsos, C. (2003). LOCI: Fast Outlier Detection using the Local Correlation Integral. *Proceedings of the International Conference of Data Engineering, 2003.*

Pawlak, Z. (1982). Rough Sets. *International journal of computer and Information Sciences,* 11, 341-356.

Pawlak, Z. (1991). Rough Sets: Theoretical aspects of reasoning about data. Dordrecht: Kluver Academic Publisher.

Pazzani, M., Marz, C., Murphy, P., Ali, K., Hume, T. & Brunk, C. (1994). Reducing misclassification cost. *In Proceedings of the 11th Intl. Conference on machine learning*, pp. 217- 225, 1994.

Phua, C, Alahakoon, D. & Lee, V. (2004). Minority report in fraud detection: Classification of skewed data, *SIGKDD explor. Newsl.*, Vol. 6, N°1, pp.50-59, 2004.

Powell, M.J.D. (1985). Radial Basic Functions for multivariable interpolation: a review. *IMA Conference on Algorithms for the Approximation of Functions on Data.* pp.143-167, RMCS Shrivenham, England.

Ramasmawy,S., Rastogi, R. & Shim, K. (2000). Efficient Algorithms for Mining Outliers from large datasets, *Proceedings of International conference of management of data (SIGMOD' 00)*, 2000, pp. 427-438.

Raskutti, B. & Kowalczyk, A. (2004). Extreme re-balancing for svms: a case study. *SIGKDD Exploration*, Vol 6, N°1, pp. 60-69.

Ray, S & Turi, H. (1999). Determination of number of clusters in k-means clustering and application in colour image segmentation. *Proceedings of 4th International conference in pattern recognition and Digital Techniques,* (ICAPRDT'99), Calcutta, india, 27-29 December 1999, pp. 137-143.

Rosenblatt, F. (1958). The Perceptron: a probabilistic model for information storage and organization in The brain. *Psycological review,* 65. pp.386-408.

Ruspini, E. (1969). A new approach to clustering. *Information and Control,* N°15, pp.22-32, 1969.

Sam, T.R. & Lawrence, K.S. (2000). Nonlinear Dimensionality Reduction by Locally Linear embedding. *Science , 290*, pp. 2323-2326.

Soler, V. & Prim, M. (2007). Rectangular basis functions applied to imbalanced datasets. *Lecture notes in computer science,* Vol. 4668/2007, Springer.

Spyrou, E., Stamou, G. Avrithis, Y. & Kollias, S. (2005). Fuzzy Support Vector Machine for image classification fusing mpeg7 visual descriptors. *Proc. 2nd Eur. Workshop Integr. Knowl. Semantics Dig. Media Technol.* London UK, pp.25-30.

Tan, T.Z., Ng, S.G. & Quek, C. (2005). Ovarian cancer diagnosis by hippocampus and neocortex-inspired learning memory structures. *Neural Networks.*Vol 18, 5-6, pp.818-825.

Tan, T.Z.; Ng, S.G. & Quek, C. (2007). Complementary Learning Fuzzy Neural Network: An approach to Imbalanced Dataset. *Proceedings of International Joint Conference on Neural Networks,* Orlando, Florida, USA, August 12-17.

Tomek, I. (1976). Two modifications of CNN. *IEEE Transactions System Man Comm.* 6, pp.769-772.

Turney, P.D. (2000). Learning algorithms for keyphrase extraction. *Information Retrieval,* vol.2 , n°4, pp. 303-336.

Vannucci, M., Colla, V., Cateni, S. & Sgarbi, M. (2011). Artificial intelligence techniques for unbalanced datasets in real world classification tasks. *Computational Modeling and Simulation of Intellect current state and future perspectives,* pp. 551-565.

Veropoulus, K. Campbell, C. & Cristianini, N. (1999). Controlling the sensitivity of support vector machines, in *Proc. Int. Joint Conf. Artificial Intelligence,* Stockholm, Sweden, pp. 55-60.

Visa, S. & Ralescu, A. (2005). Issues in mining imbalanced datasets - a review paper. *Proocedings of the Sixteen Midwest Artificial Intelligence and Cognitive Science Conference,* pp. 67-73.

Xie, Z., Hu, Q. & Yu, D. (2005). Fuzzy Support Vector Machine for classification. *Proc. Int. Conf. Adv. Natural. comput.* Changsha, China p.1190-1197.

Xu, Z. & Liu, S. (2009). Rough based Semi- Supervised Outlier Detection. *Sixth International conference on Fuzzy System and Knowledge Discovery,* pp. 520-524.

Wang, L.X. & Mendel, J.M. (1992). Generating fuzzy rules for learning from examples. *IEEE Transactions on Systems, Man and Cybernetics,* Vol 35, No 2, pp.353-361.

Wang, J. Xu, M., Wang, H. & Zhang, J. (2006). Classification of Imbalanced Data by using the SMOTE algorithm and Locally Linear Embedding. *Proceeding of 8th International conference on Signal Processing,* IEEE, Classification of Imbalanced Data by using the SMOTE algorithm and Locally Linear Embedding. Vol. 3, pp. 16-20, 2006.

Wang, Y., Wang, S. & Lai, K. (2005). A new fuzzy support vector machine to evaluate credit risk. *IEEE Trans. Fuzzy Syst.* Vol 13, no 6, pp.820-831.

Weiss, G.M. & Provost, F. (2003). Learning when training data are costly: the effect of class distribution on tree induction. *Journal of Artificial Intelligence Research,* 19, pp. 315-354.

Wu, G. & Chang, E. (2003). Class boundary alignment for imbalanced dataset learning. *Proceeding of Internaltional Conference Data Mining,* Workshop Learning Imbalanced Datasets II, Washington ,D.C.

Wu, G. & Chang, E. (2004). KBA: Kernel Boundary Alignment considering imbalanced data distribution.. *Proceeding of IEEE Trans. Knowl. Data Eng.* Vol 17, N°6, pp. 786-795.

Xie, J. & Qiu, Z. (2007). The effect of imbalanced datasets on LDA: a theoretical and empirical analysis. *Pattern Recognition,* vol. 40, pp.557-562.

Xue, Z.; Shang, Y; Feg S. (2010) Semi-supervised outlier detection based on fuzzy rough C-means clustering, *Mathematics and Computers in simulation,* 80, pp.2011-2021, 2010.

Yousri, N.A., Ismal, M.A. & Kamel, M.S. (2007). Fuzzy outlier analysis a combined clustering-outlier detection approach, *IEEE SMC 2007.*

Yu, D., Sheikholeshami, G & Zhang, A. (2003). Findout: finding out outliers in large datasets. *Knowledge and information Systems,* pp.387-412.

Zadrozny, B., Langford, J. & Abe, N. (2003). Cost sensitive learning by cost proportionate example weigthing. In *ICDM'O3 Proceedings of the Third IEEE International Conference on Data Mining,* 2003.

Zhang, D., Gatica-Perezs, D., Bengio, S. & McCowan, I. Semi supervised adapted HMMs for unusual event detection, *IEEE Computer society Conference on Computer Vision and Pattern Recognition (CVPR'05) IEEE Press,* June, 2005. Vol 1 pp.611-618.

Zou, S. Huang, Y., wang,Y. Wang, J. & Zou, C. (2008). SVM learning from imbalanced data by GA sampling for protein domain prediction. *Proc. of 9th Int. Congf. Joung Comput., Sci* Hunan, China, 2008, pp.982-987.

Section 4

Application to Image Processing and Cognition Problems

11

Fuzzy Inference Systems Applied to Image Classification in the Industrial Field

Silvia Cateni, Valentina Colla, Marco Vannucci and Alice Borselli
Scuola Superiore S. Anna, TeCIP Institute, Pisa
Italy

1. Introduction

In the last years many industries have increased the exploitation of vision systems applied to several fields. This fact is basically due to the technological progress that has been reached by these systems: the reliability of vision systems allows the industries to achieve considerable cost savings in terms of both material and human resources.

Among the most important applications of vision systems in the industrial field there are robot positioning and driving, code reading, non contact measuring as well as quality control and monitoring.

In particular quality controls are nowadays performed through vision systems in many industries; these systems guarantee reliability comparable and sometimes greater with respect to human operators, especially for a large quantity of products. In fact, vision-based automatic inspection systems allow to process a huge amount of data in a very small time with respect to human performance.

The vision systems are usually composed by several components: a set of cameras to capture the images, an illumination system and a system for the image processing and classification. These systems are able to capture images of a wide range of products in order to find defects which do not fit the quality standards of the considered industrial production process.

The present chapter deals with the application of Fuzzy Inference Systems (FIS) for the classification of images, once they have been pre-processed through suitable algorithms. One of the main reasons for exploiting a FIS to this aim lies in the possibility of approaching the problem in a way similar to human reasoning. In fact a FIS allows:

- To describe the problem in linguistic terms;
- To translate the human experience (which is very often the reference starting point in industrial applications) through inference rules. The possibility of providing a methodological description in linguistic terms is a great advantage in problems that cannot be solved in terms of precise numerical relations, especially when only empirical a priori knowledge is available.
- To perform an eventual further adaptation of the rules of the inference machine by exploiting the available data, as a neural training algorithm can be applied to tune some parameters of the fuzzy classifier.

Moreover, FIS-based classifiers provide the further advantage of a great flexibility, thanks to the possibility to add rules without affecting the remaining parts of the inference machine.

Clearly the preliminary image processing phase should be developed with the aim to extract the most suitable features from the images to be fed as input to the fuzzy system.

The chapter will be organised as follows: a preliminary generic description of the main features of FIS-based image classifiers will be provided, with a particular focus on those general applications where a preliminary ad-hoc image features extraction phase is included. The advantages and limitations of FIS-based classifiers toward other algorithms will be presented and discussed. Afterwards, some case studies will be proposed, where FIS-based image classifiers are applied in an industrial context.

2. Vision systems

In the last years the use of computer vision systems has enormously increased, especially in the industrial field, for several tasks (Malamas et al., 2003; Chin & Harlow, 1982; Nelson et al., 1996).

Traditionally human experts performed visual inspection and quality control and, in some cases, the human performance are better than the one provided by a machine. On the other hand, human operators are slower than machines, their performance is not constant through time and finding many expert operators is not easy for any industry. Moreover there are several applications where the job may be repetitive and boring (such as target training or robots guidance) or also difficult and dangerous (such as underwater inspection, nuclear industry, chemical industry ...).

Vision system are widely adopted in the control of robots for pick and place operations showing their power in very complex tasks (Sgarbi et al., 2010).

A vision system consists of electronic, optical and mechanical components and it is able to capture, record and process images. Typically it consists of one or more cameras, an optical system, a lighting system, an acquisition system and, finally, an image processing system. The object to be tested is placed in front of cameras and it is properly illuminated. The optical system forms an image on camera sensor which produces in output an electrical signal. Then this signal will be digitized and stored. Finally the image can be analysed with an appropriate software. A general scheme of a typical industrial vision system is shown in Fig.1.

The computational resources are exploited for processing the captured images through suitable analysis and classification software. One or more cameras acquire images under inspection and a lighting system is adopted to illuminate the scene in order to facilitate the acquisition of the image features (Malamas et al., 2003).

The prerequisites for the design and development of a good machine vision system depend on the application field and the task to be reached. An "universal" vision system, i.e. which is capable to fulfil any task in any application, does not exist; only after having established the requirements of the specific application the vision system can be designed.

In the last years computer and machine vision are been connected together for non invasive quality inspection. Machine vision allows to analyse video data, such as data coming from a video camera, in order to plan future operations. The automatic systems which carry out visual inspection by means of machine vision are often called *Automatic Visual Inspection Systems* (Jarvis, 1979).

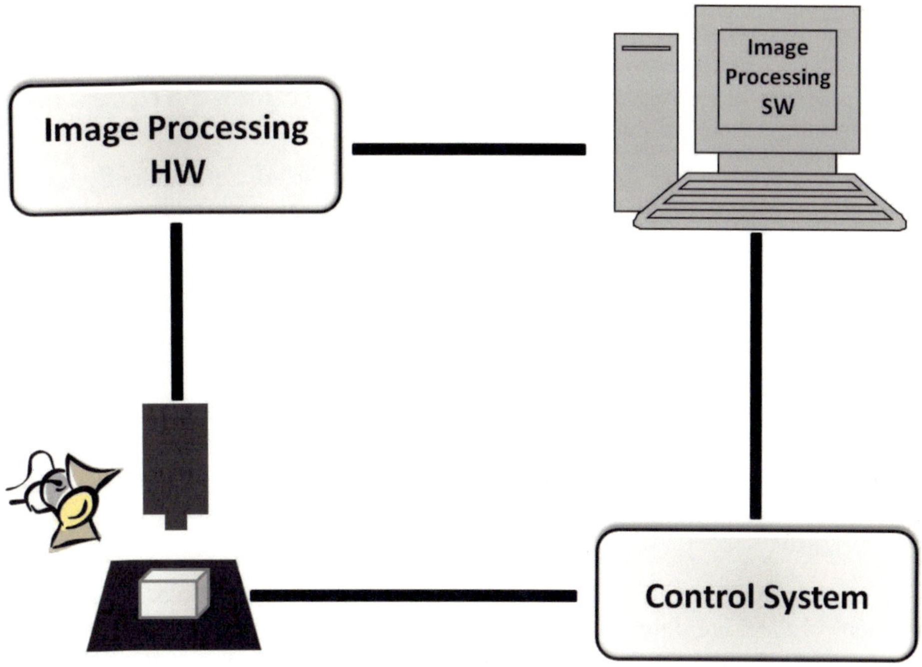

Fig. 1. Scheme of a simple industrial vision system.

Artificial vision is defined as the set of computational techniques which aim to create an approximate model of the three-dimensional world from two-dimensional projections of it. A classic problem concerning artificial vision is to determine whether there are specific objects or activities in the image. Another problem, which is solved by vision systems, is to reconstruct a three dimensional model about the scene to be analysed, given one or more two-dimensional images of it (Klette et al., 1998). The optical techniques which are widely adopted can be divided in two approaches: active methods and passive methods. Active methods regard the case where the scene is radiated by appropriate electromagnetic radiation, while passive methods regard the case where the images of the scene are the real images. Active methods are more expensive than passive ones and they are not always applicable. In contrast, passive methods have lower resolutions than the active ones. Both approaches adopted the visual cues that are used by human vision system to retrieve the depth of the scene projection on the retina, such as blurring and other optical phenomena.

There are many applications of artificial vision in industrial field such as defect detection, robot placement, robot orientation and robot guidance (Lowe & Little, 2005), codes reading, classification. In the last decades the Artificial Vision has evolved into a mature science, which embraces different markets and applications becoming a vital component of advanced industrial systems (Lanzetta, 1998).

3. Feature extraction procedure from the image

Image processing belongs to the field of signal processing in which input and output signals are both images.

Feature extraction tends to simplify the amount of property required to represent a large set of data correctly. A feature can be defined as a function concerning measurements which represent a property of a considered object (Choras, 2007). Features can be classified as *low-level features* and *high level feature.*

The *low-level features* are the features which can be extracted automatically from image without any information about the shape. A widely used approach is the so called *edge detection*, which is adopted in order to identify points in a digital image at which the image brightness changes brusquely, also edge detection highlights image contrast. The boundary of features within an image can be discover detecting contrast as the difference in intensity. Trucco & Verri (Trucco & Verri, 1998) identified three main steps to perform edge detection: noise smoothing, edge enhancement and edge localization. Noise smoothing, also called noise reduction, eliminates noise as much as possible without destroying the edges of the image. Edge enhancement produces images with large intensity values at edge pixels and low intensity levels elsewhere. Finally edge localization is used to decide which local maxima among the filter outputs are effectively edges and are not produced by noise (Roque et al., 2010).

The Sobel edge detection operator (Sobel, 1970) has been the most popular operator until the improvement of the edge detection techniques having a theoretical basis. It consists of two masks in order to identify the edges under a vector form. The inputs of the Sobel approach include an image *I* and a threshold *t*. Once the noise smoothing filters have been applied, the corresponding linear filter is carried out to the new smoothed image by using a pair of 3x3 convolution masks, one estimating the gradient in the *x*-direction (columns) and other estimating the gradient in the *y*-direction (rows).

$$\begin{bmatrix} -1 & -2 & -1 \\ 0 & 0 & 0 \\ 1 & 2 & 1 \end{bmatrix} \begin{bmatrix} -1 & 0 & 1 \\ -2 & 0 & 2 \\ -1 & 0 & 1 \end{bmatrix} \quad (1)$$

The output of the two above defined masks is represented by two images I_1 and I_2. Through equation (2) the degree of the intensity gradient is estimated for each pixel $I(i,j)$.

$$p(i,j) = \sqrt{I_1(i,j)^2 + I_2(i,j)^2} \quad (2)$$

Finally the pixels $p(i,j)$ which are greater than the threshold *t* are identified as edges.

Canny edge detection operator (Canny, 1986) is probably the most popular edge detection technique at the moment. It is created by taking into account three main purposes:

- best possible detection with no spurious responses;
- good localisation with minimal distance between detected and effective edge position;
- single response to delete multiple responses to a single edge.

The first requirement reduces the response to noise through an optimal smoothing. Canny demonstrated that Gaussian filtering is optimal concerning edge detection. The second requirement is introduced to improve the accuracy, in fact it is used to detect edges in the right position. This result is obtained by a process of non-maximum suppression (similar to peak detection) which maintains only the points that are located at the top of a crest of edge data. Finally the third requirement regards the position of a single edge point when a change in brightness occurs.

High-level features extraction is used to find shapes in computer images. To better understand this approach let us suppose that the image to be analyzed is represented by a human face. If we want to automatically recognise the face, we can extract the component features, for example the eyes, mouth and the nose. To detect them we can exploit their shape information: for instance, we know that the white part of the eye is ellipsoidal and so on. Shape extraction includes finding the position, the orientation and the size. In many applications the analysis can be helped by the way the shape are placed. In face analysis we imagine to find eyes above and the mouth below the nose and so on.

Thresholding is a simple shape extraction technique. It is used when the brightness of the shape is known, in fact pixels forming the shape can be detected categorizing pixels according to a fixed intensity threshold. The main advantage lies in its simplicity and in the fact that it requires a low computational effort but this approach is sensitive to illumination change and this is a considerable limit. When the illumination level changes linearly, the adoption of a histogram equalization would provide an image which does not vary; unfortunately this approach is widely sensitive to noise rendering and again the threshold comparison-based approach is impracticable. An alternative technique consists in the subtraction of the image from the background before applying a threshold comparison; this approach requires the a priori knowledge of the background. Threshold comparison and subtraction have the main advantage to be simple and fast but the performances of both technique are sensitive to partial shape data, noise and variation in illumination.

Another popular shape extraction technique is the so called *Template matching,* which consists in matching a template to an image. The template is a sub-image that represents the shape to be found in the image. The template is centred on an image point and the number of points that match the points in the image are calculated; the procedure is repeated for the whole image and points which led to the best match are the candidates to be the point where the shape is inner the image. Template matching can be seen as a method of parameter estimation, where parameters define the position of the template but the main disadvantage of the proposed approach is the high computational cost.

Another popular technique which locates shapes in images is the *Hough Transform* (Hough, 1962). This method was introduced by Hough to find bubble tracks and subsequently Rosenfeld (Rosenfeld, 1969) understood its possible advantages as an image processing method. It is widely used to extract lines, circles and ellipses and its main advantage is that it is able to reach the same results than template matching approach but is it faster (Princen et al., 1992). The Hough Transform delineates a mapping from the image points into an accumulator space called Hough space; the mapping is obtained in a computationally efficient manner based on the function that represents the target shape. This approach requires considerable storage and high computational resources but much less than template matching approach. When the shape to be extracted is more complex than lines and circles or the image cannot be partitioned into geometric primitive a *Generalised Hough*

Transform (GHT) approach can be used (Ballard, 1981). GHT can be implemented basing on the discrete representation given by tabular functions.

4. Industrial quality control

In the field of quality control there are two main elements which play an important role: the presence of sensors used to capture data, such as signals or images, and the adopted computational intelligence techniques (Piuri & Scotti, 2005). The quality monitoring includes the use of signal measurements or machine visual systems in order to allow a standardized and non-invasive control of industrial production processes. The computational intelligence techniques comprise the formalisation of the mechanism which allows the extraction of useful information from the images and its interpretation for the purposes the systems it is designed for; therefore it may also include components such as neural networks, fuzzy systems and evolutionary computer algorithms. A generic quality control system needs to manage techniques belonging to several scientific areas, such as depicted in Fig.2.

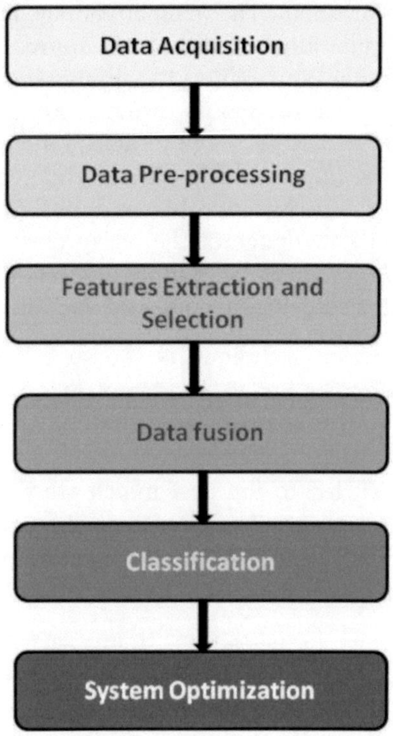

Fig. 2. Generic scheme of quality control system

In the following, a brief explanation of all the blocks included in Fig. 2 is provided.

4.1 Data acquisition

The data acquisition is a typical problem concerning measurements systems. A lot of studies demonstrate how the computational intelligence techniques can improve the performance of sensors from both the static and the dynamic point of view (Ferrari & Piuri, 2003). The sensor modules can be able to self-calibrate and also reduce the unexpected non-linearities. Also eventual errors can be detected and, if necessary, corrected (Wandell et al., 2002). Images are usually acquired by cameras in digital format.

4.2 Data pre-processing

The main aim of signal pre-processing is to reduce the noise and to make use of inherent information provided by signals. In literature many conventional pre-processing techniques have been proposed (Proakis & Manolakis, 1996; Rabiner & Gold, 1975) including computational intelligence techniques; in this context a good survey of neural and fuzzy approaches for signal pre-processing is due to Widrow and Sterns (Widrow & Stern, 1985).

If the captured data consist of an image, pre-processing phase is used to correct image acquisition and not perfect source image conditions. In each system, which implements machine vision functionalities, a pre-processing phase is recommended in order to correct image acquisition errors or to improve characteristics for visual inspection.

Image pre-processing is a phase which, through several operations, improves the image by suppressing undesirable distortions or enhancing relevant features for the further analysis tasks. Note that image pre-processing does not add information content to the image (Haralik & Shapiro, 1992; Hlavak et al., 1998) but uses the redundancy basing on the concept that a real object has similar neighbouring pixels which correspond to a similar brightness value. A distorted pixel can be removed from the image and it can also be reinserted in the image having a value equal to the average of the neighbouring pixels.

The main operations included in the pre-processing image phase are resumed as follow:

- Cropping
- Filtering
- Smoothing
- Brightness
- Detecting Edges

Cropping is introduced to remove some parts of the image in order to point out the regions of interest.

Image filtering exploits a small neighbourhood of a pixel belonging to the input image in order to provide a new brightness value in the output image.

Smoothing techniques are used to reduce noise or eventual fluctuations occurring in the image. To reach this task it is necessary to suppress high frequencies in the Fourier transform domain.

Brightness threshold is a fundamental operation to extract pertinent information. It consists in a gray scale transformation whose result is a binary image. This approach is based on the segmentation and separates objects from their background.

Edge Detection is a very important step in image pre-processing. Edges are pixels lying where the intensity of image charges roughly. In previous paragraph the edge detection method is treated in more details.

4.3 Features extraction and selection

With the previous operation all features that are processed by sensors have been fixed. Through feature extraction and selection the initial data can be reduced in order to diminish the computational complexity of the system. Moreover a reduction of features number simplifies both the pattern representation and the classifier structure; finally a reduction of features number solve the problem of "curse of dimensionality" (Roudys & Jain, 1991). The so-called curse of dimensionality problem consists in the fact that the number of instances for feature exponentially increases with the number of features itself; also in order to reduce the complexity of the computational intelligence modules under training, it is fundamental to limit the number of features to consider. Both feature extraction and feature selection are used for the reduction of the feature space. The main difference between the two approaches is that the feature extraction approach generates new features based on transformation or combination of the original features while feature selection approach selects the best subset of the original feature set (Dalton, 1996).

4.4 Data fusion

This operation combines the available features in order to obtain more significant information concerning the quality of the industrial process under consideration. A widely used technique is the so called *sensor fusion*, which combines information of different type coming from several sensors. A lot of papers, concerning the use of intelligent techniques have been proposed, such as (Bloch, 1996; Filippidi et al., 2000; Xia et al., 2002; Benediktsson et al., 1997). Data fusion systems can be composed by several elements such as sensors, data-fusion nodes, data-fusion databases and expert knowledge databases.

4.5 Classification

Once the features are fixed, they are led in input to a classifier which outputs a value associated to the classification of the quality (integer value) or a quality index (real value).

The classification can be divided into two approaches: conventional classification and computational intelligence-based classification. The computational intelligence-based approach includes statistical approach (Fukunaga, 1972), neural networks (Haykin, 1999) and fuzzy systems (Bezdek, 1992). This last issue will be treated in the next section.

4.6 System optimization

Modules belonging to the quality control system contain parameters which need to be fixed in order to improve final accuracy, computational complexity, maximum possible throughput and memory exploitation. These parameters include, for instance, thresholds, filter coefficients and number of hidden neurons in the case of use of neural network.

In order to build a satisfactory quality control system it is important to integrate all the above cited activities. In order to obtain more accurate, adaptive and performing systems the use of computational intelligence techniques are recommended.

5. Fuzzy classifier

Fuzzy Logic has been introduced by Zadeh (Zadeh, 1965) and it is based on the concept of "partial truth", i.e. truth values between "absolutely true" and "absolutely false". Fuzzy Logic provides a structure to model uncertainty, the human way of reasoning and the perception process. Fuzzy Logic is based on natural language and through a set of rules an inference system is built which is the basis of the fuzzy computation. Fuzzy logic has many advantages, firstly it is essential and applicable to many systems, moreover it is easy to understand and mostly flexible; finally it is able to model non linear functions of arbitrary complexity. The Fuzzy Inference System (FIS) is one of the main concepts of fuzzy logic and the general scheme is shown in Fig.3.

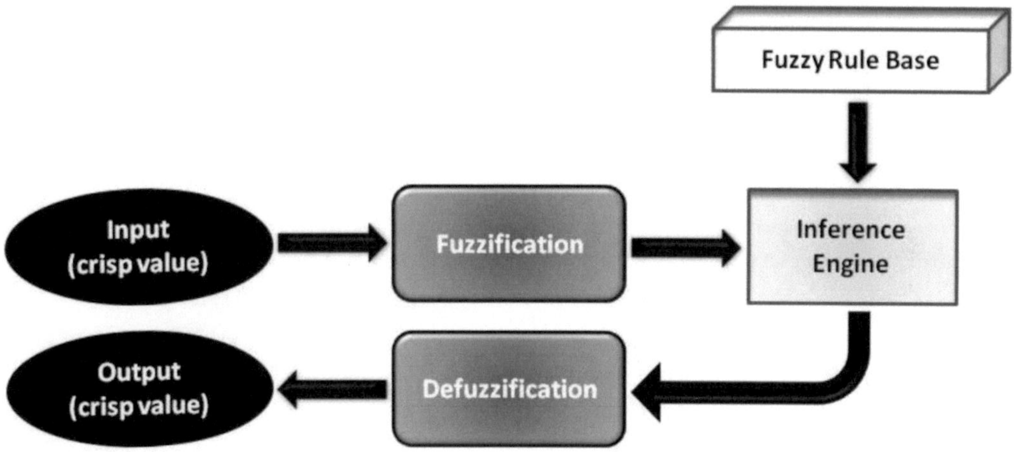

Fig. 3. FIS scheme

A FIS is a way of mapping input data to output data by exploiting the fuzzy logic concepts.

Fuzzification is used to convert the system inputs, which is represented by crisp numbers into fuzzy set through a fuzzification function. The fuzzy rule base is characterized in the form of *if-then* rules and the set of these fuzzy rules provide the rule base for the fuzzy logic system. Moreover the inference engine simulates the human reasoning process: through a suitable composition procedure, all the fuzzy subsets corresponding to each output variable, are combined together in order to obtain a single fuzzy for each output variable. Finally the defuzzification operation is used to convert the fuzzy set coming from the inference engine into a crisp value (Abraham, 2005).

Fuzzy classification is an application of fuzzy theory. In fuzzy classification an instance can belong to different classes with different membership degrees; conventionally the sum of the membership values of each single instance must be unitary. The main advantage of fuzzy classification based method includes its applicability for very complex processes.

6. Exemplar industrial applications

The quality control in industrial applications is used to monitor and to guarantee the quality of the processes.

Actually many industries have adopted vision systems for improve the quality control of products (Amiri & Shanbehzadeh, 2009; Ferreira et al., 2009). The quality control includes the ability tackling problems of several scientific areas, such as signal acquisition, signal processing, features extraction, classification and so on. Many approaches have been proposed in order to design intelligent signal and visual inspection systems for the quality control using fuzzy theory, that has been recognized in the literature as a good tool to achieve these goals. In the following a description of some exemplar fuzzy-based methods is proposed.

6.1 Vehicle classification exploiting traffic sensors

Kim et al. (Kim et al., 2001) propose an algorithm for vehicle classification based on fuzzy theory. Many approaches have been proposed in order to identify vehicles through traffic sensors; one of the most typically adopted technologies for vehicle classification is the combined loop and piezoelectric sensor system (Kim et al., 1998; Kim et al., 1999). A heuristic knowledge about vehicle speed or shape, once the vehicle length is known, is available, but in the loop/piezo detector there is not a precise mathematic association between the vehicle length and speed or shape. Also this heuristic knowledge could be well formalised using the *if-then* fuzzy rules.

The main idea of the proposed method is to modify the output length value from the loop sensor and use it to classify each vehicle. The general scheme of the proposed algorithm is shown in Fig.4.

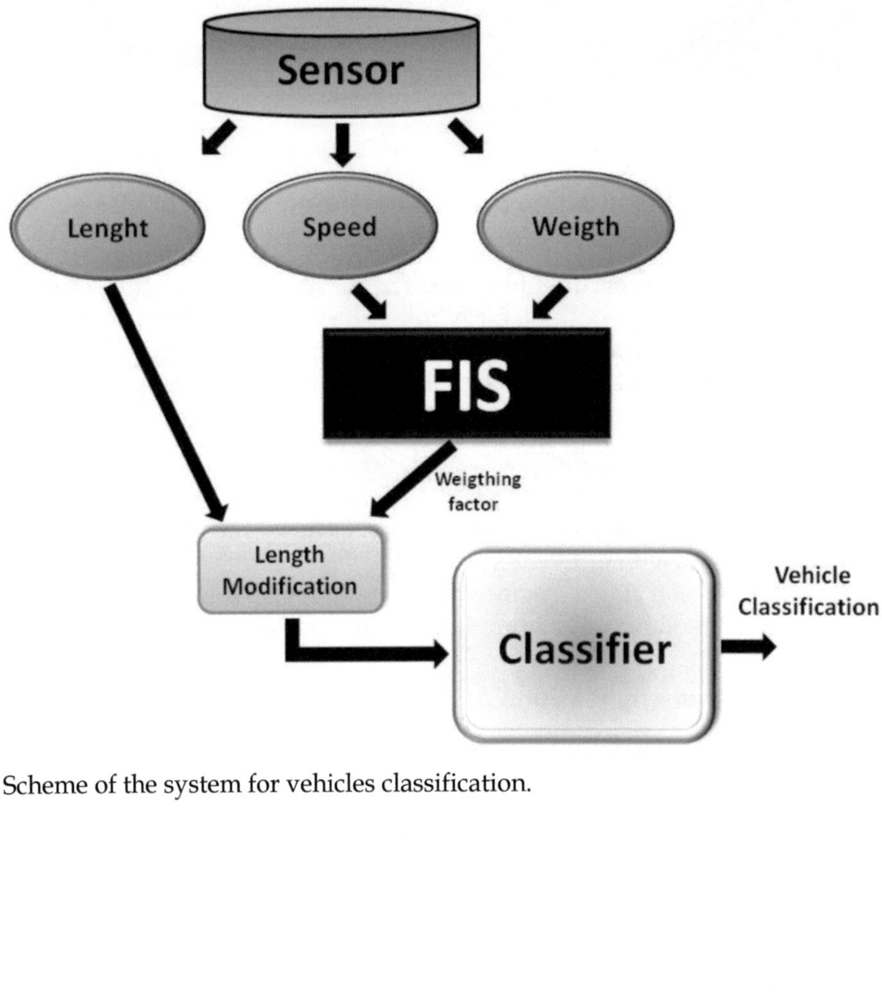

Fig. 4. Scheme of the system for vehicles classification.

Two features are selected to be fed as inputs to the fuzzy system namely the vehicle weight and speed. The output of the fuzzy system is a weighting factor which is used to modify the length value. Inputs and output are interpreted as linguistic values in this manner:

- Speed : slow, medium, fast
- Weight: very light, light, medium, heavy
- Length mod: negative big, negative small, zero, positive small, positive big.

Triangular membership functions have been defined to represent each linguistic value. Finally the fuzzy rule basis have been created with the help of expert's heuristic knowledge, which is described in Tab.1.

Speed	Weight	Length Modification
Slow	Very light	Zero
Medium	Very light	Negative small
Fast	Very light	Negative big
Slow	Light	Positive small
Medium	Light	Zero
Slow	Medium	Positive big
Medium	Medium	Positive small
Fast	Medium	Zero
Slow	Heavy	Positive big
Medium	Heavy	Positive big
Fast	Heavy	Positive small

Table 1. Rule basis

On the basis of the rules the output of the fuzzy system is evaluated through an inference system of Mandani type (Mandani, 1974) and a defuzzification operation. Finally the modified vehicle length is calculated as follows:

$$LM = L * [1 + (WF / 100)] \tag{3}$$

where *LM* is the modified length, *L* represents the measured length and *WF* is the weighting factor in output from the fuzzy system. The modified length is used as input to a classifier in order to obtain the vehicle classification. Experimental results demonstrate that the proposed algorithm using fuzzy approach significantly outperforms the conventional vehicle classification algorithm (Kim et al., 1998; Kim et al., 1999). The classification error using a conventional algorithm is 12.78% (74 errors on 579 vehicles analysed), while adopting the proposed fuzzy approach the classification error decreases to 6.56% (38 errors on 579 vehicles).

6.2 Classification of surface defects on flat steel products

Borselli et al. (Borselli et al., 2011) propose a fuzzy-based classification in order to classify a particular class of defects that can be present on the surface of some flat steel products. In the steelmaking industry a lot of steel rolling mills are equipped with an Automatic

Inspection System (ASIS) (Stolzenberg & Geisler, 2003). Such system contains a lighting system to illuminate the two faces of the moving strip and a set of cameras catch the images related to the steel surface each time a potential defect is detected. The defect is classified, when possible, and the images are stored in a database. Due to large amount of images and to the time constraints, often an on line classifier can misclassify some defects or it is not able to classify particular defects. An offline analysis of the non classified defects through more powerful although time-consuming techniques concerning this class of defects can greatly enhance the quality monitoring. In (Borselli et al., 2011) an off line classifier is proposed, that is capable to distinguish two types of particular defects called *Large Population of Inclusions* (LPI) and *Rolled In*, which are very similar. Before classification process an image cleaning is carried out through two filtering operations in order to improve the image quality. In particular a Sobel filter (Weng & Zhong, 2008) and a binarization are applied. Sobel filter is used to detect the edge while the binarization is a filter used to point out the regions having a different lightness with respect to the background. The two filters are independently applied to the original image and then the resulting images are summed in order to achieve a binary image where relevant defects are more visible. Depending on the nature of the considered defects, four features are extracted from the image which are: number of the regions where a defect is focused, the maximum width, the shape and the brightness of the considered regions. The four features are fed as inputs to classifier and the output, a value lying in the range [0,1], represents the probability that the analyzed defect is effectively a LPI defect. Finally a threshold comparison determines whether the defect belong to the LPI class or to the Rolled In class. The threshold is set to 0.5 and output values greater than 0.5 are considered LPI defects, Rolled In otherwise. The general scheme of the proposed approach is shown in Fig.5.

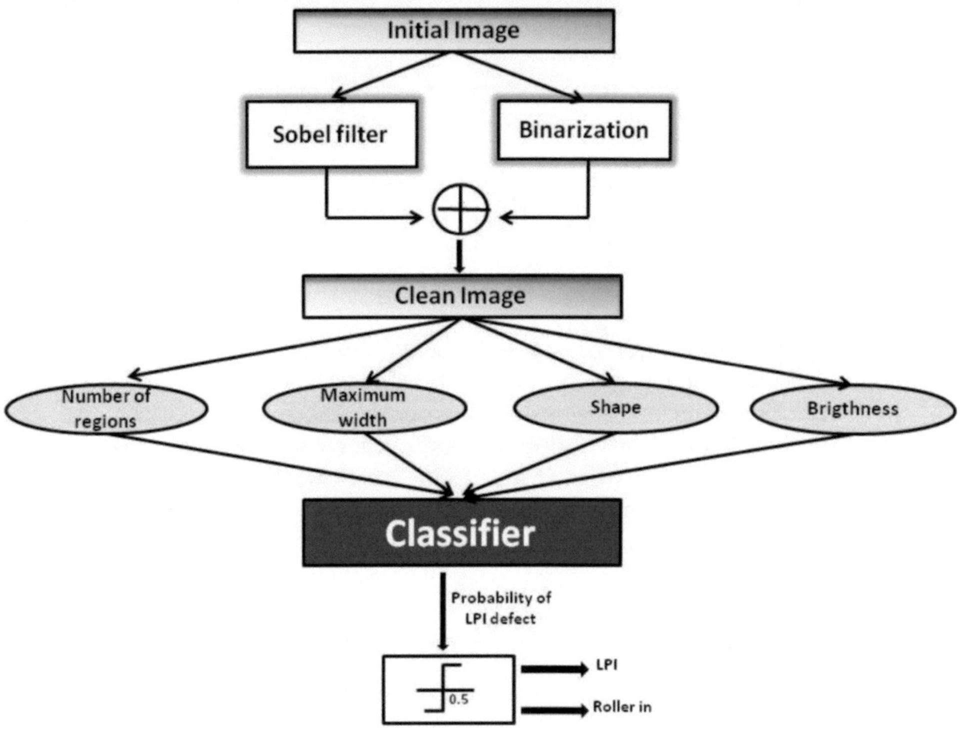

Fig. 5. Diagram of the proposed approach.

The classification is based on a FIS. Four fuzzy sets are considered:

- Number of regions: *small, high*
- Maximum width: *small, high*
- Shape: *small, high*
- Brightness: *low, high.*

The output is a fuzzy set, called probability of LPI defect, which can assume two values: *low* and *high.*

The inference rules that have been adopted are described in Table 2.

Number of regions	Maximum Width	Shape	Brigthness	Operator	Probability of LPI defect
Small	High	High	Small	Or	low
High	Small	Small	High	Or	high

Table 2. Rules

All the considered membership functions are Gaussian and are tuned by exploiting the data, as the adopted FIS is an Adaptive Neuro-Fuzzy Inference System (ANFIS) (Jang, 1991; Jang, 1993).

In order to demonstrate the effectiveness of the proposed method a comparison with other common classifiers has been made. The tested classifiers are: a Multi Layer Perceptron (MLP) classifier (Werbos, 1974), a Decision Tree (DT) (Argentiero et al., 1982) based on C4.5 algorithm (Quinlan, 1993), a Support Vector Machine (SVM) (Yan et al., 2009), a Learning Vector Quantization-based (LVQ) classifier (Elsayad, 2009). The method has also been compared to a previous system developed by the same authors (Borselli et al., 2010), which exploits a non-adaptive FIS whose parameters have been heuristically tuned.

The experimental data involve 212 images provided by an Italian steelmaking industry which have been randomly divided in two groups: a training set which includes the 75% of data and a validation set with the remaining 25%.

The performance has been quantified in terms of average accuracy μ and standard deviation σ, that are calculated on 30 tests and are defined as follows:

$$\mu = \frac{\sum_{i=1}^{N} Acc(i)}{N} \tag{4}$$

$$\sigma = \sqrt{\frac{\sum_{i=1}^{N} (Acc(i)-\mu)^2}{N}} \tag{5}$$

where *Acc(i)* is the accuracy calculated during test *i*-th. *N* is the number of tests (in this example *N*=*30*).

Results show that the proposed ANFIS-based approach outperforms the other approaches providing the highest accuracy (94.4%) and a low standard deviation values (2.1 %). This approach outperforms the other ones mainly because it is based on the knowledge of the technical personnel.

6.3 On line defects detection in Gas Metal Arc Welding

Another fuzzy application used in industrial field is proposed by Naso & Turchiano (Naso & Turchiano, 2005), who propose the development of an intelligent optical sensor for on line defects detection in Gas Metal Arc Welding (GMAW).

GMAW (Li & Zhang, 2001) is a welding process widely used in industrial field (Bingul et al., 2000) which presents many advantages, such as low costs, high metal deposition rate and suitability to automation. Also the process monitoring and defect-detections methods are very important tasks in order to improve the weld quality reducing manufacturing costs.

The electro-optical sensor includes two main modules (sensor and telescope) which are interconnected with optical fibers. This equipment aims at filtering and splitting the measured radiation into four components: infrared (*IR*), ultraviolet (*UV*) and two radiations at visible wavelengths (*VIS1, VIS2*). Photodiodes convert the resulting beams in electrical signals. The wavelength of the two signals belonging to the visible spectrum is set to tolerate the computation of the electronic temperature (*Te*) of the plasma. If *VIS1, VIS2, Te* are interdependent, then only *Te* and *VIS1* are taken into account to eliminate redundancies.

Before the on line classification operation, a signal pre-processing phase is necessary in order to improve the signal quality. The pre-processing phase includes two stages: signal filtering and extraction of the regularity indices. Signal filtering is a fundamental step in this context because a large amount of noise affects the observed signals. The Kalman filter (Brown & Hwang, 1992) has been adopted to this purpose, which provides efficient algorithms for estimating useful parameters in the stochastic environments. Regularity indices are extracted considering several factors: first of all, given a fixed configuration of the welding equipment, the signals associated to successful welding processes have the same behaviour; in contrast, signals observed during defective welds contain particularly features which are easily associable to the occurred defect. Also, it is possible to discover when the quality of the weld decreases, the cause of such downgrading and the type of defect. For the classification task the information describing the behaviour of the observed signal can be synthesized in three independent features:

1. *Normalized Signal Offset* (NSO), which is used to quantify the deviation of the signal from the expected value belonging to an ideal weld.
2. *Change of Normalized Signal Offset* (CNSO), which measures the change in signal levels between two consecutive time windows.
3. *Residual Signal Noise* (RSN), which represents the remain noise in the signal after the Kalman filtering.

The extracted features are fed as inputs into a classifier. In order to develop a classifier that directly exploits the experts knowledge a fuzzy system has been chosen. It must be noticed that signals belonging to different welds are different due to the stochastic nature of the phenomena under consideration; also the deviation of one or more indices from their expected behaviour often is due to the occurrence of a defect during the welding process. Fuzzy system, in this context, is the ideal classifier, as it is simple, it can directly use the knowledge of the experts and it can be easily reconfigured when new knowledge is available.

In order to limit the number of membership functions and rules the classification task is developed through two different fuzzy systems operating parallel. The first fuzzy classification system is used to provide a percentile index of acceptability of the weld, while the second fuzzy system detects the simultaneous signal patters directly connected with a specific defect. The first FIS gives a real time estimate of the quality of each weld, also for each time-window the system analyzes the indices through a rule-based method. Firstly a partition of the range of each observed input three fuzzy set is been made basing on the set of reference welds used as training set. The three introduced fuzzy sets are referred to quality: Optimal (OPT), acceptable (ACC) and unacceptable (UNA) and the membership functions have a trapezoidal shape. Finally the fuzzy system uses the welding time (*Time*) as an input to let the classification ignore the first seconds of process when the welding equipment is warming up. To describe the time interval a single linear piecewise increasing membership function regime (*REG*) is introduced. The output is represented by three membership functions as well. In this case the membership function are represented by three singletons as follows:

- OPT = 100%
- ACC=50%
- UNA= 0%

Once the membership functions have been defined, a few generic rules are introduced. The first rules refer to obvious conditions; then, each time, another rule is included and the overall classification performance is evaluated in order to adjust membership function and rule weights. The output is so defined as an index of weld quality, in particular 0% (UNA) indicates the occurrence of defect while 100% (OPT) represents an optimal weld, values in the range 0-100% represent intermediate acceptability. Subsequently a threshold of acceptability is introduced in order to convert the fuzzy degree of quality in a binary decision: good or defective weld.

The fuzzy rules used by the quality estimation system can be described as follow:

1. *If Time is not REG then the output is OPT. (weigth=1).*
2. *If Time is REG, NSO (IR) is OPT and CNSO (IR) is OPT and RSN (IR) is OPT and NSO (UV) is OPT and CNSO (UV) is OPT and RSN (UV) is OPT and NSO (VIS) is OPT and CNSO (VIS) is OPT and RSN (VIS) is OPT and NSO (Te) is OPT and CNSO (Te) is OPT and RSN (Te) is OPT then the OUTPUT is OPT. (weigth =1).*
3. *If NSO (IR) is UNA or CNSO (IR) is UNA or RSN (IR) is UNA or NSO (UV) is UNA or CNSO (UV) is UNA or RSN (UV) is UNA or NSO (VIS) is UNA or CNSO (VIS) is UNA or RSN (VIS) is UNA or NSO (Te) is UNA or CNSO (Te) is UNA or RSN (Te) is UNA then the OUTPUT is UNA. (weigth =0.1).*
4. *If NSO (IR) is ACC or CNSO (IR) is ACC or RSN (IR) is ACC or NSO (UV) is ACC or CNSO (UV) is ACC or RSN (UV) is ACC or NSO (VIS) is ACC or CNSO (VIS) is ACC or RSN (VIS) is ACC or NSO (Te) is ACC or CNSO (Te) is ACC or RSN (Te) is ACC then the OUTPUT is ACC. (weigth =0.2).*
5. *If Time is REG, NSO (IR) is ACC and CNSO (IR) is ACC and RSN (IR) is ACC and NSO (UV) is ACC and CNSO (UV) is ACC and RSN (UV) is ACC and NSO (VIS) is ACC and CNSO (VIS) is ACC and RSN (VIS) is ACC and NSO (Te) is ACC and CNSO (Te) is ACC and RSN (Te) is ACC then the OUTPUT is ACC. (weigth =0.8).*

6. *If Time is REG, NSO (IR) is UNA and CNSO (IR) is UNA and NSO (VIS) is not OPT then the OUTPUT is UNA. (weigth =0.18).*
7. *If Time is REG, NSO (UV) is UNA and NSO (VIS) is not UNA then the OUTPUT is UNA. (weigth =0.18).*
8. *If Time is REG, NSO (IR) is UNA and CNSO (IR) is UNA and RSN (IR) is UNA and NSO (UV) is UNA and NSO (VIS) is UNA and NSO (Te) is UNA then the OUTPUT is UNA. (weigth =0.18).*
9. *If Time is REG and RSN (IR) is UNA and NSO (Te) is UNA and CNSO (Te) is UNA and RSN (Te) is UNA then the OUTPUT is UNA. (weigth =0.18).*
10. *If Time is REG and CNSO (IR) is UNA and CNSO (UV) is UNA and RSN (UV) is UNA and CNSO (VIS) is UNA and RNS (VIS) is UNA and CNSO (Te) is UNA then the OUTPUT is UNA. (weigth =0.18).*

The second fuzzy system is used to display messages which explain the occurred defect or the anomaly operation in the considered weld. The considered events for this aim are the common ones such as current increase, current decrease, voltage variation, gases assistance decrease, contamination of with materials having different thermal properties and occurrence of hole in the metal. The second FIS is similar to the first one working with analogous membership functions and rules and provides six outputs, one for each considered defect. It is evident that a single defect could be associated to one or more causes.

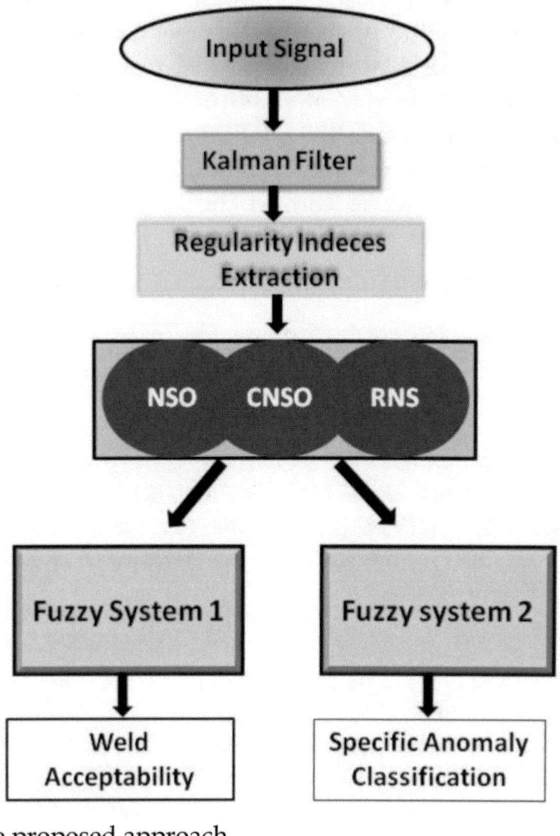

Fig. 6. Diagram of the proposed approach

Both Fuzzy Inference Systems are Mandani type and a general scheme of the proposed approach is shown in Fig.6.

The proposed approach has been evaluated with 40 different welding processes, where the 70% of processes are non defective while the remaining 30% present particular defects voluntarily induced or *a posteriori* detected with an appropriate tool. Furthermore, 60% of data are used as training set and 40% as validation set.

In order to demonstrate the effectiveness of the proposed method a comparison with a stochastic approach (Sforza & DeBlasiis, 2002) is provided. It is important consider that stochastic approach is not able to indicate the type of defect and, in order to make the comparison, the fuzzy index of quality must be convert in a binary value, also a threshold is necessary. The obtained results show that the fuzzy classification system correctly classifies all considered welds while the stochastic approach misclassifies 14% of the welds.

Finally a sensitivity analysis in order to evaluate the robustness of the proposed approach, when membership function, rules and operating condition vary, is carried out. The sensitivity investigation on the several variation of parameters leads to the following conclusion: if a proper pre-processing signal phase and a correct identification of the important features are been carried out, then the proposed fuzzy classification system can be effectively built and tuned.

6.4 Detection of wafer defects

An interesting industrial application which exploits the advantages of the fuzzy theory is due to (Tong et al., 2003). The authors propose a process control chart which integrate both fuzzy theory and engineering experience in order to monitor the defects on a wafer which have been clustered.

The wafer manufacturing process contains many step, such as alignment, etch and deposition. It is a very complex process; the occurrence of defects on the wafer surface is unavoidable and decreases the wafer yield.

Typically Integrated Circuits (IC) manufacturers use c-charts to monitor wafer defects. This technique assumes that wafer defects are randomly and independently distributed so that the number of defects has a Poisson distribution. A limit of this approach is that the real defect clustering infringes this constraint creating a non acceptable occurrences of false alarms. A modified c-chart, introduced in order to solve this problem, is presented by Albin & Friedman (Albin & Friedman, 1991) and it is based on a Neyman Type-A distribution. Unfortunately also this approach presents a considerable limit, as it can monitor only the variation in the number of defects but it is not able to detect variation located within the wafer. The authors demonstrate that applying fuzzy theory in combination with engineering experience it is possible to build a process control chart which is able to monitor the clustered defect and defect clustering simultaneously. The proposed algorithm is illustrated in Fig.7.

The KLA 2110 wafer inspection system (Castucci et al., 1991) is adopted to obtain the wafer map. This system provides in-line wafer inspection information such as number of defects, size of defects, placement of defects and, finally, type of defects. The number of defects are determined and the cluster index is calculated. Some cluster indices are provide to calculate the extent of the clustering of the defects; an efficient cluster index is due to Jun et al. (Jun et al., 1999). This particular *Cluster Index* (*CI*) does not require any a-priori assumption concerning the defects distribution. CI is calculated in the following way: let us suppose that *d* represents the number of defects occurred on a wafer, and X_i and Y_i are the coordinates of the generic defect *i* $(1 \leq i \leq n)$ in a two dimensional plane.

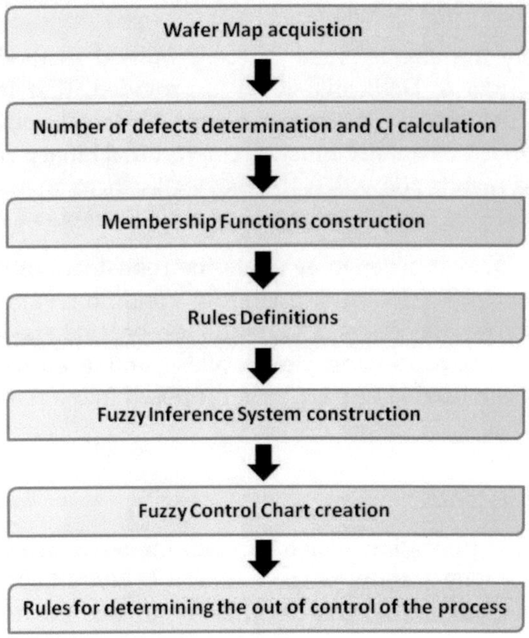

Fig. 7. Procedure of proposed approach

Sorting X_i and Y_i in ascending order, we can define $X_{(i)}$ and $Y_{(i)}$ as the coordinates of the *ith* defect. Moreover the two follow intervals A_i and B_i are evaluated:

$$A_i = X_i - X_{i-1} \quad (6)$$

$$B_i = Y_i - Y_{i-1} \quad (7)$$

Note that $X_{(0)}$ and $Y_{(0)}$ are considered null.

Finally CI can be defined as in equation (8)

$$CI = min\{\, \mu_A^2/\sigma_A^2 \,,\, \mu_B^2/\sigma_B^2 \,\} \quad (8)$$

where μ_A and μ_B are the mean value of A_i and B_i respectively, while σ_A and σ_B are their standard deviation. $CI=1$ when the defect distribution is uniform, moreover if $CI>1$ then the defects are clustered.

Once *CI* is available, the membership functions corresponding to number of defects, *CI* and output of the system are evaluated. Number of defects and clustering are important characteristics which mainly determine the wafer yield. In this approach this two variables as input of the FIS, which is Mandani type, and the output of the process represents the output of the fuzzy system. In the proposed examples the number of defected can be classified in seven classes defined as follows:

1. very low
2. low
3. medium low
4. medium
5. medium high
6. high
7. very high

Also, for each fuzzy set a triangular membership function is constructed accordingly.

Clustering phenomena is classified in ten classes and the output can be classified in ten levels as well. Finally, according to the process control a set of rules based on experts knowledge has been defined. It is important to consider that, when many defects are present, without clustering, the process is considered out of control, while when the number of defects is low clustering is significant and also under control.

The corresponding rules created to monitor the process can be written as follow:

R1: IF Defect is very high and C1 is term 1, then value is term 10
R2: IF Defect is very high and C1 is term 2, then value is term 10

.

.

.

Ri: IF Defect is medium and C1 is term 10, then value is term 2

.

.

.

R70: IF Defect is very low and C1 is term 10, then value is term 1

Subsequently a fuzzy system according to the rules and a fuzzy control chart can be designed also building eventual control limits. Once the defect data are stored, they are transformed into output of the fuzzy inference rules and a control chart which monitor both number of defects and clustering is constructed. The last important step is determine the rules which determine when the process is out of control.

The main advantages of the proposed approach include the possibility to incorporate within the fuzzy system the knowledge of experts and the experience of engineering. Moreover the proposed chart is easy and very helpful in judging real process conditions and, finally, it is simpler and more efficient respect to Poisson based c-chart and the Neyman-based c-chart.

6.5 Detection of defective products in the paper industry

A further application of a combination of vision systems and fuzzy inference is found in (Colla et al., 2009) and is related to a quality control task within the paper industry.

One of the main phases of the manufacturing of paper rolls for domestic consists in cutting a long semi-finished roll into rolls of standard length by means of an automatic machinery equipped with a fast-rotating circular blade.

These iterated cuts damage the blade of the machinery devoted to this operation due to the resistance of the paper roll. The performance of the damaged blade decreases the quality of the cut and can lead to surface defects on the roll section and on the contour of the roll itself, as shown in Fig. 8.

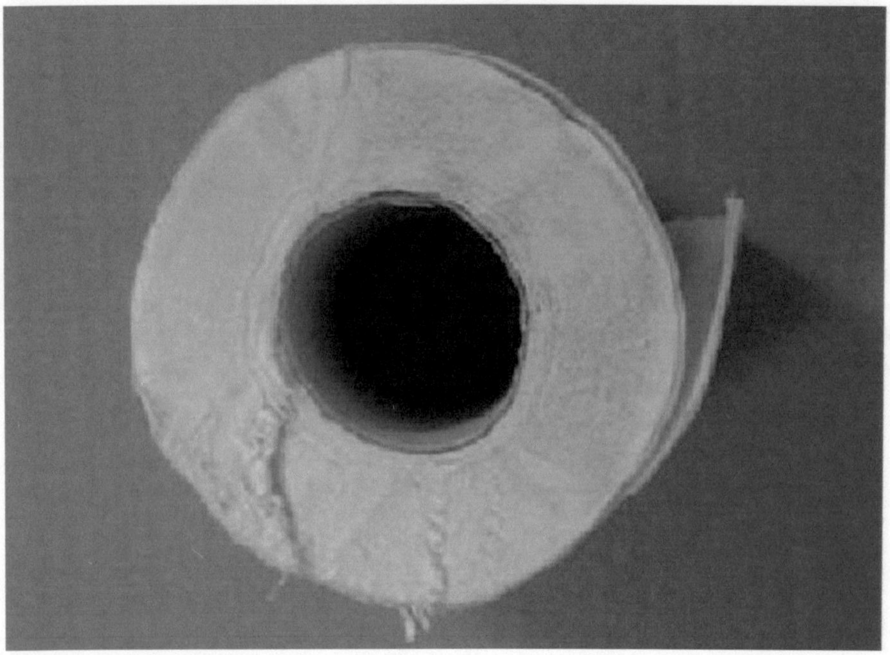

Fig. 8. Defects on the roll surface.

Unfortunately, independently on the quality of the paper itself, the presence of these defects compromises the marketability of the final product, thus a quality control step is needed in order to perform the selection of the final product. Usually this latter control is manually performed by a human operator which assesses the quality of each product, one by one, taking into account the quantity, intensity and kind of defects that are present on the roll sections. The human operator decides not only if each single roll has to be discarded or put into market but also when to stop the machinery for the maintenance of the cutting blade.

Within this context it would be desirable to automate the process of quality control for different purposes: on one hand in order to avoid an alienating task for the human operator, on the other hand in order to speed-up the control and to increase the repeatability and standardise the performance of the control operations, as, obviously, the results of the quality check are heavily affected by the experience and skills of the human operators. For these reasons a fuzzy inference-based vision system has been developed for the quality control on the previously described process.

This automatic system is placed immediately after the cutting machinery, in order to examine the rolls as soon as they are produced, while in the laboratory experimental set up, the paper roll is manually placed in front of the camera. In the real industrial operating scenario, each time a new roll is cut, a belt or a robot should place it with its circular section in front of the camera that is part of the vision system.

The vision system exploits one single static analogical B/W camera which acquires the images and digitalizes them. The decision system directly operates on the digitalized grey scale image and, as a result, provides the decision concerning the destination (market or recycling) of the inspected product.

The main goal of the developed system is to evaluate the quality of single products on the basis of the defects that are eventually present on the internal part of the paper section, neglecting the irregularity of the contour, as this latter defect can be due also to other phases of the manufacture and does not compromise the marketability of the product.

The quality control system here described implements three subsequent processing stages, which are summarized in the flow chart depicted in Fig.9.

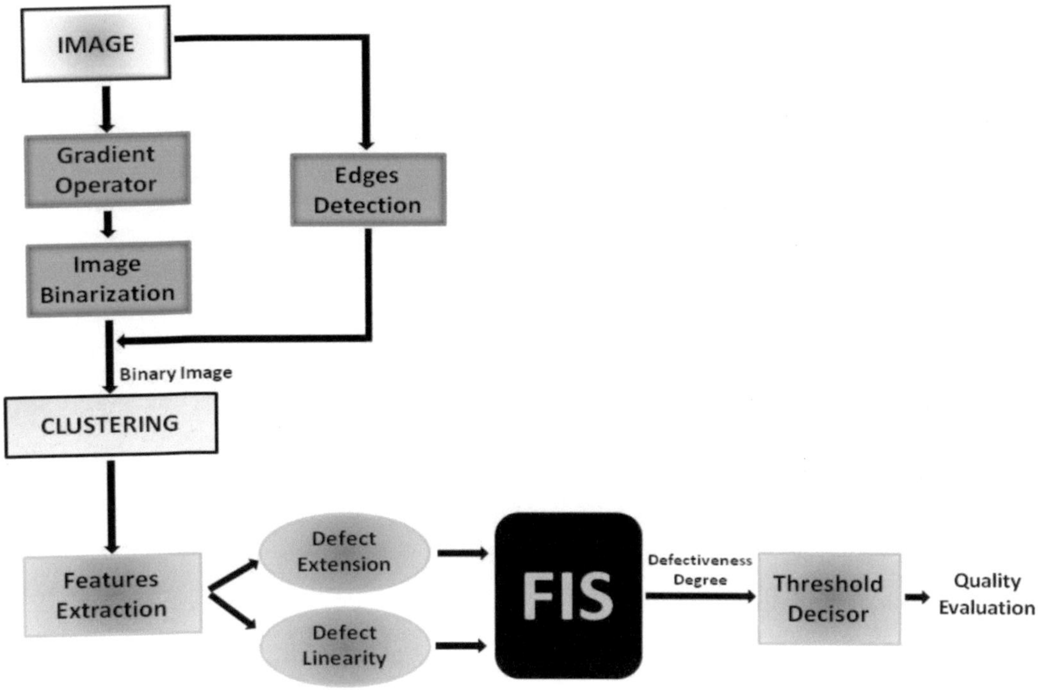

Fig. 9. Flow diagram of the quality control system for the assessment of paper rolls.

The first one performs some *image processing* operations which elaborate the grey scale image and aim to put into evidence those areas of the roll section that are affected by surface defects. At this stage, a combination of filters is used to highlight the grey level discontinuities on the images. These filters take into account the grey intensity of each specific point and of its neighbours for calculating the so-called *gradient* associated to each pixel, which is higher in correspondence of strong and abrupt variations of the image. This feature can indicate the presence of defects. In order to select only those points where the grey level change is particularly high and, by consequence, more probably belonging to a defect, a threshold operator which produces a binary image is used.

This latter operation, together with the faulty zones, puts into evidence the contour of the paper roll which has to be eliminated from the resulting image for the successive processing steps. For this reason the pixels corresponding to the borders of the roll are detected through a specific *edge finding* algorithm based on the Canny method (Canny, 1986) which achieves good results and is not sensitive to the noise present in the examined image.

The second step of the computation analyses the binary image through an ad-hoc developed clustering algorithm which groups the single potentially defective points into macro-defects which represent the potential final defects of the product. The clustering is necessary in order to perform a selection among all the highlighted points and in order to put into evidence some key feature of the potential defects. The result of the clustering is a set of clusters, each one representing a potential defect and characterized by the points it includes. A first selection among these candidate defects is performed by discarding those clusters formed by less than a predefined threshold of points. The remaining ones are passed to the third control stage for the final assessment.

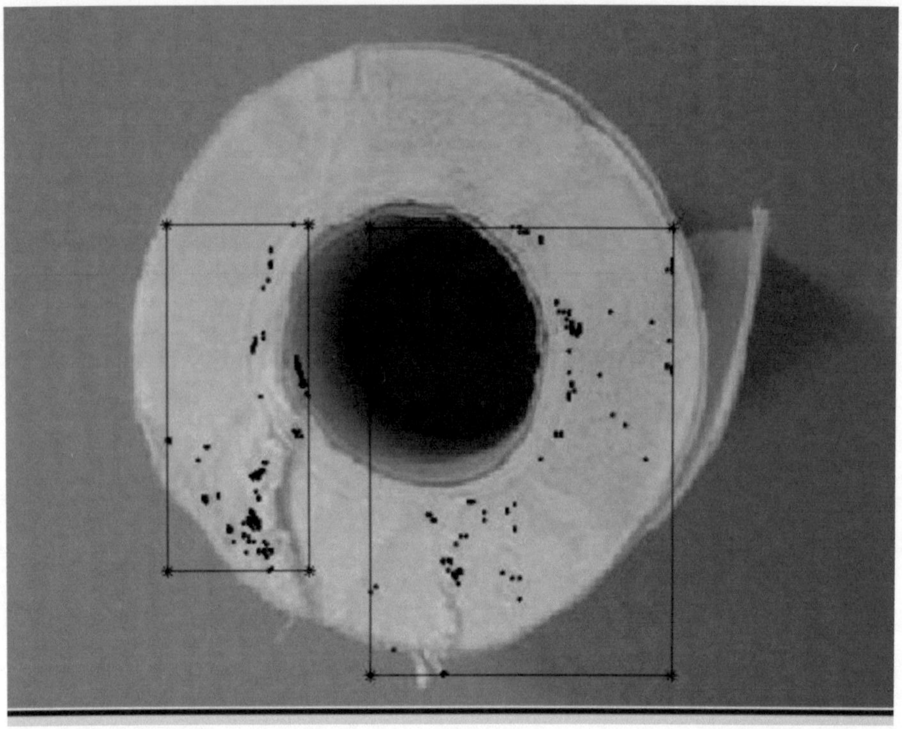

Fig. 10. The result of the image processing and clustering stage: single potentially defective points and clusters are highlighted.

This final decision is taken by means of a FIS (Mandani type) which implements the same rationale adopted by the human operators currently performing this task. In general human operators take into account two main characteristics of the identified critical regions: their extensions and the linearity of their shapes, thus the developed FIS is based on the following two input variables:

1. *defect extension* which is measured in terms of the number of pixels belonging to a cluster. Three fuzzy sets correspond to this fuzzy variable and refer to the number of pixels in the cluster: *low, medium* and *high.*
2. *linearity* is calculated as the mean square distance of pixels of the clusters from the best-fitting straight-line. Also for this variable three fuzzy sets are created: *low, medium* and *high.*

The output of the designed FIS is represented by a single variable, the so-called *defectiveness,* which reflects the decision about the final roll destination. This variable corresponds to three fuzzy sets: *not defective, uncertain* and *defective.*

The adopted membership functions are Gaussian and their domain depends on the universe where the corresponding fuzzy variable is defined (for instance, 0-200 points for the variable *extension.*

Seven fuzzy rules derived from the knowledge of expert human operators constitute the adopted inference system. The defectiveness index is evaluated for all the clusters eventually present on a single roll: if a paper roll contains at least one cluster whose defectiveness index is higher than a fixed threshold, it is discarded.

The adopted rules are expressed in Table 3.

Defect Extension	Linearity	Operator	Defectiveness
Low	Low	and	Uncertain
Low	Medium	and	Defective
Low	High	and	Defective
Medium	Low	and	Defective
Medium	Medium	and	Uncertain
Medium	High	and	Defective
High	-	and	Defective

Table 3. Adopted Rules

Several tests have been performed for evaluating the proposed quality control system. The value of the defectiveness discrimination threshold must meet two opposite requirements: on one hand the choice of high values of such threshold leads to a high number of *missed detections* (MD) of faulty rolls, on the other hand low values of the threshold rise several so-called *false alarms* (FA) which correspond to pauses on the process for the maintenance of the machinery. Both these situations must be avoided although, according to technical personnel, to avoid missed defect detections is more important, as the presence of faulty rolls can affect the commercial competitiveness of the product.

The results obtained by the proposed vision system are extremely good as, with the selected threshold, an extremely low number of defective products are missed and a satisfactory number of false alarms are risen. The best compromise is reached fixing the threshold to 0.70; with this threshold the error is percentage is 4.6, the percentage of false alarms is 3.7 and finally the missed detections percentage is 0.9.

7. Conclusions

In the last years Vision Systems in the industrial field have been widely adopted providing innovative solutions in the direction of industrial application. Vision systems improve the productivity and the quality monitoring becoming a competitive tool to industries which employ this technology.

In this chapter a brief description of vision system is provided and then the principles of industrial quality control have been treated. Several examples of use of fuzzy system in different industrial applications have been described. The results demonstrate how applicable the FISs are in industrial field: their flexibility and the simplicity make this approach an optimal solution to describe complex processes.

8. References

Abraham, A. (2005). Rule-based expert system. *Handbook of measuring system design,* John Wiley & Sons, ISBN: 0-470-02143-8, USA, 2005.

Albin, S.L. & Friedman, D.J. (1991). Clustered defect in IC fabrication: Inpact on Process Control Charts, *IEEE Trans. on Semiconductor Manifacturing,* 4 (1), 1991.

Amini, M. & Shahnbehzadeh, S. (2009). An Experimental Machine Vision System for quality Control of Industrial Colour Printer, *2nd international Conference on Machine Vision,* Dubai, UAE, pp. 225-228.

Argentiero, P., Chin, R., Beaudet, P. (1982). An automated approach to design the decision tree classifiers, *Pattern analysis and Machine Intelligence,* 4(1), pp.51-57.

Benediktsson, J.A.; Sveinsson, J.A.; Ersoy, J.R. & Swain, O.K. (1997). Parallel Consensual neural networks. *Neural Networks, IEEE Trans.,* Vol. 8 Issue 1, pp.54-64.

Bezdek, J.C. (1992). Computing with uncertainty. Comunication Magazine, *IEEE* vol.30, Issue 9, pp.24-36.

Bingul, Z.; Cook, G.E. & Strauss, A.M. (2000) Application of fuzzy logic to spatial thermal control in fusion welding. *IEEE Trans. Ind. Applicat.* Vol. 36, 6, pp. 1523-1530.

Bloch, I. (1996). Information combination operators for data fusion: a comparative review with classification. *IEEE Trans.Systems Man and cybernetics,* Part A Volume 6 Issue 1, pp.52-67.

Borselli, A., Colla, V., Vannucci, M. & Veroli, M. (2010). A Fuzzy Inference System applied to defect detection in flat steel production. *In IEEE World Congress on Computational intelligence,* 18-23 July, CCIB Barcelona, Spain.

Borselli, A., Colla, V. & Vannucci, M. (2011). Applying Surface defects classification in steel products: a comparison between different artificial intelligence-based approaches. *In Proceeding of the 11th lasted International Conference on Artificial Intelligence and Applications,* pp.129-134. Innsbruck, Austria.

Brown Grover, R., Hwang, P. (1992). Introduction to Random Signals and applied Kalman Filtering, *Wiley* New York.

Canny J. (1986). A Computational Approach to Edge Detection. *IEEE Transactions on Pattern Analysis and Machine Intelligence* 6 (November 86): 8

Castucci, P. Dickerson, G. & Backer, D. (1991) Utilizing an integrated yield management system to improve the return on investment in IC manufacturing, *Semiconductor Manufacturing Science Symposium, 1991. ISMSS 1991., IEEE/SEMI International*, 20-22 May.

Chin, R. T., & Harlow, C. A. (1982). Automated visual inspection: A survey. *IEEE Transactions on Pattern Analysis and Machine Intelligence,* 4(6), 557–573. doi:10.1109/TPAMI.1982.4767309

Choras, R.S. (2007). Image Feature Extraction Techniques and their applications for CBIR and Biometrics Systems. *International Journal of Biology and Biomedical Engineering,* Vol. 1, Issue 1.

Colla, V.; Giori, L.; Vannucci, M.; Bioli, G. (2009). A Fuzzy Inference System Applied to Quality Control in Paper Industry Chap. 13 in Modeling, Control, Simulation and Diagnosis of Complex Industrial and Energy Systems *ISA/O^{3}NEDIA* (ISBN 978-1-934394-90-8), pp. 253-272.

Dalton, J. (1996). Digital cameras and electronic color image acquisition, *Campcon'96 Technologies for the information Superhighway,* Digest of papers, 25-28 february 1996, pp. 431-434.

Elsayad, A.M. (2009). Classification of ECG arrhythmia using learning vector quantization neural network, *International Conference on Computer Engineering & Systems,*pp.139-144.

Ferrari, S. & Piuri, V. (2003). Neural Networks in Intelligent Sensors and Measurement Systems for Industrial applications.

Ferreira, M.J., Santos, C. & Monteiro, J. (2009). Cork parquet Quality Control Vision System based on texture Segmentation and Fuzzy Grammar, *IEEE Transactions on industrial Electronics,* 56 (3), pp. 756-765.

Filippidis, A.; Jain, L. & Martin, N. (2000). Multisensor data fusion for surface land-mine detection. *IEEE Trans. on Systems, Man and Cybernetics,* Part C, vol.30, pp.145-150.

Fukunaga, K. (1972). Introduction to statistical pattern recognition. *Academic Press Inc* , London.

Haralik, R.M. & Shapiro, L.G. (1992). Computer and Robot Vision, Vol. 1, *Addison Wensley,* 1992.

Haykin, S. (1999). Neural Networks. *Prentice Hall,*1999.

Hlavak, S.M. & Boyle, V. R. (1998) Image processing Analysis and Machine Vision. *PSW Publishing,* 1998.

Hongcan, Y.; Lin, C. & Bicheng, L. (2009). A SVM-Based Text Classification Method with SKK-Means Clustering Algorithm. *International Conference on Artificial Intelligence,* pp.379-383.

Hornik, K.; Stinchcombe, M & White, H. (1989). Multilayer feedforward networks are universal approximators, *Neural Networks,* 2 pp. 359-366.

Hough, P.V.C (1969). Method and Means for Recognising Complex Patterns, *US Patent 3969654.*

Jain, A.K.; Duin, R.P.W.& Mo, J. (2000). Statistical pattern recognition: a review. *IEEE Transaction on Pattern Analysis and Machine Intelligence,* Vol. 22, n°1, pp.4-37.

Jang, J.S.R. (1991) Fuzzy Modeling using Generalized Neural Networks and Kalman Filter Algorithm. *Proc. of ninth national conference on artificial Intelligence,* pp.762-767.

Jang, J.S.R. (1993) ANFIS: Adaptive- Network-based Fuzzy Inference Systems. *IEEE Transactions on Systems, Man and Cybernetics,* 23(3) pp.665-685.

Jarvis, J.F. (1979). Visual inspection Automation. *Proceeding of Computer Software and Application Conference,* 1979.

Jun, C., Hong, H., Kim, Y., Park, S.Y., Park, K.S. and park, H. (1999). A Simulation-based Semiconductor Chip Yield Model Incorporating a new defect cluster index. *Microelectronics Reliability,* 1999, 39, pp.451-456.

Kim, S.W.; Eun, Y.; Kim, H., Ko, W.J., Jung,Y.G., Choi, Y.G & Cho, D. (1998). Performance comparison of Loop/piezo and ultrasonic Sensor-based detection system for collecting individual vehicle information, *Proc. 5th world congr. Intell. Trans. System,* Seoul, Korea.

Kim, S.W.; Eun, Y.; Ko, W.J., Kim, H., Cho, I & Cho, D. (1999). A new loop detector circuit for improving low-speed performance, *Proc. 6th world congr. Intell. Trans. System,* Toronto, Canada.

Kim, S.W., Kim, K. & Lee, J. (2001). Application of fuzzy logic to vehicle classification algorithm in loop/piezo- sensor fusion systems. *Asian Journal of Control,* Vol. 3, Nà 1, pp. 64-68, March 2001.

Klette, R.; Schuluns, K. & Koschan, A. (1998). Computer Vision: three Dimensional Data from images, *Springer,* Singapore, 1998.

Lanzetta, M. (1998). 3d vision in production processes, part i - state of the art. *Automazione e Strumentazione elettronica Industriale,* ANIPLA, XLVI(2), pp. 155-164.

Li, P. & Zhang, Y.M. (2001). Robust sensing of arc length. *IEEE Trans. Instrum. Meas,* vol.50, n°3, pp.697-704.

Lowe, D.G & Little, J.J. (2005). Vision-based global localization and mapping for mobile robots. *IEEE Transactions on Robotics,* 21 (3), pp.364-375, 2005.

Malamas, E. N., Petrakis, E. G. M., Zervakis, M. E., Petit, L., & Legat, J. D. (2003). A survey on industrial vision systems, applications and tools. *Image and Vision Computing, 21*(2), 171–188. ù

Mandani, E.H. (1974). Application of fuzzy algorithms for control of simple dynamic plant. *Proceedings of the IEEE Control and Science,* 121, pp. 298-313, 1974.

Miljkovic, O. (2009). Image pre-processing tool, *Kragujevac J. Math,* 32, pp.97-107, 2009.

Naso, D. & Turchiano, B. (2005). A fuzzy logic based Optical sensor for online Weld defect detection. *IEEE Transactions on industrial informatics,* Vol. 1 , n°4, November 2005.

Nelson, B. J., Papanikolopoulos, N. P., & Khosla, P. K. (1996). Robotic visual servoing and robotic assembly tasks. *IEEE Robotics & Automation Magazine, 3*(2), 23–31.

Piuri, V. & scotti, F. (2005). Computational Intelligence in Industrial Quality Control. *IEEE Proceed. International Workshop on Intelligence signal,* pp. 4-9, 1-3 September, 2005, Faro, Portugal.

Princen, J., Yuen, H., Illingworth, J. & Kittler, J. (1992). Properties of the adaptive hough transform. *Proc. 6th scandinavian conference on Image Analysis,* Oulu Finland, June, 1992.

Proakis, J.G. & Manolakis, D.G. (1996). Digital Signal Processing : Principles, Algorithms and Applications. *Upper Saddle River,* NJ: Prentice Hall.

Quinlan, J.R. (1993). c4.5: Programs for Machine Learning, *Morgan Kaufmann Publisher.* New York.

Rabiner, L.R. & Gold, B. (1975). Theory and Application of Digital Signal Processing. *Englewood Cliffs,* NJ: Prentice Hall.

Roque, G., Musmanno, R.M., Montenegro, A. & Clua, E.W.G (2010). Adapting Sobel edge detector and canny edge extractor for iphone 3GS architecture, *Proceedings of the 17th International Conference on Systems, Signals and Image Processing,* IWSSIP, PP. 486-489, 2010.

Rosenfeld, A. (1969). Picture Processing by Computer, *Academic Press,* London UK, 1969.

Roudys, S.J. & Jain, A.K. (1991). Small sample size effect in statistical pattern recognition. *IEEE Trans. on Pattern Analysis and Machine Intelligence,* Vol.13, n°3, pp.252-264.

Rutishauser, U.; Joller, J. & Douglas, R. (2005). Control and learning of ambience by an intelligence building, *IEEE trans. on systems Man and Cybernetics,* Vol.35 n°1.

Sforza, P. & de Blasiis (2002). On line optical monitoring system for arc welding, *NDT & E Int,* vol. 35, n°1, pp.37-43.

Sgarbi, M.; Colla, V. & Bioli, G. (2010). A 3D vision-based solution for product picking in industrial applications. Cap. 10 *Intelligent Systems in Operations Methods Models and Applications in the Supply Chain,* pp. 190-208, IGI Global, USA ISBN: 9781615206056

Sobel, I.E. (1970). Camera Models and Machine Perception. *PhD Thesis,* Stanford University, 1970.

Stolzenberg, M. & Geisler, S. (2003). Status of surface inspection at steel production.*proc. of the 3rd European Rolling conference.* pp.311-316.

Tong, L.; Yang, C.; Chen, M.; Yu,H. & Wang, M. (2003). Process chart for controlling wafer defects using fuzzy theory. *Proceedings of the Third International Conference on electronic business (ICEB 2003),* 9-13 December 2003, Singapore (China).

Trucco, E. & Verri, A. (1998). Introductory Techniques for 3D computer vision. *Prentice Hall,* 1998.

Wandell, B.A. ; El Gamal, A.; Girod, B. (2002). Common principles of image acquisition systems and biological vision. *Proceedings of the IEEE,* Vol. 90, Issue 1, pp.5-17, January 2002.

Wen, M. & Zhong, C. (2008). Application of Sobel Algorithm in Edge Detection of Images. *China High-Tech Enterprise,* pp.57-62, July, 2008.

Werbos, P.J. (1974). The roots of Backpropagation, *John Wiley & Sons Inc.* New York.

Widrow, B. & Sterns, D. (1985). Adaptive Signal Processing. *New york Prentice Hall,* 1985.

Xia, Y.; Leung, H. & Bossè, E.(2002). Neural data fusion algorithms based on a linearly constrained least square method. *IEEE Trans on Neural Networks,* Vol. 13, pp.320-329, Mar 2002.

Zadeh, L.A. (1965) Fuzzy sets. *Information and Control,* Vol. 8, pp.338-353, 1965.

12

Edge Detection Based on Fuzzy Logic and Expert System

Shuliang Sun[1], Chenglian Liu[1,2], Sisheng Chen[1]
[1]*Department of Mathematics and Computer Science, Fuqing Branch of Fujian Normal University, Fuqing*
[2]*Department of Mathematics , Royal Holloway, University of London,Egham, Surrey, TW20*
[1]*China*
[2]*UK*

1. Introduction

The process of detecting outlines of an object and boundaries between objects and the background in the image is known as edge detection. It is an important tool used in many applications: such as image processing, computer vision and pattern recognition [1].

Linear time-invariant (LTI) filter is the most common method to the edge detection. On the condition of first-order filter, an edge is considered as an abrupt variation in gray level between two neighbor pixels. Then the aim is to find out the points in the image which the first-order derivative of the gray level is of high magnitude. The root mean square value (RMS) is often used as the threshold value to the input image [2].

Second order operators are used sometimes. LoG (Laplacian-of-Gaussian) [3] filter is the most commonly used. There are three drawbacks with this operator. Firstly, it produces the greater computational complexity. Secondly, it generates a continuous line to represent all edges in the input image, and is also not adequate to describe more general structures.

Fuzzy logic represents a powerful approach to decision making. Since the concept of fuzzy logic was formulated in 1965 by Zadeh, many researches have been carried out its applications in the various areas of digital image processing: such as image assessment, edge detection, image segmentation, etc [4]. Bezdek et al, trained a neural net to give the same fuzzy output as a normalized Sobel operator [5]. The advantage of the new method over the traditional edge detector is very apparent. In the system described in [6, 7], all inputs to the fuzzy inference systems (FIS) system are obtained by applying to the original image a high-pass filter, a first-order edge detector filter (Sobel operator) and a low-pass (mean) filter. The adopted fuzzy rules and the fuzzy membership functions are specified according to the kind of filtering to be executed.

2. General description composition of the fuzzy inference system

Fuzzy image processing is not a unique theory. It is a collection of different fuzzy approaches to image processing. Generally speaking, edge detection with fuzzy logic is composed of expert knowledge, fuzzification, membership modification, fuzzy set theory and defuzzification [8]. As shown in figure 1.

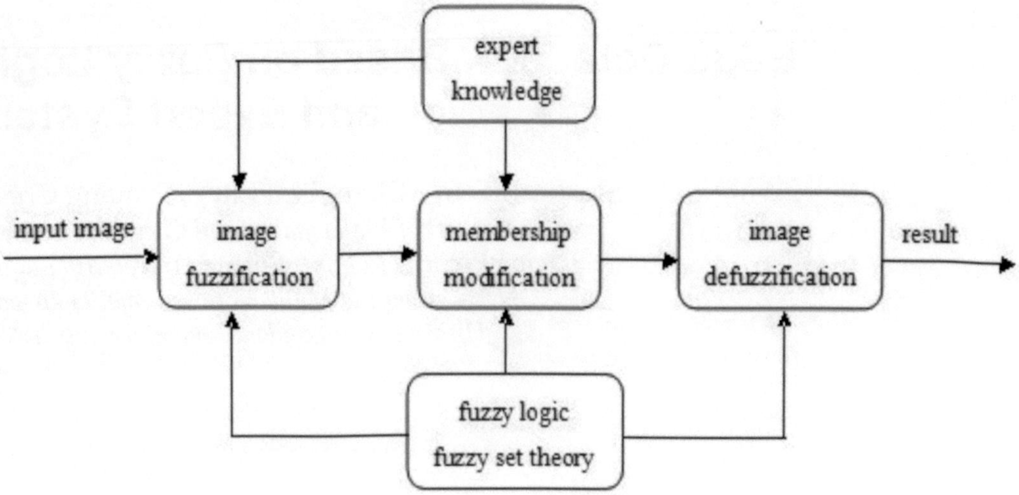

Fig. 1. The general structure of fuzzy image processing

The coding of image data (fuzzification) and decoding of the results (defuzzification) are steps that make possible to process images with fuzzy techniques. The main power of fuzzy image processing is in the middle step (modification of membership values). After the image datas are transformed from gray-level plane to the membership plane (fuzzification), appropriate fuzzy techniques modify the membership values. This can be a fuzzy clustering, a fuzzy rule-based approach, a fuzzy integration approach and so on.

Fuzzy image processing plays an important role in representing uncertain datas. There are many benefits of fuzzy image processing. Firstly, fuzzy techniques are able to manage the vagueness and ambiguity efficiently and deal with imprecise data. Secondly, fuzzy logic is easy to understand. Fuzzy reasoning is very simple in mathematical concepts.

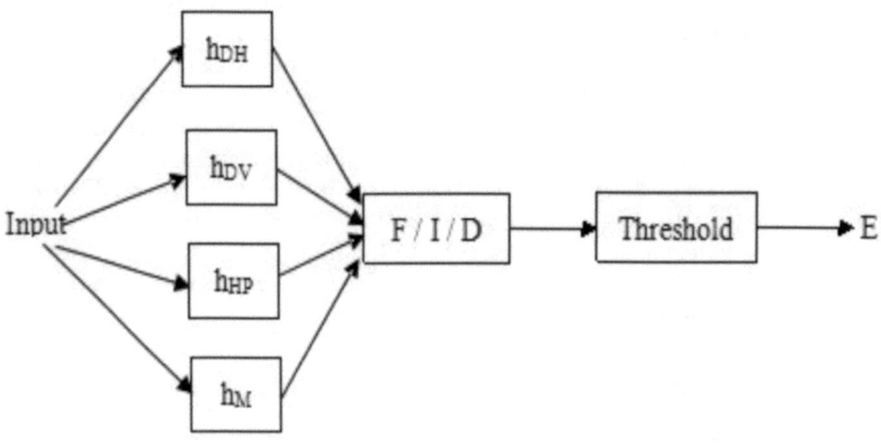

Fig. 2. Fuzzy inference system (FIS) applied to edge (E) detection

In many image processing applications, expert knowledge is often used to work out the problems. Expert knowledge, in the form of fuzzy if-then rules, is used to deal with imprecise data in fuzzy set theory and fuzzy logic. Fuzzy method will be more suitable to manage the imperfection than the traditional way.

Input of the the fuzzy inference system (FIS) is the original image and composed by a high-pass filter, a first-order edge detector filter (Sobel operator) and a low-pass (median) filter. It depicts in Figure 2.

In FIS , h_{DH} and h_{DV} are the Sobel operators used to estimate the first derivative of Image in horizontal and vertical directions. h_{HP} and h_M are the kernels of a high-pass and a low-pass (median) filters. F, I and D are the fuzzification, inference and defuzzification stages[9].

3. Edge detection with FIS system

3.1 Image pretreatment

Three linear and one non-linear (median) filters are used in this paper. A high-pass filter (h_{HP}) and a median filter (h_{MF}) are 3x3 masks.

[i-1, j-1]	[i-1, j]	[i-1, j+1]
[i, j-1]	[i, j]	[i, j+1]
[i+1, j-1]	[i+1, j]	[i+1, j+1]

Fig. 3. 3 * 3 matrix mask

Sobel operators (h_{DH} and h_{DV}) are kernels with 3x3 elements given by [10]: h_{DH} and h_{DV} are Sobel operators used to estimate the first derivative of Image in horizontal and vertical directions.

$$h_{DH} = \begin{bmatrix} -1 & 0 & 1 \\ -2 & 0 & 2 \\ -1 & 0 & 1 \end{bmatrix}, \quad h_{DV} = \begin{bmatrix} -1 & -2 & -1 \\ 0 & 0 & 0 \\ 1 & 2 & 1 \end{bmatrix} \tag{1}$$

Then the filtered images will be calculated through a bidimensional convolution operation, I is the original image:

$$DH = h_{DH} * I \tag{2}$$

$$DV = h_{DV} * I \tag{3}$$

However, the result of convolution of the two Sobel kernels is combined by computing norm-2.

$$D_{HV} = \sqrt{DH^2 + DV^2} \tag{4}$$

A high-pass filter (h_{HP}) and a median filter (h_{MF}) are defined as:

$$h_{HP} = \begin{bmatrix} -1 & -2 & -1 \\ -2 & 12 & -2 \\ -1 & -2 & -1 \end{bmatrix} \tag{5}$$

$$h_{MF} = \text{median}\{x_1, x_2, x_3, x_4, x_5, x_6, x_7, x_8, x_9\} \quad (6)$$

x_i (i =1,2,...,9) is the element of 3x3 mask.

Then the filtered images will be calculated through a bidimensional convolution operation:

$$HP = h_{HP} * I \quad (7)$$

$$M = h_{MF} * I \quad (8)$$

Laplacian operator and Gaussian function are separately defined as:

$$\nabla^2 f = \frac{\partial^2 f}{\partial x^2} + \frac{\partial^2 f}{\partial y^2} \quad (9)$$

$$h(x,y) = \exp\left(-\frac{x^2 + y^2}{2\sigma^2}\right) \quad (10)$$

Then LoG operator is formed by the convolution between Gaussian function and Laplacian operator.

$$\nabla^2 h = \left(\frac{r^2 - \sigma^2}{\sigma^4}\right)\exp\left(-\frac{r^2}{2\sigma^2}\right) \quad (11)$$

Here suppose $r^2 = x^2 + y^2$.

3.2 Fuzzy sets and fuzzy membership functions

Three fuzzy sets are made up to represent each variable's intensities; these sets are symbolized to the linguistic variables "low", "medium" and "high".

The adopted membership functions for the fuzzy sets are Gaussian function and sigmoid function. For the linguistic variables "low" and "high", sigmoid function is chosen; Gaussian function is used for the variable "medium" with the mean 127.5. As shown in Figure 4.

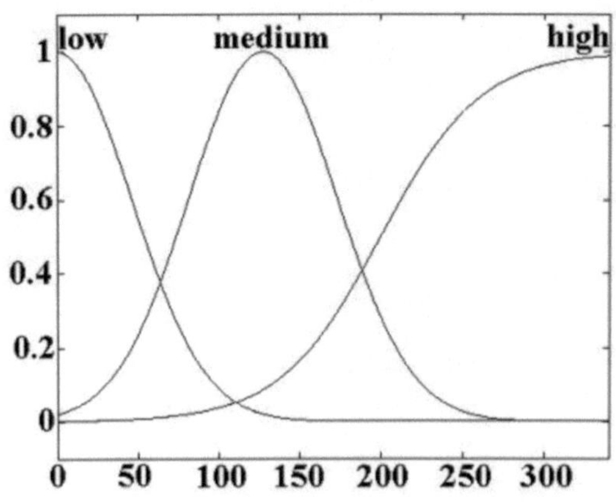

Fig. 4. Membership functions of the fuzzy sets

By the defined fuzzy rules, the output of this fuzzy system is classified to one of three classes [11, 12]. Output membership functions are shown in figure 5.

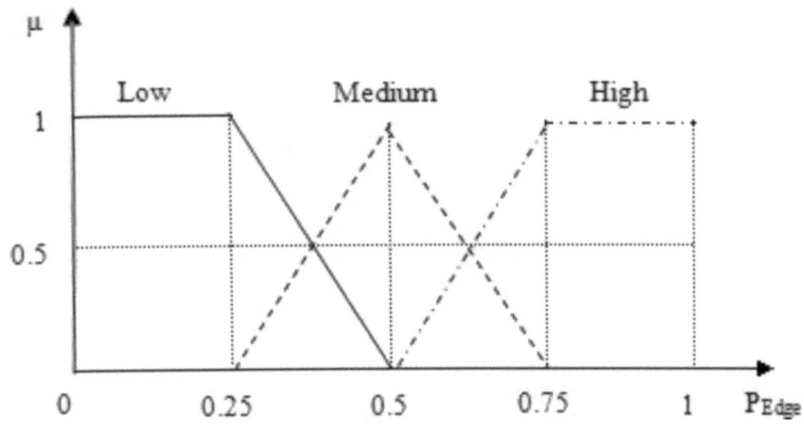

Fig. 5. Output membership functions

Fuzzy inference rules are applied to assign the three fuzzy sets characterized by membership functions μ_{High}, μ_{Medium}, and μ_{Low} to the output set.

3.3 Fuzzy inference rules

The fuzzy inference rules are defined in such a way, and the rules are shown below:

1. IF (M is low) and (h_{DV} is low) and (HP is low) THEN ("Edge" is low).
2. IF (M is low) and (h_{DV} is low) and (HP is medium) THEN ("Edge" is low).
3. IF (M is low) and (h_{DV} is low) and (HP is high) THEN ("Edge" is low).
4. IF (M is low) and (h_{DV} is medium) and (HP is low) THEN ("Edge" is low).
5. IF (M is low) and (h_{DV} is medium) and (HP is medium) THEN ("Edge" is low).
6. IF (M is low) and (h_{DV} is medium) and (HP is high) THEN ("Edge" is medium).
7. IF (M is low) and (h_{DV} is high) and (HP is low) THEN ("Edge" is low).
8. IF (M is low) and (h_{DV} is high) and (HP is medium) THEN ("Edge" is high).
9. IF (M is low) and (h_{DV} is high) and (HP is high) THEN ("Edge" is high).
10. IF (M is medium) and (h_{DV} is low) and (HP is low) THEN ("Edge" is low).
11. IF (M is medium) and (h_{DV} is low) and (HP is medium) THEN ("Edge" is low).
12. IF (M is medium) and (h_{DV} is low) and (HP is high) THEN ("Edge" is medium).
13. IF (M is medium) and (h_{DV} is medium) and (HP is low) THEN ("Edge" is medium).
14. IF (M is medium) and (h_{DV} is medium) and (HP is medium) THEN ("Edge" is medium).
15. IF (M is medium) and (h_{DV} is medium) and (HP is high) THEN ("Edge" is high).
16. IF (M is medium) and (h_{DV} is high) and (HP is low) THEN ("Edge" is medium).
17. IF (M is medium) and (h_{DV} is high) and (HP is medium) THEN ("Edge" is high).
18. IF (M is medium) and (h_{DV} is high) and (HP is high) THEN ("Edge" is high).
19. IF (M is high) and (h_{DV} is low) and (HP is low) THEN ("Edge" is low).
20. IF (M is high) and (h_{DV} is low) and (HP is medium) THEN ("Edge" is medium).
21. IF (M is high) and (h_{DV} is low) and (HP is high) THEN ("Edge" is medium).

22. IF (M is high) and (h_{DV} is medium) and (HP is low) THEN ("Edge" is medium).
23. IF (M is high) and (h_{DV} is medium) and (HP is medium) THEN ("Edge" is medium).
24. IF (M is high) and (h_{DV} is medium) and (HP is high) THEN ("Edge" is high).
25. IF (M is high) and (h_{DV} is high) and (HP is low) THEN ("Edge" is medium).
26. IF (M is high) and (h_{DV} is high) and (HP is medium) THEN ("Edge" is high).
27. IF (M is high) and (h_{DV} is high) and (HP is high) THEN ("Edge" is high).

(a) (b) (c) (d)

Fig. 6. Using different methods to detect the image with gradation of gray levels

3.4 Fuzzy logical operations and defuzzification

The output of the system P_{Final}, which is representing the probability used for final pixel classification as edge or not, is reckoned on a singleton fuzzifier. Mamdani defuzzifier method [13] is given by:

$$P_{Final} = \frac{\sum_{l=1}^{M} \bar{y}^{l} (\prod_{i=1}^{n} \mu_{k_i^l}(\alpha_i))}{\sum_{l=1}^{M} (\prod_{i=1}^{n} \mu_{k_i^l}(\alpha_i))} \tag{12}$$

where α_i are the fuzzy sets associated with the fuzzy rule base, $\bar{y}$ is the output class center and M is the number of fuzzy rules being considered.

4. Experiments

The proposed fuzzy edge detection method is simulated using MATLAB 7.0 on different images, and its performance is compared to that of the Sobel and LoG operator. In Figure 6, (a) is the original image, (b) is the image that the Sobel operator with threshold automatically estimated from image's RMS value. (c) is the image with LoG operator to detect edges, and the threshold is computed automatically. The FIS system, as shown (d), not only detects edges much better, but also makes the output image without noise.

Form above the experiments, it can be obviously shown that no matter how different images are tested, such as from bright to dim or from natural to artificial , the FIS system proposed in this paper is much better than Sobel and LoG operator in edge detection. The only disadvantage is that FIS system is not as simple as Sobel and LoG operator.

5. Conclusion

In this paper, FIS has been presented. The three edge strength values used as fuzzy system inputs were fuzzified using Gaussian membership functions and sigmoid function. Fuzzy if-then rules are used to modify the membership to one of low, medium, and high classes. Finally, Mamdani defuzzifier method is used to form the final edge image. By the simulation results, it can be concluded that though more computationally expensive than Sobel and LoG operators, the FIS system is superior in greater robustness to detect edge, and also advantage in edge detection exactly and noise removed clearly.

6. References

[1] J. C. Bezdek. (1981). *Pattern Recognition with Fuzzy Objective Functions*. Plenum, New York.

[2] M. N. Mahani, M. K. Moqadam, H. N. pour, etc. (2008). Dynamic Edge Detector Using Fuzzy Logic, *CSISS 2008*, Sharif University ofTechnology, Kish.

[3] L. Liang and C. Looney. (2003). Competitive Fuzzy Edge Detection, *Applied Soft Computing* , pp. 123 - 137 .

[4] G. Mansoori and H. Eghbali. (2006). Heuristic edge detection using fuzzy rule-based classifier, *Journal of Intelligent and Fuzzy Systems*, Volume 17, Number 5, pp. 457-469.

[5] Kuo, R. J. (1997). A robotic die polishing system through fuzzy neural networks, *Computer Industry*, Volume 32, Number 3, pp. 273–280.

[6] Tizhoosh H.R.(2002). Fast fuzzy edge detection, *Proceedings of Fuzzy Information Processing Society*, pp. 239-242.

[7] Lin, C. T., Lee, S. G.(1994). Reinforcement structure/parameter learning for neural network based fuzzy logic systems, *IEEE Trans. Fuzzy Systems* , Volume 2, Number 1 , pp. 46–63.

[8] Shahana B., Prasad B., E D Nagendra Prasad T. (2011). A New Approach for Edge Detection Using First Order Techniques. *IJCSt* , Volume 2, Number 1, pp. 78-82.

[9] Abdallah A. Alshennawy, and Ayman A. Aly. (2009). Edge Detection in Digital Images Using Fuzzy Logic Technique. World Academy of Science, Engineering and Technology 51, pp. 178-186.

[10] Cristiano Jacques Miosso1, Adolfo Bauchspiess. (2001). Fuzzy Inference System Applied to Edge Detection in Digital Images. *Proceedings of the V Brazilian Conference on Neural Networks - V Congresso Brasileiro de Redes Neurais*. April 2–5, - PUC, Rio de Janeiro - RJ - Brazil, pp. 481-486.

[11] Yujing Zhang. (2008). *Image Treatment and Analysis Technology*. Beijing, pp. 189-193.

[12] Wafa B., Fardin A. T., Om-Kolsoom S. (2009). Fuzzy Edge Detection Based on Pixel's Gradient and Standard Deviation Values. *PROCEEDINGS OF THE IMCSIT*. Volume 4, pp. 7-10.

[13] Aborisade, D. O. (2010). Fuzzy Logic Based Digital Image Edge Detection. *Global Journal of Computer Science and Technology*, Volume 10, Number 14, pp. 78-83.

13

Type-2 Fuzzy Logic for Edge Detection of Gray Scale Images

Abdullah Gubbi and Mohammad Fazle Azeem
Department of Electronics and Communication Engineering
PA College of Engineering, Mangalore, Karnataka
India

1. Introduction

Image processing is characterized by a procedure of information processing for which both the input and output are images, such as photographs or frames of video [Jain'86]. Most image processing techniques involve treating the image as a two-dimensional signal and applying standard signal processing techniques to it.[webpage1] Fuzzy Image Processing (FIP) is a collection of different fuzzy approaches to image processing. Nevertheless, the following definition can be regarded as an attempt to determine the boundaries. Fuzzy image processing includes all approaches that understand, represent and process the images, their segments and features as fuzzy sets. [webpage2]The representation and processing of the images depend on the selected fuzzy technique and on the problem to be solved [Jang'95]. Here is a list of general observations about fuzzy logic:

- *Fuzzy logic is conceptually easy to understand.*

The mathematical concepts behind fuzzy reasoning are very simple. Fuzzy logic is a more intuitive approach without the far-reaching complexity. Fuzzy logic is flexible. With any given system, it is easy to layer on more functionality without Starting again from scratch.

- *Fuzzy logic is tolerant to imprecise data.*

In real world everything is imprecise if you look closely enough, but more than that, most of the data which appear to be precise are imprecise after careful inspection. Fuzzy reasoning builds this understanding for the system rather than tackling it onto the end (precise).

- *Fuzzy logic can be built on top of the experience of experts.*

Fuzzy logic relies upon the experience of experts who already have familiarity and understanding about the functionality of systems.

- *Fuzzy logic can model nonlinear functions of arbitrary complexity.*

A fuzzy system can be created to match any set of input-output data. This process is made particularly easy by adaptive techniques like Adaptive Neuro-Fuzzy Inference Systems (ANFIS), which are available in Fuzzy Logic Toolbox.

- *Fuzzy logic can be blended with conventional control techniques.*

Fuzzy systems don't necessarily replace conventional control methods. In many cases fuzzy systems augment them and simplify their implementation. Fuzzy logic is based on natural language. The basis for fuzzy logic is the basis for human communication. This observation underpins many of the other statements about fuzzy logic. Because fuzzy logic is built on the structures of qualitative description used in everyday language, fuzzy logic is easy to use. Natural language, which is used by ordinary people on a daily basis, has been shaped by thousands of years of human history to be convenient and efficient. Sentences written in ordinary language represent a triumph of efficient communication [Webpage3].

The most important reasons for FIP are as follows:

1. Fuzzy techniques are powerful tools for knowledge representation and processing
2. Fuzzy techniques can manage the vagueness and ambiguity efficiently

In many image-processing applications, expert knowledge is used to overcome the difficulties in object recognition, scene analysis, etc. Fuzzy set theory and fuzzy logic offer us powerful tools to represent and process human knowledge in the form of fuzzy IF-THEN rules. On the other side, many difficulties in image processing arise because of the uncertain nature of the data, tasks, and results. This uncertainty, however, is not always due to the randomness but to the ambiguity and vagueness. Beside randomness which can be managed by probability theory, FIP can distinguish between three other kinds of imperfection in the image processing.

- Grayness ambiguity
- Geometrical fuzziness
- Vague (complex/ill-defined) knowledge

These problems are fuzzy in the nature. The question whether a pixel should become darker or brighter after processing than it is before? Where is the boundary between two image segments? What is a tree in a scene analysis problem? All of these and other similar questions are examples for situations that a fuzzy approach can be applied in a more suitable way to manage the imperfection.

FIP is an amalgamation of different areas of fuzzy set theory, fuzzy logic and fuzzy measure theory. The most important theoretical components of fuzzy image processing:

- Fuzzy Geometry (Metric, topology,)
- Measures of Fuzziness and Image Information (entropy, correlation, divergence, expected values,)
- Fuzzy Inference Systems (FIS) (image fuzzification, inference, image defuzzification)
- Fuzzy Clustering (Fuzzy c-means, possibility c-means,)
- Fuzzy Mathematical Morphology (Fuzzy erosion, fuzzy dilation,)

Applications of Edge Detection: Some of the practical applications of edge detection are:-

1. Medical Imaging

- Locate tumors and other pathologies
- Measure tissue volumes
- Computer guided surgery

- Diagnosis
- Treatment planning
- Study of anatomical structures

2. Locate objects in satellite images (roads, forests, etc.)
3. Face recognition
4. Fingerprint recognition
5. Automatic traffic controlling systems
6. Machine vision

This chapter spread over seven sections. Section 2 briefly describes uncertainties in recognition system. Brief description of Type-2 FIS is given in Section 3, while Section 4 deals with image pre-processing. Edge detection methods are elaborated in Section 5. Section 6 present experimentation and simulation results. Finally, conclusions are relegated to Section 7.

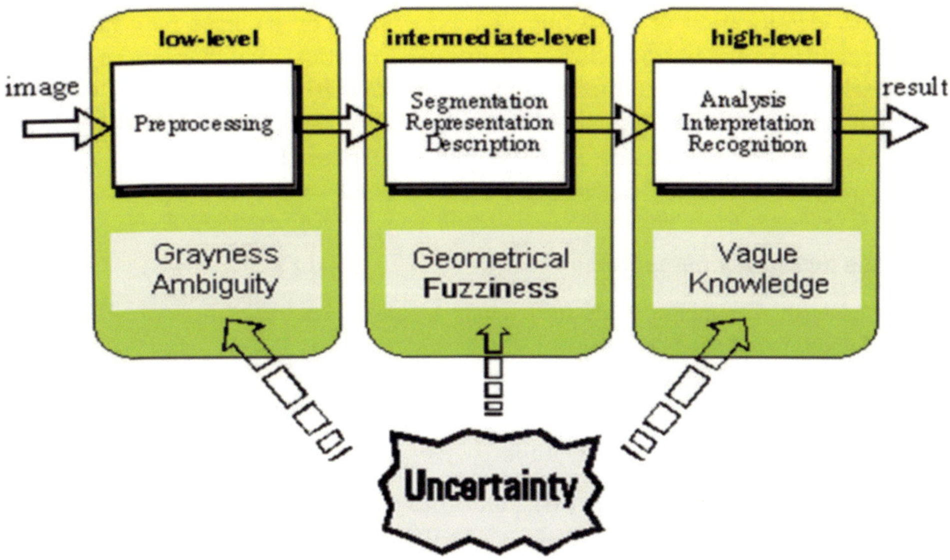

Fig. 1. Uncertainty/imperfect knowledge in image processing.

2. Uncertainties in a recognition system and relevance of fuzzy set theory

A gray scale image possesses some ambiguity within the pixels due to the possible multi-valued levels of brightness. This pattern uncertainty is due to inherent vagueness rather than randomness. The conventional approach to image analysis and recognition consists of segmenting (hard partitioning) the image space into meaningful regions, extracting its different features (e.g. edges, skeletons, centroid of an object), computing the various properties of and relationships among the regions, and interpreting and/or classifying the image. Since the regions in an image are not always clearly defined, uncertainty can arise at every phase of the job. Any decision taken at a particular level will have an impact on all higher level activities. In defining image regions, its features and relations in a recognition system (or vision system) should have sufficient provision for representing the uncertainties involved at every level.[Lindeberg'1998] The system should retains as much as possible the information content of the original input image for making a decision at the highest level. The final output image will then be associated with least uncertainty (and unlike conventional systems it will not be biased or affected very much by the lower level decisions).

Consider the problem of determining the boundary or shape of a class from its sampled points or prototypes. There are various approaches[Murfhy'88, Edelsbrunner'83, Tousant'80] described in the literature which attempt to provide an exact shape of the pattern class by determining the boundary such that it contains (passes through) some of the sample points. This need not be true. It is necessary to extend the boundaries to some extent to represent the possible uncovered portions by the sampled points. The extended portion should have lower possibility to be in the class than the portions explicitly highlighted by the sample points. The size of the extended regions should also decrease with the increase of the number of sample points. This leads one to define a multi-valued or fuzzy (with continuum grade of belonging) boundary of a pattern class [Mandal'92 & 97]. Similarly, the uncertainty in classification or clustering of image points or patterns may arise from the overlapping nature of the various classes or image properties. This overlapping may result from fuzziness or randomness. In the conventional classification technique, it is usually assumed that a pattern may belong to only one class, which is not necessarily true. A pattern may have degrees of membership in more than one class. It is, therefore, necessary to convey this information while classifying a pattern or clustering a data set.

2.1 Grayness ambiguity measures

In an image I with dimension MxN and levels L (based on individual pixel as well as a collection of pixels) are listed below.

r^{th} Order Fuzzy Entropy :

$$H^r(I) = (-1/k)\sum_{i=1}^{k}[\{\mu(s_i^r)log\mu(s_i^r)\} + \{\{1-\mu(s_i^r)\}log\{1-\mu(s_i^r)\}\}] \quad (1)$$

where s_i^r denotes the ith combination (sequence) of r pixels in I; k is the number of such sequences; and $\mu(s_i^r)$ denotes the degree to which the combination - s_i^r, as a whole, possesses some image property μ.

2.2 Hybrid entropy

$$H_{hy}(I) = -P_w \log E_w - P_b \log E_b \quad (2)$$

with

$$E_w = (1/MN)\sum_{m=1}^{M}\sum_{n=1}^{N}\mu_{mn}.\exp(1-\mu_{mn}) \quad (3)$$

$$E_w = (1/MN)\sum_{m=1}^{M}\sum_{n=1}^{N}(1-\mu_{mn}).\exp(\mu_{mn}) \quad (4)$$

where μ_{mn} denotes the degree of "whiteness" of the $(m,n)^{th}$ pixel. P_w and P_b denote probability of occurrences of white (μ_{mn} =1) and black (μ_{mn}=0) pixels respectively; and E_w and E_b denote the average likeliness (possibility) of interpreting a pixel as white and black respectively.

2.3 Spatial ambiguity measures based on fuzzy geometry of image

The basic geometric properties of and relationships among regions are generalized to fuzzy subsets. Such an extension, called fuzzy geometry [Rosefeld'84, Pal'90 & 99], includes the topological concept of connectedness, adjacency and surroundedness, convexity, area, perimeter, compactness, height, width, length, breadth, index of area coverage, major axis, minor axis, diameter, extent, elongatedness, adjacency and degree of adjacency. Some of these geometrical properties of a fuzzy digital image subset (characterized by piecewise constant membership function μ_I (I_{mn}) or simply μ. These may be viewed as providing measures of ambiguity in the geometry (spatial domain) of an image.

3. Type-2 fuzzy system

The original fuzzy logic (FL), Type-1 FL, cannot handle (that is, model and minimize the effects of) uncertainties sounds paradoxical because the word fuzzy has the connotation of uncertainty. A user believes that Type-1 FL captures the uncertainties and vagueness. But, in reality Type-1 FL handles only the vagueness, not uncertainties, by using precise membership functions (MFs). When the Type-1 MFs have been chosen, all uncertainty disappears because Type-1 MFs are totally precise. Type-2 FL, on the other hand, handles uncertainties hidden in the information/data as well as vagueness by modeling these using Type-2 MFs. All set theoretic operations, such as union, intersection, and complement for Type-1 fuzzy sets, can be performed in the same for Type-2 fuzzy sets. Procedures for how to do this have been worked out and are especially simple for Type-2 fuzzy sets [Karnik'2001].

First, let's recall that FL is all about IF-THEN rules (i.e., IF the sky is blue and the temperature is between 60 and 75° Fahrenheit, THEN it is a lovely day). The IF and THEN parts of a rule are called its antecedent and consequent, and they are modeled as fuzzy sets. Rules are described by the MFs of these fuzzy sets. In Type-1 FL, the antecedents and consequents are all described by the MFs of Type-1 fuzzy sets. In Type-2 FL, some or all of the antecedents and consequents are described by the MFs of Type-2 fuzzy sets.

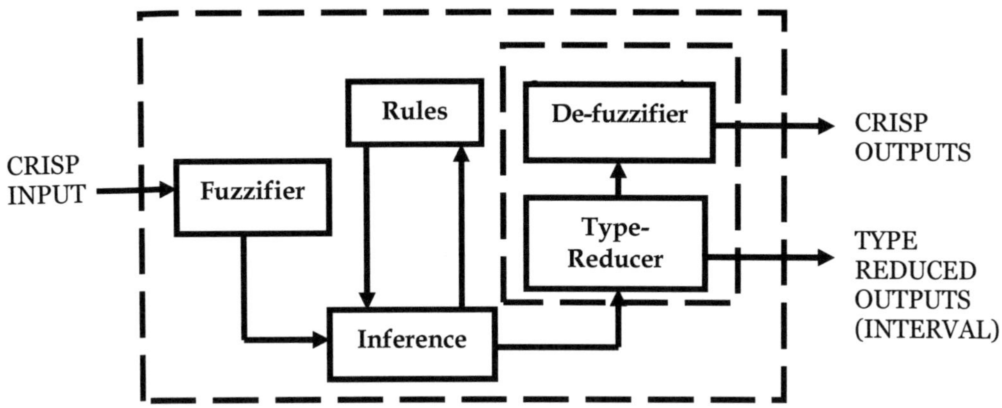

Fig. 2. Block Diagram of Type-2 FIS

The Type-2 fuzzy sets are three-dimensional, so they can be visualized as three-dimensional plots. Unfortunately, it is not as easy to sketch such plots as it is to sketch the two-dimensional plots of a Type-1 MFs. Another way to visualize Type-2 fuzzy sets is to plot their so-called Footprint Of Uncertainty (FOU). The Type-2 MFs, MF(x, w), sits atop a two-dimensional x-w plane. It sits only on the permissible (sometimes called "admissible") values of x and w. This means that x is defined over a range of values (its domain)—say, X. In addition, w is defined over its range of values (its domain)—say, W.

From the Figure 2, the measured (crisp) inputs are first transformed into fuzzy sets in the fuzzifier block because it is fuzzy set, not the number, that activates the rules which are described in terms of fuzzy sets.

Three types of fuzzifiers are possible in an interval Type-2 FLS. When measurements are:

- Perfect, they are modeled as a crisp set;
- Noisy, but the noise is stationary, they are modeled as a Type-1 fuzzy set; and,
- Noisy, but the noise is non-stationary, they are modeled as an interval Type-2 fuzzy set (this latter kind of fuzzification cannot be done in a Type-1 FLS).

after fuzzification of measurements (inputs), the resulting input fuzzy sets are mapped into fuzzy output sets by the Inference block. This is accomplished by first quantifying each rule using fuzzy set theory, and by then using the mathematics of fuzzy sets to establish the output of each rule, with the help of an inference mechanism. If there are M rules, the fuzzy input sets to the Inference block will activate only a subset of those rules usually fewer than M rules. So, at the output of the Inference block, there will be one or more fired-rule fuzzy output sets.

The fired-rule output fuzzy sets have to be converted into a number by Output Processing block as shown in the Figure 2. Conversion of an interval Type-2 fuzzy set to a number (usually) requires two steps. In the first step, an interval Type-2 fuzzy set is reduced to an interval-valued Type-1 fuzzy set called type-reduction. There are many type-reduction methods available [Karnik'2001]. Karnik and Mendel have developed an algorithm, known as the KM Algorithm, used for type-reduction. It is very fast algorithm but iterative. The second step of output processing, after type-reduction, is defuzzification. Since a type-reduced set of an interval Type-1 fuzzy set is a finite interval of numbers, the defuzzified value is just the average of the two end-points of this interval. If a type-reduced set of an interval Type-2 fuzzy set is a Type-1 fuzzy set, the defuzzified value can be obtain by any of the defuzzification method applied to Type-1 FL.

4. Image pre-processing

Image acquisition is a highly important step for the automatic quality control because it provides the input data for the whole process. The acquisition is performed by an optical sensor which is always a video camera with one line or a matrix of CCD, which provide accurate and noiseless image. Local illumination is directly linked with the quality of image acquisition because it is straight forward to demonstrate that its variations can heavily affect the patterns visibility in the image. Consequently the natural sources of light which are non-constant must not be employed and their influence should be carefully eliminated. Thus the use of a strictly controlled illumination provides good illumination control. Exclusively, one or more artificial light sources are the reasonable alternative.

Pre-processing: Before a computer vision method can be applied to image data in order to extract some specific piece of information, it is usually necessary to process the data in order to assure that it satisfies certain assumptions implied by the method. Examples are

a. Re-sampling in order to assure that the image coordinate system is correct.
b. Noise reduction in order to assure that sensor noise does not introduce false information.
c. Contrast enhancement to assure that relevant information can be detected.
d. Scale space representation to enhance image structures at locally appropriate scales

The following are the generally applied preprocessing methods.

a. Contrast adjustment
b. Intensity adjustment
c. Histogram equalization
d. Morphological operation

a. **Contrast adjustment:** The contrast of an image is the distribution of its dark and light pixels. A low-contrast image exhibits small differences between its light and dark pixel values. The histogram of a low-contrast image is narrow. Since the human eye is sensitive to contrast rather than absolute pixel intensities, a perceptually better image could be obtained by stretching the histogram of an image so that the full dynamic range of the image. After stripping away the color from an image (done by setting the saturation control to zero) the grayscale image that remains, represents the Luma component of the image. Luma is the portion of the image that controls the *lightness* of the image and is derived from a weighted ratio of the red, green, and blue channels of the image which corresponds to the eye's sensitivity to each color. The Luma component of images can be manipulated using the contrast controls in color image. Extreme adjustments to the image contrast will affect image saturation.
b. **Intensity adjustment:** Image enhancement techniques are used to improve an image, where "improve" is sometimes defined objectively (i.e., increase the signal-to-noise ratio), and sometimes subjectively (i.e., making certain features easier to see by modifying the colors or intensities). Intensity adjustment is an image enhancement technique that maps the image intensity values to a new range. The low-contrast images have its intensity range in the centre of the histogram. Mapping the intensity values in grayscale image I to new values, such that 1% of data is saturated at low and high intensities of I. This increases the contrast of the output image.
c. **Histogram Equalization:** The purpose of a histogram is to graphically summarize the distribution of a uni-variate data set. In an image processing context, the histogram of an image normally refers to a histogram of the pixel intensity values. This histogram is a graph showing the number of pixels in an image at each different intensity value found in that image. For an 8-bit grayscale image there are 256 different possible intensities, and so the histogram will graphically display 256 numbers showing the distribution of pixels amongst those grayscale values. Histograms can also be taken of color images. Either individual histogram of red, green and blue channels can be taken, or a 3-D histogram can be produced with the three axes representing the red, blue and green channels. The brightness at each point representing the pixel count. The exact output from the operation depends upon the implementation. It may simply be a picture of the required histogram in a suitable image format, or it may be a data file of

some sort representing the histogram statistics. The histogram graphically shows the following:

1. Center (i.e., the location) of the data;
2. Spread (i.e., the scale) of the data;
3. Skewness of the data;
4. Presence of outliers; and
5. Presence of multiple modes in the data.

The Histogram Equalization [wang'95] evenly distributes the occurrence of pixel intensities so that the entire range of intensities is covered. This method usually increases the global contrast of images, especially when the usable data of the image is represented by close contrast values. Through this adjustment, the intensities can be better distributed on the histogram. It allows the areas of lower local contrast to gain a higher global contrast. Histogram equalization accomplishes this by effectively spreading out the most frequent intensity values. Then probability density function (pdf) is calculated for the histogram.

d. **Morphological Operation** The identification of objects within an image can be a very difficult task. One way to simplify the problem is to change the grayscale image into a binary image, in which each pixel is restricted to a value of either "0" or "1". The techniques used on these binary images go by such names as: blob analysis, connectivity analysis, and morphological image processing (from the Greek word morphē, meaning shape or form). The foundation of morphological processing is in the mathematically rigorous field of set theory. However, this level of sophistication is seldom needed. Most morphological algorithms are simple logic operations and very ad hoc. Each application requires a custom solution developed by trial-and-error. Every texture image taken has been implemented with morphological reconstruction using Extended Maxima Transformation (EMT) with thresholding technique. The EMT is the regional maxima computation of the corresponding Horizontal Maxima Transformation (HMT). As a result, it produces a binary image. A connected-component labeling operation is performed, in order to evaluate the characteristics and the location of every object. The extended maxima transform computes the regional maxima of the H-Transform. Here H refers to nonnegative scalar [Karnik'2001]. Regional maxima are connected components of pixels with a constant intensity value, and whose external boundary pixels will have a lower value.

There are many techniques for preprocessing available in the literature. In the presented work, images are pre-processed using low pass filter whose mask is given as in eq. (5). This preprocessing is applied to remove the noise from the image. Later Image is normalized by taking account of mean and standard deviation.

$$Lp = \frac{1}{25} * \begin{bmatrix} 1 & 1 & 1 & 1 & 1 \\ 1 & 1 & 1 & 1 & 1 \\ 1 & 1 & 1 & 1 & 1 \\ 1 & 1 & 1 & 1 & 1 \\ 1 & 1 & 1 & 1 & 1 \end{bmatrix} \quad (5)$$

5. Edge detection

Edge detection is a fundamental tool used in most image processing applications to obtain information from the frames as a precursor step to feature extraction and object segmentation. This process detects outlines of an object and boundaries between objects and the background in the image. An edge-detection filter can also be used to improve the appearance of blurred or anti-aliased video streams.[webpage4]

The basic edge-detection operator is a matrix-area gradient operation that determines the level of variance between different pixels. The edge-detection operator is calculated by forming a matrix centered on a pixel chosen as the center of the matrix area. If the value of this matrix area is more than a given threshold, then the middle pixel is classified as an edge. For the of edges detection techniques normally methods like *Canny, Narwa, Iverson, Bergholm y Rothwell* [Heath'1996] are applied. Others methods can group in two categories: Gradient and Laplacian. The gradient methods like *Roberts, Prewitt* and *Sobel* detect edges, looking for maximum and minimum in first derivative of the image like the Laplacian methods find the zeros of second order derivative from the image [webpage5]Edges are extracted from the enhanced image by a two-stage edge detection operator that identifies the edge candidates based on the local characteristics of the image. Examples of gradient-based edge detectors are *Roberts, Prewitt,* and *Sobel* operators. All the gradient-based algorithms have kernel operators that calculate the strength of the slope in the directions which are orthogonal to each other, commonly vertical and horizontal. Later, the contributions of the different components of the slopes are combined to give the total value of the edge strength.

Recent techniques have characterized edge detection as a fuzzy reasoning problem [Boskovitz'2002], [Hanmandlu'2004], [Liang'2001&2003], [Miosso'2001]. These techniques have presented good and promising results in the areas of image processing and computational vision. Fuzzy techniques allow a new perspective to model uncertainties due to the uncertainty of gray-values present in the images. Thus, instead of assigning gray-values to the pixels in the image, fuzzy membership values may be assigned. Miosso and Bauchspiess [Miosso'01] have evaluated the performance of a fuzzy inference system in edge detection. It was concluded that despite the much superior computational effort, when compared to the *Sobel* operator, the implemented FIS system presents greater robustness to contrast and lighting variations besides avoiding obtaining double edges. Further tuning of the parameters associated with the fuzzy inference rules is still necessary to further reducing the membership values for the non-edge pixels. The proposed study is the beginning of an effort for the design of new edge detection techniques, using Fuzzy Inference Systems (FIS).

5.1 Calculation of the gradients

The *prewitt* operator measures two components. The vertical edge component is calculated with kernel *prewitt_y* and the horizontal edge component is calculated with kernel *prewitt_x*. The operator uses two 3×3 kernels [Green'02] and they are smaller than image size. These kernels are convolved with the original image. Convolution is a mathematical way of combining two signals to form a third signal. It is the most important technique in Digital Signal Processing. Using the strategy of impulse decomposition, systems are described by a signal called the impulse response. Convolution is important because it relates the three signals of interest: the input signal, the output signal, and the impulse response. These kernels are convolved with the original image to calculate approximations of the derivatives, one for horizontal changes, and one for vertical. If we define I as the source image, and G_x and G_y are two images which at each point contain the horizontal and vertical derivative approximations, they are computed as:

$$G_x = \sum_{i=1}^{i=3}\sum_{j=1}^{j=3}(Prewitt\_x_{i,j}) * I_{r+i-2,c+j-2} \tag{6}$$

and

$$G_y = \sum_{i=1}^{i=3}\sum_{j=1}^{j=3}(Prewitt\_y_{i,j}) * I_{r+i-2,c+j-2} \tag{7}$$

Where G_x and G_y are the prewitt mask convolved with original image, "*" is the convolution operator. The *prewitt* masks are shown as follows:

$$Prewitt\_x = \begin{bmatrix} -1 & 0 & +1 \\ -1 & 0 & +1 \\ -1 & 0 & +1 \end{bmatrix} \text{ and } Prewitt\_y = \begin{bmatrix} -1 & -1 & -1 \\ 0 & 0 & 0 \\ +1 & +1 & +1 \end{bmatrix} \tag{8}$$

Prewitt operator is applied on a digital image in gray scale. It calculates the gradient of the intensity of brightness of each pixel giving the direction of the greater possible increase of black to white. In addition, it also calculates the amount of change of the direction. Notion for G_x as DH and G_y as DV is used for FIS implementation.

The *prewitt* operator performs a 2-D spatial gradient measurement on an image. Typically it is used to find the approximate absolute gradient magnitude at each point in an input grayscale image. The *prewitt* edges detector uses a pair of 3x3 convolution masks, one estimating the gradient in the x-direction (columns) and the other estimating the gradient in the y-direction (rows). A convolution mask is usually much smaller than the actual image. As a result, the mask slides over the image, manipulating a square of pixels at a time.

For the purpose of finding out the performance of edge detection, the image is taken from the ORL face database [webpage6]. The original image is shown in Figure 3(a) while Figure 3(b) shows the preprocessed and normalized image.

The *Prewitt* mask given by *Prewitt_x* is convolved with the normalized image shown in Figure 3(b) in the horizontal direction and the obtained edges are as shown in Figure 4(a). Similarly The *Prewitt_y* is convolved with the image shown in Figure 3(b) in the vertical direction and the obtained edges are as shown in Figure 4(b) .Figure 4(c) shows the edges which are obtained from gradient magnitude, $G = \sqrt{Gx^2 + Gy^2}$. Figures 5 (a)-(c) show the histogram of the corresponding Images in Figures 4(a)-(c).

The gray scale intensity of each pixel of preprocessed image in Figure 3(b) is a value between 0 and 255. The maximum and minimum element values of the matrices given by DH, DV and G for the image shown in Figure 3(b) are listed in Table 1. These values can be used for defining the Type-1 and Type-2 Fuzzy set for antecedent variables.

Gray scale value	Preprocessed Image	DH	DV	G
Minimum	4	-828	-613	0
Maximum	204	746	725	853

Table 1. Minimum and Maximum element value of the matrices for Preprocessed Image, DH, DV and G

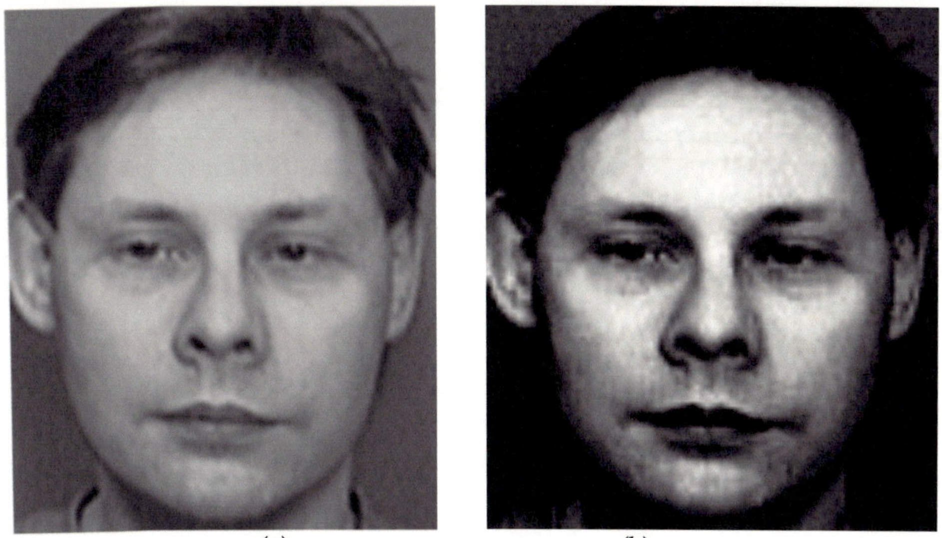

(a) (b)

Fig. 3. (a) The original image obtained from oral face data base. (b) After preprocessing and normalizing the original image.

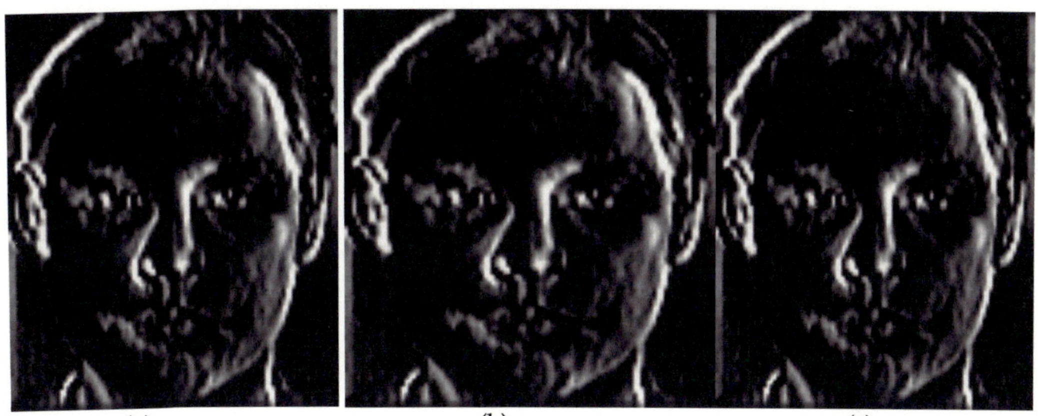

(a) (b) (c)

Fig. 4. (a) Edges obtained by *Prewitt_x* operator (b) Edges obtained by *Prewitt_y* operator (c) Edges obtained by *magnitude gradient.*

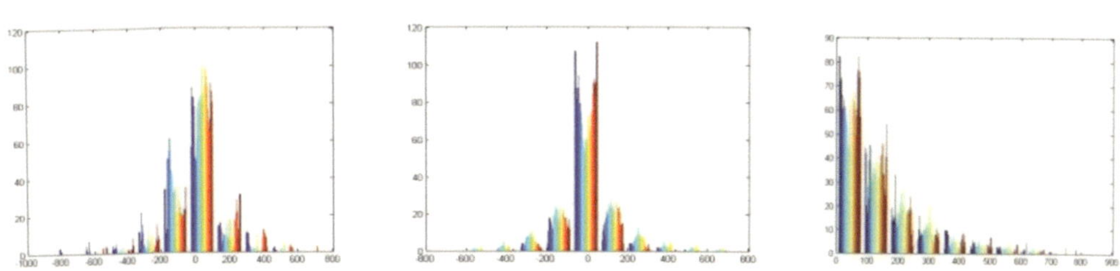

(a) (b) (c)

Fig. 5. Histograms of (a) the Image 4(a). (b) the Image 4(b). (c).) the Image 4(c)

5.2 Edges detection by type-1 FIS

The system implementation was carried out considering that both, the input image and the output image obtained after defuzzification, are 8-bit quantized. The Mamdani method was chosen as the defuzzification procedure, which means that the output fuzzy sets obtained by applying each inference rule to the input data were joined through the add function; the output of the system was then computed as the centroid of the resulting membership function [Jang'95]. Block Diagram of Type-1 Fuzzy Logic, with two inputs, one output and 10rules, using the Matlab Fuzzy Logic Tool Box [WebPage 7] is shown in Figure 6.

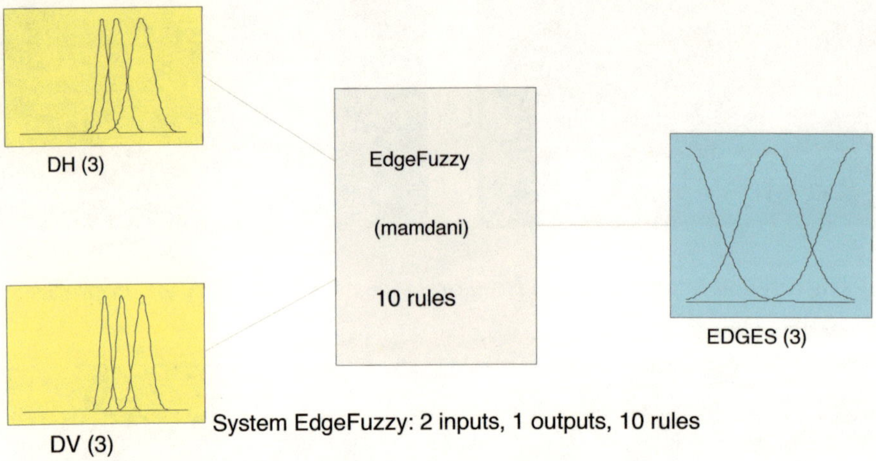

Fig. 6. Block Diagram for Type-1 Darken the lines between blocks Inference System

Since the image is preprocessed hence we use the horizontal gradient and Vertical gradient as inputs to Type-1 FIS with Gaussian member ship function For the Type-1 FIS, these two inputs are the gradients with respect to x-axis and y-axis and calculated by equations (6) and (7) which are denoted by DH and DV respectively.

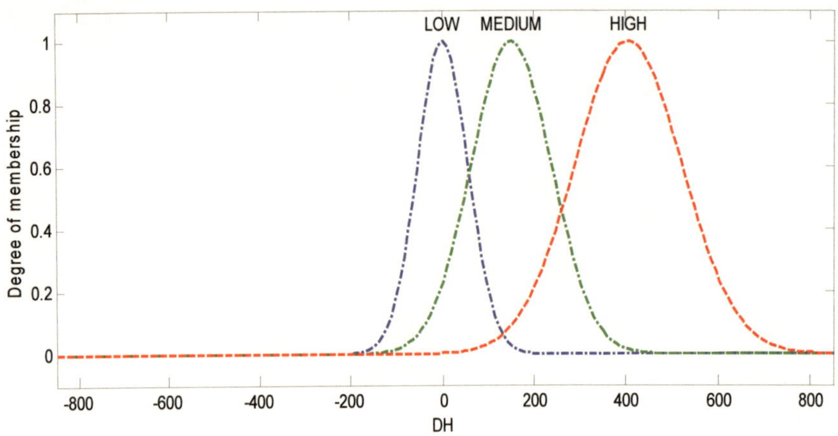

Fig. 7. Membership function for input 1 (DH)

Fuzzy 1 output image and its corresponding histogram

For all the fuzzy variables, the membership functions are Gaussian. According to the executed tests, the values in DH and DV, vary from -850 to 850, then the ranks in x-axis adjusted as shown in Figures 7 and Figure 8..The output variable , i.e. EDGES, membership functions are shown in Figure 9.

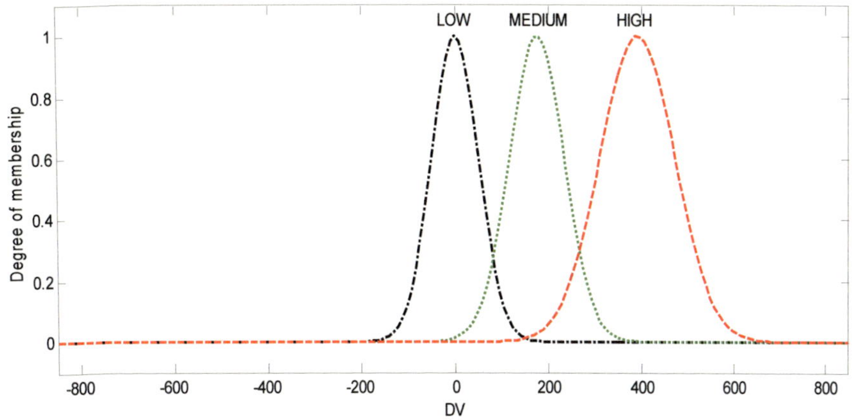

Fig. 8. Membership function for input 2 (DV)

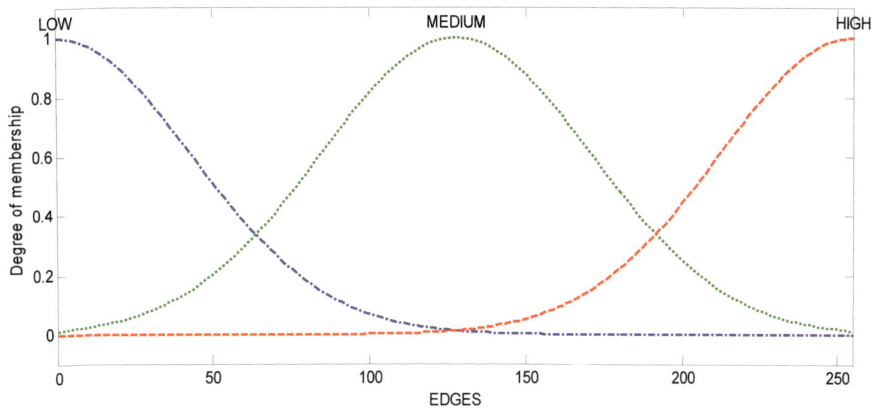

Fig. 9. Membership function for output EDGES

The ten fuzzy rules that allow to evaluate the input variables, so that the output image displays the edges of the image in color near white (255 gray scale), whereas the background was in near black (0 gray value).

1. If (DH is LOW) and (DV is LOW) then (EDGES is LOW)
2. If (DH is MEDIUM) and (DV is MEDIUM) then (EDGES is HIGH)
3. If (DH is HIGH) and (DV is MEDIUM) then (EDGES is HIGH)
4. If (DH is HIGH) and (DV is MEDIUM) then (EDGES is HIGH)
5. If (DH is MEDIUM) and (DV is LOW) then (EDGES is MEDIUM)

6. If (DH is LOW) and (DV is LOW) then (EDGES is LOW)
7. If (DH is LOW) and (DV is HIGH) then (EDGES is HIGH)
8. If (DH is LOW) and (DV is MEDIUM) then (EDGES is MEDIUM)
9. If (DH is MEDIUM) and (DV is HIGH) then (EDGES is HIGH)
10. If (DH is HIGH) and (DV is HIGH) then (EDGES is HIGH)

The result obtained from Type-1 FIS is outperform the *prewitt* operator edges as shown in Figure 10.

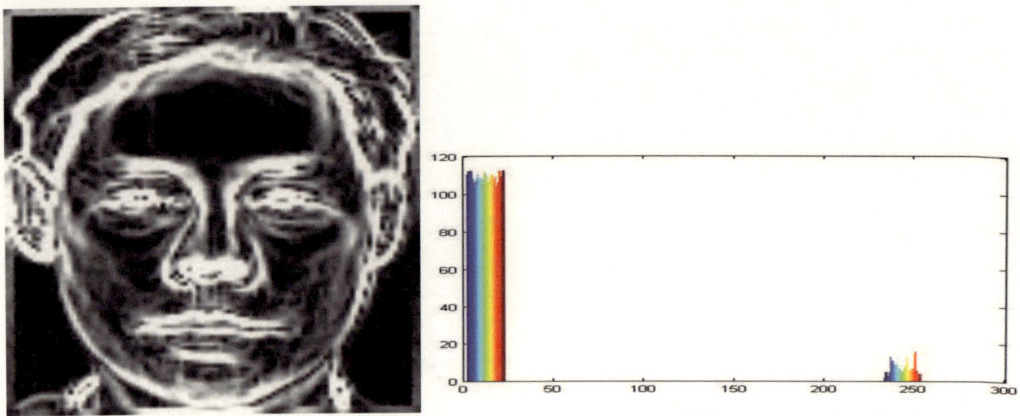

(a) (b)

Fig. 10. (a) AnEdge obtained by Type-1 FIS , and (b) its histogram.

5.3 Edges Detection by Type-2 FIS

Edge detection problems are fuzzy in the nature. The question whether a pixel should become darker or brighter after processing than it is before? Where is the boundary between two image segments? All these questions can be answered in the form of linguistic expressions known as rules. As far as rules are concern the rules do not change. "A rule is a rule is a rule…." What does change is the way in which one is going to model and process the fuzzy sets for antecedent and consequent of rules. In Type-1 FL, they are all modeled as Type-1 fuzzy sets, whereas in Type-2 FL, some or all are modeled as Type-2 fuzzy sets. In this implementation the range of pixels intensities are selected as edge pixels. This range can be obtained by Type-2 fuzzy outputs.

Type-2 FIS is implemented using mamdani model with Gaussian type membership function defined over the range of antecedent variables given in Table 1 and is shown in the figure 11 and Figure 12. The same set of rules are used for Type-2 FIS as of Type-1 FIS. Figure 6 also shows the block diagram for Type-2 FIS. The only difference between Type-1 and Type-2 FIS is the way the fuzzy sets are defined and processed for antecedent and consequent variables in this implementation. Type-2 FIS has been implemented in MATLAB using "Toolbox for Type-2 Fuzzy Logic" developed by prof(Dr)Oscar castillo [WebPage8]. The edges acquired by Type-2 FIS is shown in Figure 14. Comparing the Fig. 14 with Fig. 4 and Fig. 10, it shows that Type-2 FIS provide enhanced flexibility in choosing the pixel values. Hence, the result obtained from Type-2 FIS outperforms the *prewitt* operator and Type-1 FIS results.

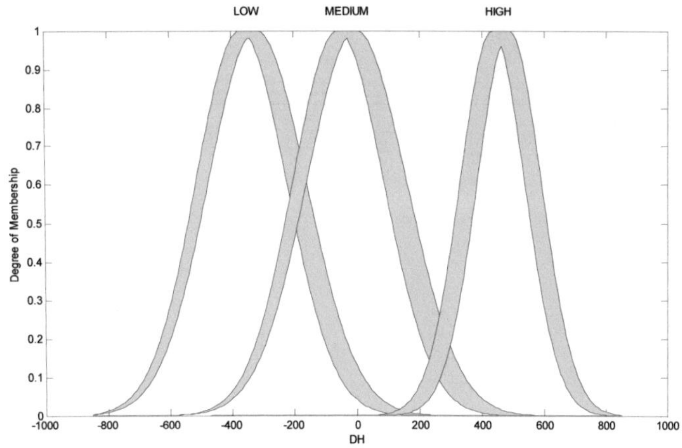

Fig. 11. Membership function for input 1 (DH)

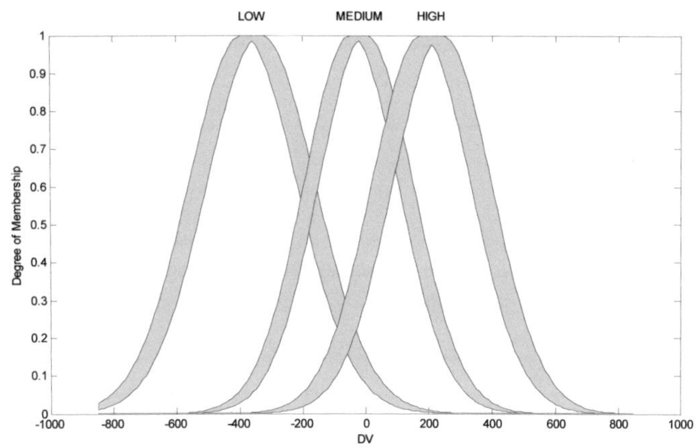

Fig. 12. Membership function for input 2 (DV)

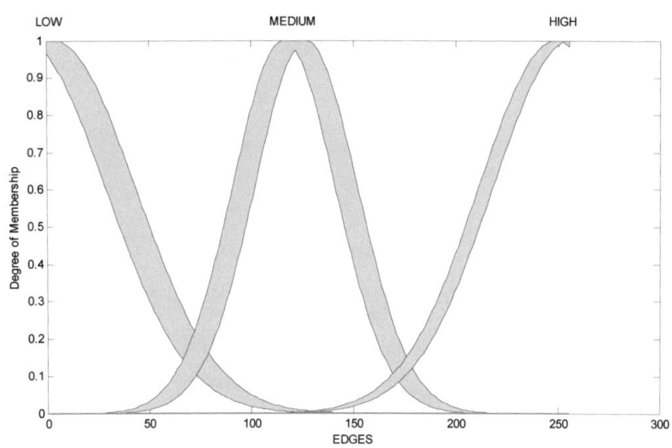

Fig. 13. Membership function for output (EDGE)

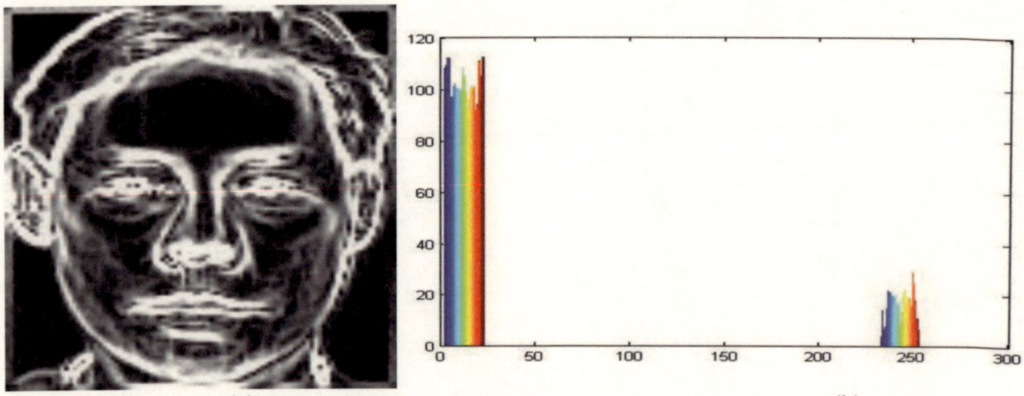

(a) (b)

Fig. 14. (a) AnEdge obtained by Type-2 FIS , and (b) its histogram.

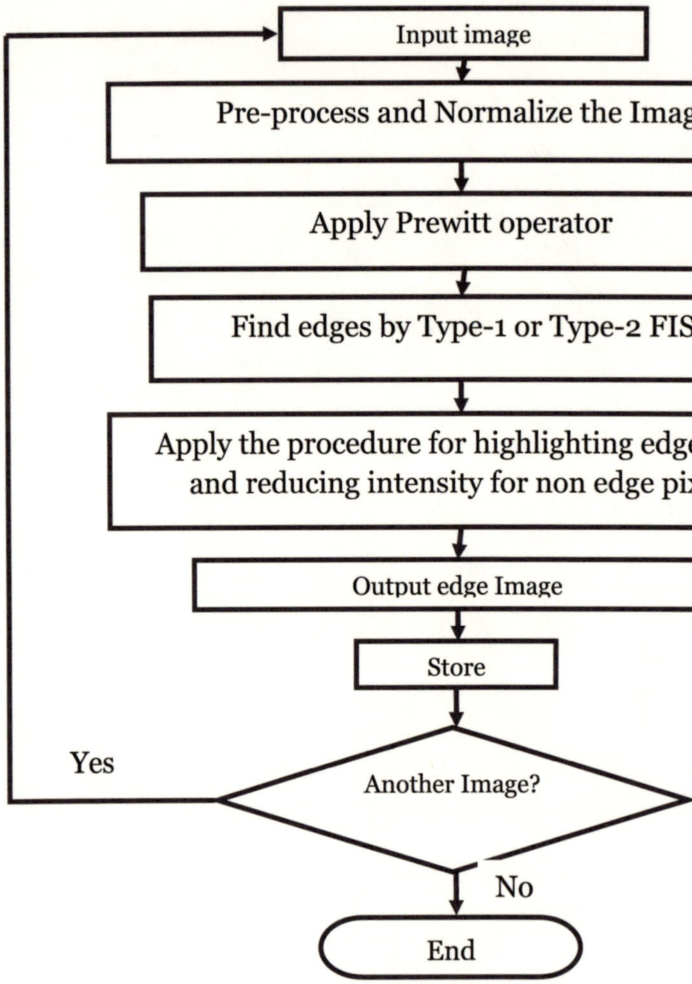

Fig. 15. Flow chart of the Edge Detection Algorithm.

6. Experimentation and simulation results

Figure 15 shows a flow chart representation of implementation procedure for acquiring the edges. A step by step implementation procedure for acquiring the edges is mentioned below.

Step 1. Transform the image into Gray scale pass is through low pass filter and normalize.
Step 2. use *prewitt* operator expressed by equation 6 - 8.
Step 3. Apply Type-1 FIS or Type-2 FIS to find the edges.
Step 4. Apply the procedure to high light the pixels which forms the edge pixels and for non edge pixels reduce the intensity value.

Experimentation of above mentioned procedure for obtaining the edges is carried on three different types of image given in Table 2. The image name are mentioned in the first column of table, while second column contains original image, third, fourth and fifth column shows the acquired edges of the images by gradient magnitude, Type-1 FIS, and Type-2 FIS respectively. The result shows that Type-2 FIS outperform *Prewitt* gradient and Type-1 FIS method.

Name	Original Image	Gradient Magnitude	Type-1 FIS	Type-2 FIS
Taj Mahal, India				
Baboon			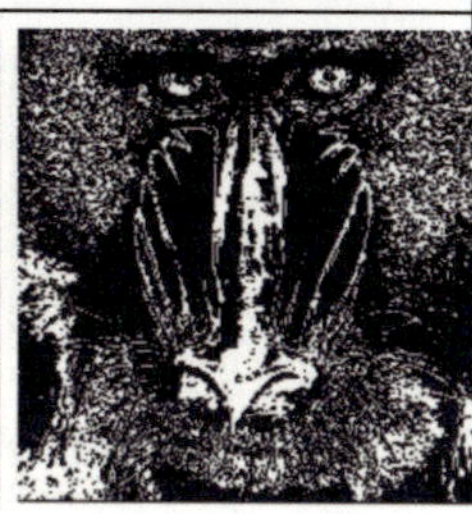	
Leena				

Table 2. Original Images, their name, and obtained edges by GM, Type-1, and Type-2 FIS

7. Conclusion

The problem of image processing and edge detection under fuzziness and uncertainty has been considered. The role of fuzzy logic in representing and managing the uncertainties in these tasks was explained. Various fuzzy set theoretic tools for measuring information on grayness ambiguity and spatial ambiguity in an image were discussed along with their characteristics. Some examples of edge detection, whose outputs are responsible for the overall performance of a recognition (vision) system, were considered in order to demonstrate the effectiveness of these tools in providing both soft and hard decisions. Gray information is expensive and informative. Once it is thrown away, there is no way to get it back. Therefore one should try to retain this information as long as possible throughout the decision making tasks for its full use. When it is required to make a crisp decision at the highest level one can always throw away or ignore this information. The significance of retaining the gray information in the form of class membership for soft decision is evident. Uncertainty in determining a membership function in this regard and the tools for its management were also stated. Finally a few real life applications of these methodologies are described.

The proposed technique used fuzzy if then rules are a sophisticated bridge between human knowledge on the one side and the numerical framework of the computers on the other side, simple and easy to understand. To achieve a higher level of image quality considering the subjective perception and opinion of the human observers.

- The proposed technique is able to overcome the draw backs of spatial domain methods like thresholding and frequency domain methods like Gaussian low pass filter. The proposed technique is able to improve the contrast of the image.
- The proposed technique is tested on different type of images, like degraded, low contrasted images.
- In this chapter we introduce the Type-2 FIS to detect edges. Type-2 FIS edge detector includes appropriately defined membership function using expert knowledge and decides about pixel classification as edge or non edge. Experimental results shown that, the proposed method extract more integrity of edges and avoid more noise than *prewitt* operator and Type-2 FIS.

8. References

[1] Boskovitz, V.; and Guterman, H., "An Adaptive Neuro-Fuzzy System for Automatic image segmentation and edge detection", *IEEE Transactions on fuzzy systems*, vol. 10, no. 2, April 2002, pp. 247–262.

[2] Celeux G.; and Govaert G.. "Gaussian parsimonious clustering models" *International journal on Pattern Recognition*, vol.28, no. 5, May1995,pp.781-793.

[3] Edelsbrunner, H.; Kirkpatrik, D.G.; and Seidel, R., "On the Shape of a Set of Points in the Plane", *IEEE Transaction on Information Theory*, vol. 29, no. 4, July 1983, pp.551-559.

[4] Hanmandlu,M.;See,J.;Vasikarla,S.;"Fuzzy edge detector using entropy optimization". In Proceedings of the International Conference on InformationTechnology: Coding and Computing,ITCC,vol.1 April 2004, pp 665–670.

[5] Jain A. K., "Fundamentals of digital image processing", Prentice-Hall, Inc., New Jersy, 1986.

[6] Roger Jang J. S. and Gulley Ned. "Fuzzy Logic ToolboxUser's Guide". The MathWorks, Inc., January 1995.
[7] Karnik N. N;. and Mendel, J. M.; "Centroid of a type-2 fuzzy set," *International journal on Information Sciences*, vol. 132, Nov2001.pp. 195-220,
[8] Liang L., Basallo E., and Looney C. "Image edge detection with fuzzy classifier". In Proceedings of the ISCA 14th International Conference, 2001, pages 279–283.
[9] Liang L. and Looney C. "Competitive fuzzy edge detection". *International journal on Applied Soft Computing*, Vol. 3, 2003, pp. 123– 137.
[10] Lindeberg .T "Edge Detection and Ridge Detection with Automatic Scale Selection", *International Journal of Computer Vision*, vol 30,no. 2, (1998), pages 117—154.
[11] Murfhy C. A. "Constitutent Estimation of Classes in R2 in the Context of Cluster Analysis" Ph D Thesis Indian Statistical Institute Calcutta (1988)
[12] Miosso C. J. and Bauchpiess " A. Fuzzy inference system applied to edge detection in digital images". In proceedings of the V Brazilian Conference on Neural Networks, 2001, pages 481–486.
[13] DP Mandal, C A Murthy. and S K Pal "Utility of multiple choices in detecting ill-defined roadlike structures" *International journal on General Systems* vol 64, no 2, June 1994 pp- 213-228
[14] Mandal, D. P.; Murthy C. A. andS. K. Pal,"Determining the shape of a pattern class from sampled points Extension to RN", *International journal on General Systems*, vol. 26, no. 4, pp. 293--320, 1997.
[15] Pal,S. K.,Ghosh, A. "Index of area coverage of fuzzy image subsets and object extraction" ,Pattern Recognition Letters, Vol. 11, (1990): pp.831-841.
[16] Rosenfeld.A., "The fuzzy geometry of image subsets",Pattern Recognition Lett. 2(1984),:pp 311-317 5.
[17] Toussaint G. T "Pattern Recognition and Geometrical Complexity". Proc. 5th *International Conference on pattern Recognition* , Miami Beach, 1980, pp. 1324-1347. MR 0521237
[18] Y. Wang, Q. Chen and B. Zhang. " Image enhancement based on equal area dualistic sub-image histogram equalization method". *IEEE Trans. on Consumer Electronics.* vol45,no1,(1999)pp: 68-75.
[20] Webpage1, Roger Claypoole, Jim Lewis, Srikrishna Bhashyam, Kevin Kelly, (Rice University, Huston, U.S.A.), Curso: "ELEC 539 - Digital Image Processing Rice University" Available:
www.owlnet.rice.edu/~elec539/Proyects97/morphjrks/moredge.html
[21] Webpage2,.http://www.wolfram.com/products/applications/fuzzylogic/examples/processing.html
[19] Webpage3,
http://www.doc.ic.ac.uk/~nd/surprise_96/journal/vol2/jp6/article2.html
[21] Webpage4, http://library.wolfram.com/examples/edgedetection/
[22] Webpage5,.http://www.owlnet.rice.edu/~elec539/Projects97/morphjrks/moredge.html
[22] Webpage6,.AT&T Laboratories, Cambridge, 2002, "The ORL Database of faces", http://www.uk.research.att.com/facedatabase.html,
[22] Webpage7, Web, The MathWorks, Inc., "Fuzzy Logic Toolbox
http://www.mathworks.com/products/matlab/,

[24] Webpage8, Michael D. Heath, (Florida, Mayo de 1996), "A Robustal Visual Method for Assessing the Relative Performance of Edge Detection Algorithms", Available: http://marathon.csee.usf.edu/edge/edge_detection.html
[26] Webpage8,. http://www.hafsamx.org/his/index.htm

14

Neuro-Fuzzy Prediction for Brain-Computer Interface Applications

Wei-Yen Hsu
Graduate Institute of Biomedical Informatics, Taipei Medical University
Taiwan

1. Introduction

The brain-computer interface (BCI) work is to provide humans an alternative channel that allows direct transmission of messages from the brain by analyzing the brain's mental activities [1–7]. The brain activity is recorded by means of multi-electrode electroencephalographic (EEG) signals that are either invasive or noninvasive. Noninvasive recording is convenient and popular in BCI applications so it is commonly used. According to the definition suggested at the first international meeting for BCI technology, the term BCI is reserved for a system that must not depend on the brain's normal output pathways of peripheral nerves and muscles [2]. It has become popular for BCI systems on motor imagery (MI) EEG signals in the last decade [8]. It reveals that there are special characteristics of event-related desynchronization (ERD) and synchronization (ERS) in mu and beta rhythms over the sensorimotor cortex during MI tasks by discriminating EEG signals between left and right MIs [9, 10]. ERD/ERS is the task-related or event-related change in the amplitude of the oscillatory behavior of specific cortical areas within various frequency bands. An amplitude (or power) increase is defined as event-related synchronization while an amplitude (or power) decrease is defined as event-related desynchronization. As other event-related potentials, ERD/ERS patterns are associated with sensory processing and motor behavior [2]. The principal objective of this study is to propose a BCI system, which combines neuro-fuzzy prediction and multiresolution fractal feature vectors (MFFVs) with support vector machine, for MI classification.

A model is used for time series prediction to forecast future events based on known past events [11]. A variety of methods have been presented in time series prediction, such as linear regression, Kalman filtering [12], neural network (NN) [13], and fuzzy inference system (FIS) [14]. Linear regression is simple and common, but it has less adaptation. Kalman filtering is an adaptive method, but intrinsically linear. The NN can approximate any nonlinear functions, but it demands a great deal of training data and is hard to interpret. On contrary, FIS has good capability of interpretation, but its adaptability is relative low. FISs are fuzzy predictions that can learn fuzzy "if-then" rules to predict data. They are readable, extensible, and universally approximate [14]. Adaptive neuro-fuzzy inference system (ANFIS) [15] integrates the advantage of both NN and fuzzy system. That is, ANFIS not only has good learning capability, but can be also interpreted easily. In addition, the training of ANFIS is fast and it can usually converge only depending on a small data set.

These good properties are suitable for the prediction of non-stationary EEG signals. Therefore, ANFIS is used for time-series prediction in this study.

An effective feature extraction method can enhance the classification accuracy. An important component for most BCIs is to extract significant features from the event-related area during different MI tasks. A great deal of feature extraction methods has been proposed. Among them, the band power and AAR parameters are commonly used [16–19]. Feature extraction based on band power is usually obtained by computing the powers at the alpha and beta bands. The features are then extracted from band powers by calculating their logarithm values [16] or averaging over them [17]. AAR parameters are another popular feature in mental tasks [18, 19]. The all-pole AAR model lends itself well to modeling EEG signals as filtered white noise with certain preferred energy bands. The EEG time series is fitted with an AAR model.

Furthermore, fractal geometry [20] provides a proper mathematical model to describe complex and irregular shapes that exist in nature. Fractal dimension is a statistical quantity that effectively extracts fractal features. In the last decade, feature extraction characterized by fractal dimension has been widely applied in various kinds of biomedical image and signal analyses, such as texture extraction [21], seizure onset detection in epilepsy [22], routine detection of dementia [23], and EEG analyses of sleeping newborns [24]. In this study, discrete wavelet transform (DWT) together with modified fractal dimension is utilized for feature extraction. That is, MFFVs are extracted from wavelet data by modified fractal dimension. MFFVs contain not only multiple scale attributes, but important fractal information.

The support vector machine (SVM) [25] recognizing the patterns into two categories from a set of data is usually used for the analyses of classification and regression. For example, the SVM is used to classify attention deficit hyperactivity disorder (ADHD) and bipolar mood disorder (BMD) patients by proposing an adaptive mutation to improve performance [26]. The SVM is used for seizure detection in an animal model of chronic epilepsy [27]. Since it can balance accuracy and generalization simultaneously [25], it is used for classification in this study.

To evaluate the performance, several popular methods, including AAR-parameter approach and AAR time-series prediction, are implemented for comparison. This chapter is organized as follows: Section 2 presents the materials and methods. Section 3 describes experimental results. The discussion and conclusion are given in Sections 4 and 5, respectively.

2. Problem formulation

An analysis system is proposed for MI EEG classification, as illustrated in Fig. 1. The procedure is performed in several steps, including data configuration, neuron-fuzzy prediction, feature extraction, and classification. Raw EEG data are first filtered to the frequency range containing mu and beta rhythm components in data configuration. ANFIS time-series predictions are trained by the training data at offline. Information from ANFIS time-series predictions is directly applied to predict the test data. Modified fractal dimension combined with DWT is utilized for feature extraction. The extracted fractal features are used to train the parameters of SVM classifier at offline. Finally, the SVM together with trained parameters is utilized to discriminate the features.

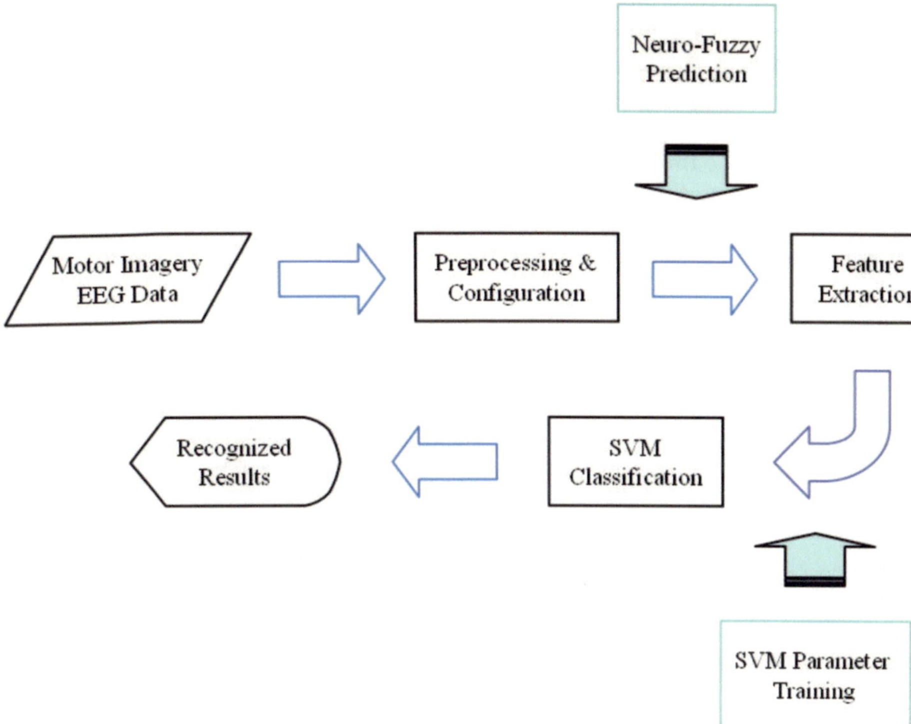

Fig. 1. Flowchart of proposed system.

3. Experimentation

The EEG data was recorded by the Graz BCI group [19, 28–32]. Two data sets are used to evaluate the performance of all methods in the experiments. The first data sets were recorded from three subjects during a feedback experimental recording procedure. The task was to control a bar by means of imagery left or right hand movements [19, 28, 30, 31]. The order of left and right cues was random. The data was recorded on three subjects - the first subject S1 performs 280 trials, while the last two subjects, S2 and S3, hold 320 trials. The length of each trial was within 8–9s. The first 2s was quiet, an acoustic stimulus indicates the beginning of a trial at t = 2s, and a fixation cross + was displayed for 1s. Then at t = 3s, an arrow (left or right) was displayed as a cue (the data recorded between 3 and 8s are considered as event related). At the same time, each subject was asked to move a bar by imagining the left or right hand movements according to the direction of the cue. The recordings were made using a g.tec amplifier and Ag/AgCl electrodes. All signals were sampled at 128 Hz and filtered between 0.5 and 30 Hz. An example of a trial for C3 and C4 channels is given in Fig. 2(a).

The second data sets were recorded from three subjects by using a 64-channel Neuroscan EEG amplifier [29, 32]. The left and right mastoids served as a reference and ground, respectively. The EEG data was sampled at 250 Hz and filtered between 1 and 50 Hz. The subjects were asked to perform imagery movements prompted by a visual cue. Each trial started with an empty black screen; at t = 2s a short beep tone was presented and a cross '+'

appeared on the screen to notify the subjects. Then at t = 3s an arrow lasting for 1.25s pointed to either the left or right direction. Each direction indicates the subjects to imagine either a left or right hand movement. The imagery movements were performed until the cross disappeared at t = 7s. No feedback was performed in the experiments. The data set recorded from subject S4 was 180 trials, while the data sets for subjects S5 and S6 were 120 trials. For each subject, the first half of the trials were used as training data and the later half of the trials were used as test data in this study.

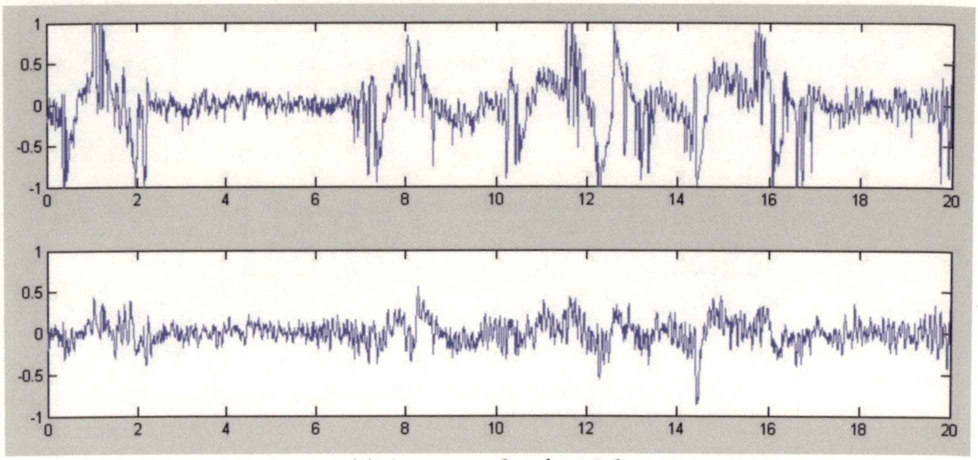

(a) An example of a trial

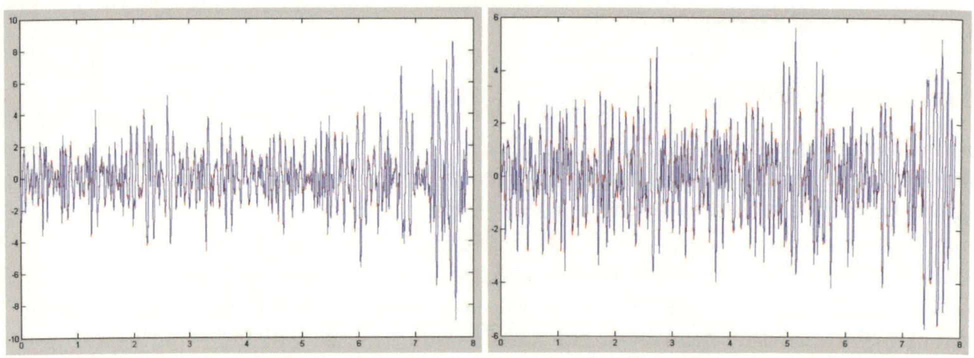

(b) Actual and predicted signals (C3) (c) Actual and predicted signals (C4)
(Actual filtered signals: Red; Predicted signals: Blue)

Fig. 2. Intermediate results.

4. Methodologies

4.1 Data configuration

The mu and beta rhythms of the EEG are those components with frequencies distributed between 8-30 Hz and located over the sensorimotor cortex. In addition, using a wider frequency range from the acquired EEG signals can generally achieve higher classification accuracy in comparison with a narrower one [33]. A wide frequency range containing all mu and beta rhythm components is adopted to include all the important signal spectra for MI classification. In this study, the raw EEG data are filtered to the frequency range between 8 and 30 Hz with a Butterworth band-pass filter.

To make a prediction at sample *t*, the measured signals extracted from the recorded EEG time-series data are used from samples *t-Ld* to *t-d*. The parameters *L* and *d* are the embedding dimension and time delay, respectively. Each training input data for ANFIS prediction consist of respective measured signals of length *L* on both the *C3* and *C4* channels, which are important for BCI works because they are located in the sensorimotor cortex [34]. The training input data are represented as follows:

$$\left[\left(C3_{t-Ld},\ldots,C3_{t-d},C4_{t-Ld},\ldots,C4_{t-d} \right)^{t} \mid \left(C3_{t},C4_{t} \right)^{t} \right] \quad (1)$$

There are event related data of approximately 5s length in each trial. All parameter selection is performed from the training data. All training data are used to train the parameters of prediction models, which will be further used for feature extraction. The test data are finally tested to evaluate the performance of the system by using the trained parameters.

4.2 Neuro-fuzzy prediction

Time series prediction is the use of a model to forecast future events based on known past events. Although all kinds of methods in time series prediction have been presented, ANFIS time-series prediction is slightly modified and adopted in this study since it integrates the advantages of NN and fuzzy system.

The ANFIS network architecture applied for the time-series prediction of EEG data is introduced. A detailed description of ANFIS can be found in [15]. ANFIS enhances fuzzy parameter tuning with self-learning capability for achieving optimal prediction objectives. An ANFIS network is a multilayer feed-forward network where each node performs a particular node function on incoming signals. It is characterized with a set of parameters pertaining to that node. To reflect different adaptive capabilities, both square and circle node symbols are used. A square node (adaptive node) has parameters needed to trained, while a circle node (fixed node) has none. The parameters of the ANFIS network consist of the union of the parameter sets associated to each adaptive node. To achieve a desired input-output mapping, these parameters are updated according to given training data and a recursive least square (RLS) estimate.

In this study, the ANFIS network applied for time-series prediction contains *L* inputs and one output. There are 2^{L} fuzzy if-then rules of Takagi and Sugeno's type [35] in the representation of rule base. The output is a current sample, and the inputs are the past *L* samples in the time delay *t*. The output of the *i*th node in the *l*th layer is denoted by O_i^l. The node function for each layer is then described as follows.

Layer 1: Each node in this layer is a square node, where the degree of membership functions of input data is calculated. The output of each node in this layer is represented as

$$O_i^1 = \mu_{M_{jk}}(C_{t-(L-j+1)d}), \quad j=1,2,\ldots,L;\ k=1,2;\ i=1,2,\ldots,2L \quad (2)$$

where $i = 2(j-1)+k$, C representing $C3$ or $C4$ is the input to node i, and M_{jk} is the linguistic label associated with this node function. The bell-shape Gaussian membership function $\mu_{M_{jk}}(C)$ is used

$$\mu_{M_{jk}}(C_{t-(L-j+1)d}) = \exp\left(-\left(\frac{C_{t-(L-j+1)d} - a_{jk}}{\sigma_{jk}}\right)^2\right) \tag{3}$$

where the parameter set $\{a_{jk}, \sigma_{jk}\}$ adjusts the shape of the Gaussian membership function. Parameters M_{jk} in this layer are referred to as premise parameters.

Layer 2: Each node in this layer is a circle node labeled Π multiplying the incoming signals together and sends out their product.

$$O_i^2 = w_i = \prod_{j=1}^{L} \mu_{M_{ji}}(C_{t-(L-j+1)d}), \quad i = 1,2 \tag{4}$$

Each node output represents the firing strength of a rule.

Layer 3: Each node in this layer is a circle node labeled N. The firing strength of a rule for each node in this layer is normalized.

$$O_i^3 = \overline{w}_i = \frac{w_i}{\sum_j w_j}, \quad i = 1,2 \tag{5}$$

Layer 4: Each node in this layer is a square node with its node function represented as

$$O_i^4 = \overline{w}_i f_i = \overline{w}_i \left(\sum_{j=1}^{L} p_{ij} x_j + r_i\right), \quad i = 1,2 \tag{6}$$

where the output f_i is a linear combination of the parameter set $\{p_{ij}, r_i\}$. Parameters f_i in this layer is referred to as consequent parameters.

Layer 5: The single node in this layer is a circle node labeled Σ computing the overall output y as the sum of all incoming signals.

$$O_1^5 = y = \sum_i \overline{w}_i f_i = \frac{\sum_j w_j f_j}{\sum_j w_j} \tag{7}$$

The architecture of neuron-fuzzy prediction in this chapter is shown in Fig. 3. The consequent parameters are updated by the RLS learning procedure in the forward pass for ANFIS network learning, while the antecedent parameters are adjusted by using the error between the predicted and actual signals. The parameter optimization for ANFIS training is adopted an approach that is mixed least squares and back-propagation method. Two

ANFISs are used to perform prediction. That is, they labeled lANFIS and rANFIS are used to predict left and right training MI EEG data, respectively. The actual filtered signals and their predicted results for C3 and C4 channels are shown in Fig. 2(b) and 2(c), respectively.

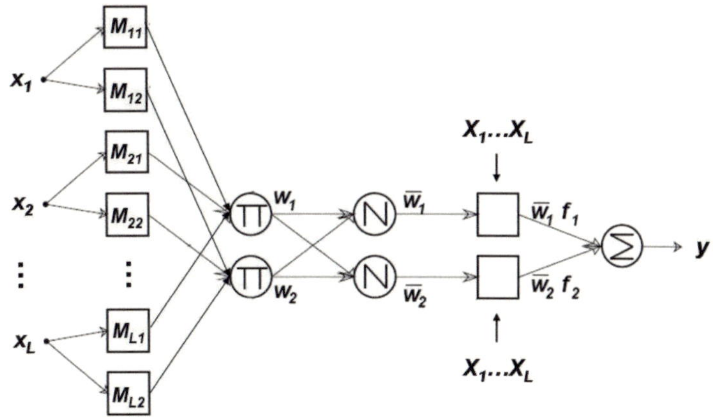

Fig. 3. Architecture of neuro-fuzzy prediction.

4.3 Feature extraction

After lANFIS and rANFIS are trained by using the left and right MI training data trial by trial respectively, they are used to perform one-step-ahead prediction. The test data are then input to these two ANFISs sample by sample, and features are extracted by continually calculating the difference of MFFVs between the predicted and actual signals as the length of predicted signals achieves 1-s window. The MFFV will be outlined in the next paragraph. In this study, feature extraction is performed on the 1-s window of predicted signals instead of directly classifying native predicted signals. A flowchart of feature extraction is shown in Fig. 4.

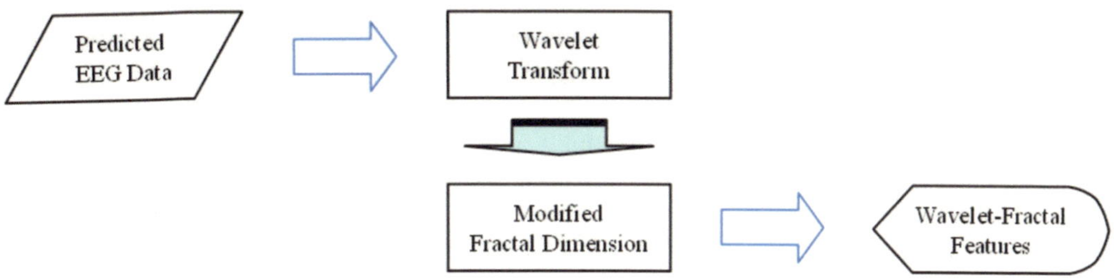

Fig. 4. Flowchart of feature extraction.

A signal is decomposed into numerous details in multiresolution analysis, where each scale represents a class of distinct physical characteristics within the signal. Wavelet transform is used to achieve multiresolutional representation in this study [21, 33, 36-39]. The 1-s segment is decomposed into numerous non-overlapping subbands by wavelet transform.

Fractal geometry provides a proper mathematical model to describe a complex shape that exists in nature with fractal features. Since fractal dimension is relatively insensitive to signal scaling and shows a strong correlation with human judgment of surface roughness [20], it is chosen as the feature extraction method. A variety of approaches were proposed to estimate fractal dimension from signals or images [21-24]. A differential box counting (DBC) method covering a wide dynamic range with a low computational complexity is modified and used in this study [33]. A MFFV is extracted by modified fractal dimension from all the non-overlapping subbands of a 1-s segment.

The MFFV reflects the roughness and complexity of non-overlapping subbands of a signal. These MFFV calculations reduce prediction cost from a 1-s window to a feature vector for each signal. Features are extracted by continually calculating the difference of MFFVs between the predicted and actual signals as the length of predicted signals achieves 1-s window. In other words, two sets of MFFV features are first extracted from the predicted and actual signals respectively as the length of predicted signals achieves 1-s window. They are then subtracted for each respective subband. Finally, features are obtained by continually calculating their difference. The left and right test data are input to both the lANFIS and rANFIS, and each ANFIS provides two predictions from the *C3* and *C4* channels. Accordingly, four sets of MFFVs can be extracted after each new set of predictions is obtained. Each time a new set of predictions is produced, the oldest one is removed from the 1-s segment and a new MFFV is then extracted from the signals within the window. Since a large window is too redundant for the real time application, a 1-s window is short and selected for feature extraction. The length of a 1-s segment is a compromise between the computation cost and event-related potential (ERP) component applications. If the window length is selected properly, the extracted MFFVs will produce the maximum feature separability and obtain the highest classification accuracy.

4.4 Classification

It can be difficult to establish stable NNs since appropriate number of hidden layers and neurons usually need to carefully choose to approximate the function in question to the desired accuracy. The SVM first proposed by Vapnik [25] not only has a very steady theory in statistical learning, but guarantees to obtain the optimal decision function from a set of training data. The main idea of SVM is to construct a hyperplane as the decision surface in such a way that the margin of separation between positive and negative examples is maximized. The SVM optimization problem is

$$\min_{w} \frac{1}{2} w^T w + C\sum_{i=1}^{N} \xi_i$$
$$\text{subject to } \xi_i \geq 0, \forall i, \text{ and } d_i\left(w^T x_i + b\right) \geq 1 - \xi_i, \forall i = 1,2,\ldots N \quad (8)$$

where $g(x) = w^T x + b$ represents the hyperplane, w is the weighting vector, b is the bias term, x is the training vector with label d, C is the weighting constant, and ξ is the slack variable. It is then transformed into a convex quadratic dual problem. The discriminant function with optimal w and b, $g(x) = w_o^T x + b_o$, posterior to the optimization form becomes

$$g(x) = \sum_{i=1}^{N} \alpha_i d_i K(x, x_i) + b_o \tag{9}$$

where α is a Lagrange multiplier and $K(x,x_i)$ is a kernel function. Generally, appropriate kernel functions are the polynomial kernel function $K(x_i,x_j) = \left(x_i^T x_j + 1\right)^p$ and the radial basis function (RBF) kernel function $K(x_i,x_j) = \exp\left(\left(-1/2\sigma^2\right)\left\|x_i - x_j\right\|^2\right)$. In this study, the latter is chosen for the SVM.

In the proposed system, classification is performed on MFFVs for recognizing the corresponding state at the sample rate. A different SVM classifier at each sample point is produced to classify each set of MFFVs for the training data. The classification sample point possessing maximal classification rate for training data is used as the standard classifier, which will be used for all classification performed on the test data. The best parameters selected from the training data are then applied to the test data to estimate the classification accuracy of test data.

5. Results

5.1 Performance of prediction methods

To assess the performance of proposed time-series prediction method, several prediction methods combined with power spectra features are implemented for comparison. They are AAR-parameter approach and AAR time-series prediction. The power spectra features are obtained by calculating the powers at the alpha and beta bands [16, 17]. The AAR-parameter method is an AAR signal modeling approach. The all-pole AAR model lends itself well to modeling the EEG as filtered white noise with certain preferred energy bands. The EEG time series is fitted with an AAR model. In the experiments, the order of AAR model is chosen as six and the AAR parameters are estimated with the RLS algorithm. To select the best value for the order of AAR model, an information theoretic approach is adopted [3]. The AAR parameters are used as features at each sample point for each trial. The AAR time-series prediction method is a time-series prediction approach, where left and rights ANFISs in the

Classification Accuracy [%]	AAR Parameters	AAR Prediction	Neuro-Fuzzy Prediction
S1	71.5	81.4	86.9
S2	66.3	76.6	84.2
S3	64.9	78.3	77.2
S4	72.6	79.6	88.6
S5	65.7	73.1	80.1
S6	61.0	77.0	79.8
Average	67.0	77.7	82.8

Table 1. Comparison of performance among different time-series prediction frameworks using power spectra features

ANFIS time-series prediction method are replaced by left and right AAR models. The lengths of windows for the AAR-parameter approach and AAR time-series prediction are all 1-s windows, which are the same as that for the ANFIS time-series prediction.

The comparison results of classification accuracy among different time-series prediction using power spectra features are listed in Table 1. The average classification accuracy of AAR-parameter approach is 67.0%, while AAR time-series prediction is 77.7% in the average classification accuracy. ANFIS time-series prediction obtains the best average classification accuracy (82.8%).

5.2 Performance of features

To further estimate the performance of proposed ANFIS time-series prediction method and MFFV features, ANFIS time-series prediction method combined with power spectra features is used for comparison in Table 2. The average classification accuracy for ANFIS time-series prediction method combined with power spectra features is 82.8%, while MFFV features under ANFIS time-series prediction method obtain 91.0 in the average classification accuracy.

Classification Accuracy [%]	Power Spectra	MFFV
S1	86.9	92.8
S2	84.2	88.5
S3	77.2	90.3
S4	88.6	93.9
S5	80.1	88.2
S6	79.8	92.0
Average	82.8	91.0

Table 2. Comparison of performance between power spectra and MFFV features under the use of ANFIS time-series prediction

5.3 Statistical analysis

Two-way analysis of variance (ANOVA) and multiple comparison tests [40] are performed in the experiments. The statistical analyses with two-way ANOVA are used to evaluate that the difference is significant or not for the two factors, methods and subjects. After analyzing with the two-way ANOVA, multiple comparison tests are used to estimate the *p*-values and significance of each pair of methods. The results of tests will be discussed in detail in the next section.

6. Discussion

6.1 Statistical evaluation of prediction methods

ANFIS combines the advantage of NN with that of FIS. Moreover, the training of ANFIS is fast and it can generally converge from small data sets. These attractive properties are suitable for the prediction of non-stationary EEG signals. Table 1 lists the comparisons of performance among different prediction frameworks using power spectra features. In addition, two-way ANOVA and multiple comparison tests are performed to verify if the prediction methods are significantly different or not. The results indicate that AAR time-series prediction method is much better than AAR parameter approach in classification accuracy (p-value 0.0007) that is improved by 10.7% on average, while ANFIS time-series prediction method is slightly better than AAR prediction method (p-value 0.0195). The classification accuracy increases by 5.1%. Accordingly, ANFIS time-series prediction has the best performance in classification accuracy among these three methods. The results deduce that ANFIS time-series prediction is the best prediction framework in MI classification.

6.2 Statistical evaluation of features

Wavelet-fractal features are extracted from wavelet data by modified fractal dimension. MFFVs are utilized to describe the characteristic of fractal features in different wavelet scales, which are greatly beneficial for the analysis of EEG data. The comparison of performance between power spectra and MFFV features under the use of ANFIS time-series prediction is listed in Table 2. In addition, two-way ANOVA and multiple comparison tests are performed again to validate whether the two features are significantly different. The results indicate that MFFV features are significantly better than power spectra features in classification accuracy (p-value 0.0030), which is improved by 8.2% on average. The results indicate that MFFV features are better. These two results also suggest that ANFIS prediction framework together with MFFV features is a good combination in BCI applications.

6.3 Advantage of proposed method

The proposed ANFIS prediction framework combined with MFFV features provides a good potential for EEG-based MI classification. Furthermore, the proposed method has other potential advantages as follows: Firstly, the MFFV features really improve the separability of MI data, because the power spectra feature extracted from the predicted signals results in poorer performance. Secondly, the MFFV features can effectively reduce the degradation of noise. In other words, the MFFV features are extracted by DWT and modified fractal dimension. The former obtains multiscale information of EEG signals while the latter decreases the effect of noise. It is because the calculation of an improved DBC method is proposed and applied to modified fractal dimension.

7. Conclusion

We have proposed a BCI system embedding neuro-fuzzy prediction in feature extraction in this work. The results demonstrate the potential for the use of neuro-fuzzy prediction together with support vector machine in MI classification. It also shows that the proposed system is robust for the inter-subject use under careful parameter training, which is important for BCI applications. Compared with other well-known approaches, neuro-fuzzy prediction together with SVM achieves better results in BCI applications. In future works, more effective prediction/features and powerful classifiers will be used to further improve classification results.

8. Acknowledgements

The author would like to express his sincerely appreciation for grant under shared facilities supported by the Program of Top 100 Universities Advancement, Ministry of Education, Taiwan.

9. References

[1] R. Leeb, F. Lee , C. Keinrath, R. Scherer, H. Bischof, and G. Pfurtscheller, "Brain-computer communication: Motivation, aim, and impact of exploring a virtual apartment," *IEEE Trans. Neural Sys. Rehabil. Eng.*, vol. 15, no. 4, pp. 473-482, 2007.

[2] J. R. Wolpaw, N. Birbaumer, D. J. McFarland, G. Pfurtscheller, and T. M. Vaughan, "Brain-computer interfaces for communication and control," *Clin. Neurophysiol.*, vol. 113, pp. 767-791, 2002.

[3] W. Y. Hsu, "EEG-based motor imagery classification using neuro-fuzzy prediction and wavelet fractal features," *Journal of Neuroscience Methods*, vol. 189, no. 2, pp. 295-302, June 2010.

[4] W. Y. Hsu, C. Y. Lin, and W. F. Kuo, Unsupervised Fuzzy C-Means Clustering for Motor Imagery EEG Recognition," *International Journal of Innovative Computing, Information and Control*, vol. 7, no. 8, pp. 4965-4976, Aug. 2011.

[5] W. Y. Hsu, "EEG-based Motor Imagery Classification using Enhanced Active Segment Selection and Adaptive Classifier," *Computers in Biology and Medicine*, vol. 41, no. 8, pp. 633-639, Aug. 2011.

[6] W. Y. Hsu, "Continuous EEG signal analysis for asynchronous BCI application," *International Journal of Neural Systems*, vol. 21, no. 4, pp. 335-350, Aug. 2011.

[7] W. Y. Hsu, "Application of Multiscale Amplitude Modulation Features and FCM Clustering to Brain-Computer Interface," accepted for published in *Clinical EEG and Neuroscience*, June 2011, In Press.

[8] L. Parra, C. Alvino, A. C. Tang, B. A. Pearlmutter, N. Yeung, A. Osman, and P. Sajda, "Linear spatial integration for single trial detection in encephalography," *NeuroImage*, vol. 7, no. 1, pp. 223-230, 2002.

[9] G. Townsend, B. Graimann, and G. Pfurtscheller, "Continuous EEG classification during motor imagery-simulation of an asynchronous BCI," *IEEE Trans. Neural Sys. Rehabil. Eng.*, vol. 12, no. 2, pp. 258-265, 2004.

[10] G. Pfurtscheller, and F. H. Lopes da Silva, "Event-related EEG/MEG synchronization and desynchronization: basic principles," *Clin. Neurophysiol.*, vol. 110, pp. 1842-1857, 1999.

[11] R. H. Shumway, and D. S. Stoffer, "Times Series Analysis and its application," New York: *Springer-Verlag*, 2000.

[12] X. Hu, D. V. Prokhorov, I. I. Wunsch, and C. Donald, "Time series prediction with a weighted bidirectional multi-stream extended Kalman filter," *Neurocomputing*, vol. 70, pp. 2392-2399, 2007.

[13] N. Stamatis, D. Parthimos, and T. M. Griffith, "Forecasting chaotic cardiovascular time series with an adaptive slope multilayer perceptron neural network," *IEEE Trans. Biomedical Engineering*, vol. 46, no. 12, pp. 1441-1453, 1999.

[14] H. J. Rong, N. Sundararajan, G. B. Huang, and P. Saratchandran, "Sequential Adaptive Fuzzy Inference System (SAFIS) for nonlinear system identification and prediction," *Fuzzy Sets and Systems,* vol. 157, no. 9, pp. 1260-1275, 2006.

[15] J. S. Jang Roger, "ANFIS: adaptive-network-based fuzzy inference system," *IEEE Trans. SMC,* vol. 23, no. 3, pp. 665-685, 1993.

[16] B. Obermaier, C. Neuper, C. Guger, and G. Pfurtscheller, "Information transfer rate in a five-classes brain-computer interface," *IEEE Trans. Neural Sys. Rehabil. Eng.*, vol. 9, pp. 283-288, 2001.

[17] C. Guger, G. Edlinger, W. Harkam, I. Niedermayer, and G. Pfurtscheller, "How many people are able to operate an EEG-based brain-computer interface (BCI)?," *IEEE Trans. Neural Sys. Rehabil. Eng.*, vol. 11, pp. 145-147, 2003.

[18] D. P. Burke, S. P. Kelly, P. de Chazal, R. B. Reilly, and C. Finucane, "A parametric feature extraction and classification strategy for brain-computer interfacing," *IEEE Trans. Neural Sys. Rehabil. Eng.*, vol. 13, pp. 12-17, 2005.

[19] C. Guger, A. Schlögl, C. Neuper, D. Walterspacher, T. Strein, and G. Pfurtscheller, "Rapid prototyping of an EEG-based brain–computer interface (BCI)," *IEEE Trans. Rehab. Eng.*, vol. 9, no. 1, pp. 49-58, 2001.

[20] B. B. Mandelbrot, "Fractal geometry of nature," *Freeman Press*, San Francisco, 1982.

[21] W. L. Lee, Y. C. Chen, and K. S. Hsieh, "Ultrasonic liver tissues classification by fractal feature vector based on M-band wavelet transform," *IEEE Trans. Medi. Imag.*, vol. 22, pp. 382-392, 2003.

[22] P. Paramanathan, and R. Uthayakumar, "Application of fractal theory in analysis of human electroencephalographic signals," *Computers in Biology and Medicine*, vol. 38, no. 3, pp. 372-378, 2008.

[23] G. Henderson, E. Ifeachor, N. Hudson, C. Goh, N. Outram, S. Wimalaratna, C. Del Percio, and F. Vecchio, "Development and assessment of methods for detecting dementia using the human electroencephalogram," *IEEE Trans. Biomedical Engineering*, vol. 53, no. 8, pp. 1557-1568, 2006.

[24] L. Rankine, N. Stevenson, M. Mesbah, and B. Boashash, "A nonstationary model of newborn EEG," *IEEE Trans. Biomedical Engineering*, vol. 54, no. 1, pp. 19-28, 2007.

[25] B. E. Boser, I. M. Guyon, and V. Vapnik, "A training algorithm for optimal margin classifiers," *Proc. 5th Annu. Workshop on Computational Learning Theory*, pp. 144-152, 1992.

[26] K. Sadatnezhad, R. Boostani, and A. Ghanizadeh, "Proposing an adaptive mutation to improve XCSF performance to classify ADHD and BMD patients," *J. Neural Eng.*, vol. 7, pp. 066006 , 2010.

[27] M. Nandan, S. S. Talathi, S. Myers, W. L. Ditto, P. P. Khargonekar, and P. R. Carney, "Support vector machines for seizure detection in an animal model of chronic epilepsy," *J. Neural Eng.*, vol. 7, pp. 036001, 2010.

[28] A. Schlogl, C. Keinrath, R. Scherer, and G. Pfurtscheller, "Estimating the mutual information of an EEG-based brain computer interface," *Biomedizinische Technik*, vol. 47, pp. 3-8, 2002.

[29] A. Schlogl, F. Lee, H. Bischof, and G. Pfurtscheller, "Characterization of four-class motor imagery EEG data for the BCI-competition 2005," *J. Neural Eng.*, vol. 2, pp. L14–L22, 2005.

[30] E. Haselsteiner, and G. Pfurtscheller, "Using time-dependent NNs for EEG classification," *IEEE Trans. Rehabil. Eng.*, vol. 8, no. 4, pp. 457-462, 2000.

[31] Graz Data Sets and description for the BCI 2003 competition. [Online]. Available: http://ida.first.fraunhofer.de/projects/bci/competition/

[32] Graz Data Sets and description for the BCI 2005 competition. [Online]. Available: http://ida.first.fraunhofer.de/projects/bci/competition_iii/

[33] W. Y. Hsu, C. C. Lin, M. S. Ju, and Y. N. Sun, "Wavelet-based fractal features with active segment selection: Application to single-trial EEG data," *Journal of Neuroscience Methods*, vol. 163, no. 1, pp. 145-160, 2007.

[34] H. Jasper, "Report of committee on methods of clinical exam in EEG," *Electroencephalogr. Clin. Neurophysiol.*, vol. 10, pp. 370-375, 1958.

[35] K. Y. Lian, C. H. Su, and C. S. Huang, "Performance enhancement for T-S fuzzy control using neural networks," *IEEE Trans. Fuzzy Systems*, vol. 14, no. 5, pp. 619-627, 2006.

[36] I. Daubechies, "Orthonormal bases of compactly supported wavelets," *Comm. Pure Appl. Math.*, vol. 41, pp. 909–996, 1988.

[37] W. Y. Hsu, P. W. F. Poon, and Y. N. Sun, "Automatic seamless mosaicing of microscopic images: enhancing appearance with colour degradation compensation and wavelet-based blending," *Journal of Microscopy*, vol. 231, no. 3, pp. 408–418, 2008.

[38] W. Y. Hsu, and Y. N. Sun, "EEG-based motor imagery analysis using weighted wavelet transform features," *Journal of Neuroscience Methods*, vol. 176, no. 2, pp. 310–318, 2009.

[39] W. Y. Hsu, "Wavelet-based Envelope Features with Automatic EOG Artifact Removal: Application to Single-Trial EEG Data," *Expert Systems with Applications*, Aug. 2011, DOI:10.1016/j.eswa.2011.08.132, In Press.

[40] F. J. Anscombe, "The Validity of Comparative Experiments," *Journal of the Royal Statistical Society. Series A (General)*, vol. 111, no. 3, pp 181–211, 1948.

Section 5

Application to Power System Engineering Problems

15

Fault Diagnosis in Power Distribution Network Using Adaptive Neuro-Fuzzy Inference System (ANFIS)

Rasli[1], Hussain[2] and Fauzi[1]
[1]Universiti Teknologi Malaysia
[2]Universiti Kebangsaan Malaysia
Malaysia

1. Introduction

Fault diagnosis in power distribution system is an initial action in preventing power breakdown that will affect electrical consumers. Power utilities need to take proactive plan to ensure customer satisfaction and continuous power supply. Power breakdown is a problem to utilities as well as energy users and there are a lot of factors that can cause interruption to the power system. Power distribution system is exposed to approximately 80% of overall faults that come from a wide range of phenomena including equipment failure, animals, trees, severe weather and human factors (Marusic & Gruhonjic-Ferhatbegovic, 2006). Whenever any of these factors befall the power system, costumers will experience power failure which will disturb their daily transactions. Since customers need smooth and reliable power supply, utilities have to develop an electrical power that has quality, reliability and continuous availability; they are responsible for the planning of power restoration properly in order to maintain high market place. Most engineers in power distribution system have decided that power breakdown is related to system reliability issues (Richard, 2009).

One problem when breakdown occurs is the long time taken to provide reenergized power after fault. To quote some examples are the power breakdown that occurred in Keningau, Sabah, East Malaysia on July 5, 2009 in which about 2 to 3 hours were taken for repairing. A power failure also happened in Lembah Klang, West Malaysia on January 13, 2005 for 5 hours that affected many industries (Fauziah, 2005). In Cameron, Middle of Africa, the engineers had taken 2 hours to detect the fault location in AES-SONEL Ngousso substation on April 2006 (Thomas & Joseph, 2009). This phenomenon has to be considered seriously by power utilities so as to overcome frequent breakdowns and provide power restoration plan effectively. If they are unable to solve the problem effectively, they will lose consumers' confidence and power system maintenance will highly increase. In addition, power system that has low reliability encourages repeated significant faults. The faults require time for restoration. There is an index to control the duration within power interruption, which is called the customer average interruption duration index (CAIDI). Therefore, power utilities are urged to aim for low index value so that the system reliability can be maintained (Richard, 2009).

The first step for implementing power restoration plan is by developing a precise and an accurate fault diagnosis in power distribution system. Usually, fault diagnosis involves several tasks such as fault types classification, fault location determination and power restoration plan. Firstly, the types of fault must be classified. Then, the fault location can be determined accordingly. The fault location in power distribution system is very important in order to plan power restoration through power system reconfiguration by using operational states of circuit breakers (CB) and line isolators (LI). With such plan, it can fully help power operators to make a decision immediately for further action in power restoration.

The remaining parts of the chapter are organized as follows. Section 1 explains the introduction of the chapter followed by the literature review in Section 2. In Section 3, the concept of adaptive neuro-fuzzy inference system is addressed clearly. Next the ANFIS design for fault types classification and fault location determination is described in Section 4. The results of fault diagnosis are presented in Section 5. Finally conclusions are given in Section 6.

2. Literature review

Many research works on fault diagnosis incorporate artificial intelligent approaches which process the information from alarms and protection relays in power distribution and transmission systems (Zhiwei et al., 2008; Souza et al., 2004; Mohamed & Mazumder, 1999; Binh & Tuyen, 2006). An expert system has been implemented in cooperation with SCADA and EMS to develop a more efficient and precise centralized fault diagnosis system in transmission networks (Sekine et al., 1992). The approach registers information such as fault location, causes of fault and identifies unwanted operation of protection devices. Voltage and current sensors are installed on transmission lines for real time implementation and this involves a high cost. Artificial neural network (ANN) based fault diagnosis method in the distribution system is then developed to locate the fault, identify the faulty protection devices and isolate the faulty sections. Fault location and fault states of lines and bus sections are obtained using the information from alarm relays (Mohamed & Mazumder, 1999). This technique provides effective information to the operator for decision making but most distribution systems are not completely equipped with alarm relays.

A combination of ANN and fuzzy logic has been used to process the information from alarms and protection relays (Souza et al., 2004) for the purpose of identifying the faulty components and line sections. A wavelet based ANN approach is developed for fault detection and classification (Silva et al., 2006). The approach uses oscillographic data from fault recorders and therefore requires communication networks between remote power system and digital fault recorders. A substation fault diagnosis system has been developed using the Petri net theory (Jingbo & Longhua, 2006). In this method, the information from circuit breakers and faulty protection devices are configured based on mathematical formulations to calculate the precise fault section. Two Petri net concepts, namely, neural Petri net and fuzzy neural Petri net are used for locating faults at the lines or sections (Binh & Tuyen, 2006). However, these methods are not suitable for fault diagnosis in distribution systems due to lack of information of alarm and protective relays.

A new and accurate fault location algorithm using adaptive neuro-fuzzy inference system (ANFIS) has been developed for a network with both transmission lines and under-ground cables (Sadeh & Afradi, 2009). It uses fundamental frequency of three-phase current and neutral current as inputs while fault location is calculated in terms of distance in kilometer. Although it gives a good performance, there are some imperfections in the fault location due to the wide range in distance. An ANN based fault diagnosis method has been implemented in an unbalanced underground distribution system (Oliveira, 2007). The method uses fundamental voltage and current phasors as inputs to the ANN for locating faults in the line sections. Another ANN based approach which combines the ant colony optimization algorithm has been developed for fault section diagnosis in the distribution systems (Zhisheng & Yarning, 2007). The method locates faults in terms of the line sections but the exact fault points are still not known.

3. The concept of adaptive neuro-fuzzy inference system

Adaptive neural fuzzy inference system (ANFIS) is based on fuzzy logic modeling and uses artificial neural network as the learning algorithm. The system can teach, change the data environment or respond to the remote stimulus for adapting to the change of data environment (Michael, 2005). ANFIS produces constant and linear target by using respective zero and first-order polynomial equations and is also known as a Sugeno-type of fuzzy inference system (FIS).

ANFIS approach targets only one output from several given inputs. The target is manipulated through the performance of the membership function curve according to a particular data input. The curve parameters are identified based on the respective weighted values via the product in between the created learning rules. A ratio between the individual and overall weighted values is calculated. The ratio is gained by using the parameters of output membership function then, finally ANFIS predicts the target by producing an overall gained value as an output. Membership function parameters in input and output sides are adjusted through a learning process to get the targeted values. ANFIS uses hybrid algorithm that consists of a combination between back-propagation and least-square estimation techniques (Jang, 1993). The techniques are implemented in artificial neural network as a learning algorithm that gives very fast convergence and more accurate in ANFIS target.

3.1 ANFIS's learning processes

The ANFIS model exhibits a predicted target whenever it is trained by using at least two columns of data. The last column is the target data and also as an output of the trained ANFIS, while the rest of the columns are the input data. Thus, an ANFIS structure has a single output with at least one column of input data. For the best prediction and high reliability of its performance, the model needs more elements in the column of the input data. However, this situation will also cause the processing time for learning to be slow. For that reason, the ANFIS has to be configured in a high speed processor. Every element in each row of the input data is called data variable in which the linguistic values of the relationship between them is by the rule of 'IF-THEN'. A total of the rule is proportional to the membership function value and the number of column data is linked by the following equation:

$$F^D = P \quad (1)$$

where,
D : Total number of column for the input data
F : Number of membership functions
P : Number of rules

The data is classified as training data and testing data in ANFIS's learning process. Testing data should be in the range of training data for the purpose of testing procedures. The number of training epoch also gives a good result in predicting the target. Accurate targets consider a minimum prediction error from the result of ANFIS training. The error can be reduced by adjusting the variable membership function (MF) and epoch parameters. With increasing in number of MF and epoch, the error will reduce accordingly. Sometimes, no reducing in error can be noticed even though the epoch was increased up to 5000 and above. This is due to the way the data is assembled. Therefore effective input data assembly will result good prediction. For this work, effective configuration of the data has been reached by preparing a wide data range between their elements and arranging the data from small to large values.

During the training process, MF parameters are varied so as to yield the ANFIS's output as target values. The minimum error percentage is a small difference between target and prediction values and it is used to measure the success level of a training process. ANFIS performs a hybrid learning algorithm in the training process which is a combination of two algorithms namely back-propagation and least square estimate (Jang, 1993). The hybrid method improves the bad features of individual algorithm and both are popular in ANN implementation.

In hybrid learning algorithm, MF parameters are adjusted to identify the best prediction value. The parameters determine the size of MF curve as shown in Fig.1. The curve of 'gbell' shape has been selected in the learning process due to its high performance in giving a precise prediction (Jang, 1993). There are MF curve in input and output parts of ANFIS model. Back-propagation algorithm takes responsibility to vary MF parameter in input side of the model, whereas least square estimate (LSE) takes into consideration on the output side as a linear line. In MF parameters, the input side varies, whereas for output, they are static and vice versa.

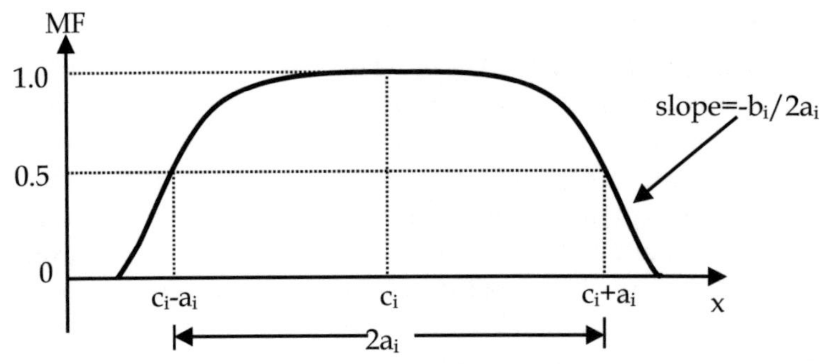

Fig. 1. Gbell shape for MF curve in input side

The prediction values are performed after the MF parameters in both sides of the ANFIS model converge the values according to the given training epoch (Mitra et al., 2008). Fig.2

and 3 show the effect of different epoch and change of MF curve's shape with respect to the prediction error in initial and final learning process.

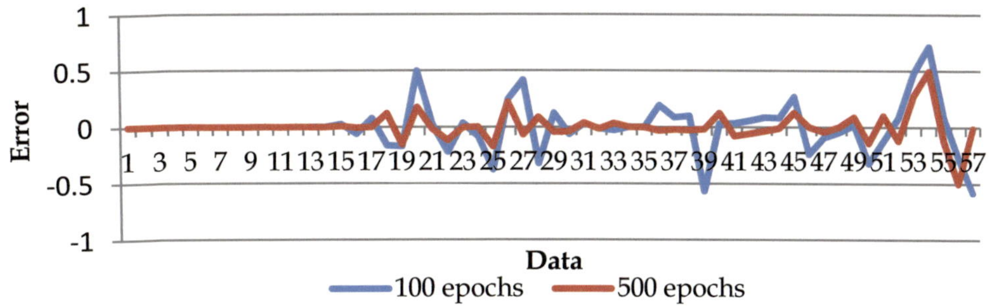

Fig. 2. Prediction errors according to different training epoch

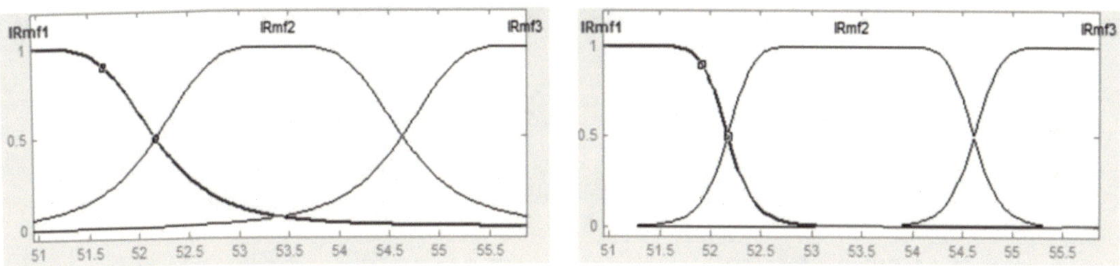

(a) (b)

Fig. 3. (a) Initial stage and (b) MF curve of input side on final stage

ANFIS's learning process can be implemented easily by using the provided source code in Matlab such as 'newfis', 'evalfis' and editfis'. A trained ANFIS model is formatted with a file extension of '.fis' to represent an ANFIS module. On the other hand, the file is represented as a module for a particular task where all modules are configured accordingly based on a hierarchy layout to form a fault diagnosis system in power distribution network. The '.fis' file is also a flexible module that can reform when the data changes or new data is added without restructuring the model physically. ANFIS has a capability of producing very fast result in prediction even when handles a large size of input data. Therefore, the system is compliable to most application especially in adaptive control as well as ANFIS in implementing fault diagnosis. Each ANFIS module for a particular task is programmed by using source codes in Matlab. The programming is developed for every task in fault diagnosis and then the tasks are integrated in another programming to perform a simulation tool for fault diagnosis in power distribution network.

3.2 Development of ANFIS model

A basic ANFIS model is shown in Fig.4 in which the model is illustrated in five blocks of learning stages. This model is an example of ANFIS development model for power restoration plan that consists of two inputs and two membership functions. So, there are four fuzzy 'IF-THEN' rules to show the relationship between fault locations in 'x, y' coordinates and it also shows the operational status of CB and LI in the power distribution network. So, the target is '1' for operating while '0' for non-operating state of the devices.

In this chapter, an ANFIS model has been developed with 27 fuzzy 'IF-THEN' rules for the task of power restoration plan as shown in Fig.5 and 8 rules in determining the fault location. Since, the number of block functions represent the rules for every input data, it is difficult to describe the operational process of the model due to lack of space. However, a basic ANFIS model is shown in Fig.4 for that purpose. There are five stages of ANFIS operational process that includes fuzzification, 'IF-THEN' rules, normalization, de-fuzzification and neuron addition.

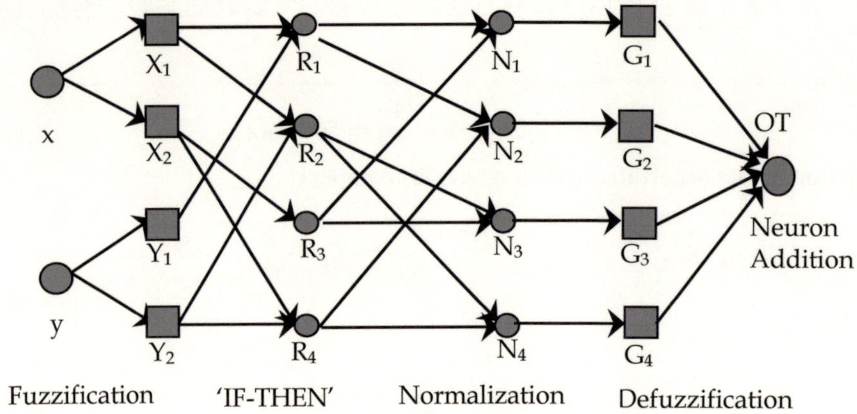

Fig. 4. A basic ANFIS model with two inputs data and two MFs.

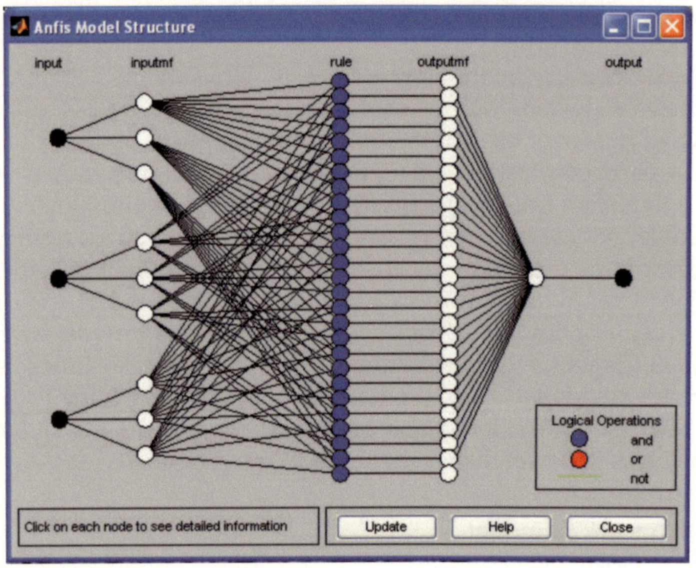

Fig. 5. An ANFIS model structure for the task of power restoration plan

3.2.1 Fuzzification

Referring to Fig.4, the fuzzification stage is located at the first stage of receiving of the input signal. Its function is to convert the input signal to fuzzy signal in which the signal is yielded via the input side of the MF curve. The curve is performed by using the following equations:

$$X_i(x) = \frac{1}{1 + \left(\frac{x - c_i}{a_i}\right)^{2b_i}} \tag{2}$$

$$Y_i(y) = \frac{1}{1 + \left(\frac{y - c_i}{a_i}\right)^{2b_i}} \tag{3}$$

where, Xi(x) and Yi(y) are fuzzied values for each input data, whereas a_i, b_i and c_i are MF parameters for respective representative of middle, width and slope of the curve as shown in Fig.1. These parameters are varied accordingly to get a suitable curve in order to get fuzzy signal.

3.2.2 Stage of 'IF-THEN' rule

An output signal from the fuzzification stage becomes an input to the stage of the 'IF-THEN' rule. In this stage, the fuzzy signal is gained by using equation (4) up to (7).

$$R_1 = X_1(x) \times Y_1(y) \tag{4}$$

$$R_2 = X_1(x) \times Y_2(y) \tag{5}$$

$$R_3 = X_2(x) \times Y_1(y) \tag{6}$$

$$R_4 = X_2(x) \times Y_2(y) \tag{7}$$

R_1, R_2, R_3 and R_4 are real values for every 'IF-Then' rule.

3.2.3 Normalization

Next, the output signal from the stage of 'IF-THEN' rule will be an input signal to the normalization stage. In this stage, every gained signal are divided to the total of gained signal by the following equation,

$$N_i = {}^{R_i}/_{R_T} \qquad i = 1, 2, 3, 4 \tag{8}$$

where, $R_T = R_1 + R_2 + R_3 + R_4$

3.2.4 Defuzzification

The next process is signal defuzzification in which the output signal from the normalization stage becomes an input signal to this defuzzification stage. In this stage, a normalized signal is gained again through a linear equation that is formed from the MF of the output signal as shown in the following equation,

$$G_i = N_i(p_i x + q_i y + r_i) \qquad i = 1, 2, 3, 4 \tag{9}$$

with p_i, q_i and r_i being the MF parameters for the linear signal.

3.2.5 Neuron addition

The last process in the ANFIS operation is called neuron addition in which all defuzzification signals, G_i are added together as shown below:

$$OT = \sum G_i \qquad i = 1, 2, 3, 4 \tag{10}$$

OT is a predicted value.

3.3 Good features of the ANFIS

The advantages of ANFIS are compared to other artificial intelligent techniques such as an artificial neural network (ANN) and an expert system (ES). The advantages are as follows; i) ANFIS gives a high precision in classification and prediction models. This precision when compared to the index error that is presented between ANFIS and ANN show the error of 0.036 and 0.32 respectively (Jang, 1993). ii) ANFIS has adaptive features to solve wrong data problem that involves new power network configuration. The scenario is rather difficult to solve using expert system due to fixed rules. iii) ANFIS has an effective learning process on the training data while considering optimization in its implementation (Jang, 1993; De Souza et al., 2003).

4. The ANFIS design for fault types classification and fault location determination

The development of fault diagnosis in power distribution network implements the ANFIS approach because of its compact structure, very fast training process and precise prediction. A developed fault diagnosis requires a compact ANFIS model development with significant tasks. The tasks involve fault types classification, fault location determination and identification of an operational state of CB and LI for power restoration plan. Every task is represented by an ANFIS model that is structured based on a hierarchy of power distribution network. Post-fault three-phase root mean square (RMS) current is applied to the model to produce the respective task at the output. For the purpose of developing fault diagnosis in power distribution network, such fault current is only used as the model input. If a measured current is more than the current without fault in a network, surely there is some fault in the power network. Fig.6 shows a block diagram of the fault diagnosis development that consists of four ANFIS modules. The modules are stated as ANFIS1 to ANFIS4 when representing the diagnosis tasks. From the figure, post-fault 3-phase current from the faulty power network is injected to ANFIS1 that is responsible for predicting the target in integer 1 to 10 when representing the types of fault.

Meanwhile, fault location is identified according to geometry coordinates. The same fault current as an input to the ANFIS1, is also applied to ANFIS2 and ANFIS3 modules in which they are developed to produce the output in X and Y coordinates respectively. In other words, the modules represent precise fault point in the power network. The technique of geometry coordinate gives better accuracy in producing the fault location compared to the cut-off faulty line approach (Butle-Pury & Moratti 2006). Furthermore, Fig.6 shows a position of ANFIS4 module for restoration power plan in the network. The input signal to this module is from fault location identification whereas the operational states of CB and LI are the module output. The states are considered for the purpose of determination of a new power network configuration. Faulty lines must be isolated before proceeding to the power restoration plan. Binary codes are used to show the states in which digit '1' represents CB and LI in 'close' whereas digit '0' is in 'open' switch.

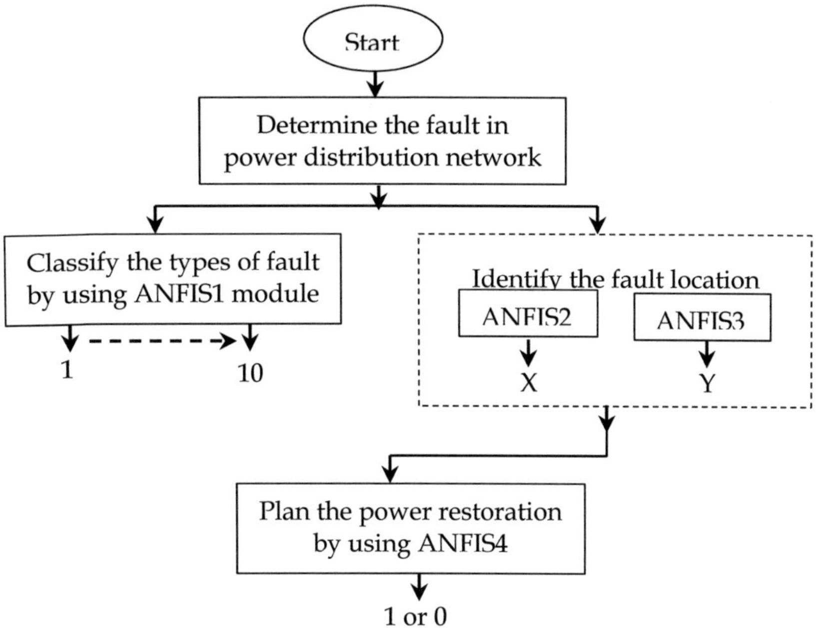

Fig. 6. A block diagram of the procedures in fault diagnosis system

4.1 Fault types classification

Usually, the types of power fault are classified accordingly such as a phase to ground, a phase to phase, two phases to ground and three-phase faults. Fig.7 shows ANFIS1 module

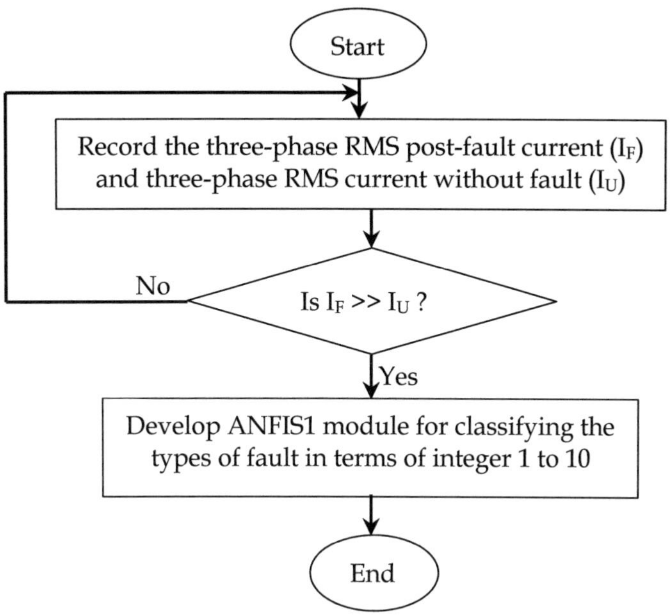

Fig. 7. A procedure in fault types classification

development that is responsible for the task of predicting various types of fault in terms of integer 1 to 10 as follows, 1- red phase to ground fault (AG), 2 - yellow phase to ground fault (BG), 3 - blue phase to ground fault (CG), 4 - Three-phase fault (3P), 5 - red phase to yellow phase fault (AB), 6 - yellow phase to blue phase fault (BC), 7 - blue phase to red phase fault (CA), 8 - red and yellow phases to ground fault (ABG), 9 - yellow and blue phases to ground fault (BCG), 10 - blue and red phases to ground (CAG).

4.1.1 ANFIS1 design for fault types classification

Fig.8 shows the design of an ANFIS1 model that is structured according to the type of fault and represented by the integers 1 to 10. The model consists of ten ANFIS modules which are labeled as ANFIS1-1 to ANFIS1-10. The first module conducts A phase to ground fault (AG) prediction in integer 1 and follows by ANFIS1-2 in integer 2 for 'BG', ANFIS1-3 in integer 3 for 'CG' and so on. ANFIS1-4 to ANFIS1-10 modules represent respective 3P, AB, BC, CA, ABG, BCG and CAG faults. Table 1 shows some relationship parameters between the input and output of ANFIS1's signals.

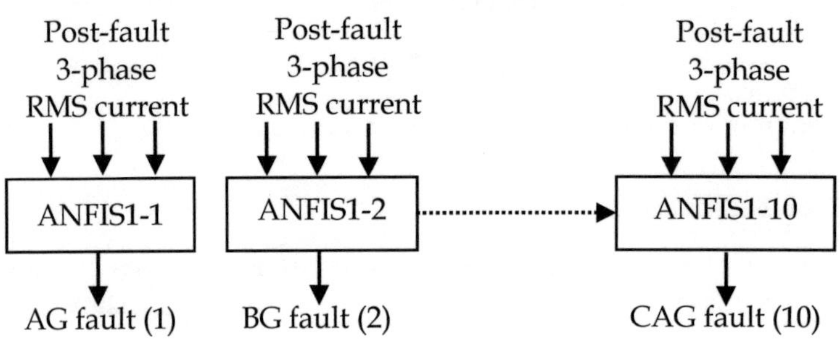

Fig. 8. ANFIS1 design for fault types classification

ANFIS modules	Input	Output
ANFIS1-1	Post-fault 3-phase RMS current	1 – AG fault
ANFIS1-2	"	2 – BG fault
ANFIS1-3	"	3 – CG fault
ANFIS1-4	"	4 – 3P fault
ANFIS1-5	"	5 – AB fault
ANFIS1-6	"	6 – BC fault
ANFIS1-7	"	7 – CA fault
ANFIS1-8	"	8 – ABG fault
ANFIS1-9	"	9 – BCG fault
ANFIS1-10	"	10 – CAG fault

Table 1. Input and output parameters from every ANFIS1 module.

4.1.2 A Procedure for classifying the types of fault

Fig.9 shows a procedure for classifying various types of fault in power distribution network through developing an ANFIS1 model. The first step is the preparation of power network in

XY coordinate layout. The selected power distribution network is a 47 buses practical system. Then, by using the commercial software of PSS-ADEPT, the network is analyzed to record a post-fault 3-phase RMS current for each identified fault point. These points are fault location in XY coordinates for every feeder and radial lines including loads. The post-fault current data is used to train ANFIS1-1 to ANFIS1-10 modules according to respective target output that are integers 1 up to 10. The integers are representative of 10 types of fault. There are 163 selected coordinates for fault points with two fault resistors in the 47 buses practical power network. Therefore, it has about 2462 simulations in generating the data set. Table 2 shows a distribution data for training, testing and classifying the types of fault in the practical system.

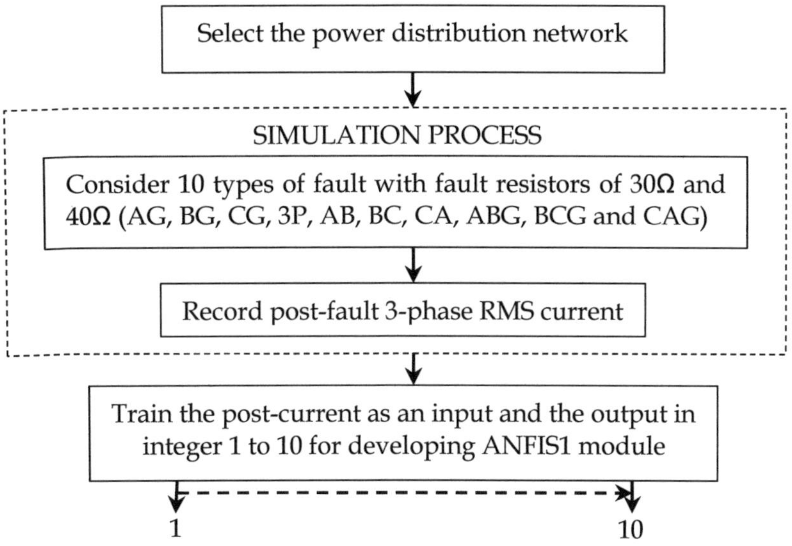

Fig. 9. A procedure for developing ANFIS1 in fault types classification

ANFIS1 module	Generated data set	Trained data set	Number of ANFIS input	Number of ANFIS output
ANFIS1-1 to ANFIS1-3	465	445	3	1
ANFIS1-4	177	157	3	1
ANFIS1-5 to ANFIS1-10	182	162	3	1

Table 2. The training and testing data for classifying the types of fault in a 47 buses practical system

4.2 Fault location identification

Referring to Fig.10, ANFIS2 and ANFIS3 are developed to identify fault location in respective X and Y coordinates. According to previous literature, most of the methods in identifying the fault location for power distribution network are in fault distance from a substation or zone. This approach considers geometrical coordinates in determining fault location in which it produces more accurate and precise fault location identification. From

Fig.10, three-phase RMS post-fault current with (I_F) and without (I_U) fault are compared to investigate the fault in the power system. If current is I_F higher than current I_U, the current I_F is recorded with the merging fault type.

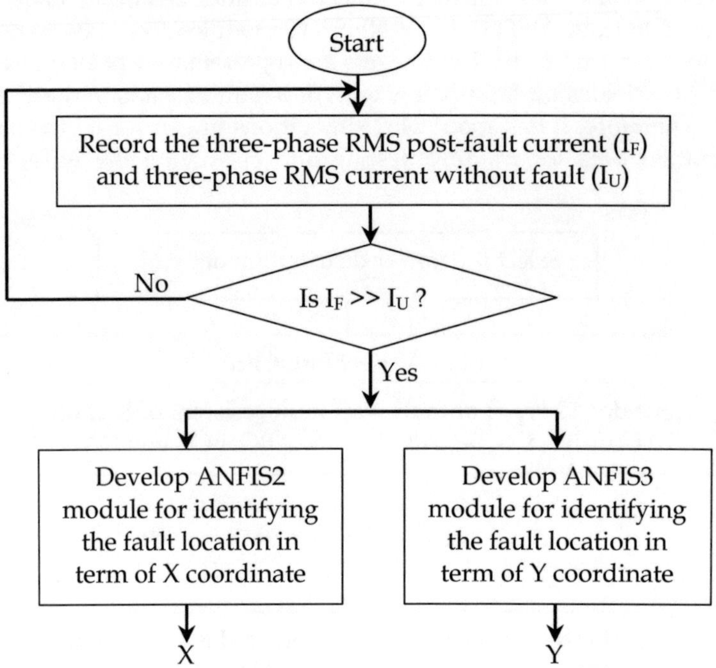

Fig. 10. A procedure for identifying fault location

4.2.1 ANFIS2 and ANFIS3 designs for identifying fault location

The structure of ANFIS2 and ANFIS3 are configured according to selected fault points as shown in Fig.11. For a 47 buses practical system, there are 163 fixed fault points with 64 'X' coordinates and 45 'Y' coordinates. Thus, the total coordinate point is 109. Those points are

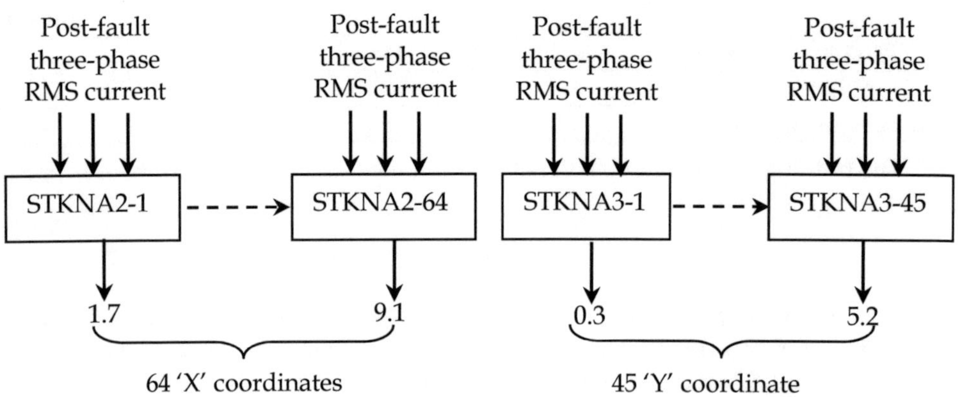

Fig. 11. ANFIS2 and ANFIS3 design for identifying fault location in a 47 buses practical system

represented by each ANFIS module. ANFIS2 consists of 64 modules that are labeled as ANFIS2-1 up to ANFIS2-64 whereas for ANFIS3, its total module is 45 from ANFIS3-1 to ANFIS3-45. The signal input to the ANFIS2 and ANFIS3 is a three-phase RMS post-fault current while the signal output is in terms of X and Y coordinates respectively as shown in Fig.11. Table 3 shows the input and output parameters of the 47 buses practical system.

ANFIS module	Input	Output
ANFIS2-1	Post-fault 3-phase RMS current	1.7
↓		↓
ANFIS2-64	"	9.1
ANFIS3-1	"	0.3
↓		↓
ANFIS3-45	"	5.2

Table 3. Input and output parameters of ANFIS2 and ANFIS3 for identifying fault location in a 47 buses practical system

4.2.2 A procedure for identifying fault location

The procedure for locating fault in a power distribution network by the implementation of ANFIS2 and ANFIS3 modules is clearly shown in Fig.12. The first stage is a selection of power network for testing. Then the network layout is drawn in XY plane for locating the selected fault points along the feeder and radial lines. Fig.13 presents an example of the layout. The detail specification of the network is in the next sub-section. This network layout is embedded in fault analysis simulation software such as PSS-ADEPT to collect the fault current data at each fault point.

Next, the three-phase RMS post-fault current is collected at the main substation through a simulation of fault analysis to the selected power distribution network. The fault analysis is applied to every point of the fixed coordinates while considering 10 types of fault and several fault resistors (R_f). For example, by using three fault resistors and 163 fault points, there are 1335 simulations for single fault to ground and about 486 simulations for double fault to ground. Meanwhile, about 643 simulations are required for phase to phase and three-phase faults. Therefore, the total simulation is about 2464 for power distribution network in the 47 buses practical system. The data collected is arranged in such a way that it has three columns of input parameters and one column of target values. The target is either X or Y coordinates in which they are used to train ANFIS2 and ANFIS3 respectively.

By identifying the fault location in terms of 'XY' coordinates, more precise and accurate location not only in terms of distance from the feeding substation can be yielded. The structure of ANFIS2 and ANFIS3 are quite simple so they undergo a very fast process in the training stage. However, the simulation process should be done repeatedly due to too much fixed fault points in selected power distribution network. If any network has more feeder and radial lines with long line distance, the fault point should also be more. Thus, the number of ANFIS models will also increase.

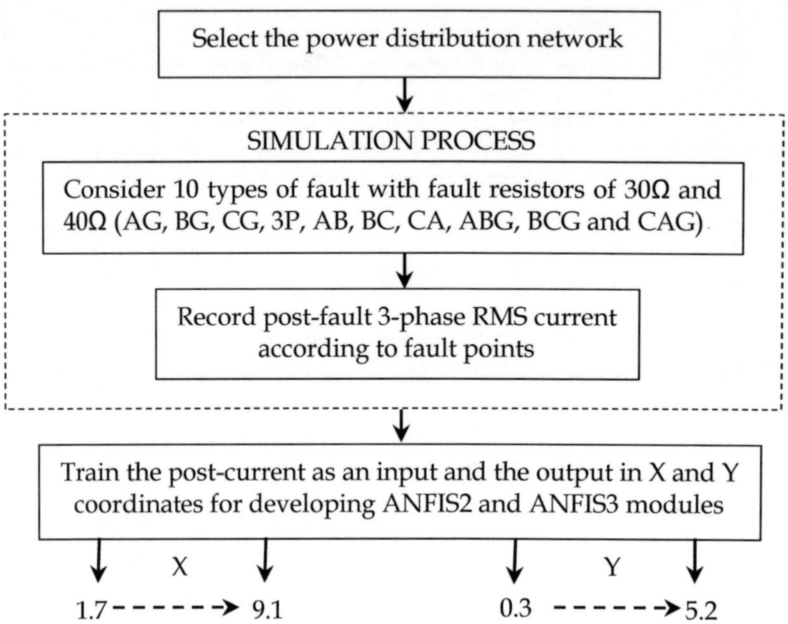

Fig. 12. A procedure for developing ANFIS2 and ANFIS3 in fault location identification

4.2.3 The 47 buses practical system

A single line diagram of the 47 buses practical system is illustrated in Fig.13. The system has seven 11 kV feeders and four 33 kV feeders including 87 CBs and 9 LIs in 11 kV feeder. In this chapter, only 11 kV feeders are used for simulating and testing in order to observe the performance of the developed fault diagnosis system. There are about 2464 line data of three-phase RMS post-fault current that is recorded during the simulation stages. Bus B1 is a power source bus in which it is located on coordinate (1, 2.2) while a monitoring bus B2 is coordinated on (1.8, 2.7). B2 is used for recording the three-phase RMS post-fault current during fault.

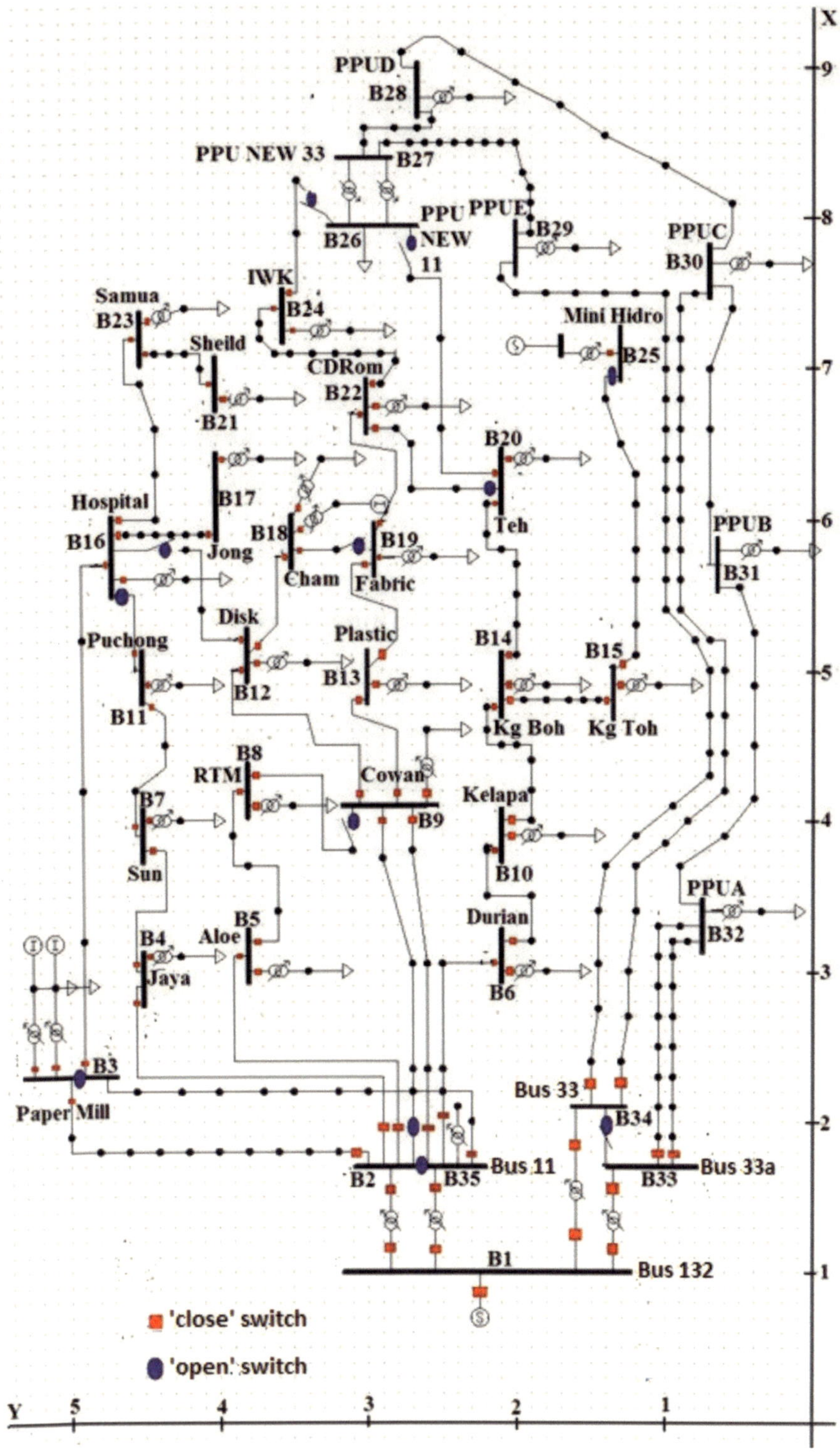

Fig. 13. A single line diagram of 47 buses practical system

4.3 Power restoration plan

Power restoration is a very important consideration in the development of fault diagnosis system especially in a distribution network. Hence, easy and fast action must be taken seriously to plan a power restoration procedure so that the power can be reenergized immediately in a safe and proper manner. This problem can be solved using the ANFIS approach by applying the operational states of CB and LI as shown in Fig.14. This simple technique uses only fault points in XY coordinates and the target is in operational states of CB and LI. These parameters are trained to develop the ANFIS4 model. The power restoration plan considers some requisite processes before developing the ANFIS4 module which are as follows: make sure the power network has a support feeder or a radial that is the nearest to fault feeders. No service loads due to line isolation (NSL) must be calculated in volt-ampere (VA). In addition, the total of loads in the supported feeder (TSL) and actual capacity of the feeder (CSF) should be defined clearly. If NSL is smaller than the differentiation between CSF and TSL, the power restoration plan will be carried to the next action.

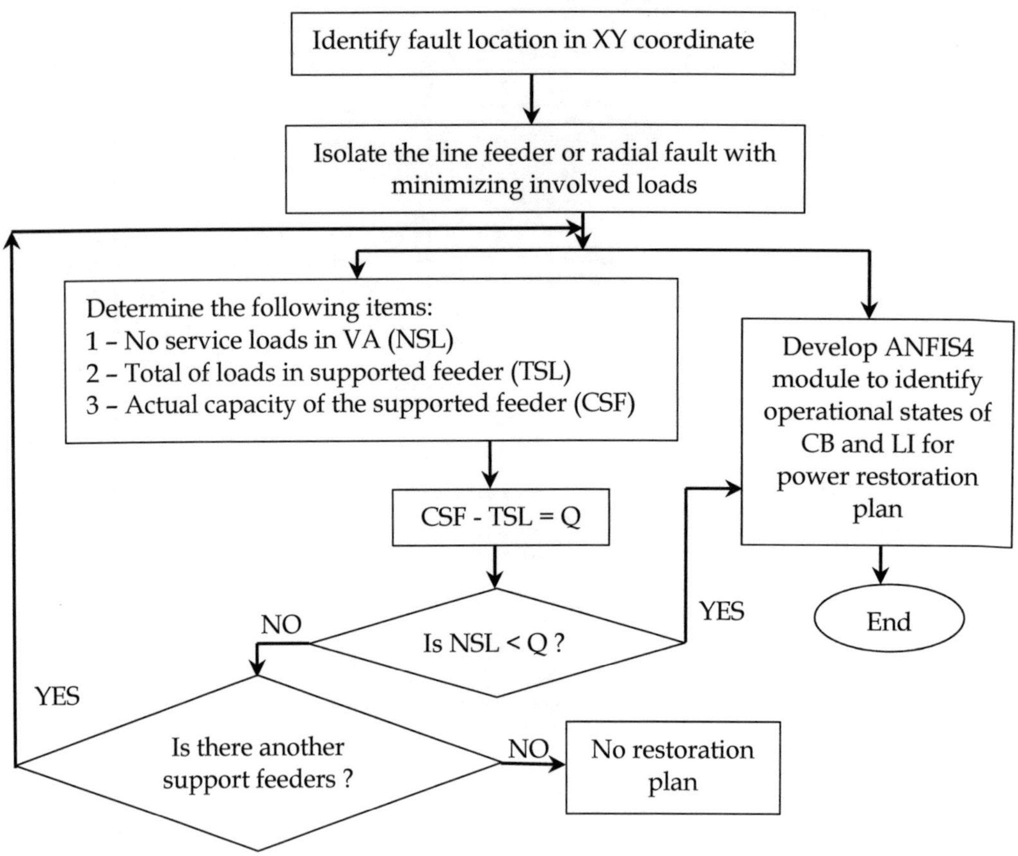

Fig. 14. A procedure for planning power restoration

4.3.1 ANFIS4 design for planning power restoration

Fig.15 shows an ANFIS4 design in a power restoration plan in a 47 buses practical system. The design has 93 modules namely ANFIS4-1 to ANFIS4-93 according to the total of CB and LI in the power network. The input and output data to the ANFIS4 are XY coordinates and binary number respectively. The binary represents the operational states of CB and LI as listed in Table 4. Digit '1' indicates 'close' position while '0' is for 'open' position.

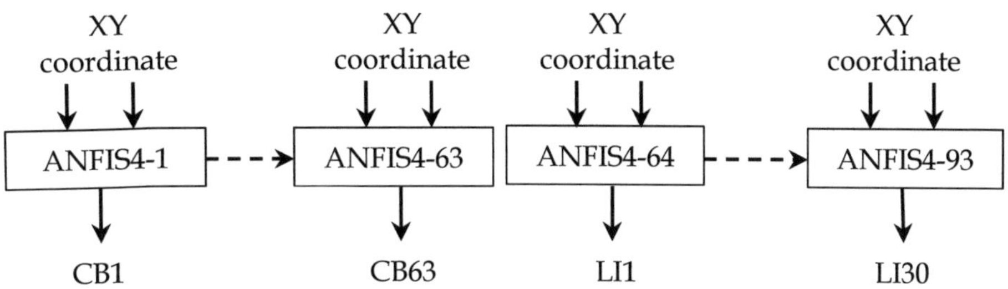

Fig. 15. ANFIS4 design for power restoration plan

ANFIS module	Input	Output
ANFIS4-1	Post-fault 3-phase RMS current	1 or 0
↓	"	↓
ANFIS4-93	"	1 or 0

Table 4. Input and output parameters for ANFIS4 module in power restoration plan

4.3.2 A procedure to train ANFIS4 for power restoration plan

There are several steps in developing ANFIS4 as well as collecting and training the data for the purpose of power restoration plan. The steps are as follows:

i. Isolate the fault feeder or radial with the minimized load.
ii. Identify the non-service loads (NSL) in volt-ampere (VA).
iii. Identify support feeder or radial that is available to the fault feeder and determine its load total (TSL).
iv. Identify the support feeder capacity (CSF) in the power distribution network.
v. Calculate the difference between CSF and TSL.
vi. If NSL is greater than the difference, identify another support feeder or radial. If the feeder is available, repeat steps (iii) to (vi). But if the feeder is not available, the power restoration plan cannot proceed.
vii. If the NSL is smaller than the difference, the plan shall be implemented with a procedure as shown in Fig.16.

In this case, a 47 buses practical system has been selected for developing and testing the ANFIS4 module. There are 59 fixed fault points in the selected network, so the collected data has about 5487 lines which includes 63 CBs and 30 LIs in the practical system. Each line consists of three rows including X, Y coordinates and the integer '1' or '0' represents an operational state of CB and LI. The point coordinates are the input signal to the ANFIS4 whereas the integer is the output. Due to the 93 devices for all CBs and LIs, the ANFIS4 modules should be developed regarding to the numbers of the device. Thus, the modules are labeled as ANFIS4-1 to ANFIS4-63 for all CBs and followed by ANFIS4-64 to ANFIS4-93 for all LIs. Table 5 shows a distribution of the data set for each module to train them.

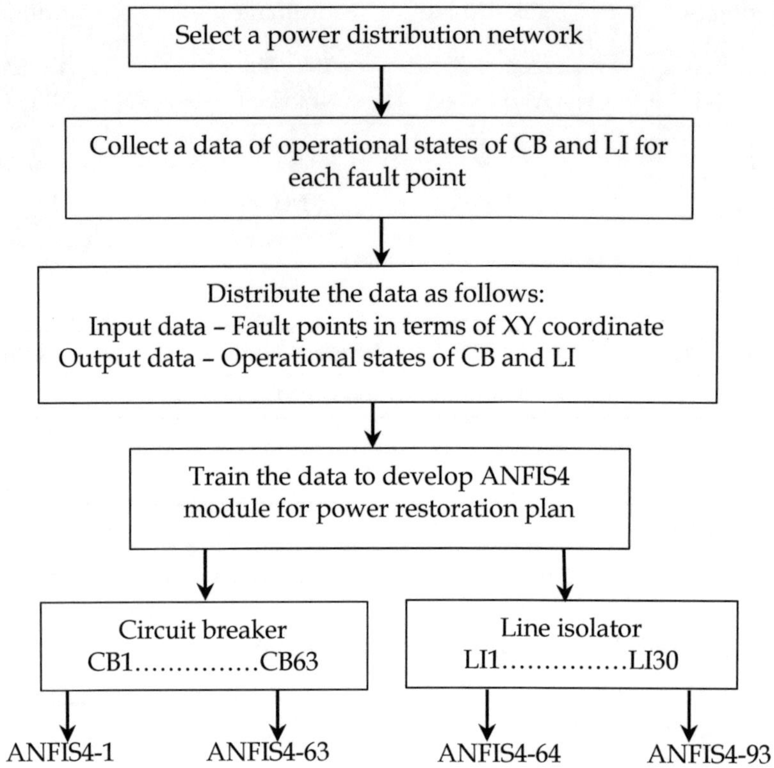

Fig. 16. A procedure for developing ANFSI4 module in power restoration plan

ANFIS1 module	Generated data set	Trained data set	Number of ANFIS input	Number of ANFIS output
ANFIS4-1	80	59	2	1
⋮	"	"	2	1
↓	"	"	2	1
ANFIS4-93	"	"	2	1

Table 5. A distribution of the data set for power restoration plan

5. The result of fault diagnosis

Fault diagnosis performance is measured through a precision and accuracy of ANFIS prediction. The measurement is in percentage error for ANFIS1, ANFIS2 and ANFIS3 while in absolute error for ANFIS4. The 47 buses practical system is used to test the ANFISs. The prediction results from ANFIS1, ANFIS2 and ANFIS3 are presented for practical systems that consist of 1232 test data sets. Meanwhile, ANFIS4 predicts about 2743 test data sets for the same system. The number of test data set is taken from 50% of overall data training.

5.1 The result on ANFIS1 prediction for classifying types of fault

Fig.17 shows the curve of a percentage error and a real target value for ANFIS1 prediction in classifying fault types in 47 buses practical system. The average percentage error for such power systems is 2E-5%. Meanwhile, the maximum percentage error for the same power system is 0.52%. From the result on ANFIS1 in classifying the types of fault in terms of integer 1 to 10, it can be said that the ANFIS module is able to show precise prediction.

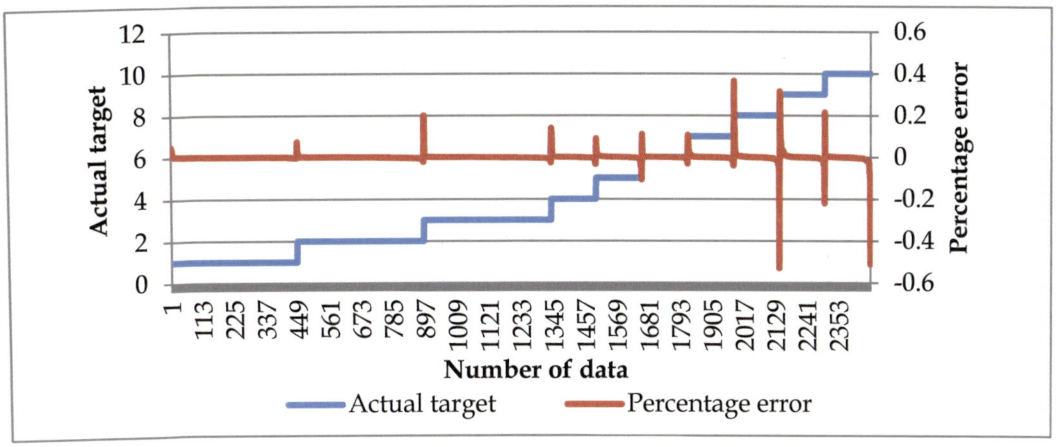

Fig. 17. The result on ANFIS1 prediction for classifying types of fault in the 47 buses practical system.

5.2 The result of ANFIS2 for identifying fault location in terms of X coordinate

The average percentage error of 1.2E-5% is the result of ANFIS2 prediction for identifying the fault location in terms of X coordinate as shown in Fig.18. From the figure, the maximum percentage error is 1.8% in the 47 buses practical system. As a conclusion based on the result, it can be seen that the developed ANFIS2 module is more precise in predicting the fault location than the developed ANN (artificial neural network) module with the same data.

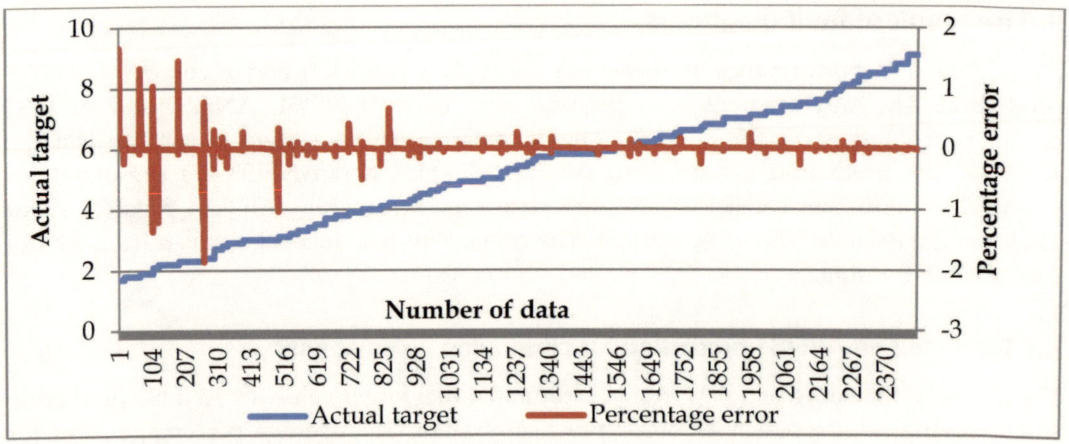

Fig. 18. The result of ANFIS2 prediction for identifying fault location in terms of X coordinate in the 47 buses practical system.

5.3 The result of ANFIS3 for identifying fault location in terms of Y coordinate

Fig.19 shows the result of ANFIS3 for identifying the fault location in terms of Y coordinate in the 47 buses practical system. It is found that about 2.1E-2% is the average percentage error and 10.7% is the maximum percentage error of the ANFIS3 prediction. As a conclusion, ANFIS3 has a high precision for identifying the fault location in terms of Y coordinate based on the average percentage error for 2464 numbers of data training in the system.

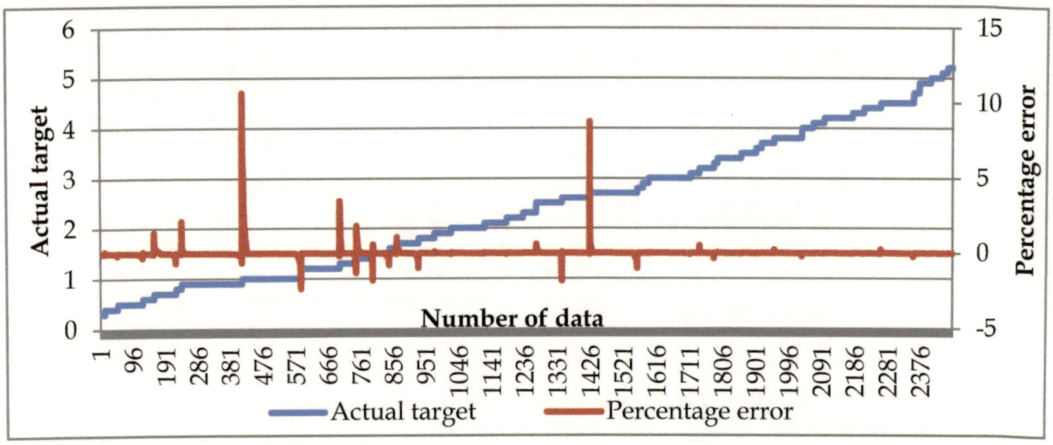

Fig. 19. The result on ANFIS2 prediction for identifying fault location in terms of Y coordinate in the 47 buses practical system.

5.4 The result on ANFIS4 for planning power restoration

Fig.20 shows the result on ANFIS4 prediction in determining the operational states of CB and LI for power restoration plan. Both devices are provided in the 47 buses practical system as a test network for the task. The result shows that the average absolute and maximum absolute errors are 1.14E-7 and 0.028 respectively. Referring to the Fig.20, B1 up to B26 represent 26 buses in the 11 KV of practical system. According to the result, ANFIS4 module gives a high accuracy in the prediction of the operational states of CB and LI for power restoration plan.

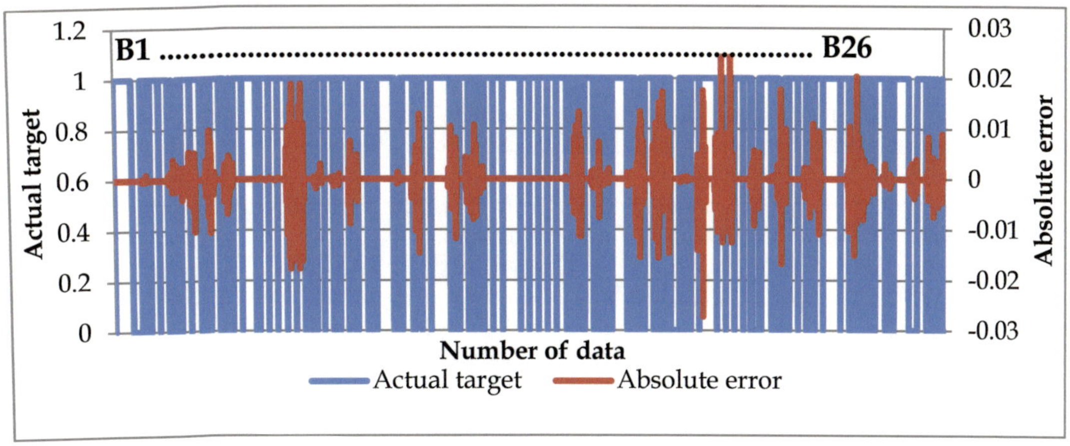

Fig. 20. The result on ANFIS4 prediction for determining operational states of CB and LI for power restoration plan in 47 buses practical system.

6. Conclusion

In general, this chapter describes an accurate method for identifying various fault types as well as the location for the purpose of power restoration plan using the operational states of CB and LI in the power distribution system. For this purpose, the ANFIS approach has been developed by using the representative integers 1 to 10 in classifying ten types of fault. This adaptive approach is also implemented to identify the fault location in power distribution system in terms of geometrical coordinates. Since the developed ANFIS modules are a useful fault diagnosis tool in completing the task, this approach is continuously developed for power restoration plan through network reconfiguration by controlling the operational states of CB and LI. The performance of ANFIS is tested on a 47 buses practical system in which it shows more precision when predicting the target for the developed fault diagnosis system.

7. Acknowledgment

This work of research has been financially supported by the Univerti Kebangsaan Malaysia (UKM) and the Universiti Teknologi Malaysia (UTM).

8. References

Binh, P.T.T., & Tuyen, N.D. (2006). Fault Diagnosis of Power System Using Neural Petri Net and Fuzzy Neural Petri Nets, *Power India Conference, IEEE*, pp. 5, ISBN 0-7803-9525-5, New Delhi, India, n.d.

Butler-Purry, K.L. & Marotti, M. (2006). Impact of Distributed Generators on Protective Devices in Radial Distribution Systems, *Proceedings of the IEEE Power Engineering Society in Transmission and Distribution Conference*, pp. 87-88, ISBN 0-7803-9194-2, Dallas, Texas, USA, May 21-24, 2006

Fauziah, A. (January 2005). PM Mahu Laporan Segera - TNB Diarah Siasat Terperinci Punca Gangguan Bekalan Elektrik, In: *Utusan Malaysia,* 14.01.2005, Available from http://www.utusan.com.my/utusan/info.asp?pub=Utusan_Malaysia&sec=Berita_Utama

Jang, J.-S.R. (1993). ANFIS: Adaptive Network Based Fuzzy Inference System. *IEEE Transaction on Systems, Man and Cybernetic,* Vol.23, No.3, pp. 665-685, ISSN 0018-9472

Marusic, A. & Gruhonjic-Ferhatbegovic, S. (2006). A Computerized Fault Location Process for Overhead Radial Distribution Feeders, *IEEE Mediterranean Conference on Electrotechnical,* pp. 1114-1117, ISBN 1-4244-0087-2, Benalmadena, Malaga, Costa del Sol, May 16-19, 2006

Michael Negnevitsky. (2005). *Artificil Intelligent: A Guide to Intelligent System,* Addison-Wesley, ISBN 0-321-20466-2, Harlow, England

Mitra, P., Maulik, S., Chowdhury, S.P. & Chowdhury, S. (2008). ANFIS Based Automatic Voltage Regulator with Hybrid Learning Algorithm. *International Journal of Innovations in Energy Systems and Power,* Vol. 3, No.2, pp. 1-5, ISSN 1913-135X

Mohamed, A. & Mazumder. (1999). A Neural Network Approach to Fault Diagnosis in a Distribution System. *International Journal of Power and Energy systems.* Vol.19, No.2, pp. 129-134, ISSN 1078-3466

Oliveira, K.R.C. (2007). *Advanced Intelligent Computing Theories and Applications with Aspects of Artificial Intelligent,* Springer Berlin, ISBN 978-3-540-74201-2

Richard, E.B.(2009). *Electric Power Distribution Reliability.* CRS Press, ISBN 978-0-8493-7567-5, USA

Sadeh, J. & Afradi, H. (2009). A New and Accurate Fault Location Algorithm for Combined Transmission Lines Using Adaptive Network-Based Fuzzy Inference System. *Journal of Electric Power System Research,* Vol.79, No.11, pp. 1538-1545, ISSN 0378-7796

Sekine, Y., Akimonto, Y., Kunugi, M. & Fukui, C. (1992). Fault Diagnosis of Power System. *Proceedings of the IEEE.* Vol.80, No.5, pp. 673-683, ISSN 0018-9219

Silva, K.M., Souza, B.A. & Brito, N.S.D. (2006). Fault Detection and Classification in Transmission Lines Based On Wavelet Transform and ANN. *IEEE Transaction on Power Delivery,* Vol.21, No.4, pp. 2058-2063, ISSN 0885-8977

Souza, J.C.S., Meza, E.M., Sebilling, M.T. & Do Corato, M.B. (2004). Alarm Processing in Electrical Power Systems through a Neuro-Fuzzy Approach. *IEEE Transaction on Power Delivery,* Vol.19, No.2, pp. 537-544, ISSN 0885-8977

Thomas Tamo Tatiesa & Joseph Voufo. (2009). Fault Diagnosis on Medium Voltage (MV) Electric Power Distribution Networks: The Case of The Downstream Network of The AES-SONEL Ngousso Sub-Station. *Journal of Energies,* Vol.2, No.2, pp. 243-257, ISSN 1996-1073

Zhisheng Zhang & Yarning Sun, 2007. Assessment on Fault-Tolerance Performance Using Neural Network Model Based on Ant Colony Optimization Algorithm for Fault Diagnosis in Distribution Systems of Electric Power Systems, *The 8th International Conference on Software Engineering, Artificial Intelligent, Networking and Parallel Distributed Computing,* pp. 712-716, ISBN 0-7695-2909-7, Qingdao, China, July 30 - August 1, 2007

Zhiwei Liao, Fushuan Wen, Wenxin Guo, Xiangzhen He, Wei Jiang, Taifu Dong, Junhui & Binghua Xu. (2008). An Analytic Model and Optimization Technique Based Methods for Fault Diagnosis in Power System. *The 3rd International Conference on Electric Utility Deregulation and Restructuring and Power Technologies,* pp. 1388-1393, ISBN 978-7-900714-13-8, Nanjuing, China, April 6-9, 2008

16

A Multi Adaptive Neuro Fuzzy Inference System for Short Term Load Forecasting by Using Previous Day Features

Zohreh Souzanchi Kashani
*Young Researchers Club, Mashhad Branch,
Islamic Azad University, Mashhad
Iran*

1. Introduction

Load forecasting had an important role in power system design, planning and development and it is the base of economical studies of energy distribution and power market. The period of load forecasting can be for one year or month (long-term or medium-term) and for one day or hour (short-term) [1, 2, 3, and 4].

For short-term load forecasting several factors should be considered, such as time factors, weather data, and possible customers' classes. The medium- and long-term forecasts take into account the historical load and weather data, the number of customers in different categories, the appliances in the area and their characteristics including age, the economic and demographic data and their forecasts, the appliance sales data, and other factors [17].

The time factors include the time of the year, the day of the week, and the hour of the day. There are important differences in load between weekdays and weekends. The load on different weekdays also can behave differently. For example, in Iran, Fridays is weekends, may have structurally different loads than Saturdays through Thursday. This is particularly true during the summer time. Holidays are more difficult to forecast than non-holidays because of their relative infrequent occurrence.

Several techniques have been used for load forecasting that among its common methods we can refer to linear-regression model, ARMA, BOX-Jenkis[5] and filter model of Kalman, expert systems [6] and ANN [1-4,7]. According to load-forecasting complex nature, however its studying by linear techniques cannot meet the need of having high accuracy and being resistant. Adaptive neural-fuzzy systems can learn and build any non-linear and complex record through educational input-output data.

Then neural-fuzzy systems have many applications in studying load forecasting and power systems according to the non-linear and complex nature of power nets. Among them we can refer to load-peak forecasting and daily network load-curve forecasting.

The east of Iran power plant consumed load information was used for simulation of consumed load forecasting system. The effect of weather forecasting information in consumed load was considered by entering Mashhad climate information gathered from weather forecasting department of the province.

2. A review of previous works

Certain days load model (formal and informal vacations) is completely different from load model of working days of week (Saturday to Wednesday), but is very similar to its near Fridays. Short-term load forecasting by using fuzzy system cannot have a good function for load forecasting of days by itself since load model of special off-days has a big difference to a usual days. As usual days load model is different regarding the surface and the shape of curve, therefore we need an expert system for adjusting the primary forecasting which apply necessary information for results correction by using an expert person's experience.

On the other hand the power price is a signal with high frequency at competitive market; multi season changes, calendar effect weekends and formal vacation) and the high percentage of unusual prices are mostly during periods of demand increase [8]. The behavior of load curve for different week days is different and in sequential weeks is similar to each other. In this paper, authors use ARMA[1] and ANFIS[2] models for power signal forecasting. A compound method is also suggested in [9] based on neural network that forecast power price and load simultaneously. In [10, 11], PSO[3] has been used for forecasting that in these papers it is in the form of long-term. In [12], the method of neural network learning and SVR[4] is presented in order to a faster forecasting. A local learning method is introduced here and KNN[5] is used for model optimizing. In [13], power load model is also mentioned as a non-linear model and a method is suggested that has the capability of non-linear map.

This paper purpose is introducing SVR with a new algorithm for power load forecasting. SVR and ANN are used for error reduction.

2.1 Short-term load forecasting methods

As we use short term load forecasting in our method, review some important methods here.

A large variety of statistical and artificial intelligence techniques have been developed for short-term load forecasting [17].

Similar-day approach. This approach is based on searching historical data for days within one, two, or three years with similar characteristics to the forecast day. Similar characteristics include weather, day of the week, and the date. The load of a similar day is considered as a forecast. Instead of a single similar day load, the forecast can be a linear combination or regression procedure that can include several similar days. The trend coefficients can be used for similar days in the previous years.

Regression methods. Regression is the one of most widely used statistical techniques. For electric load forecasting regression methods are usually used to model the relationship of

[1] Autoregressive moving average

[2] Adaptive Neural- Fuzzy Inference System

[3] Particle swarm optimization

[4] Support vector regression

[5] K-nearest neighbor

load consumption and other factors such as weather, day type, and customer class. Engle et al. [18] presented several regression models for the next day peak forecasting. Their models incorporate deterministic influences such as holidays, stochastic influences such as average loads, and exogenous influences such as weather. References [19], [20], [21], [22] describe other applications of regression models to loads forecasting.

Time series. Time series methods are based on the assumption that the data have an internal structure, such as autocorrelation, trend, or seasonal variation. Time series forecasting methods detect and explore such a structure. Time series have been used for decades in such fields as economics, digital signal processing, as well as electric load forecasting. In particular, ARMA (autoregressive moving average), ARIMA (autoregressive integrated moving average), ARMAX (autoregressive moving average with exogenous variables), and ARIMAX (autoregressive integrated moving average with exogenous variables) are the most often used classical time series methods. ARMA models are usually used for stationary processes while ARIMA is an extension of ARMA to non-stationary processes. ARMA and ARIMA use the time and load as the only input parameters. Since load generally depends on the weather and time of the day, ARIMAX is the most natural tool for load forecasting among the classical time series models. Fan and McDonald [23] and Cho et al. [24] describe implementations of ARIMAX models for load forecasting. Yang et al. [25] used evolutionary programming (EP) approach to identify the ARMAX model parameters for one day to one week ahead hourly load demand forecast. Evolutionary programming [26] is a method for simulating evolution and constitutes a stochastic optimization algorithm. Yang and Huang [27] proposed a fuzzy autoregressive moving average with exogenous input variables (FARMAX) for one day ahead hourly load forecasts.

Neural networks. The use of artificial neural networks (ANN or simply NN) has been a widely studied electric load forecasting technique since 1990 [28]. Neural networks are essentially non-linear circuits that have the demonstrated capability to do non-linear curve fitting. The outputs of an artificial neural network are some linear or nonlinear mathematical function of its inputs. The inputs may be the outputs of other network elements as well as actual network inputs. In practice network elements are arranged in a relatively small number of connected layers of elements between network inputs and outputs. Feedback paths are sometimes used. In applying a neural network to electric load forecasting, one must select one of a number of architectures (e.g. Hopfield, back propagation, Boltzmann machine), the number and connectivity of layers and elements, use of bi-directional or uni-directional links, and the number format (e.g. binary or continuous) to be used by inputs and outputs, and internally.

The most popular artificial neural network architecture for electric load forecasting is back propagation. Back propagation neural networks use continuously valued functions and supervised learning. That is, under supervised learning, the actual numerical weights assigned to element inputs are determined by matching historical data (such as time and weather) to desired outputs (such as historical electric loads) in a pre-operational "training session". Artificial neural networks with unsupervised learning do not require pre-operational training. Bakirtzis et al. [29] developed an ANN based short-term load forecasting model for the Energy Control Center of the Greek Public Power Corporation. In the development they used a fully connected three-layer feed forward ANN and back propagation algorithm was used for training.

Input variables include historical hourly load data, temperature, and the day of the week. The model can forecast load profiles from one to seven days. Also Papalexopoulos et al. [30] developed and implemented a multi-layered feed forward ANN for short-term system load forecasting. In the model three types of variables are used as inputs to the neural network: season related inputs, weather related inputs, and historical loads. Khotanzad et al. [31] described a load forecasting system known as ANNSTLF. ANNSTLF is based on multiple ANN strategies that capture various trends in the data. In the development they used a multilayer perceptron trained with the error back propagation algorithm. ANNSTLF can consider the effect of temperature and relative humidity on the load. It also contains forecasters that can generate the hourly temperature and relative humidity forecasts needed by the system. An improvement of the above system was described in [32]. In the new generation, ANNSTLF includes two ANN forecasters, one predicts the base load and the other forecasts the change in load. The final forecast is computed by an adaptive combination of these forecasts. The effects of humidity and wind speed are considered through a linear transformation of temperature. As reported in [32], ANNSTLF was being used by 35 utilities across the USA and Canada. Chen et al. [4] developed a three layer fully connected feed forward neural network and the back propagation algorithm was used as the training method. Their ANN though considers the electricity price as one of the main characteristics of the system load. Many published studies use artificial neural networks in conjunction with other forecasting techniques (such as with regression trees [26], time series [33] or fuzzy logic [34]).

Expert systems. Rule based forecasting makes use of rules, which are often heuristic in nature, to do accurate forecasting. Expert systems, incorporates rules and procedures used by human experts in the field of interest into software that is then able to automatically make forecasts without human assistance.

Expert system use began in the 1960's for such applications as geological prospecting and computer design. Expert systems work best when a human expert is available to work with software developers for a considerable amount of time in imparting the expert's knowledge to the expert system software. Also, an expert's knowledge must be appropriate for codification into software rules (i.e. the expert must be able to explain his/her decision process to programmers). An expert system may codify up to hundreds or thousands of production rules. Ho et al. [35] proposed a knowledge-based expert system for the short-term load forecasting of the Taiwan power system. Operator's knowledge and the hourly observations of system load over the past five years were employed to establish eleven day types. Weather parameters were also considered. The developed algorithm performed better compared to the conventional Box-Jenkins method. Rahman and Hazim [36] developed a site-independent technique for short-term load forecasting. Knowledge about the load and the factors affecting it are extracted and represented in a parameterized rule base. This rule base is complemented by a parameter database that varies from site to site. The technique was tested in several sites in the United States with low forecasting errors.

The load model, the rules, and the parameters presented in the paper have been designed using no specific knowledge about any particular site. The results can be improved if operators at a particular site are consulted.

Fuzzy logic. Fuzzy logic is a generalization of the usual Boolean logic used for digital circuit design. An input under Boolean logic takes on a truth value of "0" or "1". Under fuzzy logic an input has associated with it a certain qualitative ranges. For instance a transformer load may be "low", "medium" and "high". Fuzzy logic allows one to (logically) deduce outputs from fuzzy inputs. In this sense fuzzy logic is one of a number of techniques for mapping inputs to outputs (i.e. curve fitting).

Among the advantages of fuzzy logic are the absence of a need for a mathematical model mapping inputs to outputs and the absence of a need for precise (or even noise free) inputs. With such generic conditioning rules, properly designed fuzzy logic systems can be very robust when used for forecasting. Of course in many situations an exact output (e.g. the precise 12PM load) is needed. After the logical processing of fuzzy inputs, a "defuzzification" process can be used to produce such precise outputs. References [37], [38], [39] describe applications of fuzzy logic to electric load forecasting.

Support vector machines. Support Vector Machines (SVMs) are a more recent powerful technique for solving classification and regression problems. This approach was originated from Vapnik's [40] statistical learning theory. Unlike neural networks, which try to define complex functions of the input feature space, support vector machines perform a nonlinear mapping (by using so-called kernel functions) of the data into a high dimensional (feature) space. Then support vector machines use simple linear functions to create linear decision boundaries in the new space. The problem of choosing an architecture for a neural network is replaced here by the problem of choosing a suitable kernel for the support vector machine [41]. Mohandes [42] applied the method of support vector machines for short-term electrical load forecasting. The author compares its performance with the autoregressive method. The results indicate that SVMs compare favorably against the autoregressive method. Chen et al. [43] proposed a SVM model to predict daily load demand of a month. Their program was the winning entry of the competition organized by the EU Load NITE network. Li and Fang [44] also used a SVM model for short-term load forecasting.

3. Consumed load model

The load forecasting art is in selecting the most appropriate way and model for and the closest ones to the existing reality of the network among different methods and models of load forecasting, by studying and analyzing the last procedure of load and recognizing the effective factors sufficiently and maximizing each of them, and then in this way it forecasts different time periods required for the network with an acceptable approximation. It should be accepted that there is always some error in load forecasting due to the accidental load behavior but never this error should go further than the acceptable and tolerable limit. Relative accuracy has a particular importance in load forecasting in power industry. Especially when load forecasting is the basis of network development planning and power plant capacity. Since, any forecasting with open hand causes extra investment and the installation capacity to be useless and vice versa any forecasting less than real needs, faces the network with shortage in production and damages the instruments due to extra load.

Consumed load model is influenced by different parameters such as weather, vacations or holidays, working days of week and etc. in order to build a short-term load forecasting system, we should consider the influence of different parameters in load forecasting, which it can be full field by a correct selection of system entries. Selection of these parameters depends on experimental observations and is influenced by the environment conditions and is determined by trial and error.

4. Reviewing the predictability of time series by the help of lyapunov exponent[6]

Chaos is a phenomenon that occurs in many non-linear definable systems which show a high sensitivity to the primary conditions and semi random behavior. These systems will remain stable in the chaotic mode if they provide the Lyapunov exponent equations.

4.1 Background

Detecting the presence of chaos in a dynamical system is an important problem that is solved by measuring the largest Lyapunov exponent. Lyapunov exponents quantify the exponential divergence of initially close state-space trajectories and estimate the amount of chaos in a system.[50]

Over the past decade, distinguishing deterministic chaos from noise has become an important problem in many diverse fields, e.g., physiology [51], economics [52]. This is due, in part, to the availability of numerical algorithms for quantifying chaos using experimental time series. In particular, methods exist for calculating correlation dimension (D2) [53], Kolmogorov entropy [54], and Lyapunov characteristic exponents. Dimension gives an estimate of the system complexity; entropy and characteristic exponents give an estimate of the level of chaos in the dynamical system.

The Grassberger-Procaccia algorithm (GPA) [53] appears to be the most popular method used to quantify chaos. This is probably due to the simplicity of the algorithm [55] and the fact that the same intermediate calculations are used to estimate both dimension and entropy.

However, the GPA is sensitive to variations in its parameters, e.g., number of data points [56], embedding dimension [56], reconstruction delay [57], and it is usually unreliable except for long, noise-free time series. Hence, the practical significance of the GPA is questionable, and the Lyapunov exponents may provide a more useful characterization of chaotic systems.

For time series produced by dynamical systems, the presence of a positive characteristic exponent indicates chaos. Furthermore, in many applications it is sufficient to calculate only the largest Lyapunov exponent ($\lambda1$). However, the existing methods for estimating $\lambda1$ suffer from at least one of the following drawbacks: (1) unreliable for small data sets, (2) computationally intensive, (3) relatively difficult to implement. For this reason, we have developed a new method for calculating the largest Lyapunov exponent. The method is reliable for small data sets, fast, and easy to implement. "Easy to implement" is largely a subjective quality, although we believe it has had a notable positive effect on the popularity of dimension estimates.

For a dynamical system, sensitivity to initial conditions is quantified by the Lyapunov exponents. For example, consider two trajectories with nearby initial conditions on an attracting manifold. When the attractor is chaotic, the trajectories diverge, on average, at an exponential rate characterized by the largest Lyapunov exponent [58]. This concept is also generalized for the spectrum of Lyapunov exponents, λi (i=1, 2, ..., n), by considering a small

[6] Lyapunov exponent

n-dimensional sphere of initial conditions, where n is the number of equations (or, equivalently, the number of state variables) used to describe the system. As time (t) progresses, the sphere evolves into an ellipsoid whose principal axes expand (or contract) at rates given by the Lyapunov exponents.

The presence of a positive exponent is sufficient for diagnosing chaos and represents local instability in a particular direction. Note that for the existence of an attractor, the overall dynamics must be dissipative, i.e., globally stable, and the total rate of contraction must outweigh the total rate of expansion. Thus, even when there are several positive Lyapunov exponents, the sum across the entire spectrum is negative.

Wolf et al. [59] explain the Lyapunov spectrum by providing the following geometrical interpretation. First, arrange the n principal axes of the ellipsoid in the order of most rapidly expanding to most rapidly contracting. It follows that the associated Lyapunov exponents will be arranged such that

$$\lambda_1 > \lambda_2 > \ldots\ldots > \lambda_n$$

where λ_1 and λ_n correspond to the most rapidly expanding and contracting principal axes, respectively. Next, recognize that the length of the first principal axis is proportional to $e^{\lambda 1 t}$; the area determined by the first two principal axes is proportional to $e^{(\lambda 1+\lambda 2)t}$; and the volume determined by the first k principal axes is proportional to $e^{(\lambda 1+\lambda 2+\cdots+\lambda k)t}$. Thus, the Lyapunov spectrum can be defined such that the exponential growth of a k-volume element is given by the sum of the k largest Lyapunov exponents. Note that information created by the system is represented as a change in the volume defined by the expanding principal axes. The sum of the corresponding exponents, i.e., the positive exponents, equals the Kolmogorov entropy (K) or mean rate of information gain [58]:

$$K=\sum_{\lambda i>0} \lambda i$$

When the equations describing the dynamical system are available, one can calculate the entire Lyapunov spectrum. The approach involves numerically solving the system's n equations for n+1 nearby initial conditions. The growth of a corresponding set of vectors is measured, and as the system evolves, the vectors are repeatedly reorthonormalized using the Gram-Schmidt procedure. This guarantees that only one vector has a component in the direction of most rapid expansion, i.e., the vectors maintain a proper phase space orientation. In experimental settings, however, the equations of motion are usually unknown and this approach is not applicable. Furthermore, experimental data often consist of time series from a single observable, and one must employ a technique for attractor reconstruction, e.g., method of delays [60], singular value decomposition.

As suggested above, one cannot calculate the entire Lyapunov spectrum by choosing arbitrary directions for measuring the separation of nearby initial conditions. One must measure the separation along the Lyapunov directions which correspond to the principal axes of the ellipsoid previously considered. These Lyapunov directions are dependent upon the system flow and are defined using the Jacobian matrix, i.e., the tangent map, at each point of interest along the flow [58]. Hence, one must preserve the proper phase space orientation by using a suitable approximation of the tangent map. This requirement, however, becomes unnecessary when calculating only the largest Lyapunov exponent.

If we assume that there exists an ergodic measure of the system, then the multiplicative ergodic theorem of Oseledec [61] justifies the use of arbitrary phase space directions when calculating the largest Lyapunov exponent with smooth dynamical systems. We can expect that two randomly chosen initial conditions will diverge exponentially at a rate given by the largest Lyapunov exponent [62]. In other words, we can expect that a random vector of initial conditions will converge to the most unstable manifold, since exponential growth in this direction quickly dominates growth (or contraction) along the other Lyapunov directions. Thus, the largest Lyapunov exponent can be defined using the following equation where d(t) is the average divergence at time t and C is a constant that normalizes the initial separation:

$$d(t) = Ce^{\lambda 1t}$$

For experimental applications, a number of researchers have proposed algorithms that estimate the largest Lyapunov exponent [55,59], the positive Lyapunov spectrum, i.e., only positive exponents [59], or the complete Lyapunov spectrum [58]. Each method can be considered as a variation of one of several earlier approaches [59] and as suffering from at least one of the following drawbacks: (1) unreliable for small data sets, (2) computationally intensive, (3) relatively difficult to implement. These drawbacks motivated our search for an improved method of estimating the largest Lyapunov exponent.

4.2 Calculation of lyapunov exponent for time series

In order to calculate Lyapunov exponent for those systems which their equation is not determined and their time series is not available, different algorithm is suggested [45-49].

The algorithm proposed by Wolf [48], seeks the time series of close points in the phase space. These points went round the phase space or got divergent rapidly. Close points in the same direction are selected.

The differential coefficient is in the direction of the maximum development and their average logarithm on the route of phase space yields the biggest Lyapunov exponent. Suppose that series of $x_0, x_1, x_2, \ldots x_k$ is available and the interval between them is obtained as $t_n - t_0 = n_\tau$ that τ is the interval between two successive measurement. If the system has chaotic behavior, we can explain divergence of the adjacent routes based on the difference range between them, as following.

$$d_0 = |x_j - x_i| \quad (1)$$

$$d_1 = |x_{j+1} - x_{i+1}| \quad (2)$$

.

.

.

$$d_n = |x_{j+n} - x_{i+n}| \quad (3)$$

It is supposed that d_n will increase exponential by n increase:

$$d_n = d_0 e^{\lambda n} \tag{4}$$

So by calculating its logarithm we have:

$$\lambda = \frac{1}{n} \mathrm{Ln} \frac{d_n}{d_0} \tag{5}$$

There should be at least one Lyapunov exponent bigger than zero to have chaos, the existence of positive value of λ means the chaotic behavior of system. Therefore, in order to Table 1 we can expect system to forecast.

Winter	Fall	Summer	Spring
0.07563	0.05428	0.0444	0.0523

Table 1. Lyapunov exponent for seasons of one year

5. Preparing the input data

First step in the process of electricity load forecasting is to provide last information of the system load being studied. After preparing the input data matrix, it is turn of classification. The reason of this classification is the existence of completely determined models in different days that were referred to in many references. Among different days of weeks, Saturday to Thursday which are working days in Iran, have the same load model. Fridays have also their own particular model and have a low level of load. Special days have a completely different model, too. So it seems necessary at the first look that each of these classes should be analyzed separately. We consider 2 groups of features that refer to previous days; 2, 7, and 14 day ago, and 2, 3, 4 day ago.

6. Adaptive neural- Fuzzy inference system

ANFIS, proposed by Jang [14, 15], is an architecture which functionally integrates the interpretability of a fuzzy inference system with adaptability of a neural network. Loosely speaking ANFIS is a method for tuning an existing rule base of fuzzy system with a learning algorithm based on a collection of training data found in artificial neural network. Due to the less tunable use of parameters of fuzzy system compared with conventional artificial neural network, ANFIS is trained faster and more accurately than the conventional artificial neural network. An ANFIS which corresponds to a Sugeno type fuzzy model of two inputs and single output is shown in Fig. 1. A rule set of first order Sugeno fuzzy system is the following form:

Rule i: If x is Ai and y is Bi then fi = $p_i x + q_i y + r_i$.

ANFIS structure as shown in Figure 1 is a weightless multi-layer array of five different elements [15]:

- Layer 1: Input data are fuzzified and neuron values are represented by parameterized membership functions;
  - $O_{l,i}$ is the output of the *i*th node of the layer l.
  - Every node *i* in this layer is an adaptive node with a node function

$$O_{1,i} = \mu A_i(x) \text{ for } i = 1, 2, \text{ or}$$

$$O_{1,i} = \mu B_{i-2}(x) \text{ for } i = 3, 4$$

- x (or y) is the input node i and A_i (or B_{i-2}) is a linguistic label associated with this node
- Therefore $O_{1,i}$ is the membership grade of a fuzzy set (A1,A2,B1,B2).
- Typical membership function:

$$\mu A(x) = \frac{1}{1+|\frac{x-ci}{ai}|2bi}$$

- a_i, b_i, c_i is the parameter set.
- Parameters are referred to as premise parameters.

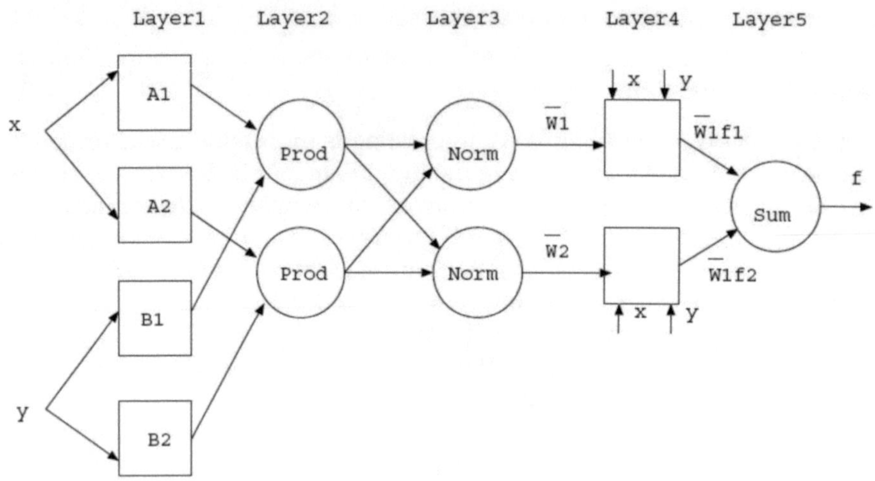

Fig. 1. ANFIS architecture

- Layer 2: The activation of fuzzy rules is calculated via differentiable T-norms (usually, the soft-min or product);
  - Every node in this layer is a fixed node labeled Prod.
  - The output is the product of all the incoming signals.
  - $O_{2,i} = w_i = \mu A_i(x) \cdot \mu B_i(y)$, $i = 1, 2$
  - Each node represents the fire strength of the rule
  - Any other T-norm operator that perform the AND operator can be used
- Layer 3: A normalization (arithmetic division) operation is realized over the rules matching values;
  - Every node in this layer is a fixed node labeled Norm.
  - The ith node calculates the ratio of the ith rulet's firing strenght to the sum of all rulet's firing strengths.
  - $O_{3,i} = \overline{w}_i = \frac{w_i}{w_1+w_2}$, i = 1, 2
  - Outputs are called normalized firing strengths.
- Layer 4: The consequent part is obtained via linear regression or multiplication between the normalized activation level and the output of the respective rule;
  - Every node i in this layer is an adaptive node with a node function:

$$O_{4,1} = \overline{w}_i f_i = \overline{w}_i(p_x + q_i y + r_i)$$

- $\overline{w}_i$ is the normalized firing strenght from layer 3.
- $\{p_i, q_i, r_i\}$ is the parameter set of this node.
- These are referred to as consequent parameters.

- Layer 5: The NFN output is produced by an algebraic sum over all rules outputs.
  - The single node in this layer is a fixed node labeled *sum*, which computes the overall output as the summation of all incoming signals:
  - overall output = $O_{5,1} = \sum \overline{w}_i f_i = \frac{\sum_i w_i f_i}{\sum_i w_i}$

The main objective of the ANFIS design is to optimize the ANFIS parameters. There are two steps in the ANFIS design. First is design of the premise parameters and the other is consequent parameter training. There are several methods proposed for designing the premise parameter such as grid partition, fuzzy C-means clustering and subtractive clustering. Once the premise parameters are fixed, the consequent parameters are obtained based on the input-output training data. A hybrid learning algorithm is a popular learning algorithm used to train the ANFIS for this purpose.

- ANFIS uses a hybrid learning algorithm to identify the membership function parameters of single-output, Sugeno type fuzzy inference systems (FIS).
- There are many ways of using this function.
- Some examples:

[FIS,ERROR] = ANFIS(TRNDATA)

[FIS,ERROR] = ANFIS(TRNDATA,INITFIS)

7. The proposed method for power consumed load forecasting

Since fuzzy methods and systems were presented for using in different applications, researchers noticed that making a fuzzy powerful system is not a simple work. The reason is that finding suitable fuzzy rules and membership functions is not a systematic work and mainly requires many trails and errors to reach to the best possible efficiency. Therefore the idea of using learning algorithms was proposed for fuzzy systems. Meanwhile learning of fuzzy network proposed them as the first goals for being unified in fuzzy methods in order to make the development and usage process of fuzzy systems automatic for different applications. Function estimation by using the learning methods is proposed in neural networks and neural-fuzzy networks.

In the suggested methods we forecast load consume and its improvement by the help of the offered method. One of the famous neural-fuzzy systems for function estimation is ANFIS model. We used this system for power consumed load forecasting in this paper too, but with this difference that we used one separate adaptive neural-fuzzy system for each season of the year. Although at the time of training these systems data overlapping is considered, because data of each season of the year is not completely independent and there is some similarities between the first days of a season with its previous season regarding the amount of load consumption. Figure 2 shows the diagram of multi adaptive neural-fuzzy system (multi ANFIS).

As it is shown too, in the Figure 2, we us a switch for any subsystem of a season be thought in lieu of that season. Therefore the time of system training and testing will decrease and the entrance of extra data is prevented.

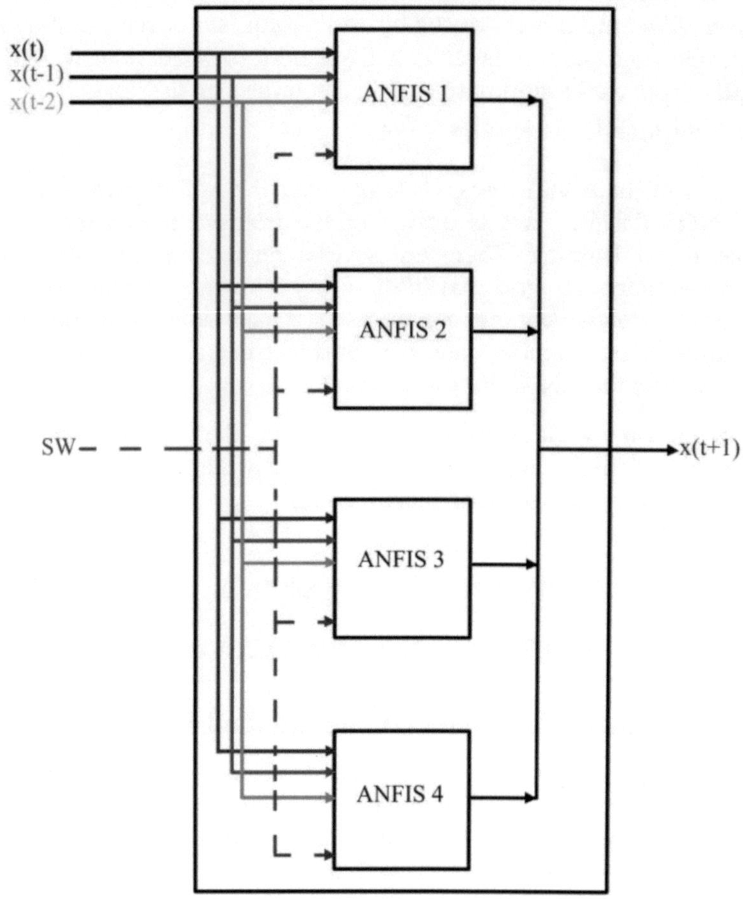

Fig. 2. Implemented Diagram of Multi ANFIS

8. Result

In the proposed method we classified day into two categories. We divide the season days into two groups of working days (Saturday to Thursday) and holidays that their load consumption is different from other days.

Here we also calculated the output of Multi ANFIS based on the features of previous day, one time with 2, 7, and 14 day ago and another time with 2, 3, and 4 day ago. You can see the results in Table 2 and 3.

The amount of the accuracy of the performance of any of calculation methods in load forecasting is determined by measuring the obtained values of system model and comparing it with real data.

Mean Absolute Percentage Error (MAPE) is used for studying the performance of every mentioned method with the data of related test. MAPE is determined by following relation:

$$\text{MAPE}= 1/\text{N} \left(\sum_{i=1}^{N} APE_i \right) \tag{6}$$

$$\text{APE}= |(\text{V(forecast)}-\text{V(actual)})/ \text{V(actual)}|*100\% \tag{7}$$

MAPE for working days	load consumption forecasting
1.5409	Spring
2.1869	Summer
2.4575	Fall
1.5116	Winter

Table 2. Power load consumption forecasting for the working days (saturday to thursday) with 2, 3, and 4 day ago

MAPE for working days	Load consumption forecasting
0.9602	Spring
0.8568	Summer
1.1392	Fall
1.3015	Winter

Table 3. Power load consumption forecasting for the working days (saturday to thursday) with 2, 7, and 14 day ago

As it is obvious of the above Tables, making working days separate from holidays with using previous days features (2, 7,and 14 day ago) yields a better result, in load consumption forecasting.

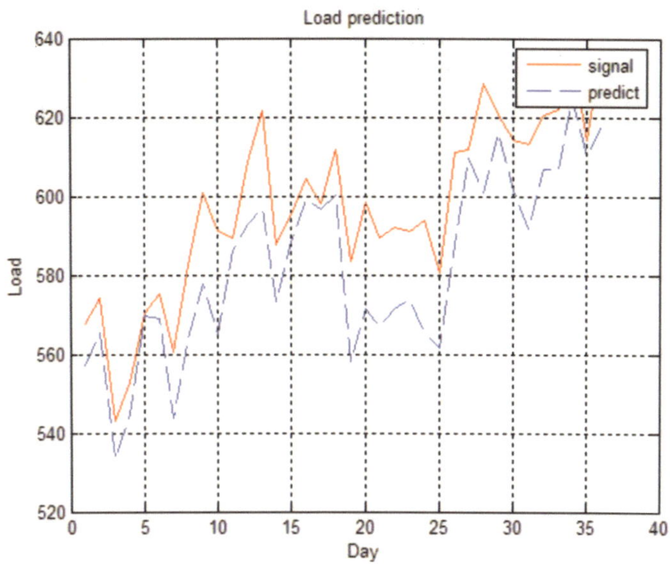

Fig. 3. Power load forecasting for Working days (Saturday to Thursday) of fall with features of 2, 3, and 4 day ago

Also in order to compare, the diagram of daily load forecasting curves for fall through both groups is shown in Figures 3 and 4. It should be mentioned that MATLAB software is used for load forecasting and simulation.

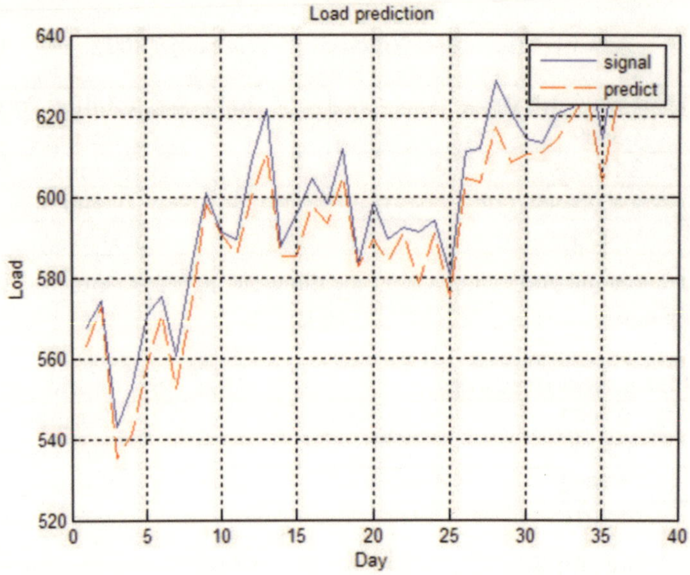

Fig. 4. Power load forecasting for Working days (Saturday to Thursday) of fall with features of 2, 7, and 14 day ago

9. Conclusion and suggestion

Comparing mentioned methods above shows that separation of working days from holidays has a better result in load consumption forecasting. As shown in Figure 5 we can

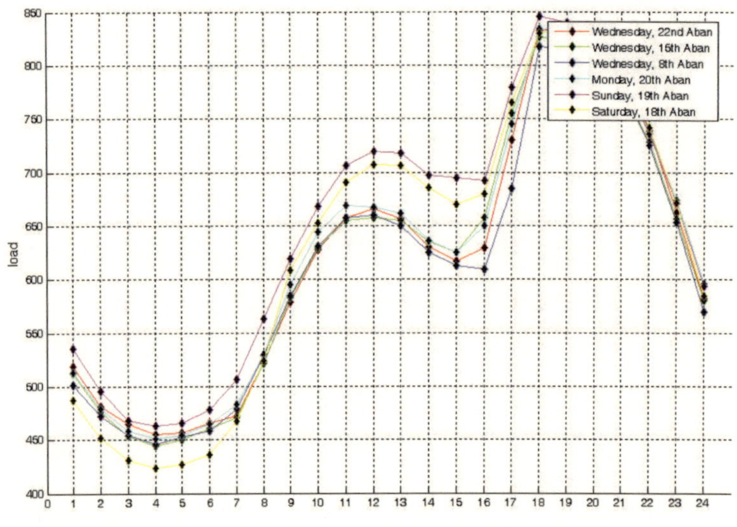

Fig. 5. Compare of the feature of 2, 7 and 14 day ago with 2, 3 and 4 day ago

see that using the features of 2, 7 and 14 day ago are better than 2, 3 and 4 day ago. A cyan and yellow line are refer to 3 and 4 day ago. We can see that these features cannot have good effect on load forecasting.

According to this that in most proposed methods load consumption time series data is used; it seems that we can obtain better results by using time series data of one or more parameters effective in load consumption [16] also with load consumption time series. Accurate load forecasting is very important for electric utilities in a competitive environment created by the electric industry deregulation.

10. References

[1] Huang, S.J. and K.R. Shih, 2003. Short term load forecasting via ARMA model identification including non- Gaussian process consideration. IEEE Trans. Power Syst., 18: 673-679.

[2] Kandil Nahi, Rene Wamkeue, Maarouf saad and Semaan Georges, 2006. An efficient approach for short term load forecasting using artificial neural networks. Int. J. Electric Power Energy syst., 28: 525-530.

[3] Mandal Paras, Tomonobu Senjyu, Naomitsu Urasaki, Toshihisa Funabashi, 2006. A neural network based several hours ahead electric load forecasting using similar days approach. Int. J. Elect. Power Energy Syst., 28: 367-373.

[4] Topalli Ayca Kumluca, Ismet Erkmen and Ihsan Topalli, 2006. Intelligent short term load forecasting in Turkey. Int. J. Electric. Power Energy Syst., 28: 437-447.

[5] Moghram, I. and S. Rahman, 1989. Analysis and evaluation of five short term load forecasting techniques. IEEE Trans. Power Syst., 4: 1484-1491.

[6] Rahman, S. and R. Bhatnager, 1988. An expert system based algorithm for short term load forecast. IEEE Trans. Power Sys., pp: 392-399.

[7] Senjyu, T., H. Takara, K. Uezato and T. Funbasi, 2002. One hour ahead load forecasting using neural network. IEEE Trans. Power sys., 17: 113-118.

[8] F. J. Nogales, J. Contreras, A. J. Conejo and R. Espinola, "Forecasting Next-Day Electricity Prices by Times Series Models", IEEE Transaction On Power Systems, Vol. 17, no.2, May 2002.

[9] Amjadi N, Daraeepour A, "Mixed price and load forecasting of electricity markets by a new iterative prediction method", Electric power systems research, 2009.

[10] Niu D, Li J, Liu D, "Middle-long power load forecasting based on particle swarm optimization", computers and mathematics with applications, 2009.

[11] Alrashidi M, Elnaggar K, "Long term electric load forecasting based on particle swarm optimization", applied enery, 2009.

[12] He W, "Forecasting electricity load with optimized local learning models", Electrical power and energy systems, 2008.

[13] Hong W-C, "Electric load forecasting by support vector model", Applied Mathematical Modelling, 2009.

[14] Jang, J.S.R., C. T. Sun and E. Mizutani. Neuro-Fuzzy and Soft Computing, Prentice Hall, Upper Saddle River, NJ, USA. 1997.

[15] Jang, J.S. ANFIS: Adaptive-network-based fuzzy inference system, IEEE Trans. on System, Man, and Cybernetics, vol. 23, pp.665-685, May/June, 1993.

[16] Souzanchi-K Z, Yaghobi M, Akbarzadeh-T M, "Modeling and Forecasting Short_term Electricity Load based on Multi Adaptive Neural-Fuzzy Inference System by Using Temterature", 2nd International conference on Signal Processing Systems(ICSPS), 2010.

[17] E A. Feinberg, D Genethliou. LOAD FORECASTING, APPLIED MATHEMATICS FOR POWER SYSTEMS Load Forecasting

[18] R.F. Engle, C. Mustafa, and J. Rice. Modeling Peak Electricity Demand. Journal of Forecasting, 11:241–251, 1992.

[19] O. Hyde and P.F. Hodnett. An Adaptable Automated Procedure for Short-Term Electricity Load Forecasting. IEEE Transactions on Power Systems, 12:84–93, 1997.

[20] S. Ruzic, A. Vuckovic, and N. Nikolic. Weather Sensitive Method for Short-Term Load Forecasting in Electric Power Utility of Serbia. IEEE Transactions on Power Systems, 18:1581–1586, 2003.

[21] T. Haida and S. Muto. Regression Based Peak Load Forecasting using a Transformation Technique. IEEE Transactions on Power Systems, 9:1788–1794, 1994.

[22] W. Charytoniuk, M.S. Chen, and P. Van Olinda. Nonparametric Regression Based Short-Term Load Forecasting. IEEE Transactions on Power Systems, 13:725–730, 1998.

[23] J.Y. Fan and J.D. McDonald. A Real-Time Implementation of Short-Term Load Forecasting for Distribution Power Systems. IEEE Transactions on Power Systems, 9:988–994, 1994.

[24] M.Y. Cho, J.C. Hwang, and C.S. Chen. Customer Short-Term Load Forecasting by using ARIMA Transfer Function Model. Proceedings of the International Conference on Energy Management and Power Delivery, 1:317–322, 1995.

[25] H.T. Yang, C.M. Huang, and C.L. Huang. Identification of ARMAX Model for Short-Term Load Forecasting: An Evolutionary Programming Approach. IEEE Transactions on Power Systems, 11:403–408, 1996.

[26] D.B. Fogel. An Introduction to Simulated Evolutionary Optimization. IEEE Transactions on Neural Networks, 5:3–14, 1994.

[27] H.T. Yang and C.M. Huang. A New Short-Term Load Forecasting Approach using Self-Organizing Fuzzy ARMAX Models. IEEE Transactions on Power Systems, 13:217–225, 1998.

[28] M. Peng, N.F. Hubele, and G.G. Karady. Advancement in the Application of Neural Networks for Short-Term Load Forecasting. IEEE Transactions on Power Systems, 7:250–257, 1992.

[29] A.G. Bakirtzis, V. Petridis, S.J. Kiartzis, M.C. Alexiadis, and A.H. Maissis. A Neural Network Short-Term Load Forecasting Model for the Greek Power System. IEEE Transactions on Power Systems, 11:858–863, 1996.

[30] A.D. Papalexopoulos, S. Hao, and T.M. Peng. An Implementation of a Neural Network Based Load Forecasting Model for the EMS. IEEE Transactions on Power Systems, 9:1956–1962, 1994.

[31] A. Khotanzad, R.A. Rohani, T.L. Lu, A. Abaye, M. Davis, and D.J. Maratukulam. ANNSTLF-A Neural-Network-Based Electric Load Forecasting System. IEEE Transactions on Neural Networks, 8:835–846, 1997.

[32] A. Khotanzad, R.A. Rohani, and D. Maratukulam. ANNSTLF- Artificial Neural Network Short-Term Load Forecaster-Generation Three. IEEE Transactions on Neural Networks, 13:1413–1422, 1998.

[33] T.W.S. Chow and C.T. Leung. Nonlinear Autoregressive Integrated Neural Network Model for Short-Term Load Forecasting. IEE Proceedings on Generation, Transmission and Distribution, 143:500–506, 1996.

[34] S.E. Skarman and M. Georgiopoulous. Short-Term Electrical Load Forecasting using a Fuzzy ARTMAP Neural Network. Proceedings of SPIE, 181–191, 1998.

[35] K.L. Ho, Y.Y. Hsu, F.F. Chen, T.E. Lee, C.C. Liang, T.S. Lai, and K.K. Chen. Short-Term Load Forecasting of Taiwan Power System using a Knowledge Based Expert System. IEEE Transactions on Power Systems, 5:1214–1221, 1990.

[36] S. Rahman and O. Hazim. Load Forecasting for Multiple Sites: Development of an Expert System-Based Technique. Electric Power Systems Research, 39:161–169, 1996.

[37] S.J. Kiartzis and A.G. Bakirtzis. A Fuzzy Expert System for Peak Load Forecasting: Application to the Greek Power System. Proceedings of the 10th Mediterranean Electrotechnical Conference, 3:1097- 1100, 2000.

[38] V. Miranda and C. Monteiro. Fuzzy Inference in Spatial Load Forecasting. Proceedings of IEEE Power Engineering Winter Meeting, 2:1063–1068, 2000.

[39] S.E. Skarman and M. Georgiopoulous. Short-Term Electrical Load Forecasting using a Fuzzy ARTMAP Neural Network. Proceedings of SPIE, 181–191, 1998.

[40] V.N. Vapnik. The Nature of Statistical Learning Theory. NewYork, Springer Verlag, 1995.

[41] N. Christiani and J.S. Taylor. An Itroduction to Support Vector Machines and Other Kernel-Based Learning Methods. Cambridge University Press, Cambridge, 2000.

[42] M. Mohandes. Support Vector Machines for Short-Term Electrical Load Forecasting. International Journal of Energy Research, 26:335–345, 2002.

[43] B.J. Chen, M.W. Chang, and C.J. Lin. Load Forecasting using Support Vector Machines: A Study on EUNITE Competition 2001. Technical report, Department of Computer Science and Information Engineering, National Taiwan University, 2002.

[44] Y. Li and T. Fang. Wavelet and Support Vector Machines for Short-Term Electrical Load Forecasting. Proceedings of International Conference on Wavelet Analysis and its Applications, 1:399- 404, 2003.

[45] Gencay R, Dechert W.D., (1992), "An Algorithm for the n-Lyapunov exponents of an n-dimensional unknown dynamical system" Physica D 59:142 57.

[46] Nychka D.W., Ellner S., (1992), "Finding chaos in a noisy system", J R Stat Soc B., 54:399-426.

[47] J. C. Sprott, "Chaos and Time-Series Analysis", Oxford University Press, USA.

[48] Wolf, A., Swift, J.B., Swinney, H., L., and Vastono, J.A., (1985), "Determining Lyapunov exponent from a time series", Physical D 16, PP. 285-317.

[49] Michael T. Rosenstein, James J. Collins, and Carlo J. De Luca," A practical method for calculating largest Lyapunov exponents from small data sets"

[50] M Rosenstein, J Collins, C Luca, A practical method for calculating largest Lyapunov exponents from small data sets, 1992

[51] G. W. Frank, T. Lookman, M. A. H. Nerenberg, C. Essex, J. Lemieux, and W. Blume, Chaotic time series analysis of epileptic seizures, Physica D 46 (1990) 427.

[52] P. Chen, Empirical and theoretical evidence of economic chaos, Sys. Dyn. Rev. 4 (1988) 81.

[53] P. Grassberger, and I. Procaccia, Characterization of strange attractors, Phys. Rev. Lett. 50 (1983) 346.

[54] P. Grassberger, and I. Procaccia, Estimation of the Kolmogorov entropy from a chaotic signal, Phys. Rev. A 28 (1983) 2591.

[55] S. Ellner, A. R. Gallant, D. McCaffrey, and D. Nychka, Convergence rates and data requirements for Jacobian-based estimates of Lyapunov exponents from data, Phys. Lett. A 153 (1991) 357.

[56] J. B. Ramsey, and H.-J. Yuan, The statistical properties of dimension calculations using small data sets, Nonlinearity 3 (1990) 155.

[57] A. M. Albano, J. Muench, C. Schwartz, A. I. Mees, and P. E. Rapp, Singular-value decomposition and the Grassberger-Procaccia algorithm, Phys. Rev. A 38 (1988) 3017.

[58] J.-P. Eckmann, and D. Ruelle, Ergodic theory of chaos and strange attractors, Rev. Mod. Phys. 57 (1985) 617.

[59] A. Wolf, J. B. Swift, H. L. Swinney, and J. A. Vastano, Determining Lyapunov exponents from a time series, Physica D 16 (1985) 285.

[60] N. H. Packard, J. P. Crutchfield, J. D. Farmer, and R. S. Shaw, Geometry from a time series, Phys. Rev. Lett. 45 (1980) 712.

[61] V. I. Oseledec, A multiplicative ergodic theorem. Lyapunov characteristic numbers for dynamical systems, Trans. Moscow Math. Soc. 19 (1968) 197.

[62] G. Benettin, L. Galgani, and J.-M. Strelcyn, Kolmogorov entropy and numerical experiments, Phys. Rev. A 14 (1976) 2338.

17

Fuzzy Inference System in Energy Demand Prediction

Thair Mahmoud, Daryoush Habibi,
Octavian Bass and Stefan Lachowics
School of Engineering, Edith Cowan University,
Australia

1. Introduction

Fuzzy Inference Systems (FIS) have been widely used in many applications including image processing, optimization, control and system identification. Among these applications, we would like to investigate energy demand modelling. Generally, developing an energy demand model is the challenge of interpreting the historical use of energy in an electric power network into equations which approximate the future use of energy. The developed model's equations are coded and embedded into a processor based system, which predicts the output when a certain type of input occurs. However, the range and quality of prediction is still limited within the knowledge supplied to the model. The major concern about the energy demand modelling is to categorize the type of prediction in short or long-term prediction. In addition, it is crucial to categorize the type of the power network to be modelled. Since identifying the useful historical operation data for setting the model parameters is crucial in modelling, the operation history of the modelled systems must to be analysed. In simple terms, modelling energy demand is the art of identifying the right modelling technique and system's operation parameters. The operation parameters differ based on the type and size of the modelled system. So, taking into consideration why the system is modelled will justify the selection of modelling techniques. Among the reasons for modelling energy demand is managing the use of energy through an Energy Management System (EMS).

For EMS, most of the Artificial Intelligence (AI) methods will lack robustness in terms of their programming and their required computation resources, especially when the EMS is designed to perform on-line quick response tasks. Artificial Neural Network (ANN) might be good candidate among modelling techniques, as there has to be a compromise between robustness of the method and its required computation resources for a specific type of modelling. However, there are a few reasons why ANNs are not suitable for our proposed discussion: their limited adaptability within limited computation resources, their training time and their models' complexity, especially when we deal with highly non-linear systems. Looking at our case study and the reasons this scenario is modelled, we have found that Fuzzy Inference Systems (FIS) are the most appropriate for modelling the energy demand in this specific system, since model development, model parameters, model adaptation capability and computation resources requirements are met. The reason behind choosing FIS to model the energy demand is the flexibility to control the prediction performance and the complexity of the model. Fuzzy modelling and reasoning systems have been widely utilised in literature because of their applicability and modelling performance. The use of Adaptive Neuro Fuzzy Inference Systems (ANFIS) gives the fuzzy modelling two extra valuable advantages: the training time and prediction accuracy compared to other modelling techniques. Fuzzy modelling has been successfully applied in different types of applications including electricity and gas demands, economics and finance, weather and meteorology studies, health and population growth, geographic information systems, traffic and transport systems, etc.

In the recent years, energy demand prediction modelling has been widely investigated, especially when its smartgrid applications have been rapidly grown, and energy price change has been rapidly correlated to the energy demand prediction. Different smart prediction mechanisms have been introduced in literature. (McSharry 2007) has developed a day-ahead demand prediction models, and (Alireza Khotanzad 2002) has introduced a new short-term energy demand prediction modelling technique which integrates the real-time energy price change in the prediction models. (Amir-Hamed Mohsenian-Rad 2010) have also introduced the real-time price environment modelling to perform an optimised residential load control, where a fundamental bid-based stochastic model is presented to predict electricity hourly prices and average price in a given period by (Mazumdar 2008). Among the prediction mechanisms we aim at addressing the use of Fuzzy Inference systems in developing short-term demand prediction models, which can be applied in SmartGrid and electronic market applications.

The objective of this chapter is to review the use of fuzzy logic in modelling the energy demand in a specific electric network after analysing its demand characteristics. This chapter will also discuss the use of FIS to improve the prediction performance and adapt the prediction to the real time effects. We consider a real electric power system by modelling its energy demand and verifying the prediction output results. The next section will consider the system's operation data while selecting the most effective modelling parameters, highlighting the use of FIS in modelling, choosing the suitable data clustering method and detailing learning, training and verification for different type of demand patterns.

2. Fuzzy modelling

Fuzzy modelling is a widely utilised and targeted modelling method. It attracts attention from academic and industrial research sectors because of its applicability and flexibility in interpreting the human decision in many complex computer controlled applications. Despite that its complexity has been mainly considered in modelling, as the number of developed fuzzy rules affects the modelling performance, fuzzy modelling is still one of the most efficient modelling techniques. Its main modelling concept is the same as that used in other modelling techniques, which is building mathematical expressions based on historical operation data for the modelled system. It is considered an effective technique to establish an FIS from a given nonlinear input-output set of data, when in fuzzy modelling, the data is partitioned in the input space and an optimal fuzzy rule table and membership functions are developed.

The data partition is performed using data clustering methods. A data clustering method is applied to partition the input-output set of data into a set of clusters. Depending on the type of clustering method, different type and number of clusters can be identified.

A range of data clustering methods have been illustrated in literature such as the nearest neighbourhood clustering method (Wang 1994), Gustafson-Kessel clustering method(Donald and William 1978), Gath-Geva clustering method (Gath and Geva 1989), fuzzy c-means (FCM) clustering method (Frank Höppner 1999), the mountain clustering method (Yager and Filev 1994) (Yager and Filev 1994), and Fuzzy Subtractive Clustering Method (FSCM) (Chiu 1994). However, the main problem of fuzzy modelling comes from the difficulties of choosing the right range of parameters which leads to the number of rules. In other words, the inaccurate parameter settings would deteriorate the prediction accuracy. Good fuzzy modelling parameter settings come from a good understanding of the modelled system and its modelling problems. The main justification for this problem is that when the number of clusters is increased, the prediction output will have strong alignment with the modelled data. As when the number of clusters equals to the number of data, the developed clusters will specifically resemble the training data characteristics, and lose the generality of resembling the system operation characteristics. Consequently, the clusters will mostly resemble a part of the operation data. Therefore, the prediction will miss other kind of operation data that differ from data modelled despite their availability within the modelled data range, which will result in a high prediction error. In contrast, when the number of clusters is reasonable, the prediction will cover the training data regions, as well as any other types of operation data, as far as they are located within the range of the training data. The prediction however will result in an acceptable range of error, which is fairly accepted by all research communities.

In other terms, a suitable parameters choice is the key solution for a successful fuzzy modelling, which will be based on an optimized number of rules and prediction accuracy level. This problem can be solved by analysing the modelled system operation history and indentifying suitable modelling parameters. In addition, having experience about fuzzy modelling will help the modelling process. However, trial and error may be applied for output tuning in most of the modelling cases.

In comparing fuzzy modelling with ANN, it has been concluded that to select the right modelling method, it is crucial to consider the type and the size of the system, the amount of system's historical operation data and the required computation resources. Regarding the type and the size of our case study, it has been found that fuzzy modelling will suit the modelling process. More details about the case study and data analysis are explained in the case study section in this chapter. Full details about the fuzzy modelling process are also explained in modelling methodology section in this chapter. In this chapter we aim at discussing the use FIS as a tuner fuzzy system. The next section describes the main operation principles of Self-Tuning Fuzzy Systems STFS and the use of FIS to improve the prediction accuracy or to adapt the prediction to the external effects.

3. Self tuning fuzzy systems

In modern automation, adaptability has become crucial in implementing smart applications. In the way, that they resemble the human sense of adaptive thinking. Usually, ANN is highly utilised in implementing adaptive systems. However, self tuning and adaptive algorithms are not restricted to ANN, they can also be implemented through fuzzy logic and other optimization techniques. The specific tuning mechanism implementation is subject to the type of the problem or the system to be processed. The tuner and main systems may share the same input parameters, or they may receive two different types of inputs from external sources depending on nature of operation. Self-tuning systems have practically unlimited applications, and they have been widely utilised in academic and industrial applications.

Basically, a STFS is an on-line adaptive output fuzzy system, where its output is changed depending on the type of input and the pre-defined knowledge in the fuzzy tuning system. Generally speaking, a fuzzy system is called tuneable when any of its parameters (input/output scaling factors, membership functions shape and type or fuzzy rules) are changed instantly. It is a combination of general and tuner fuzzy, where the tuner FIS tunes the general system' parameters. Although sometimes both systems have the same input parameters, but they still perform different independent jobs. The main reason using STFS in modelling is to perform a short term prediction and to add the safe prediction estimations to the predicted output. This can be achieved by adapting the prediction to the external effects through a pre-defined knowledge based system.

By looking at our modelled case study, it has been noticed that the model has highly non-linear characteristics. So, developing a model for a high precision prediction is a major challenge. Hence it is required to focus on the model prediction accuracy to consider its weak-points. By considering the energy demand in the targeted case study, modelling knowledge could be added regardless of its availability in the supplied operation data. Using the self-tuning fuzzy system will help in adding the missing knowledge to the operation history data. For such kind of systems, a possible design with external input parameters from external data sources to tune the main fuzzy model output based on a knowledge base could be implemented. In this chapter we aim at utilising the real-time demand change measure to investigate the FIS ability to adapt the prediction output to the actual demand change. Alternatively, in our modelling discussion we also use the main fuzzy system's input parameters to tune the prediction based on a knowledge base system. Similarly, the tuning part may use different mechanisms, e.g. rules, membership functions or output scale tuning. The Weights Adjusting Method (WAM), which is the method that adjusts the output of the main system, is derived from the process needs for adaptation. WAM is set to adjust the weights of the output of the main system and its tuner based on the needed amount of adaptation. Depending on the tuner's fuzzy rule base, a suitable WAM can be derived. Although even when different types of models are discussed in our modelled electric network, only one WAM is applied. For simplicity, we aim at utilising an output scale adaptation design. The full design details are explained in the Modelling Methodology section, whereas the results will be discussed from the prediction improvement point of view and the adaptation performance in the Summary section. In the next two sections, the details about modelling twelve-month load patterns in a real electric network are presented. Additionally, the twelve models are equipped with twelve different tuner fuzzy systems to improve their prediction accuracy or to adapt their prediction to the external effects, depending on the purpose of the modelling.

4. Case study

The electrical energy use of the power network of the Joondalup campus of Edith Cowan University (ECU) in Western Australia has been selected in this study to evaluate the robustness of the proposed modelling technique. Just like most commercial buildings that the energy demand may depend on several independent variables, each having different weightings. Accept when it comes to a university type load profile, a few extra variables may affect the load change patterns. So, it is highly advantageous to analyse the historical operation data of the modelled system to indentify the effective variables. The ECU's electric network has nine substations serving 32 buildings. The minimum daily demand in this university does not drop below 500 kWh at any time, while the maximum daily demand may go up to 3500 kWh in summer daytime. Identifying the critical issues in the network is very important before proceeding in modelling. Fig. 1 shows Load changes in the ECU's Joondalup campus in January 2009.

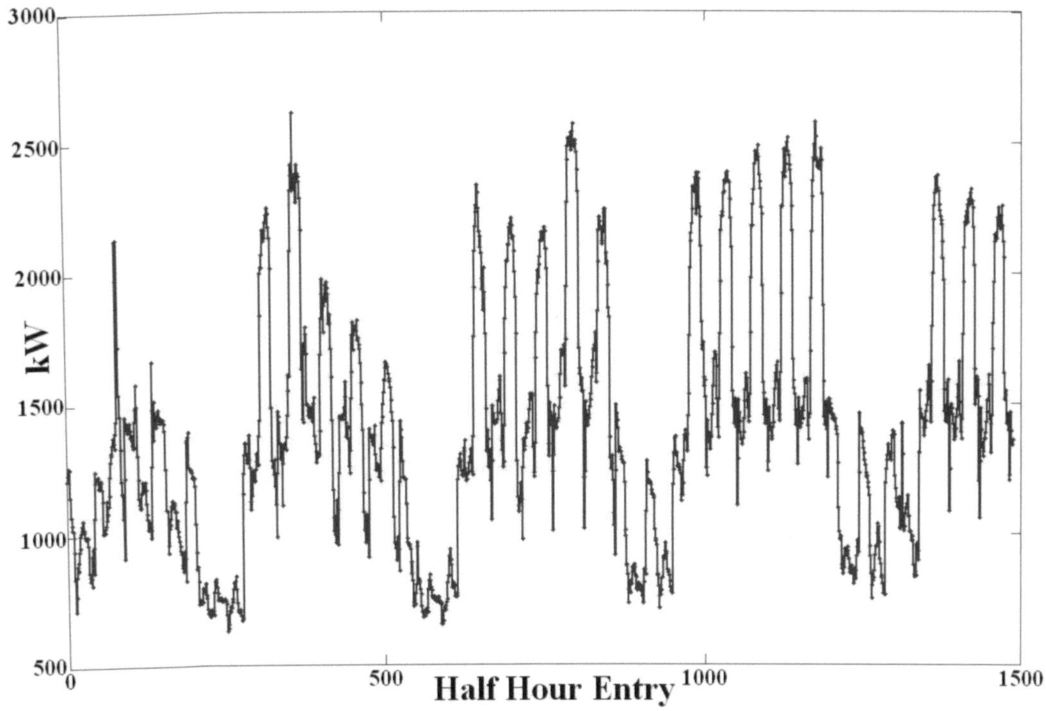

Fig. 1. Load changes in the ECU's Joondalup campus in January 2009.

By monitoring the load change in Fig.1, several load change patterns have been indentified including the weekdays, weekends and hours correlation. In addition, we can identify other important modelling factors e.g. weather, date, hours, order of the day (Monday, Tuesday,...,etc.) and type of the day (working day or weekends/holidays). It has also been noticed that big load changes are infrequent. In this modelling strategy, these big load change events are ignored. It is assumed that such big load changes need to be predefined or have warning settings assigned in order to avoid system overloads. From analysing these effective factors, we could draw a correlation picture about the load change in the ECU's Joondalup Campus and other effective parameters. For more details about load change analysis, Fig. 2 shows the correlation between a 30 minutes interval load change and other identified factors in the ECU's Joondalup campus in January 2009. Fig.2 includes 1500 entry of the correlated information data.

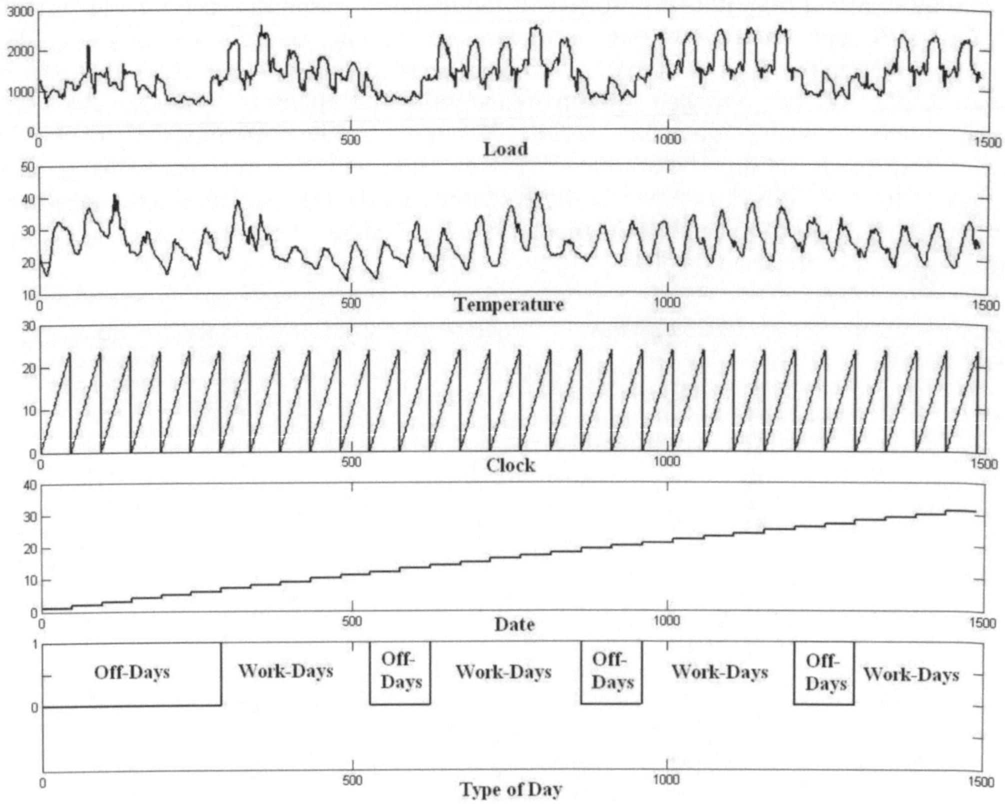

Fig. 2. Load change correlation with the effective factors for ECU's Joondalup campus in January 2009.

By spotting at the critical load change correlation among the identified parameters in Fig.2, several ideas about the energy use scenarios can be obtained. It is also noticeable that there is a big correlation between the daylight time, temperature, type of the day and the monthly order of the day. In Fig.2, only the effective load change parameters mentioned previously are illustrated. Theoretically, other load change parameters could be identified by analysing the university work hours, the nature of activities and the weekly time table in the university. From analysing the university weekly time-table, we could introduce another variable, which is the weekly order of the day. Although this parameter would have an effective load change contribution to the university's energy usage for a certain time of the year, namely the teaching period, but it rarely affects the load change in the remaining times of the year. On an average, it would require higher computation resources and would not indicate the load change effectively throughout the whole year. Therefore, it has been concluded not to consider this parameter among the modelling parameters. The next section details the modelling process and illustrates some hints about the fuzzy modelling.

5. Modelling methodology

This section covers the methodology to model the energy demand measured at 30 minute intervals in the ECU's Joondalup Campus. Basically, the model is developed by combining two modelling systems: the main FIS which is developed from modelling the input-output data using FSCM and ANFIS, and the second FIS system which is either developed by using the correlation between the energy demand and the temperature throughout the day, or by using the knowledge about the real-time demand change with its ability to achieve safe adaptation to the main model's output.

To improve the prediction accuracy and reduce the model complexity, the annual energy demand of the ECU's Joondalup Campus has been proposed to be split into twelve monthly models, represented by twelve different demand pattern models. Each model represents a one month demand model. Fig. 3 illustrates the proposed annual energy demand prediction structure for ECU's Joondalup campus, it also illustrates the possible extra added input to improve the prediction accuracy when possible.

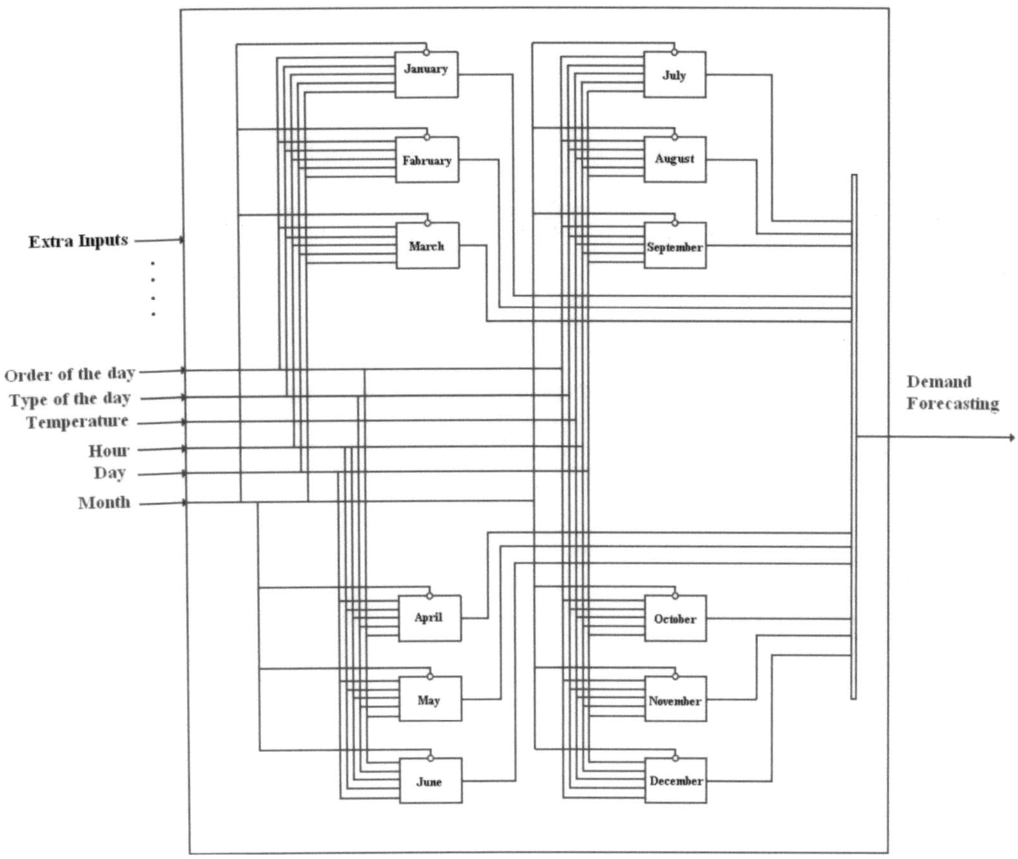

Fig. 3. The energy annual demand prediction structure of ECU's Joondalup campus

Splitting the annual demand model into twelve spilt sub-models gives the prediction the ability to cope with the twelve different load change patterns. In addition, it reduces the computation resources, when only one month model is active at a time. Thus the modelling uses twelve separate modelling methodologies depending on the load change analyses for the individual months. Regarding building the two FIS, their methodology is explained in the following subsections:

5.1 Main fuzzy system

In this subsection, we discuss the use of FIS in modelling. In this investigation, we aim at utilising data clustering methods to perform the fuzzy modelling. Data clustering methods divide the supplied data into different groups based on identified common characteristics in each group. However, these characteristics are identified based on the type of data clustering method. In literature, several types of data clustering methods have been discussed including the on-line and off-line methods. In our investigation, we aim at utilising off-line data clustering methods in modelling.

We aim at clustering the historical operation data of the targeted electric network to develop the demand prediction models. At the end of clustering, a fuzzy reasoning system will be developed. We aim at using ANFIS for developing our targeted fuzzy models. The complete modelling process is illustrated in Fig. 4.

In our modelling example, we use Fuzzy Subtractive Clustering Method (FSCM) (Chiu 1994). It is a method where each of the supplied data is tested under the condition that it has the highest density among the tested individuals. Every individual data is considered to be a candidate for the cluster centring. The individual density is evaluated as follow:

$$P_i = \sum_{j=1}^{n} e^{-\alpha\|x_i - x_j\|^2} \quad (1)$$

where

$$\alpha = \frac{4}{r_a^2} \quad (2)$$

The data density for a specific cluster centre candidate is evaluated from the number of nearer individuals that contribute to the cluster centre. The highest density is identified to become a first cluster centre. The cluster size is decided when FSCM parameters are set to cover a range of data individuals in the cluster's neighbourhood. The radius r_a , which is also referred by Range of Influence (ROI), defines the range of neighbourhood for the clusters extraction. Each of the developed clusters is a basis of a fuzzy rule that describes the system attitude, when the number of these clusters is the number of the fuzzy rules in the modelled network. When the first cluster centre is found, the next highest density is evaluated. Let the new investigated cluster centre to be x_i, and P_i be its density measure. When every data individuals is x_c, the next cluster centre is identified as follow:

$$P_i = P_i - P_{c1} e^{-\beta\|x_i - x_{c1}\|^2} \quad (3)$$

$$\beta = \frac{4}{r_b^2} \quad (4)$$

$$r_b = 1.5 r_a \quad (5)$$

Where P_{c1} is the next density point to be examined, and $x_{c1}$is the next data point to be examined. where r_b is a constant, which has the influence of reducing the density measure. r_b is defined based on the experience of data clustering. Usually, it is larger than r_a to avoid closely placed clusters. Sometimes, trial and error is used to select the best value of r_b. However, the value of r_b is set to $1.5 r_a$ as illustrated in literature (Chiu 1994), and r_a is set based on the experience about the data clustering. In our investigated cases different values were applied depending on the type of the problem. It is clearly noticed that ROI value decides the number of membership functions, thus influencing the complexity of the developed network. Table 1 illustrates the full details about r_a settings for the investigated cases.

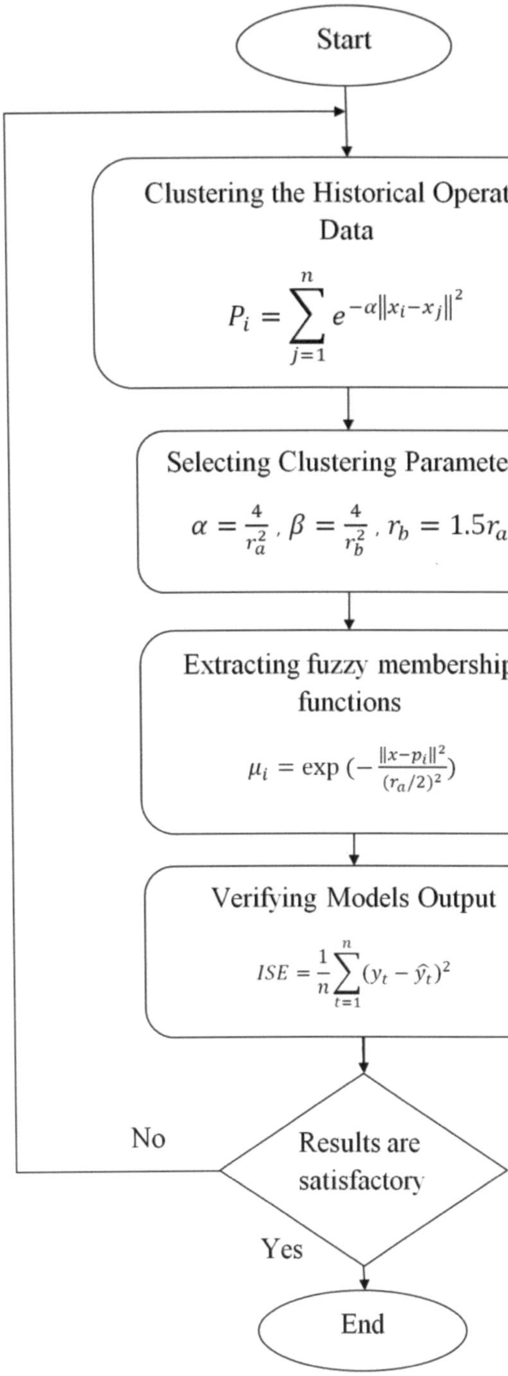

Fig. 4. Selecting suitable FSCM parameters in ANFIS modelling

The next stage is to repeat the above estimation process to identify other cluster centres. The process of indentifying clusters is repeated until the amount of new identified density is equal of less to 0.15 of the highest identified density. More information about FSCM parameters details is found in (Chiu 1994).

The identified data clusters can be easily utilised as fuzzy rules' centres in the zero-order Sugeno fuzzy models. When a data individual is located within the cluster range, a membership function between that particular data individual and its cluster centre is derived. Data affiliation to the cluster centres is derived as follow:

$$\mu_i = \exp(-\frac{\|x-p_i\|^2}{(r_a/2)^2}) \tag{6}$$

where x is the cluster centre and p_i is the input set of data.

By clustering temperature, hour, day and load change data, random FSCM parameters values e.g. Influence Range, Squash, Accept Ratio and Reject Ratio are applied.

These values selection may have strong effects on the complexity of the developed models. Table 1 shows the number of membership functions and the selected ROI values for each of the twelve month models.

Months\Membership Functions ranges	ROI	Rules	Membership Fctn.
January	0.35	28	112
February	0.4	23	92
March	0.5	14	56
April	0.33	40	160
May	0.44	17	68
June	0.4	25	100
July	0.45	20	80
August	0.48	19	76
September	0.43	18	72
October	0.5	11	44
November	0.5	16	64
December	0.41	20	80

Table 1. ROI Values and Complexity of the 12 Month Models

After clustering is made, the developed membership functions are trained. Then, when the developed network is being trained, a simple test will be carried to verify the prediction accuracy of the developed models. To increase the range of prediction in the developed models, the historical operation of three years set of data (2007, 2008 and 2009) is used. The three years data has been divided into three different groups. The first set of data is used to extract the clusters, which is taken as a 90% of the 2007 and 2008 historical data. The second set of data, which is used to train the developed fuzzy systems, has been taken as a whole set of 2007 and 2008 data. Finally, the third set of data, which is used to verify the success of the developed model, has been taken as the 2009 operation data. Fig. 5 shows the data utilization in developing the demand models in this work.

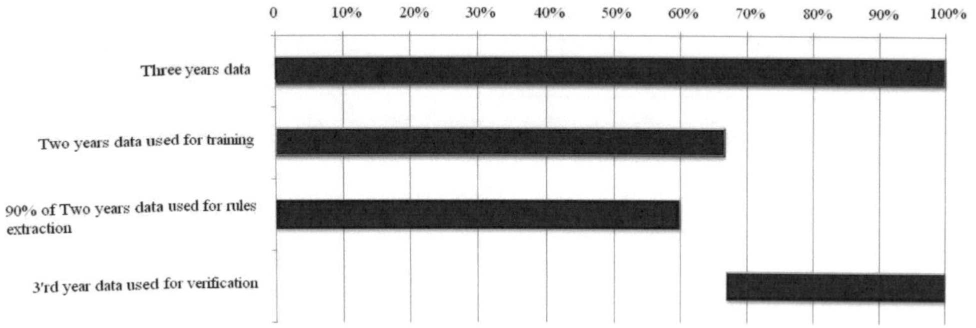

Fig. 5. Modelling data utilization for the ECU's Joondalup Campus energy consumption

After the rules which relate the input-output data have been developed, the developed clusters have been utilised in neuro-fuzzy networks to develop a zero-order Sugeno FIS, which will perform a 30 minutes ahead short-term prediction. In conventional fuzzy systems, trial and error is applied to tune the developed membership functions of the input-output universe of discourse of the fuzzy system. When ANN is used to tune the membership functions, an automated selection process based on the performance index is performed. The membership functions are trained to resemble the training data characteristics. In neuro-fuzzy networks, their networks structure is changed accordingly with the operation scenarios. Neuro-fuzzy networks however utilise the ability of learning of the neural networks to get the best tuning process with better performance and less time (Kandel 1993). Since the fuzzy systems have the property of universal approximation, it is expected that the equivalent neuro-fuzzy networks representation have the same property as well.

Adaptive Neuro Fuzzy Inference System (ANFIS) is another candidate to perform the fuzzy membership functions tuning. ANFIS structure was firstly proposed by (Jang 1993), where other models of ANFIS were proposed by (Chin-Teng Lin 1996) and (Wang and Mendel 1992). Fig. 6 illustrates the ANFIS structure with its learning mechanism.

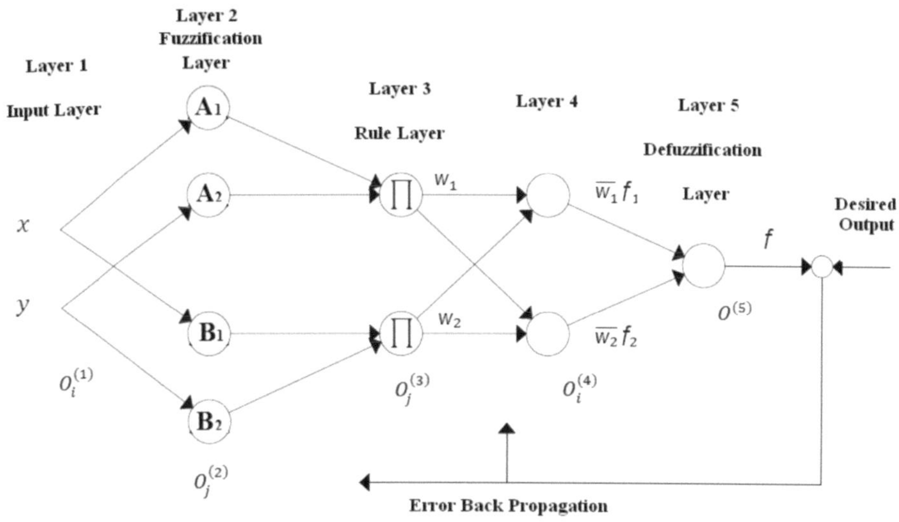

Fig. 6. ANFIS structure with its learning mechanism

where f is the output of the net, x and y are the inputs to this net. The weights of layer 3 are represented by $(\overline{w}_1, \overline{w}_2)$, and the weights of layer 4 are represented by $(\overline{w}_1 f_1, \overline{w}_1 f_2)$, where the used rules of Sugeno ANFIS in this model are expressed in the following form:

$$\textit{If } x \textit{ is } A_1 \textit{ and } y \textit{ is } B_1 \quad \textit{THEN } f_1 = p_1 x + q_1 y + r_1$$

$$\textit{If } x \textit{ is } A_2 \textit{ and } y \textit{ is } B_2 \quad \textit{THEN } f_2 = p_2 x + q_2 y + r_2$$

Where (p_i, q_i, r_i) are the parameters that are determined and referred to as the consequent parameters. More details about ANFIS parameters can be found in (Jang 1993).

In conventional neuro-fuzzy networks, back-propagation algorithm is used to adjust the network parameters, while in ANFIS the adjusting mechanism is performed by the Hybrid Learning Algorithm (HLA). HLA is basically combined of two identification methods, the least-squares method to identify consequent parameters for the forward pass in layer 4 and the back-propagation method for the backward pass to identify the premise parameters by the gradient descent in layer 2. This combination achieves faster convergence than that of the original back-propagation method. Table 2 illustrates the hybrid learning passes with their identified parameters:

Parameters\Direction	Forward pass	Backward Pass
Premise parameters	Fixed	Gradient descent
Consequent parameters	Least-square estimator	Fixed
Signals	Node outputs	Error signals

Table 2. Two passes in the hybrid learning procedure for ANFIS (J. S. R. Jang 1997).

Finally, when verification result is within an acceptable error bound, the modelling procedure is concluded. Fig. 7 illustrates the developed input membership functions for the four inputs zero-order Sugeno fuzzy system of January's operation of the ECU's Joondalup Campus power network.

From Fig 7, and from the developed Sugeno-fuzzy system for January demand prediction, the developed rules are explained as following:

If *(Temperature is Temperature in Cluster n) and (Hour is Hour in Cluster n) and (Day is Day in Cluster n) and (Day-type is Day-type in Cluster n)* **Then** *(Demand is Demand in Cluster n)*

Where $0 < n \leq$ number of developed rules.

Finally, for the other 11 months of the year, their developed models have different input-output ranges based on the pattern of operation and weather change throughout the four seasons of the year in city of Joondalup. Although other effective modelling parameters have been nominated for the proposed models, experimental investigations have been applied to use three-, four- and five-input modelling parameters for the demand prediction performance improvement, we stick to choosing the four-input modelling parameters, which has been successfully approved to be an optimal selection, from the prediction complexity and prediction improvement point of view, for the developing demand prediction models for the targeted power network.

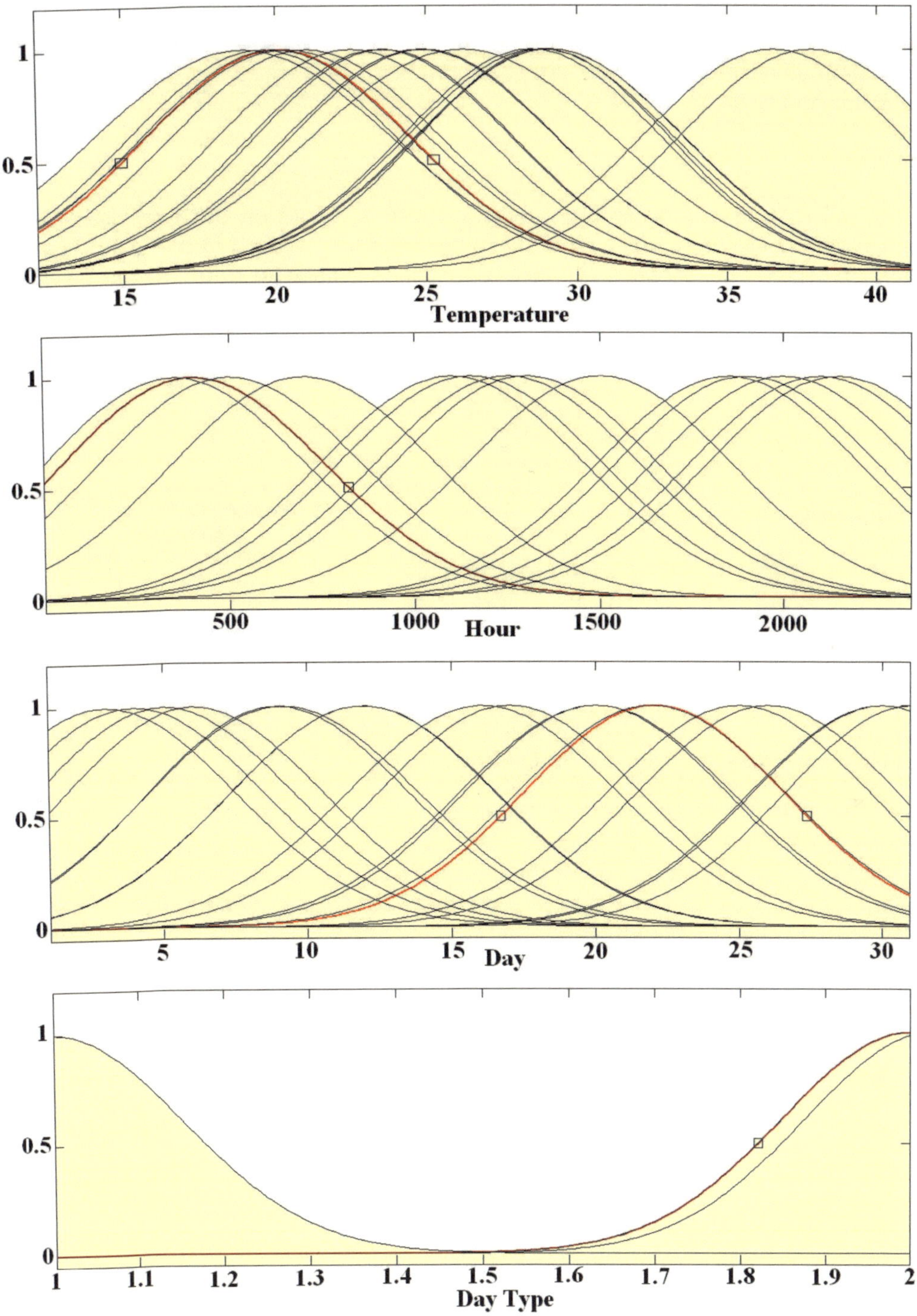

Fig. 7. The developed input membership functions for the four inputs zero-order Sugeno fuzzy system of January's operation of the ECU's Joondalup Campus power network.

5.2 The self-tuning fuzzy system

In this subsection, we aim at discussing two tuning mechanisms which have the ability to improve the prediction accuracy and adapt the prediction to the external effects such as the real-time demand change:

5.2.1 Parallel self tuning fuzzy system

First, we will look at improving our prediction results, based on our knowledge of the energy demand conditions, which could have been partially missed in the given historical operation data. We aim at using the self tuner fuzzy system to improve the prediction accuracy. Fig. 8 illustrates a main fuzzy system with its tuner fuzzy system combination.

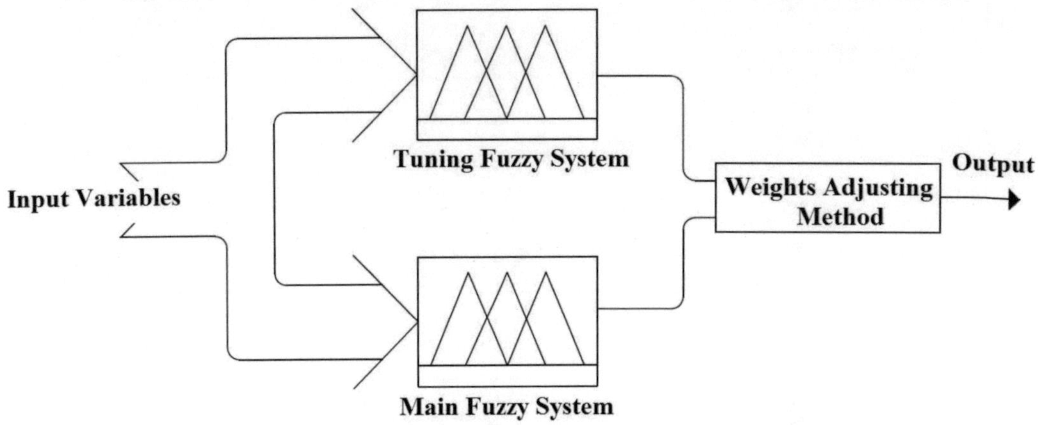

Fig. 8. Self-Tuning fuzzy system (self tuning fuzzy system)

For this system, it is required to enhance the performance of the prediction model by using the knowledge of the system performance, safe operation estimations and actual important needed decisions. In this work, two of the model inputs are selected to develop the fuzzy rule-based system. The rule-based system is developed to have a smooth transition between the specified operation cases in the decision making. In this work generally, we investigate the use of a one rule based system the twelve-month models. Table 3 illustrates the propose rule based system in this investigation.

Hour\Temperature	V. Cold	Cold	L. Warm	Room temp.	Warm	Hot	V. hot
Midnight	S. low	Normal	Normal	S. High	High	V. High	V. High
Dawn	Normal	S. High	High	V. High	V. High	Vv High	Vv High
Morning	Low	S. Low	Normal	Normal	S. High	High	V. High
Afternoon	V. Low	V. Low	Low	Low	S. Low	Normal	Normal
Sunset	V. Low	Low	S. Low	Normal	S. High	High	V. High
Evening	Low	S. Low	S. Low	Normal	S. High	High	V. High
Night	S. Low	Normal	S. High	High	V. High	V. High	Vv. High

Table 3. Self tuning fuzzy rule-based system

To cope with the operation pattern changes through the twelve months of the year, different membership functions are proposed for every month models: all twelve-month models have the same membership functions shape, but with different input/output ranges. Fig. 9 shows the proposed membership function design for the tuning fuzzy system of the January prediction.

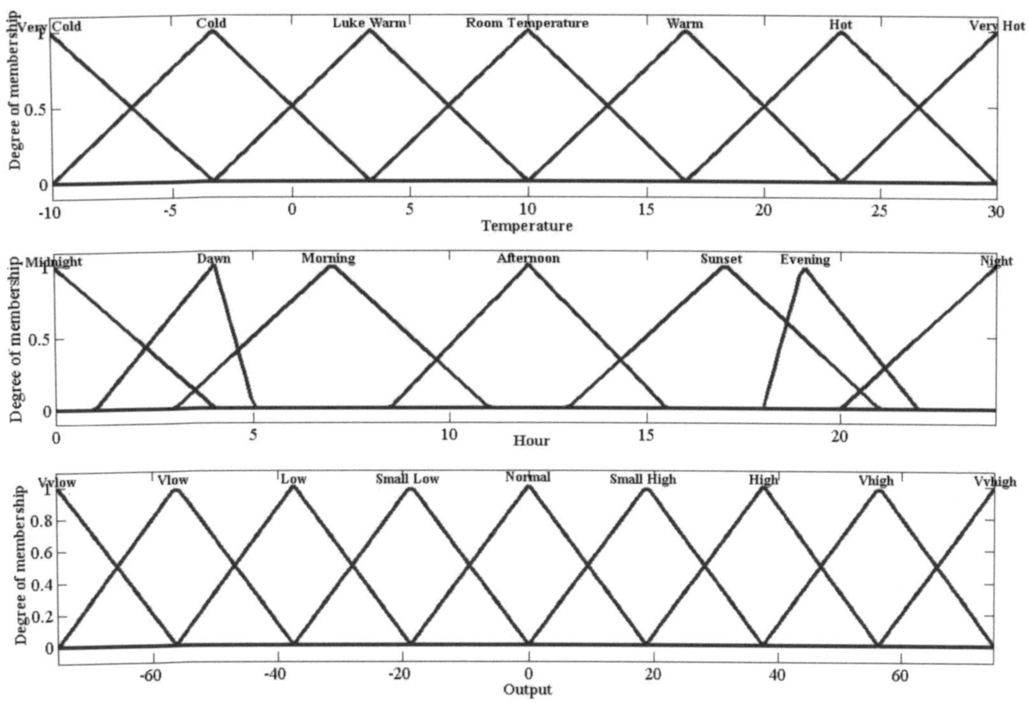

Fig. 9. Membership functions design for the tuning fuzzy system of January demand prediction model

Table 4 illustrates the membership function design for the twelve monthly prediction fuzzy systems.

Months\Membership Functions ranges	Temperature	Hour	Output
January	[-10 30]	[0 24]	[-75 75]
February	[-10 35]	[0 24]	[-75 75]
March	[-10 20]	[0 24]	[-50 50]
April	[15 35]	[0 24]	[-30 30]
May	[0 20]	[0 24]	[-40 40]
June	[0 25]	[0 24]	[-50 50]
July	[-20 20]	[0 24]	[-50 50]
August	[5 20]	[0 24]	[-30 30]
September	[-20 20]	[-4 24]	[-30 30]
October	[30 70]	[0 18]	[-200 200]
November	[10 50]	[-4 18]	[-100 100]
December	[-10 20]	[-4 18]	[-100 100]

Table 4. Membership function design ranges for the 12 monthly demand prediction tuning fuzzy systems

The twelve-month models have different self-tuning fuzzy designs. From the twelve designs, different prediction improvements are carried out. Conservatively, we would like to spot on the weakest prediction region throughout January in Fig. 10, which shows the demand prediction for the 17th to the 21st of January 2009 using ANFIS and Self-Tuning Fuzzy System. The amount of prediction improvement is calculated by evaluating the Integral Square of Error (ISE). ISE is evaluated as follow:

$$ISE = \frac{1}{n}\sum_{t=1}^{n}(y_t - \widehat{y_t})^2$$

where n is the number of entries, t is the time at each entry, y_t is the actual demand and $\widehat{y_t}$ is the predicted value. From the equation above, the results show that the self-tuning fuzzy system has an enhanced prediction accuracy error. Table 5 shows the amount of ISE in each month and the percentage of improvement achieved by the fuzzy tuning systems.

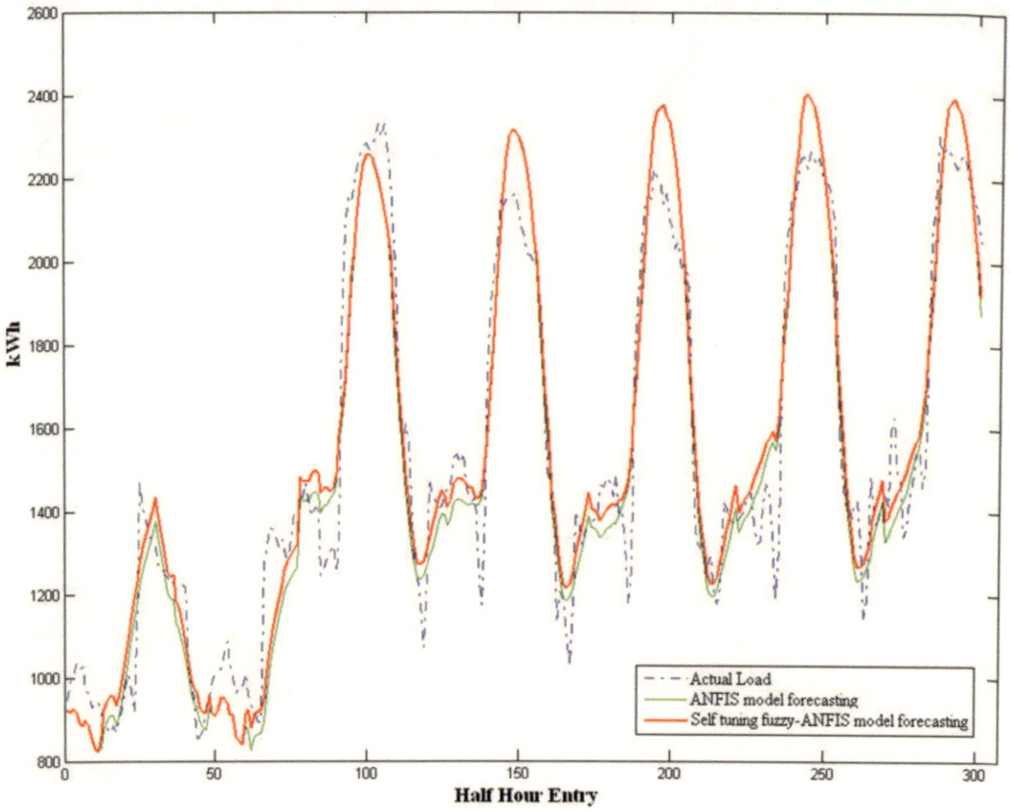

Fig. 10. Self tuning and ANFIS prediction for the 17th to the 21st of January 2009

Month\model	ANFIS ISE	Self-tuning fuzzy-ANFIS ISE	Improvement
January	29030	27230	6.2%
February	23590	22080	6.4%
March	42060	41040	2.5%
April	45300	45160	0.3%
May	27880	27760	0.4%
June	21660	21390	1.2%
July	19100	18760	1.7%
August	25030	24930	0.3%
September	24160	23760	1.6%
October	29260	28920	1.1%
November	27050	25060	7.3%
December	32890	30490	7.2%

Table 5. The amount of ISE in each month with improvement rate made by fuzzy tuning systems

5.2.2 Feedback Self-Tuning Fuzzy System

The Feedback Self-Tuning System FSTF is applied when any external effect variables such as the real load measures are fed to the model to adapt its prediction accuracy. With its adaptation mechanism, it adapts the model prediction to the external effects. The adaptation is developed based on an expert knowledge based system, which achieves successful and safe adaptation when the external effects are applied. The main principle of using this mechanism in our case study is to consider the actual instant demand change pattern change in the next subsequent prediction intervals, which provides flexibility to the model to correct its prediction path. The mechanism is built based on a feedback signal supply to allow the real demand change to enhance the prediction output.

Just like the parallel self-tuning fuzzy system, the adaptation may apply on the main fuzzy parameters e.g. membership function parameters, input-output universe of discourse or the output scale. For simplicity, we aim at utilising the output scale example in this chapter. Fig.11 illustrates the adaptation mechanism for the Feedback Self-Tuning System.

For the twelve different load change patterns in the targeted electric network, twelve different adaptation designs are required. For simplicity, one rule base system could be implemented to cope with twelve-month load change pattern. It is required therefore to tune the FSTFS input-output universe of discourse to fit its output with the load change patterns in every individual month. Out of this adaptation mechanism, different adaptation ranges may come from the twelve-month models. Table 6 illustrates the used rule based system for the proposed FSTFS.

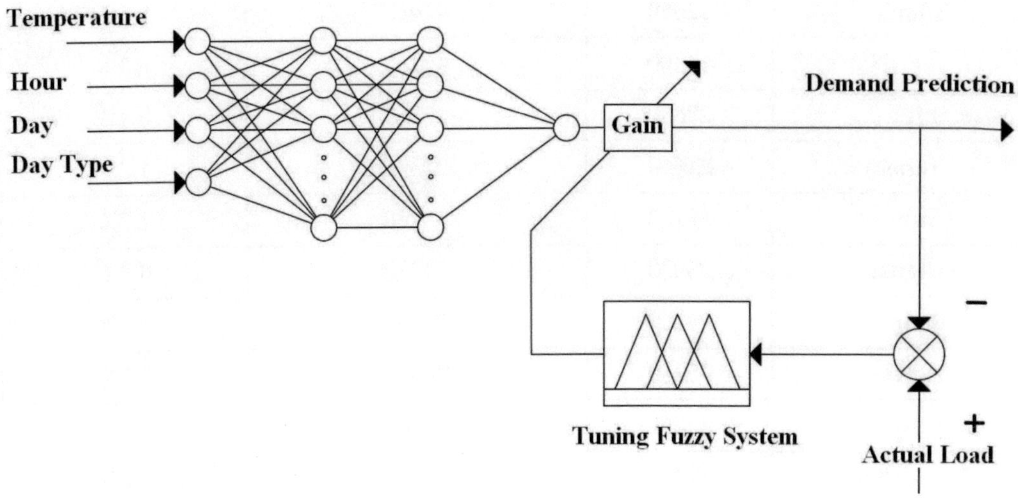

Fig. 11. Feedback Self-Tuning Fuzzy System

Error	Degree of Change
Vvery Low	Vvery High
Very Low	Very High
Low	High
Zero	Normal
High	Low
Very High	Very Low
Vvery High	Vvery Low

Table 6. FSTFS Rule Based System

Fig. 12 illustrates the FSTFS membership function design for the proposed demand prediction model.

The feedback prediction mechanism can be safely utilised in generation scheduling application or any other energy management system applications. For a safe use of prediction output, a safety margin value is added to the prediction results, which allows a flexible utilisation for the predicted demand.

To show the adaptation performance of the investigated systems, a conservative result is shown in Fig. 13, which illustrates the weakest prediction accuracy region throughout the year for the investigated electric power network.

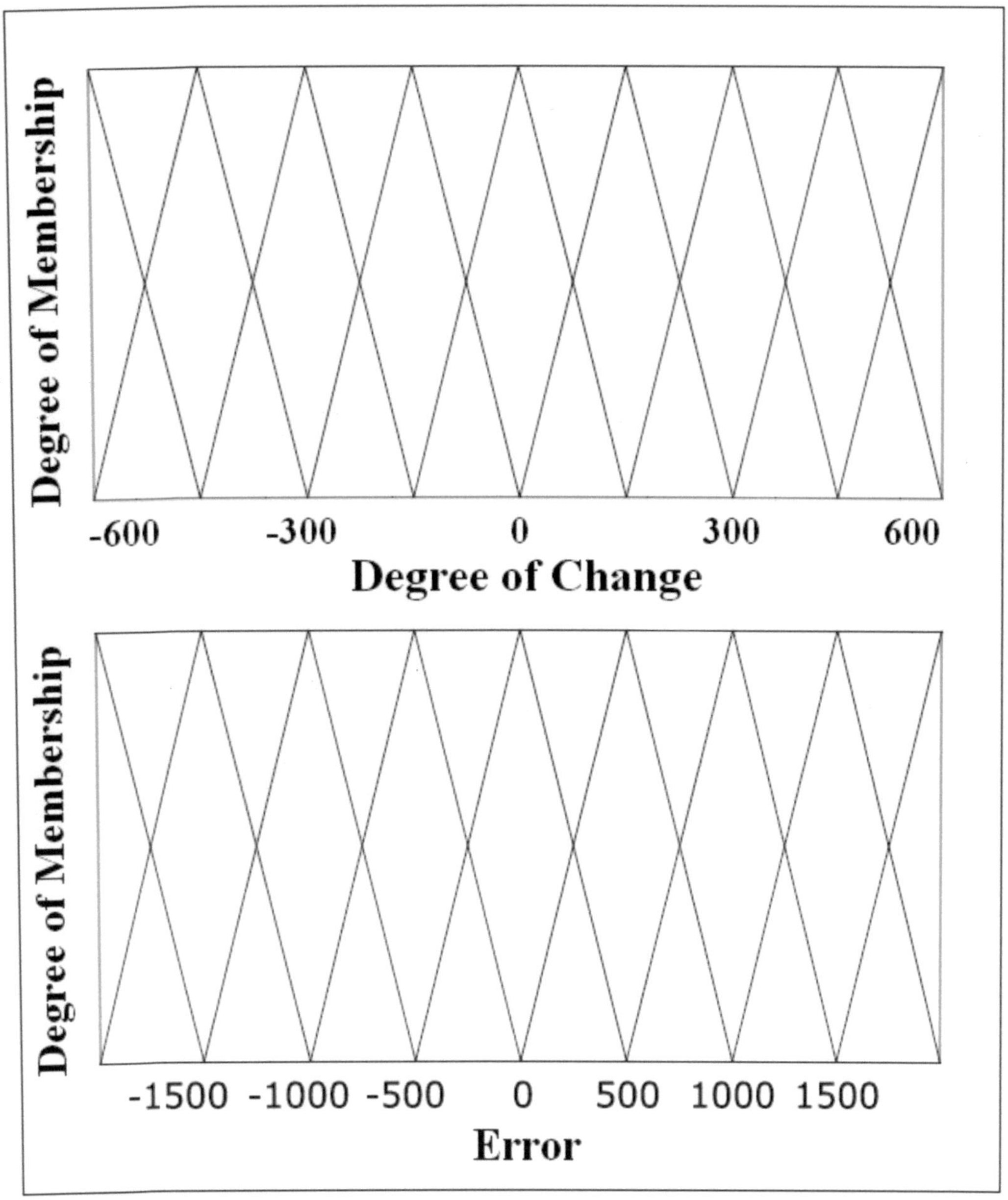

Fig. 12. FSTFS membership function design for the proposed demand prediction model

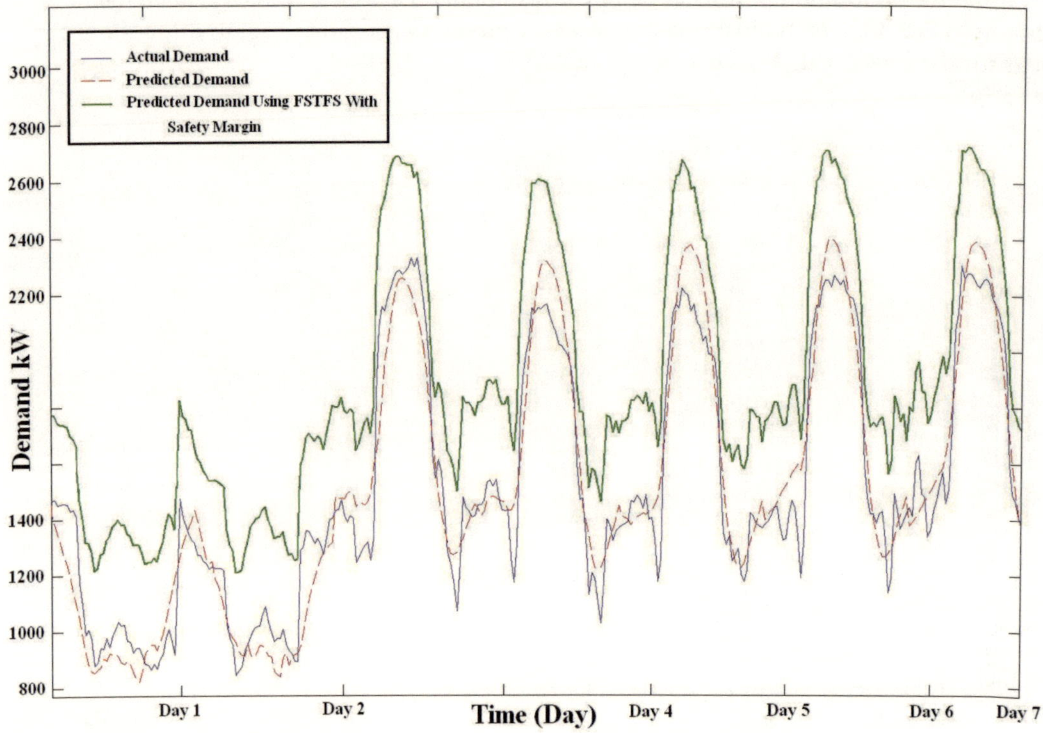

Fig. 13. Actual and Feedback Self-Tuning System Demand Prediction in the ECU Power Network for the 17th to the 21st of January 2009

6. Summary

In this chapter, the art of using FIS in modelling energy demand prediction for a specific electric network has been discussed. The type and the size of the modelled electric network has been comprehensively analysed in terms of the input-output identified effective parameters and their correlation in changing the pattern of the energy use. The identified parameters, however, were used in developing the energy demand prediction models. Fuzzy modelling process has been discussed by looking at its applications and limitations for the selected case study. In our modelling, we have utilised Fuzzy Subtractive Clustering Method to show the tips about its use in modelling, where ANFIS has been applied to develop the zero-order Sugeno fuzzy models. The annual energy demand model for the selected case study has been developed for an individual monthly basis with a specific design applied to deal with the twelve-month patterns. However, certain modifications had to be applied on each month to account for the peculiar conditions to that month.

In addition, two fuzzy tuning mechanisms have been used to improve the fuzzy models prediction accuracy. The first mechanism was used to add the safe operation assumptions to reduce the missing knowledge in the decision making for the developed models. The results from the first mechanism showed that the added fuzzy systems improved the prediction accuracy with different rates throughout the twelve months of the year. In case of the second fuzzy tuning mechanism, a real-time demand change has been added to the main fuzzy models to adapt their prediction to the real-time demand change through tuner fuzzy systems. From the twelve different demand changes throughout the year, different prediction adaptation ranges have been found. As a conclusion for these discussions, the FIS has a wide range of applications in modelling, especially when we deal with highly non-linear multiple input-output systems we have also shown throughout this chapter that several simulation studies have proved the success of using FIS in modelling, which brightens wider its range of mathematical and engineering applications.

7. References

Alireza Khotanzad, E. Z., Hassan Elragal (2002). "A Neuro-Fuzzy Approach to Short-Term Load Forecasting in a Price-Sensitive Environment." *IEEE TRANSACTIONS ON POWER SYSTEMS* 17(4): 10.

Amir-Hamed Mohsenian-Rad, a. A. L.-G. (2010). "Optimal Residential Load Control With Price Prediction in Real-Time Electricity Pricing Environments." *IEEE TRANSACTIONS ON SMART GRID* 1(2): 14.

Chin-Teng Lin, C. S. G. L. (1996). *Neural Fuzzy Systems: A Neuro-Fuzzy Synergism to Intelligent Systems*. New Jersey, Prantice-Hall.

Chiu, S. L. (1994). "Fuzzy Model Indentification Based on Cluster Estimation." *Journal of Intelligent and Fuzzy Systems* 2: 267-278.

Donald, E. G. and C. K. William (1978). *Fuzzy clustering with a fuzzy covariance matrix*. Decision and Control including the 17th Symposium on Adaptive Processes, 1978 IEEE Conference on.

Frank Höppner, F. K., Rudolf Kruse, Thomas Runkler (1999). *Fuzzy Cluster Analysis: Methods for Classification, Data Analysis and Image Recognition*.

Gath, I. and A. B. Geva (1989). "Unsupervised optimal fuzzy clustering." *Pattern Analysis and Machine Intelligence, IEEE Transactions on* 11(7): 773-780.

J. S. R. Jang, C. T. S., and E. Mizutani (1997). *Neuro-Fuzzy and Soft Computing – A Computational Approach to Learning and Machine Intelligence*. Upper Saddle River, NJ, Prentice Hall.

Jang, J. S. R. (1993). "ANFIS: adaptive-network-based fuzzy inference system." *Systems, Man and Cybernetics, IEEE Transactions on* 23(3): 665-685.

Kandel, I., & Langholz, G (1993). *Fuzzy Control Systems*, CRC Press.

Mazumdar, C. M. R. a. M. (2008). "Forecasting the Mean and the Variance of Electricity Prices in Deregulated Markets." *IEEE TRANSACTIONS ON POWER SYSTEMS* 23(1): 8.

McSharry, J. W. T. a. P. E. (2007). "Short-Term Load Forecasting Methods: An Evaluation Based on European Data." *IEEE TRANSACTIONS ON POWER SYSTEMS* 22(4): 7.

Wang, L. X. (1994). *Adaptive fuzzy systems and control: design and stabilityanalysis*. NJ, Prentice-Hall.

Wang, L. X. and J. M. Mendel (1992). *Back-propagation fuzzy system as nonlinear dynamic system identifiers*. Fuzzy Systems, 1992., IEEE International Conference on.

Yager, R. R. and D. P. Filev (1994). "Approximate clustering via the mountain method." *Systems, Man and Cybernetics, IEEE Transactions on* 24(8): 1279-1284.

Section 6

Application to System Modeling and Control Problems

18

Control Application Using Fuzzy Logic: Design of a Fuzzy Temperature Controller

R.M. Aguilar, V. Muñoz and Y. Callero
University of La Laguna
Spain

1. Introduction

The reason for using fuzzy logic in control applications stems from the idea of modeling uncertainties in the knowledge of a system's behavior through fuzzy sets and rules that are vaguely or ambiguously specified. By defining a system's variables as linguistic variables such that the values they can take are also linguistic terms (modeled as fuzzy sets), and by establishing the rules based on said variables, a general method can be devised to control these systems: Fuzzy Control (Babuška, 1998; Chen, 2009). Fuzzy control is a class of control methodology that utilizes fuzzy set theory (Pedrycz, 1993). The advantages of fuzzy control are twofold. First, fuzzy control offers a novel mechanism for implementing control laws that are often based on knowledge or on linguistic descriptions. Second, fuzzy control provides an alternative methodology for facilitating the design of non-linear controllers for plants that rely on generally uncertain control that is very difficult to relate to the conventional theory of non-linear control (Li & Tong, 2003; A. Sala et al., 2005).

Every day we mindlessly perform complex tasks: parking, driving, recognizing faces, packing the groceries at the supermarket, moving delicate objects, etc. To solve these tasks (overcome an obstacle), we gather all the information necessary for the situation (topology of the terrain, characteristics of the obstacle such as speed, size, ...). With this information and by relying on our experience, we can carry out a series of control actions that, thanks to the feedback present between the system under control and our bodies, can achieve the desired goal.

The controller receives the performance indices (reference) and the system output. To replace the human in a control process, a controller must be added. The controller is a mathematical element, and as such all of the tasks that it is able to perform must be perfectly defined. This control link is studied in Control Theory and is based on two principles:

1. The system to be controlled must be known so that its response to a given input can be predicted. This prediction task requires having a complete model of the system. This identification phase is essential to the performance of the control algorithm.
2. The objective of the control must be specified in terms of concise mathematical formulas directly related to the system's variables (performance index).

When a system's complexity increases, mathematics cannot be used to define the aforementioned points. The model cannot be defined due to non-linearities, to its non-stationary nature, to the lack of information regarding the model, and so on.

We are, however, living in rapidly evolving times where the main goal is to break the limitations that exist in our use of machines in an effort to increase productivity. The use of and advances in intelligent machines will fundamentally change the way we work and live.

To this end, we are building autonomous control systems that are designed to work properly for long periods of time under given uncertainties in the system and the environment. These systems must be capable of compensating for faults in the system without any outside intervention. Intelligent autonomous control systems use techniques from the field of Artificial Intelligence (AI) to achieve autonomy. These control systems consist of conventional control systems that have been augmented using intelligent components, meaning their development requires interdisciplinary research (Jang et al., 1997).

The emergence and development of Artificial Intelligence is of great importance. AI can be defined as that part of computer science that is charged with the design of intelligent computers, meaning systems that exhibit those characteristics that we associate with intelligent human behavior, such as understanding, learning, reasoning, problem solving, etc. Fuzzy Control is one of the new techniques in Intelligent Control, one that aims to imitate the procedure we humans use when dealing with systems (Cai, 1997). For example, when operating a water tap, if we want to obtain the desired flow rate, we reason using terms such as:

"If the flow is low, turn the handle all the way left"

"If the flow is high, turn the handle right a little bit", etc.

Precise quantities such as "2 liters/second" of "65 degrees counterclockwise" do not appear in these rules, and yet we manage to achieve the desired flow rate.

We also apply this form of reasoning to more complex situations, from regulating not only the flow rate but the water temperature, and even when driving a car. In none of these cases do we know precise values; rather, vague magnitudes suffice, such as "very hot", "near", "fast", etc.

Another important consideration is that the control can be expressed as a set of rules of the type: "For certain conditions with some variables, do these actions in others". In this structure, the conditions are called antecedents and the actions consequents.

We may conclude that human reasoning in these situations involves applying logic to uncertain magnitudes. If we want to implement this control artificially, the most convenient course of action is to use a tool that models uncertain magnitudes, this being Fuzzy Set Theory, and apply a logic to these magnitudes, this being Fuzzy Logic (Klir & Yuan, 1995). Both elements belong to a new field in the symbolic branch of Artificial Intelligence that has found in Fuzzy Control one of its main applications, even above other, more formal applications such as expert systems. The fact that it mirrors the process of human reasoning justifies the success of this new method, due to its ease of use and understanding. In a few years AI has blossomed and experienced great commercial success, eclipsing even that of expert systems.

In this chapter we will consider the fuzzy control of a liquid's temperature. This is a very simple academic problem that can be solved using various techniques, such as a classic PI control scheme (Horváth & Rudas, 2004). We will use it in this text, however, to illustrate the design and operation of a fuzzy controller.

An introduction to fuzzy control is presented first, followed by a description of the general outline. In subsequent sections we describe each of the steps in the design of the fuzzy controller: choice of inputs and outputs, rule base, fuzzy quantification, and fuzzification, inference and defuzzification mechanisms. We conclude with a simulation of the proposed temperature controller.

2. Fuzzy logic applied to control: Fuzzy control of temperature

The use of the Fuzzy Logic methodology in real systems is immediately applicable to those systems whose behavior is known based on imprecisely defined rules. This imprecision arises from the complexity of the system itself. The way to approach such a problem is to reduce the complexity by increasing the uncertainty of the variables (J. Sala et al., 2000; Yager & Filev, 1994). Thus, in problems that present non-linearities, and to which classical control techniques are hardest to apply, these techniques are very useful and easy to use (Takana & Sugeno, 1992; Tanaka & Wang, 2001; Wang, 1994).

In the vast majority of systems, be they highly complex or not, the systems' behavior can be given by a set of rules that are often imprecise, or that rely on linguistic terms laden with uncertainty. This results in rules of the type "If the volume is large, the pressure is small", which define the behavior of a system. If we focus on the rules that are defined to control the system, we can formulate different rules of the type "If the cost is small and the quality is good, make a large investment".

This last rule type is the most frequently seen in daily life. For example, to regulate water flow from a faucet, we need only apply rules of the type "If the flow is excessive, close the tap a lot", or "If the flow is low, open the tap a little" in order to carry out the desired action. Using precise magnitudes such as "flow rate of 1.2 gallons/minute" or "turn 45° clockwise" is unnecessary.

Therefore, a general knowledge base for the system is available; that is, a set of rules that aim to model the actions to be carried out on the system so as to achieve the desired action. Said rules are provided by an expert, one whose experience with handling the system provides him with knowledge of how the system behaves.

The Mandani fuzzy inference mechanism is very useful when applying Fuzzy Logic to the control of systems (Passino, 1998). If we consider a classic feedback scheme, the controller has enough information about the system to determine the command that must be applied to said system so as to achieve a desired setpoint. The idea, put forth by Zadeh, for using Fuzzy Control algorithms relies on introducing the knowledge base into the controller such that its output is determined by the control rules proposed by the expert. Said rules contain fuzzy sets (linguistic terms) in the antecedents and in the consequents, and hence they are referred to as a whole as a fuzzy control rule base.

If we wish to apply this control scheme to a real system, the fuzzy controller must be adjusted to existing sensor and actuator technology, which relies on precise magnitudes (Jantzen, 2007). The exact values provided by a sensor must therefore be converted into the fuzzy values that comprise the variables of the antecedent in the rule base. Likewise, the fuzzy values inferred from the rules must be transformed into exact values for use in the actuators. A diagram of this process is shown in Figure 1.

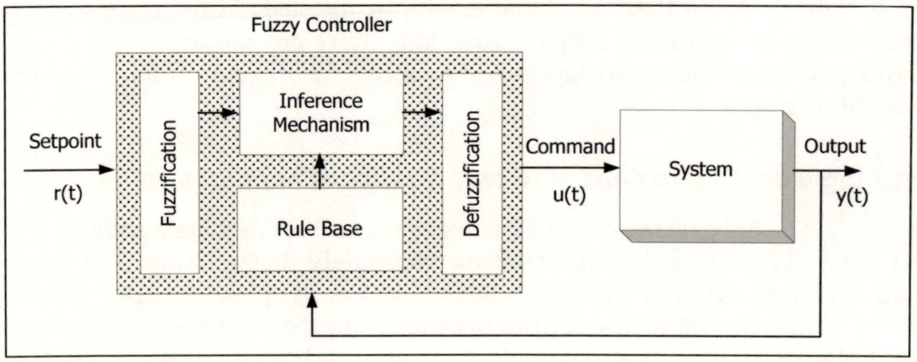

Fig. 1. Fuzzy controller

A block diagram for a fuzzy control system is given in Figure 1. The fuzzy controller consists of the following four components:

1. Rule base: set of fuzzy rules of the type "if-then" which use fuzzy logic to quantify the expert's linguistic descriptions regarding how to control the plant.
2. Inference mechanism: emulates the expert's decision-making process by interpreting and applying existing knowledge to determine the best control to apply in a given situation.
3. Fuzzification interface: converts the controller inputs into fuzzy information that the inference process can easily use to activate and trigger the corresponding rules.
4. Defuzzification interface: converts the inference mechanism's conclusions into exact inputs for the system to be controlled.

We shall now present a simple temperature control example, shown in Figure 2, to introduce each of the fuzzy controller components.

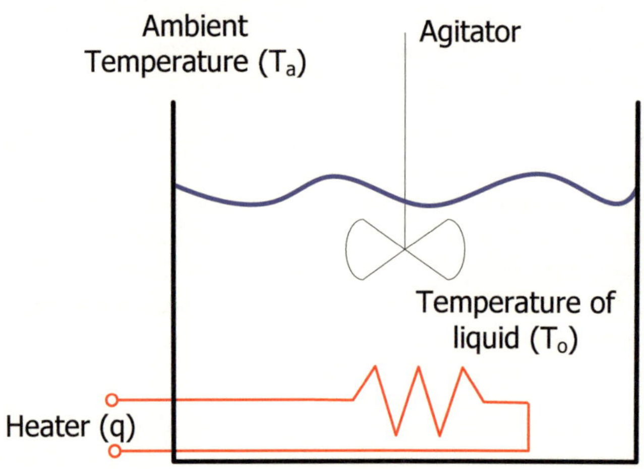

Fig. 2. Temperature controller.

Consider the system shown in Figure 2, where T_o is the temperature of the liquid that we wish to control and T_a is the ambient temperature. The input produced by the heating element is denoted with the letter q, and the desired temperature is T_d. The model for the system, keeping in mind that there are two energy sources (one generated by the heating element and one from the environment), is given by the transfer matrix that results when each of the inputs is considered separately. The expression shown in Equation 1 yields $G_1(s)$ and $G_2(s)$, given in Equations 2 and 3, respectively.

$$\frac{T_o(s)}{Q(s)} = G_1(s) * G_2(s) \tag{1}$$

$$G_1(s) = \frac{T_a(s)}{Q(s)} = \frac{\frac{1}{\mu A}}{\frac{MC_e}{\mu A}s + 1} \tag{2}$$

$$G_2(s) = \frac{T_o(s)}{T_a(s)} = \frac{1}{\frac{MC_e}{\mu A}s + 1} \tag{3}$$

where:

1. M: Mass of liquid
2. C_e: Specific heat
3. μ: heat transfer coefficient between the tank and the environment
4. A: heat transfer area
5. T_o: temperature of liquid
6. T_a: ambient temperature
7. Q: heat input

This is a simple academic problem and many techniques are available for solving it, such as a classic PI controller. We will use it in this text, however, to illustrate the design and operation of a fuzzy controller.

3. General outline of the fuzzy controller

We may conclude then that the procedure for implementing these fuzzy techniques to control systems consists of two very different stages:

1. First stage, to be completed before the control algorithm is executed, and consisting of:
a. Establishing the controller's input and output variables (linguistic variables).
b. Defining each variable's fuzzy sets.
c. Defining the sets' membership functions.
d. Establishing the rule base.
e. Defining the fuzzification, inference and defuzzification mechanisms.
2. Second stage, to be completed with each step of the control algorithm, and consisting of:
a. Obtaining the precise input values.
b. Fuzzification: Assigning the precise values to the fuzzy input sets and calculating the degree of membership for each of those sets.

c. Inference: Applying the rule base and calculating the output fuzzy sets inferred from the input sets.
d. Defuzzification: Calculating the precise output values from the inferred fuzzy sets. These precise values will be the controller's outputs (commands) and be applied to the system to be controlled.

This scheme is applied to classical feedback control techniques, as shown in Figure 3. The classical controller is replaced by a fuzzy controller, which performs the same function. The variables in lower case indicate precise values ('r' for the setpoint, 'e' for the error, 'u' for the command and 'y' for the output), while upper case letters indicate the corresponding fuzzy variables.

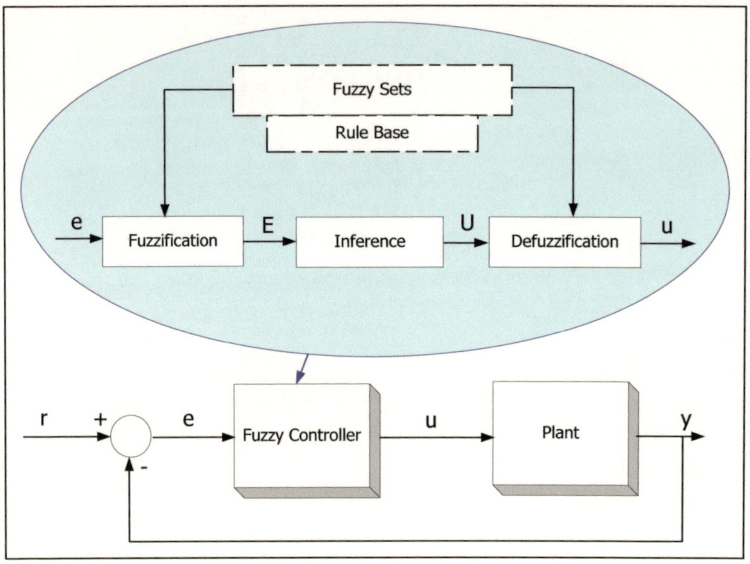

Fig. 3. Fuzzy controller in the feedback loop.

4. Fuzzy controller inputs and outputs

If we assume the presence of an expert in the feedback loop that controls the temperature system, as shown in Figure 4, then a fuzzy controller must be designed that automates the way in which the human expert carries out this control task. To do this, the expert must indicate (to the designer of the fuzzy controller) what information he receives as the input to his decision-making process. Assume that in the temperature control process, the expert observes the error and the variation in this error to carry out his control function; that is, he makes his decision based on the result obtained from Equation 4:

$$e(t) = r(t) - y(t) \tag{4}$$

Though there are many other variables that can be used as the input (e.g., the integral of the error), we will adopt this one since it is the one used by the expert.

We must next identify the variables to be controlled. For the temperature control case proposed, we can only control the amount of energy (q) supplied by the heating element.

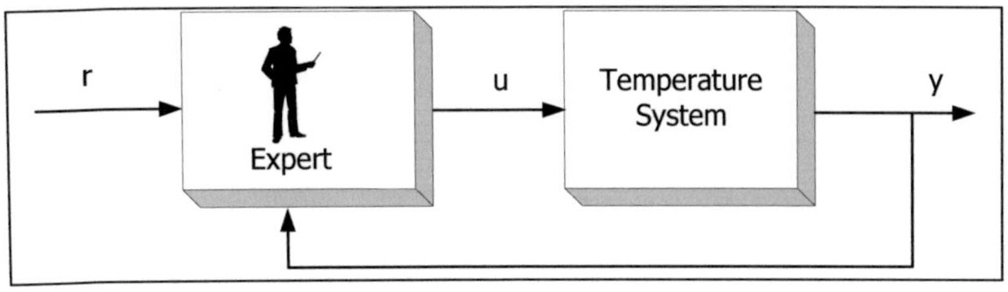

Fig. 4. Human control of a temperature system.

Once the fuzzy controller's inputs and outputs are selected, the next step is to determine the reference input desired, which in our case will be r=60 (step input of sixty).

The fuzzy control system, then, with its inputs and outputs, would be as shown in Figure 5.

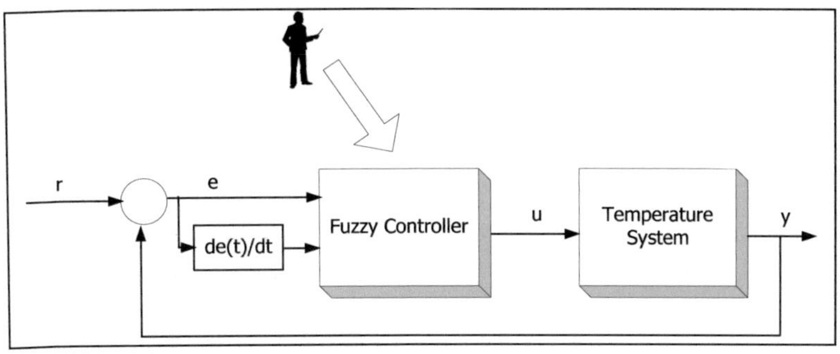

Fig. 5. Fuzzy controller for a temperature system.

5. Inclusion of control knowledge in the rule base

Assume that the human expert provides a description in his own words of the best way to control the plant. We will have to use this linguistic description to design the fuzzy controller.

5.1 Linguistic description

An expert uses linguistic variables to describe the time-varying inputs and outputs of the fuzzy controller. Thus, for our temperature system, we might have:

1. "error" to describe e(t)
2. "error variation" to describe de(t)/dt
3. "increase-energy-supplied" to describe $\Delta u(t)$

We used the quotes to emphasize how certain words or phrases. Though there are many possible ways to describe the variables linguistically, choosing one or another has no effect on how the fuzzy controller works, it only simplifies the task of constructing the controller using fuzzy logic.

Just as e(t) takes on a value, for example, 0.1 at t=2 (e(2)=0.1), so do linguistic variables take on "linguistic values", that is, the values of the linguistic variables change over time. For example, to control the temperature, we can have the "error", "error-variation" and "increase-energy-supplied" take on the following values:

1. LN Large Negative
2. MN Medium Negative
3. SN Small Negative
4. ZE Zero
5. SP Small Positive
6. MP Medium Positive
7. LP Large Positive

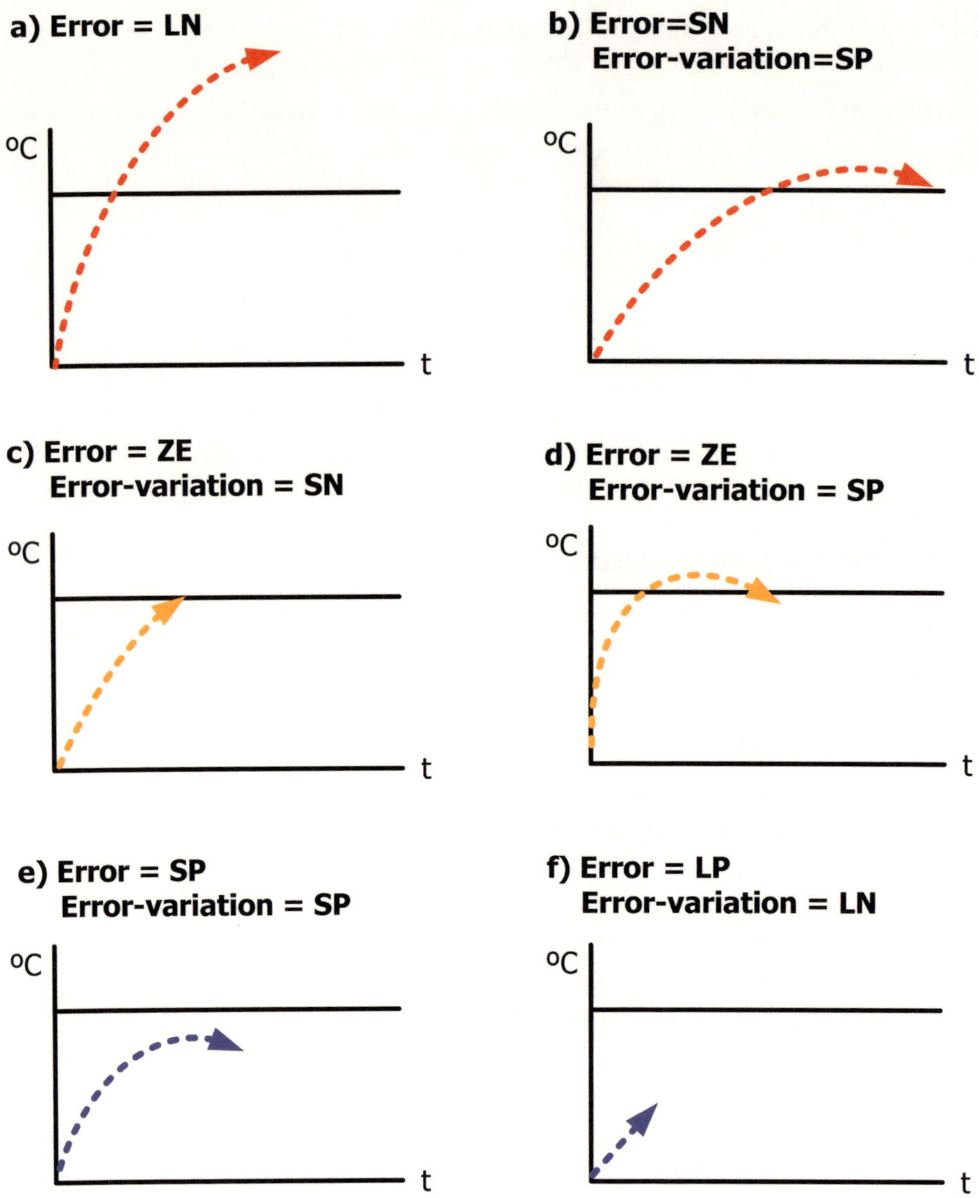

Fig. 6. Temperature system in different states.

Let us now consider how we can describe the system's dynamics based on the linguistic variables and the values they assume. In the case of the temperature controller, each of the following phrases represents different system states:

1. The error is Large Negative, indicating that the temperature of the liquid is much higher than desired, Figure 6.a.
2. The error is Small Negative and the error-variation is Small Positive, indicating that the temperature of the liquid is somewhat higher than the setpoint and dropping to the desired value, Figure 6.b.
3. The error is Zero and the error-variation is Small Negative, indicating that the temperature of the liquid is more or less at the setpoint but rising, Figure 6.c.
4. The error is Zero and the error-variation is Small Positive, indicating that the temperature of the liquid is more or less at the setpoint but falling, Figure 6.d.
5. The error is Small Positive and the error-variation is Small Positive, indicating that the temperature of the liquid is below the setpoint and dropping further, Figure 6.e.
6. The error is Large Positive and the error-variation is Large Negative, indicating that the temperature of the liquid is well below the setpoint but increasing, Figure 6.f.

5.2 Rules

Next we will use the linguistic quantifiers defined earlier to craft a rule set that captures the expert's knowledge regarding how to control the system. Specifically, we have the following rules to control the temperature:

1. If the error is LN, MN or SN, then increase-energy-supplied is LN.

This rule quantifies the situation in which the liquid's temperature is above that desired, meaning heat must not be supplied.

2. If the error is LP and the error-variation is SP, then increase-energy-supplied is LP.

This rule quantifies the situation in which the liquid's temperature is far below the setpoint (undesired situation) and decreasing, requiring a substantial heat input.

3. If the error is ZE and the error-variation is SP, then increase-energy-supplied is SP.

This rule quantifies the situation in which the liquid's temperature is close to the desired temperature but decreasing slightly, meaning that heat must be supplied to correct the error.

Each of the three rules above is a "linguistic rule", since it uses linguistic variables and values. Since these linguistic values are not precise representations of the magnitudes they describe, then neither are the linguistic rules. They are merely abstract ideas on how to achieve proper control, and may represent different things to different people. And yet, experts very often use linguistic rules to control systems.

5.3 Rule base

Using rules of the type described above, we can define every possible temperature control situation. Since we used a finite number of linguistic variables and values, there is a finite number of possible rules. For the temperature control problem, given two inputs and seven linguistic variables, there are 72=49 possible rules (every possible combination of the values of the linguistic variables).

A convenient way of representing the set of rules when the number of inputs to the fuzzy controller is low (three or fewer) is by using a table. Each square represents the linguistic value of the consequent of a rule, with the left column and the top row containing the linguistic values of the antecedent's variables. A temperature control example is shown in Table 1. Note the symmetry exhibited by the table. This is not coincidental, and corresponds to the symmetrical behavior of the system to be controlled.

error/error-variation	LN	MN	SN	ZE	SP	MP	LP
LP	LN	LN	LN	LP	LP	LP	LP
MP	LN	LN	LN	MP	LP	LP	LP
SP	LN	LN	LN	SP	SP	LP	LP
ZE	LN	LN	LN	ZE	MP	MP	LP
SN	LN	LN	LN	SN	ZE	SP	MP
MN	LN	LN	LN	MN	SN	ZE	SP
LN	LN	LN	LN	LN	MN	SN	ZE

Table 1. Rule base for controlling temperature.

6. Fuzzy quantification of knowledge

Until now we have only quantified the expert's knowledge of how to control a system in an abstract manner. Next, we shall see how, using fuzzy logic, we can quantify the meaning of the linguistic descriptions so as to automate the control rules specified by the expert in a fuzzy controller.

6.1 Membership functions

Let us now quantify the meaning of the linguistic variables using the membership functions. Depending on the specific application and the designer (expert), we may select from various membership functions.

The fuzzy partitions for both the input variables (error and error-variation) and for the output variable (increase-energy-supplied) will consist of seven diffuse groups uniformly distributed in a normalized universe of discourse with range [-1,1]. Figure 7 shows the partition for the input variables, and Figure 8 that corresponding to the output variable.

The membership functions for the controller's input variables, at the edge of the universe of discourse, are saturated. This means that at a given point, the expert regards all values above a given value as capable of being grouped under the same linguistic description of "large-positive" or "large-negative". The membership function of the controller's output variable, however, cannot be saturated at the edge if the controller is to function properly. The basic reason is that the controller cannot tell the actuator that any value above a given value is valid; instead, a specific value must always be specified. Moreover, from a practical standpoint, we could not carry out a defuzzification process that considers the area of conclusion of the rule if, as an output, we have membership functions with an infinite area.

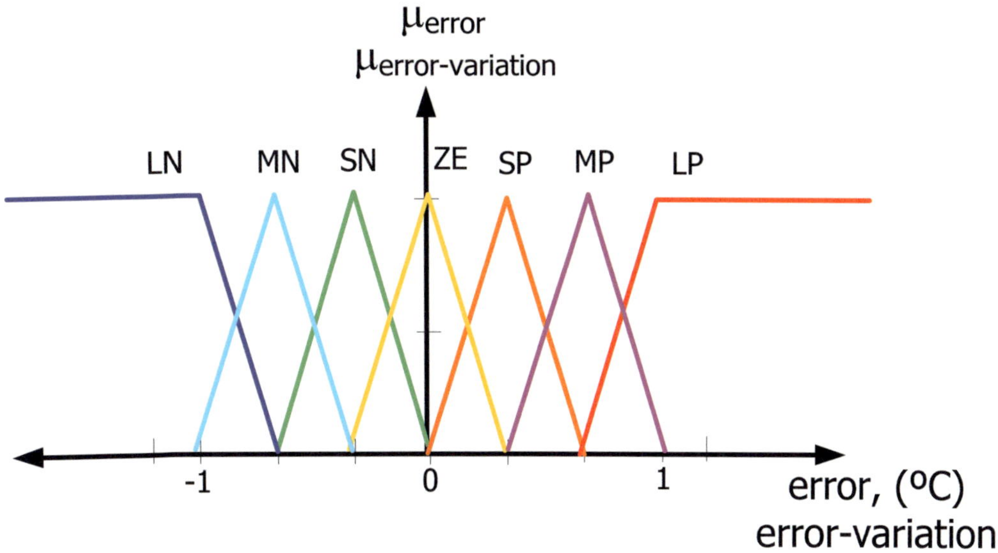

Fig. 7. Fuzzy partition of controller input variables.

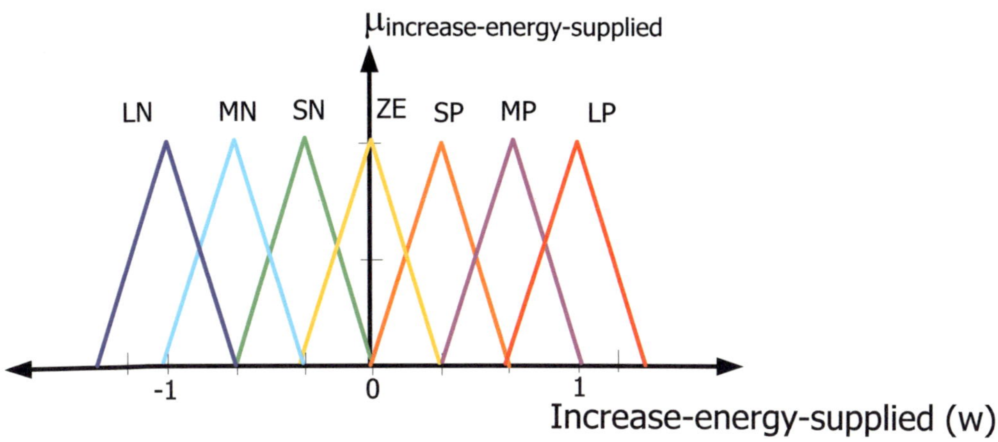

Fig. 8. Fuzzy partition of controller output variable.

7. Fuzzification, inference and defuzzification

In order to complete the design of the controller, we need to define the fuzzification, inference and defuzzification procedures.

In most practical applications of fuzzy control, the fuzzification process used is the "singleton", where the membership function is characterized by having degree 1 for a single value of its universe (input value) and 0 for the rest. In other words, the impulse function could be used to represent a membership function of this type, Figure 9. It is especially used in implementations because in the absence of noise, the input variables are guaranteed to equal their measured value. We also avoid the calculations that would be required if another membership function were used, such as Gaussian fuzzification, which requires constructing a Gaussian-shaped membership function to represent the exact value being provided by the sensor.

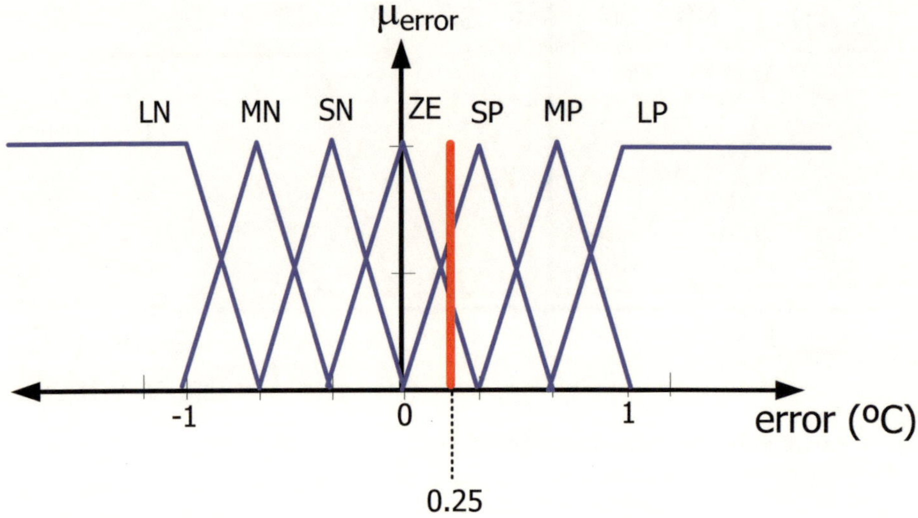

Fig. 9. Fuzzification process for the controller's input variable.

In order to define the inference mechanism, we have to determine how to carry out the basic operations. Since we are using Mandani's model, we have decided to implement the T-norm as the minimum and the S-norm as the maximum.

The last step is to define the defuzzification process. For this temperature control case, we will use the center of gravity.

8. Simulation of fuzzy temperature control

Normally, before proceeding with the implementation of the controller, a simulation is performed to evaluate its performance. The results of the simulation can aid in improving the design of the fuzzy controller and in verifying that it will work correctly when it is implemented. Such a simulation is shown below, implemented using Matlab (Sivanandam et al., 2007), specifically Simulink to simulate the control loop and fuzzy toolbox to implement the fuzzy controller.

The controller designed earlier is defined using the fuzzy toolbox in Matlab, yielding the fuzzy system shown in Figure 10. The fuzzy partition of the inputs and output is shown in Figure 11. As for the output surface, it is shown in Figure 12.

With this tool, we can see how the inference process is carried out, Figure 13.

The next step is to carry out a simulation with the temperature system to check the control system's performance. To do this, we will use the simulation tool Simulink, which allows us to implement the control loop in blocks and to use the fuzzy system made with the fuzzy toolbox as the controller. The diagram of the control system, then, is as shown in Figure 14.

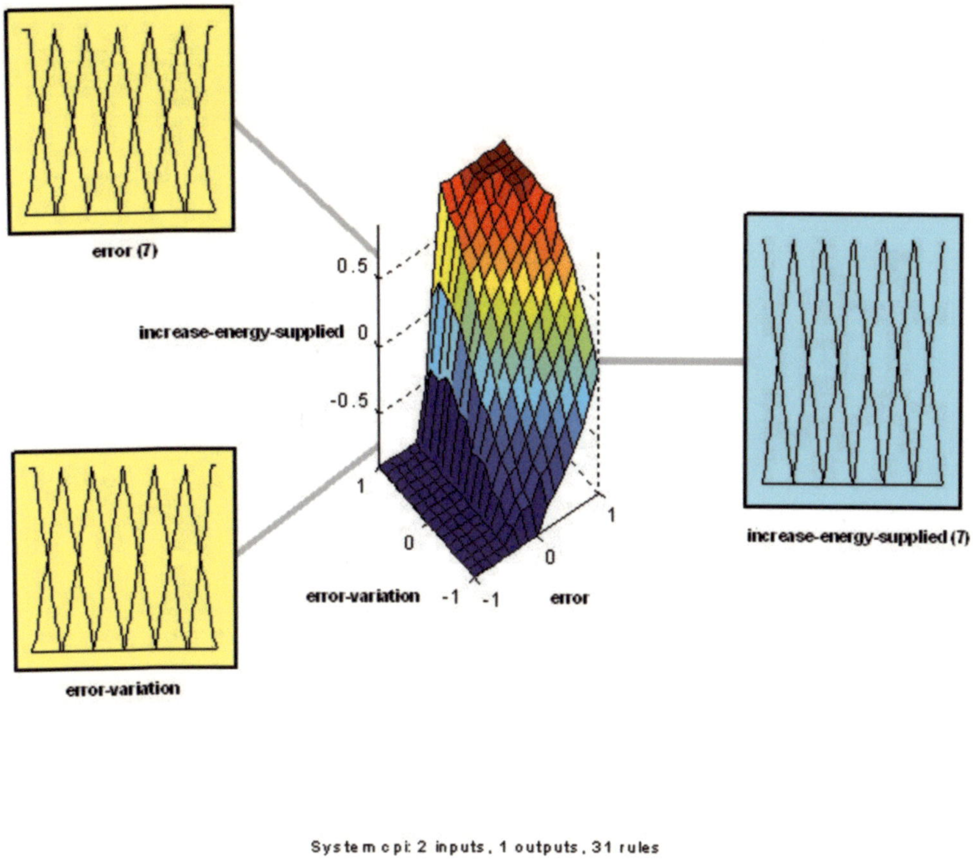

Fig. 10. Fuzzy controller for the temperature system.

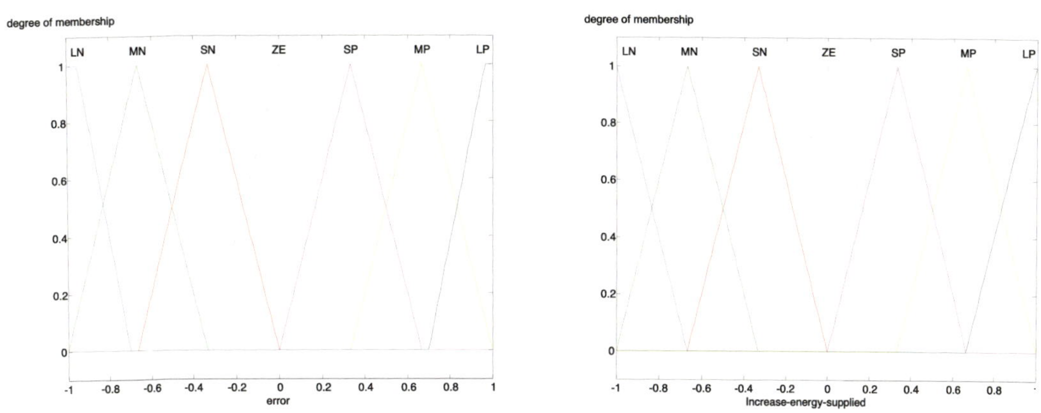

Fig. 11. Fuzzy partition of the fuzzy controller inputs (error and error-variation) and output (increase command).

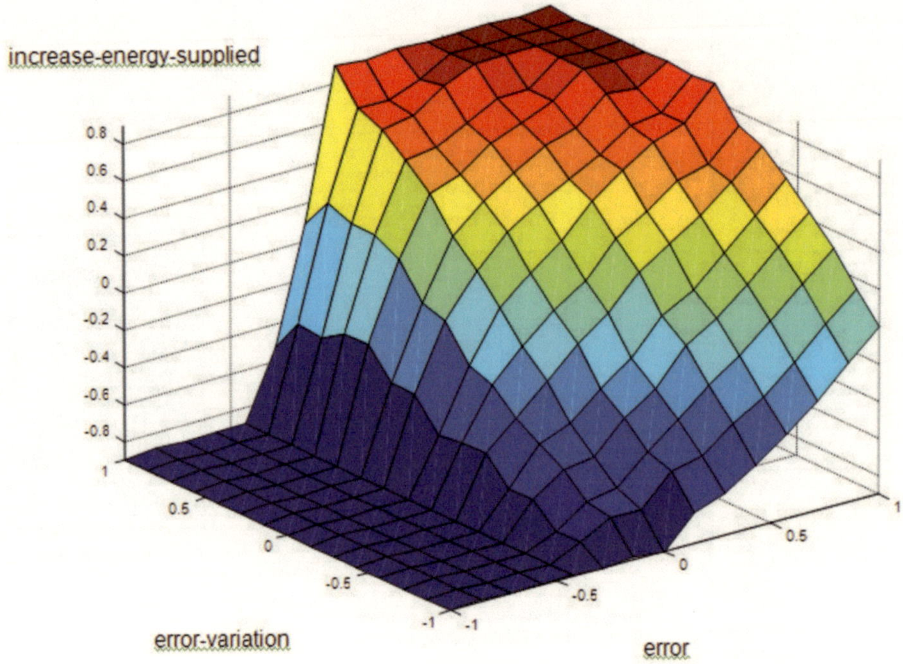

Fig. 12. Control surface.

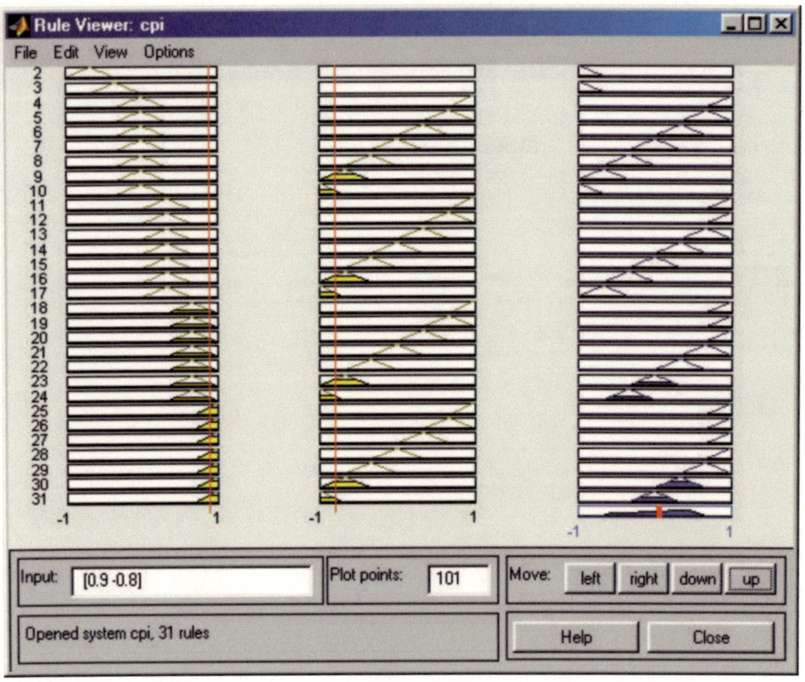

Fig. 13. Inference process for LP error (0.9) and LN error-variation (-0.8).

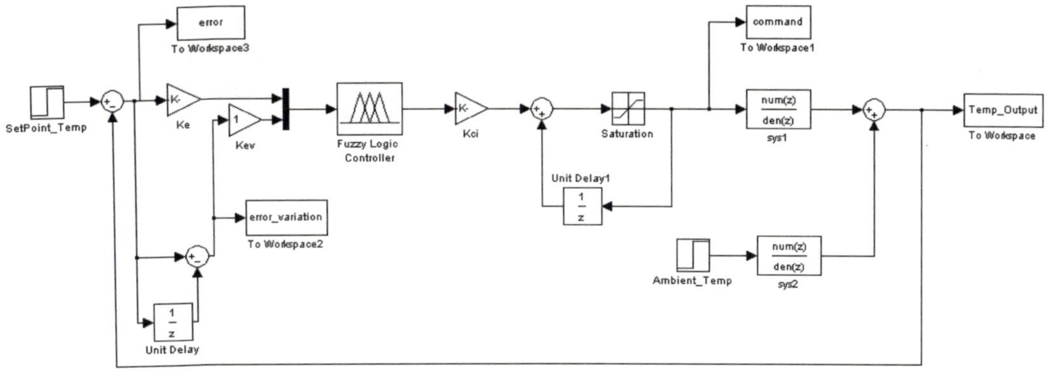

Fig. 14. Fuzzy temperature control.

A prerequisite step to studying the results of the fuzzy controller is to adjust its parameters. In other words, we used fuzzy partitions that were normalized between -1 and 1, and yet the error, the error variation and the commanded increase have to take on values within a different range. To do this, we use gains that scale these variables within the design range of the fuzzy controller, adjusting these gains to achieve the desired specifications. These gains are called gains of scale (g_s) and their effect is as follows:

1. If $g_s = 1$, there is no effect on the membership functions.
2. If $g_s > 1$, then the membership functions are uniformly contracted by a factor of $1/g_s$.
3. If $g_s < 1$, then the membership functions are uniformly expanded by a factor of $1/g_s$.

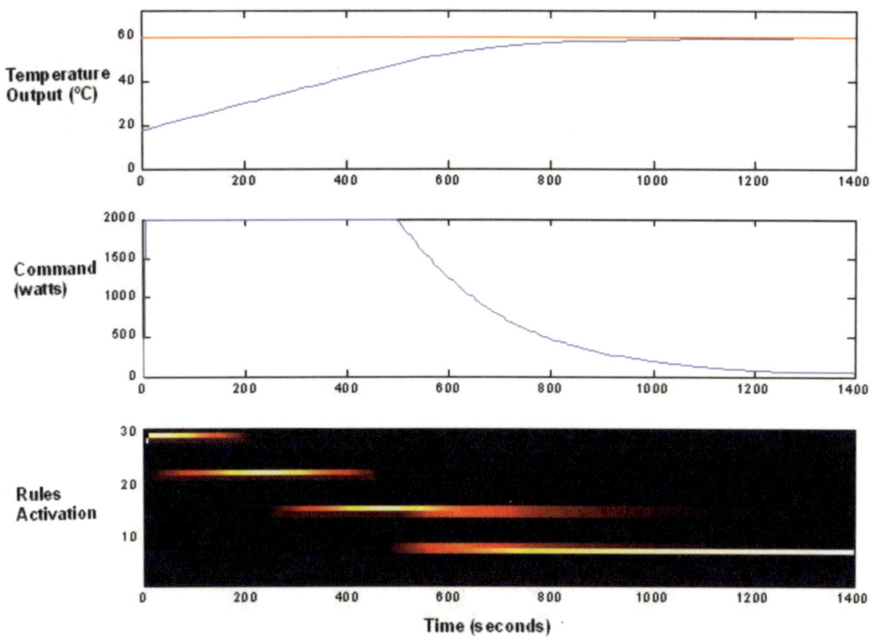

Fig. 15. Output of fuzzy temperature controller.

For the temperature controller, we have selected a gain of scale for the controller's error input of K_e=0.0238, of K_{ev}=1 for the error variation and of K_{ci}=5000 for the command increase. The values K_e and K_{ev} are needed to keep the error and the error variation bounded in the same margins. The K_{ci} value is used to match up the maximum command to the maximum value of resistance (2000 watts). The values used in the gains of scale have been selected through an adaptive method based on the results of successive simulations.

The results yielded by this system are as shown in Figure 15. By applying the maximum command (2000 watts), we can reach the setpoint value in 1000 seconds. The rules that are applied at first (trigger force equal to 0 is shown in black, with the brightness increasing to white as we progress to a trigger force equal to 1) correspond to rules 27-31, which involve LP. Then the 20-22 group takes over, these rules controlling MP errors and small error variations. Next to activate are those rules for dealing with SP errors. Lastly, rule 7, with trigger force 1, is activated for dealing with ZE error and ZE error variation.

If the setpoint is changed at t=2,200 seconds, the result is as shown in Figure 16. When the setpoint is changed, a new command is output since the MP and SP error rules are activated.

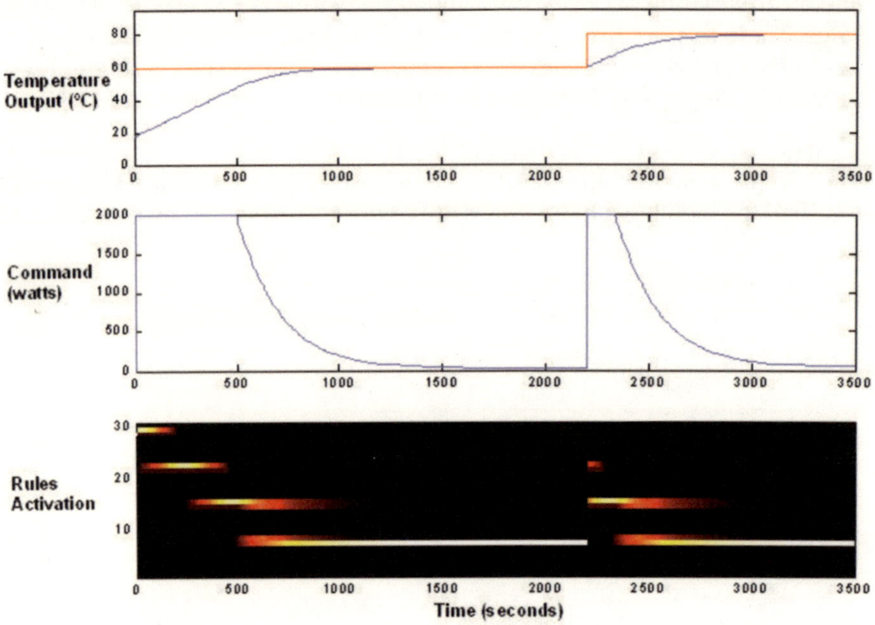

Fig. 16. Output of fuzzy temperature controller with change at t=2200 seconds.

9. Conclusions

Fuzzy logic is based on the method of reasoning that is typically used by experts to handle all kinds of systems, from the simplest to the very complex. This method (control) can be formulated with rules of the type if-then applied to inexact magnitudes such as "many", "fast", "cold", etc. Implementing this method of reasoning requires a representation of these vague magnitudes and an associated logic. These are the Theory of Diffuse Groups and Diffuse Logic, respectively.

In this chapter we have presented the steps required to implement fuzzy controllers. Such controllers, when integrated into systems that handle precise values, require a translation process before and after the reasoning method is applied. Hence the three-step structure of fuzzy controllers: fuzzification, inference and defuzzification.

The different stages were explained using an example involving temperature control. This is a trivial, academic problem that can be solved using many techniques, such as with a classical PI controller; in this chapter, however, we used this example to illustrate the design of a fuzzy controller, as well as its mode of operation.

10. References

Babuška R. (1998). *Fuzzy Modeling for Control,* Kluwer Academic Publishers, ISBN 978-0-7923-8154-9, Boston, USA

Cai X.-Z. (1997). Intelligent Control: Principles, Techniques and Applications, World Scientific Publishing Company, ISBN 978-9810225643, Singapore-New Jersey

Chen G. & Joo Y. H. (2009). Introduction to Fuzzy Control Systems, In: *Encyclopedia of Artificial Intelligence,* J. R. Rabul, J. Dorado, and A. Pazos (Eds.), 688-695, Hersh, ISBN 9781599048499, La Coruña, España

Horváth L. & Rudas I. J. (2004). *Modeling and Problem Solving Methods for Engineers,* Elsevier, Academic Press, ISBN 978-0126022506, New York

Jang J. S. R., Sun C. T. & Mizutani E. (1997). *Neuro-Fuzzy and Soft Computing,* Prentice Hall, ISBN 978-0132610667, New York

Jantzen J. (2007). *Foundations of Fuzzy Control,* Wiley, ISBN 978-0470029633, New York

Klir G. & Yuan B. (1995). *Fuzzy Sets and Fuzzy Logic,* Prentice Hall, ISBN 978-0131011717, Upper Saddle River, NJ

Li H. X. & Tong S.C. (2003). A hybrid adaptive fuzzy control for a class of nonlinear mimo systems. *IEEE Trans. Fuzzy Systems,* Vol.11, No.1, (February 2003), pp. 24–34, ISSN 1063-6706

Passino K. M. & Yurkovich S. (1998). *Fuzzy Control,* Addison Wesley Longman, Inc., ISBN 0 - 201 - 18074 - X, California

Pedrycz W. (1993). *Fuzzy Control and Fuzzy Systems,* Research Studies. Press/John Wiley, ISBN O-471-93475-5, Taunton, New York

Sala A., Guerra T. M. & Babuška R. (2005). Perspectives of Fuzzy Systems and Control. *Fuzzy Sets and Systems,* Vol.156, No.3, (December 2005), pp. 432-444, ISSN 0165-0114, North-Holland

Sala J., Picó J. & Bondia J. (2000) Tratamiento de la incertidumbre en modelado y control borrosos, *Revista Iberoamericana de Inteligencia Artificial.* Vol.4, No 10, (Summer 2000), pp. 119-126, ISSN 1137-3601, España

Sivanandam S.N., Sumathi S. & Deepa S.N. (2007). *Introduction to Fuzzy Logic using MATLAB,* Ed. Springer, ISBN 978-3540357803, Berlín, New York

Tanaka K. & Sugeno M. (1992). Stability Analysis and Design of Fuzzy Control Systems, *Fuzzy Sets and Systems,* Vol.45, No.2, (January 2002), pp. 135-156, ISSN 0165-0114, North-Holland

Tanaka K. & Wang H. O. (2001). *Fuzzy control systems design and analysis. A linear matrix inequality approach,* John Wiley & Sons, ISBN 978-0471323242, New York

Wang L. X. (1994). *Adaptative Fuzzy Systems and Control: Design and Stability Analysis*, Prentice Hall, Inc., ISBN 978-0130996312, Upper Saddle River, NJ

Yager R.R., Filev D.P. (1994). *Essentials of Fuzzy Modeling and Control,* Wiley, ISBN 978-0471017615, New York

19

An Evolutionary Fuzzy Hybrid System for Educational Purposes

Ahmed Ali Abadalla Esmin[1], Marcos Alberto de Carvalho[2],
Carlos Henrique Valério de Moraes[3] and Germano Lambert-Torres[3]
[1]Lavras Federal University
[2]José do Rosário Vellano University
[3]Itajuba Federal University
Brazil

1. Introduction

When the Fuzzy Set Theory was proposed by Lotfi Zadeh in a seminal paper published in 1965, he noted that the technological resources available until then were not able to automate the activities related to industrial, biological or chemical problems. These activities use typically analog data which are inappropriate to be handled in a digital computer that works with well-defined numerical data, i.e. , discrete values.

Using this idea, Fuzzy Logic can be defined as a way to use data from typical analog processes that move through a continuous track in a digital computer that works with discrete values. The use of Fuzzy Logic for solving control problems has tremendously increased over the last few years. Recently the Fuzzy Logic has been used in industrial process control electronic equipment, entertainment devices, diagnose systems and even to control appliances. Thus, the teaching of fuzzy control in engineering courses is becoming a necessity. In a previous work, it has been presented a computational package for students' self-training on fuzzy control theory. The package contains all required instructions for the users to gain the understanding of fuzzy control principles. The training instructions are presented via a practical example.

Although this approach has proven to be convenient in giving to students an opportunity to appreciate real life like situations, it suffers a serious disadvantage: the type of learning. In fact, students often go through a "trial-and-error" method to select an appropriate control action, such as rule definitions or membership fitting. The problem of this type of learning is a tendency from students to get the erroneous concept that corrective actions are much a matter of guess. The purpose of this chapter is to present a strategy for an automatic membership function fitting using three different evolutionary algorithms, namely: modified genetic algorithms (MGA), particle swarm optimization (PSO) and hybrid particle swarm optimization (HPSO).

The proposed strategies are applied in a computational package for fuzzy logic learning. This computer program was developed for self-training in engineering students in the theory of fuzzy control. The program contains all necessary instructions for users to understand the principles of diffuse control. In this package the main goal is to park a vehicle in a garage, starting from any starting position. The user must first develop a set of fuzzy control rules and functions of relevance that will shape the trajectory of the vehicle. The processes of fuzzification and defuzzification variables are performed by the program without user interference.

2. Description of the main features of the training package

The computational package has as main objective to park a vehicle in a garage, starting from any starting point within a pre-defined area. To this goal, the user should design a set of fuzzy control rules and also the functions of relevance that will control the trajectory of the vehicle. To set these rules, the program offers various menus with Windows and numerical routines. The processes of fuzzification and defuzzification variables are made by the program without user interference (Park et al., 1994).

Figure 1 shows the main screen to represent the problem of parking of a vehicle. This window shows the position of the garage, the existing limits (the walls) and the values of coordinated limits. Also this window presents the input variables *(x, y)* measured from the center point of the rear of the vehicle and finally, the car angle (ϕ).

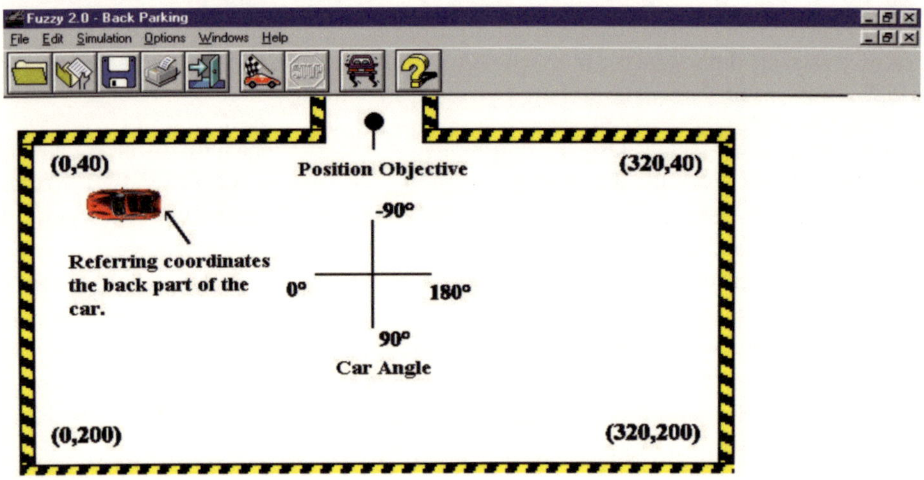

Fig. 1. Main screen of the program

For parking the vehicle, some conditions are established, and belong to two types: computational package related and linked to logical. The conditions attaching to the package represent the physical limitations, they are:

a. limits of input variables:
- position (x, y): $0 < x < 32$ and $0 < y < 20$ (in meters - parking dimensions);
- car angle of $-90° \leq \phi \leq 270°$;
- sense of the vehicle: forward or backward.

b. limit of the output variable:
- vehicle wheel angle $-30° \leq \theta \leq 30°$ (limitation of the real model).

With respect to logical limitations, they may vary according to the types of strategies employed. Some examples of these strategies can be, among others:

- minimization of the number of changes of vehicle direction (forward or backward);
- minimizing the space traversed by vehicle to the garage;
- the restriction of parts of garage for parking.

For the movement of the vehicle shall be laid down the following conditions: Acceleration equal to 1 (m/s^2) and maximum speed 1 (m/s). These two values are used as reference for all movements. To reverse the direction of motion of the vehicle there are three possibilities, which are:

a. shock against the wall: when the system verifies that the vehicle will collide against the wall in the next step;
b. rule that forces the inversion: when the reverse order is used as a result of a rule; or,
c. lack of outputs: when no rule is used by the control, i.e., if the output is zero.

The user of this computational package can define a new system by creating the roles of relevance and control rules. Initially, the user sets the number of functions of relevance for each variable. When the functions are created, they are equally spaced on the surface of the control variable. The user can modify these functions of belongingness by Fuzzy Sets Edition window. Figure 2 presents an example of editing for the x input variable.

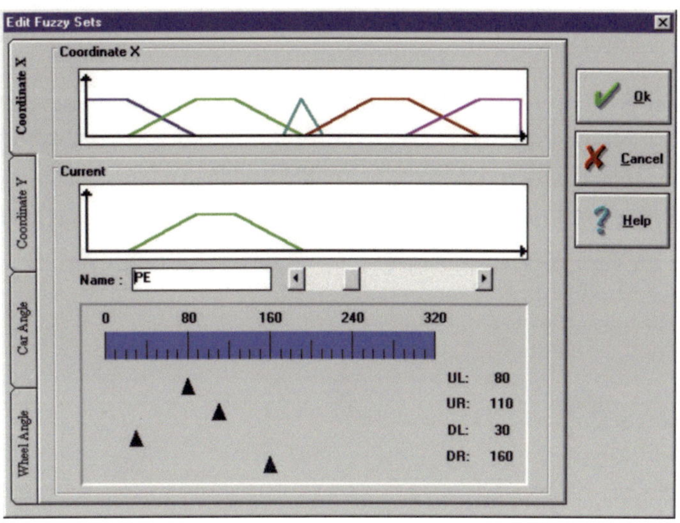

Fig. 2. Fuzzy Sets Edition window

To set the rules for the control, i.e., how the functions of relevance will be grouped, there is the Fuzzy Rules Edition window. In Figure 3, one can find two regions of interest. The first where there is the possibility of selecting the direction (forward or reverse) and coordinated corresponding to the angle of the car. The second region of interest contains the padding of the conclusion of the rule. This can be done by selecting one of the output values (or none for a rule does not set or reverse). For instance for x = LE (left), y = YT (small values), car angle = RB (right big angle) and direction = ahead (forward) values was selected as NB (negative big angle) to wheel angle, which corresponds to rule:

"IF *x* is **and** LE *y* **and** is YT **and** *car angle* is RB **and** direction of movement is *forward (ahead)* THEN wheel angle is NB."

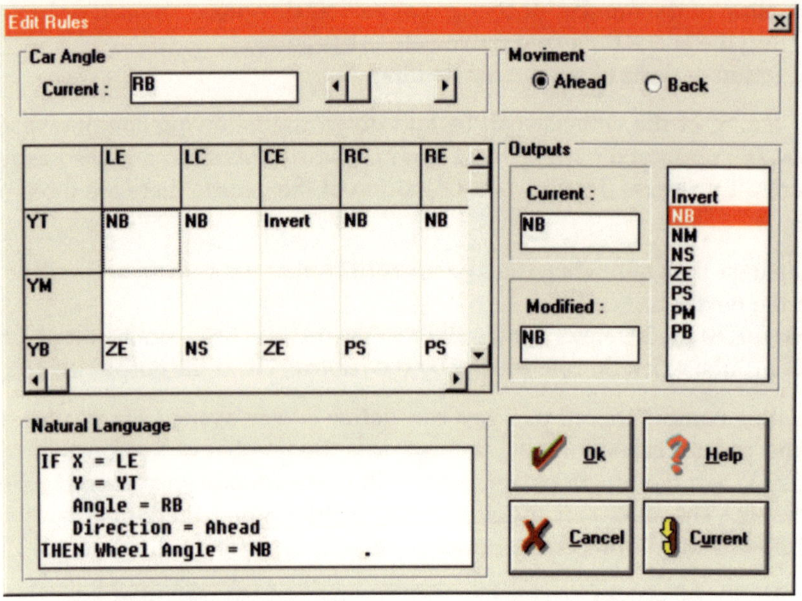

Fig. 3. Fuzzy Rules Edition window

Through the initial position of the Edition menu option the user can set a start position (x-*y* coordinates and car angle *ϕ*) to the vehicle. The simulation is started through the Start menu simulation. Figure 4 shows three possible initial positions.

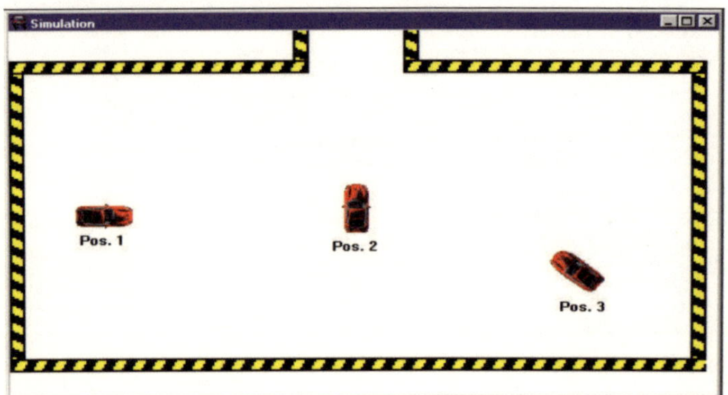

Fig. 4. Three possible start positions

In the examples of simulation in Figure 5, you can check the trail left by the vehicle during its trajectory. Each point means iteration (i.e. a full pass on the set of rules) and the count is recorded in the variables window. The first example, shown in Figure 5 (a), has produced 628 iterations; while, in the second, in Figure 5(b), for another set of rules was queried by 224 times, for the same start position. It is easy to see that the second set of rules has a batter performance than the first one for this start position.

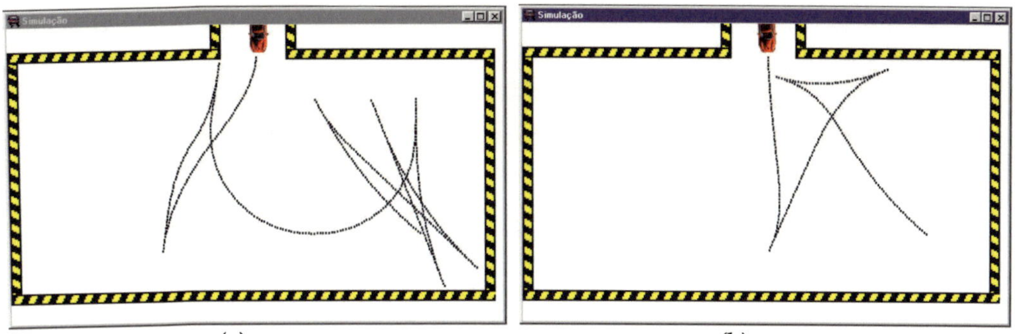

(a) (b)

Fig. 5. Examples of computational simulation package

The computational package has features that allow you to vary the size of the car between: small, medium or large. This variation creates the opportunity to verify the behavior of the control system for an outfit that has changed some of its grandeur. The computational package also has three methods of defuzzification, which are: the centroid (center of gravity), average of the areas and average of maximum values (Kandel & Langholz, 1993).

In the first version of the computational package, the learning process used is by trial and error. The user creates the functions of relevance, provides a set of rules and then performs several tests to verify the quality of control. It is known that this learning process (by trial and error) may not bring the expected results because several errors of interpretation can occur (da Silva et al., 2010).

3. Description of the evolutionary methods used in the hybrid system

The whole task of search and the optimization has several components, including: the search space, where they are considered all possibilities of solution of a given problem and the evaluation function (or function), a way to evaluate members of the search space. There are many methods of search and evaluation functions.

Search optimization techniques and traditional begin with a single candidate, iteratively, is manipulated using some heuristics (static) directly associated with the problem to be solved. Generally, these processes are not heuristic algorithmic and its simulation in computers can be very complex. Despite these methods were not sufficiently robust, this does not imply they are useless. In practice, they are widely used, successfully, in innumerable applications (Ross, 2010).

On the other hand, the evolutionary computation techniques operate on a population of candidates in parallel. Thus, they can search in different areas of the solution space, allocating an appropriate number of members to search in multiple regions.

Meta-heuristic methods differ from traditional methods of search and optimization, mainly in four aspects (Esmin et al., 2005; Medsker, 2005):

1. Meta-heuristic methods work with an encoding of the set of parameters and not with their own parameters.
2. Meta-heuristic methods work with a population and not with a single point.

3. Meta-heuristic methods use cost information or reward and not derived or other auxiliary knowledge.
4. Meta-heuristic methods use probabilistic transition rules and not deterministic.

In addition to being a strategy to generate-and-test very elegant, because they are based on social organization or biological evolution, are able to identify and explore environmental factors and converge to optimal solutions, or approximately optimal in overall levels. The better a person adapt to their environment, the greater your chance of surviving and generate descendants: this is the basic concept of social organization or biological genetic evolution. The biological area more closely linked to genetic algorithms is the genetics, and the social area is particle swarm optimization.

3.1 Genetic algorithms

In the years 50 and 60, many biologists began to develop computational simulations of genetic systems. However, it was John Holland who began, in earnest, developing the first researches in the theme. Holland was gradually refining their ideas and in 1975 published his book "Adaptation in Natural and Artificial Systems" (Holland, 1975), now considered the bible of genetic algorithms. Since then, these algorithms are being applied with success in the most diverse problems of optimization and machine learning.

Genetic algorithms are global optimization algorithms, based on the mechanisms of natural selection and genetics. They employ a parallel search strategy and structured, but random, which is geared toward enhancing search of "high fitness" points, i.e. points where the function to be minimized (or maximized) has values relatively low (or high).

Although they are not random, random walks, directed not because explore historical information to find new points of search where are expected best performances. This is done through iterative processes, where each iteration is called generation.

During each iteration, the principles of selection and reproduction are applied to a population of candidates that can vary, depending on the complexity of the problem and the computational resources available. Through the selection, if determines which individuals will be able to reproduce, generating a particular number of descendants for the next generation, with a probability given by its index of fitness. In other words, individuals with greater relative adaptation have greater chances of reproducing.

The starting point for the use of genetic algorithms, as a tool for troubleshooting is the representation of these problems in a way that the genetic algorithms to work properly on them. Most representations are genotype, use vectors of finite size in a finite alphabet.

Traditionally, individuals are represented by binary vectors, where each element of a vector (1) denotes the presence or absence (0) of a particular characteristic. However, there are applications where it is more convenient to use representations for integers as shown later in this work.

The basic principle of operation of AGs is that a selection criterion will do with that, after many generations, the initial set of individuals generates another set of individuals more able. Most methods are designed to check individuals preferentially choose majors with fitness, although not exclusively, in order to maintain the diversity of the population. A selection method used is the method of roulette, where individuals of one generation are chosen to be part of the next generation, through a raffle of roulette. Figure 6 shows the representation of the roulette to a population of 4 individuals.

i	Individual x_i	$f_i(x)$ Fitness Function (x^2)	Relative Values of Fitness Function
1	00101	25	0.04
2	00010	4	0.01
3	10110	484	0.81
4	01001	81	0.14
Total		594	1.00

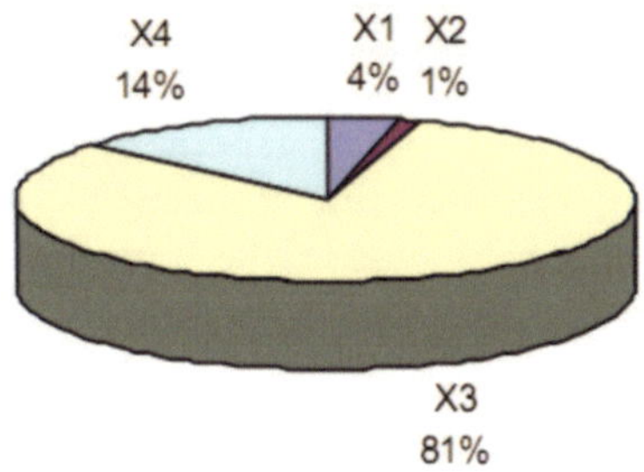

Fig. 6. Individuals of a population and its corresponding check roulette

In this method, each individual of the population is represented in roulette in proportion to its index of fitness. Thus, individuals with high fitness are given a greater portion of the wheel, while the lowest fitness is given a relatively smaller portion of roulette. Finally, the roulette wheel is rotated a certain number of times, depending on the size of the population, and are chosen, as individuals who will participate in the next generation, those drawn in roulette.

A set of operations is necessary so that, given a population, to generate successive populations that (hopefully) improve your fitness with time. These operators are: crossover (crossover) and mutation. They are used to ensure that the new generation is entirely new, but has in some way, characteristics of their parents, i.e. the population diversifies and maintains adaptation characteristics acquired by previous generations. To prevent the best individuals does not disappear from the population by manipulating the genetic operators; they can be automatically placed on the next generation via playing elitist.

This cycle is repeated a specified number of times. The following is an example of genetic algorithm. During this process, the best individuals, as well as some statistical data, can be collected and stored for evaluation.

```
Procedure AG
{g = 0;
inicial_population (P, g)
evaluation (P, g);
Repeat until (g = t)
{g = g +1;
    Father_selection (P, g);
recombination (P, g);
mutation (P, g);
evaluation (P, g);
  }
}
```

Where g is the current generation; t is the number of generations to terminate the algorithm; and P is the population.

These algorithms are computationally very simple, are quite powerful. In addition, they are not limited by assumptions about the search space, for continuity, existence of derivatives, and so on.

3.1.1 Genetic operators

The basic principle of genetic operators is to transform the population through successive generations, extending the search until you reach a satisfactory outcome. Genetic operators are needed to enable the population to diversify and keep adaptation characteristics acquired by previous generations.

The operator mutation is necessary for the introduction and maintenance of genetic diversity of the population, arbitrarily changing one or more components of a structure chosen, as is illustrated in Figure 7, thus providing the means for introduction of new elements in the population. Thus, the mutation ensures that the probability of reaching any point in the search space will never be zero, in addition to circumvent the problem of local minima, because with this mechanism, slightly changes the search direction. The mutation operator is applied to individuals with a probability given by the mutation rate *Pm*; usually uses a small mutation rate, because it is a genetic operator secondary.

Before the mutation	0 1 0 0 0
After the mutation	0 1 1 0 0

Fig. 7. Example of mutation

The crossing is the operator responsible for the recombination of traits of parents during play, allowing future generations to inherit these traits. It is considered the predominant genetic operator, so it is applied with probability given by the crossover rate *Pc*, which must be greater than the rate of mutation.

This operator can also be used in several ways; the most commonly used are:

a. One-point: a crossover point is chosen and from this point the parental genetic information will be exchanged. The information prior to this point in one of the parents is related to information subsequent to this point in the other parent, as shown in the example in Figure 8.

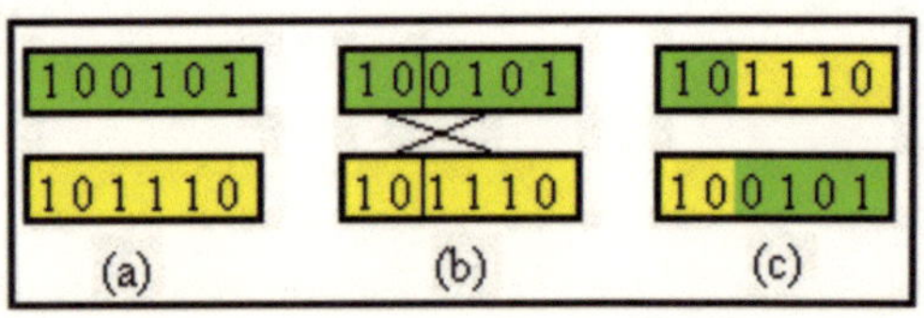

Fig. 8. Example of crossover from one-point: (a) two individuals are chosen; (b) a crossover point (2) is chosen; (c) the characteristics are recombined, generating two new individuals

b. Multi-points: is a generalization of this idea of an exchange of genetic material through points, where many crossing points can be used.
c. Uniform: don't use crossing points, but determines, through a global parameter, which the probability of each variable be exchanged between parents.

3.1.2 Genetic parameters

It is also important to analyze how some parameters influence the behavior of genetic algorithms in order to establish them as the needs of the problem and available resources.

Population size. The size of the population affects the overall performance and efficiency of AGs. With a small population performance may fall, because this way the population provides a small coverage of the search space of the problem. A large population typically provides a representative coverage of the problem domain, and preventing premature convergence solutions to local rather than global. However, for working with large populations, larger computational resources are required, or that the algorithm works by a much longer time period.

Passing Rate. The higher this ratio, the faster new structures will be introduced in the population. But if this is too high, the majority of the population will be replaced and can be lost high fitness structures. With a low value, the algorithm can become very slow.

Mutation rate. A low mutation rate prevents a given position stay stagnant in a value, and allow to reach anywhere in the search space. With a very high search becomes essentially random.

3.2 Particle Swarm Optimization

The optimization method called Particle Swarm Optimization (PSO) as other meta-heuristics recently developed, simulates the behavior of systems making the analogy with social behaviors. PSO was originally inspired by biological partner behavior associated with group of birds (Goldberg, 1989). This topic will be discussed in more detail after the basic algorithm is described.

The PSO was first proposed by John Kennedy and Russell Eberhart (1995a, 1995b). Some of the interesting features of PSO include ease of implementation and the fact that no gradient information is required. It can be used to solve a range of different optimization problems, including most of the problems can be solved through genetic algorithms; one can cite as an example some of the applications, such as neural network training (Lee & El-Sharkawi, 2008) and to minimize various types of functions (Eberhart et al., 1996).

Many popular optimizations algorithms are deterministic, as the gradient-based algorithms. The PSO, like its similar, belonging to the family of Evolutionary Algorithm is an algorithm of stochastic type that needs no gradient information derived from error function. This allows the use of PSO in functions where the gradient is unavailable or the production of which is associated with a high computational cost.

3.2.1 The PSO algorithm

The algorithm maintains a population of particles, where each particle represents a potential solution to an optimization problem. S assumed as being the size of the swarm. I each particle can be represented as an object with various features. These characteristics are as follows:

x_i: the current position of the particle;
v_i: the current speed of the particle;
y_i: the best personal position achieved by the particle.

The best personal position i particle represents the best position that the particle has visited and where he obtained the best evaluation. In the case of a task of minimizing, for example, a position that earned the lowest function value is considered to be the best position or with highest fitness assessment. F symbol is used to denote the objective function being minimized. The update equation for the best staff position is given by equation (1) using t time explicitly.

$$y_i(t+1)=\begin{cases} y_i(t) & if \quad f(y_i(t)\leq f(x_i(t+1))) \\ x_i(t+1) & if \quad f(y_i(t)>f(x_i(t+1))) \end{cases} \tag{1}$$

There are two versions of PSO, calls *gbest* templates and *lbest (the global best and the best place)* (Goldberg, 1989). The difference between the two algorithms is based directly in the way that a particular particle interacts with its set of particles. To represent this interaction will be used the symbol $\hat{y}$. The details of the two models will be discussed in full later. The definition of $\hat{y}$ as used in *gbest* model, is shown by equation (2).

$$\begin{aligned}\hat{y}(t)\in\{y_0(t),y_1(t),\ldots\ldots,y_s(t)\} \mid f(\hat{y}(t)) \\ =\min\{f(y_0(t)),f(y_1(t)),\ldots\ldots,f(y_s(t))\}\end{aligned} \tag{2}$$

Note that this definition shows that $\hat{y}$ is the best position until then found by all particles in the swarm S size.

The PSO algorithm makes use of two independent random sequences $r_1 \sim U(0,1)$ and $r_2 \sim U(0,1)$. These strings are used to give nature to stochastic algorithm, as shown below in the equation (3). The values of r_1 and r_2 are scaled through constant $c_1 > 0$ and $c_2 \leq 2$. These constants are called *acceleration coefficients*, and they exert influence on the maximum size of a particle can give in a single iteration. The speed that updates the step is specified separately for each dimension $j \in 1 \ldots n$, so that $v_{i,j}$ denotes the dimension j vector associated with the particle speed i. The update speed is given by the following equation:

$$\begin{aligned}v_{i,j}(t+1)=v_{i,j}(t)+c_1r_{1,j}(t)[y_{i,j}(t)-x_{i,j}(t)]+ \\ c_2r_{2,j}(t)[\hat{y}_j(t)-x_{i,j}(t)]\end{aligned} \tag{3}$$

In the definition of the equation, the constant speed update c_2 regulates clearly the maximum size of the step in the direction of better global particle, and the constant c_1 adjusts the size of the step in the direction of better personal position of the particle. The value of $v_{i,j}$ is maintained within the range of $[-v_{max}, v_{max}]$ by reducing the probability that a particle can exit the search space. If the search space is defined by the interval $[-x_{max}, x_{max}]$, then the value of v_{max} is calculated as follows:

$$v_{max}=k \quad X \quad x_{max} \quad \text{where} \quad 0.1\leq k\geq 1.0$$

The position of each particle is updated using your new velocity vector:

$$x_i(t+1)=x_i(t)+v_i(t+1) \tag{4}$$

The algorithm consists of repeated application of the equations above update. Below the basic PSO algorithm code is shown.

Create and initialize:
i - current particle;
s - PSO of n-dimensions:

repeat:
for each *particle i = [1 .. s]*
If *f (S_ix.x) < f (S_i.y)*
then $S_i\, y = x_i\, S$.
If $f (S_i.y) < f (s.\ \hat{y}\ )$
then $S.\ \hat{y}\ = Y_i\, S$.
end loop
Update S using the equations (3) and (4)
until *the stopping condition is* ***True***
end

The startup mentioned in the first step of the algorithm consists of the following:

1. initialize each coordinated $x_{i,j}$ with a random value in the range $[-x_{max}, x_{max}]$, for the entire $i \in 1 \ldots s$ and $j \in 1 \ldots n$. This distributes the initial positions of the particles along the search space. Select a good random distribution algorithm to obtain a uniform distribution in the search space.
2. initialize each $v_{i,j}$ with a value taken from the range $[-v_{max}, v_{max}]$ for the entire $i \in 1 \ldots s$ and $j \in 1 \ldots n$. Alternatively, the velocities of particles may be initialized with 0 (zero), provided that the initial positions are initialized in a random fashion.

The stopping criterion mentioned in the algorithm depends on the type of problem to be solved. Typically the algorithm is run for a predetermined and fixed number of iterations (a fixed number of function evaluation) or until it reaches a specific value of error. It is important to realize that the term speed models the rate of change in the position of the particle. The changes induced by speed update equation (3) represent acceleration, which explains why the constants c_1 and c_2 are called acceleration coefficients.

A brief description of how the algorithm works is given as follows: Initially, a particle any is identified as being the best particle in the group, based on his ability using the objective function. Then, all particles will be accelerated in the direction of this particle, and at the same time in the direction of own best positions previously found. Occasionally particles explore the search space around the current best particle. This way, all particles will have the opportunity to change their direction and seek a new 'best' particle. Whereas most functions have some form of continuity, chances are good to find the best solutions in the space that surrounds the best particle. Approximation of the particles coming from different directions in the search space towards the best solution increases the chances of finding the best solutions that are in the area nearby the best particle.

3.2.2 The behavior of the PSO

Many interpretations have been suggested regarding the operation and behavior of the PSO. Kennedy, in his research strengthened biological vision partner-PSO, performing experiments to investigate the roles of the different components of the velocity update equation (Kennedy & Eberhart, 1995). The task of training a neural network was used to compare performance of different models. Kennedy made use of *lbest* model (see *lbest* section for a complete description of this template), instead *gbest* model.

For this update equations developed two speed, the first by using just the experience of the particle, called the *component of cognition*, and the second, using only the interaction between the particles and called *social component.*

Consider the equation speed update (3) presented earlier. The term $c_1r_{1,j}(t)[y_{i,j}(t) - x_{i,j}(t)]$ is associated only with the cognition, where it takes into account only the experiences of the particle itself. If an OSP is built using only the cognitive component, the upgrade speed equation becomes:

$$v_{i,j}(t+1) = v_{i,j}(t) + c_1 r_{1,j}(t)[y_{i,j}(t) - x_{i,j}(t)]$$

Kennedy found that the performance of this model of "only with cognition" was less than the original PSO's performance. One of the reasons of bad performance is attributed to total absence of interaction between the different particles.

The third term in the equation, speed update $c_2r_{2,j}(t)[\hat{y}_j(t) - x_{i,j}(t)]$, represents the social interaction between the particles. A version of PSO with just the social component can be constructed using the following equation: speed update

$$v_{i,j}(t+1) = v_{i,j}(t) + c_2 r_{2,j}(t)[\hat{y}_j(t) - x_{i,j}(t)]$$

It was observed that in the specific problems that Kennedy, investigated the performance of this model was superior to the original PSO.

In summary, the term speed of PSO update consists of two components, the component of cognition and the social component. Currently, little is known about the relative importance of them, although initial results indicate that the social component is more important in most of the problems studied. This social interaction between the particles develops cooperation between them to resolve the problem.

3.2.3 Model of the best global (*gbest*)

The model allows *gbest* a faster rate of convergence at the expense of robustness. This model keeps only a single "best solution", called the *best global particle*, between all particles in the swarm. This particle acts as an attractor, pulling all particles to it. Eventually, all particles will converge to this position. If it is not updated regularly, the swarm can converge prematurely. The equations for update $\hat{y}$ and x_i are the same as shown above:

$$\begin{aligned}\hat{y}(t) \in \{y_0(t), y_1(t), \ldots\ldots, y_s(t)\} \mid f(\hat{y}(t)) \\ = \min\{f(y_0(t)), f(y_1(t)), \ldots\ldots, f(y_s(t))\}\end{aligned} \tag{5}$$

$$\begin{aligned}v_{i,j}(t+1) = v_{i,j}(t) + c_1 r_{1,j}(t)[y_{i,j}(t) - x_{i,j}(t)] + \\ c_2 r_{2,j}(t)[\hat{y}_j(t) - x_{i,j}(t)]\end{aligned} \tag{6}$$

Note that $\hat{y}$ is called *the best overall position*, and belongs to the particle called *the best global particle*.

3.2.4 The model of the best location (*lbest*)

The *lbest* model tries to prevent premature convergence keeping multiple attractors. A subset of particles is defined for each particle of which is selected *the best local particle*, $\hat{y}_i$. The symbol $\hat{y}_i$ is called *the best local position* or *better in the vicinity (the local best position or the neighborhood best)*. Assuming that the indexes of the particles are around space *s*, the equations of *lbest* update for a neighborhood size *l* are as follows:

$$N_i = \{y_{i-l}(t), y_{i-l+1}(t), \ldots, y_{i-1}(t), y_i(t), y_{i+1}(t), \ldots, y_{i+l}(t)\} \tag{7}$$

$$\hat{y}_i(t+1) \in N_i \;\; | f(\hat{y}_i(t+1)) = \min\{f(a)\}, \forall a \in N_i \tag{8}$$

$$v_{i,j}(t+1) = v_{i,j}(t) + c_1 r_{1,j}(t)[y_{i,j}(t) - x_{i,j}(t)] + c_2 r_{2,j}(t)[\hat{y}_j(t) - x_{i,j}(t)] \tag{9}$$

Note that the particles are selected in the subset N_i and they have no relation with the other particles within the domain of the search space; the selection is based solely on the index of the particle. This is done for two main reasons: the computational cost is lower, by not requiring grouping, and this also helps to promote the expansion of information on good solutions for all particles, although these are local search.

Finally, you can observe that the *gbest* model is in fact a special case of *lbest* model, when the $l = s$, i.e. when the selected set encompasses the entire swarm.

3.2.5 Considerations about the similarity between PSO and EAs

There is a clear relationship of PSO with the evolutionary algorithms (EAs). To some authors, the PSO maintains a population of individuals who represent potential solutions, one of the features found in all EAs. If the best personal positions (y_i) are treated as part of the population, then clearly there is a weak check (Lee & El-Sharkawi, 2008). In some algorithms of ES, the descendants (*offspring*), parents compete, replacing them if they are more suited. The equation (1) resembles this mechanism, with the difference that the best staff position (the father) can only be replaced by your own current position (descending), provided that the current position is more adapted to the best old staff position. Therefore, it seems to be some weak form check this on the PSO.

The speed update equation resembles arithmetic crossover operator (*crossover*) found in AGs. Typically, the intersection arithmetic produces two descendants that are results of mixing both parents involved in the crossing. The equation of speed update, PSO without term $v_{i,j}$ (see equation 3), can be interpreted as a form of arithmetic crossover involving two parents, returning only one descendant. Alternatively, the update equation of speed, without the term $v_{i,j}$. It can be seen as changing operator.

The best way to analyze the term $v_{i,j}$ is not to think of each iteration as a population replacement process by a new engine (birth and death), but as a process of continuous adaptation (Eberhart and J. Kennedy, 2001). This way the values of x_i are not replaced, but continually adapted using vectors speed v_i. This makes the difference between the OSP and the other EAs clearer: the PSO maintains information on the position and velocity (changes in position); In contrast, traditional EAs only keep information on the position.

In spite of the opinion that there is some degree of similarity between the PSO and the majority of other EAs, the PSO has a few features that currently are not present in any other EAs, especially the fact that the PSO models the speed of the particles as well as their positions.

3.3 Hybrid Particle Swarm optimization

The Hybrid Particle Swarm algorithm with Mutation (HPSOM) incorporates the mutation process often used in genetic algorithm in PSO (Esmin et al., 2005). This process will allow the particles can escape a local optimum point and perform searches in different area in the search space. This process starts by random choice in Particle Swarm and move to a new different position within the search space. The process of mutation used is given by the following equation:

$$mut(p[k]) = p([k]^* - 1) + \omega \tag{10}$$

Where the $p[k]$ is the randomly chosen particle swarm of and ω is also obtained from a random order within the following scale: $[0, 0.1(x_{max} - x_{min})]$ representing 0.1 times the length of the search space. The HPSOM algorithm has the following pseudocode.

begin
Create and initialise:
While *(stop condition is* ***false)***
begin
evalaute
update velocity and position
mutation
  end
 end

4. Integration of meta-heuristic methods with fuzzy control

4.1 Advantages of hybrid systems

The integration of fuzzy systems with meta-heuristics methods has some characteristics in common and others that complement each other, as shown in Table 1. The junction of these two techniques forms a proper way to deal with non-linear systems and data. Systems that use these techniques have improved their performance in terms of efficiency and speed of execution.

Fuzzy systems have the advantage of storing knowledge. This is a feature of expert systems so that rules, for example, are easy to modify. Fuzzy systems are an effective and convenient alternative to represent the troubleshooting when the states are well defined. However, for large and complicated systems, fuzzy systems become difficult to adjust, depending on manual methods that involve trial and error. The fuzzy relation matrix representing the relationships between concepts and actions can be unwieldy, and the best values for the parameters needed to describe the functions of relevance may be difficult to determine. The performance of a diffuse system can be very sensitive to specific values of the parameters.

	Knowledge Saving	Learning	Optimizing	Speed	Non-Linear Systems
Fuzzy Systems	✓			✓	✓
Meta-heuristic Methods		✓	✓	✓	✓

Table 1. Comparison of characteristics of fuzzy logic with meta-heuristic techniques

In general, meta-heuristic methods offer distinct advantages of optimization of functions of relevance and even learning fuzzy rules. The meta-heuristic methods result in a more comprehensive search, reducing the chance of finishing in a local minimum, through sampling of several solutions sets simultaneously. Fuzzy logic contributes with the evaluation function, stage of genetic algorithm where the adjustment is determined.

There are several possible ways to use meta-heuristic methods with fuzzy systems. A type of hybrid system involves the use of separate modules as part of a global system. The modules based on meta-heuristic methods and fuzzy logic can be grouped singly or with other subsystems of computational intelligent or conventional programs that form an application system.

Another use is the design of systems that are primarily of applications with fuzzy logic. The use of genetic algorithms aims to improve the design process and the performance of the operating system based on fuzzy system. The meta-heuristic methods can be used to discover the best values for functions of relevance when the manual selection of values is difficult or takes a long time.

There are different types of meta-heuristic methods. Among them, genetic algorithms (GA) and particle swarm optimization (PSO), which are used in this chapter. These two methods, more another variation of the PSO, called hybrid PSO (HPSO), are chosen due to their features for integration with other systems. The general procedure for using the meta-heuristic methods with fuzzy systems is shown in Figure 6. For example, a possible solution (represented by a chromosome or a bird) can be defined as a concatenation of the values of all functions of relevance. When the triangular functions are used to represent the functions of relevance, the parameters are the centers for each set widths and fuzzy. An initial range of possible parameter values, the fuzzy system is rotated to determine how much it works well. This information is used to determine the fit of each solution and to establish a new population. The cycle is repeated until you found the best set of values for the parameters of the functions of relevance.

This process can be expanded to use the population that includes information about the conditions and actions corresponding to fuzzy rules. Include them in meta-heuristic treatment allows the system to learn or refine the fuzzy rules.

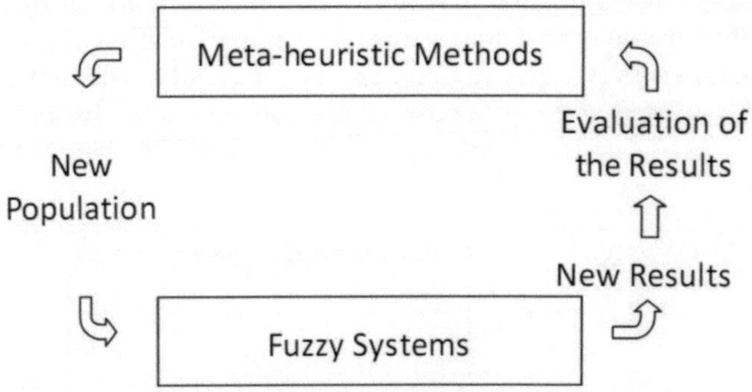

Fig. 9. Overall process for using a meta-heuristic method to improve the performance of a fuzzy system

4.2 Description of the training module

The integration of meta-heuristic methods with the fuzzy control has been implemented as follows:

a. the chromosome (or particle) was defined as the concatenation of the adjustment values of the functions of relevance
b. parameters are the centers and the widths of each fuzzy sets. The genes of chromosome (or the particles) are composed by these parameters.
c. a range of possible parameter values, the fuzzy system is rotated to determine how much it works well
d. this information is used to determine the fit of each chromosome or particle (adaptability) and establish a new population, and
e. the cycle is repeated until the number of user-defined generations (or iterations). Each generation (or iteration) is found the best set of values for the parameters of the functions of relevance.

For the meta-heuristic training, many initial positions that the vehicle will start from are defined by the user. Each initial position assesses a sub-population of the chromosomes (or particles) that represents the set of values for the parameters of the functions of relevance, seeking thus an optimization of the control not only over a single trajectory, but all possible starting positions of if from the vehicle to the parking.

After the settings makes by the user, such as number of population, number of generations (or iterations), GA values (rates of crossover, mutation, and son), and PSO values (values of r_1, r_2, c_1, c_2, and so on), the adjustment of the fuzzy membership functions starts.

The main idea behind the training is to establish the value of adjustment to the fuzzy membership functions of relevance that is how the function shifted to the left or right and how much it will shrink or expand. It is made by 2 parameters for each membership function, denoted by k_i and w_i, for the fuzzy membership function i. The value k makes a shift in the membership function, if with negative value to left or if with positive value to right; while the value of w shrink the function for negative values and expand the function for positive values. These values are included in the functions in the following way.

To describe each function of relevance of fuzzy controller are defined four parameters, they are: *LL* (lower left), *LR* (lower right), *UL* (upper left) and *UR* (upper right). In this case, all functions are trapezoids. Figure 10(a) shows the position of each these values. For setting the functions the following equations are used:

$$\begin{aligned} LL_{New} &= (LL_{Old} + k_i) - w_i \\ LR_{New} &= (LR_{Old} + k_i) + w_i \\ UL_{New} &= (UL_{Old} + k_i) \\ UR_{New} &= (UR_{Old} + k_i) \end{aligned} \tag{11}$$

Figure 10(b) shows an example of shifting membership to the following values: k = -8 and w = 2.

$$\begin{aligned} LL_{New} &= (LL_{Old} - 8) - 2 \\ LR_{New} &= (LR_{Old} - 8) + 2 \\ UL_{New} &= (UL_{Old} - 8) \\ UR_{New} &= (UR_{Old} - 8) \end{aligned} \tag{12}$$

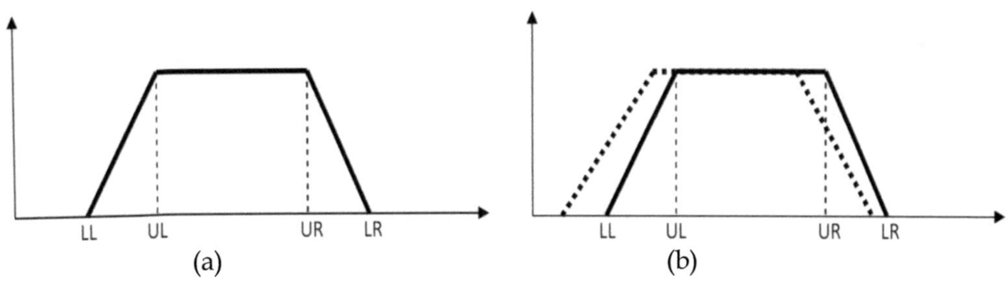

Fig. 10. Typical fuzzy membership function: (a) parameters of relevance, (b) training parameters

Meta-heuristic methods are used to find the optimal values, according to the strategy and starting points used, for k_i and w_i to the functions of relevance.

Usually a viable solution to a problem is associated with an individual (chromosome or particle) p in the form of a m vector with positions $p = \{x_1, x_2, x_3, ..., x_m\}$ where each component x_i represents a gene. Among the types of representation of individuals, the best known are: the binary representation and representation for integers. The binary representation is the classic, as proposed by John Holland (1992). However, for this development the integer code is used to represent each part of the individuals, i.e., each individual is composed by the adjustment coefficients k_i and w_i which are integer values.

With respect to the size of the chromosome, the size of each individual depends on the number of user-defined relevance functions. For a fuzzy control with a group of 18 functions of relevance for example, an individual with 36 variables (k_i and w_i where i = 1, …, 18) is composed.

The population is initialized by setting each part of all individuals to zero (functions given by the user, the coefficients are equal to zero) and the other individuals are initialized with a string of positive or negative integers in a random procedure taken into a range [-10, 10].

The evaluation function has the role to assess the level of fitness (adaptation) of each chromosome generated by algorithms. The problem goal is to minimize the trajectory of the vehicle to be parked. In case the evaluation function is given by:

$$f = \frac{1}{1+I} \tag{13}$$

where I is the total number of iterations until the final position into the park lot. According to the fitness function, the fitness of each chromosome is inversely proportional to the number of iterations.

The integration of meta-heuristic training algorithms with fuzzy model has made as follow:

1. The individual is defined as a link of the membership functions adjustment values.
2. The parameters are the centers and widths of each fuzzy set. These parameters compose the individual.
3. To check the performance of the fuzzy system it is rolled up from an initial set of possible parameters.
4. This information is used for set up each individual adjustment (adaptability) and the making of the evolution of the particle.
5. The cycle repetition is made up to complete the defined meta-heuristic method iteration number made by the user. To each meta-heuristic method iteration the best values set for the membership functions parameters is found.

5. Illustrative training examples of fuzzy control

5.1 Fuzzy control

This section presents the tests with fuzzy controls that have had their relevance adjusted using meta-heuristic methods. These tests demonstrate the efficiency of such mechanisms, allowing an objective assessment of results found. The original relevance functions are shown in Figure 11. This control has 148 rules, 15 functions relevant for the x and y input variables and car angle, and 7 output functions of angle of the wheel.

Table 2 shows the training results for the fuzzy functions shown in Fig. 11. Three initial positions have been used in this test. This table has the number of iterations that are generated by the vehicle to park using the original relevance functions.

Position	X	Y	Angle of the car	Iterations without training
1	2.5	12.0	180	330
2	16.0	13.0	-90	888
3	27.5	16.0	-40	655

Table 2. Initial positions for training and number of iterations

Figure 12 shows the vehicle in each of the initial positions. These positions were chosen according to the points where the vehicle doesn't develop a good trajectory until park and therefore generating an excessive number of iterations. The main idea is setting several initial positions will not only minimize the trajectories for these points, but as well as for other points, thus achieving a global minimization of space covered. Figures 13 show the trajectories for each initial position.

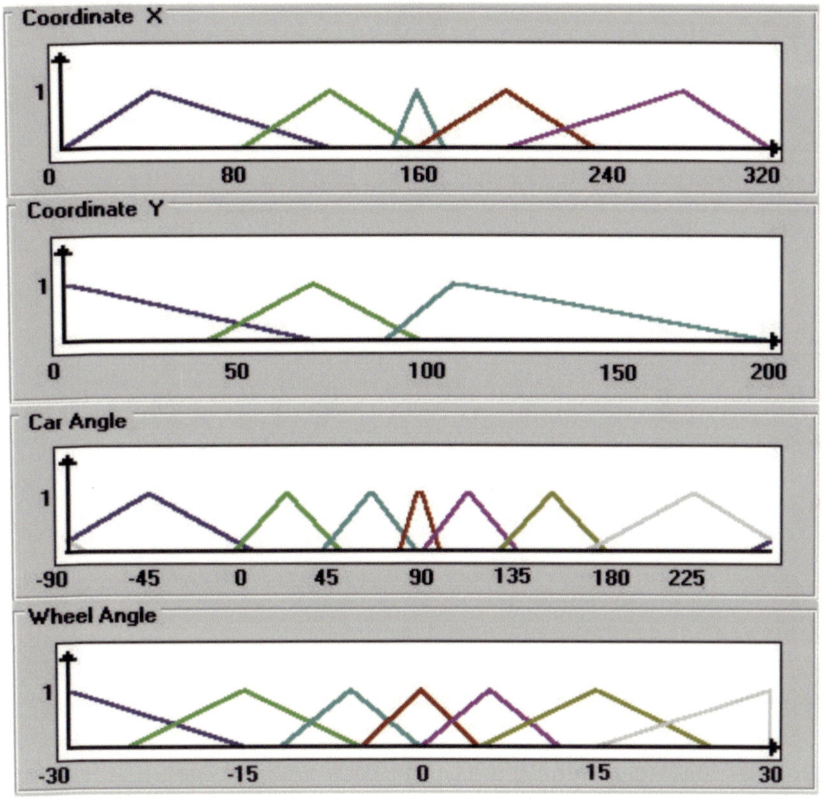

Fig. 11. Original relevance functions

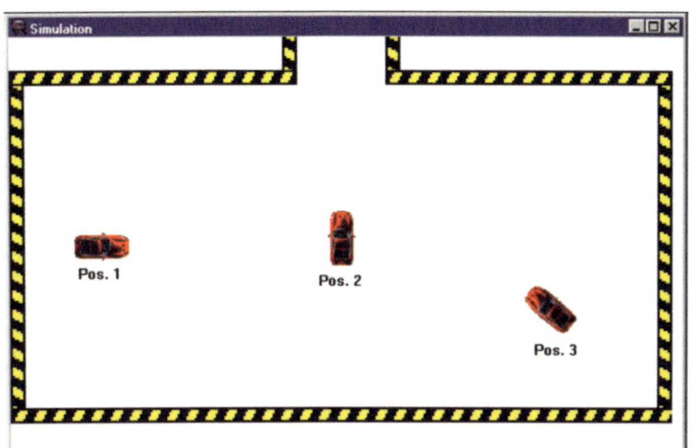

Fig. 12. Initial positions training

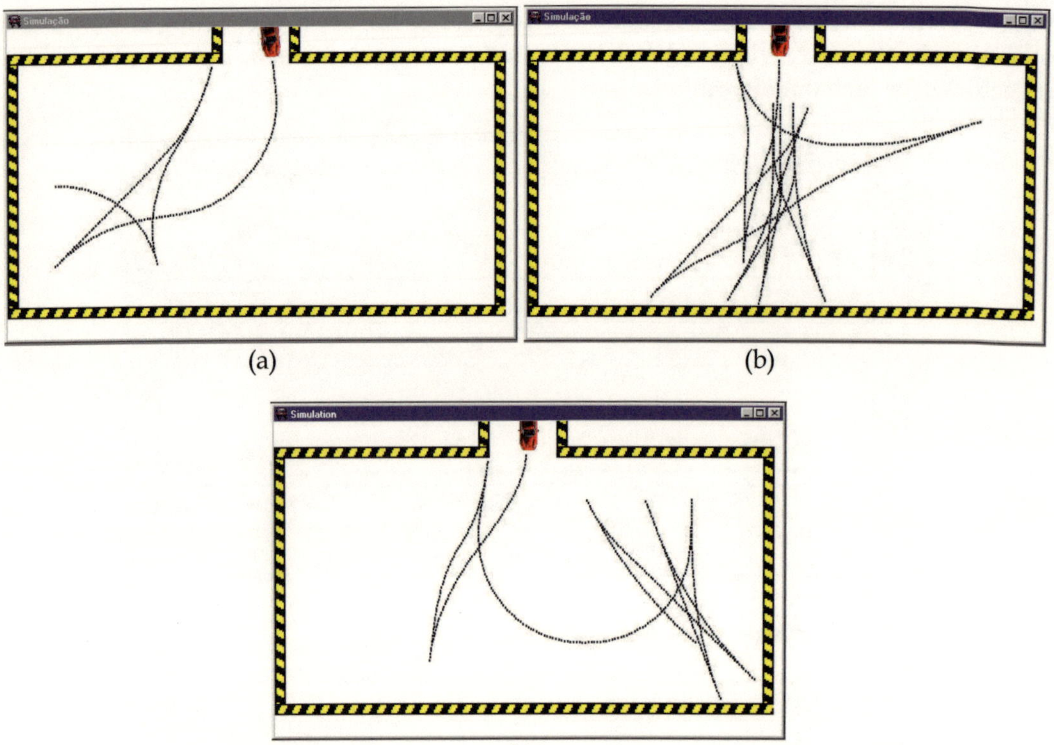

(c)

Fig. 13. Simulation results with fuzzy control without training for the following initial position: (a) position 1, (b) position 2, (c) position3

5.2 Meta-heuristic methods training fuzzy control memberships

The definition of several initial positions will not only minimize the routes referred to these points but also for other points, resulting a global minimization of traveled space. The defined GA and PSO parameters for the training are shown in Tables 3 and 4.

Population Size	14
Generations Number	30
Crossover Probability	90%
Mutation Probability	1%

Table 3. GA parameters

Size of Population	14
Number of Iterations	30
Vmax	10

Table 4. PSO parameters

After the training if the algorithm described in Section 4.2 with the fuzzy membership functions presented in Figure 11 and for three initial positions presented in Table 2, three sets of fuzzy membership are computed one for each meta-heuristic method of training (GA, PSO and HPSO). For example, the resultant GA fuzzy membership functions after adjustment are shown in Figure 14.

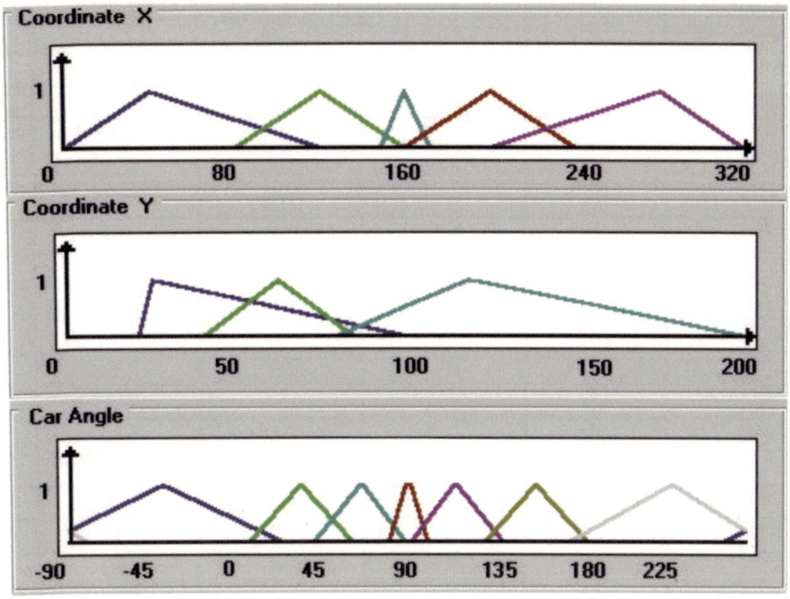

Fig. 14. Membership functions after the genetic algorithm adjustment

The generated results by meta-heuristic methods are shown in Table 5. The reduction of 941 iterations (50,2%) for GA training, 1116 iterations (59,6%) for PSO training, and 930 iterations (49,6%) were made for parking the vehicle starting from the three initial positions. These results are not optimal. Other control setups could be chosen in oder to get better results from these three initila start positions. The idea of theses simulations is presented possible adjustements of the fuzzy memberships. Also, ohter silmulations with other initial positions could create other fuzzy membership functions.

Other kind of possible simulation is to verify the quality of the resultant fuzzy membership for other initial position different from the initial position used in the training. Table 6 presents results of simulations results made starting from initial positions not used in the training for 4 types of adjustments of the fuzzy functions: human setting, and GA, PSO and HPSO trainning methods (from the functions setting by the human). The average of results of meta-heuristic methods are able to improve the better chose of the human being.

Position	Iterations without training	Iterations with GA training	Iterations with PSO training	Iterations with HPSO training
1	330	280	285	278
2	888	384	592	402
3	655	277	239	250
Total	1873	941	1116	930
Average	624,33	331.67	372	310

Table 5. Iterations after the meta-heuristic training

Case	X	Y	Car Angle	Iterations generated by Fuzzy Controls			
				Human Setting	GA Trained	PSO Trained	HPSO Trained
1	1	126	182	450	329	529	445
2	6	46	132	167	154	284	303
3	8	41	190	1000	1000	1000	1000
4	10	187	228	453	328	303	291
5	15	70	-90	318	162	282	313
6	51	112	48	278	130	128	120
7	51	112	54	280	132	126	120
8	70	95	-40	275	261	465	257
9	74	69	190	164	164	162	162
10	76	193	232	605	363	663	363
11	88	46	44	283	305	475	289
12	115	120	0	182	280	180	182
13	120	90	45	182	156	150	146
14	131	140	-72	457	292	592	512
15	141	69	-28	342	314	314	225
16	154	166	-80	863	436	980	420
17	160	135	268	1101	545	545	445
18	161	191	178	315	286	270	266
19	173	140	-72	762	590	580	544
20	208	143	244	363	310	321	312
21	217	66	-50	684	325	725	506
22	228	194	-48	830	655	855	476
23	246	169	154	312	307	507	320
24	250	180	-40	739	800	800	489
25	265	170	-40	672	329	629	483
26	290	95	-40	280	190	189	192
27	300	124	258	317	306	326	319
28	305	156	-90	350	346	340	320
29	314	73	-46	235	355	223	210
30	314	194	-44	513	744	402	388
Average				459.07	363.13	444,83	347,27

Table 6. Results of simulations for different initial position from the used to training

6. Conclusion

The fuzzy systems are a convenient and efficient alternative for solution of problems where the fuzzy statements are well defined. Nevertheless, the project of a fuzzy system may became difficult for large and complex systems, when the control quality depends of "try-and-error" methods for defining the best membership functions to solve the problem.

The meta-heuristic method training modulus provides an automatic way for the adjustment of the membership functions parameters. These techniques show that the performance of a fuzzy control may be improved through the genetic algorithms, the particle swarm optimization or the hybrid particle swarm optimization, substituting for the "try-and-error" method, as used before by students for this purpose, with no good results.

The meta-heuristic methods provided distinctive advantages for the optimization of membership functions, resulting in a global survey, reducing the chances of ending into a local minimum, once it uses several sets of simultaneous solutions. The fuzzy logic supplied the evaluation function, a stage of the meta-heuristic methods where the adjustment is settled.

7. Acknowledgment

The authors would like to express their thanks to the financial support of this work given by the Brazilian research agencies: CNPq, CAPES, and FAPEMIG.

8. References

da Silva Filho, J.I. ; Lambert-Torres, G. & Abe, J.M. (2010). *Uncertainty Treatment using Paraconsistent Logic,* IOS Press, ISBN 978-1-60750-557-0, Amsterdam, The Netherlands.

Eberhart, R. C. & Kennedy, J. (2001). *Swarm Intelligence,* ISBN 1558605959, Morgan Kaufmann, San Francisco, USA.

Eberhart, R. C. ; Simpson, P. & Dobbins, R. (1996). *Computational Intelligence PC Tools,* ISBN 0122286308, Academic Press Professional, Amsterdam, The Netherlands.

Eberhart, R.C. & Kennedy, J. (1995a). A New Optimizer using Particle Swarm Theory, *Proceedings of the Sixth International Symposium on Micro Machine and Human Science,* pp. 39-43, ISBN 0-7803-2676-8, Nagoya, Japan, Oct. 4-6, 1995.

Esmin, A.A.; Lambert-Torres, G. & Souza, A.C.Z. (2005). A Hybrid Particle Swarm Optimization Applied to Loss Power Minimization. *IEEE Transactions on Power Systems,* Vol.20, No.2, (May 2005), pp. 859-866, ISSN 0885-8950.

Goldberg, D.E. (1989). *Genetic Algorithms in Search, Optimization and Machine Learning,* ISBN 0201157675, Addison Wesley, Boston, USA.

Holland, J.H. (1975). *Adaptation in Natural and Artificial Systems,* The University of Michigam Press, ISBN 0-262-58111-6, Ann Arbor, USA.

Kandel A. & Langholz, G. (1993). *Fuzzy Control Systems,* CRC Press, ISBN 9780849344961, Boca Raton, USA.

Kennedy, J. & Eberhart, R.C. (1995b). Particle Swarm Optimization, *Proceedings of IEEE International Conference on Neural Networks,* Vol.IV, pp. 1942-1948, ISBN 0852966415, Perth, Australia, June 26-28, 1995.

Lee, K.Y. & El-Sharkawi, M.A. (2008). *Modern Heuristic Optimization Techniques: Applications to Power Systems,* Wiley – IEEE Press, ISBN 0-471-45711-6, Hoboken, USA.

Medsker, L.R. (1995). *Hybrid Intelligent Systems,* Kulwer Academic Pub., ISBN 0792395883, Boston, USA.

Park, D. ; Kandel, A. & Langholz, G. (1994). Genetic-Based New Fuzzy Reasoning Models with Application to Fuzzy Control. *IEEE Transactions on System, Man and Cybernetics,* Vol.24, No.1, (January 1994), pp. 39-47, ISSN 0018-9472.

Ross, T.J. (2010). *Fuzzy Logic with Engineering Applications*, John Wiley and Sons, ISBN 9780470743768, West Sussex, United Kingdom.

20

System Identification Using Fuzzy Cerebellar Model Articulation Controllers

Cheng-Jian Lin* and Chun-Cheng Peng
National Chin-Yi University of Technology
Taiwan, R. O. C.

1. Introduction

Being an artificial neural network inspired by the cerebellum, the cerebellar model articulation controller (CMAC) was firstly developed in (Albus, 1975a, 1975b). With the advantages such as fast learning speed, high convergence rate, good generalization capability, and easier hardware implementation (Lin & Lee, 2009; Peng & Lin, 2011), the CMAC has been successfully applied to many fields; for example, identification (Lee et al., 2004), image coding (Iiguni, 1996), ultrasonic motors (Leu et al., 2010), grey relational analysis (Chang et al., 2010), pattern recognition (Glanz et al., 1991), robot control (Harmon et al., 2005; Mese, 2003; Miller et al., 1990), signal processing (Kolcz & Allinson, 1994), and diagnosis (Hung & Wang, 2004; Wang & Jiang, 2004). However, there are three main drawbacks of Albus' CMAC, i.e., larger required computing memory (Lee et al., 2007; Leu et al., 2010; Lin et al., 2008)), relatively poor ability of function approximation (Commuri & Lewis, 1997; Guo et al., 2002; Ker et al., 1997), and difficulty of adaptively selecting structural parameters (Hwang & Lin, 1998; Lee et al., 2003).

In order to tackle these disadvantages, several methods, such as online-based clustering (Kasabov & Song, 2002; Tung & Quek, 2002) for the above-mentioned first drawback, B-spline functions (Lane et al., 1992; Wu & Pratt, 1999) and fuzzy concepts (Jou, 1992; Chen, 2001; Guo et al., 2002; Ker et al., 1997; Lai & Wong, 2001; Zhang & Qian, 2000) for the second one, and competitive learning (Chow & Menozzi, 1994), clustering (Hwang & Lin, 1998) and Shannon's entropy and golden-section search (Lee et al., 2003) for the third one, were proposed. Among these approaches, further improvements were implemented by Lin et al. (2008) with self-constructing algorithm and Gaussian basis functions.

The rest of this chapter is organized as follows. Starting from the first CMAC model in 1975 the development processes, related learning algorithms and system identification examples of the fuzzy CMACs are briefly reviewed in section 2. Sections 3 and 4 respectively discuss the self constructing FCMAC (SC-FCMAC) and the powerful parametric FCMAC (P-FCMAC). Lastly, section 5 concludes this chapter, with suggested directions of further researches.

---

* Corresponding Author

2. From CMACs to fuzzy CMAC models

2.1 The traditional CMAC models

As mentioned in the previous section, the traditional CMAC model (Albus, 1975a, 1975b) has fast learning ability and good local generalization capability for approximating nonlinear functions. The basic idea of the CMAC model is to store learned data in overlapping regions in a way that the data can easily be recalled yet use less storage space. The action of storing weight information in the CMAC model is similar to that of the cerebellum in humans. Take a two-dimensional (2-D) input vector, or the so-called two-dimensional CMAC (2-D CMAC), as an example, while its structure is shown as in Fig. 1. The input vector is defined by two input variables, s_1 and s_2, which are quantized into three discrete regions, called blocks. It is noted that the width of the blocks affects the generalization capability of the CMAC. In the first method of quantization, s_1 and s_2 are divided into blocks A, B, and C, and blocks a, b, and c, respectively. The areas Aa, Ab, Ac, Ba, Bb, Bc, Ca, Cb, and Cc formed by quantized regions are called hypercubes. When each block is shifted by a small interval, different hypercubes can be obtained. In Fig. 1, there are 27 hypercubes used to distinguish 49 different states in the 2-D CMAC. For example, let the hypercubes Bb and Ee be addressed by the state $(s_1, s_2) = (2, 2)$. Only these three hypercubes are set to 1, and the others are set to 0.

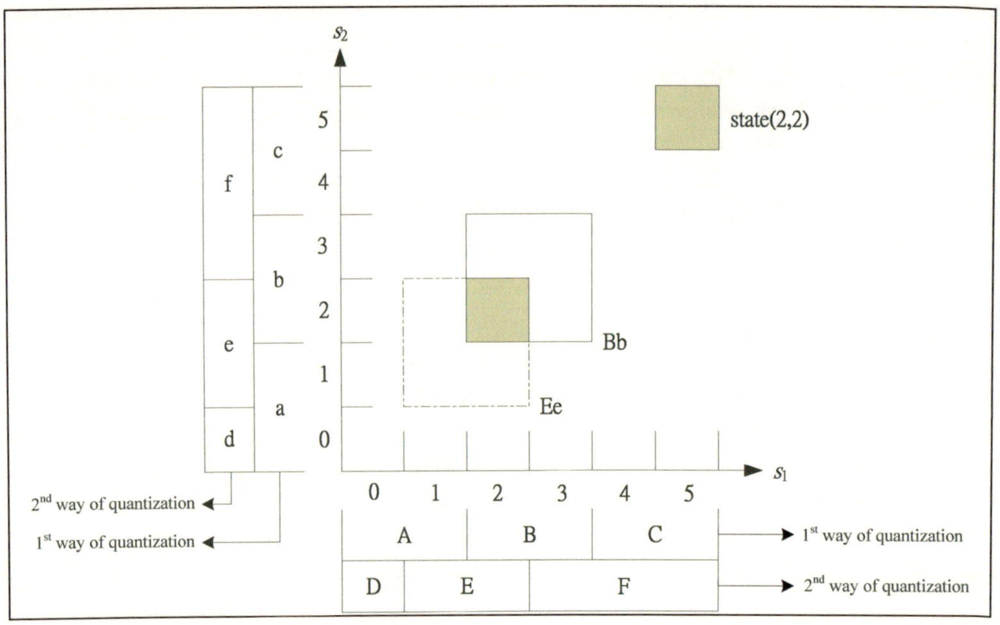

Fig. 1. Structure of a 2-D CMAC

In the work of (Mohajeri et al., 2009a) the hash coding and corresponding comparison with other neural networks for the CMACs were reviewed. There are 13 architectural improvements discussed in (Mohajeri et al., 2009a), including approaches of interpolation, numerous transfer functions (such as sigmoid, basic spline, general basis and wavelet ones), weighted regression, optimized weight smoothing, recurrence and generalization issue. Learning techniques such as neighborhood sequential training and random training were firstly considered, while the developments of other five training schemes (i.e., credit assignment, gray relational, error norm, active deformable and Tikhonov ones) were mentioned as well. In order to reduce relative memory usages, proposed approaches of hierarchical and self-organizing CMACs were reasoned, whereas the fuzzy variation of the self-organizing CMAC will be further presented in the following section of this chapter.

2.2 Fuzzy CMAC models

Many researchers have integrated the fuzzy concept into the CMAC network, such as in (Chen 2001; Dai et al., 2010; Guo et al., 2002; Jou, 1992; Ker et al., 1997; Lai & Wong, 2001; Lee & Lin, 2005; Lee et al., 2007a; Lee et al., 2007b; Lin & Lee, 2008; Lin & Lee, 2009; Lin et al., 2008; Peng & Lin, 2011; Wang, 1994; Zhang & Qian, 2000). In general, they use membership functions rather than basis functions, and the resulting structures are then called fuzzy CMACs (FCMACs).

In addition, the work of (Mohajeri et al., 2009b) provides a review of FCMACs, including over 23 relative aspects such as membership function, memory layered structure, defuzzification and fuzzy systems, was provided. Even FCMACs have originally reduced memory requirement for the CMAC, further discussions of clustering (such as fuzzy C-mean, discrete incremental clustering and Bayesian Ying-Yang) and hierarchical approaches for reducing memory sizes of FCMACs themselves were overviewed in (Mohajeri et al., 2009b) as well. Furthermore, as divided in (Dai et al., 2010), there are two classes of FCMACs architectures, i.e., forward and feedback fuzzy neural networks, which is useful for beginners to have a big picture of the basic concept for the FCMACs.

In the following sections, being the example models in this chapter the self-constructing FCMAC (SC-FCMAC, Lee et al., 2007a) and the powerful parametric FCMAC (P-FCMAC, Lin & Lee, 2009) are reviewed, in order to provide readers the insight knowledge of how these FCMAC work. Companied by their corresponding architectures and learning schemes, illustrative examples of system identification are provided as well.

3. The self-constructing fuzzy CMAC

From relative architectures to learning algorithms this section provides a brief review and discussions of the self-constructing FCMAC (SC-FMAC, Lee et al., 2007a).

3.1 Architecture of the SC-FCMAC model

As illustrated in Fig. 2, the SC-FCMAC model (Lee et al., 2007a) consists of the input space partition, association memory selection, and defuzzification. Similar to the traditional CMAC model, the SC-FCMAC model approximates a nonlinear function $y = f(x)$ by applying the following two primary mappings:

$$S : X \Rightarrow A \tag{1}$$

$$P : A \Rightarrow D \tag{2}$$

where X is an s-dimensional input space, A is an N_A-dimensional association space, and D is a 1-dimensional (1-D) output space. These two mappings are realized by using fuzzy operations. The function $S(x)$ maps each point x in the input space onto an association vector $\alpha = S(x) \in A$ that has N_L nonzero elements ($N_L < N_A$). Here, $\alpha = (\alpha_1, \alpha_2, \ldots, \alpha_{N_A})$, where $0 \le \alpha \le 1$ for all components in α is derived from the composition of the receptive field functions and sensory inputs. Different from the traditional CMAC model, several hypercubes are addressed by the input state x. The hypercube values are calculated by product operation through the strength of the receptive field functions for each input state.

In the SC-FCMAC model, we use the Gaussian basis function as the receptive field function and the fuzzy weight function for learning. Some learned information is stored in the fuzzy weight vector. The 1-D Gaussian basis function can be given as follows:

$$\mu(x) = e^{-((x-m)/\sigma)^2} \tag{3}$$

where x represents the specific input state, m represents the corresponding center, and σ represents the corresponding variance.

Let us consider a N_D-dimensional problem. A Gaussian basis function with N_D dimensions is given as follows:

$$\alpha_j = \prod_{i=1}^{N_D} e^{-((x_i - m_{ij})/\sigma_{ij})^2} \tag{4}$$

where Π represents the product operation, α_j represents the j-th element of the association memory selection vector, x_i represents the input value of the i-th dimension for a specific input state x, m_{ij} represents the center of the receptive field functions, σ_{ij} represents the variance of the receptive field functions, and N_D represents the number of the receptive field functions for each input state. The function $P(a)$ computes a scalar output y by projecting the association memory selection vector onto a vector of adjustable fuzzy weights. Each fuzzy weight is inferred to produce a partial fuzzy output using the value of its corresponding association memory selection vector as the input matching degree. The fuzzy weight is considered here so that the partial fuzzy output is defuzzified into a scalar output using standard volume-based centroid defuzzification (Kosko, 1997; Paul & Kumar, 2002). The term volume is used in a general sense to include multi-dimensional functions. For 2-D functions, the volume reduces to the area. If v_j is the volume of the consequent set and ζ_j is the weight of the scale α_j, then the general expression for defuzzification is

$$y = \frac{\sum_{j=1}^{N_L} \alpha_j w_j^m v_j \zeta_j}{\sum_{j=1}^{N_L} \alpha_j v_j \zeta_j} \tag{5}$$

where w_j^m is the mean value of the fuzzy weights and N_L is the number of hypercube cells. The volume v_j in this case is simply the area of the consequent weights, which are represented by Gaussian fuzzy sets. Therefore, $v_j = w_j^{\alpha}\sqrt{\pi}$, where w_j^{α} represents the variance of the fuzzy weights. If the weight ζ_j is considered to be one, as in this work, then the actual output y is derived as

$$y = \frac{\sum_{j=1}^{N_L} \alpha_j w_j^m w_j^\alpha}{\sum_{j=1}^{N_L} \alpha_j w_j^\alpha}. \tag{6}$$

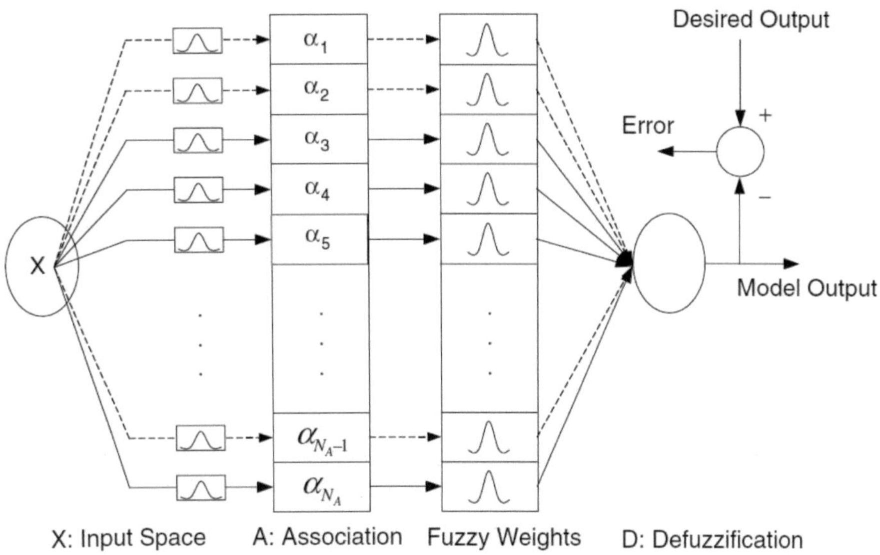

Fig. 2. Structure of the SC-FCMAC model (Lee et al., 2007)

3.2 Learning Algorithm of the SC-FCMAC

In this section, for completing the SC-FCMAC model (Lee et al., 2007a) the self-constructing learning algorithm, which consists of an input space partition scheme (i.e., scheme 1) and a parameter-learning scheme (i.e., scheme 2), is reviewed. First, the input space partition scheme is used to determine proper input space partitioning and to find the mean and the width of each receptive field function. This scheme is based on the self-clustering method (SCM) to appropriately determine the various distributions of the input training data. Second, the parameter-learning scheme is based on the gradient descent learning algorithm. To minimize a given cost function, the receptive field functions and the fuzzy weights are adjusted using the back-propagation algorithm. According to the requirements of the system, these parameters will be given proper values to represent the memory information. For the initial system, the values of the tuning parameters w_j^m and w_j^σ of the fuzzy weights are generated randomly, and the m and σ of the receptive field functions are generated by the proposed SCM clustering method.

3.2.1 The input space partition scheme

The receptive field functions can map input patterns. Hence, the discriminative ability of these new features is determined by the centers of the receptive field functions. To achieve good classification, centers are best selected based on their ability to provide large class separation.

An input space partition scheme, called the SCM, is used to implement scatter partitioning of the input space. Without any optimization, the proposed SCM is a fast, one-pass algorithm for a dynamic estimation of the number of hypercube cells in a set of data, and for finding the current centers of hypercube cells in the input data space. It is a distance-based connectionist-clustering algorithm. In any hypercube cell, the maximum distance between an example point and the hypercube cell center is less than a threshold value, which has been set as a clustering parameter and which would affect the number of hypercube cells to be estimated.

In the clustering process, the data examples come from a data stream, and the process starts with an empty set of hypercube cells. When a new hypercube cell is created, the hypercube cell center, *C*, is defined, and its hypercube cell distance and hypercube cell width, *Dc* and *Wd*, respectively, are initially set to zero. When more samples are presented one after another, some created hypercube cells will be updated by changing the positions of their centers and increasing the hypercube cell distances and hypercube cell width. Which hypercube cell will be updated and how much it will be changed depends on the position of the current example in the input space. A hypercube cell will not be updated any more when its hypercube cell distance, *Dc*, reaches the value that is equal to the threshold value D_{thr}.

Figure 3 shows a brief clustering process using the SCM in a two-input space. The detailed clustering process can be found in (Lee et al., 2007a).

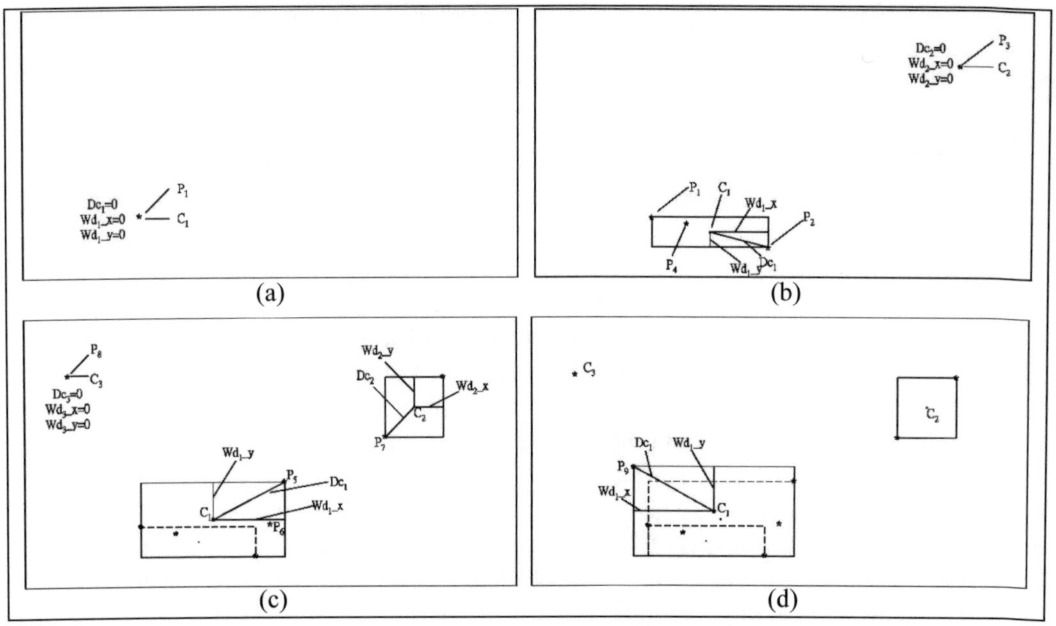

Fig. 3. A brief clustering process using the SCM with samples P_1 to P_9 in a 2-D space. (Notations: P_i for pattern, C_j for hypercube cell center, Dc_j is hypercube cell distance, Wd_j_x represents *x*-dimensions hypercube cell width, and Wd_j_y stands for *y*-dimensions hypercube cell width) (a) The example P_1 causes the SCM to create a new hypercube cell center C_1. (b) P_2: update hypercube cell center C_1, P_3: create a new hypercube cell center C_2, P_4: do nothing. (c) P_5: update hypercube cell C_1, P_6: do nothing, P_7: update hypercube cell center C_2, P_8: create a new hypercube cell C_3. (d) P_9: update hypercube cell C_1.

In this way, the maximum distance from any hypercube cell center to the examples that belong to this hypercube cell is not greater than the threshold value D_{thr}, though the algorithm does not keep any information on passed examples. The center and the jump positions of the receptive field functions are then defined by the following equation:

$$m_j = C_j,\ j = 1,2,...,n, \tag{7}$$

$$\theta_j^r = \frac{1}{\left((n_s+1)/2\right)} \cdot r \cdot D_j, \tag{8}$$

where $j = 1,2,...,n,$ and $r = 1,2,...,n_s$.

The threshold parameter D_{thr} is an important parameter in the input space partition scheme. A low threshold value leads to the learning of fine clusters (such that many hypercube cells are generated), whereas a high threshold value leads to the learning of coarse clusters (such that fewer hypercube cells are generated). Therefore, the selection of the threshold value D_{thr} critically affects the simulation results, and the threshold value is determined by practical experimentation or trial-and-error

3.2.2 The parameter-learning scheme

In the parameter-learning scheme, there are four adjustable parameters ($m_{ij}, \sigma_{ij}, w_j^m$, and w_j^σ) that need to be tuned. The parameter-learning algorithm of the SC-FCMAC model uses the supervised gradient descent method to modify these parameters. When we consider the single output case for clarity, our goal is to minimize the cost function E, defined as follows:

$$E = \frac{1}{2}\left(y^d(t) - y(t)\right)^2, \tag{9}$$

where $y^d(t)$ denotes the desired output at time t and $y(t)$ denotes the actual output at time t. The parameter-learning algorithm, based on back-propagation, is defined as follows.

The fuzzy weight cells are updated according to the following equations:

$$w_j^m(t+1) = w_j^m(t) + \Delta w_j^m, \tag{10}$$

$$w_j^\sigma(t+1) = w_j^\sigma(t) + \Delta w_j^\sigma \tag{11}$$

where j denotes the j-th fuzzy weight cell for j=1,2,…N_L, w_j^m the mean of the fuzzy weights, and w_j^σ the variance of the fuzzy weights. The elements of the fuzzy weights are updated by the amount

$$\Delta w_j^m = \eta \cdot e \cdot \frac{\partial y}{\partial w_j^m} = \eta \cdot e \cdot \frac{\alpha_j w_j^\sigma}{\sum_{j=1}^{N_L} \alpha_j w_j^\sigma} \tag{12}$$

$$\Delta w_j^{\sigma} = \eta \cdot e \cdot \frac{\partial y}{\partial w_j^{\sigma}} = \eta \cdot e \cdot \frac{\alpha_j w_j^m \sum_{j=1}^{N_L} \alpha_j w_j^{\sigma} - \alpha_j \sum_{j=1}^{N_L} \alpha_j w_j^m w_j^{\sigma}}{\left(\sum_{j=1}^{N_L} \alpha_j w_j^{\sigma}\right)^2} \tag{13}$$

where η is the learning rate of the mean and the variance for the fuzzy weight functions between 0 and 1, and e is the error between the desired output and the actual output, $e = y^d - y$.

The receptive field functions are updated according to the following equations:

$$m_{ij}(t+1) = m_{ij}(t) + \Delta m_{ij} \tag{14}$$

$$\sigma_{ij}(t+1) = \sigma_{ij}(t) + \Delta \sigma_{ij} \tag{15}$$

where i denotes the ith input dimension for i=1,2,…,n, m_{ij} denotes the mean of the receptive field functions, and σ_{ij} denotes the variance of the receptive field functions. The parameters of the receptive field functions are updated by the amount

$$\Delta m_{ij} = \eta \cdot e \cdot \frac{\partial y}{\partial \alpha_j} \cdot \frac{\partial \alpha_j}{\partial m_{ij}} = \eta \cdot e \cdot \frac{w_j^m w_j^{\sigma} \sum_{j=1}^{N_L} \alpha_j w_j^{\sigma} - w_j^{\sigma} \sum_{j=1}^{N_L} \alpha_j w_j^m w_j^{\sigma}}{\left(\sum_{j=1}^{N_L} \alpha_j w_j^{\sigma}\right)^2} \cdot \alpha_j \cdot \frac{2\left(x_i - m_{ij}\right)}{\sigma_{ij}^2} \tag{16}$$

$$\Delta \sigma_{ij} = \eta \cdot e \cdot \frac{\partial y}{\partial \alpha_j} \cdot \frac{\partial \alpha_j}{\partial \sigma_{ij}} = \eta \cdot e \cdot \frac{w_j^m w_j^{\sigma} \sum_{j=1}^{N_L} \alpha_j w_j^{\sigma} - w_j^{\sigma} \sum_{j=1}^{N_L} \alpha_j w_j^m w_j^{\sigma}}{\left(\sum_{j=1}^{N_L} \alpha_j w_j^{\sigma}\right)^2} \cdot \alpha_j \cdot \frac{2\left(x_i - m_{ij}\right)^2}{\sigma_{ij}^3} \tag{17}$$

where η is the learning rate of the mean and the variance for the receptive field functions.

3.3 An example: Learning chaotic behaviors

A nonlinear system $y(t)$ with chaotic behaviors (Wang, 1994) is defined by the following equations, i.e.,

$$\dot{x}_1(t) = -x_1(t)x_2^2(t) + 0.999 + 0.42\cos(1.75t) \tag{18}$$

$$\dot{x}_2(t) = x_1(t)x_2^2(t) - x_2(t) \tag{19}$$

$$y(t) = \sin\left(x_1(t) + x_2(t)\right) \tag{20}$$

We solved the differential Eqs. (18) and (19) with t from t=0 to t=20 and with $x_1(0)$=1.0 and $x_2(0)$=1.0. We obtained 107 values of $x_1(t)$ and $x_2(t)$ (the chaotic glycolytic oscillator, Wang, 1994) and 107 values of $y(t)$. Figure 4 shows $y(t)$, which is the desired function to be learned by the SC-FCMAC model.

The input data were $x_1^p(t)$ and $x_2^p(t)$, and the output data was $y^p(t)$, for p=1,2,...,107. For this chaotic problem, the initial parameters η=0.1 and D_{thr} =1.3 were chosen. First, using the SCA clustering method, we obtained three hypercube cells. The learning scheme then entered parameter learning using the back-propagation algorithm. The parameter training process continued for 200 epochs, and the final trained rms (root mean square) error was 0.000474. The number of training epochs is determined by practical experimentation or trial-and-error tests.

We compared the SC-FCMAC model with other models (Lin et al., 2004; Lin et al., 2001). Figure 5(a) shows the learning curves of the SC-FCMAC model, the FCMAC model (Lin et al., 2004), and the SCFNN model (Lin et al., 2001). As shown in this figure, the learning curve that resulted from our method has a lower rms error. Trajectories of the desired output $y(t)$ and the SC-FCMAC model's output are shown in Figures 5(b)-5(d). A comparison analysis of the SC-FCMAC model, the FCMAC model (Lin et al., 2004), and the SCFNN model (Lin et al., 2001) is presented in Table 1. It can be concluded that the proposed model obtains better results than some of the other existing models (Lin et al., 2004; Lin et al., 2001).

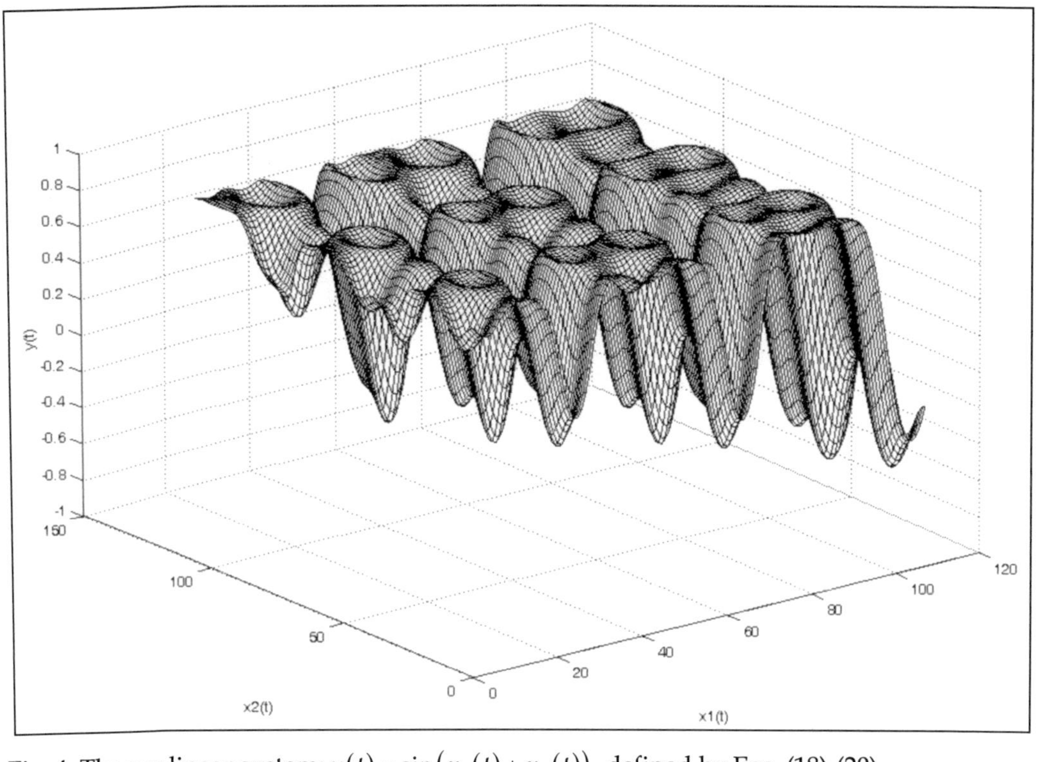

Fig. 4. The nonlinear system: $y(t)=\sin(x_1(t)+x_2(t))$, defined by Eqs. (18)-(20).

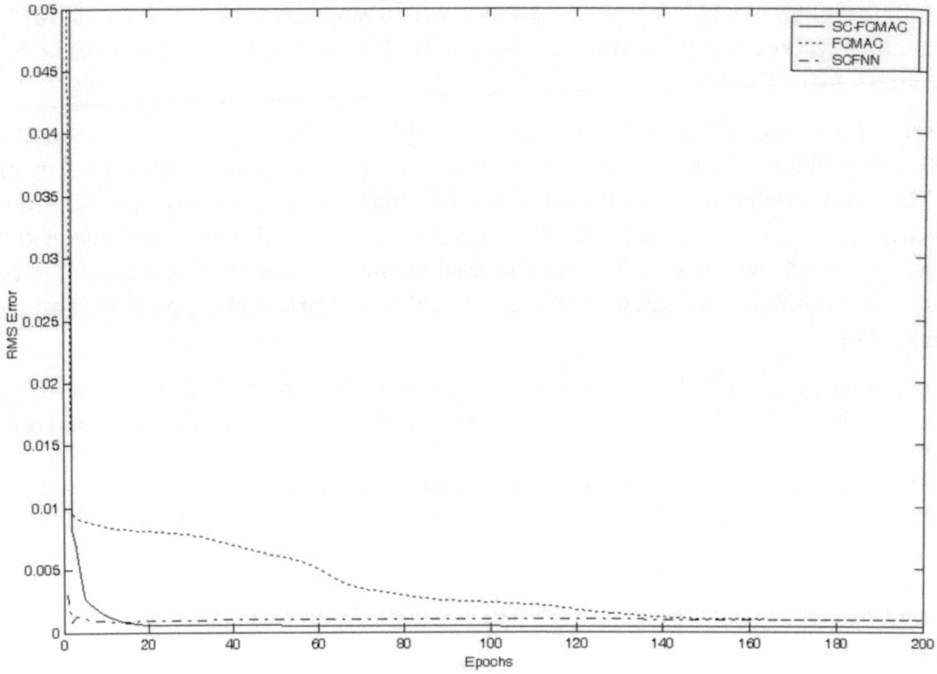
SC-FCMAC
FCMAC
SCFNN
RMS Error
Epochs
0.05
0.045
0.04
0.035
0.03
0.025
0.02
0.015
0.01
0.005
0
0 20 40 60 80 100 120 140 160 180 200

(a)

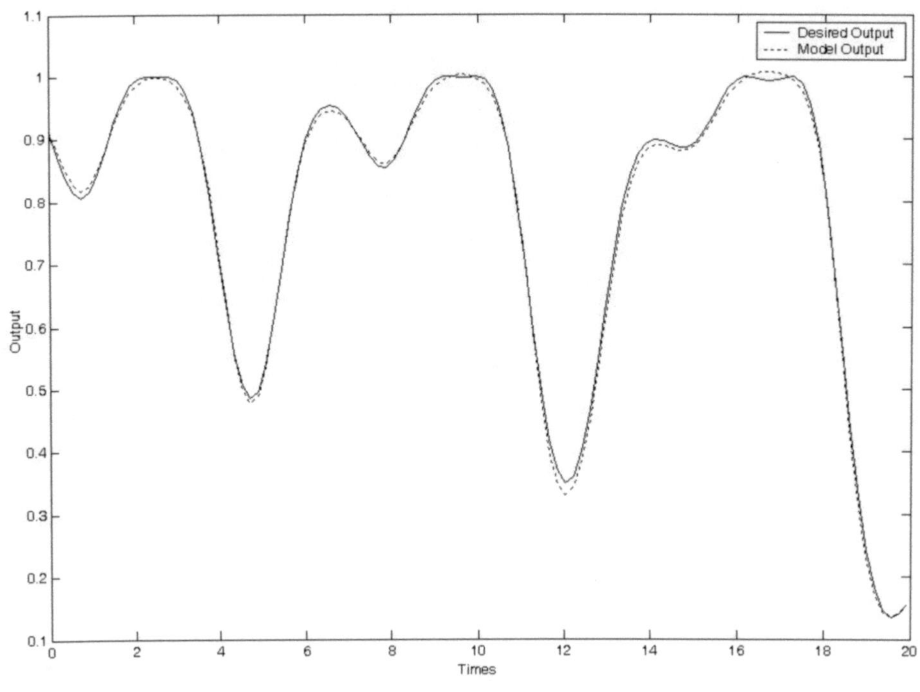
Desired Output
Model Output
Output
Times
1.1
1
0.9
0.8
0.7
0.6
0.5
0.4
0.3
0.2
0.1
0 2 4 6 8 10 12 14 16 18 20

(b)

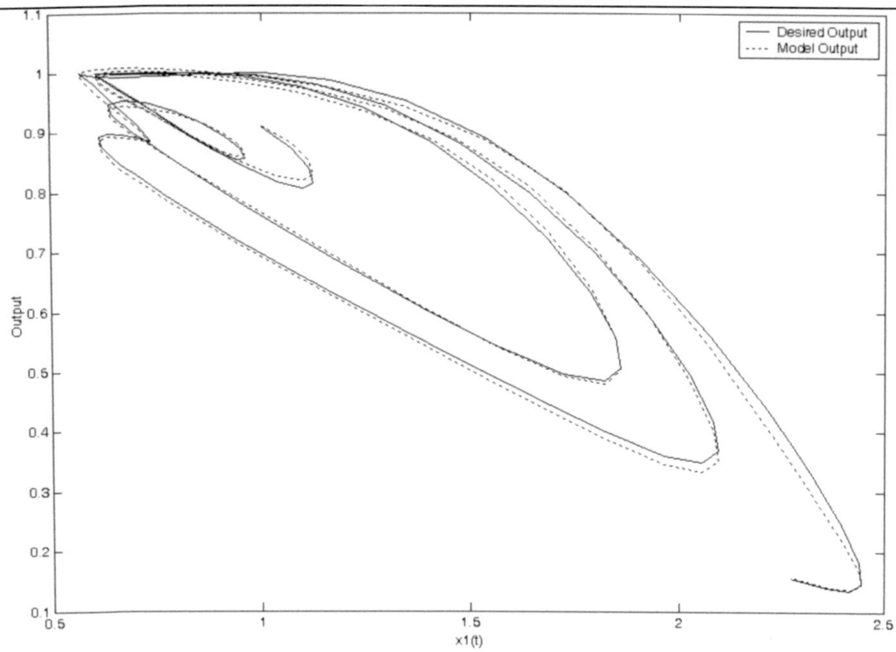

(c)

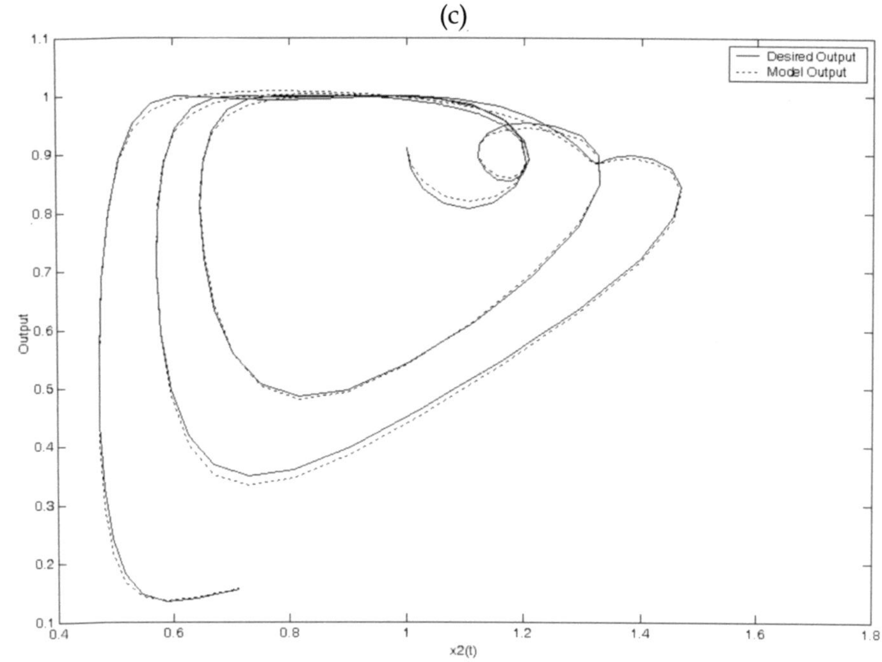

(d)

Fig. 5. Simulation results for learning chaotic behaviors. (a) Learning curves of the SC-FCMAC model, the FCMAC model (Lin et al., 2004), and the SCFNN model (Lin et al., 2001). (b) The desired output $y(t)$ and the SC-FCMAC model's output for time t dimension. (c) The desired output $y(t)$ and the SC-FCMAC model's output for $x_1(t)$ dimension. (d) The desired output $y(t)$ and the SC-FCMAC model's output for $x_2(t)$ dimension.

Items \ Models	SC-FCMAC	FCMAC (Lin et al., 2004)	SCFNN (Lin et al., 2001)
Training Steps	200	200	200
Parameters	18	18	20
Hypercube Cells	3	4	N/A
RMS errors	0.000474	0.000885	0.000908

Table 1. Comparisons of the SC-FCMAC model with some existing models for dynamic system identification

4. The parametric fuzzy CMAC (P-FCMAC)

In this section the architecture and learning algorithms of the parametric FCMAC (P-FCMAC, Lin & Lee, 2009) are reviewed, which mainly derived from the traditional CMAC and Takagi-Sugeno-Kang (TSK) parametric fuzzy inference system (Sugeno & Kang, 1988; Takagi & Sugeno, 1985). Since the SCM are inherent in the scheme of input-space partition for the P-FCMAC model, the performance of P-FCMAC is definitional better than the SC-FCMAC. Therefore, another system-identification problem is taken in order to explore the benefit of the P-FCMAC, fully and more fairly.

4.1 Architecture of the P-FCMAC model

As illustrated in Fig. 6, the P-FCMAC model consists of the input space partition, association memory selection, and defuzzification. The P-FCMAC network like the conventional CMAC network that also approximates a nonlinear function $y=f(x)$ by using two primary mappings, $S(x)$ and $P(\alpha)$. These two mappings are realized by fuzzy operations. The function $S(x)$ also maps each point x in the input space onto an association vector $\alpha= S(x)\in A$ that has N_L nonzero elements ($N_L < N_A$). Different from conventional CMAC network, the association vector $\alpha=(\alpha_1,\alpha_2,\cdots,\alpha_{N_A})$, where $0\le\alpha\le1$ for all components in α, is derived from the composition of the receptive field functions and sensory inputs. Another, several hypercubes is addressed by the input state x that hypercube value is calculated by product operation through the strength of the receptive field functions for each input state. In the P-FCMAC network, we use Gaussian basis function as the receptive field functions and the linear parametric equation of the network input variance as the TSK-type output for learning. Some learned information is stored in the receptive field functions and TSK-type output vectors. A one-dimension Gaussian basis function can be given as defined in Eq. (3). Similar to section 2.2, if a N_D-dimensional problem is considered a Gaussian basis function with N_D dimensions is expressed as Eq. (4) defined.

Each element of the receptive field functions is inferred to produce a partial fuzzy output by applying the value of its corresponding association vector as input matching degree. The partial fuzzy output is defuzzified into a scalar output y by the centroid of area (COA) approach. Then the actual output y is derived as,

$$y=\frac{\sum_{j=1}^{N_L}\alpha_j\left(a_{0j}+\sum_{i=1}^{N_D}a_{ij}x_i\right)}{\sum_{j=1}^{N_L}\alpha_j} \tag{21}$$

The j-th element of the TSK-type output vectors is described as

$$a_{0j} + \sum_{i=1}^{N_D} a_{ij} x_i \tag{22}$$

where a_{0j} and a_{ij} denote the scalar value, N_D the number of the input dimensions, N_L the number of hypercube cells, and x_i denotes the ith input dimension. Based on the above structure, a learning algorithm will be proposed to determine the proper network structure and its adjustable parameters.

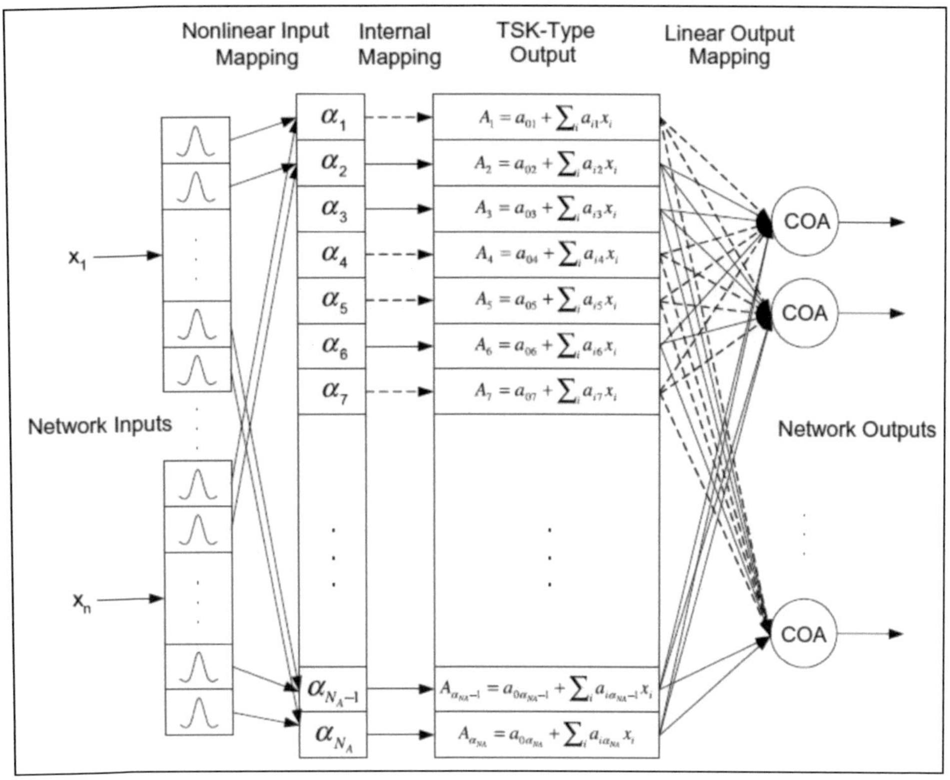

Fig. 6. Structure of the P-FCMAC model (Lin & Lee, 2009)

4.2 Learning algorithm of the P-FCMAC model

Similar to the SC-FCMAC model, the P-FCMAC's learning algorithm consists of an input space partition scheme and a parameter learning scheme. As the same SCM method was applied for input space partition, in the following paragraph the main focus is drawing to the scheme of parameter learning for the P-FCMAC, which is exhibited as in Figure 7.

First, the input space partition scheme (i.e., scheme 1) is used to determine proper input space partitioning and to find the mean and the width of each receptive field function. The input space partition is based on the SCM to appropriately determine the various distributions of the input training data. After the SCM, the number of hypercube cells is determined. That is, we can obtain the initial m and σ of receptive field functions by using SCM. Second, the parameter learning scheme (i.e., scheme 2) is based on supervised learning algorithms. The gradient descent learning algorithm is used to adjust the free parameters. To minimize a given cost function, the m and σ of the receptive field functions and the parameters a_{0j} and a_{ij} of the TSK-type output vector are adjusted using the backpropagation algorithm. According to the requirements of the system, these parameters will be given proper values to represent the memory information. For the initial system, the values of the tuning parameters a_{0j} and a_{ij} of the element of the TSK-type output vector are generated randomly and the m and σ of receptive field functions are generated by the proposed SCM clustering method.

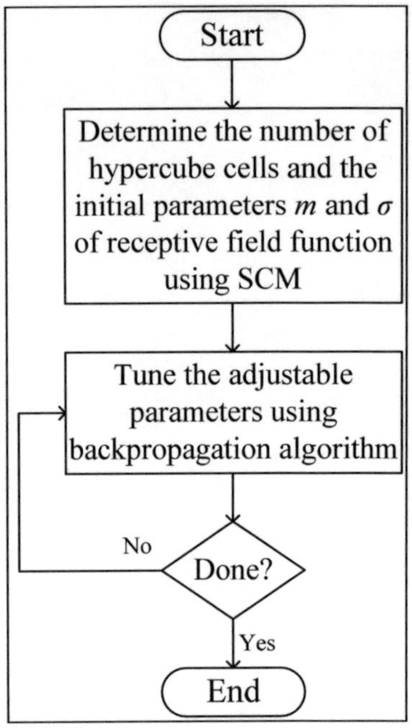

Fig. 7. Flowchart of the P-FCMAC model's learning scheme.

In the parameter learning scheme, there are four parameters need to be tuned, i.e. m_{ij}, σ_{ij}, a_{0j}, and a_{ij}. The total number of tuning parameters for the multi-input single-output P-FCMAC network is $2N_D{*}N_L{+}4N_L$, where N_D and N_L denote the number of inputs and hypercube cells, respectively. The parameter learning algorithm of the P-FCMAC network uses the supervised gradient descent method to modify these parameters. When we consider the single output case for clarity, our goal is to minimize the cost function E, defined as in Eq. (9).

Then their parameter learning algorithm, based on backpropagation, is described in detail as follows. The TSK-type outputs are updated according to the following equation:

$$a_{0j}(t+1) = a_{0j}(t) + \Delta a_{0j} \tag{23}$$

$$a_{ij}(t+1) = a_{ij}(t) + \Delta a_{ij} \tag{24}$$

where a_{0j} denotes the proper scalar, a_{ij} the proper scalar coefficient of the i-th input dimension, and j the j-th element of the TSK-type output vector for j=1,2,…,N_L. The elements of the TSK-type output vectors are updated by the amounts

$$\Delta a_{0j} = \eta \cdot e \cdot \frac{\partial y}{\partial a_{0j}} = \eta \cdot e \cdot \frac{\alpha_j}{\sum_{j=1}^{N_L} \alpha_j} \tag{25}$$

and

$$\Delta a_{ij} = \eta \cdot e \cdot \frac{\partial y}{\partial a_{ij}} = \eta \cdot e \cdot \frac{x_i \alpha_j}{\sum_{j=1}^{N_L} \alpha_j} \tag{26}$$

where η is the learning rate, between 0 and 1, and e is the error between the desired output and the actual output, $e = y^d - y$.

The receptive field functions are updated according to the following equation:

$$m_{ij}(t+1) = m_{ij}(t) + \Delta m_{ij} \tag{27}$$

$$\sigma_{ij}(t+1) = \sigma_{ij}(t) + \Delta \sigma_{ij} \tag{28}$$

where i denotes the i-th input dimension for i=1,2,…,n, m_{ij} the mean of the receptive field functions, and σ_{ij} the variance of the receptive field functions. The parameters of the receptive field functions are updated by the amounts

$$\begin{aligned} \Delta m_{ij} &= \eta \cdot e \cdot \frac{\partial y}{\partial \alpha_j} \cdot \frac{\partial \alpha_j}{\partial m_{ij}} \\ &= \eta \cdot e \cdot \frac{\left(a_{0j} + \sum_{i=1}^{N_D} a_{ij} x_i\right) \sum_{j=1}^{N_L} \alpha_j - \sum_{j=1}^{N_L} \alpha_j \left(a_{0j} + \sum_{i=1}^{N_D} a_{ij} x_i\right)}{\left(\sum_{j=1}^{N_L} \alpha_j\right)^2} \cdot \alpha_j \cdot \frac{2\left(x_i - m_{ij}\right)}{\sigma_{ij}^{\ 2}} \end{aligned} \tag{29}$$

and

$$\begin{aligned} \Delta \sigma_{ij} &= \eta \cdot e \cdot \frac{\partial y}{\partial \alpha_j} \cdot \frac{\partial \alpha_j}{\partial \sigma_{ij}} \\ &= \eta \cdot e \cdot \frac{\left(a_{0j} + \sum_{i=1}^{N_D} a_{ij} x_i\right) \sum_{j=1}^{N_L} \alpha_j - \sum_{j=1}^{N_L} \alpha_j \left(a_{0j} + \sum_{i=1}^{N_D} a_{ij} x_i\right)}{\left(\sum_{j=1}^{N_L} \alpha_j\right)^2} \cdot \alpha_j \cdot \frac{2\left(x_i - m_{ij}\right)^2}{\sigma_{ij}^{\ 3}} \end{aligned} \tag{30}$$

where η is the learning rate of the mean and the variance for the receptive field functions.

4.3 An example: Identification of a nonlinear system

In this example, a nonlinear system with an unknown nonlinear function, which is approximated by the P-FCMAC network as shown in Figure 8(b), is a model. First, some of training data from the unknown function are collected for an off-line initial learning process of the P-FCMAC network. After off-line learning, the trained P-FCMAC network is applied to the nonlinear system to replace the unknown nonlinear function for on-line test.

Consider a nonlinear system in (Wang, 1994) governed by the difference equation:

$$y(k+1) = 0.3y(k) + 0.6y(k-1) + g[u(k)] \tag{31}$$

We assume that the unknown nonlinear function has the form:

$$g(u) = 0.6\sin(\pi u) + 0.3\sin(3\pi u) + 0.1\sin(5\pi u) \tag{32}$$

For off-line learning, twenty-one training data pairs are provided in Table 2 using Eq. (31). The off-line learning configuration of the twenty-one training data points is shown in Figure 12 (a). And the on-line test configuration of the 1000 data points is shown in Figure 12 (b) that using the difference equation is defined as:

$$\hat{y}(k+1) = 0.3y(k) + 0.6y(k-1) + \hat{f}[u(k)] \tag{33}$$

where $\hat{f}[u(k)]$ is the approximated function for $g[u(k)]$ by the P-FCMAC network and $\alpha_0 = 0.3$, and $\alpha_1 = 0.6$. The error is defined as in Eq. (9)

In this example, the initial threshold value in the SCM is 0.15, and the learning rate is η=0.01. After the SCM clustering process, there are eleven hypercube cells generated. Using the first and second parameter learning schemes, the final trained error of the output approximates 0.00057 and 0.00024 after 300 epochs. The numbers of the adjustable parameters of the trained P-FCMAC network are 66.

For on-line testing, we assume that the series-parallel model shown in Figure 8 (b) is driven by $u(k) = \sin(2\pi k / 250)$. The test results of the P-FCMAC network are shown in Fig. 9(a) and (c) for the scheme-1 and scheme-2 methods. The errors between the desired output and the P-FCMAC network output are shown in Figs. 9(b) and (d) for the scheme-1 and scheme-2 methods. The learning curves of the scheme 1 and scheme 2 methods are shown in Fig. 10. Figures 9 can prove that the P-FCMAC network successfully approximates the unknown nonlinear function.

u	$g(u)$	$\hat{f}(u)$	u	$g(u)$	$\hat{f}(u)$
-1.0000	-0.0000	-0.000357	0.1000	0.5281	0.526161
-0.9000	-0.5281	-0.528020	0.2000	0.6380	0.640683
-0.8000	-0.6380	-0.628281	0.3000	0.4781	0.472271
-0.7000	-0.4781	-0.480252	0.4000	0.3943	0.400248
-0.6000	-0.3943	-0.392093	0.5000	0.4000	0.401699
-0.5000	-0.4000	-0.405011	0.6000	0.3943	0.390031
-0.4000	-0.3943	-0.390852	0.7000	0.4781	0.471195
-0.3000	-0.4781	-0.481167	0.8000	0.6380	0.648287
-0.2000	-0.6380	-0.635818	0.9000	0.5281	0.516553
-0.1000	-0.5281	-0.531204	1.0000	0.0000	0.007459
0.0000	0.0000	0.002119			

Table 2. Training data and approximated data obtained using the P-FCMAC network for 300 epochs

Table 3 shows the comparison the learning result among various models. The previous results were taken from (Wan & Li, 2003; Wang et al., 1995; Farag et al., 1998; Juang et al., 2000). The performance of the very compact fuzzy system obtained by the P-FCMAC network is better than all previous works.

Methods	Error	Methods	Error
P-FCMAC	0.00057 (Scheme 1) 0.00024 (Scheme 2)	Gradient Descent (Wang et al., 1995)	0.2841
SGA-SSCP (Wan & Li, 2003)	0.00028	MRDGA (Farag et al., 1998)	0.5221
Symbiotic Evolution (Juang et al., 2000)	0.1997	Genetic Algorithm et al. (Karr 1991)	0.67243

Table 3. Comparison results of the twenty-one training data for off-line learning.

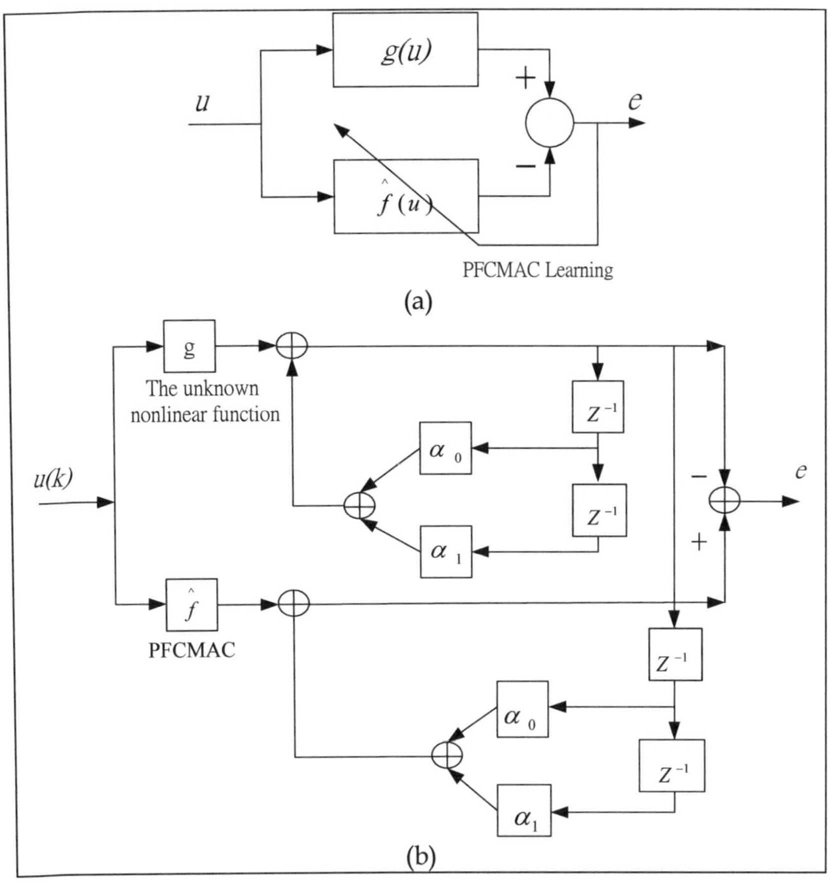

Fig. 8. The series-parallel identification model. (a) Off-line learning by twenty-one training data in Table IV; (b) On-line testing for real $u(k) = \sin(2\pi k / 250)$

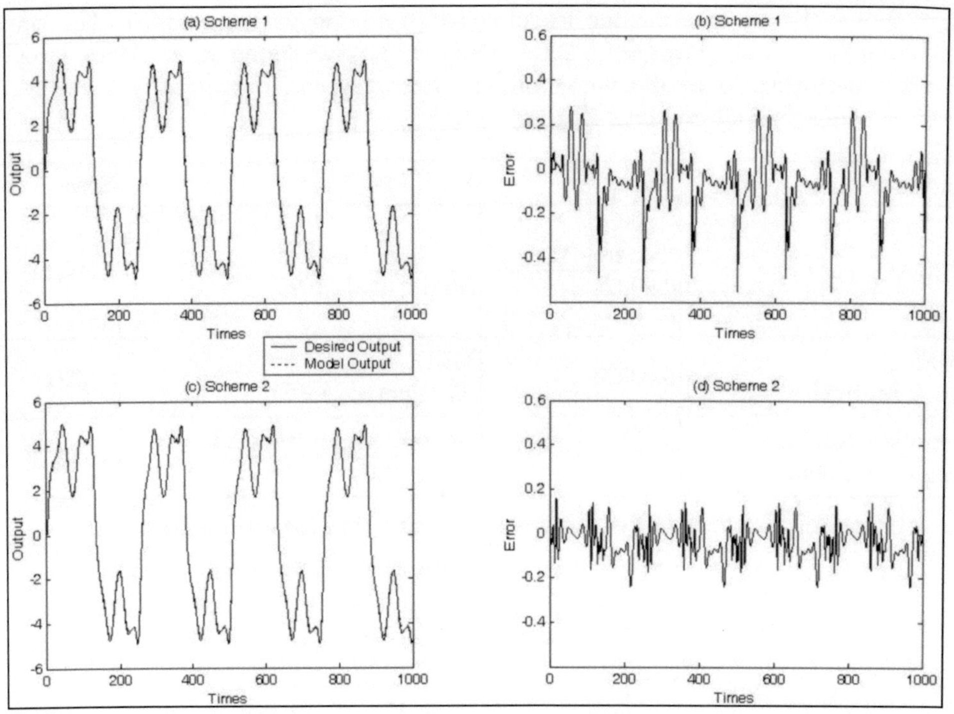

Fig. 9. Comparison of simulation results. (a) Outputs of the nonlinear system (solid line) and the identification model using the proposed network (dotted line) for the scheme 1 method. (b) Identification error of the approximated model for the scheme 1 method. (c) Outputs of the nonlinear system (solid line) and the identification model using the proposed network (dotted line) for the scheme 2 method. (d) Identification error of the approximated model for the scheme 2 method.

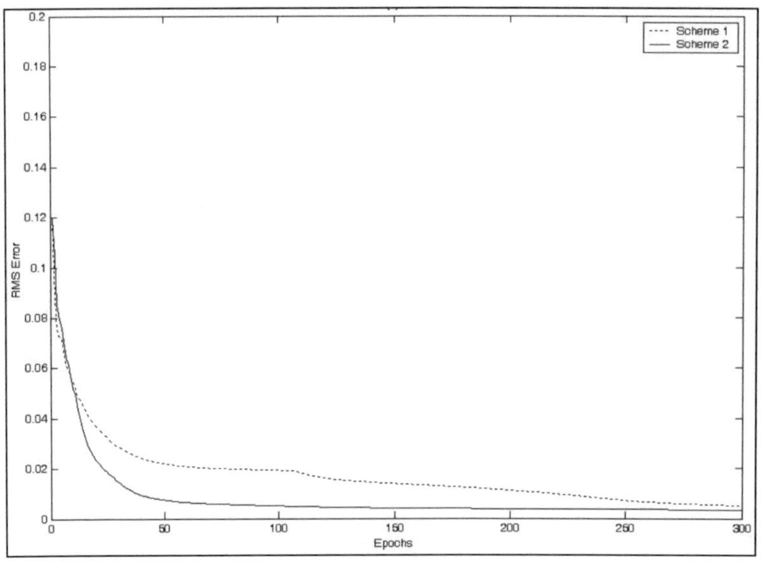

Fig. 10. Learning curves for the scheme 1 and scheme 2 parameter learning methods.

5. Conclusions

In this paper, starting from the discussion of traditional CMAC approach, two novel and latest developed fuzzy CMACs are reviewed. By summarizing the drawbacks of the CMAC model, relative improvement made in the literature have been addressed and presented. Via the exhibited self-constructing FCMAC (SC-FCMAC) and parametric FCMAC (P-FCMAC), not only the inference ability of FCMAC is demonstrated, but also presented the state-of-the art in the field of fuzzy inference systems.

6. References

Albus, J.S. (1975a). A new approach to manipulator control: The Cerebellar Model Articulation Controller (CMAC). *Transactions of the ASME: Journal of Dynamic Systems Measurement and Control*, Vol. 97, (September 1975), pp. 220-227, ISSN 0022-0434

Albus, J. S. (1975b). Data Storage in the Cerebellar Model Articulation Controller (CMAC). *Transactions of the ASME: Journal of Dynamic Systems Measurement and Control*, Vol. 97, (September 1975), pp. 228-233, ISSN 0022-0434

Chang, P.-L.; Yang, Y.-K.; Shieh, H.-L.; Hsieh, F.-H. & Jeng, M.-D. (2010). Grey Relational Analysis based Approach for CMAC Learning. *International Journal of Innovative Computing, Information and Control*, Vol.6, No.9, (September 2010), pp. 4001-4018, ISSN 1349-4198

Chen, J.Y. (2001). A VSS-type FCMAC Controller, *Proceedings of IEEE International Conference on Fuzzy Systems*, vol. 1, pp. 872-875, ISBN 0-7803-7293-X, December 2-5, 2001

Chow, M.Y. & Menozzi, A. (1994). A Self-organized CMAC Controller, *Proceedings of the IEEE International Conference on Industrial Technology*, pp. 68-72, ISBN 0-7803-1978-8, Guangzhou, China, December 5-9, 1994

Commuri, S. & Lewis, F.L. (1997). CMAC Neural networks for Control of Nonlinear Dynamical Systems: Structure, Stability, and Passivity. *Automatica*, Vol.33, No.4, (April 1997), pp. 635-641, ISSN 0005-1098

Dai, Y.; Liu, L. & Zhao, X. (2010) Modeling Of Nonlinear Parameters on Ship with Fuzzy CMAC Neural Networks, *Proceedings of IEEE International Conference on Information and Automation*, pp. 2070-2075, ISBN 978-1-4244-5701-4, June 20-23, Harbin, China, 2010.

Farag, W.A.; Quintana, V.H. & Lambert-Torres, G. (1998). A Genetic-Based Neuro-fuzzy Approach for Modeling and Control of Dynamical Systems. *IEEE Transactions on Neural Networks*, Vol.9, No.5, (September 1998), pp. 756–767, ISSN 1045-9227

Glanz, F.H.; Miller, W.T. & Graft, L. G. (1991). An Overview of the CMAC Neural Network, *Proceedings of IEEE Conference on Neural Networks for Ocean Engineering*, pp. 301-308, ISBN 0-7803-0205-2, Washington, DC, USA, August 15-17, 1991

Guo, C.; Ye, Z.; Sun, Z.; Sarkar, P. & Jamshidi, M. (2002). A Hybrid Fuzzy Cerebellar Model Articulation Controller Based Autonomous Controller. *Computers & Electrical Engineering: an International Journal*, (January 2002), Vol.28, pp.1-16, ISSN 0045-7906

Harmon, F.G.; Frank, A.A. & Joshi, S.S. (2005). The Control of a Parallel Hybrid-electric Propulsion System for a Small Unmanned Aerial Vehicle Using a CMAC Neural Network. *Neural Networks*, Vol.18, No.5-6, (June-July 2005), pp. 772-780. ISSN 0893-6080

Hung, C.P. & Wang, M.H. (2004). Diagnosis of Incipient Faults in Power Transformers Using CMAC Neural Network Approach. *Electric Power Systems Research*, Vol.71, No.3, (November 2004), pp. 235-244, ISSN 378-7796

Hwang, K.S. & Lin, C.S. (1998). Smooth Trajectory Tracking of Three-link Robot: a Self-Organizing CMAC Approach. *IEEE Transactions on Systems, Man, and Cybernetics, Part B: Cybernetics*, Vol.28, No.5, (October 1998), pp.680-692, ISSN 1083-4419

Iiguni, Y. (1996). Hierarchical Image Coding via Cerebellar Model Arithmetic Computers. *IEEE Transactions on Image Processing*, Vol.5, No.10, (October 1996), pp. 1393-1401, ISSN 1057-7149

Jou, C.C. (1992). A Fuzzy Cerebellar Model Articulation Controller, *Proceedings of IEEE International Conference on Fuzzy Systems*, pp. 1171-1178, ISBN 0-7803-0236-2, San Diego, CA, USA, March 8-12, 1992

Juang, C.F.; Lin, J.Y. & Lin, C.T. (2000). Genetic Reinforcement Learning through Symbiotic Evolution for Fuzzy Controller Design. *IEEE Transactions on Systems, Man, and Cybernetics, Part B: Cybernetics*, Vol.30, No.2, (Apr. 2000), pp. 290-302, ISSN 1083-4419

Karr, C.L. (1991) Design of an Adaptive Fuzzy Logic Controller Using a Genetic Algorithm, *Proceedings of the 4th International Conference on Genetic Algorithms*, ISBN 1-55860-208-9, pp. 450-457, San Diego, CA, USA, July 1991

Kasabov, N.K. & Song, Q. (2002). DENFIS: Dynamic Evolving Neural-Fuzzy Inference System and Its Application for Time-Series Prediction. *IEEE Transactions on Fuzzy Systems*, Vol.10, No.2, (April 2002), pp. 144-154, ISSN 1063-6706

Ker, J.S.; Hsu, C.C.; Huo, Y.H. & Liu, B.D. (1997). A Fuzzy CMAC Model for Color Reproduction. *Fuzzy Sets and Systems*, Vol.91, No.1, (October 1997), pp.53-68, ISSN 0165-0114

Kolcz, A. & Allinson, N.M. (1994). Application of the CMAC Input Encoding Scheme in the N-tuple Approximation Network, *IEE Proceedings of Computers and Digital Techniques*, Vol.141, No.3, (May 1994), pp. 177-183, ISSN 1350-2387

Kosko, B. (1997). *Fuzzy Engineering*, Prentice-Hall, ISBN 0-1312-4991-6, Englewood Cliffs, NJ.

Lai, H.R. & Wong, C.C. (2001). A Fuzzy CMAC Structure and Learning Method for Function Approximation, *Proceedings of IEEE International Conference on Fuzzy Systems*, Vol.1, pp. 436-439, ISBN 0-7803-7293-X, Melbourne, Australia, December 2-5, 2001

Lane, S. H., Handelman, D. A., & Gelfand, J. J. (1992). Theory and Development of Higher-Order CMAC Neural Networks. *IEEE Control Systems Magazine*, Vol.12, No.2, (April 1992), pp. 23-30, ISSN 1066-033X

Lee, C.-Y. & Lin, C.-J. (2005). A Self-Constructing Fuzzy CMAC Model for Learning Chaotic Behaviors. *GEST International Transactions on Computer Science and Engineering*, Vol.15, No.1, (July 2005), pp. 9-20, ISSN 1738-6438

Lee, C.-Y.; Lin, C.-J. & Chen, H.-J. (2007a). A Self-constructing Fuzzy CMAC Model and Its Applications. *Information Sciences: An International Journal*, Vol.177, No.1, (January 2007), pp. 264-280, ISSN 0020-0255

Lee, C.-Y.; Lin, C.-J. & Hsu, Y.-C. (2007b). A Parametric Fuzzy CMAC Model with Hybrid Evolutionary Learning Algorithms. *Journal of Multiple-Valued Logic and Soft Computing*, Vol.13, No.1-2, (February 2007), pp. 89-114, ISSN 1542-3980

Lee, H.M.; Chen, C.M. & Lu, Y.F. (2003). A Self-Organizing HCMAC Neural-Network Classifier. *IEEE Transactions on Neural Networks*, Vol.14, No.1, (January 2003), pp.15-27, ISSN 1045-9227

Lee, Z.J.; Wang, Y.P. & Su, S.F. (2004). A Genetic Algorithm based Robust Learning Credit Assignment Cerebellar Model Articulation Controller. *Applied Soft Computing*, Vol.4, No.4, (September 2004), pp. 357-367, ISSN 1568-4946

Leu, Y.-G.; Hong, C.-M.; Chen, Z.-R. & Liao, J.-H. (2010). Compact Cerebellar Model Articulation Controller for Ultrasonic Motors. *International Journal of Innovative Computing, Information and Control*, vol.6, No.12, (December 2010), pp. 5539-5552, ISSN 1349-4198

Lin, C.-J. & Lee, C.-Y. (2008). A Self-Organizing Recurrent Fuzzy CMAC Model for Dynamic System Identification. *International Journal of Intelligent Systems*, Vol.23, No.3, (March 2008), pp. 384-396, ISSN 1098-111X

Lin, C.-J. & Lee, C.-Y. (2009). A Novel Parametric Fuzzy CMAC Network and Its Applications. *Journal of Applied Soft Computing*, Vol.9, No.2, (March 2009), pp. 775-785, ISSN 1568-4946

Lin, C.-J.; Lee, C.-H. & Lee, C.-Y. (2008). A Novel Hybrid Learning Algorithm for Parametric Fuzzy CMAC Networks and Its Classification Applications. *Expert Systems with Applications*, Vol.35, No.4, (Nov. 2008), pp. 1711-1720, ISSN 0957-4174

Mese, E. (2003). A Rotor Position Estimator for Switched Reluctance Motors using CMAC. *Energy Conversion and Management*, Vol.44, No.8, (May 2003), pp. 1229-1245, ISSN 0196-8904

Miller, W.T.; Hewes, R.P.; Glanz, F.H. & Graft, L.G. (1990). Real-time Dynamic Control of an Industrial Manipulator using a Neural-Network Based Learning Controller. *IEEE Transactions on Robotics and Automation*, Vol.6, No.1, (February 1990), pp. 1-9, ISSN 1042-296X

Mohajeri, K.; Pishehvar, G. & Seifi, M. (2009a). CMAC Neural Networks Structures, *Proceedings of IEEE International Symposium on Computational Intelligence in Robotics and Automation*, pp. 39-45, ISBN 978-1-4244-4808-1, Daejeon, December 15-18, 2009

Mohajeri, K.; Zakizadeh, M.; Moaveni, B. & Teshnehlab, M. (2009b). Fuzzy CMAC Structures, *Proceedings of IEEE International Conference on Fuzzy Systems*, pp. 2126-2131, ISBN 978-1-4244-3596-8, August 20-24, Jeju Island, Korea, 2009

Paul, S. & Kumar, S. (2002). Subsethood-Product Fuzzy Neural Inference System (SuPFuNIS). *IEEE Transactions on Neural Networks*, Vol.13, No.3, (May 2002), pp. 578-599, ISSN 1045-9227

Peng, C.-C. & Lin, C.-J. (2011). A Self-Organizing Fuzzy CMAC Model for Classification Applications. *Innovative Computing, Information and Control Express Letters*, Vol.5, No.7, (July 2011), pp. 2389-2394, ISSN 1881-803X

Sugeno, M. & Kang, G.T. (1988). Structure Identification of a Fuzzy Model. *Fuzzy Sets and Systems*, Vol.28, No.1, (October 1988), pp. 15-33, ISSN 0165-0114

Takagi, T. & Segeno, M. (1985). Fuzzy Identification of Systems and Its Applications to Modeling and Control. *IEEE Transactions on Systems, Man, and Cybernetics, Part B: Cybernetics*, Vol.SMC-15, (January/Feburary 1985), pp. 116-132, ISSN 1083-4419

Tung, W.L. & Quek, C. (2002). GenSoFNN: A Generic Self-Organizing Fuzzy Neural Network. *IEEE Transactions on Neural Networks*, Vol.13, No.5, (September 2002), pp. 1075-1086, ISSN 1045-9227

Wan, W.Y. & Li, Y.H. (2003). Evolutionary Learning of BMF Fuzzy-Neural Networks Using a Reduced-Form Genetic Algorithm. *IEEE Transactions on Systems, Man, and Cybernetics, Part B: Cybernetics*, Vol.33, No.6, (December 2003), pp. 966–976, ISSN 1083-4419

Wang, C.H.; Wang, W.Y.; Lee, T.T. & Tseng, P.S. (1995). Fuzzy B-Spline membership Function (BMF) and Its Applications in Fuzzy-Neural Control. *IEEE Transactions on Systems, Man, and Cybernetics*, Vol.25, No.5, (May 1995), pp. 841–851, ISSN 0018-9472

Wang, D.-Y.; Lin, C.-J. & Lee, C.-Y. (2008). A New Pseudo-Gaussian-Based Recurrent Fuzzy CMAC Model for Dynamic Systems Processing. *International Journal of Systems Science*, Vol.39, No.3, (March 2008), pp. 289-304, ISSN 0020-7721

Wang, L.X. (1994). *Adaptive Fuzzy Systems and Control: Design and Stability Analysis*, Prentice-Hall, ISBN 0-1309-9631-9, Englewood Cliffs, NJ.

Wang, S. & Jiang, Z. (2004). Valve Fault Detection and Diagnosis Based on CMAC Neural Networks. *Energy and Buildings*, Vol.36, No.6, (June 2004), pp. 599-610, ISSN 0378-7788

Wu, J. & Pratt, F. (1999). Self-Organizing CMAC Neural Networks and Adaptive Dynamic Control, *Proceedings of IEEE International Symposium on Intelligent Control/Intelligent Systems and Semiotics*, pp. 259-265, ISBN 0-7803-5665-9, Cambridge, MA, USA, September 15-17, 1999

Zhang, K. & Qian, F. (2000). Fuzzy CMAC and Its Application, *Proceedings of the 3rd World Congress on Intelligent Control and Automation*, pp. 944-947, ISBN 0-7803-5995-X, Hefei, China, June 28-July 2, 2000

Section 7

Application to Civil Engineering Problems

21

Fuzzy Inference System as a Tool for Management of Concrete Bridges

Amir Tarighat
Civil Engineering Department, Shahid Rajaee Teacher Training University
Iran

1. Introduction

Bridges are important infrastructures all over the world. We have invested and spent a lot of money in constructing them. Also we assign big budgets for their maintenance, repair and strengthening annually. Since the number of bridges is increasing the amount of money needed to preserve the existing bridges at minimum standard level is considerable. In order to make decision for optimal budgeting we should know how bridges respond to various kinds of deteriorating factors and what their current and future conditions will be.

Why bridges need maintenance, repair and strengthening depend on many factors. Deterioration of bridges is due to aging, material deterioration under environmental conditions, increasing traffic volume and higher weights of vehicles. There are many factors which are responsible to make decision what the current condition and/or rating of a bridge is. Practically to make logical and defendable decisions the main action is to inspect bridges. Inspection provides a lot of collected data that should be stored and retrieved at any required time to obtain useful and practical information regarding the bridge condition and its immediate need. At this stage and by appropriate information in hand it can be possible to predict the remaining service lives of bridges.

Bridges are susceptible to many defects during their service lives. The main common defects that occur on cast-in-place concrete slab (deck) bridges include: cracking, scaling, delamination, spalling, efflorescence, honeycombs, pop-outs, wear, collision damage, abrasion, overload damage, reinforcing steel corrosion (Chen & Duan, 2000; Hartle et al., 2002). These defects are symptoms showing some kinds of deteriorations. Inspectors should report these symptoms and consequently type of deterioration(s) should be diagnosed.

Inspecting a concrete bridge deck includes visual and advanced inspection methods. The inspection of concrete bridge deck for symptoms like cracks, spallings, and other defects is primarily a visual activity. However, hammers and chain drags can be used to detect areas of delamination. In addition, several advanced techniques are available for concrete bridge deck inspection. Nondestructive methods include: acoustic wave sonic/ultrasonic velocity measurements, electrical methods, electromagnetic methods, rebound and penetration methods, carbonation and so many others if needed (Hartle et al., 2002).

Visual inspection is the primary method used to evaluate the condition of the majority of the existing bridges. Visual inspection is a subjective assessment and it may have a significant impact on the diagnosis and decisions to be made. For example a defect reported from one inspector may be different from the others. In order to overcome this unwilling fact nondestructive testing methods have been suggested for objective inspection in recent decades. Although these methods are more accurate than visual inspection, there are some kinds of problems. Interpretation of their results needs experience together with the knowledge about deteriorations of bridge material and damage types of its elements. Therefore results of visual inspection and some nondestructive testing methods are inherently uncertain and vague. It is to notify that the linguistically describing results are more uncertain and vague. Degree of uncertainty and level of vagueness depend on many parameters such as inspector's experience, definition of symptom or deterioration type, level of defect categorizations and many others.

Among many methods it seems that models based on artificial intelligence which apply soft computing methods are more attractive for dealing with uncertain and vague data in managing bridges. Fuzzy Inference System (FIS) is capable of being used in areas for decision making when data is uncertain. One of the most attractive advantages of FIS is its tolerability to noisy (uncertain and vague) data.

Based on the type of problems with uncertain and vague data, different FIS modeling types can be regarded as appropriate and easy methods for managing bridges (Tarighat & Miyamoto, 2009).

After introduction section this chapter continues with section 2 and its subsections showing the need for managing bridges and introduces Bridge Management System and Bridge Health Monitoring system. Ambiguity in diagnosis and decision making based on the collected data in above mentioned systems are discussed in section 3. Section 4 explains why fuzzy inference systems are suitable in managing systems. Its subsections are about fuzzy inference systems including Mamdani's method and Adaptive Neuro Fuzzy Inference System (ANFIS) method. Then some case studies and some typical applications of fuzzy inference system for managing bridges are included in section 5. Section 6 concludes this chapter.

2. Managing bridges

All the inspection data should be stored in inventory and inspection databases and they should be used to get information for what to do in the next step of managing bridges. Therefore a kind of managing system is required to use the data and making appropriate and logical decisions for further actions.

2.1 Bridge Management System

Bridge Management System (BMS) has great roles in managing bridges. The main feed into any BMS is inspection data. It is designed to provide information not easily available from available data. BMS can provide the following:

- Improvements in the type and quality of data that is collected, stored, managed, and used in a bridge system analysis
- A logical method for setting priorities for current needs
- Realistic and reliable forecasts of future needs
- Ways to implement changes in management philosophies and goals

It is obvious that how and to what extents the above mentioned items can be fulfilled by the available data.

In general, the condition of a BMS element is identified by condition states and corresponding condition state language. Each element has a range of minimum to maximum condition states. Information from each BMS element along with expert input to predict how the condition of that element will change over time is used in BMS computer programs. BMS programs can estimate future network funding levels based on the predicted future bridge conditions and the corresponding costs to repair or replace them (Washington State Bridge Inspection Manual, 2010).

The following outline provides a short BMS summary for a typical inspection:

- Identify the BMS elements that apply to the structure.
- Determine the total quantity for each element.
- Inspect bridge and record the deficient quantity for each element in the corresponding condition state.

2.2 Bridge Health Monitoring System

Generally in advanced BMS there is a module named Bridge Health Monitoring System (BHMS). BHMS can be considered as one of the most important parts of a practical BMS.

In bridge structures there are many different unforeseen conditions that we do not have enough information about them. Although in design codes we are forced to consider some parameters or factors affecting structural behavior there are even more items that we cannot consider them practically. Therefore it is probable to have some risk for not fulfilling the complete standards of safety. Presently health and performance are described based on subjective indices which are not precise. In addition there are some possibilities for unobserved and undiscovered symptoms, deteriorations, and damages in bridge structures due to limited or no accessibility to some elements. The immediate consequence is that the real health index is not that thought and considered. This unwilling fact impacts the effectiveness and reliability of any managerial decision irrespective of sophistication in the management process. Moreover, even experienced engineers may find visual signs of defects, deterioration and damage and cannot be able to diagnose the causative mechanisms, or their impact on the reliability of the bridge and its global health. The global health of a bridge as a whole system, inclusive of the performance criteria corresponding to each limit states is actually what is needed for effective managerial decisions. There are needs of periodic inspections to detect deterioration resulting from normal operation and environmental attack or inspections following extreme events, such as earthquakes or hurricanes. To quantify these system performance measures requires some means to monitor and evaluate the integrity of bridge structures while in service (Wang & Zong, 2002). BHMS can help managers to know about the healthiness of a bridge at any given time.

BHMS may also have other applications. For example any damage in some elements of a bridge has direct effect on its load bearing capacity especially vibration characteristics. In other words this effect can change the overall behavior of the bridge under loads which cause the bridge to vibrate. Based on this fact any method for damage detection which is capable of showing the location and severity of damage can be considered useful for bridge maintenance and repair departments (Haritos, 2000).

Bridge real time monitoring during service provides information on structural behavior under predicted loads, and also registers the effects of unpredicted overloading. Data obtained by monitoring is useful for damage detection, safety evaluation, and determination of the residual load bearing capacity of bridges. Early damage detection is particularly important because it leads to appropriate and timely interventions. If the damage is not detected, it continues to propagate and the bridge no longer guarantees required performance levels. Late detection of damage results in either very elevated refurbishment costs or, in some cases, the bridge has to be closed and dismantled. In seismic areas the importance of monitoring is more critical. Subsequent auscultation of a bridge structure that has not been monitored during its construction can serve as a basis for prediction of its present and future structural behavior. Based on these facts there are many applications for developing BHMS. As mentioned one of the most important applications of BHMS is damage detection. Among the attractive methods for damage detection problems are models based on artificial intelligence especially soft computing methods (Ou et al., 2006; Wu & Abe, 2003).

As it is used several times in above paragraphs, health can be defined as the reliability of a bridge structure to perform adequately for the required functionalities (Aktan et al., 2002). Some of these functionalities are:

- Utility
- Serviceability and durability
- Safety and stability of failure at ultimate limit states
- Safety at conditional limit states

It is not possible to quantify health and reliability of a bridge system for many of the limit states without extensive data that we often do not have. Based on a general definition monitoring is the frequent or continuous observation or measurement of structural conditions or actions (Wenzel & Tanaka, 2006). There is another definition which gives more detail: structural health monitoring is the use of in-situ, non-destructive sensing and analysis of structural characteristics, including the structural response, for detecting changes that may indicate damage or degradation [Housner & Bergman, 1997). Fig. 1 shows basic components of a typical BMS and BHMS.

In summary BMS and BHMS are used to:

- Structural management
- Increase of safety
- Knowledge improvement
- Rating the current condition of bridge or its components
- Predicting the remaining service life
- Structural/system identification
- Damage detection/diagnosis and damage localization
- Forced vibration-based damage detection
- Wind induced vibration-based damage detection
- Ambient vibration-based damage detection

- Remote sensing and wireless sensor networks
- Life cycle performance design

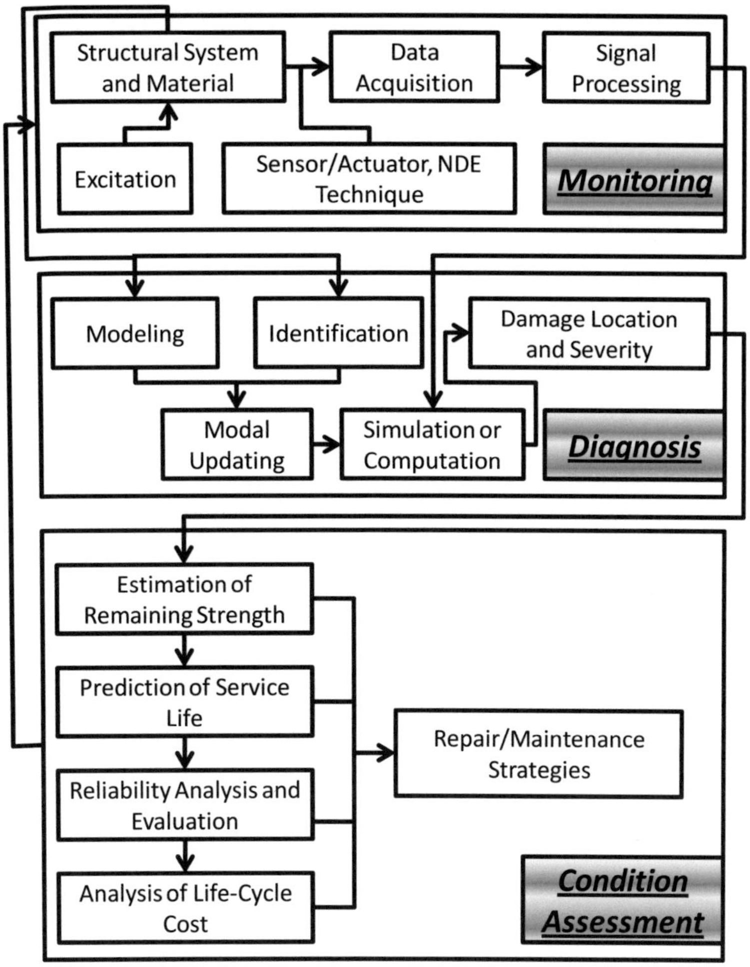

Fig. 1. Basic components of a typical BMS and BHMS

3. Ambiguity in diagnosis and decision making

Recently it is become obvious that although BMS and BHMS can be precisely used for managerial issues but there is an important fact about the collected data. Data is not perfect. It is found that the results and data-driven interpretations are prone to some degree of vagueness. Therefore, the obtained data that should be altered to information has inherently some degrees of uncertainty and vagueness (Tarighat & Miyamoto, 2009).

In managing a bridge we are concerned about condition state or standard level of a requirement. For example we want to know what the current condition state of a bridge is and to how it has been deviated from the previous and known condition state (Washington State Bridge Inspection Manual, 2010).

In most cases diagnosis is necessary to make decision for next action to return to a standard bridge condition state. Whenever we are going to diagnose, it is common to have circumstances in which we must make decision via ambiguous data and information. Practical diagnosis in managing bridges is the making of judgments about a bridge's condition state or damage detection using expert knowledge, but the observation of symptoms includes results of visual inspection and non destructive testing methods, bridge's history, and the circumstances of the diagnosis. For example, if we think about diagnosis during a regular inspection versus before a repairing operation, indications of possible deterioration or damage and need for retesting are important in the former, but in the latter, importance is placed on certainty rather than possibility. Normally a repairing operation is not performed without confirmation of the existence of deterioration or damage in the affected element of a bridge.

The words we use concerning symptoms often contain expressions of frequency and probability, such as *sever cracks* or *high corrosion*. In contrast to this kind of linguistic ambiguity, ambiguous circumstances exist in the distinguishing of the symptom, such as different inspectors' reporting differing symptoms.

When thinking about the ambiguity that originates in the characteristics discussed above, we must also consider the ambiguity that arises from the participation of experts in the bridge evaluation. In general, there is a large dependence on visual inspection results, which are subjective judgments. Since visual inspection is cheaper, faster and sometimes simpler than other inspecting methods it is more probable to have more ambiguity levels in data and interpretations (Terano et al., 1992).

Here are some more detailed explanations of the ambiguity in managing bridges. Condition rating is a judgment of a bridge component condition in comparison to its original as-built condition at a given time (Wang & Hu, 2006). Condition rating and damage detection are crucial methods and tools to conduct efficient maintenance and managing bridges. Condition rating indices are also useful for predicting future states which are completely time dependent. Based on the periodic inspections data at different time intervals deterioration rate of the material, elements and sometimes whole structure can be modeled. These models can be good tools for decision makers in future (Zadeh, 1976).

Related to condition rating definition there is another problem: what is the exact meaning of condition or health for material or bridge element in the structure? From practical point of view deterioration or damage symptoms should be easily distinguished. But in practice symptoms as signs of deteriorations cannot be easily distinguished and be reported or categorized in well-defined manner. Here, it becomes clear what the *subjective data* means. In other words the encoding of symptoms into condition rating is imprecise and involves *subjective judgments*.

Of greatest importance is the amount of variability found in the assignment of condition ratings at a given time. As an example results of the deck delamination survey conducted during some investigations indicate that this type of inspection does not consistently provide accurate results. In a case study the condition rating results analysis and the data revealed that the condition ratings were normally distributed. Table 1 shows the summary of statistical information from routine inspection for deck condition rating (Phares et al., 2000, 2001; Graybeal et al., 2001; Moore et al., 2001).

Bridge	Element	Average	Standard Deviation	Minimum	Maximum	Mode	N	Reference Rating
A	Deck	5.8	0.81	3	7	6	49	5
B	Deck	4.9	0.94	2	7	5	48	4
C	Deck	5.2	0.92	3	7	6	49	4
D	Deck	4.8	0.94	2	6	5	48	5
E	Deck	4.5	0.74	3	6	5	48	4
F	Deck	7.1	0.53	6	8	7	49	7
G	Deck	5.8	0.92	4	7	5	24	7

Table 1. Statistical information from routine inspection for deck condition rating (Phares et al., 2001).

The range of the results between min and max show the stochastic nature of the inspector's judgment. These stochastic representations show the fuzzy nature of the inspectors' judgments.

While current rating systems of concrete structures may give a fundamental understanding of structural deterioration conditions, their application is more or less limited in reflecting actual conditions. In some cases it is often difficult to cover complex structural behavior and environment in the real world. Uncertainties and fuzziness, along with complexity, add more difficulty to the estimation of condition rating by conventional methods. Therefore a better method may be a combination of logics and statistics. To take advantage of this approach in dealing with qualitative issues such as human factors, the influence of inspectors' judgment on structural condition rating and the effects of weather conditions on inspectors' judgment should be considered (Harris, 2006; Ma, 2006; Stephens, 2000; Wang et al., 2007; Yen & Langari, 1999).

Since the bridge inspection results are subjected to some degrees of imprecision and vagueness it is a good idea to use fuzzy set theory to overcome the shortcomings and problems of ordinary methods for prediction of condition of bridges. Fuzzy information or fuzzy data can be encountered in managing bridges. The main reasons for fuzzy data are imprecision in measured data and subjective judgments.

Knowledge engineering methods for dealing with uncertainty in many aspects of condition prediction are used to produce expert systems. Expert systems are expected to be effective for ill-defined problems (problems in which it is either difficult or impossible to define a method of approach).

In most cases, either the clear knowledge of ill-defined problems cannot be obtained, or completion of the knowledge set must be approached gradually. In other words, there are many cases in which knowledge is *ambiguous*. Meaning of the word *ambiguous* is also ambiguous and vague. Just as knowledge must be formulated and written down for a user to understand it, ambiguity must take some form before it can be dealt with technically. Therefore, ambiguity that is dealt with in knowledge engineering is classified and written down as follows:

- Nondeterminism
- Multiple meanings
- Uncertainty

- Incompleteness
- Fuzziness or imprecision

Uncertainty and fuzziness have a particularly close relationship with each other and systems that handle knowledge with fuzziness have been created even in the field of knowledge engineering (Terano et al., 1992).

One of the best ways of dealing with this kind of problems is the application of fuzzy inference system. Fuzzy inference system is capable of dealing with imprecise, imperfect, uncertain and vague data and information. Thus, it can be good candidate toward development of practical BMS and BHMS.

A measure of imprecision is advantageous for symptoms representation. Uncertainty characterizes a relation between symptoms and deteriorations/damages, while imprecision is associated with the symptoms representation.

4. Fuzzy inference systems and managing bridges

Fuzzy logic is an interesting and easy-to-use method for practical inference problems in engineering. It relates significance and precision to each other very well. Fuzzy logic-based inference systems enable the use of engineering judgment, experience and scarce field data to translate the level of deterioration or damage to condition rating (Rajani et al., 2006).

One of the best methods to deal with decision making problems such as condition rating of bridges is application of Fuzzy Inference System (FIS). In order to diagnose deterioration type or damage detection in concrete bridges and to increase accuracy and errors reduction caused by subjective human judgment fuzzy inferring is the appropriate choice (Wang & Hu 2006). Fuzzy sets can be used for modeling uncertainty of detection and imprecision of symptoms.

Detection support systems operate on rules with fuzzy premises, which represent imprecise symptoms. During inference fuzzy relations or implications are used, so conclusions are also represented in the form of fuzzy sets (Straszecka, 2006).

4.1 Fuzzy inference system

System modeling based on conventional mathematical tools (e.g., differential equations) is not well suited for dealing with ill-defined and uncertain systems. By contrast, a fuzzy inference system employing fuzzy *if-then* rules can model the qualitative aspects of human knowledge and reasoning processes without employing precise quantitative analyses. A Fuzzy Inference System (FIS) is a way of mapping an input space to an output space using fuzzy logic. A FIS tries to formalize the reasoning process of human language by means of fuzzy logic (that is, by building fuzzy IF-THEN rules). This *fuzzy modeling* or *fuzzy identification*, first explored systematically by Takagi and Sugeno, has found numerous practical applications in control different engineering application and fields.

Fuzzy if-then rules or *fuzzy conditional statements* are expressions of the form *IF A THEN B*, where A and B are labels of *fuzzy sets* characterized by appropriate membership functions. Due to their concise form, fuzzy if-then rules are often employed to capture the imprecise modes of reasoning that play an essential role in the human ability to make decisions in an environment of uncertainty and imprecision.

Another form of fuzzy if-then rule has fuzzy sets involved only in the premise part. By using Takagi and Sugeno's fuzzy if-then rule, we can use a relationship among variables or simply a formula. However, the consequent part is described by a nonfuzzy equation of the input variable.

Both types of fuzzy if-then rules have been used extensively in both modeling and control. Through the use of linguistic labels and membership functions, a fuzzy if-then rule can easily capture the spirit of a "rule of thumb" used by humans. From another angle, due to the qualifiers on the premise parts, each fuzzy if-then rule can be viewed as a local description of the system under consideration. Fuzzy if-then rules form a core part of the fuzzy inference system. Fig. 2 shows the general form of a Fuzzy Inference System (FIS) (Jang, 1993).

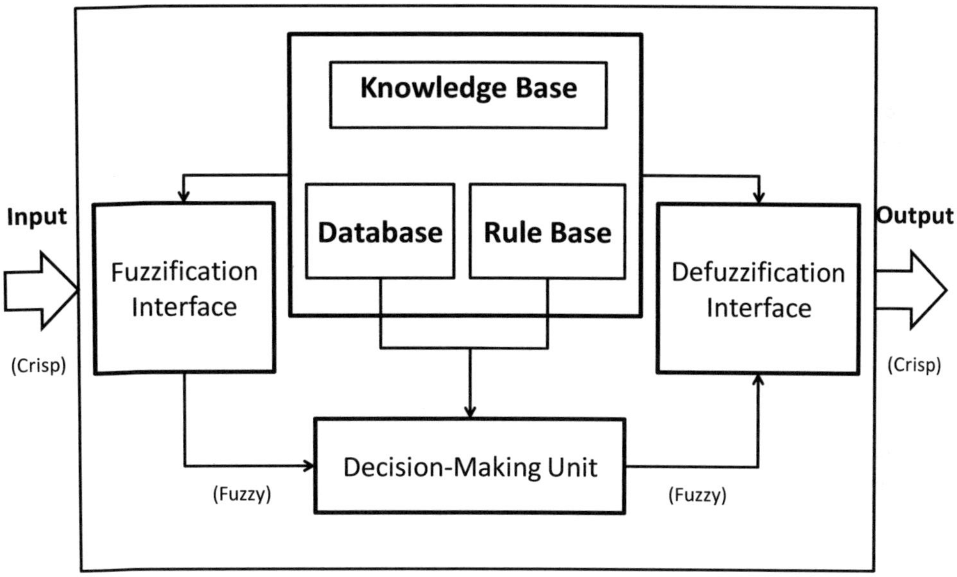

Fig. 2. Fuzzy Inference System (FIS)

4.1.1 Mamdani's method

Mamdani's method is the most commonly used in applications, due to its simple structure fuzzy calculations. This method as a simple FIS method is used to solve almost general decision making problems for practical issues.

Let X be the universe of discourse and its elements be denoted as x. In the fuzzy theory, fuzzy set A of universe X is defined by function $\mu_A(x)$ called the membership function of set.

$$m_A(x): X \in [0,1], \text{ where } \mu_A(x) = 1 \text{ if } x \text{ is totally in } A;$$

$$\mu_A(x) = 0 \text{ if } x \text{ is not in } A;$$

$$0 < \mu_A(x) < 1 \text{ if } x \text{ is partly in } A.$$

This set allows a continuum of possible choices. For any element x of universe X, membership function $\mu_A(x)$ equals the degree to which x is an element of set A. This degree, a value between 0 and 1, represents the degree of membership, also called membership value, of element x in set A. Any universe of discourse consists of some sets describing some attributes to the output. The main idea of fuzzy set theory is dealing with linguistic variables (Tarighat & Miyamoto, 2009).

A linguistic variable is a fuzzy variable. For example, the statement "a is b" implies that the linguistic variable *a* takes the linguistic value *b*. In fuzzy systems, linguistic variables are used in fuzzy rules. The range of possible values of a linguistic variable represents the universe of discourse of that variable. A fuzzy rule can be defined as a conditional statement in the form:

IF (x is a) THEN (y *is* b)

where x and y are linguistic variables; and a and b are linguistic values determined by fuzzy sets on the universe of discourses X and Y, respectively. The main and most important characteristic of fuzzy systems is that fuzzy rules relate fuzzy sets to each other. Fuzzy sets provide the basis for output estimation model. The model is based on relationships among some fuzzy input parameters (Baldwin, 1981).

All these definitions and arrangements are used to infer output based on the inputs. The most commonly used fuzzy inference technique is the so-called Mamdani method. Mamdani method is widely accepted for capturing expert knowledge. It allows describing the expertise in more intuitive, more human-like manner. However, Mamdani-type fuzzy inference entails a substantial computational burden.

The Mamdani-style fuzzy inference process is performed in four steps:

Step 1. Fuzzification of the input variables

The first step is to take the crisp inputs, $x1$ and $y1$, and determine the degree to which these inputs belong to each of the appropriate fuzzy sets.

Step 2. Rule evaluation

The second step is to take the fuzzified inputs and apply them to the antecedents of the fuzzy rules. If a given fuzzy rule has multiple antecedents, the fuzzy operator *(AND or OR)* is used to obtain a single number that represents the result of the antecedent evaluation. This number (the truth value) is then applied to the consequent membership function. Now the result of the antecedent evaluation can be applied to the membership function of the consequent. The most common method of correlating the rule consequent with the truth value of the rule antecedent is to cut the consequent membership function at the level of the antecedent truth.

Step 3. Aggregation of the rule outputs

Aggregation is the process of unification of the outputs of all rules. We take the membership functions of all rule consequents previously found and combine them into a single fuzzy set.

The input of the aggregation process is the list of found consequent membership functions, and the output is one fuzzy set for each output variable.

Step 4. Defuzzification

The last step in the fuzzy inference process is defuzzification. Fuzziness helps us to evaluate the rules, but the final output of a fuzzy system has to be a crisp number.

The input for the defuzzification process is the aggregate output fuzzy set and the output is a single number (Esragh & Mamdani, 1981).

Fig. 3 depicts the flowchart for fuzzy logic analysis based on Mamdani's fuzzy inference method (Symans & Kelly, 1999).

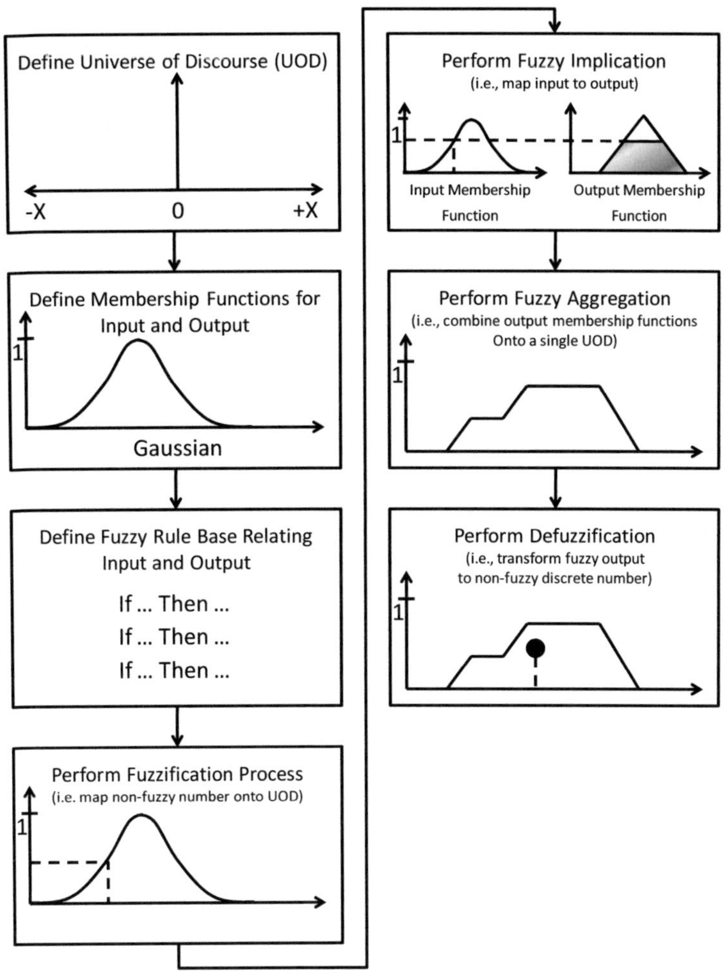

Fig. 3. Flowchart for fuzzy logic analysis based on Mamdani's fuzzy inference method (Symans & Kelly, 1999)

4.1.2 Adaptive Neuro Fuzzy Inference System (ANFIS) method

Adaptive Neuro Fuzzy Inference System (ANFIS) is a multilayer feed-forward network which uses neural network learning algorithms and fuzzy reasoning to map inputs into an output. It is a fuzzy inference system implemented in the framework of adaptive neural networks.

In order to explain ANFIS a fuzzy inference system with two inputs x and y and one output z is considered (Jang et al., 1997). In a first-order Sugeno fuzzy model with two fuzzy if-then rules we have:

Rule 1: If x is A_1 and y is B_1, then $f_1=p_1x+q_1y+r_1$

Rule 2: If x is A_2 and y is B_2, then $f_2=p_2x+q_2y+r_2$

Fig. 4 shows the reasoning procedure for the considered Sugeno model. Fig. 5 depicts the ANFIS architecture. As it is shown nodes of the same layer have similar functions. The output of the *ith* node in layer l is as $O_{l,i}$.

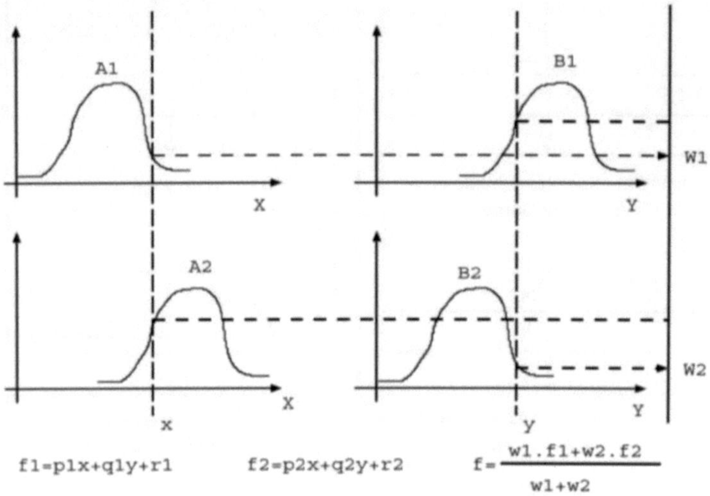

Fig. 4. A two-input first-order Sugeno fuzzy model with two rules

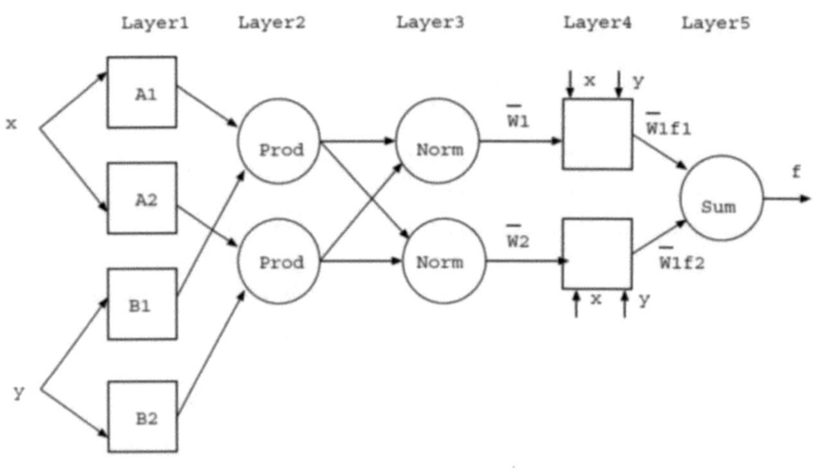

Fig. 5. Equivalent ANFIS architecture

Following few paragraphs contain brief description of the different layers:

Layer 1: Every node i in this layer is an adaptive node with a node function:

$$O_{1,i}=\mu_{Ai}(x), \quad \text{for } i=1, 2, \text{ or}$$
$$O_{1,i}=\mu_{Bi-2}(y), \quad \text{for } i=3, 4 \tag{1}$$

where x *(or y)* is the input to node i and A_i *(or B_{i-2})* is an attribute associated with this node. In other words, $O_{1,i}$ is the membership grade of a fuzzy set A $(= A_1, A_2, B_1 \text{ or } B_2)$ and it specifies the degree to which the given input x *(or y)* satisfies the quantifier A. Here the membership function for A can be any appropriate parameterized membership function such as the generalized bell function:

$$\mu_A(x) = \frac{1}{1+\left|\frac{x-c_i}{a_i}\right|^{2b_i}} \tag{2}$$

where *{ai, bi, ci}* is the premise parameters set. Changing the values of these parameters leads to change of the bell-shaped function. Therefore various forms of membership functions for fuzzy set A are possible.

Layer 2: Every node in this layer is a fixed node labeled Prod, whose output is the product of all the incoming signals:

$$O_{2,i} = w_i = \mu_{Ai}(x)\, \mu_{Bi}(y), \; i = 1, 2 \tag{3}$$

Each node output represents the firing strength of a rule. In general, any other T-norm operators that perform fuzzy *AND* can be used as the node function in this layer.

Layer 3: Every node in this layer is a fixed node labeled Norm. The *ith* node calculates the ratio of the *ith* rule's firing strength to the sum of all rules' firing strengths:

$$O_{3,i} = \overline{w_i} = \frac{w_i}{w_1 + w_2} \qquad i = 1,2 \tag{4}$$

Outputs of this layer are called normalized firing strengths.

Layer 4: Every node i in this layer is an adaptive node with a node function

$$O_{4,i} = \overline{w_i} f_i = \overline{w_i}(p_i x + q_i y + r_i) \tag{5}$$

where $\overline{w_i}$ is a normalized firing strength from layer 3 and $\{p_i, q_i, r_i\}$ is the parameter set of this node. Parameters in this layer are referred to as consequent parameters.

Layer 5: The only node of this layer is a fixed node labeled Sum, which computes the overall output as the summation of all incoming signals:

$$overall\, output = O_{5,1} = \sum_i \overline{w_i} f_i = \frac{\sum_i w_i f_i}{\sum_i w_i} \tag{6}$$

It can be observed that the ANFIS architecture has two adaptive layers: Layers 1 and 4. Layer 1 has modifiable parameters *{ai,bi, ci}* and *{aj,bj, cj}* related to the input MFs. Layer 4 has modifiable parameters *{pij,qij, rij}* pertaining to the first-order polynomial. The task of the learning algorithm for this ANFIS architecture is to tune all the modifiable parameters to make the ANFIS output match the training data. Learning or adjusting these modifiable parameters is a two-step process, which is known as the hybrid learning algorithm. In the forward pass of the hybrid learning algorithm, the premise parameters are hold fixed, node outputs go forward until layer 4 and the consequent parameters are identified by the least squares method. In the backward pass, the consequent parameters are held fixed, the error signals propagate backward and the premise parameters are updated by the gradient descent method. The detailed algorithm and mathematical background of the hybrid learning algorithm can be found in (Jang et al., 1997; Wang & Elhag, 2008).

The basic learning rule of ANFIS is the back propagation gradient descent, which calculates error signals (defined as the derivative of the squared error with respect to each node's output) recursively from the output layer backward to the input nodes. This learning rule is exactly the same as the back-propagation learning rule used in the common feed-forward neural networks. From the ANFIS architecture in Fig. 5, it is observed that given the values of premise parameters, the overall output *f* can be expressed as a linear combination of the consequent parameters. On the basis of this observation, a hybrid-learning rule is employed here, which combines the gradient descent and the least-squares method to find a feasible set of antecedent and consequent parameters. The details of the hybrid rule are given in (Jang et al., 1997), where it is also claimed to be significantly faster than the classical back-propagation method.

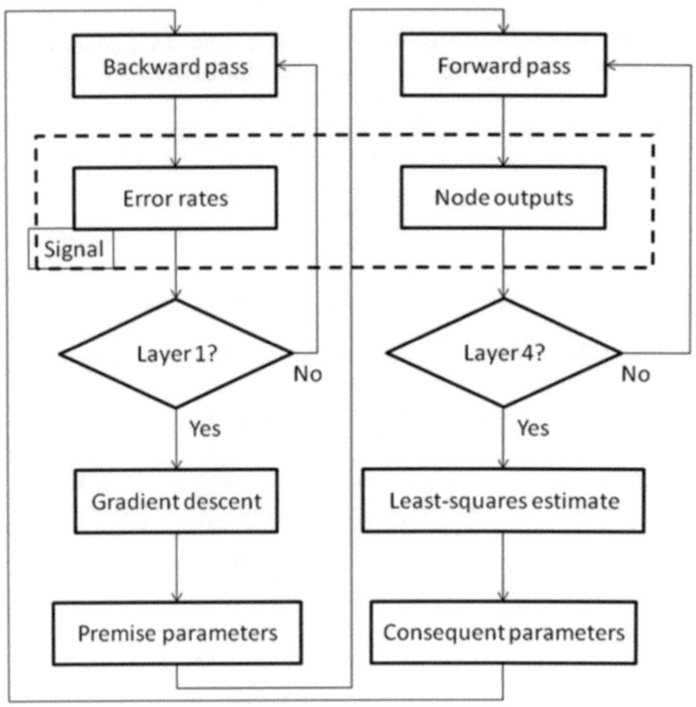

Fig. 6. Hybrid learning procedure of ANFIS

There are two passes in the hybrid-learning procedure for ANFIS. In the forward pass of the hybrid-learning algorithm, functional signals go forward till layer 4 and the consequent parameters are identified by the least-squares estimate. In the backward pass, the error rates propagate backward and the premise parameters are updated by the gradient descent. When the values of the premise parameters are fixed, the overall output can be expressed as a linear combination of the consequent parameters

$$\begin{aligned} f &= \frac{w_1}{w_1 + w_2} f_1 + \frac{w_2}{w_1 + w_2} f_2 \\ &= \overline{w}_1 (p_1 x + q_1 y + r_1) + \overline{w}_2 (p_2 x + q_2 y + r_2) \\ &= (\overline{w}_1 x) p_1 + (\overline{w}_1 y) q_1 + (\overline{w}_1) r_1 + (\overline{w}_2 x) p_2 + (\overline{w}_2 y) q_2 + (\overline{w}_2) r_2 \end{aligned} \tag{7}$$

which is linear in the consequent parameters *p1, q1, r1, p2, q2, and r2* (Jang et al., 1997; Kandel & Langholz, 1993; Li et al., 2001; Sivanandam et al., 2007). A flowchart of hybrid learning procedure for ANFIS is shown schematically in Fig. 6 (Aydin et al., 2006).

5. Case studies and some typical applications of fuzzy inference system for managing bridges

As it is mentioned in earlier parts of this chapter and is shown in Fig. 1 the main concerns of bridge management systems are diagnosis of the encountered problems (deteriorations and/or damage detection) and finding the current condition of the bridge structure. It was also discussed that diagnosis and current condition determination accompany with ambiguity. In this section some case studies and applications are presented to show how fuzzy inference system can be used in bridge management issues.

5.1 A fuzzy system for concrete bridge damage diagnosis (DIASYN system)

Bridge management systems (BMSs) are being developed in recent years to assist various authorities on the decision making in various stages of bridge maintenance, which requires, first of all, appropriate preliminary deterioration diagnosis and modeling.

Diagnosis Synthesis (DIASYN) is a fuzzy rule-based inference system for bridge damage diagnosis and prediction which aims to provide bridge designers with valuable information about the impacts of design factors on bridge deterioration.

DIASYN is supposed to be a concept demonstration system for providing the bridge maintenance engineers and the bridge design engineers with assistance to obtain preliminary but important knowledge on individual bridge defects.

The DIASYN system incorporates a fuzzy reasoning process containing a rule base with its acquisition and update facility and a fuzzy inference engine with an explanation facility, and a user interface with option selecting capacity. Fuzzy logic is utilized to handle uncertainties and imprecision involved. The rules are if-then statements that describe associations between fuzzy parameters. Given the required input data, the inference engine evaluates the rules and generates an appropriate conclusion. Users can choose to make diagnoses of new cases or to update the rule base with new training data through the user interface.

The fuzzy rules provide associations between observed bridge conditions and damage causes. They are created by a rule generation algorithm that can convert crisp training data into fuzzy statements. The training data are collected from bridge inspection records and formalized into standard vectors. In the operational mode, the system reads a state vector of observed bridge condition and the inference engine performs damage cause implication through evaluation of the rules. The output of this implication procedure is a linguistic variable that describes the possible damage cause with a confident degree. This linguistic variable can be defuzzified by the explanation facility if a crisp output is desired. In the updating mode, new training vectors are input to generate new rules together with the existing training data. New rules, if any, will be installed in the rule base before the system gives a prompting of *updating finished* as output.

Inputs of DIASYN are:

- Design factors, i.e. structural type, span length, deck width, number of spans, wearing surface type, skew angle, etc.,
- Environmental factors, i.e. humidity and precipitation, climate region, traffic volume, temperature variations, etc.,
- Other factors, such as structure age, function class and location of damages.

The inference engine in DIASYN basically executes Mamdani's original reasoning procedure. The overall firing strength of the individual rule whose antecedents are connected with an *AND* operator, the intersection, is typically determined by taking the minimum value of the individual firing strengths of the antecedents.

After system training it is ready to be used to diagnose new bridge deterioration case. Two test examples are use for system verification, one for crack diagnosis and one for spalling diagnosis. The input data of the bridge including survey and inspection information which shows that a crack occurs in superstructure with a specific condition mark, and a spalling in support-structure with another given condition mark. The inference results, along with expert opinions indicate that the particular crack was caused by 'loads and its likes' with a confidence degree of 'very true', and that the spalling was caused by 'others' with a confidence degree of very true. Both of the results are in accordance with the expert opinion, which suggests 'overloaded' and 'aging' are the causes of the crack and spalling, respectively (Zhao & Chen, 2001, 2002).

5.2 An adaptive neuro-fuzzy inference system for bridge risk assessment

Bridge risks are often evaluated periodically so that the bridges with high risks can be maintained timely. Modeling bridge risks is a challenging job facing Highways Agencies because good mathematical models can save them a significant amount of cost and time.

In this case study an adaptive neuro-fuzzy system (ANFIS) using 506 bridge maintenance projects for bridge risk assessment is introduced. The system can help British Highways Agency to determine the maintenance priority ranking of bridge structures more systematically, more efficiently and more economically in comparison with the existing bridge risk assessment methodologies which require a large number of subjective judgments from bridge experts to build the complicated nonlinear relationships between bridge risk score and risk ratings.

The 506 bridge maintenance projects dataset is randomly split into two sample sets: training dataset with 390 projects and testing dataset with 116 projects. Both the training and testing datasets cover all levels and types of bridge risks.

Inputs to the ANFIS are safety risk rating (SRR), functionality risk rating (FRR), sustainability risk rating (SURR), and environment risk rating (ERR). All inputs range from 0 to 3 with 0 representing *no risk*, 1 *low risk*, 2 *medium risk* and 3 *high risk*. Output to the ANFIS is the risk scores (RSs) of the 506 bridge projects, which ranges from 5 to 99.

With the 390 training dataset, two generalized bell-shaped membership functions are chosen for each of the four inputs to build the ANFIS, which leads to 16 if-then rules containing 104 parameters to be learned. Fig. 7 shows the model structure of the ANFIS that is to be built for bridge risk assessment in this study.

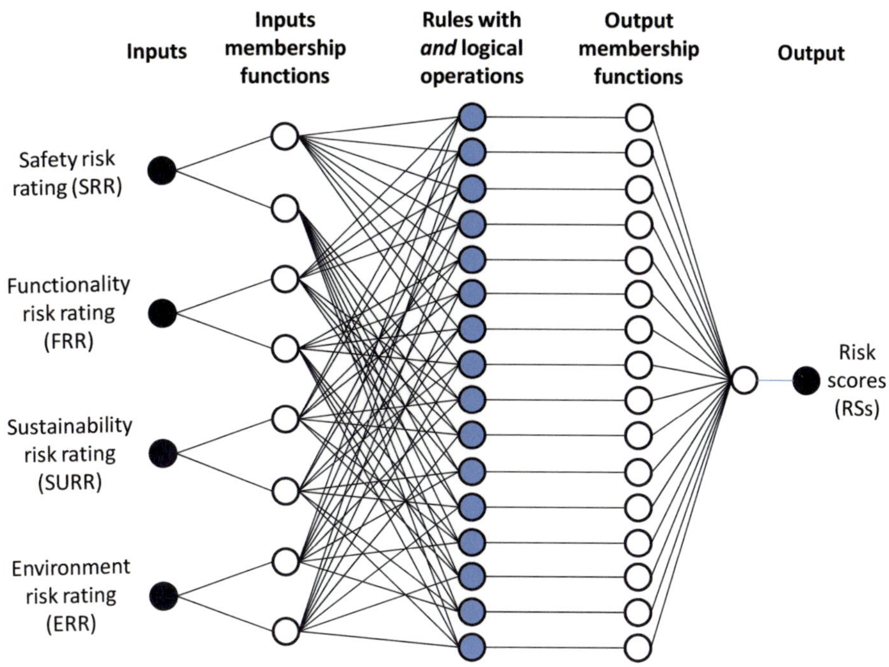

Fig. 7. Model structure of the ANFIS for bridge risk assessment

The developed ANFIS system for bridge risk assessment learns the if-then rules between bridge risk scores and risk ratings from the past bridge maintenance projects and memorizes them for generalization and prediction. It has been observed that ANFIS outperforms artificial neural networks to perform better than multiple regression models (Wang & Elhag, 2007). Differing from artificial neural network, ANFIS is transparent rather than a black box. Its if-then rules are easy to understand and interpret. In this case study the performances of the ANFIS and ANN in modeling bridge risks are compared, where the two models are trained using the same training dataset and validated by the same testing dataset. Comparison shows that the ANFIS has smaller root mean squared error and mean absolute percentage error as well as bigger correlation coefficient for both the training and testing datasets than the ANN model. In other words, the ANFIS achieves better performances than the ANN model. Therefore, ANFIS is a good choice for modeling bridge risks. Moreover, ANN is a black box in nature and its relationships between inputs and outputs are not easy to be interpreted, while ANFIS is transparent and its if-then rules are very easy to understand and interpret. But the drawback of ANFIS is its limitation to the number of outputs. It can only model a single output. In summary, ANFIS is a good choice and powerful tool for modeling bridge risks (Wang & Elhag, 2008).

5.3 Fuzzy concrete bridge deck condition rating method for practical bridge management system

Bridge management system (BMS) is a tool for structured decision making and planning/scheduling for bridge infrastructure inspection, maintenance and repair or retrofit. Any BMS is basically constructed based on data stored in inventory and inspection databases. One of the important and crucial efforts in managing bridges is to have some criteria to show the current condition of the elements of bridges based on the results from inspection data. As the results are not precise and are related to the depth and extent of the inspectors' expertise, there are some uncertainties in any evaluation. On the other side condition of bridges are rated linguistically in many cases with some kinds of vagueness in description of the bridge element conditions. Based on these facts in this case study a new fuzzy method is introduced to deal with these shortcomings from the uncertain and vague data. The fuzzy bridge deck condition rating method is practically based on both subjective and objective results of existing inspection methods and tools. The parameters of the model are selected as fuzzy inputs with membership functions found from some statistical data and then the fuzziness of the condition rating is calculated by the fuzzy arithmetic rules inherent in the fuzzy expert system. Since one of the most proven and experienced advantages of fuzzy inference systems is the tolerability for noisy (uncertain and vague) data it is believed that this proposed system can be an alternative method for current rating indices amongst many others which are almost used deterministically.

In this case study Fuzzy Inference System is used to translate the concrete bridge deck inspection results to condition rating (Tarighat & Miyamoto, 2009).

In literature the proposed rating methods are resulted from either visual inspection or nondestructive tests. Here, in order to enhance the capabilities of both methods (visual inspection and nondestructive tests) a hybrid inspection results is used to calculate the condition rating of the concrete bridge deck. Fig. 8 shows the type of inspection results.

The linguistic attributes of observed symptoms are defined as following fuzzy sets.

A1 = {No; Yes}
A2 = {NoCracks; HairlineCracks; WideCracks}
A3 = {No; Maybe; Yes}
A4 = {Firm; Moderately; Hollow; Very Hollow}
A5 = {Low; Moderate; High}

Considering Gaussian membership functions for inputs and applying Mamdani's method as fuzzy inference system Fig. 9 shows the proposed system for predicting of bridge deck condition rating. For design of fuzzy inference system 162 rules are defined based on the experts' experience and available facts from previous inspection results. Finally Fig. 10 can be used to convert the crisp condition rating result to linguistic term.

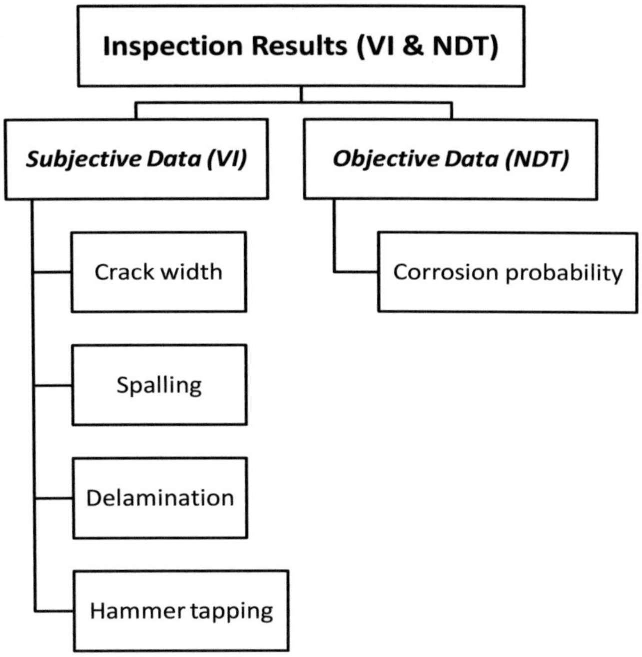

Fig. 8. Type of inspection results

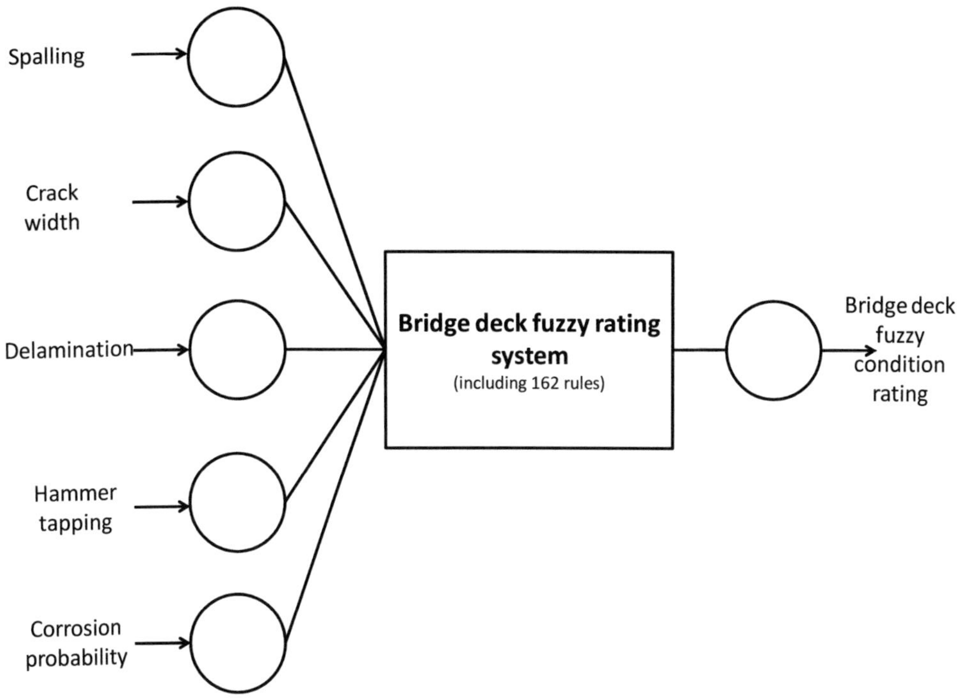

Fig. 9. Proposed fuzzy system for bridge deck condition rating.

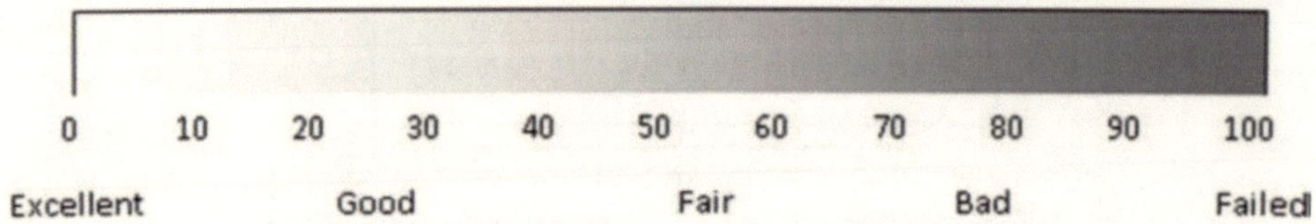

Fig. 10. Concrete bridge deck condition rating in linguistic terms.

To verify the proposed method an inspected concrete bridge deck is used. The layout of inspection is shown in Fig. 11. The proposed method is applied to the red slab and green haunch girder of the deck shown in Fig. 11.

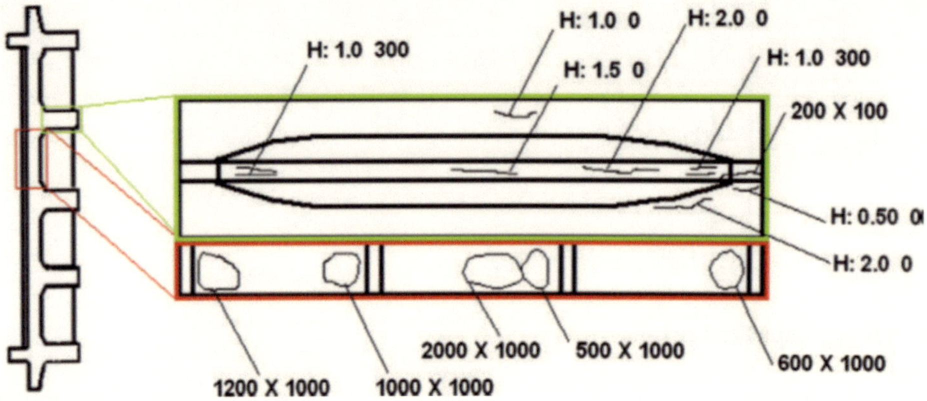

Fig. 11. Concrete bridge deck inspection layout.

Fuzzy condition rating method facilitates data collection in inspection process. No area calculation is required and it needs only the good judgment of the inspector to find out the condition rating. The inspection data is shown in Table 2. Since the symptoms and deterioration/damages of girders and slabs of a deck are totally similar the proposed model can be used for them during bridge inspection process.

Deck element	Spalling condition	Crack width condition	Delamination condition	Hammer tapping condition	Corrosion probability condition	Fuzzy condition rating
Slab (Red Area)	20	50	90	50	10	75.2
Girder (Green Area)	80	70	40	70	90	78.9

Table 2. Inspection data for typical slab and haunch girder of the reinforced concrete bridge deck.

To compare these results with a well-defined and in-use condition rating method the following seven-state rating scale, which reflects the different damage states associated with chloride-induced corrosion is used (Federal Highway Administration (FHWA), 1995; Morcous, Lounis, & Mirza, 2003). Table 3 provides a summary description of the adopted condition rating system as the benchmark.

Description	Condition rating (CR)
Excellent condition: no contamination; no corrosion; no repaired area	1
Very good condition: minor cracks, no spalls or delaminations; chloride contaminated or repaired areas 62% (of total deck area)	2
Satisfactory condition: spalls or delaminations 62%; cracked, corroded, contaminated, or repaired area 610%	3
Fair condition: spalls or delaminations 65%; cracked, corroded, contaminated, or repaired area 620%	4
Poor condition: spalls or delaminations 610%; cracked, corroded, contaminated, or repaired area 625%	5
Critical condition: spalls or delaminations 615%; cracked, corroded, contaminated, or repaired area P25%	6
Failed condition (total loss of serviceability or functionality): extensive spalling, delamination, repaired areas P30%; maintenance required	7

Table 3. Condition rating system for concrete bridge decks (Federal Highway Administration (FHWA), 1995; Morcous et al., 2003).

Based on Table 3 the condition rating for typical slab and haunch girder under consideration are 6 and 5. Scaling is required to be able to compare the results, therefore the above mentioned numbers should be multiplied by 14.28 to get a 100-based score system. Table 4 provides the comparison. It is shown that results from proposed method can estimate the condition rating very well.

Deck Component	Proposed fuzzy condition rating system		Scaled (to 100) Condition Rating based on the selected references		Absolute value Difference of the proposed method to the selected references
	Numerical value	Linguistically index	Numerical value	Linguistically index	
Slab CR	75.2	Bad	85.7	Critical condition	10.5
Girder CR	78.9	Bad	71.4	Poor condition	7.5

Table 4. Comparison of the condition ratings from two methods.

5.4 A two stage method for structural damage identification using an adaptive neuro-fuzzy inference system and practice swarm optimization

All the above three case studies are of diagnosis and assessment types. As declared earlier another important task of any BMS or BHMS is the possibility to locate damaged area or components. The present case study is about damage detection (Fallahian & Seyedpoor, 2010).

In this case study, an efficient methodology is proposed to accurately detect the sites and extents of multiple structural damages. The proposed methodology has two main phases combining the adaptive neuro-fuzzy inference system (ANFIS) and a particle swarm optimization (PSO) as an optimization solver. In the first phase, the ANFIS is employed to quickly determine the structural elements having the higher probability of damage from the original elements. In the second phase, the reduced damage problem is solved via the particle swarm optimization (PSO) algorithm to truthfully determine the extents of actual damaged elements.

Structural damage detection techniques can be generally classified into two main categories. They include the dynamic and static identification methods requiring the dynamic and static test data, respectively. Furthermore, the dynamic identification methods have shown their advantages in comparison with the static ones. Among the dynamic data, the natural frequencies of a structure can be found as a valuable data. Determining the level of correlation between the measured and predicted natural frequencies can provide a simple tool for identifying the locations and extents of structural damages. Two parameter vectors are used for evaluating correlation coefficients. A vector consists of the ratios of the first n_f vector natural frequency changes ΔF due to structural damage, i.e.

$$\Delta F = \frac{F_h - F_d}{F_h} \tag{8}$$

where F_h and F_d denote the natural frequency vectors of the healthy and damaged structure, respectively. Similarly, the corresponding parameter vector predicted from an analytical model can be defined as:

$$\delta F(X) = \frac{F_h - F(X)}{F_h} \tag{9}$$

where $F(X)$ is a natural frequency vector that can be predicted from an analytic model and $X^T = \{x_1, \ldots, x_i, \ldots, x_n\}$ represents a damage variable vector containing the damage extents $(x_i, i=1, \ldots, n)$ of all n structural elements.

Given a pair of parameter vectors, one can estimate the level of correlation in several ways. An efficient way is to evaluate a correlation-based index called the multiple damage location assurance criterion (MDLAC) expressed in the following form:

$$MDLAC(X) = \frac{\left|\Delta F^T . \delta F(X)\right|^2}{(F^T . \Delta F)[\delta F^T(X) . \delta F(X)]} \tag{10}$$

The MDLAC compares two frequency change vectors, one obtained from the tested structure and the other from an analytical model of the structure. The MDLAC varies from a minimum value 0 to a maximum value 1. It will be maximal when the vector of analytical frequencies is identical to the frequency vector of damaged structure, i.e., $F(X) = F_d$.

The key point of this case study is that ANFIS concept can be effectively utilized to determine the most potentially damaged element (MPDE) of an unhealthy structure. For this, some sample structures having the damaged elements are randomly generated based on the damage vector X as the input and the corresponding $MDLAC(X)$ as the output. In other words some scenarios are defined for damaged structures. Then, an exhaustive search is performed using the ANFIS within the available input-output data to arrange the structural elements according to their damage potentiality. Essentially, the exhaustive search technique builds an ANFIS network for each damage variable from original ones and trains the network for a little epoch and reports the performance achieved. The step by step summary of the exhaustive search algorithm for determining the MPDE of an unhealthy structure is as follows:

a. Establish the pre-assigned parameters of the intact structure.
b. Randomly generate a number of sample structures having some damaged elements within the allowed space of damage variables *X*.
c. Determine the natural frequencies of the sample structures using a conventional finite element analysis.
d. Estimate the level of correlation between unhealthy structure and each sample structure by evaluating the *MDLAC*(*X*) index via equation (10).
e. Randomly split the sample structures into two sets with some samples for training and remaining samples for testing the ANFIS, respectively.
f. Build an ANFIS model for each damage variable as the input and the *MDLAC*(*X*) as the output. This leads to *n* ANFIS models equal to the total number of structural elements.
g. Calculate the root mean square error (RMSE) for training and testing sets as:

$$RMSE = \sqrt{\frac{1}{n_t}\sum_{i=1}^{n_t}(ac_i - pr_i)^2} \tag{11}$$

where *ac* and *pr* represent the actual and predicted values of the *MDLAC*(*X*), also n_t is the number of training or testing samples.

a. Sort the structural elements according to increasing their training *RMSE* values and select the first *m* arranged elements, having the least *RMSE* errors, as the reduced damage vector, denoted here by $X_r^T = \{x_{r1}, x_{r2}, \ldots, x_{rm}\}$.
b. End of the algorithm.

Now it is time to identify damage using optimization algorithms. As mentioned above, the MDLAC index will reach to a maximum value 1 when the structural damage occurs. This concept can be utilized to estimate the damage vector using an optimization algorithm. For this aim, the unconstrained optimization problem with discrete damage variables reduced may be stated as:

$$\begin{aligned} &\text{Find} && X_r^T = \{x_{r1}, x_{r2}, \ldots, x_{rm}\} \\ &\text{Minimize:} && w(X_r) = -MDLAC(X_r) \\ & && x_{ri} \in R^d \ , \ i = 1, \ldots, m \end{aligned} \tag{12}$$

where R^d is a given set of discrete values and the damage extents x_{ri} $(i = 1, \ldots, m)$ can take values only from this set. Also, *w* is an objective function that should be minimized.

The selection of an efficient algorithm for solving the damage optimization problem is a critical issue. Needing fewer structural analyses for achieving the global optimum without trapping into local optima must be the main characteristic of the algorithm. In this study, a particle swarm optimization (PSO) algorithm working with discrete design variables is proposed to properly solve the damage problem.

In order to show the capabilities of the proposed methodology for identifying the multiple structural damages, two illustrative test examples are considered. The first example is a cantilever beam discussed in detail and the second one is a bending plate discussed in brief. The numerical results for these examples demonstrate that the combination of the ANFIS and PSO can produce an efficient tool for correctly detecting the locations and sizes of damages induced (Fallahian & Seyedpoor, 2010).

6. Conclusion

Fuzzy logic inference methods can be used for managing bridges. Models based on FIS consider simultaneously several facts or knowledge combinations as rules and indicate the final answer or guess which is very close to practical existing situation as the hypothesis of the greatest belief. The reasoning process is very clear and easy to understand by users who are not experts in the performance of decision support systems. For bridge inspection no deteriorated area calculation is needed and the only requirement is the good inspector's judgment. It should be noted that fuzzy systems can tolerate some noise to predict the outputs. This means that during bridge deck inspection if in some cases judgment is not correct, but close to real condition, the proposed method can estimate the condition very well without a major difference from practical point of view. It is clear that in deterministic methods incorrect judgment or decision changes the category of the predefined condition and overall condition rating drastically. Another point that should be notified is that FIS can be applied in areas with high nonlinearity. When nonlinearity is high the prediction accuracy is expected to be improved by using ANFIS comparing to Mamdani's method. Accuracy of the method can be improved when an adaptive optimization method is used for constructing similar model based on the training data from inspections. FIS modeling is suitable for prioritization of repairing bridges and budgeting tasks in which relatively simple and practical reasoning is required for decision makers. Even in cases that human expertise is not available, we can still set up intuitively reasonable initial membership functions and start the learning process to generate a set of fuzzy if-then rules to approximate a desired data set. The efficiency of rule-based reasoning can be improved by comparing different inference methods. Generally the inferred results are in agreement with the expert's opinion, and can provide substantial assistance to authorities in their planning.

7. References

Aktan, A. E., Pervizpour, M., Catbas, N., Grimmelsman, K., Barrish, R., Curtis, J. & Qin, X. (2002). *Information technology research for health monitoring of bridge systems*, Drexel University Intelligent Infrastructure and Transportation Safety Institute, Philadelphia, USA

Aydin, A. C., Tortum, A. & Yavuz, M. (2006). Prediction of concrete elastic modulus using adaptive neuro-fuzzy inference system. *Civil Engineering and Environmental Systems*, Vol. 23, No. 4, December 2006, pp. 295–309Baldwin, J. F. (1981). Fuzzy logic and fuzzy reasoning. *In E. H. Mamdani & B. R. Gaines (Eds.), Fuzzy reasoning and its applications*, Academic Press, London

Chen, W. F. & Duan, L. (2000). *Bridge engineering handbook.* CRC Press

Esragh, F. & Mamdani, E. H. (1981). A general approach to linguistic approximation. *In E. H. Mamdani & B. R. Gaines (Eds.), Fuzzy reasoning and its applications*, Academic Press, London

Fallahian, A. & Seyedpoor, S. M. (2010). A two stage method for structural damage identification using an adaptive neuro-fuzzy inference system and particle swarm optimization. *Asian Journal of Civil Engineering (Building and Housing)*, Vol. 11, No. 6, pp. 795-808

Federal Highway Administration (FHWA). (1995). *Recording and coding guide for the structure inventory and appraisal of the nations' bridges. Report FHWA-PD-96-001*, Washington, D.C.

Graybeal, B., Rolander, D., Phares, B., Moore, M., Washer, G. (2001). Reliability and Accuracy of In-Depth Inspection. *Transportation Research Record*, No. 1749, pp. 93-99

Haritos, N. (2000). Dynamic testing techniques for structural identification of bridge superstructures, *Proceedings of the International Conference on Advances in Structural Dynamics*, The Hong Kong Polytechnic University, Hong Kong, December 2000

Harris, J. (2006). *Fuzzy logic applications in engineering science.* Springer

Hartle, R. A., Ryan, T. W., Eric Mann, J., Danovich, L. J., Sosko, W. B., & Bouscher, J. W. (2002). *Bridge inspector's reference manual.* Federal Highway Administration

Housner, G. W. & Bergman, L. A., et al. (1997). Structural control: Past, present, and future. *Journal of Engineering mechanics, ASCE*, Vol. 123, No. 9, September 1997, pp. 897-971

Jang J. S. R. (1993). ANFIS:Adaptive-Network-Based Fuzzy Inference System. *IEEE Trans. on Systems, Man and Cybernetics*, Vol. 23, No. 3, May 1993, pp. 665-685

Jang, J. S. R., Sun, C. T. & Mizutani, E. (1997). *Neuro-Fuzzy and Soft Computing A Computational Approach to Learning and Machine Intelligence*, Prentice Hall, USA

Kandel, A. & Langholz, G. (1993). *Fuzzy Control Systems*, CRC Press

Li, H., Chen, C. L. P. & Huang, H. P. (2001). *Fuzzy Neural Intelligent Systems: Mathematical Foundation and the Applications in Engineering*, CRC Press

Ma, Z. (2006). *Fuzzy database modeling of imprecise and uncertain engineering information.* Berlin, Heidelberg: Springer-Verlag

Moore, M., Phares, B., Graybeal, B., Rolander, D. & Washer, G. (2001). Reliability of visual inspection for highway bridges. *Federal Highway Administration*, Vols. I & II

Morcous, G., Lounis, Z. & Mirza, M. S. (2003). Identification of environmental categories for Markovian deterioration models of bridge decks. *Journal of Bridge Engineering*, ASCE, Vol. 8. No. 6, pp. 353–361

Ou, J. P., Li, H. & Duan, Z. D. (2006). Structural Health Monitoring and Intelligent Infrastructure, *Proceedings of the second international conference*, Shenzhen, China, 2006

Phares, B. M., Rolander, D. D., Graybeal, B. A. & Washer, G. A. (2000). Studying the reliability of bridge inspection. *US Department of Transportation, Federal Highway Administration, Public Roads*, Vol. 64, No. 3, November/December 2000

Phares, B. M., Rolander, D. D., Graybeal, B. A. & Washer, G. A. (2001). Reliability of visual bridge inspection. *US Department of Transportation, Federal Highway Administration, Public Roads*, Vol. 64, No. 5, March/April 2001

Rajani, B., Kleiner, Y. & Sadiq, R. (2006). Translation of pipe inspection results into condition ratings using the fuzzy synthetic evaluation technique. *International Journal of Water Supply Research and Technology: Aqua*, Vol. 55, No. 1, pp. 11–24

Sivanandam, S. N., Sumathi, S. & Deepa, S. N. (2007). *Introduction to Fuzzy Logic using MATLAB*, Springer-Verlag, Berlin Heidelberg Straszecka, E. (2006). Combining uncertainty and imprecision in models of medical diagnosis. *International Journal of Information Sciences*, Vol. 176, pp. 3026–3059

Stephens, H. M., Jr. (2000). NDE reliability - human factors - basic considerations. *15th WCNDT*, Roma, Italy

Symans, M. D. & Kelly, S. W. (1999). Fuzzy logic control of bridge structures using intelligent semi-active seismic isolation systems. *Earthquake Engineering and Structural Dynamics*, Vol. 28, pp. 37-60

Tarighat, A. & Miyamoto, A. (2009). Fuzzy concrete bridge deck condition rating method for practical bridge management system. *Expert Systems with Applications*, Vol. 36, 2009, pp. 12077–12085

Terano, T., Asai, K. & Sugeno, M. (1992). *Fuzzy systems theory and its applications*. Academic Press

Wang, T. T. L. & Zong, Z. (2002). *Final Report: Improvement of evaluation method for existing highway bridges*, Department of Civil & Environmental Engineering, Florida International University, USA

Wang, J. & Hu, H. (2006). Vibration-based fault diagnosis of pump using fuzzy technique. *International Journal of Measurement*, 39, pp. 176–185

Wang, X., Nguyen, M., Foliente, G. & Ye, L. (2007). An approach to modeling concrete bridge condition deterioration using a statistical causal relationship based on inspection data. *Structure and Infrastructure Engineering*, Vol. 3, No. 1, pp. 3–15

Wang, Y. M., & Elhag, T. M. S. (2007). A comparison of neural network, evidential reasoning and multiple regression analysis in modeling bridge risks. *Expert Systems with Applications*, Vol. 32, pp. 336–348

Wang, Y. M. & Elhag, T. M. S. (2008). An adaptive neuro-fuzzy inference system for bridge risk assessment. *Expert Systems with Applications*, Vol. 34, pp. 3099–3106

Washington State Department of Transportation. (February 2010). Washington State Bridge Inspection Manual, In: *Manuals*, M 36-64.02, Available from: http://www.wsdot.wa.gov/Publications/Manuals/M36-64.htm

Wenzel. H. & Tanaka, H. (2006). *SAMCO monitoring glossary: Structural dynamics for VBHM of bridges*, Austria

Wu, Z.S. & Abe, M. (2003). Structural Health Monitoring and Intelligent Infrastructure, *Proceedings of the First international conference*, Tokyo, Japan, 2003

Yen, J. & Langari, R. (1999). *Fuzzy logic: Intelligence, control, and information*. Prentice-Hall

Zadeh, L. A. (1976). A fuzzy-algorithmic approach to the definition of complex or imprecise concepts. *International Journal of Man–Machine Studies*, 8, pp. 249–291

Zhao, Z. & Chen, C. (2001). Concrete bridge deterioration diagnosis using fuzzy inference system. *Advances in Engineering Software*, Vol. 32, pp. 317-325

Zhao, Z. & Chen, C. (2002). A fuzzy system for concrete bridge damage diagnosis. *Computers and Structures*, Vol. 80, pp. 629–641

22

Neural Network and Adaptive Neuro-Fuzzy Inference System Applied to Civil Engineering Problems

Mohammed A. Mashrei
Thi-Qar University, College of Engineering, Civil Department
Iraq

1. Introduction

Soft computing is an approximate solution to a precisely formulated problem or more typically, an approximate solution to an imprecisely formulated problem (Zadeh, 1993). It is a new field appearing in the recent past to solve some problems such as decision-making, modeling and control problems. Soft computing is an emerging approach to computing which parallels the remarkable ability of the human mind to reason and learn in an environment of uncertainty and imprecision (Jang el at., 1997). It consists of many complementary tools such as artificial neural network (ANN), fuzzy logic (FL), and adaptive neuro-fuzzy inference system (ANFIS).

Artificial neural network (ANN) model is a system of interconnected computational neurons arranged in an organized fashion to carry out an extensive computing to perform a mathematical mapping (Rafiq et al., 2001). The first interest in neural network (or parallel distributed processing) emerged after the introduction of simplified neurons by McCulloch & Pitts, (1943). These neurons were presented as models of biological neurons and as conceptual components for circuits that could perform computational works. ANN can be most adequately characterized as a computational model with particular properties such as the ability to adapt or learn, to generalize, or to cluster or organize data in which the operation is based on parallel processing.

ANN has a large number of highly interconnected processing elements (nodes or units) that usually operate in parallel and are configured in regular architectures. The collective behavior of an ANN, like a human brain, demonstrates the ability to learn, recall, and generalize from training patterns or data. ANN is inspired by modeling networks of biological neurons in the brain. Hence, the processing elements in ANN are also called artificial neurons (Rafiq et al., 2001). Artificial neural network described in this chapter is mostly applied to solve many civil engineering applications such as structural analysis and design (Cladera & Mar, 2004a, 2004b; Hajela & Berke, 1991; Sanad & Saka, 2001), structural damage assessment (Feng & Bahng, 1999; Mukherjee et al., 1996), structural dynamics and control (Chen et al., 1995; Feng & Kim, 1998) and pavement condition-rating modeling (Eldin & Senouuci, 1995).

The adaptive neuro-fuzzy inference system (ANFIS), first proposed by Jang, 1993, is one of the examples of neuro-fuzzy systems in which a fuzzy system is implemented in the framework of adaptive networks. ANFIS constructs an input-output mapping based both on human knowledge (in the form of fuzzy if-then rules) and on generated input-output data pairs by using a hybrid algorithm that is the combination of the gradient descent and least squares estimates. Readers are referred to References (Jang, 1993; Mashrei, 2010) for more details on the ANFIS. After generated input-output by training, the ANFIS can be used to recognize data that is similar to any of the examples shown during the training phase .The adaptive neuro-fuzzy inference system has been used in the area of civil engineering to solve many problems (Abdulkadir et al., 2006; Akbulut et al., 2004; Fonseca el at., 2007; Tesfamariam & Najjaran, 2007).

Most of the problems solved in civil and structural engineering using ANFIS and ANN are prediction of behavior based on given experimental results that are used for training and testing data. The matter of modeling is to solve a problem by predicting which is obtained by mapping a set of variables in input space to a set of response variables in output space through a model as represented in Fig. 1. In the box representing a model in this figure, conventionally a mathematical model is used. However, the conventional modeling of the underlying systems often tends to become quite intractable and very difficult. Recently an alternative approach to modeling has emerged under the rubric of soft computing with neural network and fuzzy logic as its main constituents. The development of these models, however, requires a set of data. Fortunately, for many problems of civil engineering such data are available.

The purpose of this chapter is to investigate the accuracy of an adaptive neuro-fuzzy inference system and neural network to solve civil engineering problems: The ANN and ANFIS are used to predict the shear strength of concrete beams reinforced with fiber reinforced polymer (FRP) bars and shear strength of ferrocement members. The performance of the ANFIS and ANN models are compared with experimental values and with those of the other methods to assess the efficiency of these models. The study is based on the available databases.

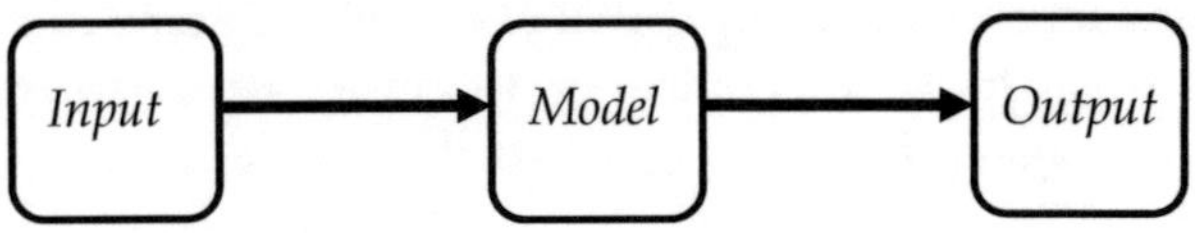

Fig. 1. An input-output mapping

2. Artificial neural network

One type of network sees the nodes as artificial neurons. These are called artificial neural network (ANN). An artificial neuron is a computational model inspired in by natural neurons. Natural neurons receive signals through *synapses* located on the dendrites or membrane of the neuron. When the signals received are strong enough (surpass a certain *threshold*), the neuron is *activated* and emits a signal through the *axon*. This signal might be sent to another synapse, and might activate other neurons (Gershenson, 2003). Fig. 2 shows a natural neuron.

The complexity of real neurons is highly abstracted when modeling artificial neurons. These basically consist of *inputs*(like synapses), which are multiplied by *weights* (strength of the respective signals), and then computed by a mathematical function which determines the *activation* of the neuron. Another function (which may be the identity) computes the *output* of the artificial neuron (sometimes independent on a certain *threshold*). ANN combines artificial neurons in order to process information (Gershenson, 2003).

Compared to conventional digital computing techniques, neural networks are advantageous because of their special features, such as the massively parallel processing, distributed storing of information, low sensitivity to error, their very robust operation after training, generalization and adaptability to new information (Waszczyszyn, 1998).

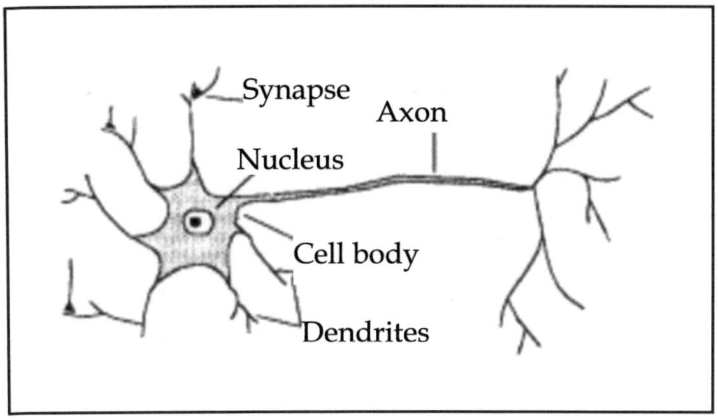

Fig. 2. Natural (biological) neurons

2.1 Learning process

An artificial neuron is composed of five main parts: inputs, weights, sum function, activation function and outputs. Inputs are information that enters the cell from other cells of from external world. Weights are values that express the effect of an input set or another process element in the previous layer on this process element. Sum function is a function that calculates the effect of inputs and weights totally on this process element. This function calculates the net input that comes to a cell (Topcu & Sarıdemir, 2007).

The information is propagated through the neural network layer by layer, always in the same direction. Besides the input and output layers there can be other intermediate layers of neurons, which are usually called hidden layers. Fig. 3 shows the structure of a typical neural network.

The inputs to the jth node are represented as an input factor, a, with component a_i (i=1 to n), and the output by bj. The values w_{1j}, w_{2j}, …, and w_{nj} are weight factors associated with each input to the node. This is something like the varying synaptic strengths of biological neurons. Weights are adaptive coefficients within the network that determine the intensity of the input signal. Every input (a_1, a_2, …, a_n) is multiplied by its corresponding weight factor (w_{1j}, w_{2j}, …, w_{nj}), and the node uses this weighted input (w_{1j} a_1, w_{2j} a_2, …, w_{nj} a_n) to perform further calculations. If the weight factor is positive, ($w_{ij}a_i$) tends to excite the node. If the weight factor is negative, ($w_{ij}a_i$) inhibits the node. In the initial setup of a neural network, weight factors may be chosen according to a specified statistical distribution. Then these weight factors are adjusted in the development of the network or "learning" process.

The other input to the node is the node's internal threshold, T_j. This is a randomly chosen value that governs the "activation" or total input of the node through the following equation (Baughman & Liu, 1995).

Total Activation: $$x_i = \sum_{i=1}^{n}(w_{ij}).a_i - T_j \quad (1)$$

The total activation depends on the magnitude of the internal threshold T_j. If T_j is large or positive, the node has a high internal threshold, thus inhibiting node-firing. If T_j is zero or negative, the node has a low internal threshold, which excites node-firing. If no internal threshold is specified, a zero value is assumed. This activity is then modified by transfer function and becomes the final output (b_j) of the neuron (Baughman & Liu, 1995).

$$b_j = f(x_i) = f\left(\sum_{i=1}^{n}(w_{ij}).a_i - T_j\right) \quad (2)$$

This signal is then propagated to the neurons (process elements) of the next layer. Fig. 4 depicts this process.

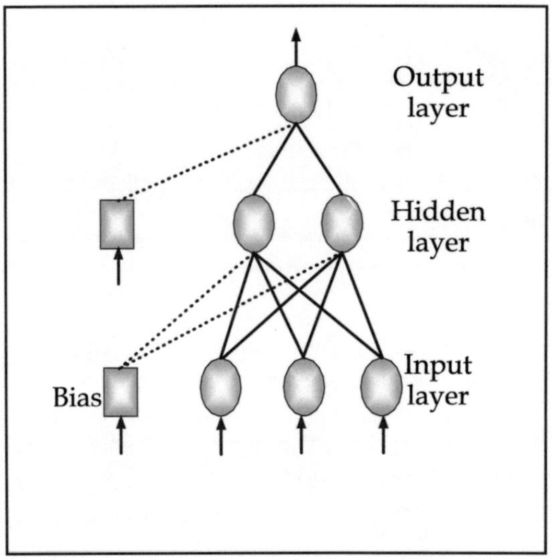

Fig. 3. Structure of a typical neural network

A back-propagation neural network has been successfully applied in various fields such as in civil engineering problems. A learning with back-propagation technique starts with applying an input vector to the network, which is propagated in a forward propagation mode which ends with an output vector. Next, the network evaluates the errors between the desired output vector and the actual output vector. It uses these errors to shift the connection weights and biases according to a learning rule that tends to minimize the error. This process is generally referred to as "error back- propagation" or back-propagation. The adjusted weights and biases are then used to start a new cycle. A back-propagation cycle, also known as an epoch, in a neural network is illustrated in Fig. 5. For a number of epochs the weights and biases are shifted until the deviations from the outputs are minimized.

Transfer functions are the processing units of a neuron. The node's output is determined by using a mathematical operation on the total activation of the node. These functions can be linear or non-linear. Three of the most common transfer functions are depicted in Fig. 6.

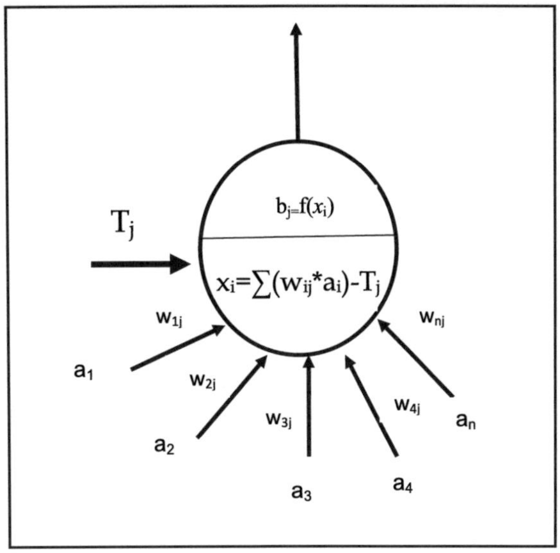

Fig. 4. A single neuron

The mathematical formulation of the functions is given as follows (Matlab Toolbox, 2009):

Pure-Linear: $f(x) = x$ (3)

Log sigmoid: $f(x) = 1/1 + e^{-x}$ $\quad 0 \le f(x) \le 1$ (4)

Tangent sigmoid: $f(x) = \tanh(x) = e^{x} - e^{-x}/e^{x} + e^{-x}$ $\quad -1 \le f(x) \le 1$ (5)

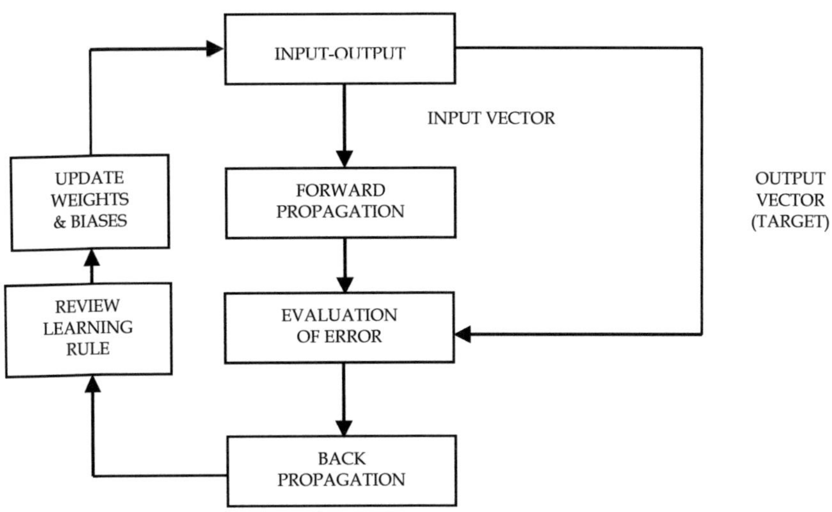

Fig. 5. Back-propagation cycle

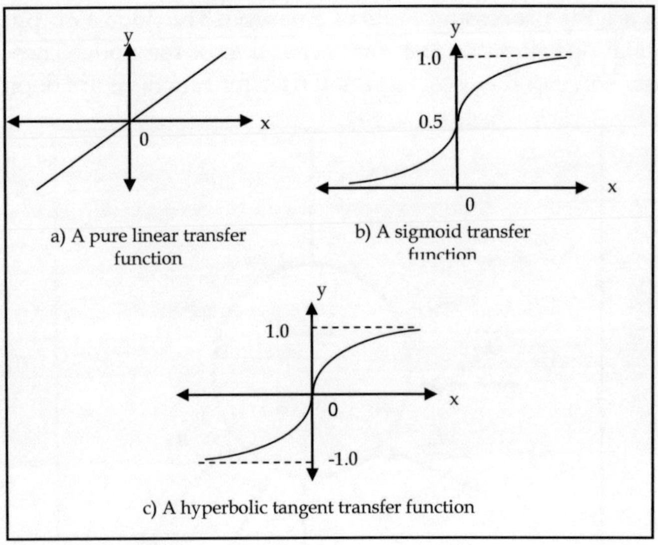

Fig. 6. Commonly used transfer function

2.2 Generalization

After the training is completed, the network error is usually minimized and the network output shows reasonable similarities with the target output, and before a neural network can be used with any degree of confidence, there is a need to establish the validity of the results it generates. A network could provide almost perfect answers to the set of problems with which it was trained, but fail to produce meaningful answers to other examples. Usually, validation involves evaluating network performance on a set of test problem that were not used for training. Generalization (testing) is so named because it measures how well the network can generalize what it has learned and form rules with which to make decisions about data it has not previously seen. The error between the actual and predicted outputs of testing and training converges upon the same point corresponding to the best set of weight factors for the network. If the network is learning an accurate generalized solution to the problem, the average error curve for the test patterns decreases at a rate approaching that of the training patterns. Generalization capability can be used to evaluate the behavior of the neural network.

2.3 Selecting the number of hidden layers

The number of hidden layers and the number of nodes in one hidden layer are not straightforward to ascertain. No rules are available to determine the exact number. The choice of the number of hidden layers and the nodes in the hidden layer(s) depends on the network application. Determining the number of hidden layers is a critical part of designing a network and it is not straightforward as it is for input and output layers (Rafiq el at., 2001).

To determine the optimal number of hidden layers, and the optimal number of nodes in each layer, the network is to be trained using various configurations, and then to select the configuration with the fewest number of layers and nodes that still yields the minimum mean-squares error (MSE) quickly and efficiently. (Eberhard & Dobbins, 1990) recommended the number of hidden-layer nodes be at least greater than the square root of the sum of the number of the components in the input and output vectors. (Carpenter & Barthelemy, 1994; Hajela & Berke, 1991) suggested that the number of nodes in the hidden layer is between the sum and the average of the number of nodes in the input and output layers.

The number of nodes in the hidden layer will be selected according to the following rules:

1. The maximum error of the output network parameters should be as small as possible for both training patterns and testing patterns.
2. The training epochs (number of iteration) should be as few as possible.

2.4 Pre-process and post-process of the training patterns

Neural networks require that their input and output data are normalized to have the same order of magnitude. Normalization is very critical; if the input and the output variables are not of the same order of magnitude, some variables may appear to have more significance than they actually do. The normalization used in the training algorithm compensates for the order-of-differences in magnitude of variables by adjusting the network weights. To avoid such problems, normalization all input and output variables is recommended. The training patterns should be normalized before they are applied to the neural network so as to limit the input and output values within a specified range. This is due to the large difference in the values of the data provided to the neural network. Besides, the activation function used in the back-propagation neural network is a sigmoid function or hyperbolic tangent function. The lower and upper limits of the function are 0 and 1, respectively for sigmoid function and are -1 and +1 for hyperbolic tangent function. The following formula is used to pre-process the input data sets whose values are between -1 and 1(Baughman & Liu, 1995).

$$x_{i,norm.} = 2.\frac{x_i - x_{i,\min.}}{x_{i,\max.} - x_{i,\min.}} - 1 \quad (6)$$

where:
$x_{i,norm}$: the normalized variable.
$x_{i,min}$: the minimum value of variable xi (input).
$x_{i,max}$: the maximum value of variable xi (input).

However, for the sigmoid function the following function might be used.

$$O_{i,norm} = \frac{t_i - t_{i,min}}{t_{i,max} - t_{i,min}} \quad (7)$$

where:
$t_{i,min}$: the minimum value of variable t_i (output).
$t_{i,max}$: the maximum value of variable t_i (output).

3. Adaptive neuro-fuzzy inference system (ANFIS)

The fuzzy set theory developed by (Zadeh, 1965) provides as a mathematical framework to deal with vagueness associated with the description of a variable. The commonly used fuzzy inference system (FIS) is the actual process of mapping from a given input to output using fuzzy logic.

Fuzzy logic is particularly useful in the development of expert systems. Expert systems are built by capturing the knowledge of humans: however, such knowledge is known to be qualitative and inexact. Experts may be only partially knowledgeable about the problem domain, or data may not be fully available, but decisions are still expected. In these situations, educated guesses need to be made to provide solutions to problems. This is where fuzzy logic can be employed as a tool to deal with imprecision and qualitative aspects that are associated with problem solving (Jang, 1993).

A fuzzy set is a set without clear or sharp boundaries or without binary membership characteristics. Unlike a conventional set where object either belongs or do not belong to the set, partial membership in a fuzzy set is possible. In other words, there is a softness associated with the membership of elements in a fuzzy set (Jang, 1993).A fuzzy set may be represented by a membership function. This function gives the grade (degree) of membership within the set. The membership function maps the elements of the universe on to numerical values in the interval [0, 1]. The membership functions most commonly used in control theory are triangular, trapezoidal, Gaussian, generalized bell, sigmoidal and difference sigmoidal membership functions (Jang et al., 1997; Matlab toolbox, 2009; Zaho & Bose, 2002).

As mentioned previously, the fuzzy inference system is the process of formulating the mapping from a given input to an output using fuzzy logic. The dynamic behavior of an FIS is characterized by a set of linguistic description rules based on expert knowledge.

The fuzzy system and neural networks are complementary technologies.The most important reason for combining fuzzy systems with neural networks is to use the learning capability of neural network. While the learning capability is an advantage from the view point of a fuzzy system, from the viewpoint of a neural network there are additional advantages to a combined system. Because a neuro-fuzzy system is based on linguistic rules, we can easily integrate prior knowledge in to the system, and this can substantially shorten the learning process. One of the popular integrated systems is an ANFIS, which is an integration of a fuzzy inference system with a back-propagation algorithm (Jang et al., 1997; Lin & Lee 1996).

There are two types of fuzzy inference systems that can be implemented: Mamdani-type and Sugeno-type (Mamdani & Assilian, 1975; Sugeno, 1985). Because the Sugeno system is more compact and computationally more efficient than a Mamdani system, it lends itself to the use of adaptive techniques for constructing the fuzzy models. These adaptive techniques can be used to customize the membership functions so that the fuzzy system best models the data. The fuzzy inference system based on neuro-adaptive learning techniques is termed adaptive neuro-fuzzy inference system (Hamidian & Seyedpoor, 2009).

In order for an FIS to be mature and well established so that it can work appropriately in prediction mode, its initial structure and parameters (linear and non-linear) need to be tuned or adapted through a learning process using a sufficient input-output pattern of data. One of the most commonly used learning systems for adapting the linear and non-linear parameters of an FIS, particularly the first order Sugeno fuzzy model, is the ANFIS. ANFIS is a class of adaptive networks that are functionally equivalent to fuzzy inference systems (Jang, 1993).

3.1 Architecture of ANFIS

Fig. 7 shows the architecture of a typical ANFIS with two inputs X_1 and X_2, two rules and one output *f*, for the first order Sugeno fuzzy model, where each input is assumed to have two associated membership functions (MFs). For a first-order Sugeno fuzzy model a typical rule set with two fuzzy if–then rules can be expressed as (Jang, 1993):

Rule (1): If X_1 is A_1 and X_2 is B_1, then $f_1 = m_1 X_1 + n_1X_2 + q_1$,
Rule (2): If X_1 is A_2 and X_2 is B_2, then $f_2 = m_2 X_1 + n_2X_2 + q_2$.

where: m_1, n_1, q_1 and m_2, n_2, q_2 are the parameters of the output function.

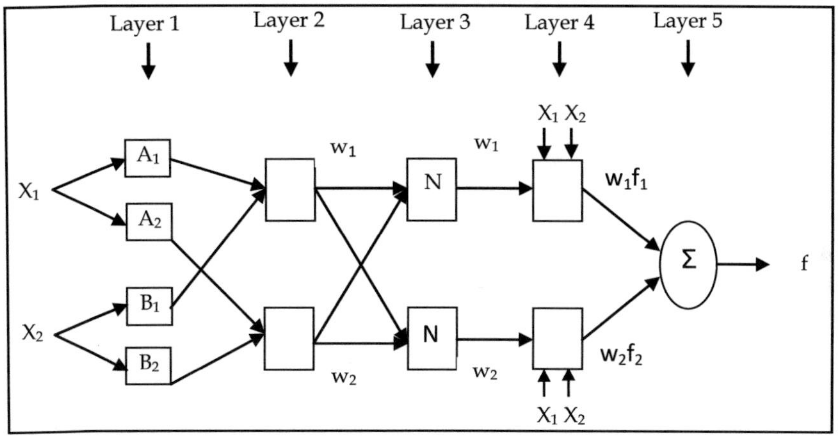

Fig. 7. Structure of the proposed ANFIS model

The architecture of the proposed (ANFIS), it contains five layers where the node functions in the same layer are of the same function family. Inputs, outputs and implemented mathematical models of the nodes of each layer are explained below.

Layer 1: The node function of every node *i* in this layer take the form:

$$O_i^1 = \mu A_i(X) \tag{8}$$

where *X* is the input to node *i*, μA_i is the membership function (which can be triangular, trapezoidal, gaussian functions or other shapes) of the linguistic label A_i associated with this node and O_i is the degree of match to which the input *X* satisfies the quantifier A_i. In the current study, the Gaussian shaped MFs defined below are utilized.

$$\mu A_i(X) = exp\left\{-\frac{1}{2}\frac{(X-c_i)^2}{\sigma_i^2}\right\} \tag{9}$$

where $\{ c_i, \sigma_i\}$ are the parameters of the MFs governing the Gaussian functions. The parameters in this layer are usually referred to as premise parameters.

Layer 2: Every node in this layer multiplies the incoming signals from layer 1 and sends the product out as follows,

$$w_i = \mu A_i(X_1) \times \mu B_i(X_2), i = 1,2 \tag{10}$$

where the output of this layer (w_i) represents the firing strength of a rule.

Layer 3: Every node i in this layer is a node labeled N, determine the ratio of the i-th rule's firing strength to the sum of all rules' firing strengths as:

$$w_i^- = \frac{w_i}{w_1 + w_2} \quad (11)$$

where the output of this layer represent the normalized firing strengths.

Layer 4: Every node i in this layer is an adaptive node with a node function of the form:

$$O_i^4 = w_i^- f_i = w_i^- (m_i X_1 + n_i X_2 + q_i), i = 1{,}2 \quad (12)$$

where w_i^- is the output to layer 3, and $\{m_i, n_i, q_i\}$ is the parameter set of this node. Parameters in this layer are referred to as consequent parameters.

Layer 5: There is only a single node in this layer that computes the overall output as the weighted average of all incoming signals from layer 4 as:

$$O_i^5 = \sum_i w_i^- f_i = \frac{\sum_i w_i f_i}{\sum_i w_i}, i = 1{,}2 \quad (13)$$

3.2 Learning process

As mentioned earlier, both the premise (non-linear) and consequent (linear) parameters of the ANFIS should be tuned, utilizing the so-called learning process, to optimally represent the factual mathematical relationship between the input space and output space. Normally, as a first step, an approximate fuzzy model is initiated by the system and then improved through an iterative adaptive learning process. Basically, ANFIS takes the initial fuzzy model and tunes it by means of a hybrid technique combining gradient descent back-propagation and mean least-squares optimization algorithms. At each epoch, an error measure, usually defined as the sum of the squared difference between actual and desired output, is reduced. Training stops when either the predefined epoch number or error rate is obtained. There are two passes in the hybrid learning procedure for ANFIS. In the forward pass of the hybrid learning algorithm, functional signals go forward till layer 4 and the consequent parameters are identified by the least squares estimate. In the backward pass, the error rates propagate backward and the premise parameters are updated by the gradient descent. When the values of the premise parameters are learned, the overall output (f) can be expressed as a linear combination of the consequent parameters (Jang, 1993):

$$f = \frac{w_1}{w_1 + w_2} f_1 + \frac{w_2}{w_1 + w_2} f_2 = w_1^- f_1 + w_2^- f_2 \quad (14)$$

$$= (w_1^- X_1) m_1 + (w_1^- X_2) n_1 + (w_1^-) q_1 + (w_2^- X_2) m_2 + (w_2^- X_2) n_2 + (w_2^-) q_2$$

which is linear in the consequent parameters m_1, n_1, q_1, m_2, n_2 and q_2.

4. Cases studies

There are two case studies considered in this chapter:

1. Predicting of shear strength of ferrocement members using ANN and ANFIS.

2. Predicting of shear strength of concrete beams reinforced with FRP bars using ANN and ANFIS.

4.1 Case study 1

In this study the back-propagation neural networks (BPNN) model and adaptive neuro-fuzzy inference system (ANFIS) are utilized to predict the shear strength of ferrocement members. A database of the shear strength of ferrocement members obtained from the literature alongside the experimental study conducted by the author is used for the development of these models. The models are developed within MATLAB using BPNN and Sugeno ANFIS.

4.1.1 Review of shear strength of ferrocement members

In recent years, ferrocement has been widely accepted and utilized. Research and development on ferrocement has progressed at a tremendous pace. Many innovative applications are being explored and constructed throughout the world. The application of ferrocement in low cost housing is well known. However, as ferrocement elements are thin, their use for roofing and exterior walls raises doubts regarding the thermal comfort inside the building (Naaman, 2000). Ferrocement is a composite material constructed by cement mortar reinforced with closely spaced layers of wire mesh (Naaman, 2000; Shah, 1974). The ultimate tensile resistance of ferrocement is provided solely by the reinforcement in the direction of loading. The compressive strength is equal to that of the unreinforced mortar. However, in case of flexure and shear, the analysis and design of ferrocement elements is complex and are based primarily on the reinforced concrete analysis using the principles of equilibrium and compatibility.

Few methods have been proposed for the estimation of the shear strength of ferrocement specimens. One of these methods is considered in this study which is given by Rao et al., (2006). They proposed an empirical expression to estimate the shear strength of ferrocement elements by considering the shear resistance of ferrocement elements as the sum of shear resistance due to mortar and reinforcement. The shear resistance of ferrocement element (V_u) was given as:

$$\frac{V_u}{b.d} = \frac{\sqrt{f_c'}}{a/d}\left\{0.0856 + 0.0028\frac{v_f f_y}{\sqrt{f_c'}}\right\} \tag{15}$$

4.1.2 ANN for predicted the shear strength of ferrocement members

An artificial neural network was developed to predict the shear strength of ferrocement. This section describes the data selection for training and testing patterns, the topology of the constructed network, the training process and the verification of the neural network results. A relative importance is carried out which is based on the artificial neural network predictions. Finally, the results of the shear strength of ferrocement members predicted by BPNN and ANFIS are compared with the results of the experimental program and empirical method. The empirical method was proposed by (Rao et al., 2006).

4.1.2.1 Selection of the training and testing patterns

The experimental data that are used to train the neural network are obtained from literature (Mansur & Ong, 1987; Mashrei, 2010; Rao et al., 2006) as shown in Table A in appendix. The data used to build the neural network model should be divided into two subsets: training set and testing set. The testing set contains approximately 13% from total database. The training phase is needed to produce a neural network that is both stable and convergent. Therefore, selecting what data to use for training a network is one of the most important steps in building a neural network model. The total numbers of 69 test specimens was utilized. The training set contained 60 specimens and the testing set was comprised of 9 specimens.

Neural networks interpolate data very well. Therefore, patterns chosen for training set must cover upper and lower boundaries and a sufficient number of samples representing particular features over the entire training domain (Rafiq et al., 2001).An important aspect of developing neural networks is determining how well the network performs once training is complete. The performance of a trained network is checked by involving two main criteria:

1. How well the neural network recalls the predicted response from data sets used to train the network (called the recall step). A well trained network should be able to produce an output that deviates very little from desired value.
2. How well the network predicts responses from data sets that were not used in the training (called the generalization step). Generalization is affected by three factors: the size and the efficiency of the training data set, the architecture of the network, and the physical complexity of the problem. A well generalized network should be able to sense the new input patterns.

To effectively visualize how well a network performs recall and generalization steps, the learning curve is generated which represents the mean square error (MSE) for both the recall of training data sets and generalization of testing set with the number of iteration or epoch. The error between the training data sets and the generalization of testing sets should converge upon the same point corresponding to the best set of weight factors for the network.

4.1.2.2 Input and output layers

In the developed neural network model there is an input layer, where input data are presented to the network, and an output layer of one neuron representing the shear strength of ferrocement member. In this study the parameters which may be introduced as the components of the input vector consist of six inputs: the total depth of specimens cross

Parameters	Range
Width of specimens (b) (mm)	100-200
Total depth of specimens (d) (mm)	25-50
Shear span to depth ratio (a/d)	1-7
Compressive strength of mortar (f_c')	26.5-44.1
yield strength of wire mesh (f_y) (MPa)	380-410
Volume fraction of wire mesh (v_f) %	0-5.7

Table 1. Range of parameters in the database

section (d), the width of specimens cross section (b),yield tensile strength of wire mesh reinforcement (f_y), cylinder compressive strength of mortar (fc'), total volume fraction of wire mesh (v_f) and shear span to depth ratio (a/d). The shear strength of ferrocement member represents the target variable. Table 1 summarizes the ranges of each different variable.

4.1.2.3 Normalizing input and output data sets

Normalization (scaling down) of input and output data sets within a uniform range before they are applied to the neural network is essential to prevent larger numbers from overriding smaller ones, and to prevent premature saturation of hidden nodes, which impedes the learning process. The limitation of input and output values within a specified range are due to the large difference in the values of the data provided to the neural network. Besides, the activation function used in the back-propagation neural network is a hyperbolic tangent function, the lower and upper limits of this function are -1 and +1 respectively. In this study Eq. 5 mentioned above is used to normalize the input and output parameters. That equation gives the required results with a certain mean square error by a small number of epochs.

4.1.2.4 Number of hidden layers and nodes in each hidden layer

The network is tested with an increasing number of nodes in hidden layer. It is found that one-hidden layer network with four nodes gives the optimal configurations with minimum mean square error (MSE). As an activation function, a hyperbolic tangent function is selected for the hidden layer and a purelin function is used for the output layer.

In this study the initial weights are randomly chosen. The network has been trained continually through updating weights until the final error achieved is $8.48*10^{-4}$.

Fig. 8 shows the performance for training and generalization (testing) sets using resilient back-propagation training algorithm, the network is trained for 420 epochs to check if the performance (MSE) for either training or testing sets might diverge. The network performance with resilient back-propagation training algorithm have been tested for training and generalizing patterns, as shown in Fig. 9 (a) and (b). A good agreement has been noted in the predicted values compared with the actual (targets) values.

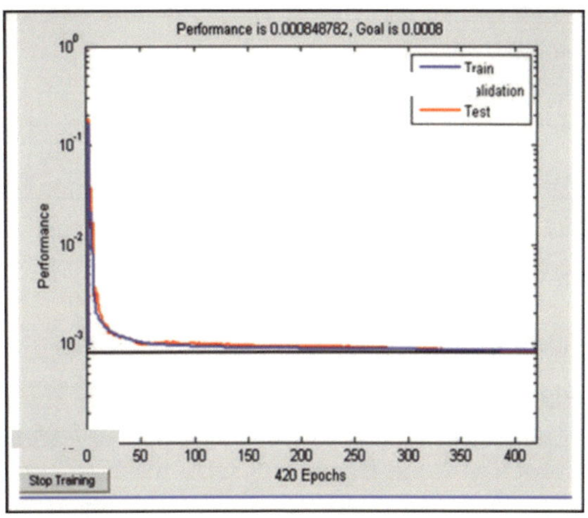

Fig. 8. Convergence of the BPNN for training and testing sets

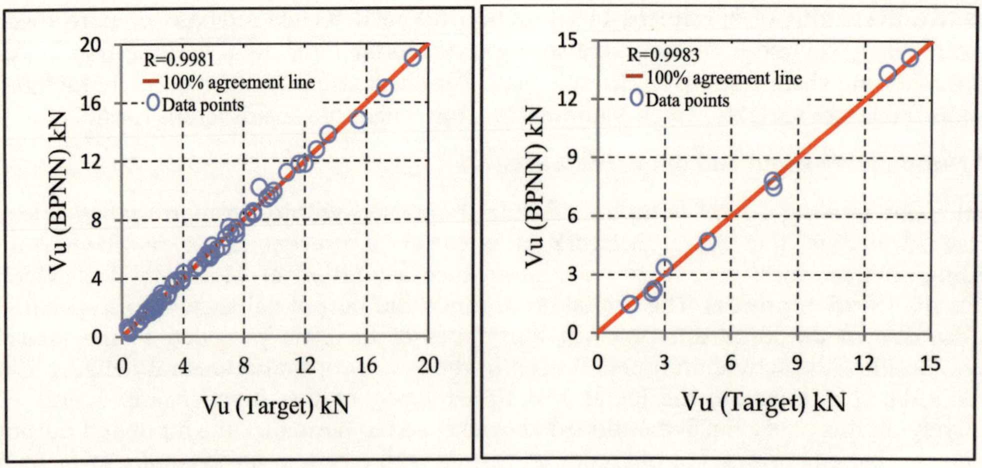

(a) For training pattern (b) For testing pattern

Fig. 9. Comparison between BPNN results and target results

4.1.2.5 Relative importance

Once the artificial neural network has been trained, a relative importance is used to investigate the influence of the various parameters on the shear strength. The effect of each parameter on the shear strength of ferrocement is clear in Table 2. After training all the data sets with the final model, the relative importance of each input variable is evaluated. The methodology suggested by Garson, (1991) is used. The relative importance of the various input factors can be assessed by examining input-hidden-output layer connection weights. This is carried out by partitioning the hidden-output connection weights into components connected with each input neuron. Table 2 lists the relative importance of the input variables in the BPNN model. It can be observed that for shear strength of the ferrocement member, the shear span to depth ratio ($^{a}/_{d}$) is the most important factor among the input variables and volume fraction of wire mesh is the second most important factor comparing with the others. Therefore, it can be concluded that ($^{a}/_{d}$) ratio has the most influence on the shear strength of ferrocement.

Input variables	b (mm)	d (mm)	f_c' (MPa)	f_y (MPa)	$^{a}/_{d}$	v_f (%)
RI (%)	7.11	20.0	8.89	5.28	38.32	20.4

Table 2. Relative importance (RI) (%) of BPNN model

4.1.3 Adaptive neural fuzzy inference system (ANFIS) model

In the developed ANFIS, six variables consisting of width (b) and depth (d) of the specimens, yield tensile strength of wire mesh reinforcement (f_y), cylinder compressive strength of mortar (f_c'), total volume fraction of wire mesh (v_f) and shear span to depth ratio ($^{a}/_{d}$) are selected as input variables to predict the shear strength of ferrocement members, which is the target variable. In this investigation the subtractive clustering technique introduced by (Chiu, 1994)with (genfis2) function was used. Given separate sets of input and output data, the genfis2 uses a subtractive clustering method to generate a Fuzzy Inference System (FIS). When there is only one output, genfis2 may be used to generate an initial FIS for ANFIS training by first implementing subtractive clustering on the data. The genfis2 function uses the subclust function to estimate the antecedent membership functions and a set of rules. This function returns an FIS structure that contains a set of fuzzy rules to cover the feature space (Fuzzy Logic Toolbox, 2009). For a given set of data, subtractive clustering method was used for estimating the number of clusters and the cluster centers in a set of data. It assumes each data point is a potential cluster center and calculates a measure of the potential for each data point based on the density of surrounding data points. The algorithm selects the data point with the highest potential as the first cluster center and then delimits the potential of data points near the first cluster center. The algorithm then selects the data point with the highest remaining potential as the next cluster center and delimits the potential of data points near this new cluster center. This process of acquiring a new cluster center and delimiting the potential of surrounding data points repeats until the potential of all data points falls below a threshold. The range of influence of a cluster center in each of the data dimensions is called cluster radius. A small cluster radius will lead to finding many small clusters in the data (resulting in many rules) and vice versa (Jang, 1997; Jonic', 1999). Membership functions (MFs) and numbers are appropriately decided when testing data set.

4.1.3.1 Database

The adaptive neuro-fuzzy inference system model is developed to predict the shear strength of ferrocement members. The same database of (69) specimens as in the previous BPNN model is used for the development of this model. The total data is divided at random into two groups (training data set, and testing data set), as shown in Table A in Appendix.

4.1.3.2 Modeling and results

The ANFIS model is developed to predict shear strength of ferrocement specimens with MFs of type (gussmf) for all input variables and linear for the output. The number of MFs assigned to each input variable is chosen by trial and error. After training and testing, the

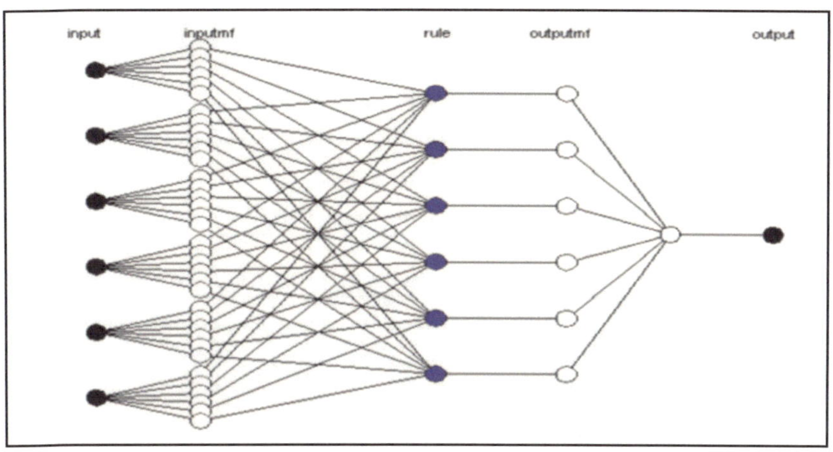

Fig. 10. Structure of the proposed ANFIS model

number of MFs is fixed as six MFs for each input variable. This is chosen when the ANFIS model reaches an acceptable satisfactory level. The structure of ANFIS model is developed as shown in Fig. 10. The basic flow diagram of computations in ANFIS is illustrated in Fig. 11. A comparison between the prediction from ANFIS and target value for each of training and testing data set is shown in Fig. 12(a) and (b) respectively. The predictions appear to be quite good with correlation coefficient R approaches one.

4.1.4 Comparison between experimental and theoretical results

The predictions of shear strength of ferrocement members as obtained from BPNN, ANFIS, and the empirical available method (Eq.15) (Rao et al., 2006) are compared with the experimental results and shown for both training and testing sets in Figs.13 and 14 and Table 3 . In Table 3 the ratios of experimental (V_e) to theoretical predictions of the shear strength (V_i) of the ferrocement specimens are calculated. The theoretical predications include those obtained by BPNN (V_1), ANFIS (V_2), and empirical method (Eq.15) (V_3). The average and the standard deviation of the ratios V_e/V_i are given in this table for both training and testing set. It can be seen that BPNN and ANFIS models give average values of V_e/V_1 and V_e/V_2 of 1.01 and standard deviations of 0.14 and 0.13, respectively for training set and the average values of V_e/V_1 and V_e/V_2 of 1.03 and standard deviations of 0.09 and 0.08, respectively for testing set , which are better than the values obtained for the empirical method. Figs. 13 and 14 confirm the same conclusion the predictions of BPNN and ANFIS

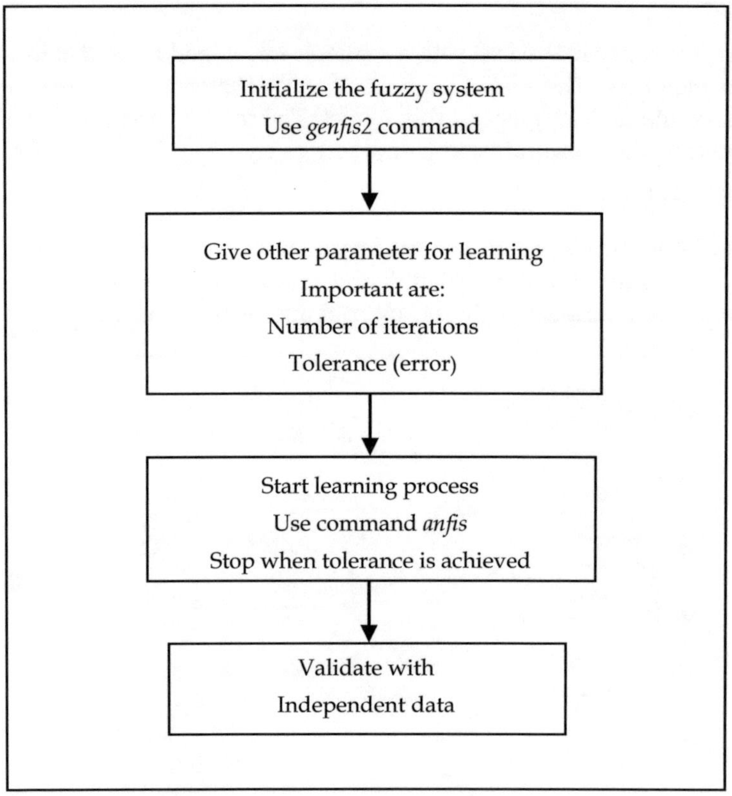

Fig. 11. The basic flow diagram of computations in ANFIS

models are better than those of the empirical method. Also in Table 3 the correlation coefficient R of predicted shear strength by BPNN, ANFIS, and the empirical method are summarized. As shown in Table 4, both ANFIS and BPNN produce a higher correlation coefficient R as compared with the empirical method. Therefore, the BPNN as well as ANFIS can serve as reliable and simple tools for the prediction of shear strength of ferrocement.

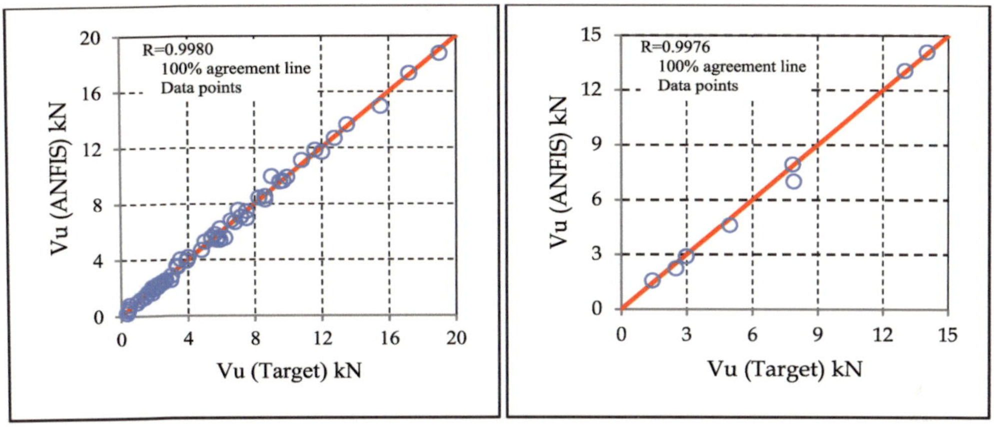

(a) For training pattern (b) For training pattern

Fig. 12. Comparison between ANFIS results and target results

Specimens	No.	Average of of V_e / V_i			STDEV of V_e / V_i		
		$\frac{V_e}{V_1}$	$\frac{V_e}{V_2}$	$\frac{V_e}{V_3}$	$\frac{V_e}{V_1}$	$\frac{V_e}{V_2}$	$\frac{V_e}{V_3}$
Training set	60	1.01	1.01	1.21	0.14	0.13	0.27
Testing set	9	1.03	1.03	1.23	0.09	0.08	0.31

Table 3. Comparison between experimental and predicted results for training and testing sets

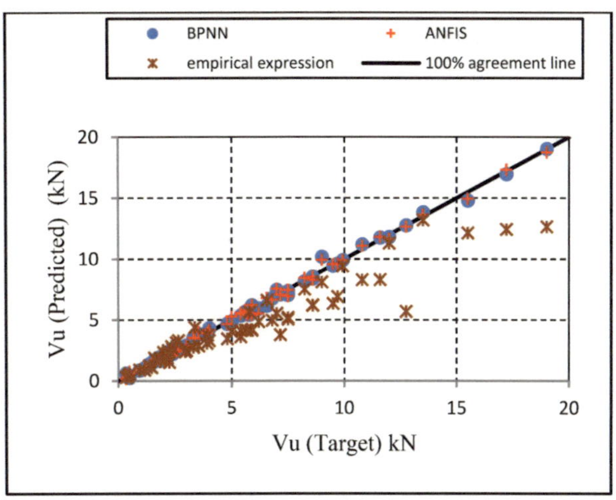

Fig. 13. Comparison experimental and predicted values for training data Set

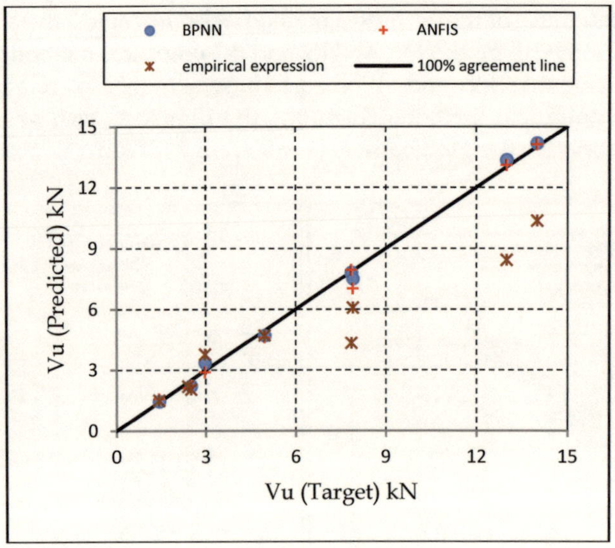

Fig. 14. Comparison experimental and predicted values for testing data Set

Type	Correlation R	
	Training	Testing
BPNN	0.9981	0.9983
ANFIS	0.9980	0.9976
Empirical Method	0.9500	0.9600

Table 4. Comparison summary of correlation R

4.2 Case study 2

In this part the PBNN and ANFIS models are developed to predict the shear strength of concrete beams reinforced with FRP bars. A database from tests on concrete beams reinforced with FRP bars obtained from the review of literature is used in this study. The structure of ANN and ANFIS models and the results of this study will be described below.

4.2.1 Review on shear strength of concrete beams reinforced with FRP bars

An FRP bar is made from filaments or fibers held in a polymeric resin matrix binder. The FRP Bar can be made from various types of fibers such as Glass (GFRP) or Carbon (CFRP). FRP bars have a surface treatment that facilitates a bond between the finished bar and the structural element into which they are placed (Bank, 2006).

During the last two decades, fiber reinforced polymer (FRP) materials have been used in a variety of configurations as an alternative reinforcement for new and strengthening civil engineering structures and bridges. The attractiveness of the material lies mainly in their high corrosion resistance, high strength and fatigue resistance. In some cases, the non-magnetic characteristics became more important for some special structures. An important application of FRP, which is becoming more popular (Tan, 2003, as cited in Al-Sayed et at.,

2005a) is the use of FRP for reinforcement in concrete structures. The use of FRP in concrete structures include: (a) the internal reinforcing (rod or bar) which is used instead of the steel wire (rod) equivalent; and (b) the external bonded reinforcement, which is typically used to repair/strengthen the structure by plating or wrapping FRP tape, sheet or fabric around the member (Wu & Bailey, 2005).

There are fundamental differences between the steel and FRP reinforcements: the latter has a lower modulus of elasticity, the modulus of elasticity for commercially available glass and aramid FRP bars is 20 to 25 % that of steel compared to 60 to 75 % for carbon FRP bars (Bank, 2006) linear stress-strain diagram up to rupture with no discernible yield point and different bond strength according to the type of FRP product. These characteristics affect the shear capacity of FRP reinforced concrete members. Due to the relatively low modulus of elasticity of FRP bars, concrete members reinforced longitudinally with FRP bars experience reduced shear strength compared to the shear strength of those reinforced with the same amounts of steel reinforcement.

Some of empirical equations have been developed to estimate shear strength of concrete beams reinforced with FRP. Most of the shear design provisions incorporated in these codes and guides are based on the design formulas of members reinforced with conventional steel considering some modifications to account for the substantial differences between FRP and steel reinforcement. These provisions use the well-known $V_c + V_s$ method of shear design, which is based on the truss analogy. This section reviews the concrete shear strength of members longitudinally reinforced with FRP bars, V_{cf}, as recommended by the American Concrete Institute (ACI 440.1R-03, 2003), Tureyen and Frosch Equation (2003), and the proposed equation by El-Sayed et al. (2005a).

4.2.1.1 American Concrete Institute (ACI 440.1R-03)

The equation for shear strength proposed by the American Concrete Institute (ACI 440.1R-03), can be expressed as follows:

$$V_{cf} = \frac{\rho_f E_f}{90\beta_1 f'_c}\left(\frac{\sqrt{f'_c}}{6} b_w d\right) \le \frac{\sqrt{f'_c}}{6} b_w d \tag{16}$$

4.2.1.2 Tureyen and Frosch equation (2003)

This equation was developed by Tureyen and Frosch, 2003. It was developed from a model that calculates the concrete contribution to shear strength of reinforced concrete beams. The equation was simplified to provide a design formula applicable FRP reinforced beams as follows:

$$V_{cf} = \frac{2}{5}\left(\frac{\sqrt{f'_c}}{6} b_w c\right) \tag{17}$$

where: $c = kd$= cracked transformed section neutral axis depth (mm).

$$k = \sqrt{2\rho_f n_f + (\rho_f n_f)^2 - \rho_f n_f} \tag{18}$$

4.2.1.3 El-Sayed et al. equation (2005a)

They applied the same procedure in ACI 440.1R-03 to derive Eq. 1 above, with some modification for proposing the Eq. below:

$$V_{cf} = 0.037 \left(\frac{\rho_f E_f \sqrt{f_c'}}{\beta_1}\right)^{1/3} b_w d \leq \frac{\sqrt{f_c'}}{6} b_w d \tag{19}$$

According to ACI 440.1R-03, the factor β_1 in the denominator of Eq. 3 is a function of the concrete compressive strength. It can be simply expressed by the following equation:

$$0.85 \geq \beta_1 = 0.85 - 0.007(f_c' - 28) \geq 0.65 \tag{20}$$

4.2.2 Shear strength database

From the review of literature (Deitz, et al., 1999; El-Sayed et al. , 2005b, 2006a, 2006b, 2006c; Gross et al., 2003, 2004; Omeman et al., 2008; Razaqpur et al., 2004; Tariq & Newhook, 2003; Tureyen & Frosch, 2002, 2003; Wegian & Abdalla , 2005; Yost et al., 2001), a number (74) of shear strength tests are used for developing the ANN and ANFIS as shown in Table B in appendix. All specimens were simply supported and were tested in three-point loading. The main reinforcement of all specimens is FRP. All specimens had no transverse reinforcement and failed in shear. These data are divided into two sets: a training set containing 64 members, and testing set comprised of 10 members. Six input variables are selected to build the ANN and ANFIS models. These variables are width (b_w), and depth (d) of the beams, modulus of elasticity of FRP (E_f), compressive strength of concrete (f_c'), reinforcement ratio of FRP (ρ_f) and the shear span to depth ratio ($^a/_d$). The output value is the shear strength of concrete beams reinforced with FRP bars. Table 5 summarizes the ranges of each different variable.

Parameters	Range
Width of beams (b_w) mm	89-1000
Effective depth of beams (d) mm	143-360
Shear span to depth ratio ($^a/_d$)	1.3-6.5
Compressive strength of concrete (f_c') MPa	24-81
Modulus of elasticity of FRP (E_f) (GPa)	37-145
Reinforcement ratio of FRP (ρ_f)	0.25-2.63

Table 5. Summarizes the ranges of the different variables.

4.2.3 ANN model and results

ANN is used to investigate the shear strength of concrete beams reinforced with FRP bars. The configuration and training of neural networks is a trail-and-error process due to such undetermined parameters as the number of nodes in the hidden layer, and the number of training patterns. In the developed ANN, there is an input layer, where six parameters are presented to network and an output layer, with one neuron representing shear strength of concrete beams reinforced with FRP bars. One hidden layer as intermediate layer is also included. The network with one hidden layer and four nodes in the hidden layer gave the optimal configuration with minimum mean square error (MSE).

The back-propagation neural network model used for this study is trained by feeding a set of mapping data with input and target variables as explained previously. After the errors are minimized, the model with all the parameters including the connection weights is tested with a separate set of "testing" data that is not used in the training phase.

The network has trained continually through updating of the weights until error goal of $15.1*10^{-4}$ is achieved. Fig. 15 shows the performance for training and generalization (testing). A resilient back propagation training algorithm is used to train the network, for 800 epochs to check if the performance (MSE) for either training or testing sets might diverge.

The network performance with resilient back propagation training algorithm have been tested for training and testing patterns, as shown in Fig. 16 (a) and (b). A good agreement has been noted in the predicting values compared with the actual (targets) values.

Based on the same idea used to study the effect of the parameters on shear strength of ferrocement members, the effect of each parameter used in the input layer on shear strength of concrete beams reinforced with FRP bars is investigated. Table 6 lists the relative importance of the input variables in BPNN model. It can be observed that for shear strength of concrete beams reinforced with FRP, the shear span to depth ratio($^a/_d$) is also the most important factor among the input variables. This result is very match with the experimental results of many papers published in this field.

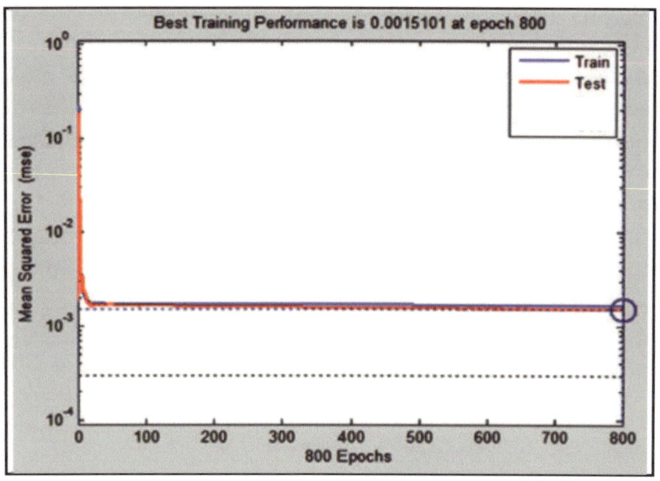

Fig. 15. Convergence of the BPNN for training and testing sets

Input variables	b_w (mm)	d (mm)	f_c' (MPa)	E_f (MPa)	$^a/_d$	ρ_f (%)
RI (%)	24.76	18.26	11.11	5.23	37.50	3.19

Table 6. Relative importance (RI) (%) of BPNN model

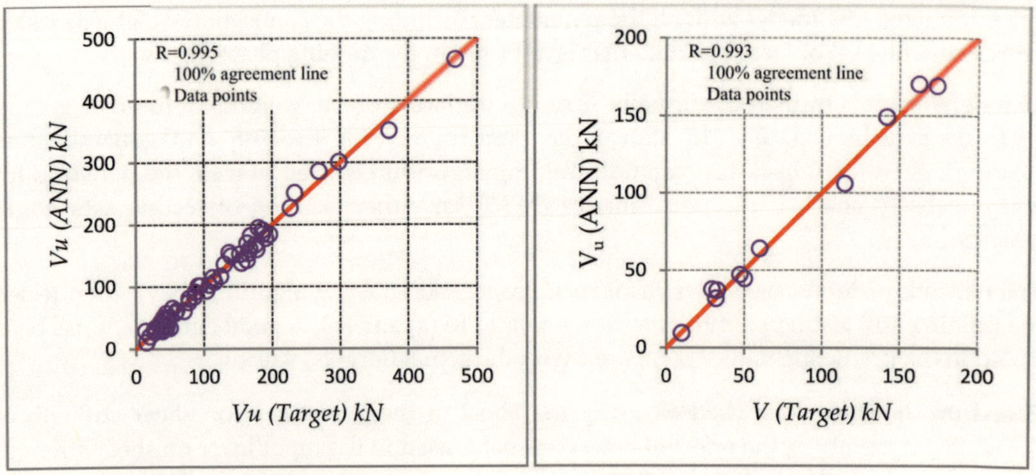

(a) For training pattern (b) For training pattern

Fig. 16. Comparison between BPNN results and target results

4.2.4 ANFIS model and results

The same technique used to build the ANFIS to predict shear strength of ferrocement members is used to build of ANFIS to predict the shear strength of concrete beams reinforced with FRP bars. Fig. 17 presents the structure of an adaptive neuro-fuzzy inference system developed to predict shear strength of concrete beams reinforced with FRP bars. The membership functions (MFs) of type (Gauss) for all input variables and linear for output present the best prediction in this study. The number of MFs assigned to each input variable is chosen by trial and error. After training and testing the number of MFs was fixed at two MFs for each input variable, when the ANFIS model reaches an acceptable satisfactory level. A comparison between the predictions from ANFIS and target value for both the training and testing data set is presented in Fig. 18(a) and(b) respectively. A good agreement has been noted in the predicting values compared with the experimental (target) values with reasonably high correlation R.

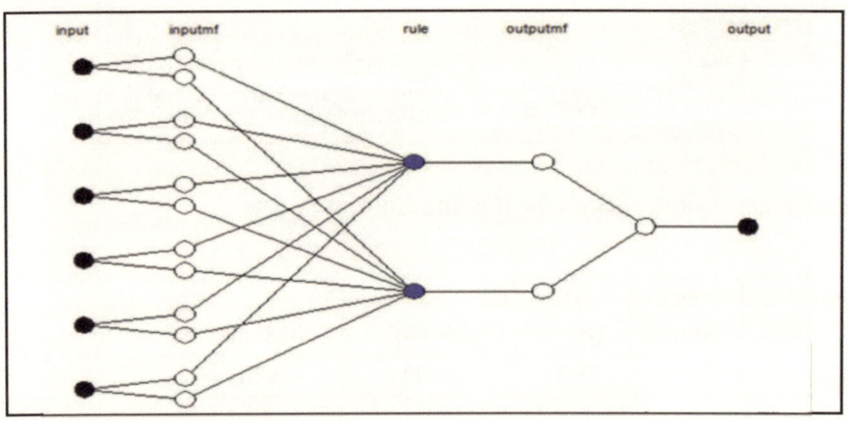

Fig. 17. Structure of the proposed ANFIS model

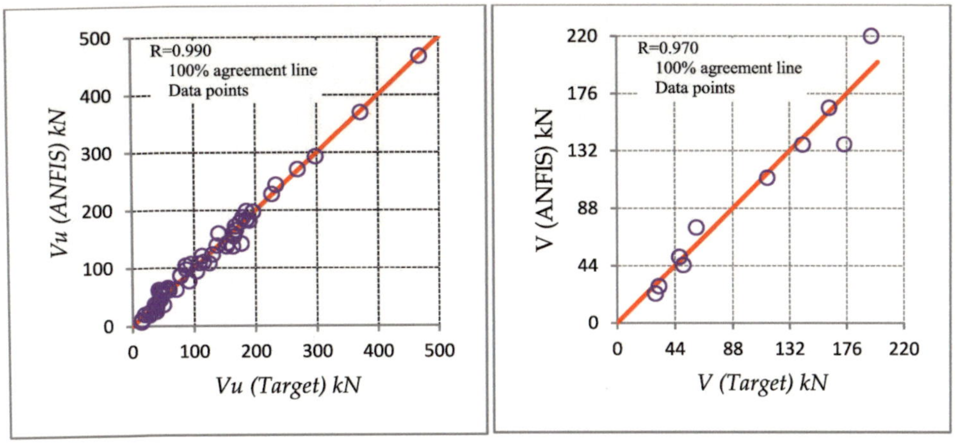

(a) For training pattern (b) For training pattern

Fig. 18. Comparison between BPNN results and target results

4.2.5 Comparison between experimental and theoretical results

The predictions of shear strength of beams reinforced with FRP as that obtained from BPNN, ANFIS, ACI 440.1R-03, Tureyen and Frosch's equation, and the proposed equation by El-Sayed et al. (2005a), are compared with the experimental results and shown for both training and testing sets in Figs. 19 and 20 and Table 7.

In Table 6 the ratios of experimental (V_e) to theoretical (V_i) predictions of the shear strength of beams reinforced with FRP are calculated, the theoretical predictions include those obtained by BPNN (V_1), ANFIS (V_2), proposed equation by El-Sayed et al. (V_3), ACI 440.1R-03 (V_4), and Tureyen and Frosch's equation (V_5). The average and the standard deviation of the ratios V_e/V_i are also given in this table. It can be seen that the BPNN and ANFIS models give average values for the testing set of V_e/V_1 and V_e/V_2 of 0.97 and 1.03 and standard deviations of 0.1 and 0.167 respectively which are much better than the values obtained from other methods as shown in table 7. Figs. 19 and 20 confirm the same conclusion that the predictions of the ANN and ANFIS models are better than those of the other methods.

Also in Table 8 the correlation coefficient R of predicted shear strength that was evaluated by BPNN, ANFIS and the other methods are summarized. As shown in Table 8, the BPNN and ANFIS produces a higher correlation coefficient R as compared with the other methods. These results indicate that the BPNN and ANFIS is a reliable and simple model for predicting the shear strength of beams reinforced with FRP bars.

Specimens	No	Average of of V_e / V_i					STDEV of V_e / V_i				
		$\frac{V_e}{V_1}$	$\frac{V_e}{V_2}$	$\frac{V_e}{V_3}$	$\frac{V_e}{V_4}$	$\frac{V_e}{V_5}$	$\frac{V_e}{V_1}$	$\frac{V_e}{V_2}$	$\frac{V_e}{V_3}$	$\frac{V_e}{V_4}$	$\frac{V_e}{V_5}$
Training set	64	1.01	1.04	2.30	5.32	3.17	0.16	0.23	2.31	3.94	2.98
Testing set	10	0.96	1.03	2.01	3.93	2.73	0.103	0.17	1.72	1.62	2.27

Table 7. Comparison between experimental and Predicted results for training and testing sets

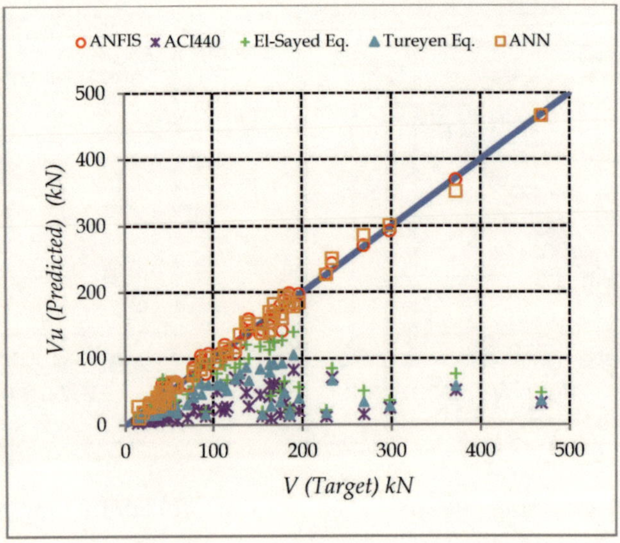

Fig. 19. Comparison experimental and predicted values for testing data set

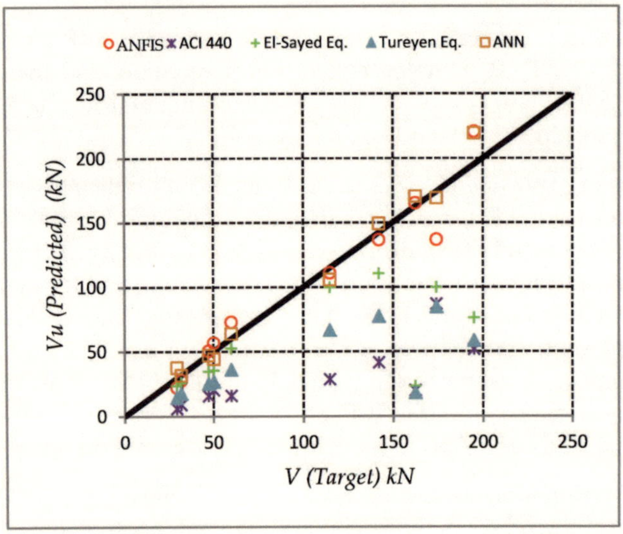

Fig. 20. Comparison experimental and predicted values for testing data set

Type	Correlation R	
	Training	Testing
ANN	0.995	0.993
ANFIS	0.99	0.97
El-Sayed's Eq.	0..32	0.63
ACI 440	0.51	0.78
Tureyen and Frosch's Eq.	0.37	0.69

Table 8. Comparison summary of correlation R

5. Conclusion

Two civil engineering applications are preformed using back-propagation neural network (BPNN)and adaptive neuro fuzzy inference system (ANFIS). The models were developed by predicting the shear strength of ferrocement members and the shear strength of concrete beams reinforced with fiber reinforced polymer (FRP) bars using BPNN and ANFIS based on the results of experimental lab work conducted by different authors. From the results of this study, the following conclusions can be stated:

1. BPNN and ANFIS have the ability to predict the shear strength of ferrocement members and the shear strength of concrete beams reinforced with FRP with a high degree of accuracy when they are compared with experimental and available methods results.
2. The relative importance of each input parameter is estimated using ANN. The relative importance study indicated that the predicted shear strength for both ferrocement and concrete beams with FRP by ANN models are in agreement with the underlying behavior of shear strength prediction based on the prior knowledge.
3. The ANN and ANFIS techniques offer an alternative approach to conventional techniques and, from them, some advantages can be obtained. Conventional models are based on the assumption of predefined empirical equations dependent on unknown parameters. However, in problems for which the modeling rules are either not known or extremely difficult to discover, such as in our problem, the conventional methods do not work well as shown in results. By using artificial neural network and the adaptive neuro fuzzy inference system, these difficulties are overcome since they are based on the learning and generalization from experimental data. ANN and ANFIS models can serve as reliable and simple predictive tools for the prediction of shear strength for both ferrocement and concrete beams with FRP of ferrocement members. Therefore, these models can be applied to solve most of civil engineering problems as a future research.

6. Nomenclature

V_u: Shear strength.
V_{cf}: The shear resistance of members reinforced with FRP bars as flexural reinforcement.
b: Width of the specimen.
d: Depth of the specimen.
v_f: Volume fraction of the mesh reinforcement (100*A_{ls}/ bd).
A_{ls}: Cross sectional area of the longitudinal reinforcing mesh
b_w: Width of the concrete specimen reinforced wih FRP
ρ_f: Reinforcement ratio of flexural FRP.
E_f: Modulus of elasticity of fiber reinforced polymers.
n_f: Ratio of the modulus of elasticity of FRP bars to the modulus of elasticity of concrete.
$f_c^{'}$: Compressive strength of concrete or mortar.
f_y: Yield strength of reinforcement (wire mesh or FRP).
a/d: Shear span to depth ratio.
β_1: Is a function of the concrete compressive strength.

6.1 Appendix

Test No.	b (mm)	d (mm)	f_c' (MPa)	f_y (MPa)	a/d	v_f %	V_u (kN)	Reference
1	100	40	35.20	410.00	1.00	1.80	8.60	*Mansur Ong*, 1987
2	100	40	35.20	410.00	1.50	1.80	5.40	
3	100	40	35.20	410.00	2.00	1.80	3.90	
4	100	40	35.20	410.00	2.50	1.80	3.00	
5	100	40	35.20	410.00	3.00	1.80	2.50	
6	100	40	35.20	410.00	1.00	2.72	10.80	
7	100	40	35.20	410.00	1.50	2.72	7.00	
8	100	40	35.20	410.00	2.00	2.72	5.70	
9	100	40	35.20	410.00	2.50	2.72	4.00	
10	100	40	35.20	410.00	3.00	2.72	3.30	
11	100	40	36.00	410.00	1.00	3.62	14.00	
12	100	40	36.00	410.00	1.50	3.62	9.70	
13	100	40	36.00	410.00	2.00	3.62	7.50	
14	100	40	36.00	410.00	2.50	3.62	5.90	
15	100	40	36.00	410.00	3.00	3.62	4.80	
16	100	40	36.00	410.00	1.00	4.52	17.20	
17	100	40	36.00	410.00	1.50	4.52	11.60	
18	100	40	36.00	410.00	2.00	4.52	8.60	
19	100	40	36.00	410.00	2.50	4.52	6.80	
20	100	40	36.00	410.00	3.00	4.52	5.60	
21	100	40	44.10	410.00	1.00	4.52	19.00	*Mansur & Ong, 1987*
22	100	40	44.10	410.00	1.50	4.52	13.00	
23	100	40	44.10	410.00	2.00	4.52	9.50	
24	100	40	44.10	410.00	2.50	4.52	7.50	
25	100	40	44.10	410.00	3.00	4.52	5.90	
26	100	40	26.50	410.00	1.00	4.52	15.50	
27	100	40	26.50	410.00	1.50	4.52	9.00	
28	100	40	26.50	410.00	2.00	4.52	7.90	
29	100	40	26.50	410.00	2.50	4.52	6.20	
30	100	40	26.50	410.00	3.00	4.52	5.00	
31	150	25	32.20	0	1.00	0	1.84	*Rao et al.,* 2006
32	150	25	32.20	380.00	1.00	2.85	8.24	
33	150	25	32.20	380.00	1.00	3.80	9.93	
34	150	25	32.20	380.00	1.00	4.75	12.00	

Test No.	b (mm)	d (mm)	f_c' (MPa)	f_y (MPa)	a/d	v_f %	V_u (kN)	Reference
35	150	25	32.20	380.00	1.00	5.70	13.50	
36	150	25	32.20	380.00	2.00	0	0.93	
37	150	25	32.20	380.00	2.00	2.85	3.92	
38	150	25	32.20	380.00	2.00	3.80	4.95	
39	150	25	32.20	380.00	2.00	4.75	5.79	
40	150	25	32.20	380.00	2.00	5.70	6.57	
41	150	25	32.20	0	3.00	0	0.49	
42	150	25	32.20	380.00	3.00	2.85	2.20	
43	150	25	32.20	380.00	3.00	3.80	2.55	
44	150	25	32.20	380.00	3.00	4.75	2.97	
45	150	25	32.20	380.00	3.00	5.70	3.36	
46	150	25	32.20	0	4.00	0	0.44	
47	150	25	32.20	380.00	4.00	2.85	1.60	
48	150	25	32.20	380.00	4.00	3.80	1.99	
49	150	25	32.20	380.00	4.00	4.75	2.35	
50	150	25	32.20	380.00	4.00	5.70	2.65	
51	150	25	32.20	0	5.00	0	0.40	
52	150	25	32.20	380.00	5.00	2.85	1.42	
53	150	25	32.20	380.00	5.00	3.80	1.86	
54	150	25	32.20	380.00	5.00	4.75	2.16	
55	150	25	32.20	380.00	5.00	5.70	2.40	
56	150	25	32.20	0	6.00	0	0.34	
57	150	25	32.20	380.00	6.00	2.85	1.37	
58	150	25	32.20	380.00	6.00	3.80	1.84	
59	150	25	32.20	380.00	6.00	4.75	2.15	
60	150	25	32.20	380.00	6.00	5.70	2.40	
61	200	50	33.80	390.00	7.00	0.25	1.16	Mashrei, 2010
62	200	50	33.80	390.00	7.00	0.50	1.47	
63	200	50	36.90	390.00	7.00	0.99	2.25	
64	200	50	40.40	390.00	3.00	0.25	2.94	
65	200	50	40.40	390.00	3.00	0.50	3.53	
66	200	50	40.40	390.00	3.00	0.99	7.16	
67	200	50	41.20	390.00	2.00	0.25	5.40	
68	200	50	41.20	390.00	2.00	0.50	7.85	
69	200	50	41.20	390.00	2.00	0.99	12.75	

Table A. Experimental data used to construct the BPNN and ANFIS for shear strength of ferrocement members

Test No.	b (mm)	d (mm)	f_c' (MPa)	ρ_f %	E_f (Gpa)	a/d	V_u (kN)	Reference
1	1000	165.3	40	0.39	114	6.05	140	El-Sayed et al., 2005b
2	1000	159	40	1.7	40	6.29	142	
3	1000	165.3	40	0.78	114	6.05	167	
4	1000	160.5	40	1.18	114	6.23	190	
5	1000	162.1	40	0.86	40	6.16	113	
6	1000	162.1	40	1.71	40	6.16	163	
7	1000	159	40	2.44	40	6.29	163	
8	1000	154.1	40	2.63	40	6.49	168	
9	250	326	44.6	1.22	42	3.07	60	El-Sayed et al., 2006a, 2006b
10	250	326	50	0.87	128	3.07	77.5	
11	250	326	50	0.87	39	3.07	70.5	
12	250	326	44.6	1.24	134	3.07	104	
13	250	326	43.6	1.72	134	3.07	124.5	
14	250	326	43.6	1.71	42	3.07	77.5	
15	250	326	63	1.71	135	3.07	130	
16	250	326	63	2.2	135	3.07	174	
17	250	326	63	1.71	42	3.07	87	
18	250	326	63	2.2	42	3.07	115.5	
19	200	225	40.5	0.25	145	2.67	36.1	Razaqpur et al., 2004
20	200	225	49	0.5	145	2.67	47	
21	200	225	40.5	0.63	145	2.67	47.2	
22	200	225	40.5	0.88	145	2.67	42.7	
23	200	225	40.5	0.5	145	3.56	49.7	
24	200	225	40.5	0.5	145	4.22	38.5	
25	127	143	60.3	0.33	139	6.36	14	Gross et al., 2004
26	159	141	61.8	0.58	139	6.45	20	
27	121	141	81.4	0.76	139	6.45	15.4	
28	160	346	37.3	0.72	42	2.75	59.1	
29	160	346	43.2	1.1	42	3.32	44.1	Tariq & Newhook, 2003
30	160	325	34.1	1.54	42	3.54	46.8	
31	130	310	37.3	0.72	120	3.06	47.5	
32	130	310	43.2	1.1	120	3.71	50.15	
33	130	310	34.1	1.54	120	3.71	57.1	
34	203	225	79.6	1.25	40.3	4.06	38	Gross et al., 2003
35	152	225	79.6	1.66	40.3	4.06	32.53	
36	165	224	79.6	2.1	40.3	4.08	35.77	
37	203	224	79.6	2.56	40.3	4.08	46.4	

Test No.	b (mm)	d (mm)	f_c' (MPa)	ρ_f %	E_f (Gpa)	a/d	V_u (kN)	Reference
38	457	360	39.7	0.96	40.5	3.39	108.1	Tureyen & Frosch, 2002
39	457	360	40.3	0.96	47.1	3.39	114.8	
40	457	360	39.9	0.96	37.6	3.39	94.7	
41	457	360	42.3	1.92	40.5	3.39	137	
42	457	360	42.5	1.92	37.6	3.39	152.6	
43	457	360	42.6	1.92	47.1	3.39	177	
44	229	225	36.3	1.11	40.3	4.06	38.13	Yost et al., 2001
45	229	225	36.3	1.66	40.3	4.06	44.43	
46	279	225	36.3	1.81	40.3	4.06	45.27	
47	254	224	36.3	2.05	40.3	4.08	45.1	
48	229	224	36.3	2.27	40.3	4.08	42.2	
49	178	279	24.1	2.3	40	2.69	53.4	
50	178	287	24.1	0.77	40	2.61	36.1	
51	178	287	24.1	1.34	40	2.61	40.1	
52	305	157.5	28.6	0.73	40	4.5	26.8	Deitz et al., 1999
53	305	157.5	30.1	0.73	40	5.8	28.3	
54	305	157.5	28.2	0.73	40	5.8	28.5	
55	305	157.5	27	0.73	40	5.8	29.2	
56	305	157.5	30.8	0.73	40	5.8	27.6	
57	150	150	34.7	1.13	134	1.55	185.2	Omeman et al.,2008
58	150	150	38.9	1.13	134	1.83	154.9	
59	150	150	37.4	1.7	134	1.83	162.3	
60	150	150	40.6	1.13	134	2.33	91.5	
61	150	150	39.6	2.26	134	1.83	185.5	
62	150	250	41.7	1.35	134	1.41	298.1	
63	150	350	37.6	1.21	134	1.36	468.2	
64	150	150	63.1	1.13	134	1.83	226.9	
65	250	326	40	0.78	134	1.69	179.5	Al-Sayed, 2006
66	250	326	40	0.78	40	1.69	164.5	
67	250	326	40	1.24	40	1.69	175	
68	250	326	40	1.24	134	1.69	195	
69	250	326	40	1.71	134	1.69	233.5	
70	250	326	40	1.71	40	1.69	196	
71	250	326	40	1.24	134	1.3	372	
72	250	326	40	1.24	40	1.3	269	
73	1000	112	60	0.95	41.3	8.93	42.6	Wegian& Abdalla, 2005
74	1000	162	60	0.77	41.3	6.17	86.1	

Table B. Experimental data used to construct the BPNN and ANFIS for shear strength of concrete beams reinforced with FRP.

7. References

Adeli, H. & Park, H. (1995). A Neural Dynamic Model for Structural Optimization-Theory. *Journal of Computer and Structure*, Vol.57, No.3, pp. 383–390, ISSN 0045-7949

Abudlkudir, A.; Ahmet, T.& Murat, Y. (2006). Prediction of Concrete Elastic Modulus Using Adaptive Neuro-Fuzzy Inference System. *Journal of Civil Engineering and Environmental Systems*, Vol.23, No.4, pp.295–309, ISSN 1028-6608

Akbuluta, S.; Samet, H. & Pamuk S. (2004). Data Generation for Shear Modulus and Damping Ratio in Reinforced Sands Using Adaptive Neuro-Fuzzy Inference System. *Journal of Soil Dynamics and Earthquake Engineering*, Vol. 24, No.11, pp. 805–814, ISSN 0267-7261

Alkhrdaji, T.; Wideman, M.; Belarbi, A. & Nanni, A. (2001). Shear Strength of GFRP RC Beams and Slabs, *Proceedings of the International Conference, Civil Construction International Conference (CCC) 2001, Composites in Construction*, pp. 409-414, Porto/Portugal

Bank .L. (2006). *Composites for Construction: Structural Design with FRP Materials*, John Wiley, ISBN 0471681261, New Jersey

Baughman, D. & Liu, Y. (2005). *Neural Network in Bioprocessing and Chemical Engineering*. Academic Press,. ISBN 0120830302. San Diego, CA

Carpenter, W.& Barthelemy, J. (1994). Common Misconceptions about Neural Networks as Approximators. *Journal of Computing in Civil Engineering*, Vol.8, No.3, pp. 345-358

Chen, S. & Shah, K. (1992). Neural Networks in Dynamic Analysis of Bridges. Proceedings, 8th Confernce. *Computing in Civil Engineering and Geographic Information System Symposium* ASCE, PP.1058–1065, New York, USA.

Chiu S. (1994). Fuzzy Model Identification Based on Cluster Estimation. *Journal of Intelligent and Fuzzy System*, Vol.2, No.3, pp.267-278.

Cladera, A. & Mar A. (2004). Shear Design Procedure for Reinforced Normal and High-Strength Concrete beams Using Artificial Neural Networks. Part I: Beams Without Stirrups. *Journal Engineering Structure*, Vol.26, No.7 pp. 917-926, ISSN 0141-0296

Cladera, A. & Mar A. (2004). Shear Design Procedure for Reinforced Normal and High-Strength Concrete beams Using Artificial Neural Networks. Part II: Beams With Stirrups. *Journal Engineering Structure,* Vol. 26, No.7pp. 927-936, ISSN 0141-0296

Deitz, D.; Harik, I. & Gesund, H. (1999). One-Way Slabs Reinforced with Glass Fiber Reinforced Polymer Reinforcing Bars, *Proceedings of the 4th International Symposium, Fiber Reinforced Polymer Reinforcement for Reinforced Concrete Structures*, pp. 279-286, Maryland, USA

Eberhart, R. & Dobbins, R. (1990). *Neural Network PC Tools A Practical Guide*. Academic Press, ISBN0-12-228640-5, San Diego, CA

Eldin, N. & Senouci, A.(1995), A Pavement Condition-Rating Model Using Back Propagation Neural Networks. *Microcomputers in Civil Engineering,* Vol.10, No.6, pp. 433–441

El-Sayed, A.; El-Salakawy, E. & Benmokrane, B. (2004). Evaluation of Concrete Shear Strength for Beams Reinforced with FRP Bars, *5th Structural Specialty Conference of the Canadian Society for Civil Engineering, CSCE*, Saskatoon, Saskatchewan, Canada

El-Sayed, A.; El-Salakawy, E. & Benmokrane, B. (2005a). Shear Strength of Concrete Beams Reinforced with FRP Bars: Design Method, ACI- SP-230—54, pp.955-974

El-Sayed, A.; El-Salakawy, E. & Benmokrane, B. (2005b). Shear Strength of One-way Concrete Slabs Reinforced with FRP Composite Bars. *Journal of Composites for Construction*, ASCE, Vol.9, No.2, pp.147-157, ISSN 1090-0268

El-Sayed, A.; El-Salakawy, E. & Benmokrane, B. (2006a). Shear Strength of FRP Reinforced Concrete Beams without Transverse Reinforcement. *ACI Structural Journal*, Vol.103, No.2, pp.235-243, ISSN 0889-3241

El-Sayed, A.; El-Salakawy, E. & Benmokrane, B. (2006b). Shear Capacity of High-Strength Concrete Beams Reinforced with FRP Bars. *ACI Structural Journal*,Vol.103, No.3, pp.383-389, ISSN 0889-3241

El-Sayed, A. (2006c),Concrete Contribution to the Shear Resistance of FPR- Reinforced Concrete beams, PhD Thesis, Sherbrook University, Canada.

Feng, M. & Kim, J. (1998). Identification of a Dynamic System Using Ambient Vibration Measurements. *Journal of Applied Mech*anic, Vo.65, No.2, pp. 1010– 1023, ISSN 0021-8936

Feng, M. & Bahng, E. (1999). Damage Assessment of Jacketed RC Columns Using Vibration Tests. *Journal of Structure Engineering*, Vol.125, No.3, pp. 265–271, ISSN 0733-9445

Fonseca, E.; Vellasco, S. & Andrade S. (2008). A Neuro-Fuzzy Evaluation of Steel Beams Patch Load Behaviour. *Journal of Advances in Engineering Software*, Vol.39, No.7, pp.535-555, ISSN 0965-9978

Fuzzy Logic Toolbox User's Guide for Use with MATLAB 2009.

Gershenson C. Artificial Neural Networks for Beginners. Cognitive and Computing Sciences, University of Sussex, Available from, http:// cgershen@vub.ac.be

Garson, G. (1991). Interpreting Neural-Network Connection Weights. *AI Expert*, Vol.6, No.7, pp. 47-51, ISSN 0888-3785

Gagarin, N.; Flood, I., & Albrecht, P. (1994). Computing Truck Attributes with Artificial Neural Networks. *Journal of Computing in Civil Engineering*, Vol.8, No.2, ISSN 0887-3801

Guide for the Design and Construction of Concrete Reinforced with FRP Bars (ACI 440.1R-03), Reported by ACI Committee 440, 2003

Gross, S.; Dinehart, D.; Yost, J. & Theisz, P. (2004). Experimental Tests of High-Strength Concrete Beams Reinforced with CFRP Bars, *Proceedings of the 4th International Conference on Advanced Composite Materials in Bridges and Structures (ACMBS-4)*, Calgary, Alberta, Canada, July 20-23, 8p.

Gross, S. P.; Yost, J.; Dinehart, D. W.; Svensen, E. & Liu, N. (2003). Shear Strength of Normal and High Strength Concrete Beams Reinforced with GFRP Reinforcing Bars, Proceedings of the International Conference on High Performance Materials in Bridges, ASCE, 426-437.

Hajela, P. & Berke, L. (1991). Neurobiological Computational Models in Structural Analysis and Design. *Computers and Structures*, Vol.41, No.4, pp. 657-667, ISSN 0045-7949

Hamidian D. & Seyedpoor M. (2010). Shape Optimal Design of Arch Dams Using an Adaptive Neuro-Fuzzy Inference System and Improved Particle Swarm Optimization. *Jornal of Applied Mathematical Modelling*. Vol.34, No.6. pp.1574-1585.

Jang, S.; Sun T. & Mizutani E. (1997). *Neuro-Fuzzy and Soft Computing A Computational Approach to Learning and Machine intelligence*, Prentice Hall, Inc. ISBN 0132610663

Jang S. (1993). Adaptive network-based Fuzzy Inference System. *IEEE Journal*, Vol.23, No.3, PP.665-685, ISSN 0018-9472

Jeon J. (2007). Fuzzy and Neural Network Models for Analyses of Piles. PhD thesis, Civil Engineering, NCSU, USA.

Jonic', S.; Jankovic', T.; Gajic', V. & Popovic', D. (1999). Three Machine Learning Techniques for Automatic Determination of Rules to Control Locomotion. *Journal of IEEE*, Vol.46, No.3, pp.300-310, ISSN 0018-9294.

Lin. C. & Lee. C. (1996). *Neural Fuzzy Systems-A Neuro Fuzzy Synergism to Intelligent Systems*. Prentice Hall P T R. Upper Saddle River, N.J., ISBN 0-13-235169-2

Lin, J.; Hwang, M.; Becker, J. (2003). A Fuzzy Neural Network for Assessing the Risk of Fraudulent Financial Reporting. *Managerial Auditing Journal*, Vol.18, No.8, pp. 657-665, ISSN 0268-6902

Mamdani, E. & Assilian, S. (1975). An experiment in linguistic synthesis with a fuzzy logic controller. *International Journal of Man Machine Studies*, Vol.7, No.1, pp. 1-13, ISSN 00207373

Mansur, M. & Ong, K. (1987). Shear Strength of Ferrocement Beams. *ACI Structural Journal*, Vol.84, No.1, pp. 10-17.

Mansour, M.; Dicleli, M.; Lee, J. & Zhang, J. (2004). Predicting the Shear Strength of Reinforced Concrete Beams Using Artificial Neural Networks. *Journal of Engineering Structures*, Vol.26, No.6, pp.781–799, ISSN 0141-0296

Malhotra, R. & Malhotra, D. (1999). Fuzzy Systems and Neuro-Computing in Credit Approval. *Journal of Lending & Credit Risk Management*, Vol.81, No.11, pp. 24-37.

Mashrei, M. (2010). Flexure and Shear Behavior of Ferrocement Members: Experimental and Theoretical Study, PhD thesis, Civil Engineering, Basrah University, Iraq.

McCulloch and Pitts, W. (1943). A Logical Calculus of the Ideas Immanent in Nervous Activity. *Bulletin of Mathematical Biophysics*, Vol.(5), pp. 115-133, ISSN 0092-8240

Mukherjee, A.; Deshpande, J. & Anmada, J. (1996). Prediction of Buckling Load of Columns Using Artificial Neural Networks. *Journal of . Structural Engineering*, Vol.122, No.11, pp. 1385-1387, ISSN 0733-9445

Naaman, A. *(2000. Ferrocement and Laminated Cementitious Composites*. Ann Arbort, Michigan, Techno Press 3000, USA 2000. ISBN 0967493900

Neural Network Toolbox User's Guide for Use with MATLAB, 2009

Omeman, Z.; Nehdi, M. & El-Chabib, H. (2008). Experimental Study on Shear Behavior of Carbon-Fiber-Reinforced Polymer Reinforced Concrete Short Beams without Web Reinforcement. *Canadian Journal of Civil Engineering*, Vol.35, No.1, pp.1-10.

Rafiq, M.; Bugmann, G. & Easterbrook, D. (2001). Neural Network Design for Engineering Applications, *Journal of Computers and Structures*, Vol.79, No. 17, pp.1541-1552.

Rao, C.; Rao, G. & Rao, R. (2006). An Appraisal of the Shear Resistance of Ferrocement Elements. *ASIAN Journal of Civil Engineering (Building and Housing)*, Vol.7, No.6, pp. 591-602.

Razaqpur, A.; Isgor, B.; Greenaway, S. & Selley, A. (2004). Concrete Contribution to the Shear Resistance of Fiber Reinforced Polymer Reinforced Concrete Members. *Journal of Composites for Construction*, ASCE, Vol.8, No.5, pp. 452-460,ISSN 1090-0268

Sanad, A. & Saka, M. (2001). Prediction of Ultimate Shear Strength of Reinforced Concrete Deep Beams using neural Networks. *Journal of Structural Engineering*, Vol.127, No.7, pp. 818-828, ISSN 0733-9445

Shah, S. (1974). New Reinforcing Materials in Concrete. *Journal of ACI*, Vol.71, No.5, pp. 257-262.

Sugeno, M.(1985). *Industrial applications of fuzzy control*, Elsevier Science Pub, ISBN0444878297, NY, USA

Topcu, I. & Sarıdemir M. (2007). Prediction of Compressive Strength of Concrete Containing Fly Ash Using Artificial Neural Networks and Fuzzy Logic. *Computational Materials Science*, Vol.41, No.3, pp.305-311, ISSN0927-0256

Tariq, M. & Newhook, J. (2003). Shear Testing of FRP reinforced Concrete without Transverse Reinforcement, *Proceedings of Canadian Society for Civil Engineering (CSCE)Anuual Conference*, Moncton, NB, Canada, 10p.

Tesfamariam, S. & Najjaran, H. (2007). Adaptive Network-Fuzzy Inferencing to Estimate Concrete Strength Using Mix Design. *Journal of Materials in Civil Engineering*, Vol.19, No.7, pp. 550-560, ISSN 0899-1561

Tully, S. (1997). Neural Network Approach for Predicting the Structural Behaviour of Concrete Slabs. M.Sc Thesis, College of Engineering and Applied Science, University of Newfoundland.

Turban, E. & Aronson, J. (2000). *Decision Support Systems and Intelligent Systems*, 6th edition, Prentice-Hall, Englewood Cliffs, NJ, ISBN: 0130894656.

Tureyen, A. & Frosch, R. (2002). Shear Tests of FRP-Reinforced Concrete Beams without Stirrups. *ACI Structural Journal*, Vol.99, No.4, pp.427-434, ISSN 0889-3241

Tureyen, A. & Frosch, R. (2003). Concrete Shear Strength: Another Perspective. *ACI Structural Journal*. Vol.100, No.5, pp. 609-615.

Waszczyszyn, Z.; Pabisek, E. & Mucha, G., (1998). Hybrid Neural Network/Computational Program to the Analysis of Elastic- Plastic Structures, *Neural networks in Mechanics of Structures and Materials*, Udine, Italy, pp. 19-23.

Wegian, F.& Abdalla, H. (2005). Shear Capacity of Concrete Beams Reinforced with Fiber Reinforced Polymers. *Journal of Composite Structures*, Vol.71, No.1, pp. 130–138, ISSN 0263-8223

Wu, Z. & Bailey, C. (2005). Fracture Resistance of a Cracked Concrete Beam Post Strengthened with FRP Sheets. *International Journal of Fracture*, Vol.135, No.(1-4), pp.35–49, ISSN 0376-9429

Yost, J.; Gross, S. & Dinehart, D. (2001). Shear Strength of Normal Strength Concrete Beams Reinforced with Deformed GFRP Bars. *Journal of Composites for Construction*, ASCE, Vol.5, No.4, pp. 268-275, ISSN 1090-0268

Zadeh L. (1965). Fuzzy sets. *Journal of Information and Control*, Vol.8, No.3, pp. 338-353.

Zadeh, L. Making Computers Think Like People. *IEEE Spectrum*. 1984; Vol.21, No.8 pp.26-32, ISSN 0018-9235

Zadih, L. (1993). Fuzzy Logic, Neural Networks and Soft Computing. *Microprocessing and Microprogramming*, Vol.38, No.1,pp.13, ISSN 0165-6074

Zadeh, L. (1994), Fuzzy Logic, Neural Networks and Soft Computing. Communication of the ACM, Vol.3, No.3, pp.77-84.

Zaho, J. & Bose, B. (2002). Evaluation of membership Functions for Fuzzy Logic Controlled Induction Motor Drive. *IEEE Journal*, Vo.1, No.pp.229-234, ISBN 0-7803-7474-6. S